BEING AND TRUTH

BEING AND TRUTH

THOMAS LANGAN

UNIVERSITY OF MISSOURI PRESS
COLUMBIA AND LONDON

Copyright © 1996 by
The Curators of the University of Missouri
University of Missouri Press, Columbia, Missouri 65201
Printed and bound in the United States of America
All rights reserved
5 4 3 2 1   00 99 98 97 96

Library of Congress Cataloging-in-Publication Data

Langan, Thomas.
   Being and truth / Thomas Langan.
    p. cm.
   Includes index.
   ISBN 0-8262-1053-8 (alk. paper)
   1. Ontology.   2. Truth.   I. Title.
DB331.L316   1996
110—dc20   96-10231
                                                                                             CIP

∞™ This paper meets the requirements of the
American National Standard for Permanence of Paper
for Printed Library Materials, Z39.48, 1984.

TEXT DESIGN: ELIZABETH K. YOUNG
JACKET DESIGN: STEPHANIE FOLEY
TYPESETTER: BOOKCOMP
PRINTER AND BINDER: THOMSON-SHORE, INC.
TYPEFACES: LITHOS, PALATINO

TO THE MEMORY OF

DR. MICHEL VAILLANT

CONTENTS

ACKNOWLEDGMENTS   ix

PART I. NATURAL FAITH

1. THE URGENCY OF THE TRUTH QUESTION   3
2. AN EPISTEMOLOGY BEYOND SUBJECTIVISM AND OBJECTIVISM   13
3. THE GUIDING PRINCIPLE OF RESEARCH AND THE UNITY OF BEING   20

PART II. THE KNOWLEDGE OF BEING

4. KINDS OF OBJECTS, KINDS OF TRUTH   37
5. IS A SINGLE WISDOM POSSIBLE?   125

PART III. TOWARD AN ONTOLOGY

6. MAN IN CONTEXTS   151
7. NATURAL HISTORY AND HISTORICAL AWARENESS MEET IN MAN   199
8. THE ULTIMATE GROUND   277
9. THE HISTORICITY OF BEING (*SEIN*)   318

PART IV. BEING AND TRUTH

10. THE ULTIMATE STRUCTURES AND THE OVERCOMING OF IDEOLOGY   343

GLOSSARY   369

INDEX   375

ACKNOWLEDGMENTS

During its ten-year gestation, this book was assisted into life by Mr. Bruce A. Stewart, who contributed many ideas and much discussion to its being. Dr. Michel Vaillant (1922–1994), a distinguished scientist and philosopher of science, to whom it is dedicated, kept a wary eye on everything I have said about nature, and Dr. Edwin Hersch, M.D., offered many psychiatric suggestions.

BEING AND TRUTH

PART I.

NATURAL FAITH

1.

THE URGENCY OF THE TRUTH QUESTION

Millennia before that critical thinking the Greeks called "philosophy," men[1] posed the question of the meaning of their existence, as the myths show. Man cannot prosper without some sense of what he is doing and how it squares with reality.

Our present planetary situation imposes three related truth questions:

1. An enhanced sense of freedom invites any who care to notice that many of our contemporaries do not face Saint Augustine's question, "What are your loves?" to assign a new urgency to the question of the rightness of what we ourselves are doing.
2. Even if the motivation for asking what we are doing and the sense of it all is in place, there remains the problem of how we can attain a certain distance from those driving beliefs giving shape to our lives. The pluralism of the planetary situation helps us see this necessity. The goal: *critical possession of the experiential grounds for our ruling beliefs, and search for what we may have been missing*. But by what method[2] can we probe the foundations in experience[3] of our ongoing, driving "natural faith," and compare it with other possibilities? A *moral* question is implied: What would motivate us

---

1. While believing serious issues of oppression of women need to be addressed, I have not found that contorting the English language to divest it of a male bias contributes enough to reforming the depths of our psyches to be worth the poetic devastation which results. I assure my readers that this does not signal any unwillingness on my part to work, in my surroundings, for justice.

2. The deconstructionists have sounded a warning. Method is not to be imported from outside the object being examined, and ideologically imposed. Eric Voegelin cautioned, as early as *The New Science of Politics* (Chicago: University of Chicago Press, 1952), that method is developed in intimate interaction with the object one is seeking to appreciate. The present work will seek to show how this can be done.

3. See Glossary. The self can distinguish between itself as reflective critical center and the self upon which it is reflecting, thus experiencing itself, including the fact that the self is much more than the center of awareness, the soul becoming better informed about the soul. Experience is always subjective, but it has a content, *that which* is experienced. This may be a mere product of imagination, or it may be a revelation about another, a thing, a person, a relation. The criteria for judging the truth of an experience must lie in what is revealed about the other, not in the experiencing itself.

to do this, and give us the character to carry out something as dangerous as a sustained critical self-examination?
3. The philosophical question par excellence, then, is this: How can we entice ourselves to widen our horizons to take into account the experiences of others, which challenge the fragile ideological structures of explanation we have built to cope with the world? As anthropological—indeed, psychological—as this sounds, I hope to show that at its base it is first of all an *ontological* question.

The rise in our time of a planetary society intensifies the old challenge of reconciling conflicting claims about how it stands with the world, and conflicting anthropologies, tearing at the foundations of society. To this situation some Postmodernist intellectuals have found a rather simple solution: Treat the large claims of the great traditions as subjectivist twaddle—even the claims of the hard sciences are not spared.

The confrontation of traditions, such as causes shooting it out in Karabakh, Azerbaijan, and the slower erosion of the sense of the Christian West as secularism triumphs are not merely theoretical questions, but practical, indeed political, even life threatening. "Truth" is not just disincarnate, formal truth but visions guiding ways of doing things. So issues of "truth" are in part questions of how to replace the civic theologies of once cohesive societies, formerly based in universal faiths, like Christianity and Islam. How does one replace such monoliths with peaceful but earnest discourse and compromising intercourse, without sinking into a pragmatic relativism that, because it destroys commitment, saps the very wellsprings of existence?

Put in this societal way, the truth challenge can be summed up thus: How to achieve a compromising, peaceful political order while retaining some seriousness (*gravitas*) in the quest to know how it really stands with being itself? Not since the birth of philosophy has the Occidental intelligentsia been so skeptical about projects of universal wisdom and so disinclined to address directly the question of being. The university may accept the need to verify certain truths, but all sense of "The Truth" is lost. However, commonsense man remains never for a moment skeptical about the reality of the things and persons with which he daily has to cope, and he infrequently questions his own sweeping judgments about them. But then, schizophrenically, he becomes a total relativist and voluntarist when someone would challenge the Big Truths of his natural faith: "I have a right to my own opinion, and you may believe what you want." The result of such a practical relativism on a wider scale is the destruction of serious conversation and the trivialization of our societies, threatening to undermine the very sense of *the serious*.

The underlying pragmatic and tolerant attitude little encourages, outside of the sciences and beyond particular philosophical and religious communities, any common pursuit of truth, and it virtually destroys the university as a community in search of truth. More troubling is the effect on the individual: The search for truth hardly seems to occupy a central place in the busy lives of most citizens. They appear to bury the lack of meaning under the heavy hand of a fideistic religion or under a mountain of goodies or both. Entertainment has become the largest single industry.

The political artisans have been remarkably successful at keeping the peace in our working, pluralistic democracies, whatever one may think of the increasing evidence of an ongoing crude manipulation of mass public opinion. The avoidance of the need for brute oppression and the freeing of people to "do their own thing" (however subtly they are manipulated in the meantime) has allowed the release of creative energy. To proselytize absolute truth claims (which many of the great traditions still do) in such a setting destabilizes this complex and tense compromise. Evangelists of all types are more than irritants. They may be dangerous to the public health!

Both the Abrahamic tradition, handing down divine revelation, and the classical philosophical tradition centered the search for truth on a foundational and unchanging being: God is the fullness of being, one and complete. For both, and for the offspring of their union, Christian thought, truth is founded in God's knowledge of himself. Success, for Christians, consists in progress in attaining wisdom and holiness, in knowing the Way, which God alone can show us and which allows his will to be done and hence his glory to shine forth, and following it, witnessing correction with one's life, not in comfortable and unruffled existence, but in exaltation and utmost seriousness.

As any Straussian[4] will tell you, the classic sense of truth has been undermined. As any Christian will also tell you, the sense of redemption—that man has to be saved from his tendencies to self-indulgence, a destructive closing in on himself which isolates him from the living wellsprings of being—has been marginalized. Replacing absoluteness of the foundation of all being is a sense of the pragmatic floating of values.

This question of valuing naturally comes to mind when we hear a contemporary thinker like Martin Heidegger declare, "The essence of truth is freedom." The widespread talk of values poses severe problems for those aware of the Nietzschean origin of the notion of valuing. Heidegger wrote several volumes attacking voluntaristic valuing and seeking to display an ontological sense of *Freiheit*.[5] Indeed, the truth question cannot be separated from the challenge of rethinking the very nature of freedom, freedom not as a psychological phenomenon of extended adolescence but as the foundation of being itself. As Cardinal Ratzinger[6] wrote in a recent article, "Jesus Christ Today," truth

---

4. The late Erwin Strauss was a tireless fighter against relativism and a proponent of returning to the foundations of classical philosophy and rediscovering Plato's sense of eternal truth.

5. The German word contains the sense of "a space to operate"—*in der Freie* means "out in the open air."

6. The prefect of the Sacred Congregation for the Doctrine of the Faith, Josef Ratzinger, the bête noire of liberal Catholics, has in fact written more profoundly about the nature of freedom than perhaps anyone in our generation other than Heidegger. The liberals are in strong disagreement about his notions of what constitutes genuine, mature liberty.

and freedom are inseparable from each other: "'I call you no more slaves but friends,' says the Lord, 'for slaves do not know what the Master is doing. I have called you friends, because all has been told to you, what I have heard from my father' [John 15:15]. Ignorance is dependency, slavery: He who does not know remains a slave. Only when one begins to know who he is, where we begin to grasp the essential, do we begin to be free."[7]

THE STARTING POINT OF ANY ENQUIRY: NATURAL FAITH

By the question of The Truth I mean the quest for the foundations of wisdom in a unified knowledge of being. In declaring this, I reveal something of my own ontological faith: at least, the principle I share with Saint Thomas and most of the thinkers in the classical philosophical tradition, "Sapientia est ordinare," which we might translate loosely, "Wisdom is about ordering things."

I have no hesitation acknowledging that these convictions about being govern my way of interpreting the pursuit of truth. One purpose in writing this book is to improve my own understanding of those presuppositions and to search critically for their foundation in experience. I am on the lookout for deeper motives, rooted perhaps in unexamined experience and even trauma, for why I see things as I do. Advance in critical self-understanding is essential to *appropriation*—making properly one's own, by becoming increasingly responsible for the traditions and experiences that have formed one's outlook.[8]

Given this goal, the present study is divided as follows. The first three chapters present an outline of my natural faith as personal starting point and framework for the inquiry, and show how my position relates to the present situation and its history. I do not intend that faith to remain a mere declaration of convictions: The remainder of the book is a search for the evidence to make the positions expressive of my lived experience credible to the reader and more nuanced. The second part, then, formed by Chapters 4 and 5, explores, using phenomenological description, how we approach the world in knowledge, and seeks to build an epistemological base for the ontology to follow. In Part III, the emphasis reverses from knowledge to being, as I lay out what I believe is known about the being of the world and our place in it, mustering evidence for the well-foundedness of this understanding. From this ontological investigation arises a better understanding of the dimensions of the truth question confronting us in its contemporary form, how the "ultimate structures" of our experience are to be fitted together in an "ecumenic wisdom."[9] This tableau—already outlined in chapter 9 of *Tradition and Authenticity*—is developed in

---

7. Josef Cardinal Ratzinger, "Jesus Christus Heute," *Internationale katholische Zeitung, Communio* (January 1990): 64.

8. Appropriation is explained at length in my *Tradition and Authenticity* (Columbia: University of Missouri Press, 1992) (hereinafter *T&A*), where it is the centerpiece of chaps. 1–2.

9. We may recall that "wisdom" was one of Aristotle's terms for first philosophy, whose object of study was being qua being.

the sole chapter constituting Part IV. It offers a charter and proper structure for post-postmodernist philosophy, hence for a pre- and post-Heideggerian thinking.

Throughout this inquiry, the distinction between epistemology and ontology is not hard and fast: How we know and what we know cannot be neatly separated. There is no subject without an object, and vice versa, nor can what is affirmed of being, of man's place in the cosmos and his destiny, be separated from the question of evidence, of how we know and establish our position on these ultimate questions.

Missing as yet is an adequate anthropology, a more sustained reflection on the nature of man, needed to carry this work forward and to found a practical wisdom, an ethics and politics combined. Much material for such a philosophy of human nature is developed along the way. Issues of sin, pathology, and redemption should be addressed from a perennial wisdom, the gift of a tradition and a living community *ek-sisting* (used in Heidegger's sense) in truth, as the source of experiences one cannot access by his lonely self. But these are experiences one's wisdom cannot do without.

WHAT IS NATURAL FAITH?

From the first moment of self-awareness we discover ourselves as always already engaged in the world, working out from a given situation, equipped with a developed view of how things stand. This governing view is the product of the ongoing interaction of our temperaments, what we have been taught, and our personal experience. These presuppositions and predispositions are woven into the horizons of interpretation we bring to our judgments of all things, and from these we draw our questions and, within those horizons, the various frames of reference we deploy in focusing on reality to answer them.

This, however, does not ruin all hope of objectivity. There is no reason to believe these interpretive horizons we bring to every knowing are inevitably false or arbitrary or seriously misleading. They are, after all, the fruit of new experience interacting with experience-tried traditions and with temperament, itself reflective of the "hard wired" being in my depths, and they are put to the test of every day's efforts to cope with things and other persons. But any interpretive horizons—as the word implies—do have their limits, not just of space and time, but of unexamined suppositions, some of which may be rooted more in deforming psychological blocks than in data from the real world successfully integrated in a wisdom.

These convictions, in the course of a lifetime, can change fundamentally and sometimes rapidly (then we speak of *conversion*). More often, though, they evolve through a long, almost imperceptible process, under the influence of life's many experiences. The chemistry of the process forming and reforming natural faith is mysterious. Despite the vital contributions of supernatural faith and grace, the overall viewpoint remains *natural* in the sense here intended: It is *natus* (born), the spontaneous result of that ongoing chemistry. No matter how important the scientific and rational component in the given individual, no matter how mature his self-criticism, the moral, the libidinous, the supernatural, and the other half-understood influences continue to work their effect. The whole of one's outlook has a *tonus:* There is a feel to the world as the individual lives it, which one can never perfectly rationally justify. It influences above all what we are willing to take seriously.

Through one's natural faith the epochal *Sein*—the light in which everything bathes and gets its sense, which Heidegger never ceased to evoke—illumines every context. From it comes the program of matters one cares about. *It is the source of one's real agenda.* The effort to state those principles explicitly—facing squarely the issue of what you want—is already a great step in focusing on the world as one begins to question the evidential foundation for these beliefs. And, at the limit, it becomes an invitation to step back behind the world.

It is not possible to lay out satisfactorily in an intellectually compelling way every aspect of one's overall view of how it stands with the world. Even the *Summa Theologiae* does not bring to adequate, explicit formulation all of Saint Thomas's implicit assumptions, nor does it explain everything in his feelings about the world. Much about *Sein*'s all-englobing illumination of his world remained unthought, even by such a master of critical reflection. This truth about "the ontological difference between *Sein* and the things it illumines," as Heidegger calls it, is why Being in the sense of Heidegger's *Sein* "gets forgotten" and why *Sein* remains so elusive. That is why, too, everyone's all-englobing position always remains to some degree a *faith,* in the sense of both a belief and a confidence in one's convictions about how it stands with the world, reflecting the surrounding mystery (*Sein*), our unthinking sympathy with the way everyone sees things, and our great difficulty in getting outside these horizons to achieve a command of being.

Because in this work I shall be moving dialectically back and forth between subjective-interpretive considerations and objective-in-itself assertions about extramental reality, I need to maintain carefully these distinctions, more complex than the ontological difference:

being, in the sense of all that is or can be, including every form of interpreting or thinking about being, hence all of nature, culture, and history;
esse, the real in itself existence of things and persons and the real relations between them, hence *esse* can be substantial or accidental, and is what it is in itself independently of interpretation;
Sein, being interpreted, the thought of real things and persons and their relations, as well as every fantastic product of the imagination, including the meaning incarnated in cultural objects, hence the origin of all culture and history.

Rendering explicit one's hold on the world has its limits. I may examine critically how it stands with things; analyze aspects of what I consider the situation to be, and how I deal with it overall; I can continue to illumine wise principles and to ground them in reflection on the whole of experience. But there is so much about the world I do not know, both because I lack information and an inability to get behind the largest structures of my thought. *Absolutes Wissen*—total knowledge—is fundamentally ontologically impossible. I cannot wish away all bad faith on my part, nor command every kind of information, much of which will become available to me only in due time, "when the hour has come."

The pervasive, uncriticized societally accepted epochal view of the world, the illumining of *Sein*, limits us through the transmission of restricted and rather strongly developed mind-sets, ways of conceiving of the world. For instance, in our era of high-technology, urbanized culture, we are in a world organized according to the rationality of efficiency. This universal mind-set establishes relationships in such a pervasive way, and it has so penetrated cultural objects—our cities with their square blocks, our telephone systems, the supermarket—that we have trouble becoming aware of it: a daily existence in the fish-and-water syndrome.

Such a framework is not only not demonstrable, in the sense of being capable of a "laying out" that would compel every person of good faith to see it; glimpsing it for oneself is difficult. It is not present so much in the form of a set of theoretical propositions as it is an atmosphere, a conditioning, threading through our judgments of what counts and in that way molding our action.

Natural Faiths and the Hermeneutic Circle of Interpretation

All this sounds very subjective. If each person approaches the world from the standpoint of his personal natural faith, forming his own little world, and if the people within a given epoch of a tradition have their own, mostly hidden agenda, reflecting social dimensions of natural faith (public opinion, what they say, *Sein*'s illumining and obscuring), what possible hope can there be of finding truth? How can reality present itself as it is in itself, if all we have access to is our own deforming interpretations of it? Does not this post-Kantian realization deliver us to the skeptical postmoderns, who promise us only the joys of suavely playing with our own fantastic mental creations?

If so, we are doomed to the trivialization of life and the gigantomachia of ideologies. But before I begin the task of recuperating all the evidence that objectivity is still possible without ideology, I want to point out, especially to the most resolute realists, that everything that has just been claimed about the hermeneutic-circle dimension of natural faith is put forward earnestly as *a universal truth claim:* One's natural faith informs the horizons of interpretation of one's world.

But how then can I, interpreting from a point of view, hold out a universally valid principle and, what is worse, present it as part of my natural faith and still claim that this is bindingly true, for everyone? In one blow, I seem to have horrified the postmodern relativists, who flee principle as ideology, and the classical realists, who can see in interpretation nothing but a relativist mistake.

Wonderful! With that map, the vessel of the Scylla and Charybdis Navigation Company can leave port, all sheets to the wind. The fun of being countercultural reaches a new peak of excitement. The captain announces from the bridge: An understandable but catastrophic mistake has been made by most modern philosophers. They assume that because all finite human knowers accede to reality from a position in time and space—that is, from a point of view or a perspective—they therefore cannot attain lastingly valid universal principles.

Suppose, while opening onto the world from a point of view, the reflective knower were to grasp a fundamental implication, a basic dimension of his own knowledge act. Neither Descartes nor Kant invalidated the project of grasping the apodeictic principle[10] in this way. Some of modern thought has been sympathetic to this, as it leaves mind grasping mind: not too much exposure to a mind-transcending reality. But I shall defend, in due course, another kind of certitude, objective in nature: the possibility of formal insight into the kinds of objective realities that present themselves, albeit in profile, but nevertheless (*pace* Kant) *as they are in themselves*.

The second point is this: When a principle is indicated as part of one's natural faith, it does not mean, just because one has perhaps not troubled to examine the grounds for holding it, or may not know very well how to draw another's attention to the grounds for holding it, that it is not true, or that there is indeed no adequate evidence for it. In any event, as Aristotle long ago showed, one cannot demonstrate a fundamental principle. That does not mean, however, that there is nothing one can do to lead another to see its truth. Upon the faith that one can, the following enterprise begins.

Take the case at hand: Confronted by such a claim in principle, *quoi faire?* The reader simply has to reflect on his own experience and see if it is not indeed the case that each human being approaches the world from a point of view, and that that point of view is formed, in part, by the personal factors that have been described. He must also face up to the reality of the vast differences in traditional, societal, and epochal outlook. The search for truth takes place within this pluralistic reality of a variety of points of view. That is the challenge of working toward what in *Tradition and Authenticity* I described as an ecumenic wisdom. Thus, in an apparent paradox, an absolute claim is made, and identified as part of my natural faith, about the relativity of our openings onto the world. The paradox is *only* apparent.

This invocation of a fundamental, universal subjective element in what we might term the transcendental truth situation by no means implies that it is "game over" for those who are convinced that *the pursuit of truth is precisely the quest for a reality transcending the consciousness that knows it*. I aim at recuperating

---

10. This is roughly what Descartes and Kant meant by "apodeictic principle": this grasp by the mind of something of its own necessary thought structure. See Etienne Gilson and Thomas Langan, *Modern Philosophy: From Descartes to Kant* (New York: Random House, 1963). The chapters on Descartes, Malebranche, Spinoza, and Kant are of most importance in this regard.

evidence for the reality of our knowledge of consistent, self-presencing, in-itself reality. I believe in a reality greater than human will, in nature, and in the Source of it, nature's God (to quote the Founders of the Republic), a reality that makes possible in the first place and conditions will's employment, and places demands on our responsibility; a reality to which human beings are beholden and to which they should strive to conform their understanding and their action, if they really desire to prosper. I shall work to gain credibility for the project of objectivity, but without losing sight of the fact of transcendental subjectivity and hence of culture and history.

Crudely put, there are two kinds of reality the lover of wisdom has to describe and then to relate correctly. First, there is the reality of all to which we can accede in knowledge, all that exists in itself regardless of what we may think about it. Then there is the reality of our consciousness' constructions, of all those great conceptual schemes we build, both to explain for ourselves the larger transcending reality and to comfort ourselves by assuaging our desires with answers and fantasies.

Relating them is a matter of clarifying how our conceptual schemes are rooted in and/or distort the experienced realities. (Classical philosophy is most often so *ravi*[11] by the real objects, it neglects to reflect sufficiently on the deformations of interpretation and the immense wealth of fantastic construction we can build from our grasp of things.) This critical process, more amply carried out, should improve the quality and reliability of our conceptual schemes' hold on the larger reality.

I want to have the cake of objectivism, classically defended by every sort of realist, and eat it, too, digesting it in the phenomenologist's stomach of interpretation. *Quel défi!* Imagine, enjoying the security of knowing real things and other persons as they are—as things-in-themselves, which Kant thought he had rendered impossible forever—and still enjoying the deconstructionists' acute sense of historicity, being able to admit that traditional views of things evolve and that sinister motives can make us good at hiding the truth from ourselves. (Yes, I acknowledge that there is much each of us does not *want* to see.) That is why the Scylla and Charybdis Navigation Company is going to be so popular: Our catering service is the only one with cake that nourishes and persists!

The mistake since Descartes has been to discount as though it were not knowledge of the thing-in-itself all knowledge that is only partial, leaving the impression that it could not achieve a respectable degree of certitude, that it could scarcely engage the future definitively in a moving world. But, I contend, our knowledge can achieve quite enough certitude to found rational human action and to justify and show the need for the pursuit of truth in a realistic sense.

---

11. To be *ravi* (from which "ravishing") is to be delightfully taken over by the object; the difference between a healthy appreciation (as in *ravissement*) and an obsession will be dealt with later.

When in Chapter 4 I begin the preliminary survey of kinds of objects and the kinds of truth we can gain about them and how the different frames of reference that give access to them relate, my perspective is phenomenological. You can see why such a method renders classical realists nervous. In the best Gilsonian tradition, they fear that once the philosopher insists on the object's being a product of consciousness, present primordially in experience and as such always limited, he has cut consciousness off from the infinite real world of which we are conscious—the bridge back to real things will never again get established.[12] Charybdis threatens our little ship. My experience, mirrored in my natural faith, tells me this is not so. The burden is on me, in the course of the phenomenological descriptions in Chapter 4, to present the evidence, from within consciousness, of the self-presencing of a transcending reality that shows consciousness reaching beyond itself to grasp what is other than itself. The success of this secures the ground for a post-postmodern but realistic ontology presented in Chapters 6 to 8.

A phenomenological method grounded in objectivistic ontological predispositions: Is that not a contradiction in terms? Is not phenomenology, by its very starting point, idealistic? Have you avoided Charybdis, dear captain, only to crash head-on into Scylla? Max Scheler, Alfred Schütz, and Gabriel Marcel did not think so. I do not believe so, as I maintained long ago in "The Future of Phenomenology." There I argued that the phenomenological method is intrinsically ontologically neutral and can serve both an idealist natural faith and one intent on showing how our knowledge yields reliable contact with the reality that surrounds and founds us.[13]

The only way to render such a claim credible is to engage in phenomenological description, guided by realistic faith. In preparation for this, I now state succinctly, without arguing it at this point, my position on this fundamental issue. This will provide a context for the posing of the truth question in all its dimensions, as far as I am able to understand them.

---

12. One can see the extreme of Gilson's terror of this in the least satisfactory book this great thinker ever wrote, *Réalisme thomiste et critique de la connaissance* (Paris: J. Vrin, 1939).

13. Thomas Langan, "The Future of Phenomenology," in *Phenomenology in Perspective*, ed. F. J. Smith (The Hague: Nijhoff, 1970), 1–16.

2.

AN EPISTEMOLOGY BEYOND SUBJECTIVISM AND OBJECTIVISM

> Quamdiu vivimus, necesse habemus semper quaerere (So long as we live, we have necessarily always to search).
> —Hugh of St. Victor, *De Sacramentis*

> Motus cognitionis in ipso remanet inquietus (The movement of cognition remains in itself untranquil).
> —Saint Thomas Aquinas, *De veritate*

> Notre nature est dans le mouvement.
> —Pascal, *Pensées*

THE REALISM PRINCIPLE

The first principle of my position refers to foundational experience in perception, and it is resolutely realistic. It affirms what common experience reveals—namely, that somehow we are able to know other persons and things as real entities, which show themselves in perception to exist independently of the knowledge that gives us access to them. That we can know persons and things in themselves, which includes knowing reliably something of what they are, is part of the foundation of the edifice of truth, of truth that can unite people in knowledge and action. But when we recall the idealist dimension, that every knowledge act is the work of the subject and hence a moment in his subjective history, and hence an opening onto the world only from a point of view, how can we really know the thing itself?

Throughout this study we shall at all times be engaged in this delicate navigation. A single false push on the tiller, and one is on a collision course with the rock of a realism that cannot make sense of interpretation, historicity, deconstruction, or else the fragile ship of philosophy will be swept into the whirlpool of an idealism that sucks the sense we enjoy in daily experience of the reality of things and persons into the maelstrom of creative imagination, where there is no compass to tell you how to sail out.

I begin by acknowledging the inherent givenness of every object of consciousness, whether thing, relations between things, or image produced by the imagination or idea produced by insight. These data provide points of orientation in reality. Every bit of otherness—other than ego as center of awareness, even the otherness of the most creative image—is to be respected, for it takes us beyond our narrow selves, the center of initiative, setting up at least that much otherness, me over against the image, which I should acknowledge if I am going to accept truth. And when what is given is more objective still than image, perhaps even data about realities entirely outside ourselves, the self-presencing of such realities alone can save us from sterilizing ourselves by becoming fixated on our own fantasies.

Whatever the question directing attention, and whatever it may be the knower brings from relevant past experience to flesh out what is just now presencing, the resultant object imposes, through its own thus allowed presence, its evidence for its distinction from consciousness and from all other things. Even the image creatively presented by the imagination distinguishes itself from the imagining activity of the mind, and this image (of this kind) from that image perhaps of a different kind. In thus showing itself, every object makes demands on the knower, it beckons to be respected, and it surprises; not all demands can be anticipated.

The father of phenomenology, Edmund Husserl, was struck by the importance of this fundamental subject-object distinction in every intentional act. Descartes, the father of modern philosophy, already glimpsed it. No matter whether I am perceiving, imagining, dreaming, or fearing, there is always present something perceived, imagined, dreamed, or feared: in Husserl's terminology a *noema*, correlative to the *noein*, the kind of conscious activity of the subject.

There seems to be a bit of a chicken-and-egg situation here. Do I not need some interest, a question, a concern, even to notice something; but how can I have an interest unless that thing somehow is already presencing? A certain dialectic is inevitable, but the valence shifts, with the emphasis in sense perception more on the passive, receptive element and, in the case of imaginative construction, more on the creative element. If I am gazing out into the garden, the robin hopping into view will call himself to my attention; involuntarily, I notice him. But if I am daydreaming about a summer cottage I would love to construct, I am free (but not totally so) to decide what is going to appear in my mind's eye to fulfill the impulses of my fancy.

No object will ever appear completely isolated and alone. To forget that is to risk reducing the full charge of intelligibility with which every object presents itself in consciousness, including always its connectedness to a wider world. The mind can to some extent disconnect it from the surrounding reality, but at the cost of a loss of the reality offered by perception. On the other hand, every intentional act is rooted fundamentally in the common horizons of the familiar world the subject normally deploys, based in his natural faith, illumined by the epochal *Sein*, and accounting for the consistency of his version of the epochal world in which he lives. Within these more embracing horizons, the particular *frame of reference*,[1] motivated by the question of the moment or the initiative taken by an aggressive thing or person pushing its way into consciousness, is deployed. Along with it comes all the subject can offer from his past experience to decipher and perhaps further construct the meaning of the object. That will include very broad notions common to the epochal world in which he lives, and its long, active traditions, not the least important being his language.

Yet see how commanding the presence of the object within these horizons of interpretation can be: I may be looking for something, and not find what I expected. The robin may appear and preempt my field of attention. I may be trying to remember something for some particular reason, and discover that involuntary associations surge up, motivated by demands made by what is already present in the imagination becoming linked to it. I may be imagining a new artwork and discover that what I have already worked out takes me in unexpected directions.

So, while acknowledging that all knowing is rooted in will acts of the subject wanting to know, looking for something, seeking some satisfaction or other, I also acknowledge that I almost always have to adjust my frame of reference to take account of what is revealed in the idea or object. If that were not so, there would occur no progress in knowledge, my images and ideas would connect with no larger reality, and all seeking would be senseless.

To sum up, this implies, then, that every intentional act transcends the initially deployed constitutive field of consciousness toward images, ideas, things, and persons that, although revealed only in consciousness and only partially (in "profile", as Husserl says), present themselves as "being in themselves." (The challenge here to Kant is deliberate and direct.) This in-itselfness can take two forms: existing real entities (things or persons) presenting an aspect of themselves as they are and as images; and/or formal intelligibilities, whether of images or of things and persons known to exist outside consciousness.

The evidence motivating *a judgment of existence*, on the other hand, demands more than what is captured in the ever-present distinction of whatness and consciousness. When evidence arises of a thing's having a reality in a cosmic time-space[2] that is independent of my consciousness of it, that is different from grasping a formal intelligibility, that is, some idea or concept the meaning of which I can understand. Clearly, a kind of evidence different from formal insight is required before I know whether a given idea expresses as well some existing reality (some *esse*). All existences presencing permit formal insight, without which I would not know what I am confronting, but not all formal insights imply existences. Any perceptual object invites further

---

1. I am not employing this term exactly as it is used in physics. I mean the particular focus or question within a world that can embrace a variety of such focuses.
2. I use "time-space" to denote a presencing, and the more familiar "space-time" in connection with physics. This will become critical in Chapter 6. As we shall see in Chapter 7, a presencing is always also a relation, and hence the primary emphasis is on time rather than space.

empirical observation and exploration; the image or ideal[3] object invites further reflection about the implications of its meaning.

This other-than-consciousness quality, this objectivity and in-itselfness, enables human beings to talk to one another by referring to the same things or the same ideas—and it is why they are able to learn. It is why they can improve their hold on the world to which we must conform our actions if we wish to avoid painful collisions with a resisting reality. At the same time we see that we can to some extent deform and reform these resisting real things through our work, but only to the extent the things allow by virtue of their *an sich* (in themselves) characteristics. If we run roughshod over this otherness, we experience ourselves doing violence either to their existence or to their intrinsic meaning, and ultimately to ourselves, because this ignoring of reality leads us down a treacherous path of lies.

THE PRINCIPLE OF CONTEXTUALITY

The second principle concerns the just mentioned contextuality of all things. It affirms the sense of connectedness of reality: Particular ideas and real things are always part of a larger whole, a context, within which they are involved with other things in many relations. That immediate context is in turn embraced by a still larger context, which in turn is embraced by a still larger context, until we consider the context of all contexts, the world. All this involvement, we shall see, weighs mightily against reductionistic Humean atomism. *Things and ideas, then, have both a sense in themselves and a sense in relations.* Each idea and each thing has a meaning interior to itself (there is an intrinsic sense to its own structure, which reflects its ontic coherence, a set of internal relations between its parts), and each is also part of larger structures or at least a larger setting—for example, the tree in the garden is domestic; the tree in the forest is wild—from which it derives further meaning.

Context is not an easy notion. Besides distinguishing the internal significance —the coherence of the thing (its meaning in itself)—and its meaning in context, we need to be aware that there are two sorts of context. There is the subjective context of the individual consciousness doing the knowing—every act of knowledge is that of a concrete subject who lives in a time-space situation, and so every act of knowing fits into the unfolding history of that subject. Then there is the objective context, that larger structure (like the refinery of which the cracking tower is part) or setting (like the garden in which the lawn chair is placed) of which any idea or thing is part, irrespective of who may be thinking about it or perceiving it at some moment in the given subject's life.

---

3. "Ideal" is used in this work in two different senses, both drawn from common usage. Here the term means simply pertaining to the realm of ideas, in contrast to the realm of real space-time things and relations. Later the term stands for a long-range goal, the conditions for attaining which have to be forged over a considerable time span. Obviously there is a connection: The condition for the possibility of having an ideal, in this second sense, is our ability to create ideas that transcend the limiting conditions of immediate experience.

Each subject has something unique to contribute to the interpretation of any idea or thing, because of the distinctness of his personal experience. The relevance of what he deploys is determined in part by the self-presencing of the thing, person, image, or idea, which, with its implications, brings its own objective context with it. The broader scene is what permits exploration, working from the thing or idea-centered core of the knowledge act toward the wider implications, calling on whatever the subject happens to know which may help illumine its meaning.

Within the objective context, structure and setting differ according to the relationships in which the object reveals itself to be caught up. Two examples will illustrate the point, which we take up in Chapter 4 when the challenge of Humean reductionism is addressed directly. First, the lawn chair, sitting in the garden, is in a certain spatial arrangement, the garden. It is a setting recognizable by kind, typical Toronto garden, because the things are arranged in familiar ways, the sense of which I am able to understand and recognize. It is not merely spatial; more is involved, including a certain aesthetic sense. Yet the lawn chair is not part of a structure in the tighter sense in which a chair's broken leg can be said to be a part: It is fastened onto the chair; its whole meaning is its supporting the chair. The chair itself can be stored in the garage or even given away without basically altering the inherent sense of the garden, understood as a disposition of lawns, beds, bushes, and trees. The cracking tower, on the other hand, is connected by pipes to the remainder of the refinery, of which larger structure it is an essential part, with some internal structure of its own, rather like an organ in the larger organism. More on this in Chapter 4.

THE CHOICE OF WORLDS

The third principle concerns the selection of our smaller worlds. The everyday real world of ordinary experience presents itself quite objectively as this or that concatenation of things existing in themselves (which confront us massively whether we like it or not), which are part of a vast, real whole, the cosmos. But our ways of approaching that world, the sectors of it we choose to inhabit, and our choices of where and on what we are going to lavish our attention—in other words, the ways in which we set the subjective context—are fundamentally influenced by the horizons of interpretation and the frames of reference each of us brings to the world out of our personal histories. These horizons of interpretation, formed by our natural faiths, and these frames of reference made relevant by the questions arising in a situation are in part the product of traditions in which we have been educated. Different traditions provoke very different questions and agendas.

The distinctiveness of traditions, including the role models that the institutions (spawned by the traditions) impose on us, as well as the particularities of individual temperament and the vagaries of experience, account for the pluralism of society, which is of an intersubjective, not just individual, kind. If we are to come to know the world of everyday social existence and my world (the way I interpret things), then a critical confrontation with the truth claims of distinctive traditions will be necessary. These claims are explicit and implicit in the various traditions—claims representing distinctive experiences and points of view and ways of living them out; claims, whether we are aware of this or not, about how it stands with being.

The central question is this: Are there criteria transcending the limitations of subjective points of view and particular desires by which the suitability of our actions and the truth claims made by those looking at the world from these various perspectives may be judged? As Plato would have put it, whence the *metron* by which the truth will be judged? This question is the spine of the present inquiry.

TRUTH AND FREEDOM

An important corollary of these principles has to do with our freedom. Ours is a finite freedom, conditioned by the limits we experience in ourselves of being able to notice, imagine, desire, and conceive and in other persons (who have their own perspectives and are centers of initiative) and things (which impose their demands and which can be the source of particular possibilities and of obstacles).

But there is another face to this: The exercise of our freedom affects what we can come to know. Plato and Aristotle both stressed the moral foundation of the search for truth; the virtues, not just intellectual but moral, which are necessary if we are to progress toward wisdom. Aristotle described these cardinal (that is, "hinge") virtues—prudence, courage, temperance, and justice. The foundation of a sound subjective context for the search for truth and for good action in the world is moral virtue, in which is founded the consistency of courses of action, the integrity of a human life, and without which there is no hope of being able to build up the rich body of needed experience, intelligibly connected, to pass on the wisdom of the traditions and to acquire the depth of character necessary for a well-thought-through reflection on the sense of what we have experienced.

But it is not just our interior dispositions that make intersubjective discourse possible: It is the self-presencing of the core of transcending, coherent, and stable givens, founding our ability to know (albeit partially and in profile) things and their settings as they are in themselves. This also motivates discussions bent on cooperatively improving our (social) understanding of things and how we deal with them.

This is necessary on an everyday basis to make possible our working together in ordinary situations. Also, it is the justification for the project of a society founded, not merely in pragmatic muddling through, but on a consensus growing out of a mutually supportive search for and experience of the truth. Without this realistic core of access to things and persons in themselves, the *communio* of larger societies and great traditions would be impossible. If things, situations, systems, settings, and structures did not present themselves with some degree of stable, circumscriptive (and symbolizable) intelligibility, we would get lost in the everyday struggle to survive and would falter in the search for meaning in our lives. Things and their settings manifest a certain ability to stand—*Selbst-ständigkeit*—which anchors (through its whatness), guides, and consolidates the never-ceasing processes of knowing.

The objectively given stabilities at the core of the objective context guide the deployment of the subjective context, because they indicate the larger structures (objective and subjective) that we need to seek out if we are to understand what is presenting itself. Many of the things we are considering allow us to go back to basic experience to verify what the things and the actions of people in their various settings have to tell us, to confirm our reflections and subjective reactions.

The interaction between revealed stabilities in the world and the searching, creating, imagining of subjectivity; between the stability of formal intelligibilities grasped by the mind and the restless processes of nature and the ravages of time, is the stuff of the dialectic of existential consciousness and is revealed by phenomenological reflection.

3.

THE GUIDING PRINCIPLE OF RESEARCH AND THE UNITY OF BEING

FROM A REALISTIC CIVIC THEOLOGY TO THE SUBJECTIVIST TURN: RESTORING THE SUBJECT-OBJECT BALANCE
The Realistic Foundation of Classical Philosophy

The ontologies of the classical philosophers had built in, long before the revelation to the Hebrews of creation came to join with philosophy, a certain optimism regarding the finding of truth: Being, Plato and Aristotle were convinced, is per se intelligible, and the human mind, of its very nature, enjoys insight into that intelligibility and can know things as they really are. Because the mind can attain something of the essence of things, the will should love what reveals itself, embracing "the already having been."[1]

I agree with the ancients that there are two reasons why this embrace of reality is needed: survival, conditioned on knowing what we are dealing with; and making sense of our existence in the midst of this world, so that our lives may somehow be joyously fulfilled. This is what that erotic striving (*philein*) toward the *sophon* meant to those "philosophers." Biblical revelation strengthened the sense that achieving such happiness is not so easy, pointing to that fallen nature, the ravages of our perversity, palpable evidence of which is hard to deny. Since man's revolt against God, our wills, claim the Church fathers, no longer follows intellect as well as will was meant to. Hence we need salvation from those prisons of lies we weave about ourselves. Salvation is the grace to know oneself and one's place in creation, a truth that cuts through our lies, offered by God's restoration of a loving relationship to the Source of our being which we severed by turning against it.

In reaction to the discovery of the damage our rebelliousness introduced, the religious man can all too easily slip into the position (from the Christian view, theologically unsound) that the human contribution—our creativity—is something Promethean, so the gods are jealous, and all human initiative is cast as rebellion. Christian revelation, on the contrary, claims that God's loving

---

[1] That is Aristotle's term for essence, *to ti einai estin*. Heidegger translates this as *Wesen als das Gewesene*. The already having been is consolidated independently of one's mind. It is what "stands," and so can be counted on as a guide for action. It is not an object of knowledge alone.

reaction to man's revolt was not to tie him to a rock and send an eagle to eat his liver, but Himself to take an initiative within history to restore our possibility to know the True Way to our salvation, and to cooperate in building the kingdom that is to result. This definitive incursion into history was prepared by the long, hard, and dramatic pedagogy of a Chosen People, the accumulation over millennia of a language of symbols and law that could carry the full charge of the divine revelation. The prophets' interventions were the means, culminating, "in the fullness of time," in the Incarnation. Jesus' teaching and example become the ultimate manifestation of the Truth that is God, in the form of the Way mankind is to follow, not a *theoria* but a community (*ecclesia*, Church).

How could the dissolution of the optimistic ancient and medieval civil theologies and the loss of the sense of searching together positively for the meaning of it all, which prevailed from the time of Athens' glory through the whole life of the Church, be so sweeping as it has become in modernity? That is a long and important story, which Etienne Gilson and I have detailed elsewhere.[2] My concern here is not so much how it happened, but how to right the resulting damage to the pursuit of truth in our time.

From the subjectivist turn with Descartes, seeking an absolute foundation for truth, through to the transcendental turn achieved by Kant, seeking to grasp consciousness' production of truth, the challenge has been to restore a balance that was destroyed: the proper balance in our understanding of what the knowing, acting subject brings to the constitution of the object, and what the object in its otherness contributes. If that can be achieved, then the quest for truth is not inevitably dissolved into skeptical historical relativism.

To be sure, our understanding of things progresses, and things themselves change. But the process of understanding is guided by the knower's respect for what gives itself, for the successive revelation of aspects of reality itself, some more stable than others. Many of these aspects may remain stable for long periods (our planet, for instance); others, abstracted through insight into inherent intelligibility, rise above time and space altogether, providing insight into many later and different experiences (for example, the concept planet as such). Principles of being itself and of all knowledge, valid transcendentally, are discovered, as we shall see (for example, every existence is of a certain kind: Existence and essence have to be considered together).

I shall examine in a moment the commonsense belief (shared by most scientists) in the unity of being, which also militates against relativism. In seeking the truth, we want to know how it stands with the one cosmos we inhabit, in which even the most changing things seem to have a relevance to the other things and to be instantiations of principles expressive of constant, overriding conditions. A sense of the unity of being motivates us not only to respect all genuine experiences but to see what light they throw on one another. If it is true that science assumes the unity of being, the same haunting

2. See Etienne Gilson and Thomas Langan, *Modern Philosophy: From Descartes to Kant* (New York: Random House, 1963).

question returns: Why have will and power, which seem to sow disunity and destruction, become so central in the thinking of our society?

Will in Descartes' philosophy (where it is viewed as the structureless abyss), as in Kant's, is destructive if it fails to submit to the discipline imposed by the form-deploying activity of transcendental consciousness. Yet the Occidental belief in transcendental consciousness as God working in us weakened: Descartes was fairly firm in this, but Kant reduced God to a practical consideration, greatly lowering the sense of objective foundation in God, whereas Hegel's Absolute Spirit was so ambiguous, so easy to confuse with our own consciousness and will, that it opened the way, as Kierkegaard grasped, to the excesses of Feuerbach, Marx, and Nietzsche. Will as a push of nature, as the source of raw energy, so to speak, little tempered by any sense of an objective, opposing reality, became central. Will, divorced from tender concern for the good of the other as other, is not love but brute power. Heretofore, in the Christian understanding, faith, as confident reception of knowledge of the other; hope, as the forward surge to fulfillment of that life within us; and love, the life force that fructifies and brings to fulfillment the already having been, are inseparable, and love was known to be the form of all the other virtues.

With Feuerbach, Schopenhauer, Marx, Spencer, and Nietzsche, the primordiality of will and praxis, understood as power, become the source of all meaning.[3] The inherent formlessness of the primordial power became an invitation to the social deployment of power to reshape mankind arbitrarily. From this came the vast, totalitarian, gnostic misadventures—the Leninism and the Hitlerism—of the past hundred years.[4]

For my part, I accept the existentialist belief that action, with will at its center, surrounded by the penumbra of uncriticized, dark life forces, is being working itself out through us. But I also believe the effort to guide this life force by the light of intelligence is part of what Being *(Sein)* has revealed as what is meant to be. Our consciousness' hold on reality—on the already having been as source of genuine possibility—reflects an essential aspect of the summit of the development and complexificaton achieved by the evolving life force itself. As a Christian, I even believe—as do Jews and Muslims, too—that the Source of this evolutive impulse *meant* for created being to develop this way. I show in Part III why I believe this. My point in mentioning it here is to explain why I take the creativity of will seriously, but do not consider it the only aspect of the evolutive principle that has to be taken into account. For me the whole program is an affair of life-producing intelligent will seeking a truth larger than

---

3. In the case of Marx, the objectified laws of history, rooted in the process of class conflict, are so determined as to make difficult the entry of individual human spiritual creativity, crushed as it is under the abstraction of collective will. This long development is detailed in Gilson and Langan, *Modern Philosophy,* and in Etienne Gilson, Thomas Langan, and Armand Maurer, *Recent Philosophy: Hegel to the Present* (New York: Random House, 1966).

4. An excellent introduction to this subject is to be found in Eric Voegelin, *The New Science of Politics* (Chicago: University of Chicago Press, 1952).

anything my will itself can produce, set in a context of seeking to grasp being as a whole, which is certainly not a product of my will or our collective wills.

THE RECOVERY OF THE SENSE OF THE UNITY OF BEING
With the Death of God the Sense of the Unity of Being Need Not Disappear

We must ask ourselves soberly what is the incentive to search, not just for pragmatic solutions to local problems, but for the wider meaning and experiential ground of our personal and social existence, for the ultimate goals toward which we should be directing our own lives and how we should together be developing society? How are we brought to divert scarce psychic energy from the pursuit of solutions to pressing practical problems, to seek instead to answer the question of the sense of it all, the question of the truth as wisdom about reality itself?

Although some 95 percent of Canadians said in the 1981 census that they believe in God,[5] there is no lack of reflective individuals in this society who doubt seriously that the world is creatively endowed with meaning and intelligibility that can guide us. Yet even atheists and astrophysicists alike seem to continue to assume that being is somehow one and, despite Kant's *Critique of Pure Reason*, to believe in the cosmos as an objective whole, not dependent on mind for its unity. That seems to imply that there exists an all-englobing objective context within which our destinies are played out.

I would suppose that most people do not worry too much how, from a limited perspective within time-space, we finite intelligences can somehow transcend the whole and conceive of a thought-embracing cosmos as a totality. They just go on believing that all things, from galactic to atomic scales, are relevant to our understanding of the whole; at the same time, they are suspicious—not without justification—of those who would too quickly press forward with a theory of being in which everything finds a cozy place.

But just what evidence is there for the supposed unity of being, and is that unity in any sense objectively grounded? Bearing in mind the natural tendency of the mind to close a gestalt, as the psychologists long ago showed,[6] we should be alert to the natural tendency to ideology, the building of a closed system of explanation to handle the grand view, and so we should be critically alert to the dangers of achieving a *factice* unified view of being. Furthermore, knowing that how we conceive of the unity of being will have a strong motivating and guiding influence on our search for wisdom, and indeed even on our daily

---

5. See *Statistics,* Canada's summary report on the 1981 census (Ottawa: Queen's Printer for Canada, 1981–1982).

6. Hans Urs von Balthasar warns that the psychologists of the Köhler school subjectivized and thus deformed the pioneering insights of Ehrenfels, who described the objective gestalten of real things. See *Herrlichkeit: Eine theologische Ästhetik,* vol. 3, *In Raum der Metaphysik,* pt. 1, *Altertum* (Einsiedeln: Johannes Verlag, 1967), 51.

agenda, I am going to be cautious about what I assert to be its form and what I take as evidence for it.

THE UNITY OF BEING
Are There Experiential Grounds for Asserting the Unity of Being?

Imagine for a moment that one approaches the truth question from an atheistic standpoint, with hostility to the idea of a preexisting Source from which the world springs, knowing itself and willing the world into existence. One's starting point would be a natural-faith belief that a finite cosmos is the ultimate reality. In the beginning an intense burst of energy somehow began to complexify and, over billions of years, as the result of an unimaginable number of permutations and combinations, to reach a degree of organization sufficient to support an interior life, culminating in the development of a higher animal capable of reflection. After a half million years of evolution, *Homo sapiens* finds itself in a situation that gives rise to the truth question: From where we stand, can we affirm that there is a single order of things, an ultimate context that we can somehow discern sufficiently so that it should serve as an (important) guide to our actions? And if so, how vital is it to us to make explicit our knowledge of it, and why?

The question is not about the subjective unity of a world of consciousness but about the objective unity of a cosmos that does not depend on consciousness, of which, on the contrary, my consciousness is only a part, and which consciousness must come to know. In a subjective sense, the world is, we admit, one: There is (for me) one transcendental subjective context; whatever is (for me) is, so far as it is (for me), in my consciousness; all the things I know and ever can know get (at least) referred to one another by being moments in the one world of a given consciousness.

But within my world of consciousness I am at once aware of evidence of more objective kinds of unity than that provided by consciousness itself, which depends on subjectivity's acts of referring. For instance, the more we learn about life on this planet, the more the various life-forms throw light on one another as stages within understandable distinctions of phyla, the more the myriads of species are seen to relate in one great process of becoming. And our planetary system is now known to be, rather than qualitatively different from the heavens, part of a larger stellar system we call our galaxy, which in turn relates to billions of other galaxies within one expanding system we call the universe. All parts of that universe, at all scales of consideration, seem relevant for understanding each other,[7] although the system is enormous, measured inferentially to be many billion light-years in breadth, and dynamic, expanding

---

7. See the physicist David Bohm's excellent discussion of "relevance" in *Wholeness and the Implicate Order* (London: Routledge, 1980), 33–36.

at nearly the speed of light.[8] In a recent article, "Particle Accelerators Test Cosmological Theory," David Schramm and Gary Steigman show how science has rejoined at the extreme limits of scale, particle physics now for the first time being used to examine the theories of cosmic becoming developed heretofore purely theoretically by cosmologists.[9]

All the evidence of an ontogenetic history, source of a certain unity of the cosmos through parentage, suggests the reasonableness of one's attempting to understand his situation in a natural, cosmic context. After pausing for a moment to consider how we form such a conception as the cosmos, I shall explain why it is important to our thinking about our human situation, even though I admit that little thought of the cosmos seems to impinge on our everyday commonsense dealings with things and with one another. (A paradox, an enigma of perspective and scale itself demanding reflection.)

How Are We Able to Form a Concept of the Cosmos?

The very fact that we can encompass the cosmos with our minds in forming a concept of it tells us something about the unique kind of thing this intelligent animal is. Grant the Kantians that it is the transcendental unity of consciousness that suggests the totality of the cosmos. Being a whole of which we are but part, the real totality cannot be experienced by us as a whole, but we can project the idea of it by hypostatically extending the unity of consciousness itself to embrace by anticipation anything and everything we may encounter. And grant further that belief in creation, accepted from revelation by most during the longest time in our tradition, reinforces the tendency to conceive of the universe as a whole even though we cannot actually so experience it. Both of these considerations—projection of world from consciousness and religious belief in the unitary origin of the world—could throw us off the trail. Nevertheless, the point is this: Neither militates against the fact that empirical researches into nature keep confirming all the kinds of objective relevance at all scales. The more closely we examine things, the more of this relevance we find in the details that mind could never produce but only discover. Every such discovery "deep down things" renders more plausible, and gives incentive to believe in and to continue to search for some sense of, a cosmic whole.

In their detailed content, the things of nature go far beyond the formalities envisioned by the Kantian categories. Kant himself acknowledges this; that is why he insists so much on the need for empirical experience. It would be preposterous to propose that the mind's organizing categories had anything essential to do with the fact that the forces known to hold together the particles

---

8. The exact size and age are still much disputed. The latest theory recoils from 14 billion years to 9, which is causing consternation as some stars seem to be 12 billion years old. My science adviser, the late Dr. Michel Vaillant, warned me in his letter of January 1, 1991, against naming any figure at this time.
9. In *Scientific American*, special issue (1991), 62–71.

in the atom's nucleus are somehow related to the force of gravity holding the planets in orbit around the sun, even if we cannot yet reduce them theoretically to one adequate explanation, illumining of all forces.[10] Or take another example: The molecules found in a certain clump of earth can be the same kind of molecules found diffused to 5 per cubic centimeter in outer space. Or background noise picked up in a radio telescope, and interpreted as evidence of the initial cosmic explosion, is interpretable roughly in the way we understand radio waves emitted deliberately by an FM transmitter.

Evidence piled on evidence keeps confirming our belief that being is somehow one. It does not and cannot establish that absolutely everything, whether of the material, psychological, or spiritual order, is ultimately relevant, that all belongs to one realm of being. But as all efforts to increase our explicit understanding of interconnectedness always bear fruit, we are constantly encouraged in our belief and motivated to keep up the quest for a unified wisdom. At the risk of being tedious, I want to point out that this does not constitute a demonstration or proof of the unity of Being.

If one could prove the existence of God, showing definitively that such a Source objectively grounds the unity of all being, one would then be intellectually obliged to make the unity of being a prime principle of all his thinking. As we shall see in Chapter 8, proving the existence of God in such an unequivocally definitive and compelling way is not a straightforward matter. Of course, for a saint, like Mother Teresa of Calcutta, whose existence is centered on the experience of a life in God, through the supernatural virtues of faith, hope, and love, what is the issue? But I am writing not for Mother Teresa, who would consider this book a waste of time, but for jaded post-modernists, spiritual counterparts of the abandoned of the streets of Calcutta!

Our Understanding within the Natural, Cosmic Context

Why is this question of the unity of being so important? Look at the negative side of the issue: In seeking harmonious existence in the midst of the cacophony of pluralistic society, one is easily tempted to hammer together an overview, a Weltanschauung, or at least to let a homemade ideology develop, to provide guidance. But if an individual is going to divert much energy to searching prudently for one wisdom, he must first believe that such a wisdom makes sense, because being itself has a unity. After all, such searching entails working at the immensely difficult task of translating the most disparate truths from different kinds of traditions and different areas of daily experience so they

---

10. Great efforts are today being expended to unite, in one explanatory theory, the four fundamental forces of physics—gravitation, electromagnetic interaction, the strong (in-nucleus) nuclear force, and the weak (electron beta emission) nuclear force. A unified field theory covering the electromagnetic and the weak forces is in reasonably good shape in terms of progress on experimental confirmation; one including the strong force has been advanced as theory, but awaits significant confirmatory experimentation. For a recent report, see Stephen Weinberg, *Dreams of a Final Theory* (New York: Pantheon, 1992).

throw light on one another. Who cares about Muslim Sufi mystics or, for that matter, the latest wild theories of astrophysics, when all energy should be poured into success at my job, and I have enough trouble just raising my children? Why must we be careful, if we do start trying to translate, not to reduce inadvertently the sense of one kind of experience to that of another, just because we already possess philosophical categories[11] derived from another kind of experience and we naturally seek to understand everything in those terms? Why is it so important to recognize the distinctiveness of different kinds of experience?[12] Why is it not enough to find a *modus vivendi* within our own little communities, without getting involved in the implied catholicity of a search for The Truth?

On the pedagogical level the greatest obstacle to starting to think responsibly about what one stands for and what life is about and how this relates to the serious truth claims of traditions foreign to one is possession of a too satisfying ideology. Many of my vaguely humanist students have worked out a voluntaristic ideology of the individual's pursuit of happiness so long as you do not hurt anyone else, with an underlying materialism justifying a self-indulgent hedonism. Among those of my Christian students who are serious about their responsibility before God, many come to the university with a natural faith built around a catechism core of well-ordered concepts, which provides the appearance of an answer to all the deep questions the philosopher might raise. Now, it is not too difficult to destroy the students' faith in what they have learned in catechism class, leaving them with nothing to guide their lives, throwing them into despair. (It is more difficult to shake libertarian and hedonistic convictions.) But most difficult of all is to lead them to begin looking into the experiential roots of what their rich tradition can furnish, the mysteries caught in the symbols they have been taught but have barely begun to appropriate personally. One cannot proceed far in any responsible appropriation of the traditions that have formed him and his situation without having to confront the question of context. That raises the issue of the unity of being in an unavoidable way. Allow me to explain.

The Concentric Circles of Situations

Commonsensically, the most elementary project of rationality imposes an effort *to understand one's situation*. The more one knows of the concrete possibilities, the clearer he will become about what is desirable and sustainable, and why—and so he sets more adequate goals, more in keeping with what the situation as a whole calls for.

---

11. See Glossary.
12. *T&A* discusses at length the distinctive kinds of truth characterizing the four genera of tradition. In Chapter 4, I inventory a variety of objects, seeking to illumine the different experiences in the midst of which they presence, and then raise problems of translating and integrating them in a single wisdom.

So, what is involved in knowing one's situation? One's personal situation forms part of ever-larger settings—family, local, provincial, national, continental, cultural, civilizational (for we are molded by our Occidental Hebraic-Greco-Roman-Christian-Enlightenment-technological civilization, with its many subcultures, producing a vast variety of institutions and ordering the landscape broadly with cities and industrial complexes and superhighways). Finally there is the "oecumenopolitan" situation, as C. Doxiades termed it, where we witness the emergence of a planetary network of institutions running roughshod over every old culture, and which are being penetrated by the world system (analyzed in *Tradition and Authenticity*).

One can think of the situation, then, as concentric circles, reaching out ever farther from the subjective, personal center. (There is no sharp line; only horizons separate the various scales.) When I consider that I am in a social situation, I must accept that two or more subjective contexts enfold the same objective setting, and that distinctive courses of action exist in the same social situation[13]—my wife may want to expand the garden we are both contemplating, but I may be letting it go to ruin. All this I have to take into consideration when I decide to act.

The same and different objective things may exist in our distinctive worlds, and our worlds meet in at least some real settings, and I meet all human actors at the very least on the large planetary scene. (We experience this fact, for instance, as regards the global environment; what each person does affects the well-being of the planet.) It is a long task to show phenomenologically how all these smaller worlds are interstitched with the various real processes and spatial relationships, some of which we know and of some we are scarcely aware. Yet all have their impact, perhaps as yet largely unperceived, on the largest, planetary setting.[14]

Each situation is formed of a network of relationships enjoying a certain intelligibility, to the degree that they show some consistency. There are usually also accidental elements that have only space-time coincidence with the more interacting factors—the table sitting in my garden is not part of the essential intelligibility of the network of relationships that constitutes the setting that is the garden—the persisting relationships themselves providing at least a temporary framework, the formal intelligibility of which can even be abstracted. (We can talk meaningfully, for instance, of the structure of George's family: father with second wife, who has difficult relationships [because of certain subjective attitudes] with the son and the daughter from the first marriage. We can name a phenomenon like that, perhaps calling it the bad stepmother syndrome.)

---

13. An objective setting is a real disposition of objects in material, cosmic time-space—for example, the road system, utility lines, and buildings in a city; they would still be here tomorrow if everyone died in a bioplasm of some sort. A situation, on the other hand, is the personal (or intersubjective) living together of subjects, at different scales, from the personal and familiar, to the national and civilizational.

14. When a consciousness grasps the sense of some setting, that knowledge becomes part of the *context* within which the particular things are known.

When we talk of understanding matters "within a situation," are we referring to subjective or objective context? One's situation obviously embraces both subjective and objective elements. The individual's interpretative horizons and the interaction of many individuals' outlooks and attitudes bring a large subjective component to any situation. But at the same time our perceptions take place in an objective, real setting, furnished with real objects—things and persons—enjoying real relations between themselves (for example, the flower pot is on the table, which is in the garden, where sit mother and son), in a time-space with dimensions other than the imaginary.

Each such situational setting is in turn a part of a larger one, from which it derives some of its meaning. It does so to the extent that factors in the more local situation are related to the flow of events (providing an objective foundation of before and after, experienced as time) and are caught up in spatial relationships, and are related to social attitudes, the well-inculturated institutions and all the processes, objective and subjective, at work on the larger scene.

The intelligibility (literally our ability to read into each setting and each situation its sense) derives both from its own internal sense and from its external sense, place as part of the larger situation(s)—its outward relations, so to speak. The internal sense is made up, in the case of settings, of the relationships between the things and the network of interrelating processes objectively within it, and in the case of situations, of the relationships between concepts, attitudes, actions, and things. The larger structure that always englobes any given setting or situation forms in regard to the smaller structure a kind of concrete universal, giving some sense to it, as the larger structure always does to all its parts.

While the greater part of the most pressing needs daily arise from the most immediate situation, wisdom demands that one recognize how factors brewing in remote corners of the largest setting can come crashing fatally into my little local world. An image from a Russian B-movie comes to mind: a young family playing in a rolling Ukrainian meadow, when suddenly, without warning, a Wehrmacht tank careens over the hill, cannon ablaze. War has crashed unexpectedly into their peaceful world.

Even the predictable end of the planet is relevant to the ultimate sense of my projects. Teilhard de Chardin suggests that if mankind really believed that all its strivings were doomed to utter and unredeemable extinction, "l'humanité fera grève," humanity would go on strike.

ECOLOGICAL AND PSYCHOLOGICAL AWARENESS AS A SOURCE OF THE SENSE OF THE UNITY OF BEING

The recent growth of ecological awareness is bringing many to realize that we must assure the survival of the fragile natural substructure supporting life. Psychological awareness is bringing us also to recognize the fragility, complexity, and mystery of the life of the soul. As we contemplate both dimensions, we begin to realize that the roots of our own personal being, which spring from the ontic structures of natural reality and the ontic and ontological structures of cultural reality, mold and influence our lives much more than we, the active, willful center, might care to believe. We like to imagine that we are in control of ourselves and our surroundings. The sad truth is, as Saint Paul reminds us (Rom. 7:15), we really do not understand ourselves very well, and this ignorance is crucial in the central issue of how our freedom works. (Which is exactly what Paul was worried about in that context; rather long before Sigmund Freud.)

It is obvious that our initiative is exercisable only within given but somewhat elastic limits. In the midst of the dialectic between the imaginative leaps of creativity, the impulses of the libido, the more or less lucid direction coming from various forms of awareness, and the impact of brute physical fact, the extent of our free self-direction remains a murky business.

The inner confusions we get ourselves into and all forms of social conflict suggest the wisdom of hanging on resolutely, as a guide for action, to any objectivity we may be able to attain, and at every situational scale, even the cosmic. It is at the large social (more than the cosmic) scale that we so easily slip into ideology, as we attempt to manipulate wide abstractions to deal with overwhelmingly huge and complex practical-political realities. At smaller scales, we tend to work out habitual, familiar *modi operandi* that function pretty well in harmony with those around us, who have to be enculturated to fairly similar views, but collisions of desires at the intimate personal level can become explosive. At both scales, mindlessness is the enemy of wisdom. The largest horizons of our natural faith can be formed more by default than through critical examination of evidence. Small-scale mindlessness is called running with the pack; and large scale, ideological commitment.[15] So it is vital, as we move out toward the ecological issues of the well-being of the planet, and down into the depths of the soul, to the vital impulses of life, that we learn how to discover and balance those fundamental realities that give rise to thoughts of being itself.

DO NOT THE LIMITS OF CONSCIOUSNESS RENDER VOLUNTARISM PLAUSIBLE?

In recognizing how limited is our knowledge of and control over our situation, I acknowledge that though much evidence points toward the unity of intracosmic being, we cannot experience the cosmos as a whole, and admit that indeed we have little grip on many factors in much more modest contexts. All this might appear to open the way to despairing of wisdom, suggesting instead the inevitability of an irreducible pluralism between human agents that only barely masks an underlying voluntarism (it is not truth that moves me but impulse. I do what I want, and there the issue rests).

---

15. The phenomenology of "everyday averageness" provided by Heidegger in *Sein und Zeit* (Tübingen: Neomarius Verlag, 1957) and by Max Scheler in *Ressentiment* (New York: Free Press of Glencoe, 1961) is relevant here.

The Voluntarist Objection

I want to try to turn this around to bring out the urgency of searching for that ultimate unity of truth, which we have been considering, while neglecting no fundamental dimension of being.

Objection: If I have no evidence for anything higher than my own creative will, if there is nothing to show me the way, or to impose an order on me definitively, no authority in heaven or on earth, why may I not respond simply to the spontaneous urgings of nature? In this way, I forge a situation of fact. I mold reality to some extent to my desires, which is acceptable if they are a kind of revelation of what nature, "the higher reason," intends of me. This implies that over against vague suppositions about the larger sense of things, I should admit the imperative facts that are my feelings enjoy a large place. Am I not free to choose my own destiny, even if it hastens my death? Is that power to choose not the source of the ultimate truly meaningful context for me, the origin of Me?

The implication of such a voluntarist position is that truth is local and partly creative, that it turns away from an illusive totality. To be sure, certain data may be imperative for the moment, ignored at my risk, but not the final interpretation.

Hanging in the background of the search for unified, overall meaning is an old question: Without belief in God, can the unity of being be founded, indeed can the objectivity of a known order be established, a realm of truth yielding knowledge of principle to which one should acknowledge serious beholdenness, and which can serve as guide to the individual's action and ground of a unified, peaceful, and free society?

The Kantian Response and the Question of the Objectivity of Our Knowledge

This need for some foundation for a unity of view preoccupied Immanuel Kant. He feared that metaphysics was built on the shaky ground of an importation of a religious belief into philosophy. Still he knew the challenge of voluntaristic skepticism should be met. He does it by founding a formal ethics on the inherent demands of mind. A doctrine of justice is based in a claim to unity of truth founded, like all of Kantian ethics, on the a priori source of unity in the transcendental consciousness, not on any state of affairs existing independently of mind. The principle of objectivity is founded in the subjectivity of the transcendental ego.

But does such a transcendental idealism really answer our dilemma? Even the resolute voluntarist has trouble ignoring the need for a certain consistency in our action, not a merely formal consideration, but a very hard-nosed factual one. Unless he is prepared to embrace a mad irrationalism, he will see that it is foolish to be pursuing courses of action that cancel each other out, or that will not help him reach the goals he has set for himself. Some distinction must be found for separating feasible from infeasible, even mad, goals. Our ends obviously have to be consonant with reality.

The question remains: By what criterion do we establish the specific course of action that we ought to follow in our lives? As our impulses are anything but consistent, we cannot escape the need to choose among them, when they send us conflicting signals. How large a context ought we, in the name of prudence and the hope of ultimate success, consult?

Where the question of consistency is raised, can the question of the foundation of consistency in an underlying unity of discourse and of being be far away? As we follow the lines of implication out from the narrowest course of action toward the ever-larger contexts our gaze discovers, where is the logical stopping point, short of all that can be known?

THE NEED FOR A GROUND IN OBJECTIVE EXPERIENCE

So, having come full circle, back to the question of unity, I shall sum up what we have seen in this tentative probing of the question of setting, situation, and the unity of being as they are relevant to action. The truth question is a question about the ground for the unity of discourse, understood as guide for action, personal and social. It is a question bound up with the issue of freedom, because it asks why and how we should acknowledge certain expressions as

1. the same, recognized, or at least recognizable, by all;
2. objectively true—that is, as enunciating a state of affairs (*Sachverhalt*) that is the same for you as for me; and
3. binding—that is, as something to the reality of which I ought, if I am being reasonable, conform my action (or, if you prefer, *good*, it being affirmed that the real is what I ought to desire).[16]

In claims about our relationships with things, with one another, and with the various scales of situation in the world, we ask how our interpretations and our initiatives fit realistically into the larger, given settings, structures, and systems of the various scales of situation.

The Interpenetration of Theory and Practice

The relationship of ontology, epistemology, and ethics is important, not just because of the need to found ethical principles, or because bad character obviously blocks the pursuit of truth, but because *being and truth are not merely theoretical*. In the course of a human life, pragmatic truth exists before theoretical truth, just as it did in the development of mankind. Saint Thomas holds that, in God, truth is not a theoretical ideal representation but *esse*, sheer existence,

---

16. I am aware of the apparent circularity here. A certain notion of rationality as a necessary good is surfacing, but I am not attempting to defend the principle. Some presupposition of some kind of rationality is obviously built in to the natural faith underlying any project of philosophy.

which we might feebly represent in human terms as knowledgeful will. That is why Christian revelation places love before faith,[17] but then understands them, with hope, to interpenetrate. God is love, declares Saint John, but He is a love that as creative origin founds all intelligibility.

This does not denigrate the theoretical in human affairs. True science is, with true love, the closest man comes to imitating God. More practically: True love is informed by knowledge of its object, and true science, as Aristotle so clearly teaches, is grounded in moral virtue, is a *philein*. Heidegger cites the need to counterwill the voluntarism that is the enemy of truth. The purest contemplation is a willed activity demanding great discipline, arrived at only after long training, and is usually found in a special social context of loving community support.

This Interpenetration Indicates the Unity of Being

This interpenetration of theory and practice in our experience is but another reflection of the unity of being. Everything in our experience points to it, despite the pluralistic impression the myriads of distinctive kinds of things make on us. We find the most disparate things all caught up in webs of causality and of meaning. All our dealings with them unfold networks of relationship, systems within systems, intelligibility and consistency everywhere we probe.

To be sure, the very richness of being has it that the wider we cast our net in the quest for an understanding of its unity, the greater the variety of fish we catch. The search for unity should be restrained from inspiring any form of reductionism.

Our research moves, then, in two directions at once: toward discovery of ever-greater varieties of natural species, of cultures, of whole levels of being, from the sub-subatomic, to the transgalactic; and toward unity, as more and more connections between all these things and levels of being are revealed as much in our practical dealings with them as in our contemplation. The richer our experience, the more confirming of our faith in being's unity.

■ ■ ■

The approach taken in the next chapter at first directs our attention away from unity and toward variety, for it is constructed in full recognition of the desirability of avoiding reductionism. There a variety of kinds of objects we commonly know and deal with are described, emphasizing the distinctive kinds of evidence they present. No exhaustive catalog of types is intended, for I possess no magic key permitting a transcendental deduction of categories. I cannot pretend to survey every possible kind of experience.

Despite an avowed pluralism in departure, we shall be brought back—never fear—to the need to search for a ground of unity. But we shall be better prepared to understand where and how in the various kinds of evidence this is to be

---

17. According to Saint Paul, "the greatest of these is charity" (1 Cor. 13:13).

sought. I shall not be shy about following lines of implication and causation wherever they lead, letting larger structures emerge from the evidence. But I have no interest in imposing a metaphysics here; rather, I want a metaphysics to reveal its outlines in reality. An impossible dream?

PART II.

THE KNOWLEDGE OF BEING

4.

KINDS OF OBJECTS, KINDS OF TRUTH

AVOIDING THE PHILOSOPHER'S CAPITAL SIN: REDUCTIONISM

What Etienne Gilson has shown about the history of ontology[1] is true of the history of concepts of truth: Philosophers have latched onto parts of reality and made them models for understanding the whole, with distorting results. In seeking to relate the various dimensions of truth, while the knower is always one and the same living subject, he has access to quite different kinds of objects, to which he relates in distinctive ways. The tree I see in my garden is a very different kind of entity from the South Seas vacation I am imagining.

Acknowledging the pluralism of our situation and with a tip of the hat to the deconstructionists, I want to avoid reductionism, driven by some hidden agenda. Gilson is right: One of these kinds of knowledge should not be made a criterion in terms of which all the other kinds of object, truth, and reality are to be appreciated. *The unity required by wisdom shall not be attained on the cheap.*

Consequently, the philosopher's task is to assemble from all he has experienced of every kind of object and relationship between objects (including significant events in history) a consistent view of being, discarding none just because abrasive to his desires. A completely unified wisdom may remain a "Kantian ideal," but in no event should it be achieved prematurely through reductionism.

Still, as we build up such a wisdom over a lifetime, we are always guided by whatever Weltanschauung has been molded in our natural faith. This overview, often in a bizarre tension with pressing everyday needs, plays an especially big role in our basic decisions ("fundamental projects," as Heidegger calls them). These life-orientations influence the choice of situations in which we place ourselves, and hence the cultural needs that will press in on me. Our largest conclusions tend to close us off to experiences difficult to accommodate to the worldview they construct—we have firmly made up our minds. In struggling against this human tendency, critical appropriators must develop a *set of habits*, a functioning part of our natural faith: Together they put into practice an attitude of allowing all genuine experience to carry its weight in the synthesis of wisdom. Required are three virtues: genuine *receptivity*, a generous openness

---

1. Etienne GilSon, *The Unity of Philosophical Experience* (New York: Scribner's, 1948), and *Being and Some Philosophers*, 2d ed. (Toronto: Pontifical Institute of Mediaeval Studies, 1952).

to all that is; *courage* to change; and intellectual *prudence*, the ability to find the proper scale within which to interpret each phenomenon and integrate it correctly into the evolving larger picture. That demands sensitivity to the degree of certitude the evidence allows.

As truth is one of the transcendental[2] predicates of being, it is necessarily predicated *analogously*. We can experience the same thing in different kinds of time-space, yielding truths of many degrees of probability and usefulness, and yet we are still able to recognize it as the same thing. This variety is reason enough why we should be in no hurry to think we have grasped definitively *the* ultimate unifying factor of reality. In Chapter 10, I show that there are several ultimate dimensions of being which must be brought into proper relation. Thinking proves daunting, to say the least.

The great pluralism in experience does not, however, present chaos. *Au contraire*, one thing leads to another, and this ad infinitum. This very fact, however, that we open onto an interconnected series of settings and systems—and this from the perspective of the different focuses of particular subjective and intersubjective worlds, with their various contexts dictated by our interests—makes it difficult to describe. For our language is abstractive, tending to build around things, concepts, and ideas of systems and settings, and constrained by discourse: Our descriptions of many things that simultaneously interpenetrate have to be spread out in time and space. The exigencies of practical life demand decision; we are pressed to base these most often on narrow selections of data. Our descriptions then jump from things through concepts to other concepts and back to particulars, usually in rather tight feedback loops. I illustrate this later by describing some typical experiences of the world, and then develop these descriptions while trying not to forget either particular or general, either natural or cultural, either subjective or objective world.

The Plurality and Kinds of Objects, and Approaches to the Same Object

Because of the things' own inherent coherence, the mind may concentrate on a particular thing in its self-standing, abstracting it from its setting. We thus consider things without the web of real relations that they have in systems. This abstractive concentration achieves *a gain of intelligibility*, as the experienced things are connected with others through the network of abstract concepts, but also results in a (temporary) *loss of intelligibility:* Nothing in reality stands alone, and the web of real relationships in which each thing is concretely caught up in its setting and systematic interactions with other things is part of its reality. The concept emphasizes only a select set of relationships.

No matter how general the resulting concept, no matter how many levels of abstraction from abstractions may be involved, the implications of every idea

---

2. Transcendent because it goes beyond all things, and even beyond the differences between things. In other words, a predicate that may be said of all things.

remain.[3] *The possibility of dwelling for a while with each thing and the concept of each sort of thing exists because different moments of our experience actually do offer some sense in themselves—they show forth their own intelligibility, rooted in the actual constitution of the things themselves.*

The following, then, require careful distinguishing:

1. the internal sense of things—their inherent stability as *this thing;*
2. their external sense in the larger whole—their intelligibility as members of a class, and the class of ever-higher genera (*species and genus*);
3. their intelligibility in a *real setting* in the world (this tree in my garden, in North Toronto);
4. their intelligibility in *real systems* of which they constitute an element or a moment (this tree draws nourishment from this soil, and so on); and finally,
5. what the mind may do imaginatively with different combinations of given intelligibilities it abstracts and reconstructs (fantasy, creative imagination).

In the case of the great conceptual structures and imaginative fantasies the mind builds for itself and into which attention (especially of intellectuals and artists) is absorbed, getting back to the real things and settings and systems that initially fed them can be complicated. That is because of the different kinds of knowledge, but also because we introduce imaginative distortions driven by desires other than the libido of knowing the truth. Confusion between types of knowledge and between knowledge and desire is the enemy of the scientific spirit.

If there is some sort of unity to being, then wisdom demands a critical understanding of the ways all possible frames of reference, founded in different kinds of desire to know, fit with one another, through various levels of abstraction. Such an investigation, I would hope, would return us ultimately to the real world from which our knowledge first derives and toward which it transcends. The peculiar rich presence of that real world to the cognitive center alone allows us ultimately to distinguish the real from the imaginary, and the already-having-been (the essence) from the not-yet (the future, the projectively sought after); and among the not-yet the "never can be" of unhealthy unfulfillable desire from the "perhaps can be" of good ideals.

The Importance of Relations

Even before I begin, *relation* is emerging as central. This is inevitable, given the finite mind that does not—as the divine Mind does—generate its own Word from itself but must find the stuff of its word given in a transcending

---

3. This allows them all potentially to be reconnected to the contexts in which they arose or to new contexts with which they fit somehow meaningfully. Similarly, we can at any moment return our regard to the experienced thing presencing perceptually in its setting, and collect new evidence of many forms of its connectedness that we have chosen to ignore or for some reason just did not notice.

reality. But it is not just our knowledge that is relational. The things themselves (including, of course, our own bodies) because they, too, are finite, and hence do not provide their own conditions, are caught up in webs of causality and other real relations, the basis of further networks of implication between abstract concepts. Only because real relations between things are visible to us and recognizable as such do we have a base for discovering the distinction between such real relations and those constructed imaginatively by the mind. The full anti-Humean implications of these declarations guide the descriptions that follow.

The Program of Research

These brief remarks show the way forward. I now sketch the program in its grand lines. By starting this epistemological survey with what objects reveal of themselves, we implicitly acknowledge that such *discovery* of relations is fundamental to ontological investigation. After we complete our *tour d'horizon* of the knower's powers of experiencing, with attention to the different kinds of objects revealed by these various kinds of experience, I describe, in Part III, the ontology, more completely the structures of being and the nature and ground of the real relations they reveal as we explore its various realms. Beginning with the question of a fundament, and asking in what sense we might find one aspect of it in the nature of the physical cosmos, we pass to the interior life of the human spirit, seeking evidence for another aspect of fundament, in the Source of all being as it is revealed to spirit and unfolds as culture and history. (It is there that we develop more fully a notion of *Sein* and relate it to the *esse* of things and real relations.) Employing as a key the relation of the distinctive frames of reference applied to that central entity, man, we propose an understanding of how these different fundamental dimensions fit together. Then, in Part IV, with the help of these open explorations of kinds of truth and realms of being, I finish with a suggestion of how the various dimensions of reality and culture relate ultimately, how they are situated within being, drawing consequences for the further pursuit of wisdom.

A note of caution about presuppositions: My deliberate refusal to spell out at the start a set of hard and fast categories does not imply that there are no categories at work in these phenomenological descriptions. Rather, I am in no rush to *systematize* these, with all the dangers that entails of ideological closing. I make no pretense at any time of possessing a principle from which to proceed to a transcendental deduction of all the categories discovered in the course of reflecting on my knowledge of the world. On the contrary, I want help in finding where any ruling concept or frame of reference is starting to close in on itself, pushing realms of experience to the margins of consideration. The same applies were I to pretend to possess the foundation in a way that dulls the surprise of the inexhaustible intimacy and creativity of the real Ground itself.

No one can have studied Heidegger seriously or have been a student of Gilson, as I have, without being keenly aware of the traps of subject-object language. I have been unable to avoid it, however, because it is the language so much of the contemporary philosophical world understands. Thus I term "objectivity" that evidence of otherness enjoyed by any and every kind of *noema*[4] of which one may be aware, insofar as it distinguishes itself, in presencing, from the subject, the one who is aware.

Obviously every objectivity enjoys some reality, in the minimal sense of an ability to distinguish itself from the knower as what he knows, and one reality—if only just one intelligibility—from another. That is true even of a hallucination: This hallucination really distinguishes itself from that one, and it enjoys this particular hold on my psyche, to the point of motivating a false judgment of existence. But I generally reserve the term "real" for that kind of being that presences objectively as a thing, the relationship between things or the concrete setting of things manifesting their existence in a time-space of their own (inserted within the cosmic time-space) which the knower recognizes as distinctive from his own being. "Real" in that strong sense contrasts with "imaginary" or "delusional" or "hallucinatory" (an imagining I misjudge as real).

The Guiding Methodological Principle

Phenomenology guided by realistic ontological convictions:[5] Rather than talking about our knowing things, as though our daily commerce with them was purely cognitive, I prefer to use the practical term "dealing" with things (*Handeln*) because most of our knowledge is neither theoretical nor contemplative, but is an active involvement with things, working with them and with other people. This awareness of the practical becomes important in the ontology of Part III, when we explore the interior life not just as the pursuit of theory but of will, passion, and desire seeking fulfillment. This living, dramatic nature of human existence obviously reveals something about being itself. Then we consider that contemplation, too, is a form of living interaction that transcends the little me.

There are realms of pure theory, of course, and the imagination is capable of soaring beyond all practical involvements. Theory and imagination (including all art) have their own kinds of temporality. Both (in the large sense) realities—the practical and the theoretical (and the artistic, which combines aspects of both)—are of fundamental import to man. But the practical revelation of reality remains central—not just what Heidegger called *Zuhandensein*, the instrumental relations we have with things, but all the moral relations we have with human beings, from manipulation to the most sublime and selfless love. All these dealings constitute a variety of kinds of relations with different kinds of things, with the different objects playing particular roles with regard to

---

4. We follow Husserl's terminology here. The *noein* (infinitive) is any cognitive activity. Its object, the distinctive presence of the knowable, is the *noema* (plural *noemata*).
5. Recall the discussion of this in Chapter 2.

one another. Some whole orders of things, such as perceptual objects, are, as Husserl showed, foundational *(fundieren)* in regard to others. Institutions are founded in people, for instance, and a sculpture has to be made out of some preexisting thing that provides the matter on which the sculptor works. Getting these hierarchical relations right is key in building a wisdom.

The Importance of Insight and Principle

Once I completed this survey, I was struck by the dominant role of insight. By "insight" I mean the brute power of intellect to grasp either the sense of perceptual givens, like the color red, or relations. I correlated the various kinds of insight that had popped into my attention with various sorts of principle that had come to notice along the way. Three truths became evident:

1. Insight is enjoyed into some objective stability or permanence (form) or consistency (as in a process, ongoing change steady enough to be grasped—as this flow of water, for instance) which presents itself in experience.
2. Every insight into such a stability, permanence, or consistency founds a principle; the knowledge of such an objective stability can lead a further process of knowledge, which beginning *(princeps)* is "that from which the rest can proceed."[6] (For instance, the concept tree, arising from abstractive knowledge of a form, becomes the principle for excluding many things from that category and for determining what rightly belongs in it, and for grouping many individual things under it.)
3. Most principles in everyday experience are part of a larger whole, which contains its own, higher (or more fundamental) principle. One may proceed thus until reaching the context of contexts, that of being itself, whose transcendental ontological principles get their sense, many believe, from a single Source, foundation of the claim of the unity of being.

Asking how we can grasp things and the significance of settings and their reality will lead us to consider the nature of insight into structure, and the relationship of structure to nature. At that point I explore in detail a nature of exceptional importance: our own human nature. The importance, for human existence, of social relations, including institutions and traditions and the kinds of truth they hand down, will become obvious. Then we reflect on the challenge of the most spiritual of those traditional claims about being, the kind that put to the critical test the whole structure of our knowledge.

THE THINGS OF PERCEPTION

It is natural to start with perception, for it is such a basic and all-pervasive mode of experience, the condition for the possibility of all our daily dealings,

---

6. Saint Thomas's definition of principle, "that from which anything in any way proceeds," derives from Aristotle.

and certainly foundational (in what precise sense we shall have to explore). "The world is too much with us," and the world is first and foremost the presencing of things and persons in concrete settings with which we are constantly being called on to cope. The all-pervasiveness of this demanding hands-on kind of experience founds commonsense man's strong realism, an element in the natural faith of all of us, on the level of our everyday affairs.[7]

The reductionist, positivist attack on this foundational knowledge, which has so impressed modern philosophy, advanced by David Hume building on notions of Descartes about "clarity and distinctness," becomes somewhat credible only at the price of ignoring this basic truth about all perceptual experience: Our perceptions are characteristically perceptions of things in settings. I do not perceive sense-data, which are an abstraction. I normally hear not a noise but a meaningful sound, like the alarming clatter of china breaking in the kitchen. Why do the positivists seek to undercut this basic experiential reality? I believe they want to dissolve perceptions into sense-data so they can claim that all structure and meaning come from the subject, thereby opening a royal path for voluntarism: If all meaning comes from mind, and I am mind, then I am the ultimate center of control.

The Self-Presencing of Things

Central to the natural faith of commonsense man is this conviction: The world presences (to the perceiving adult)[8] furnished with self-presenting, circumscribable, isolatable, basically fairly stable but also more or less active entities, which we speak of normally as things and individual persons.

Phenomenology, aided by process philosophy and relativity theory, helps us to see that the phenomenon of the present is not as simple as it seems to commonsense man. Our being present to the real things that we allow to presence to us depends on that *projective* future opening action of attending, which decides where I am going to be, and what I mean to look at, and in what selective frame of reference. Such attending is always guided by concerns and questions arising from our past. That is the source of that interpretative familiarity with everyday settings and things, and of the questions, practical and theoretical, that send us out in search of new data.[9]

---

7. In talking with my students, I discover them to be strong realists in their everyday dealings with people and things, but not concerned to draw consequences about the principles implicit in their wants and desires and courses of actions. There, they are more like Hume: happy with a reductionism that will allow them the freedom to do what they want. They therefore embrace a relativistic voluntarism, "to each his own," which experience does not really bear out.

8. The world presences differently to the newborn. The research of Jean Piaget has established the need for much experience as the prerequisite for the world presencing as it would to an adult, mature phenomenologist. See Daphne Maurer and Charles Maurer, *The World of the Newborn* (New York: Basic Books, 1988).

9. We should also note that, even as adults, we are still able to capture something of our earliest experience in this regard. Suppose you are untutored in nineteenth-century French

So important is this projective, past-recuperating activity, it evidently can take over when the passions dictate, to the point of inventing and clothing with a certain credibility a hallucination. As we are concerned throughout this study with evidence of permanence in the midst of change, of enduring realities and principles that offer guidance to life, we explore the mysteries of the temporality of being, of change that contains enough continuity to be intelligible. Anticipation, rooted in past experience, holds open the present space of awareness sufficiently to allow the real given permanences of things and settings to make their presence felt.

Perception of Real Things

Let our exploration begin. I look from my study out into the garden, illuminated by the slanting rays of the early morning sun. If I decide to focus on the experiencing of one or two distinctive things—I choose the magnolia tree and a rosebush—I must also say, if I am accurately and honestly describing the perceptual experiencing, that they appear in a setting together with a number of other distinguishable things, to which I choose not to pay much attention. Past experience, processed and sedimented to become part of my natural faith, convinces me that all perceptual objects always appear in a world—a setting of settings—furnished with other things, and that I can broaden my regard outward indefinitely, always finding more things related to the things at the center of my attention.

I am looking at the familiar setting of my garden, and I recognize the magnolia to the east of the McIntosh apple, between me and the Russian olive, which I glimpse just under the magnolia's branches, whereas the tops of the rosebushes, in late summer bloom, appear as a foreground, and the low box elder hedge before that, and the white-painted metallic table and umbrella, and the white-painted wooden chairs in the immediate foreground, just out the window. Nothing is for now out of place in this particular type of setting.

An objector might protest: "You do not *see* this bush and that hedge; you see certain colored shapes and textures that you *judge* to be this or that thing, of this or that kind." On that view, the interpreted natures would not in any sense be in the perception at the fundamental level, a revelation of the things themselves. Such an appropriate objection projects us into an epistemological dispute, rife with ontological implications, which is good, because it invites me to look more closely.

Now notice what this consideration, hauled in from the history of philosophy, is going to allow to happen next methodologically: In response to a philosophical challenge questioning that I really see what I claim to see, I focus

---

Impressionist art. You attend to Monet's *Nympheas* for the first time. Repeated encounters lead to a developing ability to perceive, which in turn opens not only additional nuance but, on occasion, massive presencing and perception of order where once there was none. (The occasions depend upon the painting's interaction with you—the richness of your other experience will make possible new profiles framed to your perception.)

my attention again on the perception, seeking to describe in words what I am actually experiencing now. Note, too, that while finding the right words is essential for directing the reader's attention, my seeing what I see and my looking more closely are not dependent on the words. The concepts I bring from past experience help me understand what I see and direct me to the words that stand for the concepts. But I see the real things shimmering in the morning light as and for what they are in themselves. (More on this later, when I attack the exaggerated language idealism of much contemporary philosophy.) A problem with language is that it is more abstract and also necessarily more discursive than the concentrated, concrete real experience I am seeking to evoke.

I am as aware as my Humean critic that I bring much to the knowledge of all these kinds of things: Processed past experience makes possible my going beyond seeing these things merely as gestalten (the outward and surface shape, more superficial than the insightful and penetrating grasp of "form"), my recognizing those gestalten as typical of a certain nature. Although I already possess vast knowledge of kinds, the perception of this rose and this magnolia at this moment triggers my entire cognitive apparatus to allow me to see this thing presencing before me for what it really is.[10] I do not just arbitrarily insert the present *noema* into a context of knowledge of roses; rather, the present gestalt determines the relevant context from the past, and then that previous knowledge enables me to focus meaningfully on what is actually presencing. It is offering aspects of itself never before caught by me and hence not contained in my concepts and previous impressions. I am *re-cognizing*, as regards type. Many factors work together to trigger deployment of the relevant knowledge: It is the whole gestalt, even though, were it reduced to the barest stylization in a pencil sketch of just the head of the rose, I would probably still be able to recognize a rose. But as I attend now to the whole bush, I see there are tight little buds, larger buds, opening blooms, fully opened blooms, all standing in familiar relationships to stems and leaves, all these parts displaying familiar colors. I learn something new every time I linger in this rose's presence, but this new knowledge largely confirms what I have already known about roses.[11]

---

10. Admitting that my phenomenological reflecting is itself always already directed (projected toward the future, which assures the investigation a present) from the (past) faith I bring to the enterprise is not tantamount to closing the door to new discovery—from new data offered by the things and from interpretative critique by co-researchers, provided I really want to see.

11. If the leaves were flaming red, the blossoms bright green, but the shape roselike, I might hesitate in my judgment: "I am seeing colored flowers shaped like roses but not colored like them," or perhaps I would judge, "These are roses, but with what weird colors." It is significant how rarely such confusions in everyday perception ever occur. The psychologist of perception, James J. Gibson, in *The Senses Considered as Perceptual Systems* (Boston: Houghton Mifflin, 1966), establishes not only that the senses grasp structure but much about the physiology of how this is accomplished. He shows how, for instance, light reflecting off a surface carries information about the thing, the structure of which influences the form the light takes. (We pursue this in Chapter 7.)

We shall come back to this question of knowledge of natures. For the moment I invite the reader to turn to his own perceiving and seek to capture that evidence in dealing with familiar things that convinces that they are indeed each presencing as the kind of thing he sees and knows each to be. Note the more closely one attends to the evidence, the more confirming of the initial snap judgment further observation tends to be. Little in our ordinary encounters is confusing. While our acquaintance with these familiar things is superficial, its sureness is due, I shall try to show, not just to the consistency of our perceptual-cognitive apparatus, but to the permanence of many things. It is not just because they change slowly, in relationship to human endurance, but because they manifest an internal coherence, an intelligible consistency in the way they hold together. If they are living, they develop in ways consistent through all members of a species. In a word, they manifest something of that essentiality Aristotle called attention to and named "form."

Too often philosophers are so impressed with the Heraclitean insight that everything changes, they underemphasize the evidence for all kinds of stability, permanence, consistency, and endurance, or displace the explanation of it too much to the side of the subject, downplaying or ignoring evidence for the objective existence of structure or form. The relative autonomy and objective stability of what we commonly call things prove central to guiding our action and anchoring our projects. We count on them to be there, and they do not disappoint us very often.

Some of the rose plants are small and fresh looking—I recognize them as newly installed—and some are tall, showing about their base old wood.[12] Each thing stands in its own characteristic[13] space, and it manifests signs of its (characteristic) endurance: I may not know that the McIntosh is all of sixty years old and that the chrysanthemums were planted last week and are probably very young, but I can see at least this much about all the trees, bushes, and plants I have singled out for attention: They are enduring enough so that I can expect them all to be there next week. If I notice one missing, I shall probably be motivated to open projectively out of this past experience a question: "What happened to the white mum bush that was here?" (The answer is that Mr. Rothman, the painter, almost totaled it. By observing closely, I can see one little twig still blooming, and two or three crushed into the ground, probably where he placed his ladder.)

The ability of each thing to reveal, in the form it imparts to the light reflecting off it, something of its being, as nature, its self-standing space, and characteristic

---

12. Again, knowledge from the past feeds this ability to notice the old wood; I can look more closely if challenged, "How do you know?" to recover reflectively the grounds of this perceptually based judgment, "This rose bush is old while this one is very young." For instance, I notice the wood is thicker, browner, and shaggier than the green, slick wood of the new bush.

13. The rose occupies a volume quite different from the hedge; it fills its space differently, less densely; and normally would be expected in a different place in the garden (the hedge usually has a dividing function).

endurance, including a certain sense as to how it will develop, comes in different degrees of aggressivity or activity on its part. The magnolia is less aggressive, as it "speaks" to me, than the cat meowing for its dinner, which in turn can engage my regard less dramatically and successfully than a child seeking attention. But even in the case of the inanimate object, see how its surface indicates a depth of inexhausted, still partly hidden while partly shining forth being. The granite boulder maintains itself, through its internal structure, against the assaults of wind and ice, holding its place and its shape even for centuries.

Here is one aspect of the perplexing question of the interplay of subjective and objective context: My own subjective present, this moment of centered awareness, opens onto a world of things, which manifest their independent endurance and their own characteristic kinds of development. Although they are present now to me, they nevertheless evidence their distinctive kinds of purchase on time, which has nothing to do with me or what I care to make of it. Barring accidents that damage or disease them, they anchor the future: I am aware that they can likely go on persisting for varying lengths of time, developing at different, to some extent understandable paces, even though I may never look at them again. The subjectivist philosophers have neglected this basic reality: Things have their own time, which has nothing to do with my human, conscious opening of time-space horizons, within which I only encounter and acknowledge their time-in-themselves.

For the tree I may be seeing for the first time, I cannot summon up familiarity from memory, but I can reason from its appearance, drawing on knowledge of like trees and many other things, to some notion of its longevity. This knowledge of the objective, cosmic endurance of the other is something quite different from my experience of my own lived time. And yet I know that the condition for my ability to open such a space-time of awareness is to continue myself to enjoy, as human body, a physical stake in that cosmic endurance, a material being in the cosmic space-time just like the tree. *Esse* precedes *Sein!*[14]

This interplay of the past-retaining future-projecting time-space horizon-opening *ek-sistenz* of the conscious living subject deploying the horizons of interpretation of a world illuminated by what Heidegger means by *Sein*, and the things with their presentation of evidence of permanence and regular development *(esse)*, is all the more complicated by the different ways in which these subjective and objective times each manifest a variety of characteristic and different thickness. The center, the present ego-point of awareness, is restricted, the immediate perceptual spatial horizon is narrow, and the time linking the just-felt with the coming into feeling is not very thick. Nevertheless, the present epochal *Sein* allows me to summon up imaginatively, if I wish, the staggering immensity of the whole physical cosmos and to range back in time to the Big Bang and out to the (possible) ultimate collapse of the cosmos

---

14. This is a fundamental ontological principle of utmost importance. It is explained more fully in Chapter 9.

into black holes, and in that way place the presencing tree into a context of previously unimaginable dimensions, very thick indeed. Likewise, the rocks of the earth present the evidence of their antiquity differently from this kind of imagining-picturing, as here-and-now traces of their genesis built into their structure.[15] We shall come back to the ontological implications of all this, in Part III.

To sum up: The stake of each thing in time-space, its "material existence" (*esse*), is manifested as enduring persistence and a certain volume, aspects of a characteristic way of developing while exhibiting permanence. So its characteristic way of being and hence acting (its nature) and its immediate relationship to other things (its setting) are veritably thrust upon us in ordinary experience, and this simultaneously: I see not only that this thing exists, here in this place and now at this moment, but something of what it is and the manner in which it is in a setting with other things. As Hans Urs von Balthasar puts it, the thing "speaks to me"[16] in all these ways at once. But then not only the thing but even the setting is eloquent. (In the case of a person, and often with higher animals as well, I also experience its personality, its own peculiar style in action-rooted habits, as we shall see.) We signify this knowledge in distinctive ways: by fabricating proper names, general nouns for kinds of things, and names for characteristic settings (for example, "garden").

That the distinctness, clarity,[17] and familiarity of these things anchor much of our larger cognitive and even imaginative constructions has enormous implications for ethics and wisdom, whatever the fans of the naturalistic-fallacy argument may think. I claim that our wide cognitive structures of explanation are saved from ideology only to the extent they are well founded in experience of concrete persons and things, offering their evidence for real structures, dynamically unfolding.

But lest all this emphasis on objective reality blind us to the subjective reality that our cognitive processes are responsible for bringing all this to be for consciousness, recall these three truths:

1. We only perceive things within the limits of our perceptual apparatus (an analytic proposition).
2. We always perceive any one thing from a profile (*Abschattung* is Husserl's term).

---

15. The present is full of mystery, complicated by the fact that I open, from my personal present, onto the distinctive temporalities of every manner of thing and of the cosmos itself. As my present concern moves out into vast space, and I begin thinking about the sense in which the light arriving to me now from a star that may have exploded forty years ago, but, being fifty light-years away, the explosion of which I shall only see in a decade, gives rise to all the difficulties on this scale, consideration of which occasioned the theory of general relativity.

16. See his beautiful descriptions of the self-presencing of things in *Theologik*, vol. 1 (Einsiedeln: Johannes Verlag, 1985).

17. Descartes ruined these terms by absolutizing them. Phenomenology must recover the sense of *relative* clarity and distinctness.

3. Consequently, our knowledge of the thing is built up synthetically from retention of different past perceptions of distinctive profiles and from anticipation of aspects we have not actually experienced, drawing almost always on previous knowledge of similar kinds of things to flesh out what is actually presencing in the senses, and perceived as the profile of the surface of something with its own mysterious depths.

The subject is most active in constituting the object as it stands in knowledge, and much of the past experience on which it draws is sedimented about ideational cores made up of signs, which help us manage conceptual knowledge of forms. But the knowledge we deploy is about the object, and the object is experienced as always making its contribution to a growing knowledge of it, never exhausted, perhaps inexhaustible.

Far from challenging the realistic thrust of our description, awareness of these subjective aspects of our experiencing reinforces the commonsense reliance inherent in such knowledge. Let us probe more extensively into the case for this.

True Waking Perceptions versus Dreams and Hallucinations

Consider the psychiatrist's bugaboo, hallucinations. Most instructive are they, as are dreams, bringing out just how active the subject is in building the object, even in normal perception. When we deliberately fantasize—for instance, dreaming up a beefsteak dinner as we lie awake during an underprovisioned camping trip—we can endow this succulent repast with all the trimmings and make it real enough to taste. So long as the awake self remains in control of the process, our enjoyable image is not mistaken for perception of a real beefsteak dinner. In a dream, one has the sense more of being swept along. In the midst of the dream, the self that controls when awake may be unsure whether I am dreaming or not, or even be convinced that the experience is of reality. It is indeed astonishing how the dream objects unfold, often with all the consistency and smooth flow of real things presenting themselves in perception. It is not just that the dreamer invests them with belief of existence; they motivate such belief through the density and consistency of their self-presentation.

How, then, do I come to recognize, "Thank God! It was only a dream"? When I wake up, I insert the dream into a larger experiential context, that of the waking world, shared on an ongoing, hands-on, intersubjectively proved-out basis with other conscious centers, and connected less voluntarily with the other, more englobing settings. The dream, with a greater emotive charge than our usual waking perceptions, tends to shift content massively and erratically as the focus of interest changes. In perception, although there always has to be some emotive element (actually moving us to attend),[18] what largely dictates

---

18. The degree of voluntariness varies. The will may dictate to the body to pay close attention (for instance, to this minutious experiment). Other times the object will crash into

content is the objective self-presencing of what involuntarily appears at the center of interest, or breaks in surprisingly from the margins.

The dream is fuzzy at the edges, indeed mostly detached from the larger context, and one cannot summon up detail at will. In perception as I move my regard to the horizons they recede, revealing a total connection to the larger setting, and although I can change focus in my imagination from, for example, the setting of this office to the setting that is my neighborhood, perceptually I can only move through a smooth, intelligible transition from one scale to another, with no breaks, no discontinuity in sense. And I can always push my research toward finer details—again, as I burrow in, the transitions are smooth, the change of scale completely intelligible, and fresh detail never lacking.

Also, because hands-on, everyday experience yields, as I work with the things, new information, their very resistance, lacking in the dream, constantly confirms their otherness. And the intersubjective nature of the experience provides constant checks as to the correctness of my ongoing interpretations: I watch what others are doing to be sure I have it right.

Like the dream, the hallucination, if it is not produced by a chemical development (natural or artificial) in the brain, is driven by desires arising from deep within the soul, often in response to a desperate need. Like the hungry camper, the abandoned old lady invents a companion and projects onto her all the reality she can muster from her experience. Remember, she desperately does not want this creation disturbed, and she is doing everything she can to insert it as successfully as possible into unfolding daily experience. The boorish psychiatrist has great trouble convincing her that everyone else is right and she is wrong for believing it.[19]

However, there are limits to the processes of verification she can deploy, if she ever wanted to. When Juan Diego first brought the bishop of Guadalupe roses in the middle of that sixteenth-century winter destined to remain decisive in Mexican history, and then the movingly lovely portrait of the Lady mysteriously painted on a material woven from cactus, the busy and jaded old cleric began to take seriously this peasant's bothersome claims about an apparition of the Virgin. As the expected fifteen-year lifespan of the cactus material became four hundred years, and reported miracles increased and persisted, belief in the reality of the apparition, which only Juan Diego witnessed, grew. If the hallucinating old lady could reach out and divest her hallucinatory companion of her jacket and hand it to the psychiatrist, the good scientist would be forced down a new line of investigation.

---

the center of attention, surprising me, and, if it is quickly adjudged dangerous, adrenaline will be discharged and the body—will or no—put on red alert for possible flight.

19. An interesting discussion erupted in class when I suggested that Dr. Edwin Hersch was right to say it is best to leave the old lady alone. To the argument "it is the lesser evil to let her enjoy the consolation of her imaginary companion" the students replied, "That is paternalistic. He is playing God. Maybe if she were helped to face reality, and if he helped her in the next stage, she might find some real companions, which would be much truer, and healthier."

The Physiological Limits of Perception and the Material Reality of Perceived Things

Commonsensically we consider the tree trunk solid. Yet its solidity does not stop all X rays, some of which radiation will find its way through the interstices in the tree's molecular structure and can be recorded on a photographic plate, offering a picture of the tree trunk that differs from the one the eye naturally offers the brain.

Some philosophers argue that my vision of the tree does not yield knowledge of the tree as it is in itself. Rather, they point out, being the product of a particular perceptual apparatus processing the stimuli of a certain gamut of radiations within the frequency spectrum we call "visible light," my present perception is but a moment interior to a stream of such experiences. Each of these gathers in only a tiny fraction of all the potential information about the things that is carried in the light. Each perception derives its value, so to speak, uniquely from its relationship to the other moments of perception. In their view, the tree's standing out is a distinguishing that goes on among perceptions, so it is with perceptions, and not things-in-themselves, that I deal.

Much in this contention is true. Indeed, what I know only partially, in profile, from a point of view, yields a contact with the tree that is always distinguishable within a wider perceptual context, both standing out in a spatial context, the perceptual valence of the tree distinguishing itself against the background of the simultaneously received perceptual whole; and distinguishing itself within a temporal flow of perceptual experiences; as well as relating to some different retained glimpses of the selfsame tree and glimpses of other things within the same and differing perceptual fields.

That is the issue: In what sense is the perceived tree really existing in the garden, and how is my consciousness able, through its own product—this sensory image—to become aware of it as not just a product of my conscious activity, but as an independent thing presencing?

The spontaneity of the commonsense grasp of the in-itselfness of real things is the effect both of the real things' speaking to me, by *in-forming* the light that reflects from them or by presenting particular tactile surfaces or sound waves formed in different ways, and of the automatic fashion in which the mind, when provoked by in-formation, releases the fruits of other relevant processed, retained information, which assists in noticing and identifying aspects of what is now presencing. If for any reason I feel the need to investigate such a spontaneously self-presenting permanence further, the collaborating investigation yields, through more deployment of the same and other senses, guided by yet more relevant information obtained in the past, a consistent witness to their characteristic and distinctive being in themselves as what they are.

Pointing out this consistently corroborating evidence is a far cry from implying a coherence theory of truth. It is, rather, calling attention to the things' ability to keep presencing when we are interested in them. Granted, these sense powers I employ are themselves consistent properties of an enduring incarnate subject, which accounts for my being able to come back to the same things again and again on the same level of interaction (or discourse) with them. This in no way weakens our sense of the reliability of our knowledge of the things' being in themselves, nor does it imply that my knowledge of the things as they are in themselves is a total, exhaustive knowledge. This evidence is accurate on its own level of perception and so far as it goes.

The permanence of the perceived thing exhibits itself as consistent within a certain time frame, drawn spontaneously from the body's own scale of consistency, and intelligible through insight into the sense of these correlated structures to the point, in most circumstances, of no ambiguity.[20] If there is need to examine the evidence, I can see many aspects of its being that found the stake it has in existence *(esse)*, its hold on the future. The physicist can explain why the half-life of certain particles is measurable in nanoseconds, why their hold on the future is so fleeting, and the biologist can partially explain why this sequoia tree has been able to endure for a thousand years.

I have no trouble recognizing that the unusual perception I now have of my apple tree from an airplane is a new angle on the same old tree. I can even synthesize intellectually the knowledge from the X-ray photograph and from a chemical analysis of some of its sap with the perceived object, this tree in this garden. When I do it, the perceptually presented real material tree serves as primary point of reference, foundation for the synthesis of other kinds of knowledge of the tree.

To be sure, the more remote from the foundation in direct perception, the more reasoning involved; as complex implications are drawn far from the foundational experiences, the more steps to bring theoretical conclusions back to the arena of direct experience for experimental verification. Error can creep in at any time. It may turn out that elements of the theory are pure creations of the imagination, in which case they will never be brought back to the experimental level successfully. But the scientist always wants to return there ultimately— and for good reason.

Some theoretical explanations propose that things are not really as they seem perceptually. But in most instances with care we can show how these apparently contradictory prospects onto the thing relate, as we come to understand how the different frames of reference themselves relate.[21] All experience points in this direction: The harder we try to understand how the objects revealed in different frames of reference come together as knowledge about the same

---

20. Interestingly, a linguistic researcher, like the eminent George Lakoff, has no difficulty seeing this "experimental reality" yielded by the interaction of these two stabilities, subjective and objective. *Women, Fire and Dangerous Things: What Categories Reveal about the Mind* (Chicago: University of Chicago Press, 1987), 297–303.

21. A reminder: Here, "frame of reference" means a particular focus, motivated by a given question, that the knower takes up from within the all-englobing world-deploying horizons of interpretation he brings with him, always animated by his past processed in the transcendental form of his natural faith.

entities, the more we see that we understand how they fit together. I offer evidence supporting this when we explore, in Part III, our knowledge of the same entity, man, viewed in different frames of reference.

The Perception of Things as Natures in Settings

Let us return to the foundation, to consider further how our more elaborate knowledge of settings and even systems[22] of things is built up. The discreteness of things should not be allowed to obscure either the setting or the grasp of things always as kinds of things, belonging to families of objects. These natures and families of objects are joined by links of ideational implication, often founded in real relations of efficient causality, especially those responsible for their genesis, however remote in natural history they may be.

The whole of philosophy has neglected the important and significant reality of settings and, worse yet, real systems. We could not manage the world of our everyday affairs, let alone attempt to steer planetary processes, without a knowledge of settings and systems. Some existentialist descriptions of particular situations imply something of this. (And it is dealt with explicitly, but with neither ontological nor anthropological depth, by the better management gurus.) But if one is interested in building up patiently a description of the whole web of experience of a cosmos, probing the significance of real things and systems of relationships between things, manifesting at many levels order, permanence, and regularity in the midst of change, then the setting and the system are important as a common level of ordered knowledge of orderly situations.[23]

There are perhaps not as many kinds of settings as kinds of objects, but they are still many, as are kinds of systems, natural and cultural. The setup of my little home office, with its computer and books and files, is a setting; so is the living room; the garden; and the neighborhood. These domestic settings are different from the classroom, the railroad yard, the broadcasting station, and so on. The oil field, for instance, can be experienced as a setting, but also understood as a system, the relationship of rocking-horse pumps, pipes, valves, and reservoirs making sense to someone who understands how the extraction of petroleum works.

Insight into the sense of a setting is, like one's grasp of an individual thing, simultaneously threefold:

---

22. See Glossary. "Part," however, signifies a situation wherein the thing in question is not structurally distinctive without reference to that whole within which it is caught up—for example, one's kidney vis-à-vis one's body. Setting, on the other hand, is more external—the houses on this block are set next to each other to form a uniform street of dwellings, but they do not interact in the same way the machinery set in a row in a factory may in composing a system.

23. Chaotic aspects of the world often show the need for the search for order to be carried out on a larger scale. Modern chaos theory shows order to exist where before common sense saw only confusion—for example, in coastlines, which viewed at a proper scale reveal an order not suspected. See, for instance, the interviews with mathematicians and scientists by Emile Noël, *Le hasard aujourd'hui* (Paris: Editions du Seuil, 1991).

1. some grasp of how the different things here relate (grasp of the *esse* of the setting as an ensemble);
2. how this might be typical (grasp of the nature of the ensemble);
3. how this immediate setting fits into a larger, surrounding setting (the living room into the house), and how a smaller system fits into a larger one (this oil field in the Saudi oil-production system); and how in a given setting one may perceive things that are themselves caught up in different systems that transcend the present setting.

Insight into a system adds understanding of how elements interact. A machine tool is intelligible in the setting of a production line and in turn contributes to our sense of that line as a system within a larger system of production; a poem read aloud is judged appropriate or inappropriate in terms of the setting in which it was read. We grasp some as characteristic stage settings in which kinds of dramas with their specific roles are played out. Within those stage settings, we grasp the sense of typical dramatic scenes within larger scenarios. A board meeting of a railway company is usually not the right place to discuss one's errant children: "The system just doesn't work that way."

But if we were not so readily able to grasp the whatness of the things in the setting or system, we would not understand the larger scene either. I recognize the distinctiveness of the thing in part through a comprehension of the particular thing's own inherent constitution and in part through comparison with things of the same kind, and in contrast with the other things' different characteristic ways of being. Along with the thing's nature goes a sense of appropriateness of certain settings. When I see the wing of a light aircraft sticking down through the ceiling of my living room, I know something is wrong. In building up our knowledge of natures and settings and systems by comparison and contrast, *analogy* plays a role.

Hegel emphasized this knowing by contrast, but tended to downplay the inherent, stable intelligibility of the thing in its own structuredness. That robs the thing of its self-standing, that ability of nature to organize itself into permanent nodules, into the distinctive sense of the basic organization of which we can enjoy some insight. We do not recognize things only as not the other things. But comparison does help us focus attention on distinctive features and thus build up our knowledge of the internal sense of each thing and its relationships to other kinds through comparison.

Many processes are involved in what philosophers too commonly lump together as "abstraction." To name just three: the elaboration of images,[24] both out of concrete experiences enjoying a texture of their own and out of generalized elements abstracted from the coming together of many experiences; the ways of manipulating such possibilities with the help of differ-

---

24. Balthasar stresses the essential intermediary role played by the image. See *Theologik*, 1:145ff. I have not gone into any detail on this, taking images' role—perhaps too much—for granted.

ent kinds of symbols; and our bringing to the fore this or that aspect of a vast pool of processed experiences and abstractions under the impulse of various emotive elements. This is a large subject inviting phenomenological illumination.

Memory of Things and Settings in Perception

Everyday experience stays close to things. It is another story when, in pursuit of a long-range goal or theoretical understanding, we build up a cognitive system, relying on abstractions from abstractions to attain a sweep of generalization based on analysis of parts of experience, and bringing together many concepts into one understanding.

The more remote from experience the deliberately fabricated cognitive tools—concepts, symbols, signs—the easier it is for the theorizing consciousness to get itself into traps that ordinary practical experience never knows. This awareness of the difficulties of theory building ought not reverberate back skeptically on ordinary experience, where it may, uncritically, weaken faith in the soundness of that close-to-things experience.

Just now I hear a sound in the kitchen. I do not know whether it was the mail coming through the slot in the door, the cat getting on the counter, or our boarder coming down for breakfast. Because I am familiar with the real setting of my house (including its social setting unfolding in daily routines, commanded by certain social systems, such as the need to be on time to work), I can remain in my office and speculate about what happened. Ah, now I hear sounds of the toaster, so I am certain it is the boarder, as the cat rarely takes toast, thieves do not have time, no one else is in the house, and Oumar does like his breakfast.

Here I am using knowledge of a familiar setting to interpret the sound. Note, I really did hear the toaster. In the context of the house, I recognize the distinctive metallic sound of the handle being pushed down. If I were standing out in a railroad yard, an identical sound would not trigger the same response from experience, even if it turned out somehow (bizarrely) that a toaster was activated, perhaps by a conductor in a caboose.

The point here is to emphasize how real that objective context is, how independent of what I may think about it or of any action on my part. The house is an isolating, independent interior space, within which a limited number of things is to be found, arranged in certain ways, which are intelligible—indeed, identification of them is familiar and easy. My deployment of the fruits of past experience is given a strong objective steer by the limited, permanent, and objective *an sich* context, within which things may come to be arranged differently while the cadre stays the same; confirmation of their various relationships is made possible by the articulated data presented by each of the things.

Not all contexts are as physical as the one in our example. Sometimes, especially when intersubjective action is the concern, large elements of a relevant context may be quite psychological and spiritual. The more it is, the more important the steering effect of the objectively given typical elements. We consider examples of this later.

The Flexibility of Mind in Perception: An Indication of Our Freedom

It should be noted with what flexibility and incredible powers of abstraction, reference, and reconstruction in different contexts the human mind is able to proceed in the perceptual realm, remaining all the while soundly oriented by the relative stability and the identifiable types of the things themselves, so that the mind operates with astonishing accuracy within this sphere of competence. Both the subjective and objective sides of the equation must be kept in mind and in balance: The mind, motivated by our desires and needs, can range around like a lion, seeking what it can devour; and this subjective activity is neither a purely arbitrary nor a purely creative process, for the powers of interested cognition are guided by what there is to be known as it really is in itself. When the subjective devouring lion, for indefensible reasons, chooses to ignore or to twist evidence, bent as it may be on fashioning the world to its liking, mischief results. But that belongs more to the realm of pathology than epistemology, so I reserve it for later.[25]

It is the grasp of the sense of structures that founds our power to reconstruct and rearrange things and to change successfully (in terms of our desires) whole milieux, including inducing, through work, real changes in objective things. Our sense of what we can and ought to do depends on our ability to move around the landscape, choosing what we want to notice and study. Animals can move surely in familiar settings and show some ability to compare things, but their behavior manifests no signs of reflection, little ability to symbolize, and hence they do not possess the full range of our ability to generalize and abstract, hold in symbol, and, as a result, rearrange things imaginatively. Thus they cannot alter rapidly their cultural setting. This limit to their cognitive ability absolves animals of responsibility and any beholdenness to an ought they cannot grasp.

But we also must not exaggerate the scope of our freedom, limited by the insufficiency of our knowledge, by the resistance of the natures of the things and the persons with which we have to deal, and by our lack of detachment. Our inability to be detached and objective is shown when certain objects obsess us. "Things [including frailties of our own bodies] are too much with us" when in the midst of the finest spiritual meditation a fly, as Pascal reminds us, distracts us. Our freedom is closely bound up with our ability to presence where we will and to focus on different objects, in different frames of reference, as it is by our ability to achieve (limited) distance from our interests.

---

25. Pathological behavior is a reality, too, consideration of which is perhaps not all that unimportant for a *sophia*. Anthropology without pathology is a gnostic dream.

The Role of Time/Space

"Moving freely about the landscape" is not a metaphor. Time/space has been woven throughout our descriptions. (I say "Time/space" to signal the existential interrelation of the two.) Time and space are first and foremost experiences of the person, who is a body of a certain size and duration operating in the world, which body provides a natural *metron*. But that world opens onto a cosmos, which gradually yields evidence of its own expanding enormity and its long duration, while englobing things of many sizes and durations. My natural *metron* and all objective distances and durations interact in complex ways. In terms of cosmic space, Montreal and Toronto have not budged; they are still 539 kilometers apart as the train flies. But now Montreal is much "closer" than it was when one was obliged to go by canoe, and people in Montreal can be instantly present electronically, at least as voices and moving pictures. Another kind of spatiality—call it "spiritual distance"—also enters the picture. My friend in Carinthia who prays for our family every day is closer to us than our next-door neighbor who was dying from cancer for six months before I ever found out about it. As lived, existential time and space are about presence, and because presence is spiritual as well as physical, the use of the term "near" here is analogous, not equivocal.

We may then distinguish three kinds of time/space: the real, objective cosmic expanse-endurance, which is what it is, whatever we may think about it or whether we think about it at all, beyond all changing theories of physics, the full truth of which is only gradually being discovered; the space/time of convenience, so that time in the dentist's chair moves slowly; and the spiritual space/time of presence—the student sitting next to you in class is very close cosmically but, as you ignore him completely ("you have no time for him"), might as well be on another planet.

The first foundation of our freedom is our physical existence, our stake, through *esse*, in the cosmic time/space. But decisions to be present and judgments about convenience so dominate the other two time/spaces, they can lead me to ignore two facts: other people and groups active as institutions have their time/space agendas, which I had better respect; and concentration on my own convenience can lead to becoming unrealistic about the inevitability of death. We shall see as we progress the impact of this truth on the exercise of finite freedom, which demands the ordering of spiritual and cosmic time/spaces.

Insight into Structure

The grasp of the sense of a given time/space is a structural insight. The much-abused term "structure" is sufficiently useful to justify my staying with it, for it is general enough to stand for the product of every kind of insight into wholes. By "structure" I mean, then, just that: any perceived or imagined or conceived whole, into the sense of which the mind enjoys an insight, that is, can grasp the characteristic way in which the parts of the whole *belong* to one another.

Perception of a gestalt is not necessarily insight into structure: I am simply confronted by a coherent figure seen or a tune played, and grasp it—largely perceptually—as a figure. The comprehension of structure requires something more: insight into the sense of the whole sufficient to throw light on how the parts belong. A *mixtum-gatherum* pile of things does not constitute a structure; the individual things are not parts, just elements in a heap or a chaos; the only information is the spatial boundary and the collection of forms.

Not all insight is intellection of how parts belong together in a whole—for example, insight into the color blue is brute grasp of the essence of a perceptum; or into the number One, of an idea of number. But much of our knowledge does arise from insight into wholes, ranging from complex real things in perception, through grasp of the sense of settings, to the great models we build in science of whole immense systems, like the human body or the galaxies. Note, too, that knowledge of structures is an *ens mentis*, phenomenologically a *noema*. Because it is the product of insight, structure is formalizable, and such form is abstractable.

Insight into structures may arise from perception of real things; perception of real relations between things (and persons); reflection on creative images in the mind; or from ideal conceptual constructions.[26] The intellect's ability to see how the parts of the thing belong in the whole founds the elementary knowledge of the nature of the real thing. This insight may occur at many levels, from perception of the order of parts in a superficial gestalt (even a child can grasp something of the relationship of head, trunk, and limbs in a human body, and see that the snake is put together differently), to profound understanding of the role, for instance, of vital organs in a higher organism, or various operating parts of a sophisticated machine. The idea of a real nature results most commonly from the abstraction arising from formal insight into the (superficial) sense of the structure of the concrete thing presencing in perception. Real systems too vast and/or too hidden beneath the surface to be glimpsed easily, or even reconstructed from a series of perceptions, require elaborate, reasoned building of a complex network of concepts (a model) that yields an understanding of the big real structures.

Structures are either static or dynamic, and both may be either open or closed. A static structure is either the form of a relatively slowly changing thing, viewed at the scale of perception as unchanging; or it may be permanent at its core until shattered and destroyed, as an atom; or it may be a fixed setting; or an institution with well-established roles, consistently played out by well-enculturated actors, so that we consider the set of relationships as basically static. (This would be a form of stable social system.) Most static structures are closed, but some may be seen to be open, in the sense of visibly incomplete, like a house lacking a roof.

---

26. The imaginary structure may use elements abstracted from formal, ideal intuitions, whether mixed with elements abstracted from perception-based insight or not.

A dynamic structure, a process, is a network of relationships between perceptively changing elements, which relationships are shifting rapidly enough, yet with a consistency in the interrelationships that allows us to recognize a process. Such a dynamic structure may be either ongoing, hence open, or finished, hence closed (the process of draining the lake went on for years, but now the lake is drained). A dynamic structure may be either stable, if the process is consistent and entirely predictable, or unstable, if consistent enough to be grasped as a process, yet erratic enough to show ups and downs, and perhaps even to escape sure prediction. To grasp a dynamic, open structure—an ongoing process—the mind must have some insight into the *vector* of the change and how the various changing aspects of the thing or of a variety of changing things caught up in the process relate, that is, how they belong in the process.

The grasp of the sense of a process delivers to the mind something rather like a modest version of Hegel's concrete universal. The whole process is comparable to a universal in relation to those moments and the distinguishable but related parts that get their sense from their setting in respect to one another and in the overall development, the way particulars get related to one another through the mediation of an abstract concept. Only, remember, the process is concrete, its moments and the distinguishable things caught up in it are concrete, but the process as a whole imparts meaning to the parts, in the sense of the setting of understandable relationships, an order.[27] Grasp of the vector of a process allows extrapolation. We have, for instance, the sense of an individual life: We see increasing dissipation, or increasing preoccupation with earning money.[28]

Excursus: Structure, Beholdenness, and Freedom

Why the tendency throughout the history of modern philosophers to convince us that mind does not recognize order, but rather imposes, produces, alters it? I believe that the principal reason, which is an aspect of the *Sein* of modernity, is sinister: the hubris that lies behind the drive, since at least Montaigne and Hobbes, toward libertinage, bound up with the release of entrepreneurial and exploratory drives, which themselves are not necessarily sinister at all. Libertinage is the release of will from reason's supervision. It was seen by every Founder of the Novo Ordo Seclorum as the greatest menace to the new Republican.[29] I have been bringing out the extensiveness

---

27. Processes may be of vastly different scales, from the running of water out of my garden hose, to planetary-wide, centuries-old developments of immense complexity, made up of many large subprocesses, intertwining in systems (for example, industrialization). See *T&A*, chap. 6.

28. Grasp of such regularity in nature and even of the free in human behavior is important to the practice of virtue and the building up of wisdom, and vital to our dealings with other people, since we have a sense of the various roles they are playing and judge their character.

29. Thomas Pangle, in "Lecture Series in Christianity and Culture" (conference held at St. Michael's College, Toronto, 1992), documents this extensively.

of our beholdeness to experience of kinds of things and kinds of situations. Forms impose an obligation of rationality to heed them as funds of possibility but also as constraints, the form of human nature especially. The very whiff of this classical notion offends the active center's wish to be God: The perpetual adolescent in us resists admitting that we cannot do what we wish when we wish with complete impunity. To some extent reality, like an authoritarian parent, demands that we toe the line by acknowledging the real forces and structures in the world. The children of Adam and Eve don't want any of it.

This sense of beholdeness is softened when the truth, that concepts are constructions of the mind, is not accompanied by the truths that every *noema* transcends the center of awareness as object, and that many forms grasped in insight refer to real ways things and situations are actually put together in the world, and that such real structures ground the truth of our subsequent conceptual grasp of them.

These possibilities of objective knowledge of natures and processes will help orient us as we seek to adjudicate competing truth claims put forward by distinctive traditions in the world system. But even on another level of achieving a social order, it is a life-and-death matter to rehabilitate the objectivity of conceptual knowledge and for pedagogues to reintroduce into education a respect for the mind's ability to discover universal truths, valid for and guiding of all. In preparation, let us consider this question of formation of concepts in more detail.

CONCEPTS AND SYMBOLS
Insight into Concepts

When the mind enjoys an insight into the sense of a structure, the resulting formal intellection can be abstracted and held as knowledge of an unchanging form, that is, as a concept. Such a concept can be symbolized and held in the mind even if no exemplars of that kind of structure now exist in external time-space—for example, dinosaurs—or as with any imaginary object.

The steps in the process of concept formation, although in practice interpenetrating to some degree, can nevertheless be distinguished. Suppose, in the case of a perception, some real thing for some reason manages to call itself to my attention. In the profile through which it presents itself to me as a gestalt, I see that it is some sort of whole—not just an outline, but something complex and substantial. The moment my mind grasps the sort of whole it is, however superficially, I can fix its form. The mind is able to discriminate (an abstractive judgment) and leave behind the particularities that appertain to its being this exemplar but not to its basic constitution: The mind grasps it as a type and forms a concept, for which a verbal symbol can be created to help in its storage, usable for relating it to other concepts and for its ready recall.

Even most of the stable things of our experience are changing somewhat at every moment, even perceptibly. The apple tree, for instance, is moving slightly in the breeze. The mind fixes the more stable aspects of its nature, the continuing features, and distinguishes them from more accidental aspects. What is perceived as changing so rapidly and overall as to merit being considered a process is nonetheless also frozen by formal intellect, the form resulting from the insight into a type of relatedness—for example, industrialization, or depression, or even rising temperature, or, more abstractly (more formally and simply) yet, increasing.

The real stabilities manifested, at the gross scale of our biophysiologically established commerce with them,[30] should not be confused with the mind's insightful ability to produce an ideal stability by fixing in a concept what manifests itself as changing rapidly enough to be a process. The tree really presents basically the same appearance, day in and day out, over a time span long enough to justify my treating it as the same big old McIntosh. In this case the mind acknowledges a permanence that continues in the world independently of what mind thinks of it. If someone denies the fact of its stability, he is wrong. When, in contrast, the mind, through insight into the sense of a process, fixes it in a concept, intellect achieves, for purposes of dealing with the process, a stability, which the process, as changing, itself enjoys only as an ongoing consistency of connectedness between its moments unfolding one into another.

The stable structure or the process from which a form may have been abstracted can as well be a product of the imagination—the idea for a painting or the flow of a musical theme. So long as it is a self-presenting structured object, present in consciousness with at least a minimum of stability or, in the case of a process, consistency,[31] abstractive insight into the way its parts and/or moments belong together can take place.[32]

The human mind is able to symbolize these aspects of being at many levels, one symbol standing for the concrete stable thing (George), another for a moment in a process (George's fourth birthday), another for the given process (George's aging), another for a formalized kind of process held as typical (the human aging process), and so on.

Reflection on this discriminating, abstracting, comparing, contrasting enhances our sense of beholdenness to objective reality. It implies (*pace* Hume) the reality of relationships between things (including the causal connections that are the foundational reality of many processes) and the real organization within them—form—that grounds the truth of the formal insight into the sense of given structures, at different levels of abstraction. The ontological reality

---

30. I stress this scale, for, at the atomic scale, one must elaborate on the sense of things maintaining their structure. More on that in Part III, Chapter 6.

31. See Glossary.

32. Because of the wide range of possible kinds of structure, notions of form vary as well. When form symbolizes a real principle of identity and permanence keeping an organism whole and prosperous, it is obviously entitatively different from the form giving coherence to a collage of images I have combined to structure an imaginary work of art existing only in my fantasy.

of such natures is considered in Part III, Chapter 6. But I prepare the way by considering our knowledge of a particularly important kind of object—ourselves, as human nature.

Deconstruction and reconstruction in imagination can reinforce the same realistic point. Because we can distinguish really given parts in experience and in abstractions, understanding the objective relationships between these various aspects, parts, perspectives, at different levels of abstraction, we can rearrange them in our imaginations, moving freely from one level of generality to another. We do this for the joy of pure fantasy, and to map out plans for changing the world through work.

Here are some examples, to build credibility for my realistic contention that our mind's inventive adventures with the data derived from things are solidly anchored in the possibilities suggested by the real being of those things.

From Physical to Spiritual (1): The Presence in a Glance

I start with a rapid perception of an everyday setting, then reflect on some of the concepts implied in my quick grasp of that setting. When I first pursued this reflection, I found, looking back over the result, that I had moved effortlessly from things seen quickly, through consideration of different levels of abstraction implied by the concepts involved, to certain concepts presupposing a vast set of human relationships—social relationships, revealing how fundamental is our ongoing notion of human nature in any effort to grasp the real, the human world.

The example: Flashing by on the commuter train, I notice a new suburban neighborhood under construction. I see that it is going to be a large development, of lower-middle-class houses, and that it is scarcely begun, just a few houses beginning to take their final shape. Now, what has happened in my perceiving all that in a flash, roaring past at 110 kilometers per hour?

I have somehow been able to interpret a glimpse of half-finished streets, great holes excavated in the ground, and frames of buildings going up in rows and a few almost-finished houses as a new neighborhood, of a certain type—classified by income,[33] lower middle class—under construction. From perception of a moment in the development of that area, I have been able to infer a process of construction and, because it is typical, foretell exactly what will become of it in the next little while.

Obviously my mind has been able to apply the fruit of all the individual experiences, gained in no methodic order, casually and with little reflection, of North American frame, brick-veneer houses going up. I grasp the sense of the process running through all the stages, from hole in the ground, through concrete foundations, wood frame, roof, exterior finish, and landscaping. So,

---

33. Or by socioeconomic status, if you prefer. Technically, they are classed by the relationship of quality of construction, quantity of space in and around the dwelling, and offering price, all of which—as a result of banking and mortgagor practice and the set of alternatives available for housing in the metropolitan area—become related to income.

KINDS OF OBJECTS, KINDS OF TRUTH   63

on this occasion I am able to recognize in the one profile providing a glimpse of one slice of the process in what stage it now is: scarcely begun.

Consider this one small move by way of example of what the mind can do through insight: my understanding the development from digging a large hole in the ground (intended for the basement) to the pouring of the basement-bearing walls. Sorry, Hume, we here see real causal connections. In fact, my mind intuits the reason for digging the hole and the relationship between that act and the pouring of the bearing walls, then the later act of setting the wood bearing walls of the first floor upon the thus-secured foundation. Within an understanding of the overall design I grasp the (intelligible) connection between these acts and the elements they produce. Together they are grasped as a process of house construction.

Take another example of interpreting holes: A large, newly excavated hole in the middle of a vast field might remain a puzzle; the setting does not provide hints as to what it may be intended to become. If I am interested I must await further developments. Time passes, the hole fills with rain. Cattle are introduced into the field and come to drink from the hole. I judge, reading into the coming to be of this cultural object, the human intention behind it: It was built as a watering hole. Then the cattle are taken away, the hole is finished in a different shape, lined with concrete, and provided with a diving board. An attractive ranch house is built in front of it. Now I understand: The excavation was for some reason carried out early, then used temporarily as a watering hole, but was intended all along to become a swimming pool.

In each of the judgments involved in grasping the sense of these things, there is some movement beyond the immediately given data, drawing on knowledge of similar settings and things, and extrapolating the sense of the process forward, but also retrojecting back to the motivating intention. There is no other way, because I have no access to the principals, I can get at the intentions lying behind these artifacts. Such fallible judgment is correctable by the evidence from further events and by comparison with similar processes. Schematically:

1. Guided by the present perception of the things in question, the mind, calling on relevant past experience, judges basically what is at issue;[34]
2. it then turns back again to the things for further observation;
3. it moves (retro) to judgment of intention; on that basis,
4. it extrapolates further developments.

How do I judge the subdivision to be a large one? I have been able to retain impressions of all the developments I have seen, processed into a set

---

34. What may appear a chicken-and-egg situation is actually a case of the spiritual interpenetration that occurs in all human knowledge: The perceiver at once recognizes (which means he is deploying the processed benefits of past knowledge) what he is looking at, but to recognize it he has had to access that relevant past knowledge.

of comparative orderings; using the rough average as a standard, I now judge the present development to be a large one. On the same basis of comparative experience, I judge it as well to be lower-middle class. This last judgment brings out especially well the flexibility and subtlety of the process. The very imprecision of the category lower-middle class serves to make my point. What may be less clear is how objectively grounded is this inference, for all its imprecision.

I am prepared to defend the claim: There really are neighborhoods built rather consistently of houses of various degrees of elaborateness, reflecting social class differences. The large, well-designed, beautifully landscaped houses in North Toronto attract astronomical prices for good reasons. They are spacious (a relative but meaningful term); with excellent distribution of the spaces (again, many comparative judgments hidden in that concept); with carefully crafted details; and they exist in a setting of like quality.[35]

The neighborhood's spaciousness, quality, and homogeneity have attracted certain types of people, with particular cultures. This localized society interacts with the architecture and landscaping to produce and maintain a homogeneous result: Myriads of individual actions, because the agents had all been enculturated to similar views and desires, some of which are rooted in human nature, have left an objective, consistent result written into the landscape. The result is inscribed in matter, occupying a definite cosmic time-space, for all to perceive who know enough to interpret correctly. It now provides a well-furnished and easily interpretable stage setting for certain kinds of character to play appropriate roles within scenarios appropriate to this kind of neighborhood. If the Langans were to move in, real-estate values would plummet.

Some highly abstract concepts are at work in our recognition of what kind of neighborhood is under construction. But we could not manage our everyday affairs, let alone the world system, without them. Much of the struggle for truth, including the gigantomachia of ideologies, draws its breath in the rarified atmosphere of just such concepts. We branch off to follow an example of one such, to get a better notion of what is involved.

Take the economic concepts high income and low income. Though remote from any perceivable entities, they nevertheless play a role in our perceiving the neighborhood to be lower-middle class. What are our ultimate experiential grounds for such a vast generalization, and how are we able to predicate such a spiritual concept of the two contrasting neighborhoods? Spiritual? In what sense?

Consider income groups. Monetary systems exist largely in the mind. They do not occupy a material time-space out there in the physical cosmos. Rather, they enjoy an intersubjective objectivity. Although money is largely in the

---

35. Again, the quality of the detailing can be compared, and although aesthetic judgment is involved, it need not be arbitrary. Cases are to be argued on the perceptible evidence embedded in the crafted detail, moldings, door designs, hardware, and so on, which a given interlocutor may or may not be educated enough in these matters to appreciate.

mind, it profoundly affects the spirit, so much so people will kill for it. Some have objected that I should term an object like money "mental" rather than "spiritual." Mental it is, indeed, but I persist with my choice of term not at all innocently, but for ontological reasons, and drawing knowingly on the history of Occidental thought. As we shall see in Part III, I wish to call attention to a gradation of ontological states from the altogether material toward the altogether spiritual, the human mental being only one grade or aspect of spirituality. To prepare the reader to think in these terms (which, like all terms used for the most basic realities, have their history and so their limits, to be sure), I use it—provocatively—here.

From Physical to Spiritual (2): A Loan from the Bank

A monetary system's effect on material reality occurs only through the actions of human beings motivated by the conceptions they share about a particular system of debits and credits, when they then elect to exchange goods or pursue work "for money." The foundation of the Being *(Sein)* of the monetary system resides in the minds of the collectivity. Signs of the system exist in the form of bank notes, coins, and recorded entries (all having *esse*) that serve to keep track of credits and debits. Credits and debits, which will be noted on computer tapes and ledgers, are aspects of that monetary system and exist, again, only in the minds of those extending and recognizing them. They are a familiar and generally agreed-upon system of contractual arrangements, which are intelligible will acts. Because these will acts are spiritual, they must be expressed and witnessed. I can pick up the phone and agree to buy one hundred shares of IBM at $98.25 per share, and that will be binding, upheld, if necessary, by a court of law, exercising the will of the community. Note, within the imaginations of the relevant agents, these commitments have a certain peculiar time-space of their own, other than material existence. This Hasmonaean bronze putah no longer has a direct purchasing power, because the society for which it was meaningful is dead; but its numismatic value may exceed by far any purchasing power it had under the Maccabean kings. The loan I have just taken out is credited to me for three years, and is extended by the North York branch of the Toronto-Dominion Bank, its place of record. It concerns a kind of spiritual space between me and my estate, and the bank and its owners. We measure years using a planetary rotation as basis, but the notion of the interest to be charged per time period resides in the mind entirely. Where the debit resides is a matter of administrative convenience. By mere fiat, it can be shifted from the branch to the main office of the T-D Bank, or the loan can even be sold to another bank.

Monetary systems work through consensus, persons deploying the same *Sein*, sharing the same world. Where they translate into reality—the ultimate bottom line, if you will—is in the action through which human beings offer a service or a desired object in exchange for being credited with an agreed number of units, which can in turn be used to convince someone else to render a service or surrender possession of a thing.³⁶ Much stability is presupposed for such a spiritual system to be viable and intelligible:

1. A constancy of human nature, founding a further stability of culture. We assume that human beings will, in the setting of a developed culture, understand an abstract system of measures for facilitating exchanges. (Persons who, educated into the system, fail to live up to the obligations they have freely assumed are treated as cranks, mentally handicapped, or criminals.)
2. We accept the reality of the inculturation of the system in all the agents, and expect the agents in certain institutions vital to the system to play their respective responsible roles. Failure can lead to loss of confidence, to inflation of the currency.
3. We presuppose the endurance and recognition of the typical things exchanged, and the consistency and dependability of certain quality of service, based in habit.

Consider some of the different levels of abstraction involved in a typical financial transaction, and then we shall trace these concepts back from the mental world to real things. This introduces a basic feature of action: role playing.

Suppose I address my branch bank for a loan of $22,000, to purchase an automobile, and the loan is for five years at 11 percent. Four concrete things are involved: a human being, the borrower; the loan officer; the assistant manager who has to give final approval; and—although none of the agents at this point is concerned actually to see it, so it is present only in their imaginations—the car itself. Perception of each of the persons is focused by the particular spiritual undertaking in which we are involved. The agents are interested not in the other as a person, but only in the function of a restricted role each is playing. I do not care that Mr. Hussein Salah, the loan officer, is a Shiite, and he cares nothing about me as the author of *Being and Truth* (so long as it is producing effectively no revenue). Each is trying to size up the other, on the presently available perceptible data. The shadowy figure of Mr. Mackenzie, the tough old Scot who is the assistant manager, is hovering over the affair like a menacing spirit, but he is present, like the car itself, in the imagination, and

---

36. Without the anchor of actual goods and services, these measures would have no sense. What does it mean to say that the marquis d'X received rents of 457 louis d'or in 1685, if one has absolutely no idea of prices or wage rates in seventeenth-century France? The economic historians establish roughly the prices of a basket of typical goods and services. One is then able to know what the louis d'or was really worth. In the equation is presupposed, of course, the social agreement to render the services and surrender the goods at approximately those prices, that is, at a reasonably consistent and specific rate of exchange as between these actions and things. As is reported in *The Story of English* (R. McCrum, W. Cran, and R. MacNeil [London: BBC Books/Faber & Faber, 1986], 280), the Cockney argot of London's East End delivered precisely the opposite—one price to those who knew how to follow the dialect, another (higher) one to those who could not.

again as a restricted function. The concrete perceptible natures of the agents and the car are precious guides to what we are about in this essentially spiritual operation.

"Spiritual" again? Consider what kind of entity the loan is. It is neither an abstract nor a cosmic thing. It is a concrete spiritual relationship (not just mental, for it involves the whole person's power to engage, and the sheriff who may show up to seize the car will do so as a physical force). It assumes the sincerity and responsibility of both contracting parties. Such an agreement can be made entirely verbally and, if witnessed, is binding in law. Because the agreement binds more than me as this human person and the agent of the bank—it binds, to be exact, my legal person, including my estate after death, and lays a condition on the ownership of my car and the assets of the Toronto-Dominion Bank, with obligations accruing to the corporate legal person—it is not sufficient, as it would be in the case of an informal personal loan, just for Mr. Salah and me to know it. Paradoxically, the extreme spirituality of my legal person and estate and the fictive corporate person of the T-D Bank makes it necessary to symbolize the relationship in a form that can be preserved and passed around the bureaucracy.

This ability to extend a spiritual time-space larger than that of any one person enhances man's power, harnessing our cooperative action beyond the lives of the presently contracting agents. But, I would emphasize, for all this, the loan, with this bureaucratically noted time-space, is spiritual, not perceptible, yet not abstract; concrete, not real in the primary sense, but real spiritually.

The written document is only a symbol, counting as evidence for the larger community that the agreement took place and rendering precise its terms. While the agreement is both spiritually intersubjective and concrete, what about another consideration, my credit worthiness? That is based on an estimation by bank officials, a judgment, founded in some general guidelines capturing the fruit of the institution's experience over the years as to what constitutes, in their eyes, the personal conditions under which it is safe to enter into a loan agreement. For this general class of loans, where repossession of the car is not difficult, the criteria will be fairly easy ones, quite functional, we may say, focused on ability to pay: Can mortgage payments on my house be met, taxes paid, food provided, with enough left over to allow progressive retirement of the auto loan?

But business loans require a more sweeping, more spiritual judgment about an individual's ability to assure successful management of a concrete business situation. Some very large general judgments will be made about the situation: Oil prices, in the next ten years, will not stay below $10 per barrel for long, and will produce the cash flow necessary to support the level of loan the bank is advancing Mr. X in his takeover bid for an oil company. Within that scenario, Mr. X can be counted on to manage the property in a trustworthy fashion, he will not be milking the company in ways our auditors will be unable to detect in time, and anyway, he would never do that kind of thing.

Behind the judgment on the price of oil during the loan period lies a large econometric model of oil production and demand, worked out according to various scenarios. Behind the judgment of Mr. X's character and ability lies long personal experience with Mr. X and how he operates, judged against the loan officers' own personal experience with human and especially managerial behavior.

Huge structures of analysis and synthesis residing on relatively limited experiential bases are a fact of everyday life. We are forced to skate on thin ice, so we become defensive when challenged. "Just how well do you know Mr. X really?" "Why, I have known him for years—I have been involved in making loans to him for fifteen years." In fact, when I stop to think about it, I know little about his personal life; I may be downplaying a disturbing incident I know about (he strong-armed an associate); I conveniently overlook that he has been successful in acquiring and selling manufacturing companies and in fact has never had anything to do with oil and gas. The complexity of such judgments, replete with delicate balancing of impressions, and their remoteness from experience to which I can return in a serious way leave me wide open to manipulation and self-deception.

This is one of the reasons why and how the will, moving toward what the agent really wants, can massage reality, to present a picture that accords with desires, not how things really are. When a person says he does not see a table right in front of him in broad daylight, we know that he needs either glasses or a psychologist. But as soon as the notions being manipulated are complex and remote from direct experience, then the knower's ongoing construction of an imaginary mental scene is desire driven, much more than in perception, where the valence is reversed in favor of the immediately present things' imposing their reality on him.

From Physical to Spiritual (3): A Collision of Time-Spaces

The example at hand shows this. Consider the background: During the period of the oil crisis, when unprecedented sums of money were being recycled from the Persian Gulf through American and European banks to Third World countries, many bank officers had to psych themselves into believing they were acting in the banks' interest. Someone with a little detachment could easily see the disaster they were brewing. I recall a dinner in 1980 with a vice-president for foreign operations of an old Boston bank, and a lawyer drawing up sovereign[37] loan agreements for a Canada-chartered bank. We were having fun at his expense: "You don't honestly expect ever to see a dollar of that money come back, do you?" His rationalizations were comical. What was going on in this rather typical case of massive self-delusion?

Well, what happens all the time in all institutions: There was a difference between the bank's real interest, long-term, and certain officers' own personal interest. (Note that "real" here means not material time-space existence, but

---

37. That is, to foreign governments or quasi-governmental organizations.

the enduring continuity of the institution, the fuller context.) Those particular officers' interest was to push money through the bank at good interest rates this year and next year. Their time-space was different from the bank's long-term interest. When the going would get rough, they could only hope they would be hidden in bureaucratic obscurity. The juridical person, the institution of the bank, would be stuck in continuity with the time-space of the loan agreements and would have to start taking write-downs, to the detriment of the equity holders.

Given that often, humanly, we are not too eager to get back to the real data, or we are only willing to return to it selectively, we see that verification may be psychologically more complex than a positivist would care to think. Existentialists have always kept will more in their view, and so have not forgotten that getting at truth somehow requires a wise attitude of the whole person.

I attempt now to draw more schematically the distinctions between kinds of notions as regards remoteness from the data.

Some Kinds of Notions and Their Relations to Experience

Let us begin with two entities accessible, at least on the surface, by direct perceptual experience. We shall see that our ways of relating to them commonly are in fact already quite different.

First, the Finished House in the Subdivision. I can return to the perception of the house for fresh experience anytime I want, and I shall find a thing that, being only mildly active (compared, for instance, with Mr. X), will have changed little over the span of a couple of years, and whose individual character is not very pronounced. This goes with the fact that the spiritual depth—the interiority—of the house is not very profound. Its reality is that material kind of time-space characteristic of all the things, living and dead, that we encounter daily, the great exception being the higher animals and those spiritual subjects, human beings, whose greater depth shows readily on the surface. Much of the reality of the house lies below the perceived surface. Even so, I know this much negatively: Upon laboratory examination no inner thoughts will be discovered, no conscious projects hidden beneath the brick. Because a house has no soul, it changes, compared to most living things, slowly and hence furnishes a rather stable point of reference.

In contrast, consider the other perceptually accessible thing, Mr. X. Granted, he is a thing, and so I can also go back to direct experience of him. The notion I have built up of him is synthesized from many different experiences in a variety of settings, although in most of them he played basically the same role, that of entrepreneurial manager and investor. The house is always in the same setting, the neighborhood where it plays, properly speaking, no role, but does carry out a given function as part of a stage scene intended by the developer. But the house itself knows nothing about any of this; unlike Mr. X, it cannot play along.

But see what a different reality is involved when I attempt to read various actions of Mr. X to figure out the role he is playing, and whether in the unfolding scenario he is playing it very well. If a question arises about some aspect of his inner self, I cannot straightforwardly initiate an empirical investigation to clear it up. I recognize that he plays a number of different roles, that some of them may be in tension, that he may deliberately dissimulate, and that, anyway, he is more than the sum total of his role playing. He is, after all, this center of awareness with the ability to know he is playing roles. I may have to wait to catch Mr. X in the act, which will clear up the question about him. Or I can ask him what he thinks he is up to, or what he believes about this or that, but his self-deception may be even more skillful than his leading others down the garden path.

All external perception captures glimpses of what lies below the surface. Depending on how developed is the interiority of the species and the individual and on the particular appearance *(Erscheinung)* the perceiver has to work with, the penetration allowed will get more or less beyond the surface. Also we have developed instruments for deeper physical penetration: An X ray tells me things about the skeleton I could not learn just looking at the skin, and the electron microscope things about the molecular structure an ordinary X ray cannot manifest. The human being is different from every other entity as regards its interior. An involuntary narrowing of the eyes may tell me more about Mr. X than his carefully dyed hair and impeccable clothes, and perhaps a pious declaration he has just laid before me. At his core lies an interaction of creative initiative (freedom) and hard-wired structures of the psyche, some genetic, some acquired, which have to be read as functions through the evidence presented by his courses of action as he plays out roles in a series of scenarios.

Dynamic, indeed. Note that every being does something, and by observing what it does, we come to understand more about its being. "Agere sequitur esse," says Saint Thomas. But the higher animals are very complex actors, and their interiority is revealed in many ways by courses of action informed by a project. In man, many different courses of action may be brought into relationship with one another and derive their form from an enveloping role the actor has to some degree freely assumed. They are roles in a scenario, they are theater: they interrelate in an intersubjective scenario within some situation or spiritual setting, such as our being together in the same institution.[38] All these roles and interrelationships are rife with intelligibility as we read the living being through our perception of many actions.

Coming to know people in their roles is a process of coming to see into the sense of a process; but the resultant insight, the intellectual grasp of the unity that threads through a series of acts, makes it possible for one to see them as bits of evidence of a character at work.

---

38. See the brilliant analysis of the history of the idea that "all the world's a stage" in *Prolegomena*, the introductory volume to Hans Urs von Balthasar's seven-volume *Theo-Dramatik* (San Francisco: Ignatius Press, 1990).

KINDS OF OBJECTS, KINDS OF TRUTH 71

Much experience is brought to this reading-in, indispensable to knowing what is going on. This foreknowledge and predisposition may also function as misleading prejudice,[39] expectations may cause me to miss subtle but important differences in the way Mr. X plays a typical role. My complex notion of Mr. X is a collage of insights into his playing of different roles, perhaps without much concern for how these come together, what the significance of certain inconsistencies might be. All this forms, despite the deficient unity, a kind of concrete universal. All knowledge I have of him is referred to the common center, the concrete material entity, of which I am reminded every time I see Mr. X. This concrete point of reference becomes the anchor for assembling all the relevant knowledge I have of him. It here functions rather like a universal, in that it gives significance to all the moments and the particular processes as characteristics of Mr. X. Grasp of their significance occurs by my bringing together those moments insightfully, similar to the way a universal spreads its revealing umbrella over many individuals. Perhaps this concrete universal might better be called "a concrete totality," a little world (cosmion) with its own inherent consistency. Or, sometimes, lack of it, as when I lament, "I cannot figure Mr. X. How can he be such a good father and such a sleazy businessman?" We expect the pieces to add up.[40]

Verification of my views on Mr. X cannot be secured by a few glimpses. The truth about this person is the result of elaborate reasoning, which moves up into abstractions and between abstractions (Mr. X is a typical Canadian, a generous soul, and so on), illumined by the *Sein* of the world in which he and I operate. This is not only the very diffuse *Sein* of the contemporary high-tech epoch, but in this case the *Sein* of the lesser world of oil and gas and of banking. But however wide-ranging the categories, the reference is still ultimately to the concrete person, Mr. X, perceptible so long as he still lives and acts.

The truth I have built up about this cosmion reveals a kind of essence, a *Wesen;* not an abstract generalization, but a concrete knowledge of how this person remains consistent with what he has always been. My grasp of this concrete consistency, quite beyond that of the human nature he holds in common with all other men, founds a cautious extrapolation: My interaction with him demands that I foresee what I can expect of him, although I acknowledge that he is also changing subtly in ways that generally make some sense. If he were pure spontaneity, such that I could await anything from him at any time with no expectation of continuity, there could be no truth of Mr. X, I could have

---

39. All the relevant previous knowledge I bring to reading the present situation is, if you like, prejudgment. It helps me to understand what is going on in the present instance, but it also can guide me to overlook that for which it does not prepare me. This is a permanent feature of our finitude.

40. I have found that colloquial expressions capture considerable everyday insight into human affairs. That is why I employ them often, and not for the sake of achieving a breezy style. Consider, for instance, apropos of those cosmiota the expression "He has not got his thing together."

no hope of dealing on a reasonable basis with him, there really would be no essential Mr. X at all.

So his already-having-been *Wesen* to some degree is seen to engage the future; it is what he will actualize in exercising his freedom. His freedom is rooted in his personal *Sein*, that fund of concrete possibilities inherited from the past, out of which he projects a future, into which is received, mysteriously, the new. There are profound implications here for the nature of human, finite freedom. The fidelity of man, to himself and to the other, has its limits, because we, unlike God, who Scripture says is "ever faithful," can be perverse. Sometimes man's inconsistency is good: It can mark an act of creative freedom from a bad course of action, what the Christian tradition calls "conversion." Often, though, in our inconsistency we are being untrue to ourselves, thereby causing those who love us distress.

Consider an example of my categorizing Mr. X—he is so typically Canadian in his willingness to compromise. I attempt to find what I can count on in him by bringing it into comparison with something I already know about a class of people. We make these kinds of judgments frequently. But what experience lies behind my abstraction, the typical Canadian?

How rarely everyday life obliges critical examination of the foundations of our sweeping judgments! We indulge ourselves in them—sexist, racist, classist, nationalist as they may be—unchallenged. Here is a merit of formal appropriation: It invites me to call some of these judgments to account.

Now, if I reflect on my own symbol, trying to clarify the concept that lies behind it, I see that I really mean not Canadians in general but more specifically middle-class WASPish English Canadians. Then I acknowledge that most of my experience of such individuals has been with central Canadians—indeed, residents of Toronto—and I might want to pause to ask whether this is appropriate in the case of Mr. X. After all, he lives in Calgary, and I do not know many Albertans. Perhaps they are different. And even if they are not, how dare I place much confidence in this gradually built-up and very anecdotal and general notion? How many have I known, and how widely distributed in various milieux? What is to prevent Mr. X from being significantly different from his class and race? Perhaps he is completely intransigent, without a drop of compromise in him.

I realize that people have told me for twenty-five years that compromise is the national tradition, which concrete instances have largely confirmed. There are exceptions: the fanaticism of both sides in the abortion or Québec separation debate, for instance, and considerable ideological hardness in the university. But are these exceptions so exceptional, or are we here seeing what happens when Canadians confront an issue where the sense of one's deepest natural faith about the meaning of human life or nation comes to the fore? In those instances, Canadians do not appear so bland. And then I recall how valiantly Canadians fought in both world wars.

There exists no natural form, the central, middle-class Canadian, that I can intuit; there is no unambiguous instantiating individual, the way the house in my neighborhood is indeed solidly typical of the species middle-class Central Canadian housing. Yet here is a broad abstract category, a universal concept, middle-class Canadian of Central Canada, the sense of which is gradually built up, illumined by the vague national and class *Sein*, and related in obscure ways to whatever supporting data there may be for it. Alas, this is typical of many of the concepts through which we do much of our thinking. What possibilities this leaves for emoting on the subject in place of hard critical analysis of the substance of the issues hidden behind its casual employ!

Note, too, that in most situations I probably have no motive to engage in serious, responsible research and reflection on the subject. Many of our concepts are formed in the process of a kind of emotional management of experience, with little intention of achieving fairness, accuracy, and depth. Truth and justice are not the prime motives. Blowing off the steam of resentment and superficial encounter often is.

This type of generalization is so unreliable as a source of truth about the things of which it is predicated, one is tempted to ask whether we ought not dispense with this kind of thinking altogether, if that is psychologically possible. Wittgenstein made this very point.[41] Racism, social class prejudice, every sort of ideological mischief is fed by just such wide-sweeping generalizations based on vague processing of spotty experience, wrapped in emotional preoccupation with my own problems. At least we should be more cautious in applying them. We should examine the emotional needs that invite us to irresponsible judging, and cultivate the habit of reminding ourselves that there are so many exceptions to some of these generalizations, we should be careful in labeling any individual.

Consider trustworthiness, an abstract concept involved in our loan transaction. I do not recall ever, until now, asking myself what this really means, not to speak of inquiring what experience may lie behind my own concept of it. The next paragraph will change all that.

Often the term occurs in a restricted context. If the banker assures his superiors that Mr. X is trustworthy, they are considering not his relationship with his wife, but that in a business context he says what he means, and he

---

41. Wittgenstein wrote to Norman Mauser in 1944: "Whenever I thought of you I couldn't help thinking of a particular incident which seemed to me to be very important. You & I were walking along the river towards the railway bridge & we had a heated discussion in which you made a remark about 'national character' that shocked me by its primitiveness. I then thought: what is the use of studying philosophy if all that it does for you is to enable you to talk with some plausibility about some abstruse questions of logic, etc. & if it does not improve your thinking about the important questions of everyday life, if it does not make you more conscientious. You see, I know that it's difficult to think well about 'certainty,' 'probability,' 'perception,' etc. But it is, if possible, still more difficult to think, or try to think, really honestly, about your life & other people's lives. And the trouble is that thinking about these things is not thrilling, but often downright nasty. And when it's nasty then it's most important" (quoted by Norman Malcolm in *Ludwig Wittgenstein: A Memoir* [Oxford: Oxford University Press, 1958], 39).

does what he says he will do. In a business scenario, he is not always trying to lay a trap for his partners.

To clarify the notion, I contrast Mr. X with Professor Y, whom I consider to be a liar. Why? Because he never lays his cards on the table. You can talk for hours with him about a difficult, disputed issue in university politics, during which he will be understanding and accommodating. Then you discover the next day, from his actions, that he has not bent an inch and was only listening for things he might quote against you. I wonder if he sees what he is doing; the confusion seems to come from deep within him.

Whence my insight into Mr. X's trustworthiness? To form the base of the general concept, trustworthiness, I have abstracted from a concrete situation its sense, which I now treat as typical: Anyone entering into an agreement, or pursuing a common interest with another, may relate to the other by laying his cards on the table and then carrying out the stated or implied obligation. The structure of the typical scenario is then further abstracted, following an insight into how the various parts (acts by different role players) of the dynamic scenario structure relate. One symbol can express the quality required for the situation to be possible: trustworthiness. Trustworthiness is a state of accidental being imputed to a person who is in the habit of engaging the future unequivocally, and who has the character necessary to be able to act: the honesty to remember what he has agreed to[42] and the courage to carry it through. The possibility of a self-liar's being trustworthy is undermined from the beginning by the confusion in his soul that clouds his vision of what he has in fact agreed to. He is forever rewriting history.

Suppose something happens that causes Mr. X's trustworthiness to come into question. He entered into a deal with Johnson in Edmonton to buy that oil-well-valve manufacturer without saying that the owner was his brother-in-law's son. He took a small minority interest and led Johnson into paying too much for it. The story does check out—here indeed is a smudge on Mr. X's reputation. What does one think then? One might suppose that this was an exception, that he was subject to unusual pressures, and conclude that in special circumstances (perhaps ill defined) you cannot entirely trust him. Or one can suspend judgment in this regard and begin acquiring wider knowledge of Mr. X's conduct in other deals. Just as in science, a single anomaly can throw the governing theory into doubt, so knowledge of a single flagrant act can motivate a search for more evidence.

The principle was deliberately made vague, mirroring the imprecision of the experiential base. Consistent behavior is a sign that two conditions are present: a continuing attitude governing ongoing decisions in a set of typical situations, and the force of character necessary for the individual to be able to act in keeping with his underlying convictions. But we have experienced the eruption of the exceptional. Sometimes this can result from the person's being placed

---

42. The dishonest person so conveniently forgets what he has agreed to or has been told. The relationship of lie and pathology and sin is intimate.

in a radically new situation, which tests his resolve as never before, showing on that occasion that it was not as well founded as one thought. (The move from familiar scenarios requires fresh thinking—for instance, he may have suffered a momentary disorientation. In a deliberate plot, like the sale of the valve manufactory, confusion cannot be the plea.) Or perhaps he was under the influence of alcohol. Then we must broaden the inquiry to discern whether he gets into that state very often. Or perhaps he just acted erratically, inexplicably. Still, the judgment seems to me inevitable: If he can do it once, he can do it again. The underlying idea is that this one exception shows that there is more to the person's entire attitude and character than we thought. In many concrete situations we recognize as comparable (an abstracting generalization based in comparison of situations), the agent will act in a similar, and hence predictable, fashion. We bring in our more generalized knowledge of human behavior to build in a caveat, not to overshoot in the degree of certitude we throw behind our extrapolation: Given the nature of human freedom, the possibility of an erratic act can never be ruled out absolutely.

■ ■ ■

This discussion was provoked by the need to move, in our example, from the perception of things like holes and half-finished houses, to the reality of the social situations that are at work behind judgments like lower-middle class. We saw that the founding experience is of a social reality of interacting role playing, in which we make judgments about the personalities and character involved. These are made possible by certain stabilities of culture and institution, more transcendentally of *Sein*, which in turn presuppose a fundamental stability in affairs human, that basic dimension we just mentioned: human nature (mirrored in what Heidegger calls the *Ek-sistenzialien*, the ongoing structural features of *Dasein*'s projection of world). So, preliminary and spotty as these reflections may have been, they serve to introduce us to the question of our forming a notion of human nature. With this preparation, let us then turn to that all-important object of our knowledge.

NATURES
Basic Knowledge of Human Nature[43]

The complexity both of the being of humans and of our knowledge processes, which must work laboriously to build up an adequate notion, precludes a simple, onetime attack on the question, How do we form a knowledge of human nature? Today one encounters resistance to the very notion that there is

---

43. I am indebted to Bruce A. Stewart for much of this section. In a recent article, "The Limits of History: Ontology, Anthropology and Historical Understanding," David J. Levy shows that the notion of a continuity in the form of a human nature is not at all foreign to the phenomenological tradition, citing in its defense such distinguished phenomenologists as Nicolai Hartmann, Max Scheler, and Hans Jonas. *Journal of the British Society for Phenomenology* 20:2 (May 1989): 150–65.

a human nature. The morning I started to work on this draft I happened onto a newspaper article by a homosexual reporting on a new homosexual men's group and their weekend get-together:

> There is one good thing about it. It is very sex positive. It seems to encourage the eroticization of everyday life, and does so outside the bounds of the traditional couple. It thrives on group eroticism and sex. I like that. It is, however, profoundly antisocial, and is so because it abandons irony and artifice, and embraces sincerity and nature. Human society, after all, is elaborated through artifice, and surely represents a flight from what Wilde termed that "dreadful universal thing called human nature." It is because we are in fact all brothers and sisters under the skin that I already know what you're going to tell me about your hopes, your fears, your dreadful family life, your need for closeness, your fear of intimacy. It is your lies I want. I already know your truths.[44]

Such declarations remind us we live in a time when a thinking person cannot presume that much about human existence; nothing in the old commonsense wisdom goes without challenge, even when, as in the quotation, one may admit there is a human nature of some sort.

The question of human nature cannot be avoided. Here I ask how we come to know ourselves as a kind of being, and then in the ontology of Part III, a fuller exploration of the nature that we know ourselves to be is undertaken, with attention to its cosmic setting, and its reality as an organism, as this affects our total understanding of what and who we are.

We have recognized two types of stability in human beings:

1. The personal, my own individual, personal persistence, as this embodied aware person and as this personality, a concatenation of temperament and character and enculturated roles manifest through all the vicissitudes of my life. (These considerations touch on the question of knowledge of personal identity, much discussed by philosophers since Hume.)[45]
2. The similar reality in others around me, who have an identity not only of their own but of "the same nature," including a reasonable inference that this kind of stability, this great likeness of kind in many individuals, proceeds back through our forebears and forward through our offspring.

The perception of real relations will be examined momentarily; that will bring us up against Hume's challenge to the reality of relations. Humeans among my readers are no doubt already eager to attack my unsophisticated recognition of both a personal identity and a continuing nature in those of our kind, given the Scottish sage's attack on all belief in the in-itselfness of perceived continuity and his contention that structure is imposed by the mind, the core of what was to become the great Kantian faith ruling over nineteenth- and twentieth-century philosophy. My answer here is simply put:

---

44. Gerald Hannon, in *Toronto Globe and Mail*, Apr. 4, 1992.
45. Personhood is given from conception; the personality of the person is developed historically-culturally throughout life.

No matter what changes do occur in our lives, we continue to find ourselves there. Even the amnesiac is convinced that there is something about his past that he ought to be able to remember. The compelling nature of that search, and his joy at remembering, shows that we do experience a continuity in ourselves—the *Sein* of a personal history—that is founded more deeply (and mysteriously!) than our conscious belief in our own personal continuance. That "bundle of perceptions," which Hume says constitutes me, contains a far deeper congruence of perceptions taken by us as continuous than Hume's own argument allowed for. We appear therefore to be justified in our self-understanding—as justified as we are in taking the world commonsensically, as even Hume indicated he did when he stepped down from his philosophical study.

Having seen that there is at least some rational underpinning available to us for our taking human beings as stabilities, what else can we discover about the scope of this knowledge of stability? We are able to recognize as human beings persons drawn from all parts of the globe. From the streets of Toronto to the upper reaches of the Amazon we seem to have no difficulty knowing the difference between our kind and others. Certainly we see this here in Toronto, which UNESCO has labeled as the world's most cosmopolitan city and which contains communities of creatures we take as being like us regardless of their origin (107 countries). Color and background seem not to be a barrier, then, to a common humanity.

But, it may be argued *en riposte,* what of the many differing views about human nature, with even Aristotle defending the institution of slavery and the categorization of some as subhuman *barbaroi?* Does not the historical record show us that various human beings have banded together to classify some of ourselves as the people and others as not the people? Indeed, does not the very real existence of national feeling act as further evidence that the question of who are we generally, as man, does not admit of such a simple reply as we have suggested?

Although I have no hesitation in calling Aristotle wrong for failing to recognize the humanity of all peoples, the point I raise should not be dismissed: the challenge to determine more closely what is of nature in the human being and what is acquired by enculturation. All men, everywhere and at every time, have had a *habitus* toward categorizing their fellows as similar and yet different. This need for a love of the particular, which has expressed itself in many ways,[46] shows something common to all men from earliest tribe to present communities. Moreover, the love of the particular itself takes on a variety of forms concurrently, from familial ties to political and traditional compositions, but always demonstrating, as Diotima indicated in Plato's *Symposium,* the human being's ability to love various particular communities simultaneously and to reach for the more universal loves open to him in doing so.[47]

---

46. For example, families (Chinese), castes (Indian), fellow citizens of the *poleis* (Classical), co-religionists (Levantine), and fellow nationals and citizens of the state (Western).

47. We return to this question in Chapter 7.

We may draw a first tentative conclusion: Man's ever-changing circumstances do not appear, on this evidence, to be a convincing argument against a common human nature, despite the rather thick veneer of historically based condition laid upon us all, from the so-called Stone Age Putumayo Indians to the self-styled technocratic elite of Western civilization. Hence two guideposts for any study of human nature. First, in evaluating the evidence, take care not to dismiss part of human nature by too hastily classifying it as the result of enculturation. As we have seen, we ought to investigate empirically just how widespread the condition experienced is. Second, take care not to add to human nature parts that really are peculiar to one particularity of mankind over another.[48] Be careful not to ascribe to human nature an overstability, recognizing that the human species, while enjoying a form that gives its present kind of reality a certain permanence, is itself something that came into being and that something can evolve from it, which would then have a different form.[49] Human beings as we know them might come to live side by side with post-humans of another species. But even if human beings died out, their present form would always be intelligible as what it is.

With these provisos in mind, let us look for further evidence for a human nature. Consider our ability to enter long-dead civilizations through the findings of archaeology. The Code of Hammurapi,[50] the Sumero-Akkadian king of Babylonia, is readily understandable today. Likewise, although the cave paintings of Les Eyzies precede writing, we find empathy and commonality with them. We may find facets of other cultures and civilizations today difficult to enter into fully—Asian music forms, for instance—but this is not much more challenging than training one's eye, ear, and expectations for the various forms of Western music and painting. Certainly, for the unconvinced, the sheer fact that the Abrahamic traditions have reached from their humble beginnings outside of Ur almost four millennia ago to embrace so many all over the planet, while remaining accessible to all these historically conditioned groups of people, stands as evidence of that common core within humanity that the Abrahamic revelation claims YHWH created.

So, then, what may we say in a basic way of this nature? Ours, like all natures, must be an intelligible permanence, grasped by our reading-in *(inter-legere)* to those consistencies seen in the midst of change manifest by real human beings, in real situations, their sense—that is, the form of human nature.[51]

---

48. We have occasion to take this up again, beginning in Chapter 6.

49. Likewise, we must be careful not to ascribe to human nature anything that is particular to a tradition, no matter how ancient, unless we are able to explain why, if whatever it is supposedly makes up part of human nature, it was not evident in other traditions. A full discussion of this would require a complete philosophical anthropology, which is beyond the scope of this book.

50. Died ca. 1750 B.C. I give the more recent transliteration of his name.

51. The concept of nature as founded in a form is not only as venerable in philosophy as Plato's ideas and the *morphē* of Aristotle, it is inevitable . . . and very dangerous. The concept form retarded for fifteen hundred years careful investigation into how this nature or that

But this answer does not begin to deal with the questions that animate humans, in real settings. Who is a human being? How do we conduct ourselves, given this reality about ourselves? (No, G. E. Moore's naturalistic fallacy is not being ignored, but is eventually challenged. See below.) What do we do with the cases at the margins: the not-yet-born,[52] the near-neonatal baby, the severely disabled, those who are dying? What, too, of the possibility of the technical forms of Man that, so far, have been the province of science fiction: the android, the cyborg, the artificial intelligence of a self-modifying computer program with holistic and inductive capabilities? We shall say something about this shortly. First, however, the central issue must be dealt with: that of the stability of the species itself.

Although we have recognized, not just endurance in the midst of change, but intelligible regularity in the development of different kinds of things,[53] that leaves open the question of the kind of permanence the human species manifests. How can one say, with confidence, in what consists the continuation of type-of-being from generation to generation, and a commonality within generations? Are there not those who worry whether there really is such a persistence as a species (as we commonly understood it), which could have a nature?

The evidence from scientific inquiry into natural variations[54] provides us with a high degree of confidence in our arguments for a human nature. Certainly the resistance to Platonic-style eternal forms encourages us to downplay the idea of everlasting permanence in the stabilities of the world, just as I resist a Platonic overplaying of the existence of forms in an intelligible heaven. Yet we must not be blind to such persistences as do offer themselves in evidence—such *permanences*, not just a brute factual endurance but an intelligible organization of a distinctive, identifiable kind achieving coherent lasting being, thanks to some regulative principle in the thing, passed on through reproduction, and so achieving permanence in the species too. On what evidence, for instance, might I claim that I (in unity) persist, yet that my species is a fiction? Such continuities as are apparent to us, in terms of man's ability to procreate with his kind in any

---

really works, requiring the devastating meat-ax attacks in the era of Galileo to free a space for empirical investigation of how this or that kind of thing is actually constituted. That led both to the loss (temporary, I trust) of finality and natural law and, in recompense, to such modest discoveries as depth psychology and DNA, for instance. Thought cannot do without a notion of form, but we must be very careful to think in every instance whence it comes and how it functions, and we should remain aware of how superficial is our grasp of the form of a real species.

52. In the various modes from spermatozoa and ovum, through zygote and embryo, to fetus.
53. See Chapter 2 and Chapter 4.
54. Ofttimes known publicly as the theory of evolution. We should, however, be proper and realize that the theory we presently consider capable of best explaining all the known evidence is a theory of natural variations, not an evolutionary theory. See Etienne Gilson, *D'Aristote à Darwin et retour* (Paris: J. Vrin, 1971); *From Aristotle to Darwin and Back Again*, trans. John Lyon (Notre Dame: University of Notre Dame Press, 1984).

country and in terms of the communality with the rest of humanity both living and deceased, argue for the long enduring permanence of the human species qua species.

Consider some of the most short-lived of species: The geneticists' favorite, *Drosophila melanogaster,* comes to mind. One human being, working over a lifetime, can readily observe fifteen hundred generations. In human terms, this represents thirty thousand years of existence. Even with such a long species' time passing, *Drosophila* has had only very minor variations observed and has never become so unstable as to be considered the progenitor of a new species of fruit fly.

This is not to deny that random mutations and natural selection can, over immense periods of time, produce some profound differences. The silver fox of the Canadian North, for instance, cannot impregnate the Feneek fox of the Sahara. But no evidence laid before us has suggested that man is somehow different in this respect from *Drosophila* or any other species; change, yes, but slowly, amid a huge coefficient of permanence. The great difference of man lies, it has always been seen, in his spiritual dimensions, not his kinship to the other living things of this planet. The incredible rapidity (on a geologic scale) of humanity's expansion is due, if you like, to a distinctive mechanism of evolution, the Lamarckian.[55] The notion that acquired characteristics may be passed on genetically may still be a matter of dispute, but it happens among humans by means of language: "Today still an Innu can take off his furs to beget a baby with a Sahalian Tourreg."[56]

We may, therefore, reasonably claim that there is such a thing as a human species persisting in time, and that it can have a common nature identifying its individuals, despite man's accelerated evolution in terms of symbols and culture and the claims of relativization that the recognition of this *geschichtlich* (historical) facet of his existence has brought.

This last point is important. Our ability to create a potentially species-wide memory through the use of symbols has afforded us the opportunity to effect a more visible rate of change while simultaneously masking our common nature behind a large variety of rapidly evolving cultures. The differences in symbols, their interpretation, and the cultural objects and institutions they help form have led to man's common understanding of small groups as an us and the bulk of mankind as a them. We should recall that *barbaroi* are, in the end, outsiders and able to be enslaved precisely because they do not share the culture and symbolism of the *poleis*. This implies that they are not men, who are political animals. The stabilities found in traditions, institutions, processes, symbols,

---

55. Indeed, our predilection for nominalist solutions is driven by the overemphasis on both the material and the spiritual—the object and the subject, if you prefer—caused by their Cartesian sundering. Our own sense of alienation and inauthenticity as an isolated subject in a world of objects conceived of as resources for our instrumental use should not rule unchallenged. See the discussion of the authentic self in *T&A*, esp. 29–51.

56. Dr. Michel Vaillant, letter to author, February 3, 1991.

and so on, have a life span much shorter than the permanence of the species in time: The transformation of these less stable elements of human existence can be observed within a single person's living memory.

None of this implies that the human species may not, one day, vary to the point of a change in its essence, leading to a new species. Nevertheless, this much is true: As long as human beings continue to propagate themselves, their nature will remain basically the same. Moreover, given their unique reflective self-consciousness, a certain spiritual continuity, assured by cultural symbols, might carry across any significant biophysiological change, provided it leaves that awareness capability intact. Even if such a change occurred, even if somehow it broke the spiritual continuity of mankind's memory through symbol, I repeat that it would forever be true that man and human nature had existed and as a kind of form would remain inherently intelligible, if only to God.

An examination of what makes up that nature will give us a more comprehensive means of dealing with the marginal cases mentioned before. We now explore in a preliminary way how we recognize nature and distinguish it from the cultural. Later, we go into the question on both sides, especially when, in building an ontology, we investigate man's place in the cosmos as a whole.

Stable Natures and Unfolding Tradition

What mankind has been able in this short time to achieve and pass on in the form of a variety of traditions, handing down maturing wisdom, is literally *vital* for us. Without it, neither the lengthening life expectancy nor the sustenance of nearly six billion people on earth could continue. These traditions provide the heritage of meanings, captured in complex symbol systems and incarnated in acculturated institutional arrangements of often vast societies, without which our capabilities would be severely diminished. These traditions manifest both continuity and evolution. Without the unchanging dimension of man's nature during this historical time span, we would be unable to make much sense out of the symbols handed down by the ancient traditions, and there would not be the underlying continuity of institution we experience, institutions that mold us to play intricate social roles.

This continuity and change is reflected in the individual. Consider again the three levels of stability we earlier recognized, which contribute to the makeup of one's ongoing natural-faith understanding of oneself and which enable us to recognize and classify types on all three levels: (1) The permanence presented by the recognizable limits of a nature. The commonality of human nature is augmented with knowledge of certain subtypes, including sexes, races, and ages, some of these typical classifications being vague and sometimes misleading. Our typological insights are not infallible penetrations into real structures; sometimes they mix real structure and projection of fantasy about those structural elements in response to some psychological need. (2) Stability in the enduring features of a personality. One generalizes to types of personality, where temperamental givens are stressed; remember the tradition of the choleric, the melancholic, and so on, based on the humors? (3) The stability of established moral character—a set of moral habits (virtues and vices)—that flesh out and give consistency to the temperamental givens of a personality. The consistency and stability provided by the habits of the last two together constitute what has often been called "second nature."[57] All three levels of stability add constancy to human action and, hence, consistency to human customs and institutions.

The Fund of Common Knowledge of Human Nature

In ordinary experience, we normally have little difficulty recognizing the presence of a human being, or even the evidence that human beings have been at work in a given setting. Only marginal situations drive us to closer analysis, forcing us to clarify what we mean by human and which traits lead us to recognize the presence of a human being. It is at the margin that we begin to see how unclear this knowledge of human nature can be. Common kinds of experience of human beings at the margins are the unborn and newborn babies, the very old in a state of advanced decline, and the severely handicapped.

Because we are organisms passing through a course of familiar development that includes primitive states (the newborn can scarcely do anything but suck and sleep and scream) and decline, we readily predicate human nature for individuals whose performance is far below the optimum we see in mature, healthy individuals. Nevertheless, in acknowledging humanity in the newborn infant, just as we recognize a diminished human being in the old man lying in a coma but whom most would regard as still fully a person, we respect their humanity.

In the first case, we see, from experience of humans going through all phases of development, the presence of a life principle, which the Greek philosophers called (as regards all living things) a soul, at work guiding the helpless little organism toward adulthood.[58] In the case of the declining old man, it is a soul lingering on amid the body's much decreased ability to perform. In the severely mentally handicapped, it is a human being that cannot reach full development, but this is not to be confused with mere animal existence. (In all

---

57. Individuals and the great human systems evolve—the symbol systems (natural languages, liturgical forms, artistic symbols, philosophic-scientific symbol systems), customs, and the institutions all change. In our search for wisdom, we are obliged to study the interactions between these various processes: between restlessly changing individuals and the symbol systems and institutions that mold their character and guide their action, which influences the further development of both the symbol systems and the institutions; between different systems of symbol (science and religion); between symbol systems and institutions (science and the state). We must study not only all of these in particular traditions but as they happen differently in distinct traditions; and we must study how these traditions are to be brought together in a single wisdom.

58. *Psyche* is Plato's term, which the Roman philosophers translated as *anima* (the animating principle).

but the severest cases we recognize some human activity—a smile or a properly human frustration.) We honor such a person because his parents are human, and he has a human body, however defective. Even if there is not a glimmer of a human regard, no communication, the rest is enough for us to project onto this defective specimen all our sense of the importance of the human.

This is not the place to launch into the important question of the metaphysical reality of personhood,[59] nor do I want to preempt discussions about the sense of the humanity of the person on life-support machines, which enters into the ethical decision to turn off the machine. I only want to call attention here to how we recognize and acknowledge fellow human beings and their activity, because this example of how we come to know this type or essence, which is so important to us, enriches our understanding of how we form all knowledge of natures.

If I discover on my porch an infant asleep in a basket, how do I recognize it as a human being rather than a monkey? In this instance, the judgment is triggered by perception of externals, the combination of gestalt, smooth skin, hairlessness, the baby's crying, and of course, the setting: all the trappings of the classic baby-abandoned-on-the-doorstep scenario. I have stored away enough experience of what human babies look like typically so as to have no hesitation in the present instance recognizing what this unwelcome phenomenon really is.

But consider a more marginal case. Suppose a maniac, rather good at imitating a gorilla's movements, is let loose in my neighborhood dressed in a gorilla outfit. I may at first be fooled into mistaking for the real thing what is in fact a man acting like a gorilla. In this case, the normally important reality of the setting does not help—neither madman nor gorilla is a likely occurrence in North Toronto gardens, although drunks are more common than monkeys. For that reason, the very uniqueness of the setting, gorilla-in-garden, alerts me from the first glimpse to be suspicious of what I am seeing. (Knowledge of types of settings gives clues to the unusual.) I draw on my limited experience with gorillas, looking for the slightest clue in this thing's behavior, in order to discern its identity. Remember, everything is being done to send me the perceptual signals that normally trigger remembrance of gorillas. I will have to observe sharply, and it will help if I know much of gorilla behavior. A child is more likely to be deceived than an adult, who has a surer knowledge of what to expect in given settings, and of how gorillas act.

When we seek to infer whether humans have been present from the imprint they have left on things, more overt reasoning enters into the process. Suppose that in an African setting we discover a cave large enough to accommodate man or gorilla. Upon examination, we find two silexes the ends of which have been chipped by a sharp object to make them into arrowheads. *Voilà!*—evidence of human beings. We are sure, because we know that such tool-using requires

---

59. See Albert Shalom, *The Body/Mind Conceptual Framework and the Problem of Personal Identity: Some Theories in Psychoanalysis, Philosophy and Neurology* (Atlantic Highlands, N.J.: Humanities Press, 1985), for an excellent introduction to the question.

human intelligence. Gorillas have been known to sharpen sticks, but not go so far as to use an instrument to make another instrument.

Regardless of the differences in education and sophistication, there is a kind of common fund of knowledge we expect in all mentally healthy adults in the same culture. Usually, when we invoke common sense, we mean this core of a culture's shared experience. But there is also a basic core of knowledge we expect of adults regardless of culture, even those coming from remote societies. If we encounter Colombian Stone Age men, we have reason to hope that they will recognize us to be men and not strange beasts, although here we indeed are operating at the margin: Their experience is not typical, as they are among the few humans left on the planet who have never seen people not of their tribal grouping.

Normally, we can count on this core of common knowledge enough to be reasonably sure that if we act in certain ways, we can provoke a predictable reaction. If we are menacing, the other will assume a defensive stance; if we signal good intentions, this will be understood across language and even gesture barriers.

Distinguishing Human Nature and Culture

To what extent does our common knowledge help in discerning acts that support the ends of human existence, from those unworthy of human beings or destructive of human good?

The challenge is compounded because there are many actions peculiar to certain cultures or even to certain epochs, perhaps even widespread within those limits, that today would be considered completely passé and in some instances condemned: the practice of slavery. There are others that have been almost universally judged deleterious to well-being, even when they may be done frequently—for example, lying because one lacks the courage to assume responsibility for what one has done. Who is without guilt in this department? And I doubt that any of you is very proud of it.... We may judge that lying is human, but it is nonetheless evil, that is, not conducive to the proper development of the human potential. It is indeed confusing that we recognize "to err is human," and yet condemn any complacency about error.

How do we distinguish what is proper to the full development of human potential? How do we separate what belongs to nature from what is cultural only, and how do we relate these, since cultural inventions that are human-potential developing must somehow not be against nature? And how do we distinguish the cultural overlay that gives a particular style to almost any act, however rudimentarily ethical or unethical it may be?[60] Finally, how do we distinguish an unalterable fact of nature from that which can be modified by education? Unless one thinks back behind the history of *Sein,* answers are bound to be dangerously inadequate.

---

60. This will be explored below.

In sum: These questions can only be dealt with adequately by developing the anthropological foundation for an ethics. Such a base is itself founded in an ontology, implicit or explicit, usually a mixture of both. To be philosophically adequate, an anthropology requires judgments, based on evidence of what, in given areas, is culturally developed and what belongs to the human kind as such.

The present study makes a preliminary ontological contribution to this daunting edifice (ontology, anthropology, historical critique, ethics), but stops at barely outlining those foundations. (Complaints about the length of this tome have resulted in its reduction by one-third already!) I close this introduction to the epistemological dimensions of this anthropological challenge with a few hints, all that I can manage for now without first completing the needed ontology followed by appropriation of the central tradition formative of my own culture and of my beliefs about man.

Suppose one is confronted with acts that truly go against nature, harmful to the perpetrator or to a victim to no noble purpose (not like the harm embraced in sacrifice for defense of one's country), and this not because they run afoul of changeable circumstances but because they touch the constitution of the human. Imagine a man peaceably cutting off his own fingers, one by one, in the quiet of his room. If the police found out after the first finger was cut, he would be forcibly prevented from continuing his ghastly operations. Why does society seek to prevent people from mutilating themselves?

Certain tribes engage in minor mutilation. The cultural anthropologist understands the cultic or status purposes, but even then, today's Christian missionaries will not try to integrate such customs into Christian ritual, because they believe that those customs fail to recognize the full dignity of the individual person, mirrored in respect for the integrity of the body.

The first case is much less ambiguous than the second. In the first, the motive is the satisfaction of an individual's unusual desire for self-mutilation. It is not common for people to mutilate themselves just for the fun of it. "Not normal" means more than that most people do not do it. We understand that it is out of keeping with the essential human need for self-preservation (a need common to all organisms) for someone to derive pleasure from an act that diminishes the person, removing a finger, or in Van Gogh's case, an ear. In most of our experience, pleasure-drives are associated with needs that sustain the person and the species, if they have not become deformed by an addiction or obsession or distorted by patterns of weak self-indulgence. Here we find a drive that seems reversed.

When the diminution brought on by a perverse form of a drive is minor, gradual, and hence not so obvious, the contra-natural character of an act is more disputable—for example, smoking or seriously overeating. In the first, we recognize the power of a strong addiction, perhaps originally begun when a person gave into the need for social acceptance in a setting itself at once very common and not a little perverse. In the second, overeating, we recognize a natural need not kept in balance with other factors in one's health.

The ritual mutilation is more arguable than the finger amputation because the otherwise diminishing act has a purpose other than a response to an irrational impulse: to please the god, or to mark oneself off as a dedicated person, or whatever. What would otherwise be a bad action having no excuse is here done at least with honorable intentions. Similarly, overeating is understandable, either as a failure to keep in check the response to attractive foods, or as a grotesque response to a perverse desire for self-destruction—understandable, but rationally condemnable as harmful to one's being as a human.

In the cases, say, of rape and murder, or a senseless act of self-mutilation, it is clear that they are harmful to the perpetrator or to those who are recipients of its effects. We believe we know human nature well enough to recognize at least in these cases what tends to fulfill its potential and what diminishes it. This common knowledge might well be formulated as a principle: A human being is meant by nature (a certain grasp of teleology is here indeed intended) to live out a life through the normal course of development, with the help of all the faculties nature has given him (even all his ten digits).

Where a fact of nature is involved, then, one is tempted to begin a process of persuasive reeducation. But suppose pathology is suspected. Either the trauma permits therapy; or it is judged incurable, because of a genetic abnormality or because the personality has become so deformed as to defy effective healing.

Interestingly, most people in our society would resist the idea of a lobotomy to alter behavior, even if obtaining the desired result were assured. A minority seem more disposed to aggressive interventions, against the individual's will. One might argue that the intervention is meant to remove physically a block to freedom. Most remain skeptical whether such an intervention is anything but a dream: Can surgeons enhance genuine freedom by cutting at the brain?

Force and violence to bend another to one's will, no matter how high the cause, are generally rejected in our society, because of what we understand human nature to demand.[61] The one exception is society's restraint of the individual who would harm himself. In Ontario, only the signature of two physicians is required to commit a suicidal pathologue.

Let us see how this consideration of respect of the other's freedom comes into play in an area of daily life. This will help us understand that talk of human nature has consequences. Take as an example the protection exercised by society to prevent sexual attention forced on those who are too young to give informed consent. The proposition that nature intends that intercourse take place only between consenting adults can be rationally defended.[62] The nature argument

---

61. The slow discovery of the fullness of this truth, and this within the "enlightened Occidental" tradition, reveals how difficult the disclosure of a nature can be. Some noble churchmen understood the tragic flaw underlying inquisition, but many did not, and Christian kings should never with calm consciences have authorized torture.

62. Not everyone agrees. I once sat fascinated at breakfast in the Rockefeller Villa in Bellagio, listening to a professor from the University of Toronto defend the legitimacy of intercourse with young children. The government of Ontario, however, does agree about harassment, passing new legislation to clarify consent to intercourse.

is that sexual intercourse is inherently such a serious involvement, it should take place only freely. Societies differ, to be sure, in their understanding of when adulthood begins and what constitutes consent situations. But wherever they see those limits, they will work to discourage at least the "too young" from free expression of their natural sexual instincts before they can understand what is involved.

This particular sort of sexual mores, I suggest, constitutes less a case of culture reshaping nature than an exercise, with cultural variations, of the full human nature, including reason's ability to encompass the whole situation of persons. This fuller nature exercises guidance over sexual drives. Nonetheless, there is room for disagreement as to what is most healthy and most moral—what respects all the givens of the natural and cultural situation and best balances them prudentially.

In all this argumentation, we depend once again on insight into what we know human beings to be. One problem with insight into natures is that it is impossible to argue someone into enjoying the insight who does not agree that a particular aspect is indeed given in experience as claimed. We have already agreed with Aristotle, one cannot demonstrate principle. Insight into a given nature present in experience or summoned up in an image yields essential principle. So what does one do in the face of denial? One attempts to draw the other's attention to the reality by description that in the final analysis must be verifiable in his own experience[63] and must somehow impress him with its evidence. Often one descends to use of the device of *reductio ad absurdum*. Human beings can refuse to see what they do not want to see; we often fail to see things that might cause us to give up a way of life we enjoy. Take, for instance, the insight that nature intends that one should strive to keep the body healthy. So a second purported insight, basically a deduction from the principle, is that pleasurable acts that risk undermining health go against nature and therefore ought to be avoided.

Can one argue someone into seeing that an organism normally fends off enemies to its optimum functioning? For an organism knowingly to undertake to compromise its ability to function well is bizarre, unless undertaken

---

63. Experience is not immanent but transcendent. It takes place in my consciousness, but it is experience of the presencing of an other-than-that-consciousness. Eric Voegelin puts it well in the context of explaining what happens in a genuine outburst of transcendence, revelation of God: "The experience signifies an ontic event. It is a disturbance in being, an involvement of man with God by which the divine Within is revealed as the divine Beyond. What is achieved by it is immediacy of existence under God; what is discovered by it is the existence under God as the first principle of order for man. Moreover, the principle is discovered as valid not only for the man who has the experience but for every man, because the very idea of man arises from its realization in the presence under God" (Eric Voegelin, "What Is History?," in *What Is History? and Other Late Unpublished Writings*, vol. 28 of *The Collected Works*, ed. Thomas Hollweck and Paul Caringella [Baton Rouge: Louisiana State University Press, 1990], 49). Voegelin's claim about the inseparability of man's experience of himself and his experience of God is substantiated scientifically from evidence in history, throughout the five volumes of *Order and History*, as well as in many essays, such as the one cited here.

for the sake of some higher good, such as fighting to save others, or in nature where organisms are normally sacrificed for the good of the hive or the species.

The second insight is more complex, containing as it does some implicit reasoning: The organism's long-term good functioning is a higher good than the pleasure of the moment. The suggestion that health can under certain circumstances be sacrificed implies that this foundational good is not the ultimate good. Health can be sacrificed for the immediate saving of a life, and health and life may be sacrificed to save the society, or to save honor, or to witness to God. Each such claim involves further purported intuitions of the relative importance of good. That seems like a lot of intuiting all based on insight into human nature, coupled with reasoning to relate insight to insight!

Consider the basic insight founding the principle that it is natural for an organism to be healthy. A child can notice the difference between a sick old man lying sallow with hollow eyes and a strapping young athlete. He compares, which obviously means going beyond the brute perception of each. But does he yet grasp much of the significance of the contrasting sights? The concept health is built up by comparing many experiences, including living through periods of being under the weather. Yet, when experience has brought us to understand the difference between health and illness, we are still required to grasp by insight that the one state is better than the other and is what the organism's very organization intends for it.

The necessity of building out of our general knowledge of human nature our notions of what is permissible and what is illegitimate—in other words, an ethics—is further complicated because many of our concerns are social. It is not just what the individual does to himself that is at issue; there are also questions of desirable and fruitful human interaction, including, especially, something like what classical philosophy defends as the common good. When we consider that kind of object—social relations—we shall see that there again insight is at work grasping types of relationship.

Cultural Transformation of Natural Things

While acknowledging as foundational our daily dealing with things, we paused to consider explicitly that these are culturally transformed entities. The familiarity of the demands of daily life (founded in the *Sein* of our milieu and epoch) helps make intelligible the situations in their respective contexts. Even the plants and trees in my garden have been pruned and set out according to a contemporary notion of the urban English garden. One learns to read in the things and their disposition the signs of various typical milieux, including even epochal styles, for example, this is a baroque chair. Their having been humanly transformed (or domesticated) gives them at least a familiar surface. That distracts us from attending either to their depths or to the origin of the *Sein*'s charge of familiarity.

Merely skin deep, this familiar surface is nonetheless real and reliable, as far as it goes.⁶⁴ Consider how objectively a smokestack-industry environment is written into an urban, industrial landscape. A Bushman from the Kalahari would have trouble making sense of it, although he could wander in and out of the buildings, step over the tracks, and avoid the open manholes. He would have to acquire experience as to what these things are all about, just as the average Occidental passing an oil refinery can identify pipes and walkways, but does not understand cracking towers and heat exchangers.

OBJECTIVE SPIRIT

We can distinguish what is actually formed into things by human intention—objective spirit, in Hegel's terms—from all the results of natural processes. What has been imprinted in them culturally nonetheless resides in them objectively, affecting them in themselves, whether any human being comes along to decipher its significance or not. For example, I can distinguish in this wood picnic table the natural wood, dried and sawed though it may be, from the humanly induced shape, and I can interpret the design as typical of cheap twentieth-century Canadian picnic tables. The distinctive kinds of evidence are easy to separate in this case.

The truth of those objects is not just the intelligibility of their internal structure, the familiar surfaces of which we can comprehend, but their setting, those various objective contexts, in which the human spirit is actively involved. There would normally be no picnic table in the chancel of a church, for instance. In the setting cultural objects play a role as parts, tools, moments, dimensions, and so on.

This holds as well for our knowledge of those perceivable things that we ourselves happen to be: human beings, who present to external examination a natural and a culturally formed dimension.⁶⁵ The added complication is that we also know both ourselves and our kind from the inside, subjectively, and we are able to project that inner experience onto another, interpreting what we see on the outside as signs of what may be happening in the heart.

THINGS IN THE IMAGINATION: CREATIVITY AND INFERENCE

When we think about things in the absence of the guiding control of actual perception, we are freer to move them about—the root of our freedom to create. Still, the real structures of things remembered continue to dominate our discourse, even the most imaginative kind. It is not easy to break the hold things, situations, institutions, and symbol systems have on us. Nor should we think of creativity just in terms of breaking free. Often the greatest creativity is a

---

64. Perhaps not always skin deep. When IBM scientists deposit single molecules in the thinnest possible lines for microchip circuits, they have penetrated fairly deeply into nature with their humanizing activity.
65. Abraham Lincoln said a man past forty is responsible for his face.

deepening within the already rich forms one has inherited. Creativity operates within the constraints, as well as on the basis of the positive possibilities, offered by real things, settings, and situations. This is so, even in those instances where, not only deepening the grasp on what has been vouchsafed, the creative impulse is able to open into territories lying beyond the old limits.

Most of our imagining consists in taking known things apart and rearranging them. We are beholden in this mental work to the structures suggested to us by the things and situations we encounter that exist independently of us. Nevertheless, it is in the imagination that the eros of unfulfilled desire has the freest time rearranging the world as we would have it. In the absence of the imperious presence of the perceived things, the valence of representation-to-thing shifts: the greater the generalization or the more restricted the part that the imagination wrenches free from the whole, the more remote the control actual reality has over us. Concepts and symbols take on more of a life of their own. We begin to float in a dream world of symbolic forms. Even then, if we are careful to respect their referential truth, we can build vast and apparently remote models out of them, and then re-descend toward the perceptible world to verify whether they guide us to new discoveries of real aspects of things. Such exploratory model building is at the heart of modern sciences.

We do something similar, in a less formal and indeed much less rigorous way, in building our daily knowledge of persons, groups of persons (races, nations, classes), institutions, and so on, needed for navigation in the world. And in art, what is more pleasing than the artist's imaginative construction that achieves a kind of necessity—the feeling that he has yielded to the sense of the materials from which he is building, and has found a form of great complexity that he has made intelligible by pulling the materials into a near perfect harmony, invoking a coherent world that may have never existed outside of our communing imaginations.

There is another lesson to be learned from attending to the artist's creative freedom. In expressing myself artistically I choose my medium—for example, ink on paper. I select a twenty-by-fifteen-inch piece of paper, which then is my field. Once a sinuous line, say, is posed on the paper, I can either build upon or around it, ignore it (at the cost of the sense of the work), or decide to throw the paper away and start over. But that line has limited my choices. Each additional stroke adds to the demands of the already-having-been: I must respect the emerging essence *(Wesen)*[66] of the work. Every artist has experienced how the work takes over.

PERCEPTION OF REAL RELATIONS

All things are revealed existing within a web of relations. To transform the

---

66. A coherent having-been, static in the case of a finished painting, dynamic in the case of a sonata. It also has an essence *(essentia)*, it belongs to recognizable (cultural) species and genera of artworks. However original, however much it represents a breakthrough, this particular work has a *form*, its having come to be founds an intelligible permanence.

last utterance of Bernanos's Curé, "Tout est relation!"[67] But Hume distorted much of modern philosophy's discussion of this vital issue; that is one reason why my insistence on the *reality of connectedness* will not be well received in some quarters.[68] Hume's claims about the subjectivity of the causal connection have been amply refuted, by Thomists, phenomenologists, process philosophers, and others. In my view, anyone who persists in denying that any real relation can be perceived as objective, existing independently of mind, simply wants to believe this, as part of an ideological agenda. So more work is needed to restore this basic component of our knowledge.

An Example: One Bush Encroaches on Another

When I sit on the veranda, I can see that the Russian olive tree has overgrown the mock orange, largely blocking it from view. This is the result of a miscalculation when I planned that part of the garden. My visitor is unaware of this until I point it out, explaining that I had intended a nice mixture of colors and textures, but I had no idea the Russian olive would grow so large. Now the whole affair *(Sachverhalt)*, of no concern to either bush, gets its sense from my project as "landscape architect, last class." The adopted point of view is mine, and the design is conceived in terms of what one might see from the veranda.

All very subjective. And yet there is obviously much in this situation that is objectively factual, that does not depend on how someone looks at it. Moreover, these objective givens guide the whole mental process of projecting the design, observing actual rates of growth, planning action to rectify miscalculations. Come look—you can see that the Russian olive *really* is crowding into the space of the mock orange.

But wait. "Crowding in" is a concept implying a judgment about proper space, a judgment that obviously involves an element of conscious appreciation. But it has an objective ground as well. I have been able to perceive, over time, that the Russian olive grows much faster. Even though measuring relative rates of growth is an activity of mind requiring memory, by using both perception and memory I am able to acquire accurate information about what is really going on in the garden, independently of consciousness. The Russian olive does grow faster than the mock orange, sneakily, even when no one is around to notice or to cut it back.

I leave it to the reader to pursue his own phenomenological reflection on the interweaving of processes of perception and memory, of projective and factual dimensions (present perception of profiles of the actual bushes themselves providing guidance to the whole complex epistemic process) in a situation such

---

67. The curé, in *Diary of a Country Priest*, breathes his last in the cry of hope, "Tout est grâce!" It occurs to me, if indeed "tout est relation," then Christianly understood this is the same as saying no finite thing gives itself to itself—therefore, indeed, "Tout est grâce!"

68. To what extent did Hume grasp how effectively his move was destroying any hope of a Christian philosophy? This has long intrigued me.

as this. In doing so, note that all the following dimensions must be brought into proper descriptive relation:

Identifications
[p] a factor primarily in consciousness
[i] a factor recognized as existing independently of consciousness, although when we are aware of it, it is also in consciousness.

Dimensions
1. The project of my initial plan [p].
2. The work of planting the two bushes [i].
3. Perceptual observations at moments $t_{1,2,3,\ldots,n}$ of the fullness of each bush [p] (although the actual size of each was at the moment of observation an [i] factor).
4. Memories and comparisons of same [p].
5. Comparisons required intellection into the different rates of growth implicit in the disparate series of observations of sizes [p], but these are verifiable through repeated measurements of the actual bushes at given moments [i].
6. Observation of encroachment by Russian olive on the mock orange [p], yields
7. Fact of actual imbrication of the one upon the other and its obscuring the view from a certain angle [i], with a [p] element of appreciation of the point of view.
8. Understanding present state of affairs as a deviation from original project remembered, with new project for work [p].
9. Throughout, the actual bushes, at whatever stage in their development, are real things [i].
10. Rectification would require a new project [p], followed by actual work—for example, trimming [i].

I intended only to open here the vast subject of perception of relations. There are so many different kinds of relations, each deserving attention. In beginning anew a phenomenology of our knowledge of them, one might return to Aristotle and Saint Thomas, resurrecting the distinction between real major and minor, and ideal major and minor distinctions, and the analysis of the four causes. One would need to bring this into relation with all the discoveries about intentional relations, such as those of "internal time consciousness," contained in the work of Husserl. The resulting vast tome, *De relationibus*, would be an important philosophical contribution.

Hume on Causal Relations

Before pushing on, however, I would point out a truth or two about the perception of a particular type of relation that comes under attack from Hume, what the tradition calls a relation of efficient causality. Hume's example of

KINDS OF OBJECTS, KINDS OF TRUTH 93

the billiard balls is cleverly chosen. The two entities are visibly compact, and of course one does not see, in the narrow sense of enregistering, thanks to impulses from the eyes, a separate entity, force being transmitted from one ball to the other. And yet, I contend against Hume, it is neither mindless habit nor deployment of an a priori concept, but insight—a cooperation of senses and intelligence—into the structure of a dynamic situation that permits perception of the causal relationship. I mean the grasp of the sense of the whole setting.

First, it is not true that I ever just observe one billiard ball slamming into another. In reality, I am in a billiard room with friends, playing a hotly contested game. George takes up his cue for a crucial shot, aiming to dodge the eight ball, hoping to propel the four into the nine at just the angle to send it off at 23.2 degrees into the northwest pocket. When I then see the four ball whizzing with a reverse spin smack the nine and stop while the stationary nine ball takes off at the wrong angle, I spontaneously, without reflection, *com-prehend* the situation as one ball imparting to another, not just motion in general, but this precise motion of this exact vector.

Now, should the genuineness of my insight be challenged by an eager disciple of the Scottish sage, I return to the situation reflectively, to see if I have indeed been victim of an illusion. It seems reasonable, given the challenge, to compare similar situations, gathering further evidence.

A good billiard player notices that there is an exact and invariable relation between the angle and velocity at which the first ball strikes the second and the path and speed of the recipient ball. It is significant that the mind is not only able to comprehend the concrete situation of the motion of this ball and the motion of the ball that receives its hit. The mind can also reach out, not to impose a ready-made form on different situations, but to encompass a series of like given events, comparing strikes as to angle and velocity, and thereby to induce a rough but serviceable principle—wonderfully put to use by my opponents whenever I play. The mind is able to do this because, strange as it may seem, the balls really do affect one another visibly as described. A mass in motion is seen to stay in motion until retarded, and when it is suddenly retarded, we can see that its impetus is transmitted to another mass, which is set in motion, not randomly, but exactly along the vector requiring the least change of conditions.

More Insight into Insight

I have responded to Hume with yet another assertion of insight. I am starting to appreciate more why Bernard Lonergan entitled his main work simply *Insight*. I earlier acknowledged insight to be a central reality, so now before we proceed, let me consolidate what we have learned about this brute power of mind.

A dog and a man both witness a thrown ball tracing a ballistics curve through the air. The dog leaps up and catches the falling ball in his mouth, which suggests that he has been able to anticipate the object's course. Clearly the higher animal's perceptual system, including his brain, is already a very impressive instrument. But nothing else the dog does authorizes us to believe that he can form a concept (ballistics curve) or grasp a relationship (inertia, air resistance, and gravity).

A man can watch balls thrown a thousand times and learn to catch them, yet have no insight into a ballistics curve. Then suddenly, mysteriously he understands that there is a point to the regularity of the curve. He has had an insight into this regularity, which means he has somehow grasped the sense of the curve as a distinctive kind of process. He may then set out to discover the forces at work, seeking an insight into their rapport. Insight follows insight, with reasoning tying together the resulting concepts into a larger structure of explanation,[69] with factors such as gravity, air resistance, and momentum becoming part of the explanation for the typical form of the trajectory.

The intellect is able to plane above the many experiences unfolding in time and read into them the sense of the form that manifests its continuity through the myriad of disparate experiences. We saw that earlier with our knowledge of organisms: They go through a building-up phase, a mature phase in which they best hold their own against the environment and put their imprint upon it, and a declining phase, ending in their failure to maintain their integrity, their elements becoming absorbed into other structures. The mind arches over the sense of the whole process.

Influenced by the Greek principle that science is of the universal, the medieval philosophers were impressed by our knowledge of types, but paid insufficient attention to intellection of singulars—not just perception here and now of this thing, but the built-up knowledge of personality or unity of style, the production of concrete universals like my knowledge of Mr. X.

This is a question not just of psychology but of ontology when I struggle to understand how individual human beings work. My most fundamental experience of being coming to be is through my own living out my life, a bundle of processes through which courses the permanence and the orderliness of development provided by my nature. This is experienced in interaction with other human beings, of like nature.

---

69. By "structure" I mean any perceived or imagined or conceived whole, into the sense of which the mind enjoys an insight, that is, can grasp the characteristic way in which the parts of the whole belong to one another.

a. Stable structure provides insight into natures. See (2) above.

b. Dynamic structure, or process, relates to ongoing knowledge of an individual subject to continual becoming. See (1) above.

To grasp a dynamic, open structure—an ongoing process—the mind must have some insight into the vector of the change and how the various changing aspects of the thing or the variety of changing things caught up in the process relate, that is, how they belong in the process. The mind, through insight into the sense of a process, can fix that sense in a concept: It achieves, for purposes of dealing with the process, a fixity, a stability, that the process, as changing, itself enjoys only as an ongoing consistency between its moments unfolding one into another.

Knowledge of individuals and of natures is not composed merely of a set of lifeless, formal abstractions. Such abstractions play a part, of course, because we do formalize, abstracting and fixing, to provide frames for our embracing many individuals. But much is built up, within those frames, of accretions of experience, partly analyzed, partly merely clothing our schemes with affectivity that those experiences trigger, precipitated about certain images that provide a kind of core. Most of my practical life is taken up not with the concept of woman but with interaction with the one woman who is my wife and the four others who are my daughters and the one who is my daughter-in-law. Of each of them I go on evolving a notion into which is folded the fruit of reflection on many thousands of disparate experiences. I stress reflection, although I realize that there operates a less-than-fully-aware chemistry, a concrete interaction between us, molding my overall impression of each. Yet I do sometimes mull over their personalities, their character—I have ideas of what is typical of that unflappable Claire, or Clara can be counted on to react thus and so, which is what you would expect of someone of aristocratic Korean culture, and so on. Each is related in my knowledge to my general understanding of human nature, but also to woman. Then each gets related to other categories that apply to individuals—Claire to chemical engineers and IBM managers; Noëlle to cardiologists and professors of medicine; the biochemist, Clara, to highly educated mothers who elect to stay home with their little children.

Insight is so all-pervasive one might be tempted to consider it simply coterminous with knowledge. But that is not correct. Aspects of our cognitive activities may be pre-insightful and others may call on the fruits of past insight without adding any new "Ah ha!" But the philosophers from Plato to Husserl and Lonergan who reflect on insight are correct in seeing in it among the best evidence of man's spirituality. Every gathering-up *intelligere* achieves a command over, and in some instances a veritable transcendence of, time and space. Ideational insight is formed without reference to time or place and remains, as idea, eternally valid.

The implications of this absoluteness of formal intelligibility have overwhelmed philosophers. Why have they reflected so little on that kind of formal insight that grasps the sense of processes? At least Whitehead and Lonergan have here left the Greeks behind, as Husserl was struggling to do when he reflected on time consciousness.

Insight plunges intellect into perception, giving rise to the "ah ha" of recognition. (Plato's point, in *Meno*, that all knowledge *[episteme]* is recollective in nature, points to this, although not with the same intent, given his ontology.) It is an experience of the in-form-ed structure/situation one is dealing with. Without the relation between parts, which I have pointed to as structure or form being itself objectively present, such in-form-ation could not take place, and the experience could not proceed. (Form presences either through perception of formed data or through imaginative re-collection.) Those who, with Hume, claim that relation cannot be, also make of insight—including their own insights—nothing more than hallucination. They deny the objectivity, all givenness of form. So I sum up one last time all the kinds of insight we have discovered.

We have insight

1. into the ongoing unity of the dynamic structure of familiar individuals.
2. into the particular kinds of things.
3. into particular settings.
4. into kinds of typical settings.
5. into structure.
6. Averaging.
7. Ontological principle.

SOCIAL RELATIONS AND THEIR REPRESENTATIONS

Social relations are what life is all about. No finite entity exists alone; rather, things found and sustain one another. All life is cooperative. Human social considerations pose their own kinds of truth problems. I come to know myself mostly in contrast to others and in playing roles conjointly with them.[70] Social relations are at the origin of the traumas that forge pathological behavior, and they are the source of inspirations that keep us going.

One can isolate individual acts passing between people (and sometimes a single act can be either traumatic or horizon opening), but in everyday life, acts tend to fall into meaningful constellations. These both build up and are guided by sets of habits and by objective stabilities in the setting (the family home) and situations, recurrent (every Christmas we do this . . .) and ongoing (older sister has lived at home since December, changing the valence in family relations).

Much of the stuff of actual daily existence is constituted by this pattern of courses of consistent action,[71] personalities, roles, schedules, cultural and class traits, and so on. Without these patterns, existence would—given human creativity—be such a chaos we would be unable to cope. Some of these we have occasion to notice explicitly, and we may even label them, the symbols representing them becoming manipulable: Mother regularly cleans the house and prepares the meals; father mows the lawn; mother is consoling, father is grumpy. (Recall the example of Mr. X's trustworthiness.) Others we know implicitly, bending with the steady wind they represent. We only reflect on them when a break in the familiar occurs, or the winds become gusty. Some are poorly grounded in experience, representing prejudices that have been passed to us

---

70. The Fichtean *Anstoß* comes to mind: the more culturally ample the persons with whom I interact, the richer my self-revelation. However, we must not go to the extremes of some post-Lacanian psychologists who apparently to want to reduce the self to a mere point of *rencontre* of such influences from others.

71. Corresponding to the Thomistic notion of habitual intention.

on the conceptual level, "Mexicans are lazy," "Canadians love compromise," and similar folk tales, some salvageable, some just old unexamined lies.

We recognize persons and individual things in their familiar gestalten and through their familiar acts. So knowledge of acts is an important part of our lives. An act is not a thing, but something a thing or person does, either to itself or to another (the Russian olive grows—that is what it does to itself—but it also grows into the space of the other bush). Many acts are sharply discrete in time and space; others manifest themselves as continual processes, such as growing. An external action is perceptible by others; internal acts, only by the agent, if he is reflective. Acts such as growing, which occur within, also show partly on the surface.

The full sense of an act can only be known from its context. The intention of a reflective actor is only one element in that context, objective elements of which may render his intention inappropriate or suggest, perhaps, that the expression of it is less than honest. Because it occupies a discrete time-space, an act can be enumerated (even a growing process—This cat grew and grew until it reached a certain size, at about age two, but now he is full grown—one continual process, graspable in terms of a time and a space) and, with its setting usually typical, classified as to kind. An act, then, is intelligible in two ways: from the sense derived from its context, and through relation to other acts of the same kind.

A Further Comment on Role Playing

Patterns of intentional (or human) acts rooted in a persisting motivation and a consistent reading of a stable situation are often evidence of the role-playing[72] we commented on earlier. Mother is not just this empirical entity, but the person who, having accepted a responsibility for this baby, consistently and dependably does motherly sorts of things, as demanded by this situation and within settings chosen for their appropriateness and/or imposed by circumstances.

The long-term engagement of will the existentialists term "fundamental project" is the vital source of directed energy feeding the consistent course of action, which in turn builds the habits that make it easier to stay on the chosen track. That consistent action is able to sustain itself because it harmonizes with the relevant reality, the roles the others in the situation are playing, and the physiological realities (say, of the baby's dependence), and the general social expectations in the particular worlds—of family, neighborhood, company, university, church, and general society. Mother does what is expected of her both because she has been enculturated a certain way and has accepted (or partly goes along mindlessly with) that vision, and because she observes the physical, biological, and social realities of the evolving situation with which she must cope. She has developed in interaction with that reality the habits ("virtues") necessary to sustain her course of action.

---

72. As *T&A* discusses this at length, so I here provide only a sketch of relevant points.

Institutions

Institutions, conjunctions of people playing coordinated roles in view of a basic common end, are one genus of complex social relations, coordinating roles, which plays a particularly large part in our lives.[73] People accept and play related roles, because their fundamental projects entail working together toward a common end. These projects may be explicitly adopted; others are implicitly enculturated into the persons involved, largely by imitation and as a result of growing up in an institutionalized situation that they continue tacitly to accept.

We saw earlier, in considering the bank, one's motives for accepting a role may be different from the goals of those in the hierarchy who set the institutional role demands. I may accept employment in an industrial corporation to receive a monthly paycheck, but to earn it I must accede to playing the role that management sees contributing to its goal, which is to produce and market a certain line of products or furnish a service profitably.

This conjunction presupposes a considerable commonalty of shared horizons of interpretation, constituting what Voegelin calls "little worlds" (cosmiota), much more detailed than the ultimate epochal setting Heidegger terms the *Seienden im Ganzen* (things taken as a whole), the characteristic way the world is organized in a given epoch. The implications of these all-englobing horizons, into which everyone in a given society is enculturated, are then necessarily woven into their horizons of interpretation and so all share them. (For example, in our technological epoch, persons enculturated to the modern world know, almost by instinct, how to work with machines and how to fit their courses of action into a planning mode. Everyone knows in a general, nonreflexive way what is expected of role players in a modern urban environment. But only chemical engineers share the vision, the concepts, the jargon of that mixture of science and art that constitutes the little world of chemical production. The epochal *Sein* illumines all the cosmiota, but the *Sein* of the world of chemical engineering, while participating in the epochal *Sein* and adding the *Seienden* it illumines to the epochal whole, does not directly illumine the whole planetary epoch.)

One recognizes that an institution is at work, either from the bottom up—by observing the purposeful concomitance of actions in a situation of concerted action too complex to be either coincidence or merely casual agreement; or from the top down—by being told the explicit intentions motivating a social project of concerted action, perhaps seeing a mission statement and a table of organization. The visible signs of the institutions impress: the university campus, or Petro Canada's filling stations. But these owe their existence to, and are supported by, the *habitus* of the enculturated people who keep the ongoing processes of the respective institutions intact, those illumined by its

---

73. How the *Sein* and *Seienden* of the cosmiota feed the substance of the epochal *Sein* is a question that needs exploring. I am doing that in a work in progress examining the essence of the present high-tech epoch.

Sein. Signs of this consistent role playing are perceptible in the regularity of performance, the skill displayed in carrying out certain courses of action, and so on.

There are two kinds of truth of institutions. First, a kind of intelligibility—an observer can discern what they are about, the underlying cooperative project, the ways the roles mesh, and how they interact with the necessary instrumental things—the streetcars, the bus stops, the garages, and so on, in the city transportation system. And second, a certain appropriateness or loyalty on the part of individuals who are true to the institution. (What certain key role players in an institution are actually up to is one thing, and the explicit stated intention, or the institution's more widely understood intention and the tradition it serves, may be another. An unscrupulous churchman may, for instance, subvert the power of the Church for his own purposes; he is thus untrue to the Church, which continues, nevertheless, to have its truth, its own goals and intelligibility. These can of course become hollowed out if too many of its agents become untrue to it.)[74]

Neither of these kinds of truth of institutions should be confused with a third kind of truth: the truth claims handed on by institutions in the service of traditions. These usually have a sense in themselves, transcending the work of the institution charged with teaching them. Again, an institution whose agents have become untrue to it will cease to be effective in handing on, unblemished, the truths for which it is supposed to stand. In extreme cases, the old truth claims can persist—for instance, in texts—even when all institutions teaching them have died out.

The difference between the ideal and the reality poses a problem in understanding an institution: the more acute, the greater the ideal. An ideal is a vision of a longer-range goal, conditions for the realization of which have yet in part to be created. The ideal may reside only in the consciousness of the principals. Or it may be expressed in an elaborated set of symbols, some of which could have been worked out over a long period, and which expressed vision may have been commented on and amended over years, perhaps even centuries—for example, the *sunna* of Islam. Such an explicated vision serves to enculturate each new generation.

Where the ideal has not been expressed, an outsider has to infer it from the principals' action, and even the insider knows it more in his bones, by going along with the *commedia dell'arte* of everyday role playing. Where texts exist showing the evolution of the ideal over time, it becomes possible to consider the diversion of practice from the ideal. Given that mixed goals are at work in any institution, it is important to understand the tensions between noble goals and less uplifting practice or, put less cynically, between noble ideal before and after the hard lessons of experience.

---

74. See *T&A,* chap. 4, for an analysis of faithful and unfaithful institutions in the service of good and bad traditions.

Hence the importance of the second kind of truth, the question of one's being true to the institution, loyal to its ideal. Assessment of this is dependent on knowledge of the first kind of truth, an understanding of what the institution is all about. One can be a true and loyal SS man—that makes sense, even though almost all humanity would agree that is sad, because the ideals of the *Schutzstaffel* were damnable. The appropriateness of an action in terms of the institution's goals is not the question of the appropriateness of the institution itself with its truth claims, which have to be judged in the larger setting. The large context raises questions pertaining to the search for wisdom itself. The ultimate context for these larger truth questions is sought in the ultimate structures of Being. I address these fundamental ontological dimensions at the end of this study, when all the pieces are in place.

Traditions

Because traditions, as well as institutions, were extensively discussed in *Tradition and Authenticity*, I will limit the discussion here to the question of truth claims that traditions can pass on—especially traditions of revelation, where the problems of verification and approach become most acute.

Chapter 6 raises truth claims of another kind of tradition—our scientific-philosophical one. Although the ongoing battles with Hume and Kant are more familiar to most philosophers, the epistemic challenges raised by traditions of revelation are less so, and yet I believe they are also singularly important. That is why I deal with them here.

Traditions mold our lives, whether directly, as in the case of true believers, (IBM's influence on our engineer-daughter, Claire, not just as institution but as a set of implicit and explicit traditions), or indirectly (the way Christianity and the scientific traditions affect every person acculturated into Western civilization). In *Tradition and Authenticity*, I proposed an important but fuzzy distinction, that between *implicit* and *explicit* traditions. Implicit traditions, like those inculturated, largely by imitation, within the family, permeate everything. However, they tend to be local, or at best national-ethnic and diffuse. But the great explicit traditions—the ones formulated in well-worked-out symbols, whose vision the institution passes on, sometimes over vast spaces and long reaches of time—influence transcultural and international situations.

The explicit traditions, through the extent and often the intensity of their influence, are easier to discern, since they incarnate themselves in large and well-articulated institutions and a treasure-house of symbols. Implicit traditions are harder to study, for one must first make explicit what is implicit, inferring from observation of action the underlying motives. That is a central work of the social sciences.

It is imperative, if one is to understand the pragmatic reality of the present world situation, to appreciate the dynamics of the great traditions and the institutions they have spawned; and it is essential to the pursuit of wisdom to confront critically the truth claims with which they challenge us.[75] The question of truth arises on two different levels: (1) the level of everyday experience, where the issues that confront us are existentially situation-bound, with attention focused on this person or this little group and these instruments I have to use to achieve my tasks, running life's errands; and (2) the ideational level, the world of larger visions, populated by wide conceptual and imaginative constructions, full of abstractions from abstractions ("Canada," "my Church," "defense of Western civilization"), emotion-driven, because our way of navigating in these ideational worlds is motivated by our larger desires. The praxis of everyday immediate existence, however, where, to be sure, emotion is indeed present, reacts more to concrete acts of individual persons present here and now, and the things at hand—this doorway, these tools—that exercise a certain restraint on the imagination.

In *Tradition and Authenticity*, I identify four genera of explicit tradition, and show that each has its own characteristic kind of truths, which are handed down and are verifiable in different ways. These four genera are artistic tradition; scientific/philosophic tradition; tradition of association (such as clubs, industrial corporations, and so on); and tradition of divine revelation (confined to the old religions in the Abrahamic tradition and, in a looser sense, to be found in Hindic and Buddhist traditions). Traditions of various types can of course interrelate. The Catholic Church, for instance, is a social reality, a gathering, analyzable therefore as a tradition of association, with the relevant kinds of truth being the intelligibility of the institution and loyalty to its ideal. But the Church is handing down a divine revelation, and hence is subject to the peculiarities of that kind of truth claim, a claim of passing on nothing less than the Word of God. In the course of doing this, the Church has spawned many artistic traditions and many theologies, different kinds of symbol systems, which themselves are subtraditions of the first and second genera, respectively.

Our concern here is truth as knowledge of being, so we should first note the complex interplay of the following elements in any actual situation in which one finds oneself within an influential tradition: There is a founding vision, which is grounded in a "privileged experience of Being" and which is caught and transmitted through a set of symbols. Those symbols have been successively elaborated over time. Then, too, there are the operations of the transmitting institution, motivated in part by the vision embedded in the handed-down symbols, but influenced as well by the present epochal horizons *(Seienden im Ganzen)*. The institution is engaged in social action, guided by the transmitted symbols and by the personal goals of its agents, which modifies the world and the symbols themselves as the result of interaction in the situation with the world.

The transmitted symbols, and the institution, mold present action, which becomes a kind of ongoing incarnation of the truth of the vision. The experience

---

75. Either through successive documents or through historic deconstruction of a principal text, the influences of successive ages embedded in the symbol system can be discerned.

of the living community modifies the sense of the symbols, distorting (when it is motivated ingenuinely) and/or adding to their truth (when it is sound action).

Truth Claims from a Tradition of Revelation

In preparation for Part III's endeavor to assemble all the dimensions of being, we have been working from the ground up, securing a base for the structure of our wisdom in appreciation for how we know the things and persons of everyday experience with some objectivity. Now we are jumping to the other end of the spectrum, as I survey a vast ideational world of a great tradition. Ultimately the critical issue has to be faced: How do everyday experience and vast ideational vision connect?

Having become aware in our planetary situation of these competing wisdoms, how can we responsibly avoid taking the measure from the top down of what these traditions claim we can know? And we need to see how the transmission of this knowledge is bound up with the very human reality of the institutions assuring its transmission. All this throws precious light on the human condition and on being itself.

At the same time, this investigation of the truth at work in the living-out of traditions underscores the reality that much of the most significant truth is not theoretical but practical, hence obviously moral in its foundation, even when the greatest theoretical wisdom structures are involved. Every interpretive act involves the whole person of the interpreter: He has to will to interpret, and his virtues or vices found his willingness to see or his desire to obfuscate. In our ontology, the question of the foundation of truth in freedom, posed by the existentialists, will be explored.

So now we leap to the most sweeping kinds of truth claims. These, too, are fundamental, because they contribute to building the ultimate context, the foundational truths of theology and politics and physics mold subtly the largest frames we deploy, our epochal transcendental horizons of interpretation, in the great space/time opened by the epochal *Sein*. In Part III, we will see how daily experience and the greatest intellectual constructions relate. But here we start with the most difficult: the knowledge involved in accepting claims of revelation, the ones that have caused the clash of whole civilizations.

To illustrate these, I choose basic claims from the tradition that has formed much of Western civilization, Catholic Christianity. Like those of Platonism or Newtonianism, they are bound up with the development of our science, our civil society, and our innermost spiritual lives.

Each of the four genera of explicit tradition put forward different kinds of truth claims, requiring distinctive forms of critique. Traditions of revelation not only pose peculiar problems of verification, but the claims can radically challenge natural-faith convictions about the very sense of existence. Therefore they cause resistance, if nothing in one's experience prepares for them, or if existential engagements entail not wanting to have anything to do with what they imply. (We can be much more detached in studying Plato or Newton.)

Hence a dilemma: The truth question has not been examined so long as the claims of the traditions of revelation, and the rich cultures and whole civilizations they have helped mold, are ignored. To ignore them is to dismiss the whole challenge of Western civilization, not to speak of Islam, the Confucian societies, and so on. That positivists and other reductionists do this merits Eric Voegelin's condemnation as "pneumopathological."[76] Yet it is hard for the reader who has never believed a tradition of revelation to take the whole business seriously—just as it is hard for Muslims to take Christianity seriously or vice versa. I do not minimize the difficulty in either case.

The truth question itself has been raised explicitly and scientifically first in the Abrahamic civilization, which adds urgency to appropriation of that tradition. Until the rise of modern science, nothing could challenge those truth claims in intensity and extent of overall influence on the Western world. Subsequently, so many in our society have become alienated from the roots of their own civilization—a truth that itself requires reflection and indeed has received it from Voegelin, among others.[77]

As one who enjoys this experience of living within a community of supernatural faith, I consider it a duty, in my effort to advance toward wisdom, to understand better what the experiences are that ground such acceptance. So I can offer a vicarious glimpse of a realm that to many remains a closed book (but, for the good of our society and civilization, should not). After all, the Christian confronts the same dilemma when he approaches the other Abrahamic traditions, Judaism and Islam, which should not be for him a closed book either. If Voegelin is right in his claim that all the great "outbursts" of transcendence reveal *foundations of order* of relevance for all men, then the pursuit of wisdom demands inquiry into what he means by "history," which entails appropriation of all the great traditions.

The Witness to Truth Claims of Revelation

If we consider the truth claims contained in the Symbolon of the apostles, the creed handed down since the early days of the Church, we see that it contains affirmations about the origins of the world; about the incarnation of God's Son in a historical person; about the Church; and about the present reign of the

---

76. See throughout *The New Science of Politics*. Recall as well the fundamental claim, cited above, that man's very self-definition comes to be in relation to his discovery of God, and God's discovery of himself to man. "What Is History?," 49. See also Henri de Lubac, *The Drama of Atheist Humanism*, trans. E. M. Riley (London: Sheed and Ward, 1949); Cornelio Fabro, *God in Exile: Modern Atheism—A Study of the Internal Dynamic of Modern Atheism, from Its Roots in the Cartesian Cogito to the Present Day*, trans. A. Gibson (Westminster, Mo.: Newman Press, 1968); and Etienne Gilson and Thomas Langan, *Modern Philosophy: From Descartes to Kant* (New York: Random House, 1963).

77. See Voegelin, "What Is History?" I am wary of Voegelin as a guide to the full sense of revelation as Christians understand it. A contemporary thinker of like scope, a Henri Cardinal de Lubac or above all Hans Urs von Balthasar, is a needed corrective to Voegelin's deficient reading of Christianity.

Holy Spirit and the eschatological destiny of man. The Symbolon itself offers no grounds for believing these things, beginning as it does simply with the affirmation, "I believe." But it is called the Symbol of the apostles, because these are truth claims handed down on the authority and witness of certain persons "who have been sent forth" (*apostolein* in Greek). This is characteristic of the foundation of the truth claims of all three branches of the Abrahamic tradition: These things are believed on the authority of, and because of, the prophetic witness of those who were present at certain events and who hand down what has been made known through those events.

That does not mean that these claims are to be swallowed whole, without any sort of corroborating evidence. The Catholic tradition has held that one seeks throughout one's experience for evidence that these truths put in practice bear good fruit, and for any light that reason, drawing on all the resources of "philosophy,"[78] can offer that will help penetrate into the mysteries: "Fides quaerens intellectum" (Saint Augustine). The question, however, remains: On what grounds could one believe what purport to be prophetic revelations from the Source of all reality about aspects of reality we could not know otherwise? If this is not to be dismissed as imagination—myth, the human consciousness striving to transcend toward God by imagining—then the nature of the evidence proffered is critical.

I cannot speak for Jewish or Muslim faith experience. When I appropriate these traditions, I shall be careful to listen to their own witnesses, avoiding projecting onto their symbols a Christian experience. But when I ask myself for the most basic ground for believing such things, I see clearly in my own experience that without the witness of holiness in the Church they would never have been believed, and should that witness fail to be convincing, they would not continue to be believed.

Holiness as Ground for Witness

I hear a murmur from puzzled philosophers: Now what sort of grounds for accepting truth claims can that possibly be—the holiness of those witnessing to their truth? In the case at hand, the witness is that of the apostles as to what Jesus Christ said and then did to found the credibility of his staggering claim to speak perfectly for God, a witness then handed down through the centuries by means of an apostolic teaching office, and the radiance of the saints, put forward as a kind of experiential ground for believing the continued validity and reality of what these truths express. It is indeed startling to the positivist mentality to suggest that holiness could possibly have something to do with determining the truth.

With this question, we would appear to have left the scientific realm of philosophy altogether. But that prejudges what philosophy is expected to take note of. Recall Plato's *Apology*: The moral witness of Socrates was central to the

---

78. The fathers of the Church called their theological reflections "philosophy."

sense of the truth he incarnated. It is at least a historical fact that this is a central Christian claim. According to the New Testament, this moral measure of truth is the very one explicitly offered by Christ, who himself claimed to be "the Way, the Truth, and the Life": "By their fruits you shall know them" (Matt. 7:16). The "fruits" are moral achievements: love, compassion, justice, peace. These do, indeed, hold a certain importance for ordinary human lives. We daily advance truth claims in this realm: "That was unjust," "He is untrustworthy," "You should have been more compassionate." The truth we are concerned with here is testimony to living experience of personal interaction with the very Source of life itself and with one another, which makes up much of the real stuff of everyday life.

The very symbol holiness is off-putting to many of my students, some of whom I have seen stumble over the word "spiritual" as well. Significant, especially when you realize that large segments of our society, despite what the media, portraying "the dying churches," would have you believe, still consider the pursuit of holiness to be what we are here on earth for.[79]

If there were no witness of holiness in the Church, then what credibility would exist for declarations about such love relationships as it basically deals with? What would be the sense of these experiences if there were no evidence of God as Person having touched human persons at the very center of their being, an encounter of freedoms in a way that makes a real difference, one that all can see, for instance, in the face of a Mother Teresa of Calcutta?[80] What precisely is holiness and how is it experienced? We must for a moment jump ahead to establish the ontological sense of the key credential.

Holiness is not just dedication. Stalin, after all, was single-minded in his pursuit of the consolidation of all state power in his own hands. Holiness is experienced in another as a kind of radiance, a glory that affects the lives of those around the saint.[81] But a power of will emanated out from Hitler

---

79. The Catholic Church is growing worldwide; there has been a steady increase in religious vocations to the priesthood and religious orders every year since 1978, when Pope John Paul II ascended to the Throne of Peter, in every part of the world except Oceania, and recently a remarkable upswing in conversions of educated persons in North America. I mention this simply to put straight what I believe is a deliberately distorted record. See *Annuario Pontifico* (Vatican City, 1994).

80. The recent encyclical on the foundations of Christian morality, *Splendor veritatis* (1993), recalls the Church's tradition that this radiance of holiness is found in all traditions where persons of good will live according to their consciences. (Bad jokes about Catholics thinking they are the only ones in heaven are disinformation.) In this witness to the absoluteness of the moral, good Christians are not alone: They are supported by the moral sense in peoples and by the great religious and sapiential traditions of East and West, from which the interior and mysterious workings of God's Spirit are not absent. The words of the Latin poet Juvenal apply to all: "Consider it the greatest of crimes to prefer survival to honor and, out of love of physical life, to lose the very reason for living" (para. 94).

81. The desert fathers were third-century hermits in Egypt who went out to the wilderness to seek a closer relationship to God. When word of their holiness reached the cities, people streamed out to be near them, and without their desiring it, communities grew up around them. The resultant monasteries exist to this day, testimony to the radiating power of their

and Stalin, too. Witnesses speak of the fascination they felt in the Führer's presence. A kind of perverse integrity in those fanatics gave them a moral force in dealing with others. History witnesses to this: whole nations bent to their will. Nietzsche was not foolish to nominate *Wille zur Macht* as the prime expression of the life force coursing through human beings.

Christianity, on the other hand, opposes "the powerlessness of love" to the power of egoistic will, which voluntarists of every stripe exalt as the ultimate reality—"the Cross versus the *Hackenkreuz*,"[82] a Christian once put it, unfairly. But there you have a pretty blunt collision of truth claims!

The radiance that streams from the saint is due to his selfless devotion to doing, not his own will, but what Scripture symbolizes by the expression, "the will of the Father." The glory manifest in holiness is supposed to be not the saint's, but the Lord's.[83] But *philosophically*, what can that possibly mean, "do the Lord's will"?

Holiness is another name for the integrity of being. It corresponds, on the level of action, to the Parmenidean insight that being *is*. If by "God" is meant the unique source of all that is—pure *esse*—and this is understood[84] as the purely constructive, hence absolute goodness, then only God is holy without qualification, and all else is holy only insofar as it has being and is therefore in some sense participating in the constructive power of God.[85] The radiance of the participating, limited thing is the shining-forth of Being itself.

Because only human beings, with the reach of their intellects and the power of their wills, can achieve integrity of considerable scope, it is in a certain kind of power in human lives that we most centrally experience holiness.[86] But watch out—this is not command power. Nature can communicate a sense of holiness to us as well, in the radiance of form, the harmony and exquisite balance of complexity, or the physical power of vast material structures. God, after all, first chose to incarnate himself as nature, the cosmos became his body, to show forth his *Herrlichkeit*, which, it cannot be denied, includes the incomprehensible energy found in daunting transformations. But the most perfect icon of the Father is his own Logos become man: the scope, creativity, and nuance of

---

love. And think of the enormous Franciscan Order, which sprang up about a reluctant *poverello*.

82. Few voluntarists like in fact the swastika and all it stands for, but often they fail to think through the implications of the philosophy of will for its own sake, which they have adopted in their individualistic self-centered lives. The Nazis, in choosing this ancient pagan cross, were well aware that Christianity was the ultimate enemy.

83. The Hebrews spoke of God's *shekinah*, God's glory; the German word for it is *Herrlichkeit*, which contains the word "Lord." It is the title Balthasar chose for a seven-volume meditation on the beauty of God.

84. For reasons to be reviewed in Chapter 8.

85. And hence is God-like. That is why Christ ordered his disciples to "be perfect as your Heavenly Father is perfect" (Matt. 5:48); there is no limit to be put on the constructive; growth in being is to continue indefinitely; we are to become "Sons of God."

86. The most faithful dog, whom we love mightily, will never strike us as holy; neither will an infant who as yet has little chance to exercise freedom.

human intellect and will, functioning without perversion or disharmony, with sovereign freedom ("a death he freely chose," says the canon of the Mass at the moment of consecration), embracing powerlessness, in total *kenosis* (emptying out), show forth being better than even the stupendous galaxies.

The saint's openness to all reality, experienced as an accessibility, *une disponibilité*, in the word of Gabriel Marcel, to *l'exigence de l'être*, to what being demands of him,[87] is a kind of healing power, the ability "to make whole again what has been broken." It is the antithesis of the will exercised in fanaticism, which always closes, dividing and destroying relationships.

Because it accompanies a will to reach out to all, holiness manifests its own kind of temporality: It confronts, rather than ignores, limits and hence does not flee the mystery of death. The saint testifies to a relationship with God's Word, which declares death vanquished: Death confronted, paradoxically, becomes death overcome. Our earthly demise is no longer all there is to the story; rather, death itself, as limit, gets its sense now from a larger context of life. Accordingly, the saint lives very much in this world, but is never captive of it. Remember the Socrates of *Apology*, who shows this detachment admirably. And the Christian sense of the *communio sanctorum:* the saint living in this world draws on the wisdom of the fathers and doctors of the Church and prays for the intercession of those who have preceded us, as well as for the sinners being purified in "purgatory." What the atheist, standing outside the community, sees as a great fantasy to escape the harsh realities of a life doomed to final destruction, the saint experiences as a grand *accompagnement:* He knows what he cannot well communicate, how much he daily draws on the resources of others, living and dead, and he suffers not the least doubt about the potential for lasting fruition of all human striving, as he experiences its growth in the Church. That is what is meant by the Christian virtue of hope.

Just as I was wrestling with how to express these things, I happened upon a passage from Hans Urs von Balthasar, writing of the polarization that has grown worse in the postconciliar Church:

> Where should one look to see a dawn? One should look to where in the tradition of the Church something truly spiritual appears, where Christianity does not seem a laboriously repeated doctrine but a breathtaking adventure. Why is all the world suddenly looking at the wrinkled but radiant face of the Albanian woman in Calcutta? What she is doing is not new for Christians. Las Casas and Peter Claver did something similar. But suddenly the volcano that was believed extinguished has begun to spit fire again. And nothing in the old woman is progressive, nothing traditionalist. She embodies effortlessly the center, the whole.[88]

■ ■ ■

---

87. Marcel, *Journal Metaphysique* (Paris: Gallimard, 1927), 178–79.
88. Hans Urs von Balthasar, *Kleine Fibel für verunsicherte Laien* (Einsiedeln: Johannes Verlag, 1980); *A Short Primer for Unsettled Laymen*, trans. Sr. M. T. Skerry (San Francisco: Ignatius Press, 1985), 17.

When a holy person arises in our midst, a faithful following gathers about the saint. Crowds may be attracted, but they never constitute the faithful following. The masses turn away at "the hard sayings" (John 6:60). Our perceptual knowledge is not only a firm ground for action, it can become, paradoxically, an obstacle to a deeper seeing. "What have you seen? The blind see, the lame walk, the lepers are cleansed, the deaf hear" (Luke 7:22). "You, Thomas, have believed because you have seen," says the Risen One after the skeptical apostle has placed his finger in the wounds. "Blessed are they who have not seen and have believed" (John 20:29). (The Gospels contain an elaborate dialectic of seeing and not seeing.)

The faithful following always turns out to be a few who yield to the demanding conditions of the saint's life and the intellectual exigencies of his prophecy, above all to obedience to the Word. Mother Teresa has millions of admirers, but only a few thousand religious sisters and brothers have entered her order and really do follow her healing example, in strict obedience to Christ's commands. They do this primarily because they believe the truth to which she witnesses by her life.

Few Christians are privileged to know personally a great saint, although most have been influenced at critical moments in their lives by the examples of exceptionally devoted people, often priests or sisters who have dedicated their lives to serving God, but few of whom achieve publicly recognized sanctity. Nevertheless, such people enjoy credibility when they mediate to us the example of Christ and the lives of the saints. The fact that one experiences in the Church many people who are trying to lead holy lives, who are attentive to the Word of God, who gather to celebrate the liturgy, who devote attention to the sacraments, and who join together to carry out works of charity, frequently heroic in extent, and this in faithful continuity with the apostles over millennia, gives flesh to what might otherwise seem a somewhat distant, if not unattainable ideal.

But if the good seen in the community reinforces, should not the mediocrity and the sinfulness have just the opposite effect? Obviously, scandal does not nourish faith. That is why Christ was so severe with the scandalous: "It were better a millstone were tied about their necks and they were cast in the water" (Matt. 18:6). What is more common, and more discouraging—for the scandalous can serve at least as a dramatic reminder of the seriousness of the struggle of good and evil—is the relentless grind of mediocrity. God himself seems to have trouble: "Here is the message of the Amen, the faithful, the true witness, the ultimate source of God's creation: I know all about you: how you are neither cold nor hot. I wish you were one or the other, but since you are neither, but only lukewarm, I will spit you out of my mouth" (Rev. 3:14–16). But curiously enough, that sinfulness, which one experiences first of all in one's own rebelliousness against reason and reality, one's own immaturity and lack of self-discipline, turns out to be less harmful to one's faith than might at first appear logical. That is in part because there is such a clear place foreseen for it within the tradition. The Hebrew Scriptures begin with man's revolt disturbing the order of God's creation. The sense of one's absolute need of forgiveness and grace is nourished by the humbling experience of needing help against his own worst side, against the drag of our mortality and the rebelliousness of perpetually adolescent wills.

The nonreligious person often misunderstands what Christians mean by "humility." Nietzsche saw in this virtue nothing but the self-deprecation of the mediocre, and his remedy was "Give yourself grace!"[89] Humility, a virtue of realism, is the acquired ability—and the courage—to face reality, even when it is not pleasant. That includes those sad situations when, either because we have painted ourselves into a corner morally, or because we simply lack something, we do not suffice unto ourselves. Pride, on the other hand, is mistakenly believing our self-sufficiency, implying that we are the ultimate reality; it is fantasizing that we have unrestricted freedom, that we can do what we will.

The religion that takes as its preferred symbol the Just Man, the archetypal icon (Balthasar's term) of God, nailed so unjustly to the cross, that cross itself, stretching throughout the cosmos, symbolizing the *pleroma*, the fullness of being in its very emptiness, is obviously not shy about confronting the mystery of evil, the unavoidable evidence that—bizarre as it may seem—we often choose the path of destruction over the Way of Being.

Why Philosophers Ought not Ignore Holiness

The philsophers' rumble grows louder: Religious belief is not something philosophers talk about; as irrational acts, beliefs do not yield to the universal discourse of reason. Wasn't Heidegger wise, qua philosopher, to set aside all *Glaubenssachen* (matters of faith), banishing them to the night of outer theology?

Recall the context. Traditions conflict in their distinctive truth claims, put forth as universal, binding on the intelligence, and constituting the center of the living experience of hundreds of millions. To ignore them implies that they are not worthy of consideration, that they are legends, myths, sick fantasies. (Freud thought these sick fantasies dangerous enough to devote two books to them.) The philosopher may of course not really mean to be so negative. Standing outside of a tradition, one does not know what to make of it all, or how to begin to approach it. (I certainly feel that way about the Hindu traditions.)

But ignoring a tradition that has centrally formed our own civilization is another matter, especially if hostility rather than indifference were to blame. The growing tradition of anti-Christian thought in the modern West was documented by Eric Voegelin.[90] The status of truth claims of each of the relevant

---

89. *Morgenröte,* in *Werke,* vol. 2 (Munich: Carl Hanser, 1969), 79.
90. Eric Voegelin had written a history of political ideas, which he abandoned in the 1940s upon realizing the larger, more comprehensive structure of symbolic interpretation whose analytic program he announced in *The New Science of Politics* and made the subject of *Order in History.* As a part of *The Collected Works of Eric Voegelin* (34 vols. projected), the Louisiana State University Press will be issuing this work and supporting essays, which trace

traditions demands the philosopher's attention. Even if convinced that certain great old traditions are massive purveyors of error,[91] he owes it to himself to offer some explanation of how benighted human nature can continue to indulge in such destructive nonsense.[92] If history confronts us with what are in effect social complexes, how is this extensive social pathology to be explained and what is to be done about it responsibly?

So the philosopher cannot responsibly sidestep so central a phenomenon as the claim of the experience of holiness as formative of our own civilization. It has been a prime motive force in Western culture, from the zeal of the prophets and apostles, to the fanaticism of the Puritans, passing by way of fifteen hundred years of Benedictine monasticism, the urban presence of the Mendicant orders, the worldwide activity of the Jesuits, and so on.

What Kind of Knowledge Can One Have of Holiness?

It has been hinted that a certain disposition is required in the perceiver for holiness to be able to presence. What kind of knowledge is this? Truth is not all theoretical; it can be about *being* taken as an active participle, a way. I claim that there is no knowing of any kind without a disposition of the knower, an attitude *(Verhalten)*, the taking of a stance, which alone allows a certain kind of object to presence. "The essence of truth is freedom."[93]

To perceive mere physical being more than fleetingly, I have to consent to stay and look. The perception of every form of personal presence beyond the minimum physical gestalt requires more than just opening one's eyes. *Disponibilité* is a condition of actively presencing, as a person, in a certain way. If one goes to an art gallery when one is not in the mood,[94] then little of the beauty of the paintings will penetrate. There can be no giving of a gift without the willful act of receiving, *re-sponse* (*spondeo* = I commit). One will

---

these developments in modern European thought. Voegelin further altered his program after vol. 3 of *Order and History,* because he recognized the need to open the field of historical consideration to embrace all the mature civilizations (see the foreword to *The Ecumenic Age* [Baton Rouge: Louisiana State University Press, 1974]). See also Michael J. Buckley, S.J., *At the Origins of Modern Atheism* (New Haven: Yale University Press, 1987); and Richard Tarnas, *The Passion of the Western Mind* (New York: Harmony Books, 1991), for parallel discussions of the same transformation.

91. With the spiritual beauties of Islam being equated with the wild excesses of an old Shiite ayatollah, Christianity with Salem witch burnings and Spanish Inquisitions, Judaism with the fanaticism of the Ultraorthodox of Gush Emunim, the entire Marxist-socialist endeavor with Stalin's Gulag, and liberal democracy with hedonism and addiction, there never having been a significant tradition without its fanatics, they provide an easy target for unsympathetic critics.

92. The positivists did offer explanations—Auguste Comte, for instance, with his three stages, the Religious, the Metaphysical, and the Positivist. So did Feuerbach, who claimed that the gods were but human inventions, and Marx, who saw in all religion mystification by the oppressor class.

93. Heidegger, *On the Essence of Truth* (Frankfurt: Klostermann, 1949), 3.

94. The German expression is better—*keine Stimmung haben.*

never discover holiness, any more than love, if one does not go looking for it, and one cannot do that if he does not bother to try to have an idea of what it might be.[95] That is why the very experience of holiness itself, like that of love or of certain forms of aesthetic beauty, is a grace, a gift: It must be given to one to suspect that there can be such a reality as condition for the possibility of openness to the notion when you encounter it.

Such a principle, that kinds of knowledge are rooted in a sort of grace, is disturbing to the natural positivism of common sense. And yet this experience is verifiable every day. Who is more likely to appreciate a sophisticated work of art, the child who has had the good fortune to be raised in a home where art was part of life and who has been educated, little by little, to see, or the truck driver's son who knows nothing of these things? The fortunate child brings capabilities of seeing and a comportment (another translation of *Verhalten*) because he has benefited from many gifts of education in this realm.

Take a kind of experience with which almost everyone is familiar: How do you recognize love in another? From this consideration, we can work back to holiness by way of analogy. I know a young mother whom I suspect of loving her second child, a daughter, more than her first, a son. I am obliged to acknowledge that this (tentative) judgment is based more on things she has said, in different contexts, than on anything she does, although she is more short-tempered with the son than with the daughter. But one hears constantly what a delight the daughter has been and how much more difficult the son. And she has explicitly stated that she resented the son's coming into her life so soon after marriage. The father dotes on both children unstintingly, but both parents set reasonable rules, and a calm, consistent, fair discipline is exercised. Nevertheless, the son is clearly pestier, more complicated than the girl.

Does the mother really love the girl more, or does she simply take more delight in her? Her devotion to both children is exemplary, and I would not hesitate to declare that she manifests love for both children. "Love" here means something more than just a kind of loyal devotion due from one who has elected to play the role of mother. It is concern for the well-being of both children, quite independent of any pleasure or recompense of any sort the mother might receive.

On what basis do I judge that her comportment manifests an element of *benevolentia* for the children? One observes uncomplaining attention to the children's needs. Because we cannot look into another's heart, I cannot be certain that her motives are pure. Perhaps she is just yielding to social pressure, from her husband, from her parents, from friends, to do the right thing. The motive of avoiding criticism may be mixed with a genuine desire for the children's own well-being.

Ambiguity attends most of what human beings do: Motives are rarely pure, because we neither have matters well thought through nor have the character

---

95. It is no accident that during five years of teaching the present text, I was never asked about holiness.

to stay a decided course without deviation to local temptations. Nothing marks the love of the saint more than its integrity, manifest not only in perfect service but in his vision: able to see Christ in the beggar, in whom others see nothing but the loser, and filled with a nearness to God and a vision of him that is a closed book to the person without grace. It is no coincidence that the prayer Mother Teresa has propagated throughout the world begins "O Lord, give me a heart so pure that I may see you in the poorest of the poor."

Often the word of Christ is the voice of plain good sense: "Judge not, lest you be judged" (Matt. 7:1). We cannot even judge ourselves. Who would be so bold as to consider his own motives perfectly pure, or to be certain that he sees truly to their core? "Those eaten by spiritual pride," might be the response. And yet in some sense we need to judge—at least we need to know if we are on the way to holiness. One seeks out the holy person as spiritual director. At the heart of Christian anthropology is the belief that such is our vocation: Every person is called by the author of his being to the fullest possible realization of self, to full Being, the most perfect possible unity with the *pleroma*.

The ruling conviction of all who adhere to traditions of revelation is that the path of salvation has been made known, that the Source of all Being does not leave us without the means to achieve that fulfillment of our being for which every reflective being yearns. Contrary to the charge of escapism, it is not an easy path: "Take up your cross and follow me!" scarcely promises a rose garden. But if it is true, it should prove joyous—"My yoke is easy" (Matt. 11:30)—however real the suffering in authentic human existence.[96]

Why, then, do so many, including some raised in these ways, profess to know of no such vocation? Because, answer these traditions, the grace of the *disponibilité* for the presencing of the evidence is missing, perhaps neglected or refused. But why should something so vital as the relations between such a person and his God be hidden deep in mystery?

We could put the question this way: Why is something so vital as the love between persons hidden deep in mystery? It was Aristotle, not Saint Thomas Aquinas, who, with his master Plato (and Socrates) before him, first insisted on the moral foundation of the quest for truth. But the Christian revelation adds: Truth is rooted in the infinite divine creative freedom and the human receptive finite dependent freedom. Conversely, how severely psychological blocks can interfere with seeing—human beings possess a frightening capacity to refuse to see what is staring them in the face. We cannot possess the freedom to move about the mental landscape without the freedom also to flee what we consider hard realities. Given the bad traditions we build for ourselves, rooted in bad habits (vices), it is no wonder that important things can pass us by. Why does the young soccer player from Québec politely refuse to turn away from the cheap movie to look down on the splendors of the Greenland glaciers as we fly over?

---

96. The paradox of a cross that turns out to be an easy yoke is intended. Mother Teresa wants no sour faces in her order.

On the other hand, we also have a capacity to imagine realities—delusion dogs our course through life. Again, we could not project a future without imagination. The ideal is the "not yet" that proves reasonable to work toward. The delusory is that part of the "not yet" destined never to be. Often we do not know for now which it is. Discerning the genuine holiness of authentic prophets from the spellbinding pretensions of false prophets is no easier than discerning true love from selfish passion. In all such instances of what we may call spiritual discernment, the criterion remains long term: "By their fruits you shall know them" (Matt. 7:16).

Just as selfish desire, if it fails to grow into love, does not secure the happiness of either the desiring or the desired one, so spiritual pride, self-torture in the name of the gods, and every form of rigorism guarantee misery. The peace of true communion with ultimate Being is absent. Instead of that emptying out of destructive ego in favor of true service to the other, resentment, manipulative threats of eternal damnation, and exalted arrogance usurp the spiritual place.

The living out of a tradition of revelation is an enduring exchange, resulting in growth. But when spiritual pride takes the place of love, there is the diminution of personality, tyranny of delusion, and manipulation of an ingenuine community.

How Is the Living Truth of a Tradition of Revelation Experienced?

How does the individual come into contact with the societally lived truth of such a prophetic tradition? How does an experience of God get transmitted concretely through the holy witness of a community that gathers about the prophet? This is philosophically important information, for two reasons. The philosopher needs to understand how these traditions work, because they are essentially formative of entire civilizations. More fundamental yet, it is another way for the philosopher to glimpse what Plato understood so well: However "eternal" insight into the Ideas may be, the human being encounters truth in a living way. Existentialism has emphasized the human and vital nature of truth. The great religious traditions, especially the Abrahamic, are all about love and hence truth as lived together in community, far from our sense of truth as theoretical, as mathematics. (But even mathematics is discovered by concrete persons in certain situations, and passed on through devoted communities of learning.)

The experience will be somewhat different in each tradition. Rather than generalize about the common denominator, I will attempt to capture something of the dynamics of transmission in the community (the Church) of the tradition I do know personally. I do not now attempt to discern what is peculiar to that tradition and foreign to all others. If my students are representatives, many readers will find this difficult and eye-opening enough.[97]

---

97. I consider the elements of Christianity twice: in the present epistemological context, looking at them as a way in which truth is transmitted; and in Part III, as dimensions of a way of being.

In the early communities, overwhelmed by the presence of the great prophets—Moses, David, Isaiah, Jeremiah, Muhammad—and for the early Christians, the nearness of the Christ event, the believers were swept along by the charismatic presence of the Holy One of God. Muhammad, like Gautama the Buddha, enjoyed a quarter century to put his personal stamp on his little community. Jesus, however, had only three years of public life. But how are these beliefs then sustained over millennia?

In Catholicism one sees a high degree of codification of doctrine, passed on in catechism, reinforced by preaching: The vision has from early on been developed into a coherent theology. This process began with the writing down of the prophets' utterances, starting almost three millennia ago, which evolved into the compilation and canonization of the Scriptures, which had added to them accounts of Jesus' deeds and teaching, and apostolic directions (letters), all of which evolved into the canon of the New Testament. The emerging theological vision was elaborated and commented on by the fathers and the doctors of the Church "mobilizing for the defense of truth the arms of the intellectually superior and for that reason most serious competitor, of Hellenistic-Roman philosophy," as Voegelin puts it.[98] The pluralism of immense orthodox theological traditions can get reduced in popular catechetics to a pat teaching, easily deformed into an ideology by teachers who mouth it but do not live it in sanctity. But one need not allow the worse-case scenario to blind one to the beauty and clarity of the best catechetics.[99] Protestants and others who do not understand Catholicism misplace the locus of the primary experience of the tradition. It is not in Holy Writ, but in experience of the living *communio* in liturgy and good works.[100]

In the liturgy (which means literally, "the work of the crowd"), one participates in the "communion of saints," which is not just the witness of this

---

98. Eric Voegelin, "The Beginning and the Beyond," 184, which his editors, Thomas Hollweck and Paul Caringella, term "the most important of Voegelin's unpublished writings." This late essay, intended for an Aquinas Lecture at Marquette University, was recently published in *What Is History? and Other Late Unpublished Writings*, 173–284.

99. The idea of writing catechisms was Martin Luther's. The recently issued *Catechism of the Catholic Church*, the first universal catechism in four hundred years, strikes me as avoiding ideological patness in a splendid fashion.

100. Voegelin, who presents one of the most penetrating analyses of the prophetic experience, is one of those who miss the point of Catholic experience. I keep glancing toward Voegelin because I see this powerful thinker so close to much that I am trying to bring out here, and yet distressingly far. In his analysis of the primary experience of the divine, the emphasis is noetic, in the sense of what is expressed in the word as the divine surfaces in the psyche, the sensorium of the primal encounter. He does emphasize this as an ontic event, but then shows hostility to dealing with it in the public domain, seeing it as codification that "closes the apophantic field," as objectivization, an effort to manipulate and control divine things. To be sure, every misuse of the divine through inauthentic expropriation of it for one's interests degenerates into such objectification. But the living out of truth in community as liturgy and common good works, as well as all sense of sacrament, eucharist, and *ecclesia*, seems little appreciated by Voegelin. See his most important statement, "The Beginning and the Beyond."

particular crowd piously devoting their time to go to Mass. Rather, the age-old ritual and the words of Holy Scripture here find their proper place, in the liturgical cycle of the year. It is an ongoing work, with the prophets of old, the evangelists and the apostles, and the saints. That is an experience of living truth, in harmony with the cosmic seasons and unfolding the life of God with us in the old dispensation and in the center of history, the Incarnation of his Son in Jesus Christ. This praise and thanksgiving is the central work for which man was created. In the monastery one can witness what a life centered in liturgy is like, a forecourt of heaven. The casual Sunday Mass goer can miss the whole point of the liturgy, even after a lifetime of practice. The Mass reenacts the great events of Christ's life and of all human history, the sacrifice on the cross and the victory over death, accompanied by the prayers, psalms, and prophetic utterances, ranging from God's word to Abraham—promising him that he would become "the father of many peoples"—to the priest's contemporary application, in the sermon, of these lights to our current situation, a prophetic utterance guided by the charism of the priestly office.[101]

The eucharist is, then, at once a prayer, a prophetic utterance through the medium of the apostolic office, and a sacrament that supernaturally makes present again the central event of history. The epistemic character of each of these elements requires explaining. The religious believer experiences them, after all, as prime sources of Truth. I shall try to invoke summarily something of this experience.

Living in the Tradition (I): Prayer and Prophecy

All religious people would agree on this: Prayer is the primary means of communication God has himself established; it is built into our nature and his; no one who does not pray can experience God richly.[102] *The Catechism of the Council of Trent* defines prayer as "the turning of the heart and mind to God." The turning of the mind is a willing to be present. You can have no friendship with a person if you never will to do something together. Like any other reality, with the exception of the most aggressive physical presences crashing in on us, God can occupy no place in our conscious life unless we strive to hold open a time-space for him.

---

101. Because Voegelin remains a prisoner of that Protestantism which he calls, in *The New Science of Politics* (Chicago: University of Chicago Press, 1952) "gnostic" (his worst insult) and thus this brilliant searching "eye" sees nothing more in sacrament and office than an "objectification" that destroys the "tenuous tension in the sensorium of the psyche" in communion with the divine, Voegelin's fascinating insights into religious experience stand in need of a completion. For this I suggest the work of Hans Urs von Balthasar, whom the young Voegelin once so much admired.

102. Voegelin, who loved the psalms and who, I am told, asked to have a psalm read to him as he lay dying, despite the sensitivity he shows in seeking to recuperate what happens in the sensorium that is the soul of the great prophet, says nothing about the same thing happening in the ordinary believer unspectacularly as he truly prays every day.

The turning of the heart is a *con-versio* away from our self-centeredness as we become willing to love another—in this case, God. As with any love, it is the willing of God's good, which here entails the unqualified acceptance of his will (which, because he is good and the source of all goodness, turns out to be the willing of our own true fulfillment). When we love a human being, we are still obliged, in respect for the truth, to hold back a little: We must discriminate critically between what the other wills that is genuinely good and what is deficient, sometimes even evil. We can deliver ourselves into God's will with total confidence, for he wills for us, and all his creation, only what is best, given what is meant by "God" here: He is not only initial source of all that is positive and constructive, as Providence he reveals himself as continuing to counteract the dragging elements of entropy and the aggressive destructiveness brought on by perverse acts of finite will.[103]

When *Gaudium et Spes,* a key document of the Second Vatican Council, says of Christ that "he reveals man to man,"[104] the seemingly paradoxical statement is clear to Christians: we often do not face up to who we are; we have obscured, through our abusive actions, the sense of our own best interest. We are at war with ourselves, as Saint Paul reminds us, and in letting God reveal to us again who we really are, he dis-covers us to ourselves.

To a person who has no experience of prayer life, it must seem that the religious person, in praying, is simply talking to himself, a projection of his desires in the form of a superhuman personage, a father or mother figure, with whom he then holds a dialogue. That indeed happens. Nor does the praying person always know whether and, if so, how his prayers have been answered. People of prayer, however, insist that their prayers are answered. Where is the truth in this? Again, the criterion "By their fruits." If the result of a prayer life is increasing fidelity to Christ's teaching, greater personal integrity, greater love of neighbor, more profound confidence in God and hope of salvation, richer insight into being, peace, in one and around one,[105] then every Christian would say that indeed, one's prayers have been answered.

Still, there appears to be much sterile prayer, going through the motions without much visible effect on the lives of the churchgoers. Perhaps those of us who fit this description would be even worse if we did not keep going through the motions. We cannot judge, any more than we can be certain, much of the

---

103. Commonsensically, we recognize the effective enemy of truth: every tendency that blocks us from maximizing our own good, even when we know what it is. Gabriel Marcel has a beautiful description of how enjoyment, self-centered and narrow, can block the achievement of joy, true fulfillment: "That enjoyment of self is not joy, for joy is not a satisfaction but exaltation" (*Le mystère de l'être* [Paris: Aubier, 1949], 2:121).

104. *Gaudium et Spes,* in *Documents of Vatican II,* ed. Austin Flannery, 2d ed. (Grand Rapids: William B. Eerdmans, 1988), 22.

105. To take a couple of extreme cases: the (to date) ninety thousand dying persons taken in from the street by Mother Teresa's brothers and sisters say something, and she declares it would never have been possible without the Eucharist and prayer. Jean Vanier's sixty L'Arche communities ministering in love to the most severely handicapped speak volumes. If these are the fruit of self-delusion, then let us have more of it.

time, what effect our most heartfelt appeals are having on the people with whom we are striving to have communication. The religious person believes that where grace has apparently produced little fruit, the rocky ground of our own hearts, and not the good grain of the generous sower, is to blame.

But there we touch what Saint Paul calls the *mysterion,* the workings of grace and free will. The atheist encounters this mystery, at least in terms of natural human grace: Why does offering ourselves to another often fall on rocky ground, and why on other occasions do we discover ourselves or the other opening up, dropping our defenses? "Le coeur a ses raisons que l'ésprit ne connaît point" (Pascal).[106] This central mystery of the heart is at the heart of ontology, alas. Without purity of heart, neither truth nor peace will ever be lastingly attained . . . small truths, yes, and moments of respite and temporary satisfaction, but not peace.

Christian prayer life should not be considered in isolation from the entire sacramental and teaching life of the believing community. The answer to prayer comes from liturgical life, from Scripture, from meditating on the life of Jesus Christ, from a sermon, from spiritual direction (a "spiritual work of mercy," one of the good works inspired by the Holy Spirit), including Confession, from the examples given by the saints, including the few great ones we may be privileged to know personally. Prayer and prophecy, therefore, are inseparable: One prays to the God who has let himself be known, and in so many ways.

The impact of such concrete direction, of having a model in the life of Christ, a teaching presence in the Church, the rich instruction of Scripture, is that the Christian usually knows all too clearly what is expected of him; he is aware of how far short of the demanded perfection he falls. The nature of his relationship with God in the Church is evident in the sacraments.

Living in the Tradition (II): The Eucharist

Sacramentality is characteristic of the life of the most incarnational of all religions. This sense of sacramentality corresponds with a distinctive Catholic anthropology, one that—against Platonism and tendencies in certain Protestant traditions—accepts that we are not spirits, but incarnate spirits: The body is good. Catholicism is not puritanical.

The idea of the Source of the cosmos entering into history, through concrete action on flesh-and-blood people, to achieve the ultimate purpose of his creation is central to the Abrahamic traditions. His prophetic initiatives are all unexpected—indeed, astounding—none more so than his willingness to presence in the midst of human history, to show us what his human creation was meant to be, before the first man and woman twisted it by succumbing to the temptation to be envious of God. This incarnation of the saving Truth shows us the Way and conquers sin and death in an ultimate triumph of Life itself.

---

106. "The heart has its reasons which the mind does not know at all."

If one accepts that astonishing series of claims, which the whole history of Israel is witness to—"This is a hard saying," as the gospel puts it (John 6:60)—it reveals God's intimacy with his chosen people, that Christ willed to associate mankind with his sanctity, to incorporate us as continuation of his presence. It also reveals the community of believers to be an extension of his work, faces of Christ, a "mystical Body." The sacraments give flesh, or continuing social reality, to this unique ongoing presencing of God in Christ: the humble matter, work of human hands, bread and wine, he chose as vehicles of this unique presencing, and through this, a slow, painful divinization of our sinful humanity—a purification of our hearts—is effected.

This reciprocal relationship of moral practice and idea, of heart and mind, that we see here is not a revelation made only to Hebrews and Christians, but a clear teaching of Plato and Aristotle. Forgive the seeming materialism of this declaration: Truth that is not grounded in enfleshed experience is floating tenuously in the imaginative, manipulable spirit. Evil, too, gets incarnated, as it tends to leave the realm of the fantastic to enflesh itself in destructive acts, breeding addictions, obsessions, unbridled passions, domination, and corrupt institutions.

Critique of Truth Claims: Reason, Emotion, and Principle

A nonbeliever, looking in from outside the liturgical-evangelical-patristic-charitable experience given spirit by the four-millennia-old wisdom of the living community (*ecclesia*), may have difficulty making sense of the claims of this revelation. When he tries, probably the best one can hope for is something like a Jungian reading of archetypal symbols for what they reveal of the strivings of the psyche. Carl Jung himself considered such an endeavor scientific and urgent. But he warned that anyone lacking the relevant psychic experience—in this case, because they are religious symbols, the religious experience—could not possibly know what he pretended to research.

Recently a group was discussing the passage where Jesus says that he will give a new *manna* that will hold the secret of eternal life, his own body and blood, and many of the disciples found this too hard, and so ceased following Jesus. Christ turned to his inner group and asked them if they, too, were going to leave him. As always, Peter answers, "Where would we go, Lord, for you have the words of eternal life? We have believed and have known that you are the holy one of God" (John 6:68–69). A young Anglican said that as impossible to understand as all these things are, she finds that it helps strengthen her faith to reason about them, and that when she does they make ever more sense. They really are "words of a sort which should be intriguing to the philosopher, the whole idea that life can in some way come from words, or better, from the word, the Logos." A medical doctor replied that when she is being bombarded from all sides by "Enlightenment" attacks against her religion, she draws strength from a root faith that it is not possible to understand, but her whole experience tells her that at its core it is true. To all this, yours truly commented that faith is like that: as Saint Augustine said, it seeks understanding, "fides quaerens intellectum," and efforts to deepen the understanding of what is revealed and experienced produce light. But at the same time it is the grace of faith at the core that is nourishing the quest for understanding, even the very desire to try to understand. (Remember with what ease the positivist dismisses the whole affair, unimpressed by the experience of billions.)

It was agreed by all present that the experience of God in faith should not be confused with emotion; that emotions, while always telling us something, at least about ourselves, are treacherous to interpret and are involved also in the projection of an imaginary God, tailor-made to respond to certain needs. The masters of the spiritual life, counseling use of the imagination, also warn against basing anything finally on emotion—the critical element must be present.[107] Although one may pass through a state where emotions play a role, maturing in the spiritual life demands rising above mere feeling.

Truth claims—and not just ones about religious matters—are often founded in experiences that are difficult to conceptualize adequately, that require the gifts of the poet to invoke for others. Consider how hard it is to get across to someone who has never experienced it some particular form of love, or an experience of suffering under a load of pathological guilt, or the beauty of a Bach fugue. Yet these are all common, undeniable, and important realities of human existence.

Our search through kinds of objects, kinds of truth has, in a strange way, brought us back to where we began—with our elementary encounter with reality, in experience. But now that we have surveyed widely different kinds of experience and the kinds of objects they yield, we are better prepared to deal with the critical element in all such encounters, the element necessary to appropriate all this philosophically.

As Husserl helped us understand, every experience (*Erlebnis*, literally "something lived") is true, in the sense that when one is enjoying an experience, it is indeed happening to one, in some way or other revealing something. The experiencer, in being able always to distinguish himself from what is experienced, stands over against the objectum, judging the meaning of its content, and potentially, if he elects to reflect critically on it, exercising explicit critical judgment of its truth. Critical judgment is distinguished from the more implicit ongoing judgments we make in practical experience by virtue of the methodic will to look at the phenomenon in the appropriate and adequate context.

What a particular experience can tell about reality is a foundational critical issue.[108] To sort out sound from dubious conclusions about the significance of

---

107. Balthasar, in *Herrlichkeit*, vol. 1, affirms that the Christian experience is not psychological or emotional, but dogmatic. By this, he means that it is about the truth experienced in Christ.

108. Balthasar, *Herrlichkeit*, points out that the German word for experience, *Erfahrung*, is built on the root *fahren* (to travel). An experience always moves us forward; it is a living reality, directing us toward the experienced, which itself is caught up in webs of dynamic process.

what I experience, I must draw on the totality of my wisdom, partially held in the form of principles. Critical reflection must discriminate between experiences dominated by emotions fed by unsupportable and even psychologically unhealthy desires and experiences that result from a genuine perception.[109]

The feeling of emptiness, which I experience as need, is real enough but often vague as to what might requite it. It can be untrustworthy in representing what would be respectable for assuaging it. Moreover, some desires are not healthy requirements of my being, real needs, but are perversely nurtured fantasies. Any feeling can feed in me an inclination to be ruthless in my effort to satisfy it. The tradition has consistently warned of impure desires—for example, those of what Saint Augustine termed the *libido dominandi*. Plato and Aristotle discoursed on the need for reason to discriminate among and to control potential consequences of acting under the tutelage of the emotions.

Just as emotion requires judgment, reason requires the contribution of experience, and experience is always orchestrated by feeling. The feeling that is part of perception is body coming into contact with something. Reason cannot set down in advance what is going to count as real, but must be at the service of experience, for only in external and internal experience can the real be revealed, and I can learn of its qualities by becoming engaged with them and by sorting out the elements and judging their meaning.

Principle and the Deconstructionists

In carrying out its discriminating work, critical reflection moves back and forth between various subjective and objective contexts, comparing, analyzing, and judging experiences, as it seeks to set what they reveal into the largest and most complex possible context. In doing this, it disengages principles (by insight and by insightful deduction from first principles) and in turn is guided by previously grasped principles.

Hume was convinced that principle resulted from the ordering mind's imposition of all structure. That would transform the reality of principle into a product of mind, driven by will. The deconstructionists claim that such will has been largely deployed in bad faith, in support of vested interests.

To be sure, vast principles, such as God, the Almighty Creator of all, have been invoked on many an occasion as the excuse for meting out some rough treatment in protection of ill-gotten gains; and certain epochal mind-sets, such as the famous technological mentality, have immense and largely uncriticized consequences when, as cultural predispositions, they mold the civilization. Efforts to see the abusive manipulations to which they can lead are legitimate. The deconstructionists have helped raise awareness of this. But to suggest that all knowledge of principle is nothing but projection of desire does not hold up, as Kenneth Schmitz has shown very well.[110]

---

109. And they may include an emotive dimension.
110. Kenneth L. Schmitz, "From Anarchy to Principles: Deconstruction and the Resources of Christian Philosophy," *Communio: International Catholic Review* 16:1 (spring 1989): 69–88.

Having come back full circle to experience, we shall finish this survey with a reflection on the kinds of principles we can know, because nothing better presents the phenomenon of thought coming to grips with the structures present in reality as it reveals itself to the experiencing, reflecting mind. This should also counteract any impression, which may have grown despite my intentions, that in an essentially dynamic world, approached by active, changing subjects always from a point of view, lasting truth cannot be attained. Every discovery of the knowledge of principle we have made along the way gives the lie to relativism. Let us see how and why.

THE CONCLUSION IS THE BEGINNING: PRINCIPLE DEFENDED IN PRINCIPLE

Principle, following Saint Thomas, was defined as "that from which anything in any way proceeds," *princeps*, the first. Now a cause, condition, or situation can be first in a given definable order; as a genuine starting point it is a relative absolute, so to speak, in that limited domain. One cannot go back behind it, unless one leaves that order. Or a principle can express an absolute absolute, a first principle of being itself; the domain is without limit, transcendental.

There are many ways in which a thing, cause, condition, or situation can be an *archē*, an originator. If it is not an absolute first principle, this first, or *archē*, will itself receive a certain sense when considered in a wider frame of reference, embracing a larger (but still finite) order, revealing that the principle itself has its own anterior origins.

To illustrate this, and to see how lesser principles constitute foundations for intelligibility, let us glance back over some of the different kinds of principles we have come across in this exploration.

The first time I had something to say about principle was to confess that I possessed no principle from which I could work a transcendental deduction of the categories[111] governing the selection of kinds of objects and kinds of truth we would discover, which admission dooms us to a somewhat haphazard adventure of discovery. That implied something about the way we discover and hold first principles of being: They are not truths from which the experientially distinguishable orders of being are to be deduced. I will address this after we survey the less demanding kinds of principle.

The first of these was the mention of soul as a principle guiding the development of an organism: an effective organizing factor at work in each and every living thing, following a specific course of development, securing their healthiest prosperity. We could add that every kind of formal cause is a principle of being for the thing thus formed.

How do we know that there really is any such principle or "formal cause," as Aristotle called it? By insight into our experience of how individual things

---

111. Transcendental deduction would derive all principles from one, by logical progression. Kant thought he could do that.

maintain their evident integrity, we proceed from experience by abstractive, generalizing insight, which yields a sense of their characteristic type of being. The knowledge yielded by this brute exercise of mind is lasting. No matter when this particular organism came into being or when it may be destroyed, it will always be true (forever[112] in a world of ideal insight) that so long as it lasted a principle of internal organization was at work overseeing the subprocesses of alimentation, cell building, excretion, reproduction, and so on. To understand the generation of the soul and why it continues a tradition of the same kind of organism, we must look beyond to its principles.

To acknowledge that some principle reigns over the orderly development of the organism does not of itself yield information about the precise ways in which it carries out this organizing function. At the present stage of empirical investigation of how in various kinds of living thing this governance works, we remain somewhat in the dark. The soul is not a thing but a coordinated set of functions and relationships that secure an observable unity in the overall process of the organic thing's self-maintenance.

The second mention of principle found us moving from the principle of soul toward a very general principle of how life is meant by nature to be lived: The dynamic of every living thing carries it forward, unless interfered with, through its natural course of development. This insight constituted an intermediary step from "is" to "ought." The implication was that those organisms which can reflectively grasp the sense of their own natures can (and ought to?) see (by insight) that they are the kinds of things which normally come to maturity and consequently (a step in reasoning, again requiring insight), when faced with a choice of actions, ought to choose those which favor the intended maturation. This is recognition in principle of the *telos* built into the soul.

At that point we encountered another kind of principle of knowledge: Certain kinds of knowledge (grace and love and knowledge of art were examples) presuppose a corresponding kind of experience without which, although communicated verbally, they are empty of meaning. This is a broad principle, an assertion of the primordiality of experience, drawn from reflection on how our knowledge is built up. This principle of experience is broad enough to bring us to the question of how we grasp the broadest of all, transcendental principles, the first principles of Being. I promised earlier to say something about this.

I take a realistic stand on this absolutely fundamental question. Mind is not self-constituted as the god that is meant to dominate all that is.[113] As power of

---

112. I have hesitated to say "eternal," to avoid some sort of Platonic world of forms. The ideal world of forms yielded by insight is not the cosmic time-space of perceptual experience, but a realm interior to consciousness. This is not some kind of everlasting real world from which the forms of concrete things are derived, as Plato thought.

113. Hence our dependence on experience (*Erfahrung*). We are always *unterwegs, homines viatores* (as Marcel says), *Eksistents* (in the word of Heidegger), standing out toward the future. Experience—the past—points the way forward. This is also reflected in revelation: Christ in proclaiming himself the divine Truth in the same breath claimed to be the Way and the Life,

insight, mind contains no built-in content-laden criteria of the real, but must learn of it in experience. This always includes experience of itself experiencing, although its inherent intentional dynamic carries the fullest force of its attention out toward the object and not reflectively back to itself. Even the mind's grasp of self-evident principles such as the principle of contradiction is the result of the whole person's interaction with surrounding reality, in the encounter with which the power of mind is able to grasp aspects of being's basic intelligibility, in the subject and the object. The notion that something cannot be and not be in the same respect at the same time is not the result of a quirk in how mind is constituted but an acquaintance in experience of the way things are, a grasp of the reality of persistent stability and structure, an acknowledgment that things have an identity and that relations between things can be stable and meaningful. As being manifests itself in the form of identifiable discrete things manifesting a characteristic whatness, existing in settings that quickly show themselves, with experience, to be dependable, like "home," mind encounters this otherness and permanent whatness. A child will grasp this and act accordingly, expecting mother to be mother, and distinguishing persons from animals, and knowing what belongs in his home long before the adult animadverts explicitly to the principle of noncontradiction.

Mind opens onto a transcending reality that reveals its own structures, the logical demands of which have to be met or we cannot proceed to deal with them successfully. This is so, whether "we" is my ego, intersubjective transcendental ego, or even the sum total of accumulated human experience held in the symbols and institutional structures that constitute the wisdom transmitted by the traditions. Reality is greater than any of these and continues to reveal itself to all consciousness—personal, intersubjective, and stored in traditional symbols.

This is the spirit of humbly recognizing the limits of our reason—its dependence on the passivity of experiencing—in which we should interpret Saint Athanasius' much misunderstood expression, *sacrificium intellectualis*. He did not mean that the Christian should crucify reason; rather, the intellect should recognize its limits when in the presence of transcending mystery. Balthasar is excellent on this: "The principle always held up by ecclesial theology [is] that the article of faith embraced in a living faith must be the basis and point of departure for a deepened rational reflection—just as the attempt to understand a work of art better must always proceed from its entirety."[114]

"Reason" remains, in all this, the term for that brute ability of intellect to see and to distinguish analytically among the parts of what presents itself in external and internal perception. But it is dependent on the gifts of perception, the gifts of experience, in order to have something to see and to discern. In the next chapter, we examine the problem of translating distinctive experiences

---

and bids us "Take up your cross [which we can interpret as the suffering, *passio*, of receiving "the slings and arrows of outrageous fortune"] and follow me."

114. Balthasar, *A Primer*, 36.

captured by different traditions. We argue there, once again, the importance of our objective knowledge of things and principles as guide and anchor for our more ethereal mental constructions, and for the need to recuperate every phase of experience as ground for critique of those constructions.

5.

IS A SINGLE WISDOM POSSIBLE?

STRIVING FOR A UNIVERSAL DISCOURSE: PHILOSOPHY

Arguing against settling down definitively in a live-and-let-live pluralism in which traditions would comfortably reside in their separate worlds, I urged formation of a wisdom. But communication between traditions implies a unity of discourse, a function of an underlying project of reason, and hence translatability of all experiences. Given the variety of kinds of truth, is that credible? And does not the problem already exist at the personal level, as each of us has unique experiences, our own natural faith—each lives in his own world?

Are All Experiences Expressible in Translatable Symbols?

In one sense, no experience is exactly translatable into any other, precisely to the extent that each yields some distinctive facet of reality. (My experience this evening of this unique sunset is different from that of my friend, standing at my side and admiring the same scene.) On the other hand, to the extent that every experience yields a facet of a transcending reality, which itself is related to other realities, and relatable through concepts to other intelligibilities, and through expression of the same intelligibilities can be the focus of attention of several centers of awareness, it can be integrated into ever larger structures of meaning and shared between subjective worlds. (My friend and I have no difficulty oohing and aahing at this display of God's artistry, confident that we are discussing the same sunset.)

To the extent, then, that the various kinds of experiences and ideas are somehow relatable to one another, however remotely—capable in some sense of being integrated (not just dumped in the same mind like a container) into a single world of discourse—the question of how, and through what manner of translation, confronts us, even on the perceptually verifiable level of everyday experience. If conversation is possible, people who have enjoyed similar experiences of the same things must be able to forge linguistic symbols adequate to explaining how the distinctive experiences are different and yet relate to the same thing, and how that thing relates to other things experienced. Finally, they should be able to situate reflectively the phenomena expressed within the different histories of the distinctive worlds, subjective and objective.

The vital role of objectivity in all this seems obvious to me, and, founding it, reality: When there exists outside consciousness some thing or situation to which several can have access, then one uses his experience as a base for finding the appropriate symbols to direct the other's attention to the same aspects of the same or similar kinds of things or situations. He can do this because in themselves these external realities transcend all individual consciousness, presenting their evidence for their own endurance and spatial location and/or formal type, or their place within the peculiar time-space of an imaginative construction.[1]

In the case of common objects of perception, that all seems clear (convincing everyone but resolute skeptics). But the possibility of transmission of experiences of things to which the other has no direct access and radically different from any he has ever enjoyed—that is another matter!

Because reality, presencing in experience, offers its own measure, the question of translatability is in some way an issue of the commensuration of the criteria revealed in different realms of experience. In pursuing translatability and commensurability, we could explore any number of kinds of truth to see the challenges of putting them in communication—for example, the problem of translating the most culture-bound experiences. *Salon* is not exactly "living room," and the French experience of how a *salon* is set up and of what goes on there does not evoke the same resonance as the casual lounging around in a Canadian living room. Although there is no term-to-term correlation, one can circumlocute the problem, as I just did, pinpointing the difference. Or there is the problem of translating the mathematical symbols of physics into ordinary language.[2] Or regions of desire: the conflict between the architect's desire to fashion a beautiful building and the company's desire to keep costs down; or determining the cost-effectiveness of safety devices; or apportioning medical resources—how much is one willing to spend to save a life?

In *Tradition and Authenticity*, while considering the kinds of truth characteristic of the four genera of explicit tradition—the artistic, the scientific/philosophic, the associational, and the revelational—some start was made on the question of integrating truths of disparate experiential origin into one wisdom. Now it is necessary to go farther, to make the project of wisdom more credible.

The Most Difficult Challenge: Fundamental Truth Claims

I propose to face the difficulty by continuing my reflection on the most demanding claims of all: the truths brought forward by traditions of revelation.

---

1. In class I often invoke an imaginary object, made up and described on the spot, and then ask the students to describe it back to me. Focusing their attention on the (via language) shared objective-imaginative intelligibility, they are able to respond accurately to questions about it. Objectivity and reality (in the reductionist cosmic sense), remember, are not the same.

2. David Bohm, the physicist-philosopher, once assured me that any theory in physics is entirely translatable into terms ordinary educated people could understand. And Albert Einstein is reported to have said that, until he could explain his theory of general relativity at a level comprehensible to a six year old (obviously with some loss of detail, but nevertheless in broad outline), he didn't really understand it himself (anecdote via B. A. Stewart from Rev. Hal Stockert, who claims to have heard it from Einstein during 1954).

They are the most difficult because, not only do they pronounce on ultimate matters, but, clearly, they have more to do with faith than other things appear to have (they, too, have their element of faith, recall). They purport to be revelations of how it stands with being itself offered by the mysterious, personal Source of all reality. Everyone can see that we will never com-prehend either being or God.

But the incomprehensibility of being and of God is no excuse for not bothering ourselves with either. Even if an ultimate dimension of experience—God—is to be reduced, through psychological and sociological deconstruction by Feuerbach, Marx, and Freud, at least this massive reality of the human cultural scene is not simply ignored as it is by the practical atheist. The project of a genuine ecumenical wisdom demands more: finding reasonable ways to bring these great claims about being itself into discussion and ultimately to fit them together critically in a nonreductionist ontology. Such a wisdom must be able to interpret all valid experiences communicated by whatever kind of symbol, including those most demanding of all symbols, the ones put forward with the staggering claim that they are the Word of God himself. I am taking up this challenge, at least in a preliminary way, here, before proceeding to the ontology, to get a reading of the full dimensions of the epistemic task facing the lover of wisdom—a better idea of what knowledge is required to secure an adequate ontological base for that wisdom.

Because of the supernatural component in my own natural faith, I am open to claims about experience of being that has wide and deep dimensions. But can the believer make sense to the nonbeliever who does not share in religious experiences and so thinks that those who indulge in such visions have left genuine experience behind and flown off into myth? But if the religious and the nonreligious can talk to one another, what is the appropriate, mutually meaningful form of discourse? Under what conditions would it be appropriate to undertake such discussion?[3]

The world holds out hope in this regard. Sustained ecumenical discussion between believers in different traditions is going on, especially under official Church patronage. Because a base of similar experiences in the sphere of the divine is available to all believers, the most serious dialogue is proceeding between various branches of Christianity, and, less intensively, between Muslims

---

3. Few in Canadian society are eager to talk about experiences of the divine (or any experience touching what is really serious). These are personal matters, it seems, except of course for the religious fanatics, who importune one to ask if one is born again. Bruce Stewart points out that experiences of the divine *(ho theos)* are difficult to express without immediately, before any effort to enter into the experience one is trying to communicate, applying the traditional language from the Abrahamic traditions, which have formed our Western civilization. As Voegelin says, a noetic revelation of the divine gets lost under the pneumatic language. He suggests that many thoughtful persons have moved to living out their convictions as a means of communication instead of attempting discussion. See Voegelin, *Order and History*, vol. 4, *The Ecumenic Age* (Baton Rouge: Louisiana State University Press, 1974), for an extended discussion.

and Christians, and between Jews and Christians. Rev. Ignatius Hirudayam, S.J., the leader of twenty years of Hindu-Catholic dialogue in the ashram he founded in Madras, reports that this, too, has been a fruitful exchange.[4] And I have participated in long-running fruitful discussions with atheists.

Translation between traditions must pass by way of philosophical discourse, that is, aim at universality of assent. But there is no philosophical language *an sich*, perfectly transparent, encouraging every dimension of being to show itself. The very idea of philosophy is of Greek, not Hindi origin. Think of "philosophy" here as standing for a motivation and a comportment, rather than a given method and a language floating above all cultures. The *philein* in *philosophia* has to be widened to embrace not just a theoretical wisdom but the reality of what may at first seem to us barbarous: the other (which is what the Greek *barbaroi* meant) as really different from all I have as yet experienced.[5] I will never make the effort to enter into his world unless I learn to love him, which I can only do if I am also striving for purity of heart (read: getting away from defensive egoism). Think of the *sophon* as the intended non-exclusion of any dimension of being to which one can have access in any kind of experience whatever; plus the critical element, aware judgment of the genuineness of all elements and how all dimensions fit together, with attention to the *metra* implied by commensurability. This includes the wisdom to recognize destructive, inherently unintegratable elements as well, with a critique that reveals their core anti-being.

THE MORAL BASE OF PHILOSOPHY: THE COMPORTMENT OF CONFIDENCE

This moral base is presupposed: the will to open a credit that all sides have worthwhile experiences to contribute, so that each can learn from the other,

---

4. Traditions of revelation with extensive explicit materials to share afford the best opportunity for such dialogue (as I pointed out in *T&A*, chap. 3). A dialogue would be far more difficult when dealing with one whose tradition is fully oral, such as that of the Dalai Lama. If there are also "atheistic traditions of revelation," as Bruce Stewart suggests, dialogue would be more difficult still—the Dalai Lama's tradition at least speaks to some similar concepts of how it is with being and the world. When I press for an explanation, Stewart points to the noetic revelation of the divine that Voegelin discusses in *Order and History*, vols. 2 (*The World of the Polis*) and 3 (*Plato and Aristotle*), and to which he returns in vols. 4 and 5. "Atheistic" here refers to the failure to move from the noetic to the pneumatic forms. See Paul Caringella, "Voegelin: Philosopher of Divine Presence," in *Eric Voegelin's Significance for the Modern Mind*, ed. Ellis Sandoz (Baton Rouge: Louisiana State University Press, 1991), 174–205. Voegelin remains a prime discussant throughout the present volume, because I believe his insights into religious experience to be at once among the most fertile and the most subtle (and hence) dangerous deformations of the tradition, as I, a Catholic, understand it.

5. The Greek was most dismissive of anything foreign to his "superior" civilization, just as, within the structure of the *poleis*, citizens of one *polis* were equally dismissive of anything foreign to their own city. Saint Paul, on the other hand, announced the "good news" that in Christ all otherness is taken up and lovingly unified, all barriers introduced by otherness are dissolved: "There is neither Jew nor Greek, master nor slave, male nor female" (Gal. 3:28).

a con-fidence (literally, "faith together"), and a sense that no one possesses the last word, a resolutely nonideological attitude. Naive? No: I acknowledge, humbly as regards myself, compassionately as regards others, my limitations and even, as the Christian would say, "sinfulness": those irrational elements of hatred and destruction that leave their ugly traces of anti-being on every tradition and each personality, reducing openness. Fruitful conversation requires the grace to overcome these. Communication is difficult—how rare are the privileged loci of real dialogue. They abound in philosophy departments, of course—about as much as irony is understood today! Achieving the right comportment of genuine disponibility, what Heidegger calls the appropriate *Verhalten*,[6] is part of the lifelong moral struggle to build character. To take another instance, I have found dialogue with some Muslims difficult because few of those with whom I have talked think Christianity has anything to teach them. They say that Islam superseded Christianity, which, while "a religion of the book," distorted Jesus' message, which the Qur'an presents in all its purity, for it is the one message of the one God. In the Islamic-Christian encounters in Tunisia, the Christians acknowledged that there are treasures in Muslim spirituality from which the Christian can learn, but a certain suspicion about Muslims in general remained, too. Perhaps an element of fear exists, because the simplicity of the Muslim monotheist faith attracts many over against the sophistication of Christian Trinitarian theology. I offer this sour note as an illustration that the moral conditions making possible such exchanges are obviously easier to describe than they are to realize. Love always seems in short supply, even in the most intellectual circles!

One has to be authentically secure to respect the other and to allow the possibility of the genuineness of his experience,[7] one has to have taken responsibility for what he is by critically examining his own vision.[8] The foundation is secured in truth, not ideological obduracy. Pursuit of authenticity must be accompanied by progress in holiness, banishing the lie as one struggles to bring his actions into line with what he has been able to know is true. Such integrity achieves security because one is no longer afraid of reality, any reality, for one's life is now built on a minimum of indefensible fantasy and a maximum of genuine experience of the good. That experience is, at its summit, interpersonal.

Aristotle was clear about it: True dialogue, like the friendship he so well described, can only take place between what the Philosopher called *spoudaoi*—mature persons, the Greek equivalent of holiness.[9] Without that maturity, there

6. Further discussion of comportment is in Chapter 10.
7. See *T&A*, chap. 2, for a discussion of personal authenticity.
8. The Balthasarians may be wondering: "Is not *appropriation* terribly 'existentialist'? For the Christian, appropriation gives way to expropriation of one's ego by following Christ, so that God's will, not my own *ek-sisting*, reigns." No one can make sense of such a claim without first entering into and following the supernatural way of the Gospel.
9. *Nicomachean Ethics* 1113a29–35. See Voegelin's excellent discussion of this passage, in *Order and History*, vol. 3, *Plato and Aristotle* (Baton Rouge: Louisiana State University Press, 1957), 300f.

is only combat and put-down, sin and pathology, not searching discussion and a mutual questing for truth and living it out together.

COMMUNICATING PRIVATE AND PUBLIC EXPERIENCES

At issue is the very possibility of communicating experiences to another. I say "experience" because what the symbols of religion capture are the fruits of lived interpersonal relationships, not mere descriptions of things, nor principles derived from things.

I sense that my friendship with George is not going well. Each time we meet we argue; he seems progressively more withdrawn. I tell a mutual friend about this: Something is wrong with George. His strange attitude seems more basic than just some undiagnosed problem in our relationship. Suppose the friend has not noticed anything. What can I adduce as evidence? I can only recount what I have experienced. If my friend is going to learn about the situation, to which he personally has not been a party, he has to trust that my witness is accurate. I am confronted with the poetic challenge of finding the concepts to analyze and the words to describe the patterns of incidents from which the relationship gets its substance. I can recount anecdotally significant events; I can describe how I was affected by things George said or failed to say, providing some sense of the context. My reactions form a large part of what is going on. These are my intuitions into the whole tenor of the situation, "intuition" here meaning vague, perhaps not very well grounded judgments about interconnections between events, forming patterns, which may reveal in the telling as much about me as about George—indeed, the mutual friend may notice this, but be too discreet to mention it.

Objective Events, the Experience of Them, and the Communication via Gospels

Obviously, when a believer is testifying about an intimate experience that he thinks involved God's action in his life, the listener must rely on his confidence in the reporter's discernment and on his own familiarity, if any, with like experiences. This intimate experiencing and the recounting of it can be very tenuous. Fortunately the witness given by those in the Abrahamic traditions is not all or even principally about such private experiences. I return to the example of this tradition, because of the special challenges with which it confronts mankind, hence its key role in the ecumenical effort. But also, and here I agree with Carl Jung, to talk about how experience can be transmitted, it is better to start with experiences one has himself enjoyed.

The Gospels witness to wondrous public events, in which Jesus' power was manifest to the multitude, and to his teaching, much of it public. Even the more difficult parts of that teaching were shared with the twelve apostles, although only the inner three—Peter, James, and John—witnessed the Transfiguration, the moment on Mount Tabor, where Christ's divinity was allowed to shine forth. That teaching, as the observer in the synagogue said after hearing Him, was delivered "with authority." The risen Christ, the New Testament claims, was seen by many, and the church he founded grew to be a vast historical enterprise, the work of an apostolic community, with a long tradition of authoritative teaching and of charitable works. But it was also a sinful community, as its traditions, from the Gospels on, explicitly point out. This lends credibility to the human reality in what is being attested to. All these claims are about events in the public domain, not about intimate interior experiences.

That is what is at the center of the Symbolon of the apostles: the figure of the historical person, Jesus of Nazareth, claimed to be the Christ and the continuing reality of his church. As Saint Irenaeus, second-century bishop of Lyon, declared, that community has from the start jealously guarded "the wholeness of the truth about Jesus Christ, about what He said and about what He did." That is a historical claim about what has in fact been taught, from documents subject to critical scrutiny. The issue for the Christian is truth, indeed the whole of the truth. That is the sense of the *catholou:* The universality claimed by the Church is less its mission to all humanity than its sacred obligation to transmit the whole of the truth that is Jesus Christ.[10] The early community—and it was a community endeavor—produced four complementary (and not always perfectly consistent) versions of the Gospel in an effort to mirror many facets of an inexhaustible public experience. The Gospel of John ends with the declaration, "This disciple is the one who vouches for these things, and we [the community] know that his testimony is true. There were many other things that Jesus did; if all were written down, the world itself, I suppose, would not hold all the books that would have to be written" (John 21:24–25).

At the center of the great religions stands a colossal figure, a person, acknowledged to be only a human being, but one who has been singled out as the exceptional channel for the expression of truth. K'ung Fu-tzu, Lao-tzu, Gautama the Buddha, Zoroaster, Moses and the other great prophets, Socrates, Muhammad: They teach with authority, many with deontic authority, that is, what they say imposes itself by the sheer brilliance of the wisdom it expresses, backed up by the living example of the purity of the great personage's own life. Some teach with the authority of prophets—Muhammad, for instance, is expressly the Messenger of God, who passes on what the Angel Gabriel reveals to him to be God's will. The prophet, too, is expected to authenticate what he teaches by the living example of his own purity. In some ways, Socrates is such a seminal figure for philosophy, one not totally devoid of a prophetic element (there is the mysterious business of the Athenian's daemon), and whose life and martyrdom provide what *martyrein* means: witness. Plato's Academy was

---

10. Is the collision between Voegelin and the Catholic tradition as great here as I think? He seems to me to hold as a weakness—on overobjectification—what the Church considers its sacred trust: to teach "everywhere and at all times the same truth," to paraphrase Vincent of Lerins, the fifth-century monk, "the whole of what Christ revealed."

a little *ecclesia* of lovers of wisdom following Socrates' way. That wisdom constituted a theo-onto-logia.

Often, again as in the case of Socrates, the Buddha, and Jesus, the seminal figure himself writes nothing. Rather, his teaching is captured, elaborated, and passed on by the disciples, and his example followed. Much mythological embroidering can go on about the historical kernel. At issue may be truths about the cosmos and about things generally, but central to each tradition are always experiences of a personal nature.

That fact, and the pervasive influence of the great personal religions in molding the history of mankind, makes me believe that philosophy should not depersonalize reality. Post-Cartesian science so tends, the positivists holding up as a triumph depersonalization (with some justification, to the extent that careful measurement and mathematical symbolization have led to progress in the exact sciences). Others have combated this notion when it has been extended to all experience. Think of Blaise Pascal; Wilhelm Dilthey, who contrasted the *Geisteswissenschaften* with the *Naturwissenschaften;* the student of evolution Henri Bergson; the mathematician-philosopher Alfred North Whitehead; the psychiatrist-philosopher Karl Jaspers; the philologist and linguist Martin Buber; the personalists Gabriel Marcel, Immanuel Mounier, René La Senne, André Marc, and Maurice Merleau-Ponty; the political philosopher Eric Voegelin; the phenomenologists Immanuel Levinas and Paul Ricoeur; the biologist and anthropologist Pierre Teilhard de Chardin; Henri de Lubac; the theologian Hans Urs von Balthasar; and the personalist philosopher Karol Wojtyla. May we not legitimately add Heidegger to that list? The present work is in the line of all these thinkers who recognized the personal dimension of reality, striving to capture the sense of personal experience as the highest being, and to see how varieties of such experiences can be integrated into a single wisdom.

The Most Difficult Claim: That about Jesus Christ

But the claims made about Jesus are different, more demanding than many of the claims about the great founders of other religions. About no other has such an unequivocal and uncompromising claim of divinity been made and at the same time of complete humanity—he is affirmed by the Council of Chalcedon to be "wholly God and wholly man."[11] This places the phenomenon of Jesus—as the prophetic challenge always does, but this time in the most demanding form—at the dividing line between the familiar (but mysterious) human and the unfamiliar (but mysterious) divine.[12] The transcending Source of all does

---

11. My lack of study and dialogue with the rich Hindu traditions makes valid comparison impossible, but the Bhodisatvas seem, to one peering in superficially, shadowy in the claims made of their humanity and what they incarnate by way of divinity. My point here is positive, that Chalcedon's claim about Christ is disconcerting because so clear.

12. By the divine is meant something more than whatever is more perfect in its mode of being than man. That larger and vaguer sense is more properly designated, following recent

not on this occasion just communicate with man through a chosen human being, as in prophecy, but comes into our immanent history to share, through our own human mode of existence, in its joys and tribulations, to assume them unto himself and thereby to sanctify human existence through his personal making it holy. He is claimed to have shown his divine power, to have been rejected by his own people ("He came amongst His own and His own knew Him not"; John 1:11), to have been treated as a criminal ("was crucified, died and was buried"). In the ultimate public manifestation of his divinity, he conquered death, for himself and for us all, as, continuing the words of the Symbolon of the apostles, "He rose again from the dead and ascended into heaven, where He sits at the right hand of the Father, from whence He will come to judge the living and the dead."

Now there is indeed a challenging truth claim. Just as the Muslim considers the truth claim, "There is but one God, and Muhammad is his prophet," so the Christian believes the claim of the Incarnation and redemption through the risen Christ the most important truth claim of all history. These kinds of truth claim ought leave no one indifferent. If they were the result of some small sect in Oregon getting high on mushrooms, they could be dismissed with the disdain some secularized people now treat them to. But because Christianity and Islam are the central beliefs of close to half of mankind, and the heart of civilization-spawning traditions, that dismissal is dangerous to the health . . . of mankind. After all, if true, the central Christian claim would indeed be the hinge of all history. Enough people have believed it for it to have inspired the transformation of the Roman Empire and then the great civilizations of the Orthodox East and the Latin West, and to give a basic cast even to European modernity (why is science Western?),[13] leaving as a legacy in postmodern times strong, renewing Christian communities, embracing close to a quarter of mankind, in every part of the world, still generating intriguing new cultural expressions and many purported insights.

Although I believe it, I fully appreciate why non-Christians wonder how any serious person can possibly take such an enormity seriously, or at least wonder how such delusional fanaticism can forge whole civilizations. The Christian is in the same situation vis-à-vis Islam, wondering at the Meccan merchant's power of belief, which in twenty-five years forged such a strong *umma,* able rapidly to transform entire parts of the world.[14] We treat the vast claims of others as beautiful (often meaning "crazy") myths, and then shake our heads at the fruits they produce.

---

usage, "the sacred." The more distinctly Christian sense of the divine entails a claim of God's absolute transcendence and of infinite personhood in God.

13. See Stanley Jaki's convincing argument, in his Gifford Lectures, on the Christian origins of modern science, *The Ways of Science and the Way to God* (Chicago: University of Chicago Press, 1978).

14. In some ways Jewish belief is even more problematic for the Christian, for the coming of the Mash'iah—the Christ—opens an issue of continuity that Islam does not pose.

Those engaged in ecumenical dialogue suffer from the absoluteness of the Christ claim: Is it not the greatest of all stumbling blocks to unification of the truths of the traditions? But "stumbling block" is precisely the term the tradition itself has applied to the enigmatic figure of Christ, and especially his crucifixion, since one of the first Christian written documents, Saint Paul's first letter to the Corinthians (1:23): "a *skandalon* for the Jews and madness for the nations"—a definitive stumbling block, I would say, to traveling together the path to a unified wisdom of mankind. But the Jewish claim to be a Chosen People and the Muslim claim that Muhammad is the Seal of the Prophets are stumbling blocks, too, although, I would say, smaller boulders.

The secularizers see demythologization as the only way to clear the path to truth: boulders into sand traps! Only with secularization will mankind be free of "transcendental mortgages" and will find itself, not these projections of human imagination, at the center of all reality. That has been the cry since Feuerbach and Marx, and the tendency of most Enlighteners long before.

For perspective, remember that it is not just the great religions that confront us with stupendous claims that shatter the complacencies of ordinary experience. There are, for instance, some pretty hard-nosed astro-physicists putting forward claims that strike common sense as incredible: the cosmos, now believed to be more than ten billion light-years in width,[15] was hurled from a central point of energy; and in the first seconds of this unfolding reality, the entire mass was contained in a ball of tiny dimensions weighing its present unimaginable weight; and in the further unfolding of the process, all the exquisite complexities grew up and achieved their respective precarious balances. (Or try to imagine what this claim means: In Andromeda there is a black hole, thought to contain a mass ten thousand million times that of our sun.)

But there is another difficulty with a claim like that about Jesus: Hegel, Jung, Teilhard de Chardin, and Balthasar are not talking about exactly the same experiences. Different experiences get referred to the same object, Jesus Christ. That is no reason for not taking these various claims seriously, but it does impose the need to clarify what in a given instance one is reflecting about.

The community of those sent forth by Christ demands attention by professing to speak in his name. Interestingly, no such apostolic authority is claimed by the other religions—not even Islam, at least not since the demise of the caliphate.[16] The apostles, however, declared that Christ had charged them, "Whatsoever you shall bind on earth shall be bound in heaven" (Matt. 16:19).

---

15. Differences in evaluating the available evidence for the evolution of the universe—especially in the first few seconds—account for the great variations in the estimates by various astrophysicists. Recently (August 19, 1991) I read in *The Economist* that the age may be as low as twelve billion years.

16. The *khalifa*, as head of the *umma*, with authority descended from the Prophet, ruled the community, but even in the heyday of the caliphate, the caliphs were modest in their claims of participating in the Prophet's authority. At least, that was so in the tradition of the way, the Sunna ("rule," "course," "law"). The *shi'ah Ali* ("party of Ali") claims a strong authority by divinely sanctioned prophetic descent from Muhammad, which reaches

"The Maximum of Differentiation of Experience"

To my argument that these extravagant claims to authority are to be taken seriously at least because of their historical importance, the eminent political philosopher Eric Voegelin adds another. Inquiring into man's quest for social order, Voegelin put forward as a scientifically justifiable claim that the Christian consciousness represents "the *maximum of differentiation* of experience through the revelation of the *Logos* in history."[17] By this he means that through theological reflection on the Christ event, rising to a summit in the West in the theological syntheses of Saint Augustine and Saint Thomas, it was given to mankind to achieve the fullest, most thoroughly articulated, and best-balanced understanding of how man relates to God, to nature, and to one another.

This is not the last word; indeed, subsequent breakthroughs have been significant. Rather, the tradition came closest to a proper and well-thought-out framework, a detailed overall vision of how what I have called here "the ultimate structures" relate.[18] Voegelin contends further that modern "gnostic civilization" represents a regression from this maximum, and a loss of the sense of "the openness of the soul"[19] in moving toward reductionist atheism. Because men could not live with the "uncertainty of faith,"[20] they sought to substitute for divine revelation of man's situation systems of thought through which they could feel secure in their commanding vision of how it stands with Being. Starting with the eschatological speculations of Joachim of Floris at the end of the twelfth century, this kind of speculation became, in modern times, progressively secularized, to end in the great voluntaristic and necessitarian systems of Marx, Lenin, and the Fascists.

Voegelin warns in his letter to Alfred Schütz, in which he speaks of "maximum differentiation," that the Christian claims must be approached historically; they must be understood in the context of the time in which they exploded

---

enormous proportions in certain Shia sects, the Mahdiy ("he who is rightly guided") being a figure reminiscent of the Christ of the Second Coming.

17. Voegelin to the phenomenologist Alfred Schütz, January 1, 1953, in *The Philosophy of Order*, ed. P. Opitz and G. Sebba (Stuttgart: Klett-Cotta, 1981), 454.

18. That it is a sophisticated and complex differentiation quite capable of absorbing into its ample horizons all that modern thought also has to offer I can attest, as I work my way through the seventeen large, dense volumes of Balthasar's theological trilogy, *Herrlichkeit, Theo-dramatik, Theologik,* which is based in that classical Augustinian-Thomistic treasure-house.

19. Eric Voegelin, *The New Science of Politics* (Chicago: University of Chicago Press, 1952), 164. This theme constitutes the subject of research in his five-volume *Order and History,* begun subsequent to the Chicago lectures, a work I consider essential for anyone struggling today to understand the dimensions of the truth question.

20. Voegelin is at odds with Balthasar on the nature of the experience of faith—a grave difference between them, as it was between Balthasar and the early Barth. Later, Barth grew closer to Balthasar's position, perhaps in part as a result of the long discussions they had together in Basel. For Balthasar, the experience of faith is not "uncertain"—he is no Kierkegaardian.

The Barth-Balthasar debate is well summarized in Georges de Schrijver, *Le merveilleux accord de l'homme et de dieu: Etude de l'analogie de l'être chez Hans Urs von Balthasar* (Leuven: Leuven University Press, 1983), chaps. 7–9.

onto the scene, in order to get the measure of the challenge they pose to contemporary thought.[21] He goes on to explain the status of what he calls "dogmatics":

> What the men of the eighteenth-century Enlightenment held against Christian dogmatics (enlightened thinkers are repeating it today), namely that theological statements—unlike statements concerning sense perception—are meaningless because they cannot be verified, is the very starting point of Christian theology. On this point Thomas would agree with every Enlightener. Dogmatics is a symbolic web which explicates and differentiates the extraordinarily complicated religious experiences; furthermore, the order of these symbols is a descriptive system, not a rational system capable of being deduced from axioms. (We must note the insistence of Thomas that Incarnation, Trinity and other doctrines are rationally impenetrable, i.e. rationally meaningless.) Here, it seems to me, lies the greatest value of Christian theology as a store of religious experiences amassed over more than a thousand years, which has been thoroughly analyzed and differentiated by Church Fathers and Scholastics in an extraordinary cooperative enterprise. To set up against this treasure hoard (without having exhaustive knowledge of it) philosophical speculations of a monotheistic, pantheistic, dualistic, or any other kind,[22] speculations which inevitably rest on individual thinkers' very limited experiences, seems to me, I am bound to say, brash mischiefmaking, even if the mischief is committed by thinkers such as Bruno or Hegel or William James.[23]

We have barely begun to scratch the surface of the challenge of the truth claims mediated to us in religious symbol.[24] Other than a few remarks on holiness and sacramentality, and an effort to place both in the context of a living tradition, I do not attempt in the present volume to explore the nature of religious experience. And I have limited comment to a single religion.

Having already written nineteen hundred pages in my own effort at appropriating this same tradition, I can comment on its richness and complexity. But after fifteen years, I still feel I am only beginning to grasp something of the dimensions of that "treasure-hoard of symbol." That is why I have felt compelled to plunge into Balthasar's seventeen-volume unnamed synthesis, looking for help to reach a greater depth of understanding.[25] But at least I can

---

21. *The Philosophy of Order*, 454.
22. Christianity, for Voegelin, is none of these: it is Trinitarian.
23. *The Philosophy of Order*, 456.
24. *T&A* superficially catalogs the great explicit traditions of religious and philosophical truth. It is a long list (see Appendix C).
25. Behind those seventeen volumes lies the work of his lifetime: eighty volumes of theology; one hundred volumes of translations from the fathers and doctors of the Church and modern sources he considered essential—from Péguy, Bernanos, and Claudel to works of spiritual mystics; and eighty volumes of dictation from Adrienne von Speyer, the medical doctor-mystic whom he considered a full collaborator in his own work. Add five hundred articles, the founding of a religious institute, and thirteen editions of the review *Communio*, and you will get some idea of the scope a really serious effort at appropriation can attain! Voegelin, incidentally, acknowledges the influence that young Balthasar had on his own early formation. Eric Voegelin, *Autobiographical Reflections*, ed. Ellis Sandoz (Baton Rouge: Louisiana State University Press, 1989): "So far as I remember, I became aware of the problem

now appreciate Voegelin's remark that it is hubris bordering on folly to think one can invent one's own system of thought to compete not with a millennium but with three millennia[26] of uninterrupted reflection and elaboration on the symbols of revelation by the greatest minds and the most gifted poets and the greatest saints of an entire suite of civilizations.[27] When I look back through that inheritance, trying to discern the dynamic lines of its unfolding essence, I am daunted by the thought of what awaits the worldwide community of sages as they bring all the traditions loyally into dialogue.

When Voegelin speaks of this tradition as an "extraordinary cooperative enterprise," he reminds us that the pursuit of truth has been from the earliest prophets and philosophers a community undertaking. The leaps of individual creative genius should not be underestimated. But if the Church has a Saint Augustine in its midst, it is because of a Saint Monica, his mother, and a Saint Ambrose, his teacher. Saint Thomas without Saint Albert, and Albert without both the Dominicans and all those lesser scholars and translators who made it possible to recover Aristotle, could not have happened. Moreover, the religious experience was mediated to all of them by the whole Church, hierarchical and of popular piety, the flesh-and-blood community, struggling against its sinfulness.

The Christian is called upon to find the measure[28] of the genuineness of his personal religious experiences in the bosom of the Church. Because fundamental interpersonal relationships are the issue, the person pursuing the spiritual life is urged to find a spiritual director, a person experienced in matters of the soul and a guardian of the orthodox tradition, that is, of the whole truth (*catholou*). Spiritual experience of "the transcendent entering into the human time-space within the sensorium of the soul" (Voegelin) does not provide the

---

of Gnosticism and its application to modern ideological phenomena for the first time through the introduction of Hans Urs von Balthasar's *Prometheus*, published in 1937" (66). Voegelin also cites "the great work by Ferdinand Christian Baur on *Die christliche Gnosis; oder, die christliche Religionsphilosophie in ihrer geschichtlichen Entwicklung* of 1835." This is a work Balthasar knew well.

26. I do not understand why Voegelin says "a thousand years." The elaboration of symbols of revelational origin began at the time of the Sinai experience, very probably with Moses himself, that is, circa 1300 B.C., and continues today. With the patriarchal materials that have been taken up into the process, the tradition of handed-down and ever-more-elaborated symbols is at least thirty-five hundred years old.

27. Balthasar's having completed more than one hundred books of translations of the fathers and doctors of the Church, of mystics like Saint Theresa of Avila and Saint Theresa of Lisieux, of poets like Calderón de la Barca, Claudel, and Bernanos—the enormity of this enterprise of recuperation—gives some idea of the dimensions of that "treasure-hoard of symbol," of which Voegelin writes. And it raises the question: Can a tradition become *too* rich, the very enormity of its store of symbols and the insights and experiences they contain perhaps becoming a block to the simplicity of actually living in the tradition? Balthasar would answer that the primordial form of the living experience is the witness of the saint. Mother Teresa of Calcutta manages to be guided by these rich traditions without losing any of her simplicity. As one who had the privilege to know him personally, I must tell you that Balthasar's own disarming simplicity, total lack of arrogance, and radiant kindness gave the same witness.

28. Saint Paul calls Christ the *metron* (Eph. 4:13) of the fullness of reality.

kind of object that can be subject to communal experimental verification, like the discovery of a new virus. But such experiences are subject to a kind of test by communal wisdom: There is long experience of such matters by those who are masters of the spiritual life. The community has learned the hard way about the pathology of false prophecy, and the masters know the rigors of genuine spiritual cultivation of an interior chamber wherein the graces of a special participation in the divine life can be accommodated.[29] And these deontic authorities of the spiritual life are backed up and consolidated by the *ex officio* apostolic authority of the Church, to whom historically Christ granted the power of discerning and, it is believed, his Holy Spirit the charism to do so correctly, at least in the main and in the long term.

With this immense experience in the community of the Spirit, the Catholic insists that Christian ecumenical dialogue be conducted in communion with the Church, and under the guidance of the Christ-ordained hierarchical pastoral leadership. As a Catholic, I think it fair to suggest to adherents of other traditions that they too take care to represent truly not just their own views but their communities'. Although their institutions may not be as highly articulated as the Catholic Church, the focus of authoritative interpretation of communal experience being then less clear, still it is not just the opinion of an isolated individual that is interesting but the fullness of the truth of the tradition.

How Can Symbols Nurtured in One Tradition Be Translated into Those of Another?

This sense of a treasure-house of symbols being built up through the cooperative work of a tradition over millennia and of traditions of spiritual discipline—of ways of life—returns us to translatability. Can we bring the experience of one tradition, caught in characteristic, historical, linguistic, liturgical, and artistic symbols, illumined by the *Sein* of a particular world with its own history, over into the symbols of a foreign tradition, themselves domesticated over many centuries, and illumined by a different *Sein*, without losing the essential genius of the tradition? Can the historical *Sein* of one tradition somehow meld with the *Sein* of another or illumine the phenomena of that other tradition? Does *Sein* exclude *Sein*, so that we are left with many solitudes?

The problem is further complicated because we are, inevitably, discussing the issue through the medium of a given modern language, American English. The Christian treasure-house received its linguistic deposits originally in Hebrew, and a Hebrew of many epochs; in Aramaic, the dialect spoken in Jesus' milieu; in both classical and Koine Greek; in classical and later barbarian and then more refined medieval and finally Renaissance Latin; and in German, French, Spanish, Italian, and English.[30] It is important to keep in mind as well

---

29. A better idea of this will come with examination of San Juan de la Cruz's *Ascent of Mount Carmel* (London: Baker, 1928), in Part III, Chapter 8.

30. It bemuses me to see a great German father, Hans Urs von Balthasar, reading one of the other great modern fathers, John Henry Newman, in a new language of the tradition, English.

that key symbols of the tradition are not linguistic at all: They are liturgical, architectural, pictorial, and musical; even institutional forms have a symbolic charge. And artistic matters are especially difficult to capture in language. Poetry itself risks losing its essential feel when inept critics talk about it. There are masses of translation challenges within this, as in any tradition—never mind translating between traditions.

Sobered by this last thought, I take refuge in common sense: If some degree of translatability were not possible, there could be no long-lasting traditions. A few of the more skeptical brethren have indeed suggested something of the sort. What better way to free us from the drag of the past than to say that we have no real access to it. Our translations are interpretative projections of the *Sein* of our own worlds back onto dead worlds. The being of those worlds is lost forever, although subterranean influences of the past affect my present constructions.[31] And professional deconstructionists will reveal them at work in my bad faith.

The skeptics' complaint is not without substance. Everyone does project beliefs, partly formed from later experiences in ways that distort and misrepresent the past, uncritically back onto what they believe has been. All the more reason, drawing on our evidence for objectivity, to try to sort out how we can translate from present idiom to re-present past reality. Any success in doing this will stand us in good stead as we seek to understand how we can translate across lines not just of epoch but also of tradition.

When a symbol expresses an experience that both interlocutors have enjoyed in essentially the same way, or refers to a thing or a situation to which they can have largely the same kind of access, then the only issue is one of accuracy of reference: We must be sure we are referring to the same thing, kind of experience, or situation. From all that we have seen in our previous descriptions, this is not a problem. "Jo-Ann totaled her husband's car by spinning out on the superhighway." The symbols come from such a common, familiar world, in the *Sein*-light of which we both bathe so thoroughly, I know exactly what you are telling me. The difficulty begins when you use a symbol, or a cluster of symbols, to invoke an experience of something with which I have no familiarity, so that your expression becomes a means of my vicariously acquiring at least some notion of that experience.

If symbols, indeed all cultural objects, were unable to capture something of the sense of the world, and of the *Sein* of which they are somehow an expression, then it would be impossible to recuperate any *Sein*, and we would be confined to the horizons of our present world. In that case, scholarly effort to build a picture of life in the thirteenth-century Sorbonne would be an exercise of creative imagination with no possible rapport with the *Sein* of that milieu. Effort on the part of a gifted journalist to evoke a feeling for what is going

---

31. A Spengler and a Lawrence Brown promote this attitude when they overemphasize the distinctiveness of worlds, East-West, pre- and postmedieval, pre- and postmodern, within the Christian tradition.

on among the *fellahin* of the Nile delta would be a waste of time, at least as an enterprise in communicating the truth of another world. In such a poetic task, the scholar or the journalist manipulates symbols in which are captured experiences of things, attitudes, or situations familiar to one's audience, to get them to extend the sense a bit in order to glimpse by analogy the reality they have not experienced but which the poet is trying to evoke for them.

I offer some additional grounds for this implied huge charge of realism in language and symbol, without pretending to lay here the foundations for a theory of language, a necessary part of a complete theory of truth—logic, epistemology, and ontology being inseparable. In this preliminary exploration of the truth question, it is wise at least to inventory the main issues regarding language, symbol, and being, in dealing with translatability. In Part III, we begin to explore what is there called, following Plato, "the depths of the interior life" and, with the ontological base better secured, return to a fuller encounter with the question of how symbol can communicate being.

FIRST GLANCE TOWARD A THEORY OF LANGUAGE

An ontology-epistemology that starts from a natural faith beyond subjectivism and objectivism implies a theory of language and symbol able to offer some explanation of how the symbols capture and relate both the reality symbolized and the light of the *Sein* without which those realities would not appear as they do.

All symbolization is a subjective enterprise, showing the spirituality of the human being. The subject is able to use one part of matter (a sound, or lines impressed in clay) to signify another (the desire for a drink of water or a bushel of wheat). It shows an ability on the part of the subject to transcend the object of its signification, so as to seize it as object, as something that stands out over against (ob) the knower. It does not matter whether it be a thing completely separate in its being from the perceiver seizing it, or an attitude of the subject itself that he can ob-jectivize, circumscribing it sufficiently to represent it by a symbol—having identified the object in some way, he creates a sign to stand for it. This implies the subject's ability to understand relationships between things and between perceivers and things; states interior to the perceiver; and relationships between perceivers. And the subject can represent all manner of such relationships by signs. Between these symbols the poetizing knowers are able to weave a complex web of linguistic or other symbolic relationships, and even to play wistfully with these spiritual creations, as one does in pure poetry.

When one reflects on the mind's eye soaring from intuition to intuition, and molding the possibilities that have already been caught in previous symbols, our ability to weave exquisite lyrical poetry and to build musical structures, one might be tempted to consider the resulting spiritual world, the interior scene, as somehow autonomous, with a minimum to do with things-in-themselves. The symbolized impressions would then become the prime reality, because man lives in the Word and the humanities become an end in themselves.

But however capricious may seem the relationships between the bits of matter seized to represent aspects of reality, these symbols are meant to signify the other: things, attitudes, and relations between things and attitudes. What is represented are not signs or symbols, but entities or states of soul, some transcending toward entities, symbolized or signified. Mostly the speaker is seeking to invoke the reality in itself of what is signified, and pays little attention to the flow of linguistic instruments that make it possible for him to express the things he wants. Our symbols are able to do this so successfully that we can weave patterns of meaning between them.

Look how difficult it is to invent pure nonsense sentences. One can, of course, if one is "doing philosophy" and so needs an example: "The doorjamb treed house under over, with blue whippets." I had to make a concerted effort to break from familiar grammatical structures, all of which have been formed over millennia to accomplish a certain mirroring of reality.[32] Those forms are founded in our experience of reality. (In the real cosmos, something cannot usually be in and on the house at the same time.) On a base of the intended and the successfully signified, it is possible to play the further spiritual games of poetic construction.

This is clear in the case of imaginary entities, a negative number or the concept of a perfect circle, both arrived at by flights of intellectual construction. Working back from the concept of positive numbers representing units of any kind of thing, we construct, by insight, but drawing on the experience of debts, the notion of a deficit, of a lack of units that will have to be supplied to come back to a balance at zero. No matter how far the imaginative conceptualizing gets from directly perceived reality, it retains a reference to it, even though it may become more and more remote.

This is clear when one seeks to represent the unperceived through symbols drawn from ordinary perception. The psalmist sings: "High over all nations, Yahweh! His glory transcends the heavens! Who is like Yahweh our God? enthroned so high, he needs to stoop to see the sky and earth!" (Ps. 113:4–6). Some of the most impressive objects of our experience tower over us: the snowy mountain range, the life-giving sun, the mysterious pale moon. The great king sits on an elevated throne. So, when seeking to symbolize the Source of the universe, understood not as fundamental substrate or the basic component of all things, but as that which is beyond all things and all substrates as their total author, we naturally represent him as "plane-ing" above all things, even the highest, the most impressive, the heavens themselves. He is represented as the king, enthroned on high, but so high as to have to bend over to see even the heavens below his throne.

---

32. That would be my realistic working hypothesis about "deep grammar." If I were to respond to the Chomsky challenge, it would be in the direction of an investigation of how the deepest grammar discoverable operating, so to speak, underneath the various languages, works. These languages do capture certain aspects of the way things are and relate; we operate on and with them.

Although the psalm is written in ancient Hebrew, I have not worried about the translation, because the things at issue are so straightforwardly available to ordinary experience,[33] the notion of something's being high over something else, or of "all nations," or even "the heavens"; I know what a throne is, and the graphic notion of having to stoop to see the sky is clear enough. The difficult notions are "transcend" and "Yahweh our God." For "transcend" one might want to consult a Hebraicist, but even that is easy to grasp on a primitive level, as simply meaning that something goes beyond something else. "Yahweh our God" is precisely the difficult notion the psalmist is trying to get us to appreciate through mustering all this imagery. The obvious shortcoming of his effort is that in presenting Him as a king on a throne of unprecedented grandeur, he is caught within anthropomorphic bounds. The problem is not that the notion is unclear; it is too clear, in the sense of being related to a limited human experience, inadequate to its task.

The following from a political article can show the realism: "There are three ways a government can extract money: by force, by persuasion, by fraud. The first is called taxation; the second, borrowing; the third, inflation. If spending is not offset by taxation, one of the other two methods must make up the shortfall." The structure of the set of relationships takes the form of an equation: There must be as much money coming into government coffers in any time period as going out. On the output side, the author is lumping all expenditures together as spending; on the input side, he is claiming an exhaustive inventory of the possibilities: taxation, borrowing, inflation (which is explained subsequently as inflating the money supply, that is, "printing money").

How do we form from experience so abstract a notion as that of a dynamic equation, in this case the insight of input-output equilibrium between a set of processes? I would suggest, quite concretely: I observe the flow of water from a hose into a full tub, and I see that the inflow equals the outflow. By insight, I grasp the sense of this relationship, and the mind is able to abstract it from the particular circumstances of material flow, coming to see the underlying sense of any equilibrium flow equation.

That is, then, the conceptual framework within which these three sentences function. The propositions in the paragraph contain two main assertions and three of lesser importance. The central message is that if governments fail to raise sufficient revenues by taxation, then one of the other two ways of extracting money (or a combination of both) will inevitably come into play. This assertion depends on the truth of the other main proposition, that there are only three ways. It is presupposed that input (generation of money) must equal output (expenditure of money). The proposition that because there are only three sources of input, if government lacks, one or a combination of the other

---

33. At a Liberty Fund seminar on the psalms, we were assured that indeed the matters are straightforward and the language simple, so that translation is unusually easy, and great accuracy as to the psalmist's meaning is almost always forthcoming.

two must provide, is analytic (that is, self-evident). The three other propositions of lesser importance are that taxation is governmental extraction of money by force; that borrowing is extraction by persuasion; and inflation, by fraud.

The key proposition is the contention that these are indeed only three ways money can be extracted, by force, by persuasion, by fraud. The sentence is centrally about a process, that is, money extracting. The notion of extracting is an abstraction from a common experience of drawing something out of a larger ensemble, for example, blood being squeezed from a turnip. One word, "extracting," signifies the process; another, that which in this case is extracted—money; yet another, who is doing the extracting—government. From whom it is extracted is understood but not said—the people. From the meanings of the terms, the reader easily distinguishes who is doing what, in respect to which commodity, to whom. But there is an additional assertion, that this can occur in only three ways. The mind grasps easily the notions: (a) that there are different ways of carrying out a given process; and (b) that there may be a limited set of modes or ways for a given process.

If what is claimed in a given instance is put forward as a complete disjunction, it implies an insight that grounds this claim to exclusivity. We experience instances of this in common perceivable settings: I can eliminate these weeds in my garden by pulling them up, hoeing them under, or killing them with an herbicide. I dimly perceive why this is a complete disjunction. It is no great task for the mind, having abstracted the formal notion of a limited set of distinctive modes of carrying out a process, to apply it to much more "spiritual" processes, such as money extraction.

Borrowing—a spiritual act—is distinguished from stealing or buying, on the one hand, by the fact that there is no exchange and, on the other, by the intention of eventually returning the thing borrowed. I experience it often quite physically: I go over to Robinson and ask if I may use his electric lawn mower for a few minutes. The mind grasps the structure of this relationship of temporary, permitted alienation of an object from its owner with intent to restore it. The sense of that relationship can be intuited in a money transaction. Money was once more physical, initially being itself an object agreed to have a certain value of exchange. In its present disincarnate state, it is a numerical entry recording a credit. From the computer I am presently writing on I can, by telephone, instruct the debiting of my bank account at tax time and the crediting to that of the receiver general of Canada, to avoid a visit from the police. Nothing changes hands; there is, however, a shift of idea among me, my bank, and the government's bank. Mankind has progressively spiritualized these relationships of credit.

How does the mind know whether it is indeed true that these are the only three ways money can be extracted by governments? Is this really a complete disjunction, for if it is, then the underlying structural insight should be in view.

I find myself casting about, trying to think up a fourth or fifth alternative. My mind is running through memory of all the ways in which I have experienced money being obtained. This seems to be in some ways an automatic process, once I have programmed the memory by means of a certain question to respond. It either presents me with a challenging instance or it does not. In this case it does: How does one normally obtain money? By working for it, or selling something, whether material things or ideas. Governments can provide services for which people are willing to pay, functioning in this case like any business, and they can sell assets.

Why did the author not think of this? I can assume he is sloppy, and let it go at that, or assume that he may have thought of these possibilities and not retained them. In the latter case I then look for plausible reasons for not including them with taxation, borrowing, and inflation. They are not hard to find. Operating like a business, selling services, while it may go on, is hardly typical of what government is for. Most often it provides services that the private sector cannot, because they are unsalable at market rates. And it can sell assets, to be sure, but assets are few, and most are needed to do the job. So neither is as fundamental and endemic as the other three.

At this point, I am inclined to search for some ground of the intuition of complete disjunction. Government gets money from people either given willingly or not willingly (that is, by force)—that is a disjunction, by principle of contradiction—and if in neither of these overt ways, covertly, by setting into motion another process that less obviously results in a transfer of value inflation. The mind often works in this way, by setting up contrary possibilities.

This realism encourages belief that language stays in close contact with reality. But it should not breed a false confidence: Perfect translatability is often not possible because represented in the foreign tradition's symbols are some experiences that are not common to mankind and not readily accessible to another. These are difficult to represent in poetic symbols that are perfectly understandable on a common basis. I can remember a Jewish friend, who had been bought out of one of Hitler's camps just before the war, trying to communicate to me his feeling and insight during the Six-Day War in 1967 when it began to look as though Israel was going to be overrun and destroyed. The thought that once again a large part of the Chosen People was to be slaughtered in another holocaust changed in a flash, he recounted, his whole attitude to Judaism. "You cannot understand what it is to feel that this people, whom you believe with every fiber of your body to be called by God to a special role among the peoples, is again condemned to massive slaughter."

It is hard to participate in the pains and joys of others. I believe I understand up to a point what he means. But can a non-Jew, who has not lived the Jewish experience of the trials and exaltations of this unique people, grasp more than a shadow of the experience by trying to imagine what it would mean to oneself if the most cherished ideal, incarnated in my own case in the Church, were menaced with massive destruction in a way that might even shake one's faith in God's support of his people?

Interestingly, as I was seeking an example of an untranslatable experience, I had to pause and think fairly hard to find this Jewish one, so broadly common is our human experience. The universality of human nature grounds the feasibility of a high degree of translatability. Beyond these general terms, one can only proceed to the experience of cross-cultural communication, to feel the limits of the possible. They cannot be set down a priori.

A BRIEF INTRODUCTION TO THE WORLD SYSTEM AS AN ENTRÉE TO ONTOLOGY

This brief introduction to the truth questions raised by one tradition of revelation, along with an evocation of the problem of capturing such things in symbols and then of their translation, in bringing it into dialogue with other traditions, is sufficient to return us to the starting point of this entire reflection on the truth question: the planetary situation's bringing the traditions into unprecedented intimacy. Recognition that proponents of their truth claims sometimes collide on the battlefield has led some modern thinkers to affirm relativism. Not a new reaction: The discovery of other cultures was a factor in producing Renaissance skepticism.

Fortunately, something else is happening at the same time: Appreciation of the great traditions as cultural treasure-houses is increasing. With the growth of oecumenopolis have arisen the first signs of an ecumenical spirit. One section of *Tradition and Authenticity* has been dedicated to exploring this planetary setting of the truth question.[34] The title refers to the world system[35] to call attention to the challenge presented by the phenomenon of the planetary scope of the emerging situation, with its intertwining world-scale institutions and the need to develop instruments of thought for getting at the truth of this reality. I there distinguish five kinds of elements in the world situation: world and regional processes; institutions; systems of signs and symbols; events; and traditions. (That these relate to the types of objects and truths encountered in Chapter 4 is clear.)

World and regional processes are large-scale, ongoing changes, important enough and sufficiently persisting and consistent to call themselves to our attention. Classifying them according to C. Doxiades' "ekistics functions" grid, I have been able to identify about a hundred such processes and to suggest, for each, measurable criteria for estimating the vector, rapidity, and intensity of change.[36]

Recognition and understanding of these processes is a step toward partial control of them, a task that falls largely to institutions. The institutions were identified as instruments for the transmission of the traditions and as devices

---

34. *T&A*, pt. II, chaps. 6 and 7.
35. My research group, working on an analysis of the present planetary situation, now sees that the world system is a large part, but part only, of the *Sein* that we humorously call the HTX, High Tech X = no name, and that it xes out cultures and civilizations—X as in Xmas, or, asked a wag, is it perhaps the "anti-X"?
36. An indication of the extent to which a world system has already emerged is that my students were able to find in the University of Toronto library statistical data pertaining to about eighty of these processes, from various agencies of the United Nations Organization and the World Bank.

for attaining leverage over some of the large-scale processes. Required also is identification of the institutions strategically placed to control those processes that, if left to run amok, threaten systems breakdown.[37] The truth of what is happening in these processes and the truth contained in the ideal visions transmitted by the traditions are brought together by the responsible institutional agents who have to act accordingly: Guided by the vision, their task is to manage the processes prudentially to bring them into line with what is to be sought according to the ideal. Easy to say, but management, everyone knows, requires getting sinful human beings to cooperate:[38] this requires a bundle of skills not easily found.

The symbol systems, which include not only scientific and ordinary languages but the treasures of artistic and liturgical symbols, are the means of expression of the traditions and of communication and inspiration by society and its institutions. As expressions of ethnic cultures, the everyday languages become centers of emotional investment of whole peoples; their defense can be at the root of some of the important processes and events.

Events, which change the course of the significant processes, being particular acts,[39] are not subject to universalization. They cannot be dealt with by science, but nevertheless become part of the intelligibility of a given line of development.[40] My efforts in the HTX study are directed at clarifying the relationships between these elements and at showing how data can be gathered about them and their dynamics studied, with a view to understanding how one can live humanly in this situation.

It would be a tad ridiculous if I pretended to be able to understand anything so vast, new, rapidly changing, and complex as the HTX. *Tradition and Authenticity* showed that the world modelers have to date produced little more than hopelessly abstract world econometric models. Even Johann Millendorfer's Laxenberg model with its vaunted one hundred thousand connections is the merest skeleton. Little has as yet been done to integrate most of the world and regional processes my students have been able rather easily to identify and even to quantify.

---

37. It is possible to identify kinds of potential "systems breakdown." This is mentioned in several places in *T&A*: chap. 5 (as ingenuine and unfaithful behavior), chap. 6 (reasons for studying the world system), chap. 7 (specific examples), and in the preface, where I discuss the reasons why one ought to take up efforts of this kind.

38. Patrick Haggerty, then chairman of Texas Instruments, once said to me, sighing, "It is difficult to get ninety thousand people to do what you think they should do."

39. Not just isolated acts of one individual, but those concatenations of many agents that produce, not the smooth flow of a long-lasting process, but the critical mass of a battle, war, stock market crash, or whatever marks epochal breaks in process flows.

40. On the sense of development, see *T&A*, esp. chap. 2. A typology of events is feasible, to a degree, but I am not sure it would be worthwhile for every kind of process. Obviously, much study is expended on trying to understand the onset of an economy's downturn, but is recession an event or a direction in a process? The invasion of Poland in fall 1939 is an event, marking the outbreak of a world war. But can one usefully generalize about "war outbreak events"? It is the concrete event, often having a massive impact on many processes, that interests us practically.

But the problem of coming to grips with the emerging world system is pressing. Man's relentless searching has produced an emerging world-scale system of intertwining institutions in which truth claims are put forward and courses of action pursued, the genuineness[41] of which has to be evaluated, if we are to be responsible. We can of course ignore it, and just wait and let happen what will happen, or we can learn how to study it, and cautiously build institutions to improve the quality of our understanding and control of the processes spawned by it.

Given how far from the ideal is the modern university, which should be a place of appreciation and rational dialogue between traditions, one is tempted to think that the kind of rationality presupposed for knowing the world system is unrealistic. Individuals are too much driven by short-range, fanciful desires, and too little involved in appropriating their own traditions to enjoy the security necessary for appreciative encounter with the other. Still one ought not be too pessimistic. The evolution of international law, the various UN organizations, the European Community, and many kinds of new international institutions, and indeed growth of scholarship, scientific work on all the traditions, and the new initiatives of ecumenical dialogue, all show prudent intelligence at work on the regional and even planetary scale. We recognize the inadequacy of our conceptual tools for planetary-scale analysis, and all the problems of cross-cultural translation; our information is massive but uneven.

To launch immediately into coming to grips either with the state of the world system or with any of the major traditions or institutions shaping it, based solely upon abstract "knowing of being" yielded by epistemological reflection alone, would invite bogging down in an ideological defense of our own position. Reflection on a wide enough range of experience with actual being as it struggles to unfold in the many dimensions of the real world is necessary.

The various parts of the world that have emerged during this survey need to be examined and related in light of a metaphysical inquiry as well. This alone can provide a framework within which the distinctive dimensions of being are correctly situated in relation to one another. But ontological theory offers no guarantee of the kind of prudence and good judgment that come from varied, clear-sighted experience in the world received by a person of "maturity" (Aristotle). But elaborating an ontology does give one the opportunity to reflect more methodically on experience and thus to penetrate more into the wisdom transmitted by the traditions, as he seeks to see how the various regions of being throw light on one another.

Enhanced sense of the ultimate context is protection against that undue absolutizing of any part, which Etienne Gilson showed in *The Unity of Philosophical Experience* has plagued the history of thought. This is the task we undertake in Part III. We return, after traversing a path leading from the outermost reaches

---

41. As explained in *T&A*, chap. 4, genuineness means "basically in keeping with the facts of the case." Those interested in more detail on the world system are referred to *T&A*, pt. II.

of the cosmos to the innermost center of ourselves, to the question of the interpenetration of epistemology, metaphysics, and ethics (raised in Chapter 3), seeking to avoid reductionism and ideological stances.

As one looks for lines of order in the midst of this fluid reality of a dynamic and complex world situation, traditions appear a hopeful focus. They maintain, with the help of the institutions they spawn to perpetuate themselves, an essential intelligibility, sometimes for millennia. Into that intelligibility are gathered the effects of vast series of events, which inspire the coherent action of many coordinated subsidiary institutions. These institutions mold significantly the existences of millions of human beings, they influence cultures and even entire civilizations, and so are a key to the way the individuals behave and the cultures evolve. My faith that the appropriation of man's traditions, including a critique of the deviations from the ideal in practice—of the hypocrisy of real existence—is a fruitful way of discovering significant order in history and of producing insight into being, has informed the discussion of my own Christian tradition by way of example in these chapters now concluded.

But without the ontological inquiry that is to follow, on what grounds could I argue for, not my tradition alone, but the relevance of the riches of the world's heritage in terms of truth to be appropriated? Despite all the territory we have covered, the challenge of Chapter 3's voluntarist remains with us: We have not yet completed our rebuttal of the voluntarist stance. I believe it poses the greatest threat to contemporary Western civilization, which I see courting the risk of death in its hedonistic, selfish pursuit of will-to-power. We have to argue farther the ontological soundness of taking the truth claims of all the traditions with critical seriousness.

PART III.

TOWARD AN ONTOLOGY

6.

MAN IN CONTEXTS

OUR STARTING POINT
A Methodological and Terminological Foreword

Why proceed toward an ontology rather than defend here a full-fledged ontology?[1] The theoretical construction of an ontology must be critical, philosophy's equivalent of experimentation and contrary-to-theoretical-expectation data. Because of the interpenetration of ontology, epistemology, and ethics, these disciplines have to be co-developed, and not theoretically only. The investigator, as Aristotle told us, must come to possess certain moral and intellectual virtues without which appropriation of the wisdom of the traditions cannot advance toward the truth. To develop such a character, he must know and practice a sound ethics, a condition for becoming a *spoudaios*, a mature man.[2] Such a person must not only work out a sound theory of human knowledge, he must prove adept, by engaging in the ongoing way (*meta ton hodon*, "method") of inquiry—he must actually learn by doing how to advance in wisdom. That requires a rich and varied experience[3] methodically and critically reflected upon—what he mirrors in his speculation and how he does it matter. He must grow in his ability to reflect on being, through active participation in it, in every department of life.

---

1. I have chosen the seventeenth-century word "ontology," rather than "metaphysics," with its long history reaching back to Simplicius' cataloging of Aristotle's works, because it signals my intention, like those modern philosophers, to rethink the evidence of the fundamenta of all reality. I hope to remain sensitive to many dimensions in the historic unfolding of a perennial wisdom about being, which the post-Cartesians did not. On the history of these words, see Voegelin, "The Beginning and the Beyond," in *What Is History? and Other Late Unpublished Writings*, vol. 28 of *The Collected Works*, ed. Thomas Hollweck and Paul Caringella (Baton Rouge: Louisiana State University Press, 1990), 197.

2. Aristotle meant a male. Your author, having met in Mother Teresa the maturest and wisest of all men, and being married to a woman more intelligent and educated than himself, can honestly continue to mean by "man" what the English language means: all human beings.

3. That is why Aristotle thought no one under fifty could be a true philosopher, and it is why I doubt that academic "philosophers" who have scarcely left the classroom will have the breadth of experience necessary. On the other hand, I should point out a difference here between the Aristotelian and the Christian ideal. As Balthasar says, the Christian seeks not to grow old, wise, and resigned, like the Pagan, but to remain "eternally young, childlike, not childish," drawing on the always surprising newness of the Source of life revealed through Jesus Christ. See *Man in History*, trans. William Glen-Doepel (London: Sheed and Ward, 1968), 264–66.

There is worse yet: We have already indicated that a prerequisite for adequate understanding of the ethical component is a well-worked-out anthropology. Both because this investigator still has much to learn of the interior life through efforts to develop one; and because work on the anthropological component is not yet far advanced, to claim that I had already developed a worthy ontology and that I am ready to defend it here would be hubris. What is to be presented here is more than a mere prolegomena or a *Grundlegung*—the work is neither introductory nor programmatic, but on the way, though the journey will not end here. This palace of beings under construction has some wings roofed, some even furnished, but other parts of the foundation are barely dug. The outline is visible, even though the foundation is not completed. At least I have avoided the temptation to complete the structure ideologically!

Examining One Entity in Many Frames of Reference

The question is how the various dimensions of being revealed by different foci can be brought together into a wisdom. I begin by examining one key thing to see how various aspects or dimensions of being are revealed when one examines it in various frames of reference. Our laboratory animal is chosen because it is high up the chain of development, so that as many realms of being as possible can be found mirrored in it.

It will be seen in such different ideational lights as to seem at first not to be the same thing at all, yet reflection reveals it to be refracted in different perspectives and objectivized through distinctive kinds of analysis, one type of thing becoming many different kinds of object, but all embraced within the same englobing epochal *Sein*. We recognize this sameness, because we are able to bring the focal points of the different frames of reference into intelligible relationships with one another.

By now, I hope this claim is a credible working hypothesis, for which phenomenological evidence has already been mustered. I showed how one moves intelligibly from one frame of reference to another, keeping track of how the resulting kinds of consideration refer to the same thing or setting.

My example enjoys a privileged position from which to look out on all other things, and it uniquely offers direct phenomenological access, even to its interior. It alone gives access to important realms of being that a merely objectivistic examination of an entity separate from us could not offer. Moreover, every reader is familiar with this kind of thing, whereas the mysteries of subatomic particles or the inner life of the Trinity may not be everyone's cup of tea. The choice is obvious: *the human being*. My first focal point is a real live one, caught in the flagrant act of actually existing: myself at the moment I am writing. Another advantage: It introduces us, in more depth, to the *metron* of all else, the inquirer himself. I am not becoming Protagorean; I am preparing a criticism to transcend this natural tendency for the knower to make himself the final measure. For speculation can discover the dimensions of being that transcend the human, and are beyond all human measure.

Without pretending to exhaust all frames of reference, I nevertheless produce a long list, with a sample from each mode of my being, from organism, through social being, to interior life. Working along different lines of involvement, I show some of their interrelatedness, catching glimpses of as many ultimate dimensions of being as I can.

Following the exploration where it leads, without a preestablished road map (but with my natural faith inevitably guiding me in the general direction of where I want to come out), is like Chapter 4's exploration of kinds of knowledge. In our search for ultimate dimensions of being, the foundations, the broadest and most basic perspectives, these ultimate contexts will provide that ontological outline of which I spoke.

MYSELF AS BIOPHYSIOLOGICAL ORGANISM

I start by adopting an objectivistic point of view on myself, that of biological science. Later I adopt a subject-oriented point of view on the same entity and compare the results, discerning the merits and limits of both kinds of reflection. The organism that I am is (a) a material thing, (b) with a starkly delimited space, (c) an easily focusable gestalt, and (d) a definite kind of permanence. Consider each of these.

As a Material Thing

First, I am a thing—a bit of matter of certain mass and a particular form, energy complexified in a distinctive way, charges harmonized sufficiently to allow a form to stand out of the surrounding chaos or noise of uncoordinated molecules rushing hither and yon in random collision, and distinguishing itself from other things and other kinds. (Thing here signifies a systemic harmony of interactions maintained at least for a while, a typical kind of permanence, not everlasting but with a provisional regularity in development, and thus an intelligible coming into being, maturing and declining, with final disaggregation surely awaiting all finite entities more complex than the isolated molecule.[4]

As a Material Thing Manifesting Complexity

The biochemists Charles Thaxton, Walter Bradley, and Roger Olsen offer a distinction among kinds of things, important for understanding evolution:

---

4. Of the ultimate fate of all atoms and molecules, which physics theorizes did come into being, science informs us not. The durability of all atoms, with only the radioactive disintegrating measurably, is known; the unimaginable strength of the "strong force" binding nuclei astonishes us. When one reflects that the nuclear force released at Hiroshima was equivalent to what is found in less than a spoonful of sand, one realizes that (a) this is not imaginary and (b) this is unimaginable. Note, too, that all matter is informed matter, and that there are forms within more comprehensive forms. Thus a single free-standing atom of hydrogen has a form, the structure of which is partly described in the definite, distinctive kinds of relationships between the particles of its nucleus and the single electron in orbit about it.

"order" (for instance, in a crystal) and "complexity" (in amino acids and in DNA, constructed from nucleotide building blocks). Both manifest form, but of two different levels of being: The order of a crystal provides only a minimum of information in the midst of what can be a very large assemblage of molecules, because they are arranged in a periodic structure, the same arrangement being simply repeated over and over again,[5] reminiscent of Hegel's "bad infinite." But the complex entity has an irregular but specified structure, and when this is found, as in DNA in a specific sequence, this can be the basis of transmitting much information (over a billion letters in a written text).

As a Complex Thing That Processes Information

In the human being, such "order out of chaos"[6] does not stop there. Into this ordered center, it can receive information, not just rigidly according to a set pattern, but with flexibility allowing interpretation. This in turn permits the human to formulate and communicate information deliberately. Because of being able to form new, indeed unprecedentedly creative information, man can impose on the noisy environment, through work and through messages to other workers, more order of a highly complex kind.

This "energy forming and information transmitting" way of thinking prepares us much better than the Newton-inspired mechanics of the nineteenth century to understand what we are. (And because we are that way, being itself is informational.) This basic model is drawn from information theory—new since the horizon-opening papers of Claude Shannon—working within the general ideational context of post-Einstein physics. Though that theory respects the two laws of thermodyamics,[7] it also agrees with those, like Prigogine, Gatlin, and others, who suggest that we should start to think in terms of the existence of a third law, the inherent tendency of matter in open systems to complexify. This encourages looking for the dynamics of "emergence"[8] (though still, as

---

5. Charles B. Thaxton, Walter L. Bradley, and Roger L. Olsen, *The Mystery of Life's Origin: Reassessing Current Theories* (New York: Philosophical Library, 1984), 129.

6. The title of the book of which Nobel laureate Ilya Prigogine is co-author. Thaxton, Bradley, and Olsen, commenting on Prigogine and Nicolis' earlier work (*Self-Organization in Nonequilibrium Systems* [New York: Wiley, 1977]) warn against his notion that, when driven far enough from equilibrium, certain systems can achieve spontaneous ordering. For instance, heat conduction in gases normally occurs by the random collision of gas molecules. Under certain conditions, however, this may occur by a heat convection current, a coordinated flow of molecules, just as the normally random movement of water molecules may become a swirl down the drain. In thinking something like this happens at the origins of life, Prigogine, Eigen, and others fail to distinguish order and complexity: You can have all the order in the world, but little information, if the order is periodic. Information requires, on the contrary, a highly irregular but specified structure.

7. The first is the law of conservation of energy: In energy transformations, the total cosmic energy quantity remains constant. The second is the law of entropy: Energy tends to flow downhill toward equilibrium, that is, maximal formlessness.

8. For a popularized summary of the considerations arising in different spheres—Shannon's information theory, depth grammar, genetics—see Jeremy Campbell, *Grammatical Man* (New York: Simon and Schuster, 1982), esp. chap. 9.

Jeremy Campbell reminds us, something of a dirty word in many scientific quarters).[9]

As a Thing Manifesting Psychic Energy

Two terminological caveats: Many psychiatrists[10] are leery of any notion of psychic energy. Some take refuge in terms like "psychodynamics," little defined and not very illuminating. A term like "psychic energy" has to be distinguished from the modes of transformation and interactive permanences of energy found throughout all the rest of nature. I am looking for what is different in human operations, the unique spirituality of those operations. Psychic energy, originating in the soul and formed in the human brain, has a unique kind of existence. Just how unique can be highlighted by the question, Do the laws of thermodynamics apply to it at all? If I love immensely my first child, and a second comes along, I do not have to divert some of that love to him; rather, I find in my soul the ability to love him just as intensely. You see the problem with calling this an "energy," a term drawn from physics.

Here the second caveat becomes important: I have chosen the term "spiritual" to characterize this human form, rather than "mental." I will show reasons for employing a continuum from the purely material to the (unexperienced, putative) purely spiritual. I have sought to develop a concept of psychic energy that can go with higher spiritual forms. This will, I hope, prove useful here.

Terms like "energy" have been evolving in their philosophical sense since Aristotle, and "entropy" since the German physicist Clausius (1865) first used it in a scientific context. "Entropy" within thermodynamics refers to reversible, measurable processes in closed systems (whereas deployments of psychic energy, achieving symbolized information and order within souls—within intentional systems that are open—may accomplish certain irreversible results, not mathematically measurable). Already Claude Shannon and his followers stretched the sense of "entropy" considerably in developing information theory. Initially I sought to use it extensively, along with psychic energy, but the metaphor proved more confusing than helpful. Now my employment of it is circumspect. "Form," too, has not ceased to wander in meaning since the days of Plato and Aristotle. Not much in vogue in physics or biology, it is poised for

---

9. Scientists do not stop at the exterior grasp of form, but look for the causes of the interactive stabilities traditional philosophy means by "form." They look either for instructions, encoded or otherwise inculturated (in the case of highest organisms), or for molecular bondings in lower things, the coming into existence of which is explained in terms of particular interactions. Post-Einsteinian physicists, please do not be scandalized by the "pop" use I make here of terms that, in your specialized, sophisticated musings, have more precise definitions than they do here. I acknowledge the dangers of using terms like "energy," "entropy," and "information," which have carefully defined senses in certain scientific papers. There is both the risk of my becoming too narrowly fascinated with the terms, and the certainty that my use of them will differ from that in one or another physics context.

10. Thanks to Edwin Hersch, M.D., for what follows.

a comeback.[11] How can theoreticians speak of in-formation without meaning something by "form"? Here, because rethinking first things, I am obliged to re-form in-formatively the notion of form, relating it to a notion of in-formation, psychic energy, and a certain sense of order, that all in-form one another. While keeping an eye on contemporary information theory, I do not know physics well enough to engage the discussion on that level. The sense of in-formation developing here works out of an ontology of form and energy that is forming before the readers' eyes. Translation of this ontology and recent physics into a language where they can meet is at this point beyond my capabilities.[12]

My Spatial Contexts

Am I a big or a small thing, and so what? Does it matter if I am big or small? Compared to the size of the cosmos as we now know it, I am an indescribably small speck. I cannot imagine magnitudes like 10^{10} kilometers, or ten billion light-years. That the enormity of the cosmos[13] does not faze everyday man is due to the distortion of perspective from "existential myopia." I am impressed by the scales imposed in daily practical projects, where my garden, my neighborhood, and the distance from North Toronto to downtown preoccupy me.[14] When I strive to imagine the physical cosmos, what I create has much the emotive content of any pure poetizing. Yet my ultimate physical context is ten-plus billion light-years, is true—that whatever I may feel about it.[15]

---

11. Balthasar's *Herrlichkeit: Eine theologische Ästhetik* (Einsiedeln: Johannes Verlag, 1961), is an immense meditation on form. See esp. vol. 1.
12. The late Dr. Michel Vaillant, a scientist capable of aiding such a translation, critiqued what I have written here to help me avoid creating obstacles through egregious misunderstanding of the scientific issues touched on.
13. The size of the expanding universe is not known accurately. That it is more than ten billion light-years in expanse was considered highly probable, but new data from the Hubble telescope now suggest it is younger.
14. Suddenly, I have to go to Europe. With what ease I change my scale: "France is not really far; it is only a seven-hour plane ride." The *metron* here is more hours of travel discomfort than physical distance. An hour's walk to the store, when my car is broken down, is far. An hour's ride out to the golf course is a piece of cake.
15. When I have difficulty imagining what is meant by God, I might remember the strict unimaginability of what we know to be the size and complexity of the physical cosmos. Those big galaxies out there, are they comprehending me or am I comprehending them? In one sense, they are all in me, as the consciousness that enfolds them in thought; in another, I am supported by the biosphere of one planet of one medium-sized star in one average-sized spiral galaxy among billions, a planet that requires the whole expanding system as ground of its having come to be and is dependent on certain delicate balances within the solar, galactic, and cosmic wholes, only sketchily understood, that tolerate its tenuous hold on existence, its temporary resistance to entropy. At the same time, this precious planet means nothing to the material cosmos as such, which, apart from men considering men, appears deaf and dumb. (A theological perspective can call that judgment into question too.)

But the cosmos does mean something to me, through us it is enfolded in and illumined by *Sein*. And that is all the difference. We will never, no matter how far science advances, control even the environment of this one little planet, not even the more than three hundred compounds in a vat of wine I am attempting to vinify, let alone the health of my own body.

Yet all those galaxies themselves are dynamic structures with less internal complexity than an ant.[16]

Let us change perspective now, adopting as scale that of organisms on this planet: From that angle, I am rather big. Few animals are larger, and none is so complex. (Even the other primates lack the exquisite neurological system found in the outer cortex of our brains.) Combined with a temporal-evolutionary factor, this truth about size becomes meaningful.

My Temporal Contexts

The whole of evolution is in a sense subsumed into me. I contain atoms that emerged in the first seconds after the Big Bang, some near others now billions of light-years away. Every phase in the history of life is mirrored in my genes, the product of the meeting of two lines of genetic inheritance reaching back to the emergence of life.

From the fertilization of the ovum until disintegration reaches that point of entropy we call "death,"[17] there is a permanence, marked by a typical consistency of development, assured by the working of the basic genetic information, DNA and RNA, overseeing the constant regeneration of cells, and with a continuity of history, of experience, being written into the preservation and conservation organs of the body. Those ancient atoms become a part of a life and enter into human history. When my actions diminish the quality of the genetic material, and were I to decide not to reproduce, this would have implications for the future of mankind and hence too of the cosmos.

Because we can shift frames of reference, producing views of times within times, the temporal context of man is complex. Consider the different scale of each of these frames of reference:

1. the temporal horizons of my immediate practical preoccupations (which themselves shift focus and scale as I move through my practical everyday errands);
2. the span of a long-range course of action—for instance, my plan for a career—and I engage in many such fundamental projects;
3. the whole of my life span, a permanence assured by natural form, which raises questions about the foundations of my life, my destiny, and the sense of my life;
4. my personal history and its relations to the history of my family, nation, culture, civilization (each with ever-larger time horizons);

(The science of oenology has a handle by now on about fifteen of them.) The thought of our influencing seriously the unfolding of even one galaxy is ludicrous.

16. Hence with a lower form. The physicists tell us that our every thought radiates an electromagnetic wave that goes to the ends of the cosmos and geodesically bends back, spreading throughout the expanding system like the waves from a pebble move to the edges of a pond. Chaos theorists enjoy contemplating the thought that the movement of a butterfly's wings over Australia displaces (very slightly, indeed) an anticyclone over the Azores.

17. Which is, for the moment, difficult for medical science to define with perfect precision.

5. the endurance of the human race, its coming to be perhaps seven hundred thousand years ago, and the when and how of its eventual extinction;
6. the endurance of the cosmos.

Despite scale difference, one center of awareness grasps them all: that "present" which I am, but with the help of my memory and imagination, I can live on all these various scales. Thus the past and the scope of my projection effect and affect the present in distinctive ways. My ability to move with ease between them is a hallmark of my freedom.

My Social Contexts: Territoriality

Biologically a human being is born into a family, and that family may be part of a closely knit clan, or it may be dispersed in the urban jungle. My space does not have to be that confining area of a village; I may roam along fairly well established tracks in the urban area, and my most absorbing concerns, being a citizen of oecumenopolis, may see me daily in contact with New York and Hong Kong. I may have concerns about my nation and even about mankind as a whole. I can question my place in the cosmos. Strange organism, strange territoriality, compared to all other living things.

Consider several levels of human territoriality. First, simply as organism: The organism, despite its intense centeredness, is interactive with and dependent on a certain milieu. Despite this essential dependence—change a single parameter not all that much and the organism will die—the organism has the striking ability to absorb selected material from its surroundings and use that material for its own well-being, and even, in the case of higher forms of life, to arrange the milieu to be more propitious: The center does, after all, get its way—up to a point.[18] What distinguishes man is, first, the reach of his territory, which he has historically extended, to the point that now he brings raw materials from thousands of miles to build his habitat, and, second, the complexity and comfort of his habitat, the great modern industrial agglomeration, the metropolis.

In achieving its own orderly development, the organism, for all the freedom shown by man, manifests clearly that it is somehow preprogrammed, containing from conception the information necessary to pursue a state of maturity and to persevere in it for what appears to be a preset longevity. The ancients rightly saw more in this than the moderns, who conflate *finis* and *telos*. Aristotle emphasized the element of perfection, of maturity showing forth the fullness of possibility of the form, the striving toward which is that pursuit of the *telos* (a principle) related to form, and not, like the *finis*, simply an end state.

---

18. I leave out of consideration that, from the point of view of certain cells, the organism is simply a friendly environment used by the cell (Lewis Thomas, *The Lives of a Cell: Notes of a Biology Watcher* [New York: Penguin, 1974], 71ff.) and that every higher organism serves as a well-heated apartment house for small organisms by the millions. Neither fact distracts from the sense of what we are exploring here.

Telos bespeaks a sense of development in time, and it introduces an element of ripeness, including a certain control over milieu as an element of one's destiny, which affects the quality of territoriality.[19]

We see this especially when we consider social territoriality, with the various degrees of spirituality characteristic of the different natures of organisms. Higher animals sense the need to defend a territory vital to their survival. Only man shows such a variety of domains conceived by this one species in different cultures and epochs. Contrast tribal struggle and street smarts.

The more insecure the individual or the group feels, the more prickly he or they will be about invasions. A vast subject. But as a starter, let us look at how the human organism absorbs others for his self-sustenance and his role in sustaining others, to clarify something of these territorial relationships at a basic level.

A Note on Personal Identity

In preparation for this, the issue of personal identity in the midst of various contexts requires a preliminary remark. Personal identity has a material base in organic continuity, most mechanisms of which can today be elucidated. How far this principle of unity in genetic material penetrates to the core of spiritual reality, which must be included in the whole form of the human being, is the subject of ongoing investigation—a question with psychological and metaphysical implications. We have already alluded to it in counting biophysiological makeup and inherited temperament as factors affecting one's natural faith.

That tiny speck of a human organism is vast in at least this sense: hundreds of billions of cells, of hundreds of kinds (one hundred billion brain cells—neurons—alone), each a complexity of molecules so numerous as to constitute a busy city within the nation that is the body (each cell contains information equivalent to $2 \cdot 10^{10}$ bytes, roughly equal to one hundred sets of the *Encyclopedia Britannica*), each organ being—to continue the metaphor—like a state or a province. This, the most complex assemblage in all the world, has to function as a whole. In polar contrast to the democratic state, the whole is not there to assure primarily the well-being of each of the parts; rather, each cell, each molecule, is to a point subservient to the center, from which emerges the focused beam of awareness and will. Microbiologists tell us that this subservience is imperfect, uneasy, that many cells and many microorganisms within the host body tend to look after themselves. When this "separatism" gets out of hand, the symptoms we recognize as disease manifest themselves.

But, all in all, the centering of this immense conglomeration can hardly be imagined to be greater, especially when one thinks how complex it is, a unification exceeded only in pure spirit. Squaring this centrifugal self-centeredness of the bodily rooted reality of the individual agent with the centripetal reality

---

19. This is one of several insights for which I am grateful to K. L. Schmitz.

of our social existence and the exigence of that disappropriation we call love will preoccupy us as we struggle to situate man.

MYSELF AS INFORMATION PROCESSOR
Taking Lower Forms into Higher: The Role of Information in Man

The evolutionary complexifying-unfolding of being involves at each stage an ever more far-reaching capability of gathering, processing, and storing, not just minerals and organic matter, but information. It is curious how slow developing has been our awareness of information as an essential ingredient of life, despite the biblical revelation of God's creative activity as word. Even in the construction of the walls of individual cells there is encoded information, which guides the organism in absorbing the relevant materials and in restructuring them, and which instructs it in how, once built up, these accomplishments are to be passed on reproductively.

Information capability is one of the best indexes of an organism's degree of spirituality. The correlation between the highest information-processing capability and the deployment of *Sein*—a certain level of interpretation with its correlate degree of freedom—is a fundamental ontological issue, for the relationship of *Sein* and logos holds a key to the peculiar nature of humankind. The relationship of being, *Sein*, and information, with the fresh light this throws on freedom and spirituality, is indeed a most recent discovery.

It is not easy to determine the exact point at which life begins in the evolutionary chain, and we as yet know little about how it actually came about.[20] The threshold has certainly been crossed at the moment metabolism begins, the point at which freedom and necessity make their appearance in unmistakable form. Organisms need mobility in order to obtain sustenance, and they need sustenance in order to move. With every increase in this ranging about, a new distance requires a new mediation, and new possibilities and new risks are created. In the process, as Hans Jonas points out, the sense of sight emerges and eventually becomes primary, a step toward that ultimate and freest degree of seeing we call *theoria*.[21] "With the appearance of metabolism we can see the beginning of a trajectory in which freedom and necessity move in tension along an arc toward insight, reflection and moral responsibility."[22] With every increase in information, mobility, and freedom, the nature of territorial relations becomes more complex. At certain points, whole new ranges of possible activity become evident, and new forms are manifest, which demand their own new kinds of social organization, with a concomitant new kind of information.

---

20. Anyone who believes that we know pretty well how life evolved should read Thaxton, Bradley, and Olsen, *The Mystery of Life's Origin*. These biochemists demolish the pretensions of the best efforts to reproduce the start of life in the lab.
21. Jonas, *Phenomenon of Life: Towards a Philosophical Biology* (New York: Dell, 1968).
22. I am grateful to Mr. G. Lewis for these formulations, in a note to me dated October 24, 1989.

Once a new species has emerged, one generation of organisms, the parent(s), somehow gets programmed to produce seed containing the information necessary for launching and guiding the development of the next. This programming determines the type of complex relations of cooperation with its own kind, with things of different species, of exploitation and being exploited, with information being deployed to sustain all these relationships.

Much information is transmitted, in higher animals, from the external perceptors, keeping it aware of the immediate environment, to and through the central memory-processing unit, the brain, and much from one organ to another, preshaped, structured, as it radiates (whether as light, sound, or heavy molecules received by the olfactory glands and taste buds) or reflects off an object, and then is further shaped through the nervous system. In this doubly shaped form it affects the way in which and that about which the awareness center is aware, and it operates automatically, below the level of conscious awareness as it triggers various information-processing activities in the brain and nervous system, in a way relevant to what is actually being received. Physiological and temperamental givens and even habits work in this forming and shaping way, resulting in varying degrees of murkiness and lucidity in the in-forming of the transmitted material. All this shapes substantially the sense of the animal's world.

This internal shaping and enriching of the presently received information in no way undermine commonsense realism. If the elaborate information-processing capabilities of the animals did not respond to (as well as being the evolutionary product of) real conditions in their milieu, then they would not survive. The wages of inadequate or perverse interpretation is death. Ill-conceived fantasy kills.

In man, the critical aspect of the center of awareness is greatly enhanced. It modifies the influences of instinct and to a degree physiological limits and molds temperament and modifies enculturated, habituated, and institutionalized traditions. Man's ability to analyze his own bodily and cultural-habitual being, to ob-jectivize it and then play it off dialectically against whatever objectivity appears to him from the outside, and to improve the truth of his view of the environment, shows in the nature of the information processing and hence in the organism-environment relationship a radical difference from that characteristic of all other organisms. None other enjoys his unique ability to appreciate what is other than himself and even to anticipate developments in it. For these reasons his territoriality and his temporality take a quantum leap in complexity. All organisms seek to control their territories. Only man can also relate to others noncontrollingly, thus nonterritorially, in love.

Within the interaction between the already given organism[23]—a thus-far-given dynamic but consistent structure—and the stimuli presently being reacted to, it is difficult to distinguish, at all levels from the cellular to the

---

23. Genetically encoded instructions in the cells and the good viruses, organs made up of cooperating cells, indeed the organism as a whole.

full central nervous system, what has been genetically transmitted, what has been developed in the individual history of the particular cell or organism's interaction with a specific environment, and the impact of new input. After all, that new input results in some new development (from mutation to new learning experience) in which new and old are inextricably linked.

The difficulty is compounded, in the case of man, by the scope of his ability to react creatively, to imagine, anticipate, conceive, to launch into the not-yet (or perhaps even the never-to-be). So we are often unsure, when we move beyond immediate sense perception, what in the present mixture belongs to reality out there and what to fantasy, the not-yet. Even in perception, it is not always easy to distinguish what the stimuli coming from the object are offering and what the perceiver contributes from memory to flesh out the stimuli.

Certain stimuli are reacted to in a predetermined way; they are given much of their sense by the fixed structure of the organism to which they convey, because of the receiver's limits, highly selective information. The most rigid, almost mechanical level of receptivity is the lock-and-key arrangement of cellular receptors to the RNA that happens along (or, as is often the case, has cleverly been sent along when and as needed). At a higher level, rigid, species-typical behavior is a symptom of this kind of limited genetically determined information processing. Not much freedom there (although recent research is turning up evidence of considerable adaptability even at the cellular level).[24] The higher animals have enhanced abilities, not just to receive passively, but to scan. Human beings can probe the object in different ways (even inventing instruments to increase his information-gathering range and quality) and receive certain information into different contexts at will. But even a cat has some leeway to focus and interpret in terms of the interests of the moment. Thus the object can take on different senses, without the in-itself intentional value of the raw information transmitted by the stimuli being destroyed.

So nature has evolved mechanisms capable of transcending the punctuality of time and space to achieve long-lasting and spatially extended organizations —forms—thus making it possible for species to endure for thousands of years and for others to extend their social structures over large territories and, in the case of man, the entire planet. It is as though the whole species cooperatively achieves a territory. When we recall that for breeding, bringing up the young, and feeding the flock a certain command (limited, to be sure) of often wide territory is necessary, we recognize that we are brushing the surface of large issues—individual versus species good, information and territoriality, and the whole interplay of species rivalry within the as yet poorly known story of evolution. The evolutionary-territorial struggle goes on in our time, all over this planet. Philosophers of nature, such as Konrad Lorenz, have barely opened this fruitful new line of investigation and reflection.

---

24. The cells are programmed by their DNA to very complex acts of harmonious cooperative interaction with other cells, and the enormous redundancy in DNA allows for a radiation to mutate part of the code, making possible something new, without necessarily always compromising the code's ability to assure the cell's base traditional activity.

As incomplete as our knowledge remains, the following is basically true: Evolution unfolds in the direction of an ever greater conquering of space and time. Each higher organism can operate not only as an individual over a longer time span than, say, the insects but over a much larger territory, and the social capability of some insects and higher animals allows vast cooperative management of territories.[25] In the most complex form of being known, modern planetary human society, the role of information generation, transmission, and storage occupies up to 60 percent of work time.[26] This base is becoming a launching pad for playing with the cosmos as a whole.

By means of information, energy is concentrated and directed, increasing the power of the informed to control structures stretching far and wide and enduring for long periods of time. The relationship of power, energy, and information has been recognized for a good while to hold one of the keys to the sense of being. (The symbols Almighty Father, Son as Logos, and Holy Spirit as animator,[27] which are two thousand years old, display already, even before the *patres* go to work on them, evidence of an inside understanding of power, information, and life.) Only recently understood are some of the mechanisms by which information is generated, stored, and used in the service of life and form. It is literally vital that we go more deeply into just what is meant here by information. Ultimately, we will have to relate what we learn about it to the ancient Greek and biblical and patristic understandings of Logos and to Heideggerian sense of *Verstehen* and *Sein*.

The Nature of Biological Information

Given the form of a particular kind of molecule, it will bond with other kinds of molecules within a determined range. Every such bonding is an event, requiring an expenditure of energy: Indeed, it takes energy to achieve any sort of (temporary) stability,[28] at all levels. At higher levels of complexity, not only is energy required for initial bonding, but flows of informed energy, or information, all throughout the system are required to keep it functioning consistently. At the highest levels—those of human society—flows of information, appreciation, and love require expenditure of energy formed by psyche, a symbol that stands for what is unique about the human form these events

---

25. Monarch butterflies may migrate from Canada to Mexico, but their hold on the territory at each end is most tenuous. The lion pride does not migrate far, but it maintains a pretty firm hold over its modest territory. Human communities can command vast territories, with supreme sovereignty, often ruthlessly (often stupidly) stamping out thousands of other species.

26. As Bruce Stewart tells me, on the leading edge of symbolic analytical work, 90 percent is not unusual. The limiting factor, it appears to him, is inherent not in being-complexification, but in institutionalized organizations' less-information-intensive requirements.

27. An animator makes possible the not-yet in each individual situation and, simultaneously, knows the "to be" of the whole. Hence the Spirit that makes the Incarnation come to be and also the Paraclete are within the tradition.

28. In thermodynamics, confusingly, what we here call a stability is an "instability": The energy needed to maintain things is available for work. Coal, for instance, is burned to release heat.

take. At all levels, from the energy expended in molecular binding through to the devotion of psychic energies, much remains unknown, and at the highest level, the philosopher encounters profoundest mystery. (A human being, for instance, can be physically exhausted and yet manage somehow to pour out love for those around. That psychic energy, if we presuppose that the physical base remains at least minimally intact, does not itself take the form of physical energy, with its measurable heat flows.) There can exist no form without such a balanced flow of energies in complex equilibrium, assured by the in-formed functioning of an information system. This assures the typical integrity of the organism internally, its defense against predators, its acquisition of needed supplies from outside, and its social functioning within larger systems developed to maintain a milieu for the benefit of a society of beings of the same species.

The predetermination constituted by the molecule's nature is nothing like the information in a cell in which is preprogrammed an elaborate set of algorithms[29] governing steps of development. In the molecule the preprogramming is a function of the way the respective electrical charges are disposed in the rings of the various atoms in the molecule, and how it operates dynamically as a whole, given its atomic makeup.[30] DNA, on the other hand, is a code disposed to trigger a schedule of operations, aimed at achieving a certain maturity, a fullness of development in the sense meant by Aristotle when he wrote of the *telos*; it is not, then, just about dumbly enduring as a fixed structure, but about reacting over time through a set of planned, scheduled initiatives, played out in every healthy member of the species. To be sure, the code itself, even its redundancy, is a set series of codicils, each of which is one of the four coding bases from which (so far as we know) all the genetic instructions in the universe are built up. From this narrow, determined base (reminiscent of the narrow base of letters in an alphabet, but here the entire coding potential is contained in only four "letters"), unimaginably elaborate operations can be guided (just as they can from arranging arrays of off-on switchings, following the binary code based on Boolean algebra—there we are down to two "letters").[31]

To think of the encoded instructions in RNA and DNA as nothing but a more complex version of the same phenomenon of predisposition by virtue of makeup would be to miss a central reality of our world, a truth about form: The stages of being are a matter not just of greater complexity but of new kinds of operation, splendid reorganizations of harmonized energy, manifesting admirable glories in the form of capabilities one could never have supposed would come out of the lower achieved levels of operation.

---

29. An algorithm is a special method of manipulating symbols—a standing instruction, if you will. It is named for Al-Khowarizmi, a member of Baghdad's ninth-century House of Wisdom, who devised abstract rules of procedure for organizing mathematical expressions. See Campbell, *Grammatical Man*, 130.

30. Any chemist will tell you that molecular bonding is extremely complicated.

31. As impressive an evidence of the simplicity achieved by human spirituality as one can imagine, this ability of the mind to penetrate the structure of information to the point of, first, alphabetization and then representation of all numbers and letters by two letters, arrays of off and on.

Form here becomes command of a process, a structure of unfolding: The information is disposed to establish algorithms on how the organism is to prepare complex substructures at the right moment, including the further local reception, processing, and transmission of new forms of vital information to other organs within the whole entity. The DNA and RNA molecules are distinguishable from the rest of the cell and the whole organism, and so can be detached and manipulated by man, who now is learning how to de-form and re-form the species. For this to be possible entails, as Thaxton, Bradley, and Olsen put it, a molecular arrangement of "an aperiodic nature but with a specified sequence."[32]

The very limited, fixed structure of a single molecule severely restricts the space it can command. In a sense, there is no detachability of the information, which is essential to longer-range communication. The simpler molecules enjoy longevity, as do the atoms less heavy than the radioactive—in fact, more longevity than any organism. But this obdurate hanging in there contrasts with the cells'—and the organisms'—intelligent command over time, the command of developmental process.[33] (On the higher levels of operations of the most complex organism, this reaches the complexity of habit, symbol system, institution, culture.) The individual organism may be short-lived compared to most molecules and all atoms, but the species may live long.

Consider, in rough chronological order of their discovery, mankind's efforts to improve command of information:

the invention of spoken language
the inscribing of cave and rock symbols
the late discovery of writing
the abstract analysis of the alphabet
the creation of mythological, mathematical, and philosophical symbols, able
    to embrace large sectors of reality
the reception of the revelation of God-given images, including the revelation
    of man himself as *imago Dei*
the application of mathematical and philosophical symbols to the close
    measure and analysis of aspects of nature
the recent invention of cybernetics—the scientific awareness of information
    processing and the triumph of machine language, based in Boolean
    algebra.[34]

---

32. Thaxton, Bradley, and Olsen, *The Mystery of Life's Origin*, 129.

33. It takes a great blast of energy to split the atom. All higher entities pay a price of a certain fragility for their complexity. But the quality of their space-time command is greater. The life expectancy of organisms of different degrees of complexity varies apparently not at all as a function of complexity. At the opposite end of the scale, borrowing a vision from theology for contrast, the saint achieves an invulnerability and eternal life through allowing grace to purify his heart so he becomes, like Christ, integrable into the whole of Being, without losing personhood; there is no way to get at him through the cracks, for he has perfect integrity.

34. A caution, however, on jumping too fast with claims about the prospects for this cybernetic advance. See Roger Penrose, *The Emperor's New Mind. Concerning Computers, Minds*

The very fact that man can express just about anything in linguistic symbols, that these can be reduced to writing, that writing can be alphabetized, and that an alphabet can be represented, along with spaces and punctuation, by arrays of on-off switchings, working at close to the speed of light, which makes word processing possible, tells us something basic about natural being: The possibility that the mind analyzes the most complex wholes into symbolizable elements, from which the whole can be reconstituted with little (but some) loss of meaning, is rooted in the very structure of nature itself (including the structure of mind). The world is to some degree inherently analyzable, symbolizable, and therefore calculably capable of these operations.

This does not imply an inevitable reductionism. I may be able to express a symbol, employing the three-letter word G-O-D, a meaning, retained in no machine but only in that most impressive computer, the human brain. (It is also a reference to all the elaborate discussions to be found in the relevant literature down through the ages.) That symbol is capable in ways that remain largely mysterious of serving as an instrument of thought, which thought of God, in the mind of a theologian like Balthasar, is not exhausted by sixty volumes. This incarnation and transcendence of meaning in and from the material symbols into which it is encoded for purposes of triggering *memoria* in the brain will occupy us later in this work.

PURPOSE AND MEANING IN NATURE?
MAN IN THE GRAND SCHEME
Are the Many Kinds of Organism
and Their Hierarchy for Something?

It is rather difficult, in the case of all other organisms than man, for us to discern what they are for—if the question even makes sense. Before the myriads of organisms, many types serving to feed other types or to provide beneficial environmental conditions, one might be tempted, with the nihilist, to say that there is no overall purpose in this amusing zoo. Is nature just an accumulation of accidents as a senseless life force exuberantly pushed forward, producing forms struggling to survive? But to close one's eyes arbitrarily to so much evidence of a design we glimpse but do not entirely understand would be to incline to embrace ultimate senselessness. I consider it a form of mental laziness and a failure to love, a lack of gratitude for the beauty of the universe.

Keeping our calm, let us first inventory what is certain, or near certain. That a great evolutive life force is at work and that it has produced species in seemingly limitless variety in response to different environmental challenges now seems rather evident as we scan the vast but still spotty data. Many lower forms obviously serve to support higher entities. We can affirm that without entering into the treacherous teleological questions of whether they are meant

---

and the Laws of Physics (London: Vintage, 1989). Cybernetic problems for mankind are more likely to come from social organization and the use of sociopolitical and economic power than from our success in programming computers, at least in the near future.

to do that. Some believe that it is only a matter of power, that this species extends its dominion at the expense of others, which is, *tant pis*, the rule of the stronger. Some Neo-Darwinian philosophers have ill-advisedly extended this principle to the human sphere, as though nothing more is at work there than the laws of biology. Once beyond the descriptive level of matters of fact, one cannot pronounce with much certitude on these questions. There is indeed a struggle to survive, but also signs of cooperation here and there, from bacterium to hive to lions' den, and human society is replete with cooperation.

We glimpse in nature something like what we humans experience as purpose in our action, in the individual organism's success in interacting with an environment—it "means" to maintain itself—and in the way higher forms use lower ones (purpose mixed with will-to-power and survival of the fittest), to some extent remolding the environment into a friendlier territory.

Not being very intelligent, and hence poorly in-formed about its milieu, the maple has to waste huge quantities of seed and depend on the winds in an often vain hope to extend passively the territory of its species. Poor control over a noisy environment leads the maple to resort—in keeping with Claude Shannon's rules—to wildly extravagant redundancy. In contrast, the alert surveillance by the Canada goose while his mate broods on her nest of just six eggs is a picture of good targeting and of effective devotion for the purpose of assuring future progeny on the part of individuals in a species that operates over vast distances: When big enough, the young geese will fly away with the parents to a winter haven thousands of kilometers away. Life clearly "means to go on" in the forms attained in all these species. (Imagine the level of information gathering and processing it requires for our geese to navigate from the Canadian tundra to Louisiana.)

But what about the hierarchy in all this? In some species, specialized types occupy definite positions in a coordinated social structure, such as the beehive. All work for the whole. If they get any pleasure from what they do, it is because they are hard-wired to receive enjoyment for responding to the necessity built into their natures. Freedom is at such a low degree as scarcely to merit the name, except that the clever worker's skills as, returning, he does his dance to in-form the others of vector and distance to the sweetest nectar, and his great radius of action contrast favorably with the lowly earthworm's limited abilities, range, and information.

And between species? When one species feeds on another, when the gander gobbles up maple seeds, the sense that it is "meant" to be this way has occurred to mankind spontaneously. Even the animal-rights people today emit no cries of outrage when the wolf eats the cute little marmot, only when man eats the steer. Only recently, it seems, has anyone considered that to decapitate the hierarchy, under the influence of nihilistic ideologies, would denigrate man in an effort to save the planet. But the sincerely concerned animal-rights people and the ecologists are raising questions that must be thought about. Because nothing less is at stake than our understanding of our own place in nature, we had better look a bit closer.

What does "mean" mean when common sense suggests "It is meant to be thus"? Perhaps we are glimpsing aspects of an overarching plan, in which everything in nature (without knowing it) somehow serves the grand design. This does not entail achievement with perfect economy—the design can allow for some (perhaps even much) waste, provided the englobing cosmic *telos* is eventually achieved. (Is there not a great deal of redundancy observable in the operations of every organism, part of nature's design, with less well informed means, to assure a degree of success through materiality, that is, huge redundancy? At the high end of the scale, with humans, not one individual is considered to exist just for the sake of the group. Although there may be some redundancy, in the sense of a high birthrate among primitive peoples with a high infant mortality rate, still every individual is treasured, especially in the highest traditions, where each is understood to be a unique point of view on the world, and that touches our sense of the ultimate end of the whole cosmic affair.)

There is so much intricacy, hierarchy, unfolding purpose (for example, the geese are doing everything in their power to hatch those eggs and then to teach the tricks of the trade to the goslings), and so on, that man has always quite spontaneously seen the whole of nature as the work of a great artist. Even if one concludes that the cosmological argument for the existence of God is not rigorously compelling, one can scarcely fail to glimpse in the whole organic hierarchy a certain intelligibility that makes not only complex proteins available as building blocks for higher organisms but beasts of burden available for man. We can glimpse fragments of sense, without anthropomorphizing; we can see how within organisms extremely complex devices carry out clever functions, and how between kinds of organism relations of "making good use of" exist. Cunning adaptation and successful improvisations, which become established and encoded, abound everywhere.

Man in the Context of the Organic Hierarchy

So we humans, looked at from the organic frame of reference, have evolved in such a way as to need the complex proteins other organisms are sacrificed to provide us. We use the wood from trees and the vegetables from plants. We put higher animals to work for us, and we raise them for our food, seeking variety in tastes for mere pleasure. We use antibiotic organisms and armored horses to fight off predators, from microbes to invading Huns. And we depend on one another: for generation, for raising the vulnerable young, for help in infirmity and old age, and for the joint realization of great works. This exploitation of our position in the organic hierarchy has allowed our species to extend its territory to the entire planet, and we are now "domesticating" the atmosphere, which bears our aircraft; the deep seas, which harbor our territory-protecting submarines; and even the exosphere, where we orbit our satellites. And consider our conquest of time: Not only do we live from treasures of wisdom, and probe nature back to the first nanoseconds after the Big Bang, but the aura of rich layers of history with which we enwrap our cultural and linguistic productions is the glory of our race.[35] As in war nothing is so precious as information, information is also central to that unique ability in man—the opposite of war—appreciation.

What does the fact of this superiority have to tell us about how we should, in consequence, act? How do we relate truths gained from an organic frame of reference to the aspects of our being discovered from other kinds of analysis, especially the cultural?

The Nature and Mandate of Man's Superiority

If one asserts that man is superior to other organisms, it is important to be clear about the criterion according to which the better is measured, and how that *metron* fits into the whole understanding of being.

My students are nervous about this claim of superiority. As the grounds for acknowledging it seem to me, for reasons I am developing here, rather obvious, this resistance has puzzled me. It is not just that they are worried that man abuses his power, ruining the environment instead of husbanding it, lording it over[36] the animals instead of respecting their right to a good life, even when they are being raised for our consumption. No, they are worried about hierarchy because affirming something as better than something else implies a *metron*, to which a rational man would then be bound. And, scandal! we would be caught moving from is to ought. If, for cultural reasons one is caught in the throes of a libertarian ideology, the ultimate horror is: to be beholden to anyone or anything. The ultimate idol: One has to be free at all times and in all ways to do one's own thing.

Paradoxically, what at first looks like great humility (man is not superior, only different; all animals and even plants have rights) hides an arrogance: Who can pretend to tell me I cannot do what I jolly well feel like doing? What is masquerading as anti-elitism is the tyranny of the crowd, a mindless egalitarianism manipulated by the clever in the absence of any standards at all. I do not think it accidental that so many animal-rights advocates are also pro-choice: They worry (with good reason) about man's inhumanity to chickens in a mass poultry operation, but think little about tearing tiny human beings out of the womb. This illogic reveals a shuffling off of responsibility.

I return to the charge: By what criterion do we judge man superior to the other things of our acquaintance? First, man is by far the most complex.[37]

---

35. Keeping this conquest is not assured. As a self-important *petit bourgeois* sneers at the pretender to the Hapsburg throne, finding him intrinsically of no interest, we see in this failure to respect our collective past in its present incarnations the death of culture and the dehumanization of man. Democracy's slide into manipulated resentment and egalitarianism is a tragedy for humankind.

36. The expression is from Genesis, where it is explained, that as a result of sin, the husband will lord it over his wife; by extension, the good stewardship intended by God degenerates into stupid domination. Gen. 3:16.

37. Might one not argue for Gaia, the earth, as an even more complex individual, a system in which man is but a part—to be sure, the most complex of these—but also perhaps the

Compared to the highest animals, his brain, with the intricacies of the outer cortex reaching new heights of electro-organic harmonics, operates on a plane nowhere else achieved in nature. Of course, complexity as such is not an obvious virtue, but complexity devoted to achieving a higher quality of operation is, since complexity opens the way to a vast well-defended territory and to something far higher: the possibility of a saving kind of simplicity; a self-identity that is unassailable and leads to that ultimate kind of freedom, the ability to appreciate.

In what ways, then, are man's operations, his information and the use to which he can put it, qualitatively superior to those of other organisms and even more to inorganic entities, however gigantic their space-time extension, be they even black holes with a mass ten thousand million times that of our sun?

Higher than the control the human mind permits is mysterious appreciation. Appreciation is an activity of glorifying in the other, indeed in the whole cosmos, and in its Author in which humans engage and which they experience as truly and absolutely fulfilling. Both the ability to control and the ability to appreciate have been englobed indiscriminately in the same term, "freedom." But at first glance they seem qualitatively different.

MAN'S FREEDOM IN THE SCHEME OF THINGS
The Superiority of Human Freedom and the Need to Grasp the Sense of Its Deployment in History

However grand and noble human freedom, it is finite. To the extent that man is preprogrammed in ways he cannot alter, he is obviously not free in the libertarian sense. He cannot do whatever he can imagine, many things he can do bring bad consequences, and there is much that lies beyond his imagination. Like any other organism, he is caught up in a line of genetic inheritance, as well as being dominated by aspects of his past that are now ingrained. (Some of these influences, like psychic traumas, are now involuntarily present in consciousness, perhaps unalterably. Addictions and deeply ingrained habits get well installed in our being.) And he is materially, spatially, territorially, and temporally bound to an environment, which for humans is not just natural but cultural.

Like all limiting factors, this unfreedom is, as Saint Thomas said, a metaphysical *malum*, a boundary on our ability to be. All sentient entities experience these limits as painful—this dependence is our *passio* (receptivity), which is a suffering. And, Thomas further points out, any finite being can suffer as

---

most menacing to the well-being of the whole? See James Lovelock, *The Ages of Gaia: A Biography of the Living Earth* (New York: Norton, 1988); also his previous book, *Gaia* (Oxford: Oxford University Press, 1979). The perspective taken in *Ages* threatens to render man at best incidental. There is much to criticize in Lovelock's position—for the Gaia hypothesis to reflect an organization and an individual of sorts, man's place must be systemic, not systematic as it is portrayed—but he does help us grasp the sense of the planetary system as a complex ecological whole.

well physical (from *phusis*—the kind of form he possesses) *malum*, when it is lacking something normally found in its kind, like sight in man, which *malum* we term "blindness." But there is another side to this inevitable limitedness of our finitude—metaphysical *malum* and a particular kind of *phusis*. After all, the living thing's genetic inheritance is a painfully arrived-at treasure-house of organic developmental capabilities, perpetuating the line and helping the individual achieve automatic development of his body. And the sedimented biophysiological results of past acts form a given base in habit, a formed capability rendering future action "surer and easier" (Aristotle). (That is why good habit is termed "virtue," from *vir* = man, hence power.)

Now among the possibilities transmitted in that genetic inheritance are those that permit growth of the sensory system, the central nervous system, and the brain. These along with an acquired culture of methodic reflection empower the individual to discover aspects of his own inheritance and to act in consequence of the discovery of a (finite) range of possibilities among which he can deliberately discriminate.

This embodied past is a mix of weaknesses (some self-inflicted, some traumas inflicted by others) and strengths, memories, emotive engagements, language, vices and virtues so deeply ingrained as to form an apparent given, a second nature, influencing his natural faith and hence all future action. Self-control is a kind of personal territorial imperative, a struggle to achieve integrity: All his life long, the psychologically healthy individual[38] strives to extend the imperium of his conscious center of awareness, guided by his highest ideal, over the darker and more unyielding aspects to the extent that these seem obstacles to his fullest development. Through this struggle, he informs his every action with principles of order, thereby accumulating good fruits of endless outpourings of constructive energy—new knowledge and reinforced virtues. This building (the Germans call it *bilden*[39]) of character and wisdom is the acquisition of culture. (English has taken over the more agronomic word, from *cultivare*, to work the fields. The German term, *Bildung*, expresses better the sense of accumulating capability.)

We have been emphasizing one remarkable aspect of that ability: the human individual's capacity for discovering reflectively that he is viewing the world from different perspectives, from frames of reference, and for integrating the resulting in-form-ations into a single wisdom, which should yield a ruling ideal. This discovery, which itself is a form of appreciation, keeps him from being captive to any particular frame of reference. He may call all of them into question, deliberately relate them, choose among them, but also integrate their

---

38. "By no means common," commented psychiatrist Dr. Hersch, upon reading this.
39. Suggesting not just building up but creation of a form, *Bild* = image. The Old English *bilden* meant to construct a dwelling place. The character we build for ourselves and our natural faith are constitutive of our dwelling on earth. See Heidegger's essay, "Building, dwelling, thinking," in *Poetry, language, thought*, trans. A. Hofstadter (New York: Harper and Row, 1977), 143–61.

intelligence, and then act, with integrity, in light of the thus revealed wise ideal. Through the vital information this affords, he is able to influence his loves and to navigate around all manner of obstacle, including many which he himself is, which might otherwise block him from becoming all that, ideally, he could.

Now see how superior to that of other organisms is man's capability. He can, somehow, partially objectivize his own situation: It can become for him an object of inquiry. That is a source of power. He can elect to become increasingly in-formed about his own form, and about his situation, at many scales and many levels of depth, even to the point—exceptionally—of stepping back behind the becoming of *Sein* itself, to think the sense of this unfolding history of meaning. Holding the key to order permits appreciative reordering. He can inquire critically into the givens of his own natural faith, he can deabsolutize his own time-space situatedness, relating it imaginatively to the different time-spaces of other individuals, and even other traditions and civilizations. As this becomes information for him, he can choose to alter aspects of the objective givenness of his situation, in two ways: through his work and by convincing (or overpowering) others, and thus getting them to try to realize his goals and ideals. He can decide to change place, electing perhaps even to emigrate from his native land. The whole world is his playing field. Although he cannot be in other than the present objective moment in time, he can alter the effective content of that moment to an extent, by inserting it into the wider meaning drawn from remembered past and fantasized future. By electing to immerse himself more in certain ongoing processes and to extract himself to the extent possible from many others, the content of his effective existential time—the *Sein* of his personal world—alters considerably, and with that his future, and thus how his past is molded in fact. I choose to immerse myself in certain kinds of experience and to abstain from others. That has a great effect on who I become.

This freedom to presence objectively and imaginatively and then to work in many ways on the object gives the individual some control over his destiny. We become, says Aristotle, what we know. But also we project ourselves onto the world, in many forms of both control and appreciation. (As we shall see, appreciation, too, changes the world.) How we mold the *Sein* of our personal world is affected by and in a small way affects the epochal *Sein* of the larger world.

Freedom and *Sein*

So central to human existence is this building up of experience and our deployment of its fruits projectively, interpretatively, laboriously, and appreciatively, it is no surprise that Heidegger made the thinking of *Sein* the foundation of his ontology. He declared that "the essence of truth is freedom."[40] It is not

---

40. "Das Wesen der Wahrheit ist die Freiheit." This is the central theme of the essay Heidegger worked on for thirty years and considered a keystone of his work, *Vom Wesen der Wahrheit* (Frankfurt, 1954); "On the Essence of Truth," trans. J. Sallis, in *Martin Heidegger: Basic Writings*, ed. D. F. Krell (New York: Harper and Row, 1977), 117–41.

so paradoxical that he is also always alert to the dangers of voluntarism. In reflecting on the human existent's deployment of the interpretative horizons, Heidegger emphasizes that these are basically the fruits of the collective interpretation *(verstehen)*, Being's gifts, deposited deep in the natural faiths of all who share the same tradition. This is true even of a tradition as old and vast as the metaphysical tradition of the Occident. These gifts of Being have molded the cultural things and objective systems of relationships that ground our civilization much more than the present interpreters' willful contribution.

These gifts are not just in the collective memory. They are also written into the ways things are ordered and organized in a given era. They are in the language. They are in the collectively lived institutional interpretations. Finally, they are in all the ways these various dimensions mesh so flawlessly that we do not notice the omnipresent, all-shaping illumining of *Sein*. So we are only dimly aware of their dynamics and influence, and we are only slightly in control when we deploy the horizons of interpretation as they have been influenced by our everyday experience and continue to harmonize with it and with the cultural objects which furnish every setting. We are to a large extent so unaware, we are not authentically ourselves.[41]

Heidegger considers essential to the full living out of our freedom the step back behind[42] the historical suite of such epochal horizons: Then we can interrogate the sense that is hidden in them, and thus begin to take critical hold, on the deepest level, of those possibilities that we ourselves are.

The element of the unknown and the mysterious in what is thus revealed resides in the unpenetrated depths of the object and in the unappreciated elements in the horizons of interpretation and the limits of the point of view deployed in allowing the object to presence, the unthought in what is thought. Perhaps the deepest mystery lies not in the depths of the Beginning, hidden in the already having been *(Wesen)* of things and horizons, but in the breaking into the hermeneutic circle from the Beyond of the genuinely new in the moment of discovery and of creative leap.[43] My own personal limits are at work throughout. The core of the life of free consciousness lies, then, in this: Awareness of what is unpenetrated in the objective reality and what is obscure on the side of *Sein* itself allows critical penetration of the assumptions of interpretations and varying points of access to the object. This permits ever new access to its reality. It is that appropriation of who we are which, as authenticity, is what makes mankind unique—and superior.[44]

---

41. On authenticity—that critical taking possession of the concrete possibilities that make up the *autos* (self)—see *T&A*, 2–3, 6, 11, 38, 98–100.

42. This is explained in his critique of Hegel, "der Schritt zurück" being contrasted with *Aufhebung*. See Heidegger, *Die onto-theologische Verfassung der Metaphysik in Die Frage noch dem Ding* (Tübingen: Niemeyer, 1962).

43. Voegelin, as noted in the article of that name, shows the antiquity of the symbols Beginning and Beyond.

44. The relationship between authenticity and appropriation as the search for truth is the subject of *T&A*.

Summary

Our exploration of the thing that I am, beginning with consideration of it as an organism, has discovered two terrains to conquer: an exterior territory, in which I, operating in part on behalf of the species, impose my plans on others, as does any other organism, as I struggle to enhance my position. My natural imperialism is restrained only by that of other individuals and resisting species. A kind of will-to-power struggle seems built into nature.

Unlike all other organisms, man has an interior terrain to conquer, where the issue is self-control and appropriation. That requires, first, awareness of who I am (my taking the step back—to start with back behind myself; then, in ultimate thinking, back behind the world to think its *Sein*) and discriminating choice among my loves. Real freedom comes from authentic self-possession as condition for the possibility of the fullest gift of self. In all this is a new kind of dimension, not present among other organisms: encounter—appreciation of the other for himself, because he also is being, and my being wants in some way not just to fend off threatening being (anti-being) but to unite to all fructifying being in achievement of the richest and most satisfying order. It is by giving myself (knowingly) that I find myself.

Categories of information, power, and control, though essential to understanding who we are, no longer seem entirely adequate. It is no accident that at the very moment the world system is emerging, as the HTX transforms its Euro-American parent civilization and infiltrates from urban nodes all other civilizations, we see ethnic groups everywhere ready to fight off some neighbor identified as the enemy, as they make an idol of their culture and nationality. The political scientist Benjamin Barber cleverly dubs this tension "Jihad vs. McWorld."[45] In the next chapter we will start to see better why information and control are not enough—"What does it profit a man to gain the whole world if he loses his soul?" asked the Nazarene two millennia ago. We will search for the frame of reference needed to deal more adequately and ontologically with the great tension between control and appreciation that our reflection has uncovered.

IN WHAT SENSE IS NATURE FOUNDATIONAL TO ONTOLOGY?
Warnings of Reductionism

If the physical-organistic is indeed fundamental, but not the only fundamental dimension, an ontology based on it alone would be reductionistic. We must not treat man as though he were only an organism. I accept the warnings of the physicist-philosopher David Bohm, in his seminal work, *Wholeness and the Implicate Order*,[46] about the need to be wary of analysis. Analysis, which is an inevitable moment in scientific procedure, and indeed in all information

---

45. See his article of the same name in the *Atlantic* 269:3 (March 1992): 53–65.
46. David Bohm, *Wholeness and the Implicate Order* (London: Routledge and Kegan Paul, 1980).

processing, in singling out any element for attention, abstracts that element from the whole of which it is part, which all-englobing whole is not only, in Bohm's words, "ultimate context, but fullness of meaning." The whole that must be kept somehow in view, Bohm reminds us, is the "intra-cosmic fundament," to which we must be prepared to restore every element we have singled out. At the same time, different conglomerations, different things do present themselves—here he agrees with common sense—evincing varying degrees of autonomy ("self-law," as Bohm reminds us the word means, different ways of resisting entropy, or, in classical language, different forms or natures). This *autonomia* makes valid our separate knowledge of them without the necessity of explicit reference at all times to the whole, to the "implicate order," enfolding all moments.

In nature the elements in the more complex entities can be distinguished and indeed are found existing relatively independently of larger compounds (for example, free-floating atoms and molecules). But modern physics considers these to be not totally independent but caught up in fields. Though subatomic particles must be treated, quantum theory says, in certain contexts as particles, the ultimate analyzed elements are, in explaining other relations, represented by wave functions.

Here is a physicist warning us, then: We should not leap to conclusions about how the larger structures are built up. We should avoid the trap of ever thinking that the higher compounds have nothing added, as though form is built up merely by joining elements.[47]

Because our knowledge of the becoming of the cosmos is so limited, obscurity still surrounds the ways in which the building up of this or that kind of form actually occurred, and even about how the more complex forms still come to be.[48] Little is yet known about the coming to be even of the single cell. A popular science writer, Lewis Thomas, somewhat extravagantly says, "Tell me all about how the cell came to be and I'll tell you how the universe works."[49] Recent inventions like X-ray spectroscopy are helping rapid advances in this knowledge. Still, as we shall see in Chapter 8, efforts to render chemical evolution of life plausible, through reproducing supposed conditions at the time when certain spontaneous leaps up the evolutionary chain happened, have yet to produce convincing results.[50]

---

47. In the case of the building up of a human artifact—for example, a house—we actually experience form being brought in from above by the builder, so that it regulates the selection and progressive disposition of constituent materials, determining not just the gestalt of the building but the interior disposition, the aesthetic sense, everything about the resulting structure.

48. H. J. Morowitz has advanced an entire thermodynamic theory hypothesizing that the incoming energy from the sun must complexify on earth before breaking down and dissipating in the cold reaches of space. *Energy Flow in Biology: Biological Organization as a Problem in Thermal Physics* (New York: Academic Press, 1968).

49. Thomas, *The Lives of a Cell*, 71.

50. This is the burden of the analyses in Thaxton, Bradley, and Olsen, *The Mystery of Life's Origin*.

As long as we know as little as we do for sure about how the more complex entities were initially and still are built up from the elements, and how the teleological regulative principle works in organisms, much uncertainty remains about the exact sense in which the lesser forms are foundational for the higher. We should definitely not assume, for instance, that things are built up at every level of complexity in the same way.[51]

Even after Darwin, an evolutive push from below achieving nothing more than another, higher step of complexification does not seem enough of an explanation, first of all, for the coming to be of the long-encoded information of DNA,[52] but even more for what some describe as the spirituality of man's highest operations, the mind's ability to soar beyond time and space to embrace all but infinite being and to pull everything together in a single wisdom, down into which the infinite can reach.

When one watches spirit being communicated from parent to child, as language and social customs are learned, programming the brain, one can observe that a certain level of physiological readiness, providing the matrix of formed abilities, has first to be reached, and then that the elder in some sense pulls up the learning-ready child into the already existing cultural, spiritual world through "leading him out"—the literal meaning of e-ducation—and at the same time in-ducting and ac-culturating him into the accumulated riches of an already existing language and culture (into the light of *Sein*), by communicating attitude and information.

Obviously, if there is evidence of something like a cosmic intelligence at work all along in the creative process, that would incline one to be even more open to the thought that something in man may come from a special initiative of the Source from on high, as well as what has been built up from the evolutionary push from below.[53] The atheist is unsympathetic to any hint of such initiative from on high, of course.

Still I do not agree with Bohm, the least reductionist physicist I know, that the "implicate order" as "intra-cosmic" constitutes the whole field of our reflection.

Is Physics Inherently Reductionistic?

That brings me to the other possible reductionism I am worried about. There is a kind of assumption that is the reverse of the organicist reductionist's—the notion that because we live our lives on the level of that higher synthesis which is the human, understanding of the lower levels, while useful for practical technical control, is not all that significant philosophically and spiritually. This attitude is often joined to a feeling that modern Western physics, because of its essential use of mathematical analysis, is too abstractive in what it chooses to

---

51. This assumption badly damages the cosmological philosophizing of Steven Hawking in *A Brief History of Time* (New York: Bantam Books, 1988). More on this shortly.
52. We go into this question in Chapters 7 and 8.
53. The Bible, for instance, is built around a divine pedagogy—God's hard (and unrewarding) work in struggling to educate a people to carry out his mission.

measure, limiting itself to the temporally and spatially measurable. It is devoid of feeling for all that in nature could be present in a richer, broader, more humane (although, to be sure, less exact) physics—variety of form, fullness of form, hierarchy of form, teleology, interiority, the use of a wider range of symbols to capture more of what we experience. This sense, a kind of poetic and commonsense appreciation for the richness of nature, has much to be said for it, and operates independently of the *Seinsmysticizmus* about which I am also worried (I explain why later).

What these objections call for is not so much a justification for indulging in reductionist Western physics, as an argument for why the ontologist should take seriously the complex notion(s) of the cosmos constantly evolving from the discussions among these physicists, despite the fact that their methods do indeed appear limiting.

To start, I want to explain my sympathy for the objectors on several points. First, our Western physics is just one tradition, the biases and limits of which we must strive to keep in mind. *Sein*, in illuminating the world in this Occidental tradition of which mathematical physics is part, dissimulates as well, distracting attention from dimensions of this world that are more readily recuperable from other epochs in this tradition and perhaps from other traditions, where *Sein* has illumined things differently.

Second, the reductionism, resulting from the instruments of measure and mathematical analysis and assemblage, is indeed severe. Goethe tried to develop a more ample physics.[54] These limits, whatever the gains to be had from submitting to their discipline, should never be lost to mind. On the other hand, we study Western physics because it is our tradition, and so has affected our Occidental natural faith, and because it has concentrated attention on basic facets of the universe, led to new explorations, invited the production of powerful and accurate instruments of measure, and thus has been extraordinarily successful in discovering a vast array of truths that have transformed our picture of the cosmos, and so must find their rightful place in an unreduced ontology.

Third, it is true, as Bohm points out, that each level of being has its own intelligibility, so that the biologist can make significant progress in taxonomy, for instance, without knowledge of particle physics, the musicologist can examine the evolution of the sonata form without knowing much about acoustics, and the theologian can fruitfully reflect on the internal life of God as revealed in Scripture while remaining within a Ptolemaic cosmology. More disconcerting is that the speculations of the astrophysicists, the arguments of the evolutionist biologists, and the researches of the clinical psychiatrists, are generally of little importance in the decision making of everyday existence, and altogether constitute a tiny part of the content of human history, all of which radiates Being.

---

54. Johann Wolfgang von Goethe, *Farbenlehre* (Theory of color [1805–1810]), *Entopische Farben* (On entoptic colors [1820]), and *Metamorphose der Pflanzen* (The metamorphosis of plants [1790]), are works variously regarded today, but together recognized as an imaginative effort to develop a different kind of science, less reductionistic than Newtonian mechanics.

At each level in the hierarchy of complexification, there is a kind of consolidation, with life being led in the world in a way consonant with the degree of interiority that has been attained, in the characteristic mental landscape: the garden slug's world is very different from the cat's. And there is nothing more important in ontology than illumining all grades of autonomy. That includes the autonomy of various regions, or subworlds within the human world, without which everyday action would be impossible. Imagine if our grocery shopping were dependent on our first working out some of the paradoxes of physics.

Still, from the summit of this hierarchy the ontologist seeks to situate all that we have learned of the various dimensions of being, at all levels of this developmental hierarchy. He seeks to bring it into a single wisdom reflective of the putative unity of being, a thought structure in which all frames of reference are correctly related to one another. Each thing and every aspect under which we regard the same thing enjoys its proper *Stellung im Kosmos*, its place in the whole. Surely, then, the ongoing results of investigation at the foundational level of knowledge, by which we attempt to get at both the smallest building blocks of the entire material edifice—the particles and radiation waves—and at the outer limits of the material universe and to see how these relate, will have to be at least one of the dimensions synthesized in that wisdom.

But does not the reductionist nature of the tools of mathematical analysis and computation and model building become a special problem when we assess the exact sense of what is constantly emerging from the debates within physics? Of course it does. But then every form of knowledge poses its critical, epistemological challenges. Figuring out just what great music, or architecture, or painting reveal of Being, and how they are to be integrated into traditions of theology and philosophy, is just as challenging.[55]

Let us take notice of several of the epistemic problems of contemporary astrophysics, quantum mechanics, and their marriage in cosmology. This will assist us in assessing the sense of what this science permits us to know of the physical-organic fundament.

The underlying problem is that here the theoretical researchers are probing at the limit of the experimental. Trying to work back from (very imperfectly known) present cosmic conditions and the (imperfectly known) structure of particles, the physicists must infer what might have happened, during the first nanoseconds after the initial explosion of energy, under conditions wildly different from those we know—for instance, at unimaginable temperatures and densities. Whatever they theorize has to square with all that is known about the present behavior of every kind of radiation and all particles-entities the existence of some of which has never been empirically confirmed.

Our spiritualist ontologist, convinced that reductionistic physics is not so relevant, might interrupt: "Why bother with trying to include such wild

---

55. On the kinds of truth characteristic of the different genera of traditions, see *T&A*, chaps. 3 and 4.

speculation into my understanding of being, when it is so tenuous and bound to change in important respects from year to year. In any event, it isn't going to change what I do."

Remember the resistance the Aristotelian ontologists displayed toward Galileo and Newton? It adversely affected the overall truth of their ontologies, although Galileo remained, for 80 percent of his positions, Aristotelian. Much in Aristotelian philosophy remains relevant for contemporary wisdom.

Today I believe it is reasonable to integrate into a contemporary wisdom what, to the best of our knowledge, we judge to be the elements of perennial truth contemporary physics has established well enough to demand to be taken seriously by all thinkers. It is the same with Aristotle: Philosophers should continue to recuperate lasting insights from the ancient sage, from Newton, from whomever, wherever and whenever in history they occurred. We can be mistaken, taking as settled and true discoveries of astrophysics and particle physics and efforts to relate them, which may later prove to have been projections from theories not as sound as we now believe. But that is a risk inherent in all thinking on the frontier—indeed, even of common sense.

Here are some aspects of the cosmos I think are true, and hence should be integrated into any modern wisdom: There are clumps of galaxies, moving away from one another; the whole spectrum of now well known radiations; existence of atoms, free standing and combined in molecules; molecules, free standing and combined in larger entities, inorganic and organic; and many kinds of subatomic particles (not all are definitively established—from quarks to all forms of antimatter). Development of more complex from less complex entities—that is, evolution in some form—the phenomenon of complexification is now, as far as I can see, firmly established, although caution is in order when drawing philosophical conclusions from it and when considering claims of what happened and how.

The question of the ontological significance of physics entails the issue of mathematical analysis. Unfortunately, as mathematicians and physicists tend to be dazzled by the results that exact science has been achieving, most who engage in debates about the significance of mathematical analysis come with natural faiths very different from the nonreductionist, deliberately open faith, which motivates my own eagerness to retain truths garnered through all forms of valid experience. The obsessive myopia that leads to C. P. Snow's "two cultures" is inimical to the project of wisdom. My own myopia is due to ignorance of modern mathematics; I am excluded from the debate, a grave limit to my ontological efforts. This much I will hazard, however, hoping those better situated will correct me if even in these modest proposals I am off track.[56]

Measures of volume, duration, vector, velocity, and intensity of stable entities, and vectors, frequencies, and intensities of consistent radiations yield information about aspects of those things that do relate to one another in ways

---

56. I was fortunate to be able to submit what follows to two excellent mathematicians, Mr. Arturo Portoraro and Dr. Michel Vaillant, and I thank them for their criticisms.

that are intelligible to us, and in many kinds of relations. When we manipulate the symbols by means of which we have a hold on these dimensions and relationships, we can unpack implications of their relationships, extrapolate the sense of processes thus discovered, and build pictures (models) more complete than the view at the starting point of inquiry. And this is accomplished without losing the exactness and clarity of the beginning factors. When we return from the higher stratosphere of manipulation back to the complete field of primordial observation and measurement, we can verify whether the extensions are confirmed by what we then further observe. On the basis of the knowledge that is thus built up, we can do new things with many kinds of familiar entities. All of this—the cohering with further measurement and the utility of applications—alerts us that we are acquiring true knowledge of these things, true as far as it goes.

The mischief begins (as it can with any kind of knowing) when and if the physicist leaps from the basis of this knowledge to conclusions not entailed in what has been soundly established and/or not subject to further verification. This, however, is not a fault of mathematics. It is an error in physics, a misapplication of the mathematical tool.

To sum up, the physical cosmos is fundamental to us in at least this sense: It is a basic part of our setting, constituting an outer (and ever-expanding limit) to the synchronic and diachronic setting of experimental knowledge, and it enters into our make-up, as human beings, insofar as we are space-time, organic entities. Taking account of scientific knowledge about it is a fundamental dimension of a wisdom.

Experimental and Revealed Knowledge

The qualifier "experimental" is important, meaning what is accessible to us as a result of our willful probing of nature. Non-experimental knowledge—revelation, whether natural (between humans) or supernatural (between God and man)—cannot be extended by any willful probing on our part, because it depends on the freedom of another, who must will to open the hidden interior of its subjectivity; our coresponding is the will to receive this gift. The experimental is in the order of conquest and defense, the reception of revelation in the order of appreciation and ex-propriation. Accepting the love of God or that of any human person requires con-fidence in the testimony of the other about his own inner being. But even in the empirical probing of nature, the breakthrough intuitions are experienced as gifts. I now elaborate on the way the physical cosmos is foundational to experimental knowledge, diachronically and synchronically.

Diachronically, physical research reaches back to the beginning by today hypothesizing—through elaborate reasoning about background noise, red shifts, and what is known about the various structures of nebulae—an initial surge of energy from an unimaginably dense constriction of energy.[57] It is

---

57. I do not believe one should use the term "point," at least not in its mathematical definition. All evidence leads back, according to present theory, not to an infinitesimal point,

important to note that this cosmological theorizing does not really go back to the beginning. Stephen Weinberg can write excitingly for 150 pages about "the first three minutes." He does not pretend to attain empirically the start of the first second of the first minute.[58] Nor can we know about a hypothesized big crunch at the end of a previous cosmos, because all information would have been destroyed. All the evidence upon which the cosmologists are working is placed within time, after whatever constituted the initial moment of the present cosmos. Even what is hypothesized about what happened during the first seconds is highly inferential and uncertain. Pierre Julg points out that the perspective of cosmology does not authorize a leap back beyond time to proof of a creation, although the biblical revelation of creation has culturally enticed Western scientists to have thoughts of time as having a beginning.[59]

Synchronically, the cosmic setting of our actions and interests reaches out to the expanding limits of the galaxies hurtling away from one another, although at this scale any practical sense of synchronicity melts away, as the theory of relativity shows. The most amazing phenomenon at this scale, measured in billions of light-years, is, I firmly believe, the ease with which one kind of tiny entity within the vast cosmos can conceptualize such enormities. Teilhard de Chardin is correct to point out the central scientific significance of this phenomenon. It took mankind perhaps seven hundred thousand years to arrive at the present truth about the enormity and expansion of the universe, yet here we are in fact, embracing such a vast entity, holding it in our minds.

Just as astonishing is the relative unimportance such questions assume in most persons' daily lives. Mankind did, after all, get on for almost a million years without knowing either that the cosmos is so enormous or that it evolved and expands. Now that we do, what Teilhard de Chardin calls "the illusion of nearness" still reigns supreme in our lives as we actually lead them. Is that unimportance nothing but an error in judgment, or does it tell us something profound and significant about *la condition humaine* and perhaps even about the very fundamentality of the cosmos?

For the little speck that I am to survive mentally in an uncaring cosmos of unimaginable gigantism, surging up as I do from nowhere and destined very soon to be swallowed up in the black hole of death, I have had to be equipped by nature with a certain myopia that helps sustain an illusion of self-importance. So believe many of our contemporaries, and they are not altogether wrong, for that is part of the story. The rest depends on the truth of our personal and interpersonal existence, especially our relationship with the caring Source of this uncaring cosmos.

---

but to a kind of unimaginably concentrated plasma, of temperatures and densities heretofore unthought of. Contemporary physics is also disputing whether this moment constitutes a "singularity." See Hawking, *A Brief History of Time,* chaps. 9 and 10.

58. Stephen Weinberg, *The First Three Minutes: A Modern View of the Origin of the Universe,* updated ed. (New York: Basic Books, 1993).

59. Pierre Julg, "Au commencement du temps: Cosmologie scientifique et Dieu créateur," *Revue catholique internationale, Communio* 13:3 (May–June 1988): 54–69.

I believe it is safe to conclude at least this about the cosmos: The distinguishable parts of the universe, whatever they are and however they maintain their integrity, are not just set here and there in time-space, their relations come not just from being embraced and ordered by mind, but from interacting physically (united in the same field, in the language of physics—we are all particles); symbiotically (in the case of plant and animal life); emotionally (in the case of the higher animals); and socially (acting together in common projects, ranging from the bees' construction and maintenance of the hive to some human social projects that embrace in their intention, as religious and ontological projects do, all that is and can be). Consciousness—the ability of mind to relate freely to different things and to the relations between things—is just one, albeit a terribly important one, of these intracosmic relationships, and is itself a further deployment of the fundamental energy.[60] A certain psychic formation of that energy is a condition for the possibility of the illumining coming to be of *Sein*.

I cannot share the optimism of Steven Hawking, that combining quantum mechanics with general relativity will permit science to reach the goal he describes as "discovery of laws that will enable us to predict events up to the limits set by the uncertainty principle."[61] Hawking underestimates the dilemma posed by one of the three of time's arrows he identifies: the apparent movement against entropy represented by complexification. Even when he points out that every act of memory, whether by human or computer, expends considerable energy and hence adds to entropy, he fails to ask whether and how this achievement of form manifests a dimension of becoming reality that the laws of thermodynamics cannot account for. What I am calling "the order of appreciation" seems not to have occurred to this great appreciator! The question has been posed clearly and insistently by Teilhard de Chardin and much later by chemical physicists such as Prigogine. The astrophysicist-turned-ontologist, Hawking, downplays it unscientifically.

There is a further problem. The many holes in our knowledge, many of them quite evident and gaping, make impossible anyone's being sure whether the leaps in the evolutionary process are real or apparent. Teilhard de Chardin interpreted what evidence there was in the 1940s when he was writing *The Phenomenon of Man* in an effort to show them to be real gaps. The point is, we can examine those differences in behavior and establish by this means the distinctiveness of man, but we are not in a position at this time to understand from phylogenetic evidence just how life emerged and then eventually mankind emerged from these kindred life forms, if "emerge" turns out in both cases to be the right term. Phylogenesis may never answer the question.

To declare on the basis of a materialist faith interpreting the incomplete evidence that the initial conditions did contain the principles necessary to

---

60. Whether it may involve another characteristic, inexplicable in terms of the measurable energies of the cosmos, is a question we leave open for now while remaining alert for any evidence regarding this putative psychic energy.

61. Hawking, *A Brief History of Time*, 173.

account entirely for the present state of affairs, without addition (new input—for example, in the initial encoding of DNA)[62] or without the kind of "attraction" Teilhard hypothesizes, requires more than a leap of faith. It entails a blind commitment to a naive materialism, which seems to me arbitrarily closed to all evidence of distinctive, higher kinds of organization and everything the tradition has called "spiritual." The ontological issues become simplified, but distorted; empirical method becomes universal, but on the unscientific basis of arbitrary decision.

On the other hand, to embrace as scientific a Teilhardian hypothesis about the attraction of the Omega Point pulling the process forward to new plateaus of greater complexity demands a considerable leap beyond the evidence.[63] I am certainly willing to allow the grand mystic-poetic Teilhard de Chardin to lift my sights and keep me open to nonmaterialist possibilities. But when I integrate some elements of the Teilhardian synthesis into my ontology, I am cautious to include only those with some solid scientific evidence behind them and to avoid declaring them more certain than they really are.

Questions to Put to the Cosmos

There are many such questions, and it is hard to fathom their significance without interrogating one's entire ontology. And so there is a problem of knowing when, in building up a more explicit expression of one's ontology, is the best moment to pose them. Here are a few that I carry with me, questions on the cosmic scale, several of which have already been touched upon, and all to be kept in mind as we trudge along our ontological way, *meta + hodos*—method!

Regarding the Beginning. Suppose Hawking and associates succeed in combining quantum mechanics with general relativity in a way that makes credible Hawking's proposal that "space and time together might form a finite, four-dimensional space without singularities and boundaries, like the surface of the earth but with more dimensions." This could account for the arrow of time (although not, I repeat, the repeal of the second law), leaving us with "a universe completely self-contained, with no singularities or boundaries." Then if "this leaves nothing for God to do but to choose the initial conditions," and

---

62. We will see in the next chapter an argument that this is unthinkable, the probability of such encoding happening by chance is simply beyond credibility.

63. Teilhard de Chardin, in *The Phenomenon of Man*, trans. Bernard Wall (New York: Harper, 1959), was ill-advised to present his hypothesis as though it were so largely based on analysis of the empirical cosmological evidence. His interpretation is motivated by revelation, as he cheerfully admitted in earlier works, not designed, as was the *Phenomenon,* to convince materialistically inclined scientists to look further. That is how his work should be treated, more as an inspired vision growing out of a life of contemplation imbued with experience of God flowing from sources quite different from laboratory analysis, rather than as a hypothesis subject eventually to adequate empirical verification. Taken in this spirit, the Teilhardian vision retains a capacity to steer our regard. It does not close off avenues of investigation—indeed, it invites new ones—and it is filled with optimism about the meaningfulness of human life and about our salvation.

this in a narrow band of possibilities that can make a unified theory intelligible, the question remains, in Hawking's words: "What is it that breathes fire into the equations and makes a universe for them to describe? The usual approach of science of constructing a mathematical model cannot answer the questions of why there should be a universe for the model to describe. Why does the universe go to all the bother of existing? Is the unified theory so compelling it brings about its own existence? Or does it need a creator, and, if so, does he have any other effect on the universe? And who created Him?"[64]

I cite Hawking, not because I intend him to be philosopher for a day, but to illustrate the significance of the questions we put to the cosmos about its overall structure as these affect the very sense of a beginning. The tradition of Hebrew and Christian revelation confronts us with one kind of *archē*, physics with another. The biblical *archē* ("In the beginning God created the heavens and the earth" and "In the beginning was the Word") has its own strong, rich meaning, with origin and intelligibility of all we can experience placed in a Source outside time-space. If the meaning of the world, the sense of its own structure, does not lie within it, but the cosmos points to its transcending Source, then man's efforts to discover the sense of his existence through his own immanent experiencing of the cosmos will be insufficient. The *archē* of physics also lies beyond analysis, but in a different way, because of the lack of information in the plasma of the first picoseconds. In the search for wisdom, we struggle to understand how these two senses of the *archē* relate without dismissing any valid indication of what may lie behind them.

Regarding the End. The end (in the sense of *finis*) for us human inquirers will come long before the end of the cosmos in its present form; our planet will no longer support human life millions of years before the sun dies out. Long after that, the cosmos as a whole will either implode, destroying all information, or become cold and poor in information. This raises two questions. The first, experimental physics cannot answer: Will something in human life escape the conditions bound to total or near total destruction of all information? The other concerns the possibility of something happening after the cosmic end—be it the big crunch or just lifelessness. If a big crunch prepares a new big bang, then from an informationless state, form and information must again evolve.[65] Is there anything in our knowledge of present evolution to prepare us to believe that this might happen, and to suggest whether it must again produce conscious life? Have we really come at all close to an understanding of what in matter accounts for its complexifying?

Regarding the Present Form of the Cosmos and Its Calculability. Man's beliefs about himself were shaken by the Copernican revolution and again by the discovery that even our planetary system is small potatoes. Looked at from this cosmic perspective, man appears insignificant. Two considerations attenuate

---

64. Hawking, *A Brief History of Time*, 173, 174.
65. I am told that among physicists today the tendency is to believe that the present development from the Big Bang is a onetime event.

that impression: first, the realization that in relativity theory there is, properly speaking, no center, or (to put it the other way around) the center is wherever an observer is constructing a model for com-prehending the universe. Second is the anthropic principle, especially with a Teilhardian twist. It is not just that the study of the universe's becoming should be centered on the conditions allowing the development of the one entity able to pose the question, it is that in that thinking alone is the cosmos gathered up into a whole and permitted to show forth a meaning. This is tantamount to affirming that spirit in its highest manifestations is superior to matter organized at a low level, suggesting that what the whole becoming of being is all about is the realization of spirit, appreciation, love.

Hawking asks why, if the creation was meant to produce man, so many hundreds of billions of galaxies? That seems wasteful and unnecessary. There are theological answers to that. God shows forth his infinite glory and power by allowing to break out from the initial explosion a finite universe of staggering proportions, the least inadequate, purely material icon of his glory. And Teilhard's scientific response deserves attention: the need to produce a vast panoply of lines of probing development to optimize the opportunities for the millions of successive breakthroughs required to arrive at just the set of unimaginably complex conditions that make possible the coming to be and the enduring support of intelligent life. Behind both answers lies the same intuition, that quality—progress in complexifying form—is more significant than sheer quantity. There is a power to form that escapes the brute forces comprehended in the laws of thermodynamics. Form achieves being in another way than the mere clumping and splitting of particles. The possible lesson for everyday human life in such a consideration is that there may be more being in Mother Teresa's picking up a dying beggar than in all the parades of the Red Army on May Day.

The humbling truth of our ignorance suggests a most basic question about the very possibility of exhaustive physical knowledge of the universe, which the mathematicians themselves are raising anew. I cite a popularized report in *The Economist*.[66] At the core of physical science is the assumption that nature conforms to certain mathematical laws. But what if some laws of nature are noncomputable? Dr. Robert Geroch of the University of Chicago and Dr. James Hartle of the University of California at Santa Barbara, in attempting to work out the effects of quantum mechanics on the shape of space, which requires considering all possible trajectories of particles and all possible topologies (shape of space), worry that the resulting mathematics may be inherently noncomputable. Others, like Dr. David Deutsch of Oxford, argue that the phenomena of nature are so analogous that there is no real difference between what a computer does and what nature does. Any actual computer has to work within the laws of physics. So, what is computable is dictated by the structure

---

66. *Economist*, September 16, 1989, 89–90.

of the physical world. But there is a problem, for instance, in computing the size and age of the universe. One limit to the size (and thus the power) of computers is the amount of matter in the universe out of which computers could be fashioned. Similarly, the duration of the universe sets an ultimate limit to the length of calculations (unless, as some cosmologists think, the universe in its final moments would shrink so small so fast that an infinite number of calculations could be squeezed in).

The article concludes with this statement: "There is a crucial self-consistency in which physics and computable mathematics mutually support each other. Mathematicians have proved that there are far more non-computable functions than there are computable ones. It is lucky that the ones needed to apply most to physics seem to be computable."[67]

I cite this discussion as a caveat: it brings out well the likelihood of ultimate limits to our knowledge of the finite cosmos itself.

MAN CONSIDERED FROM A SUBJECTIVIST POINT OF VIEW

Our reflection on the thing I am as a kind of organism within a vast and complex physical cosmos has led us, as we sought to understand this kind of fundament, into a reflection on the very enterprise of physics itself. Now as we return to our subject, man, let us consider him anew, shifting our perspective radically, this time adopting the perspective of me, the individual subject, actually doing the reflection, working out to the larger intersubjective structures in which I find myself involved. I shall start again, then, more phenomenologically, as befits this more subjectivistic perspective, with myself grasping my own ontic being through ongoing awareness as I sit here before the amber screen, reflecting on myself.

As time-space center, this point of perceiving-reflective awareness, to whom all that is perceived gets referred, I determine the angles and disposition from which all that is received is taken in. This does not conflict with my ability to see that the perceived things have time-space volumes of their own. Hence I can consider relationships from their point of view, as we do in physics. I should take into account their perspective in and of themselves; otherwise, I risk ignoring truth and thus sowing chaos, as self-centered persons always do.

The father of gestalt psychology, Wolfgang Köhler, was startled during his experiments with the bright chimpanzees of Tanganyika to observe their inability to do this. One of his most intelligent subjects could not solve the problem of obtaining a bunch of bananas by first pushing it away from himself with a stick, out of a three-sided topless box, the open side pointing away, so that he could subsequently pull the bananas around the side of the box and back through his bars. This inability is related to the chimps' limited capacity for forging and understanding symbols.

---

67. Ibid., 90.

Certain psychic disorders limit the human capacity to order things normally in space. Merleau-Ponty cites the schizophrenic who could not hold objects at a distance—a hairbrush would refuse to stay over there on the window sill, and he would feel it pressing into his scalp. And self-centered persons show a limited capacity to see things from another's point of view.

In the present moment when I am reflecting on myself, this ability to project is what makes it possible for me to exit imaginatively from my present position sufficiently to imagine myself from out there, necessary if I am to conceive of myself as a human body and distinguish Thomas Langan from Michael Robinson.

Is this freedom to soar above all perspectives and to project oneself into other points of view not perhaps something that breaks with the determinate preprogramming of all lower life forms? Does it not manifest the power of a radically different kind of ability to generate, process, and apply a very different quality of information? These abilities to objectivize and reflect are "gifts of *Sein*"; the individual has to be educated to them, and the tradition has to develop and pass on the possibility for them, including the sophisticated language needed to deal with them.

Recognition of Types and Essences

More modestly, consider another aspect of our objective knowledge of ourselves. We here encounter again that important kind of permanence: the ability to recognize, not just distinctive individuals, but objective types, essences *(essentiae)* realizable in many individuals. We pause here to consider the existence and recognition of natures because they are a significant objective guide to the deployment of relevant frames of reference and to our finding our way about within even the most spiritual realms of being.

The division of the cosmos into many types of entities with distinctive forms is a striking feature of reality. Knowledge of natures is crucial to consideration of our own lineage. But more than any practical consideration, something of the glory of the cosmos is somehow bound up with its constitution as an array of forms, each manifesting, in the case of living forms, a striving to reach a certain maturity of its own distinctive sort.

We see that the cause for the similarity of metal nails in a pile is their having all been stamped from the same gauge wire by the same machine. Before I may have occasion to think about the cause, however, I have formed by casual observation the universal concept of two-centimeter slender nail. This concept is produced starting with the perception of a characteristic gestalt. Then, by bringing knowledge from the past and by insight, I abstract the form from perception of the one nail, perhaps refining the notion by comparing the many nails spread out on the table. Each nail does exhibit its own nature, its essence as already having been *(to ti einai estin)*, consisting of a certain kind of metal shaped a certain way. The universal exists in the mind, and by a further mental operation, a further abstraction, I can rise to the concept of nail in general. I recognize the function of a nail, and so implicitly grasp that the exact quality of metal can vary, and though all nails have a pointed end and some kind of head for hammering, I learn (and I understand) that they can be little, big, thin, fat, spiraled, and so on. While this comparing takes place in the mind, the individual nails existing materially in time-space are recognized to be really similar in themselves, and the causal ground for this, as we saw, is not far to seek.

But those nails are artifacts; their natures come from no inner organic growth. The metal, from the moment it was smelted, does indeed have an inner molecular structure, a nature of its own, an inner binding necessity. And the stamped-on form must marry with this inherent structure of the steel, natural form receiving and resisting but yielding to the demands of cultural form.

Take the case of two objects of nature—for instance, this granite boulder in a field and a granite infusion in a basalt outcropping many kilometers away. My knowledge of a nature is being built up in this case largely through comparison of appearances of things recognized as belonging to the very general sort, rocks. The geologist who understands igneous mineralization, and knows under what precise conditions of cooling this granite and that granite came to be, sees more in the boulder and the outcropping, and enjoys a richer and more profoundly grounded concept of granite, rooted in his understanding of its causes.

The movement of thought from comparison of surface appearances to knowledge of causes for those similarities is a movement in depth, which at once also permits a broadening of the frame of reference. The scientist is able to embrace the boulder and the outcropping in one explicatory view. He knows the boulder had to have been carried to the field by a glacier; the outcropping granite results from an infusion of magma into the interstices of the basalt. His categorical scheme is rich and subtle, enfolding a whole history of igneous becoming.

In the realm of living things, we build up many of our concepts of different kinds of natures through superficial comparison of appearances, including casual observations of characteristic ways of behaving, largely commanded by practical projects of limited range. Normally, there is little I need to know about squirrels, so my knowledge of them is built up from superficial, piecemeal observation. The squirrel for me is a characteristic gestalt, expected to dash about and turn in spastic ways as it heads for safety up the nearest tree. Superficial, and yet quite true, as far as it goes.

If we have reason to reflect more seriously on the mysteries of the coming to be and maintenance of phyla, or if we have some reason to begin noticing differences and similarities within families and down through the generations, then a new kind of thinking comes to be: We become interested in genetics and so start thinking about how the information on the continuation of the species and the information on the transmission of some persisting particular differences relate. We are then in a different world, and the history of *Sein* has advanced, which illumines things now in a new way. New kinds of things, in the sense of new notions about the old familiar plants and animals, come to be.

Much of our insight into kinds and natures, at different levels of abstraction, happens so spontaneously and flawlessly, the extent of the learning process involved in our sometimes struggling to recognize even the existence of a certain type of thing (for example, a virus) is lost on commonsense man. It becomes obvious when one reflects on art appreciation, where deployment of considerable knowledge is clearly necessary to unlock the full riches of the object. We have to learn how to listen to a Bartók quartet.

The resulting concepts are effective guides to further knowing and to action because they reflect similarities that in most instances are founded in like processes bringing such things about, or common genetic inheritance. In the case of artifacts, and in the case of human beings, we enjoy as well inside information: By making artifacts and by being humans ourselves, we are acquainted with how these things work and how persons behave. The diffuse aura of familiarity with the vast variety of things and typical events that animate the different worlds where we live our lives is an important aspect of that "illumining by *Sein*" which makes them accessible precisely as noncontroversial actors and props in the drama of everyday life. They fit together mostly flawlessly because nature, and we in cooperation with nature, arrange and design them this way and forge a consistent language able to express all these kinds of things and the many relationships woven between them.

To sum up: The world, then, is not just a random clutter of kinds of things. We discover causal bonds between things of the same nature, and causal relations, if only far back in time, between different species of the same genera. We are able to discover explanations for why different kinds of things have become as they are, either through evolutionary forces or human intentions.

The mind is able to observe similarities at different levels of generality, often without knowing the history of the causal relations that are at the origin of these apparent similarities, through perception of gestalt likeness, with no depth of understanding as to why the gestalts should appear to be same or similar. Sometimes the mind will form categories and relate things within them on the basis of similarities that may be purely happenstance and thus misleading.

Three levels of this knowledge of kinds of things can be distinguished: *Perceptual*: a gestalt, for whatever reason, distinguishes itself from its surroundings (background); *Intellectual*: if for whatever reason I am predisposed to ask about the internal constitution of what has perceptually distinguished itself as gestalt, I by insight grasp something of the internal sense of the thing as structure, and thus grasp it as form. But in most instances I do not press any deeper; my demands to know what this is are superficially satisfied. It takes special motivation—an event or a shock—to cause me to probe more deeply into its constitution. When I do I engage in theorizing, which can even lead to *Scientific rational analysis*: how and why are the molecules bonded as they are; what is the atomic makeup of the molecules? How is this machine constructed? How is this organism programmed to develop as it does and with the schedule it has of interaction with the environment? How does this art object fit into the milieu from which it garners its expressive capability? and so on.

Network of Parental and Personal Relationships

When we change our frame of reference from the directly perceptual to a conceptual consideration about humankind, fed by more remote empirical data, about parentage and family, we have to consider the causal foundation for this typological knowledge. We add other personal relationships and then include various wider social frames of reference. Types and natures will play a guiding role as we discover that this individual which I am is not a lonely or isolated phenomenon but part of a family, member of a large society, supported in its being by many social structures. It is all very well to talk, as does much recent philosophical literature, of autonomy, but my good is linked up essentially with the good of many others, my *nomos*—law—is in large measure group or social *nomos*, my *autos* is forged by traditions and illumined by the epochal *Sein* shared by everyone in the Occident. This consideration pushed Aristotle to declare that "man is by essence 'an animal of the city'" (*zoon politikon*).[68]

What Aristotle terms efficient causality[69] is at work here, the agency, the activity of a thing or of some general process, such as a great movement of the planet's plates, that brings another thing or a whole new state of affairs into being, whether it be artifacts (the stamped-out nails), natural products of telluric forces (the granite boulders), or members of species of living things. Even if I had never known my parents, I would be aware, once the notion of parenting is explained to me, that I must have had a father and a mother, four grandparents, and eight great-grandparents, quickly reaching back to an impressive number of predecessors with many genetic lines of inheritance all coming together in me. One recognizes here the long line of relevant efficient causality, which founds the commonality of natures and my very existence as an entity.

Note a distinction, then, between two possible kinds of inheritance: a genetic transmission of instructions to the bodily processes of physical and mental development that inform in detail how they are to unfold (the mechanism behind the regulative operation of human "form"); and a cultural-traditional passing down, through education, explicit or implicit, of knowledge of things and ways of behaving. The causality involved is obviously different. And one sees the complex interplay within the individual between the effects of these two streams of dependency, genetic and environmental, source of age-old arguments about human character formation.

That there is a causal link, a "handing down" (*tradere*), is obvious: in biological transmission, by means of RNA and DNA;[70] and in culture by imitation and symbols. The handing-down is in both cases a transmission of formed

---

68. *Politics* 1253a3.
69. *Metaphysics* 983a.
70. Personal relations and relations with in-laws through marriage, in contrast to lineage relationships, are founded only in acts of the will.

MAN IN CONTEXTS **191**

energies, of information, producing the linkage objectively for the continuity achieved across generational lines.

It is not only into orders of lineage that every individual is pulled involuntarily, but also into social orders of many kinds. I enter some, of course, voluntarily, once past infancy; and once adult, I remain in all by acquiescence.[71] Many of these social supports are of utmost importance to my being. I was born into a natural[72] society—family, social class, *ethnos*—interacted with it and was largely formed by it, long before I grew to an awareness enabling me to take some critical distance from it.[73]

A large range of possible shifts in frame of reference is feasible and objectively grounded (ultimately in the real forms of the foundational things—the human beings interacting) and subjectively realized in societal reality. Ask any psychologist about the scale and scope and intensity of these various societal influences he has to deal with in helping patients.

To understand in a general and more overtly ontological way this kind of intersubjective being, I will describe one typical social stability. That will suffice to show how complex and involving these social realities can be, and how formative of my personal being. This will improve our understanding of the proper place of social stabilities generally within the totality of being.

Adopting a perspective on myself as citizen of this municipality, I ask what kind of being has such a municipality, and how am I in it, how does this intersubjective reality containing objective elements—human beings, their houses, streets, and so on—to some extent mold my being while enjoying being in itself?

THE BEING OF SOCIAL STABILITIES

An event calls my status as citizen to my attention. (See how the circumstances of daily life propel the quest for truth!) I was approached to stand for the town council of Rome, Ontario, by a group dissatisfied with the municipality's ineffective resistance to a provincial road-widening project.

So the question of my duty gets thrust upon me. What am I doing here in Rome to start with? For no very noble reason, I moved ten years ago, with little explicit commitment: I found a house on a quiet street, at a price I found viable.

---

71. Unless, of course, as a citizen I would be shot down if I tried to escape beyond the borders of my fatherland.
72. In the sense—*natus*—used in Chapter 1 in the notion of natural faith, that is, functioning largely without reflective agency. *Natus* implies that I am "thrown" into it. Much that is thus naturally acquired is in fact cultural in origin.
73. The question of how extensively events in the life of an individual can affect the genetic code and get passed on is presently under investigation. But there is no doubt that events do affect my biophysiological being. Take a gross example: Suppose I was raised in an alcoholic family and given to poor eating habits, which resulted in my sharing the family tendency to obesity. Compare this rotund child now with the offspring of health-conscious, well-off trend followers who dances at the National Ballet School.

(My being-there, in Rome, is the result of a will-act, motivated by a set of self-centered desires molded by my natural-faith disposition to live a certain way. The *Sein* embracing and illumining the entire working environment and urban-suburban scene is taken for granted.) Until now I took the town for granted basically as an institutional arrangement responsible for delivering certain essential services, and extracting taxes in exchange. But neighbors have asked me to contribute to the municipal common good. Some larger communitarian reality has been invoked, which I shall not go into here, because I want to concentrate on the less taxing frame of reference, the being of the town.

The Being of Rome: Geographical and Juridical

Like many social relations, this one is partly defined by geography. (We are bodies, after all.) We can distinguish, with a slight change of reference, the geographical boundaries of the agglomeration, determined by the actual physical structures of buildings, roads, utility lines, and the juridically defined town limits. (Like most agglomerations, Rome has outgrown its juridical boundaries on one side, though there remains vacant land within the town lines on the other.)

Note the ease of shift of reference: I am in Rome one way physically, another juridically; as a body dwelling there; and as a citizen eligible for certain privileges and implying certain duties. Note also the ease with which their respective objects can be correlated, the material network of structures, an external reality, with the juridical *ens rationis*, with a spiritual time-space of its own in the minds of those who know and acknowledge the system of law. They are smoothly illumined by the same *Sein*, and they affect one another.

Because the juridical reality depends on the implicit willingness of the larger citizenry, province and nation, to accept the law defining the township limits, Rome is a territory the *Sein* of which is grounded in imagination—but imagination related to an expanse of actual land—and accepted through a fundamental intersubjective existential project by all relevant, enculturated agents, sharing the *Sein* of a society that takes for granted the rule of law.[74] Habitually informed intention, rarely thought about, is at the foundation of this social stability, jurisdictional territory. The agglomerational limits, on the other hand, are physically what they are, whether anyone recognizes them or not, running to where the streets and utility lines stop. I can only leave this real objective spirit by physically passing beyond these time-space-engaging real structures.[75]

---

74. Look what can happen when, for instance, the government of Iraq refuses to accept the boundaries of state entities drawn by colonial overlords at the end of another era. The United Nations was persuaded to enforce the legality of those boundaries, and when Iraq did not accept the will of that body as representative of the larger community's will-founding law, you know what occurred.

75. The Great Lakes Megalopolis stretched objectively from the western shores of Lake Michigan to Quebec City long before C. Doxiades called attention to the heretofore ignored

The juridically established town will likely outlast the physical endurance of most of its parts. Two hundred years from now there may remain nary a physical trace of today's Rome, but the juridical entity may well live on, embracing a fresh set of utility lines and buildings. Or it may become a ghost town, but still not be taken off the legal survey books—an interesting interrelationship of territorialities.

The Institutional Reality of the Municipality

The juridical reality is not just an idea, however; it lives, incarnated in a number of ways. Central is the ongoing functioning of that institution, the municipality, able to operate because of the role playing in its various subinstitutions by people enculturated into the different roles, all illumined by the *Sein* of this little municipal world, and who, because they bathe in its light, both implicitly and explicitly accept the laws, regulations, and other forms of guidance given by the members of the institutional hierarchy. I mesh my actions with the role playing and rules of the game of the traffic and taxing authorities. Often this suits my purposes; other times, even though I am furious at a parking ticket, I take the course of least resistance. I am not prepared to take on the municipality, trying to force some change in their intersubjectively governed behavior. Whether I realize it or not, when I conclude that you cannot beat City Hall, what I am really discovering is how elusive, all-pervasive, and impervious to any individual or group's voluntary efforts to change is the *Sein* of this little world. Just as the physical agglomeration gives a certain flesh to the town, and the juridical reality can be considered in some sense its soul, so the institutionalized habits provide a kind of nervous and muscular system.

But the soul of the community, in part structured by these municipal considerations, material and institutional (just as my soul is influenced by being the soul of *this* body of mine), is greater than that, surpassing the juridical as well. It resides also in a set of ongoing attitudes and relationships we can label the *ethnos* of the town, a kind of second nature. It gives Rome, along with the texture of its architecture and landscaping, its ultimate feel, its collective personality.

In changing frame of reference to describe certain features of Rome ethnically, I summon up a different kind of being from the rationally well defined juridical, institutional, and physical being of the town. Here we encounter matters that make hard-nosed philosophers nervous. But our lives are filled with these kinds of considerations. Before reacting with an "alas," it would be wise to grapple with the ontological significance of the more emotive aspects of intersubjective being.

---

objective reality. Forty million people lived in the megalopolis, with objective networks of transport, utility lines, and commercial exchanges, and did not even know it. See Doxiades and T. B. Douglas, *The New World of Urban Man* (Philadelphia: Philadelphia United Church Press, 1965).

Ethnic Reality

On the west end of town lies the small, poor neighborhood. Predominantly, this run-down area is occupied by people of old Canadian stock, descendants of early, modest English, Scottish, and Irish settlers, and a couple of Italian and German families. There are several single-parent families; there is evident too much alcoholism. East of the center lies the good neighborhood: several blocks of stately Victorian-era houses, which have gone through tough times, but now are appreciated again so that they are inhabited by the bank manager, the doctor, and several affluent commuters, mostly Anglicans. The remainder of the town is remarkable for neither poverty nor wealth, and is heterogeneous in racial, religious, and occupational mix.

From what experience am I rising abstractly when I declare that most citizens of the poor part are of old Canadian stock? In everyday life, we are usually in situations of casual description (being not motivated to a social-sciences survey). From spotty observations of physiognomic types, memories of bits of behavior, including the way premises are kept, we link up with our personal storehouses of relevant kinds of information, illumined by the same *Sein* as the present world in which I find little Rome, to arrive at a loose general judgment.

Given how erratic and piecemeal the process, it is startling that some such judgments can be as true as they are. If need be, I can verify that in fact almost no families of Pakistani, Chinese, or African origin are living in that neighborhood, although I may discover that some of what I took to be the lower-class WASP families are in fact Ukrainian, whose physiognomic difference I never noticed. They are basically as pale and thin, or wildly obese and pale as the rest—and their living patterns fit into the class surroundings very well.

Both institution and *ethnos* are *Mitsein*, but there is a difference in their way of being. The well-regulated, bureaucratic running of the municipality is clearly defined, a set of nonnatural, agency structures, tables of organization, and procedural customs, which are formally taught. The implicitly knit set of attitudes and behavioral habits and naturally transmitted physiognomic features that enter into formation of an *ethnos* may be enduring, but it constitutes a weave of factors harder to put your finger on. In this realm, energies are much more spontaneously and unpredictably reactive. Indeed, many of these features, though often found together, are disassociable in other situations.[76]

I, too, am caught up in some aspect of this ethnic life, circulating in a certain social class, with my own kind, much affected by their attitudes, their notions

---

76. Ethnicity exists at different levels: tribal, regional (Breton-French), national (French), international (consider the cross-border characteristics, racial type, and behavior patterns of the international European high aristocracy). And the connection between "race," in the loose sense of a set of physiognomic characteristics shared by a group, and language, custom, and religion that contribute to the sense of belonging ethnically varies across a spectrum from an extreme of pure race conception (as in Japan) to the very tolerant acceptance of racially different people one finds in a country good at assimilation, like France, where just about all types are tolerated, except North Africans (because of *pied noir* resentments, fear of Muslim intransigence, and pressure of numbers).

of what is done. My psychological identity gets partly molded and defined in this way, through the passing on of largely implicit traditions illumined by the same *Sein* that guides the mostly unspoken attitudes toward me. Much that is attractive and destructive operates on this implicit all-enveloping and often elusive level of *Sein*'s illumining of an entire milieu.

The tenuous nature of our knowledge of these ethnic social relationships and of the ground of their being (they are fluid situations, mixtures of consistencies and the erratic) should not be confused with the reality *(esse)* in which they are founded—the ground, in things, of what consistency and endurance really exist, founding whatever certitude our patchy knowledge of them may enjoy. For instance, certain physiognomic aspects of the Chinese family living at 110 North Railway Street persist as long as the individual members of the family exist. Certain patterns of paternalistic behavior of this East Indian father are thoroughly enculturated habits that govern departments of his life. Many of them he is not likely to change at all. The attitudes and habits that account for 234 West Secord Street being an eyesore are also unlikely to change, although conversion is in this case possible, but the East Indian family cannot turn white.

Habit as Ontological Ground of Social Patterns

Such an entropy-lowering pattern of habitual behavior is foundational to much of human being, individual and social. That is why Aristotle, in the *Nicomachean Ethics* and the *De Anima*, put so much emphasis on habits informing the various powers. Although impressed by the Heraclitean nature of modern physics, we should not lose sight of a basic Aristotelian insight about form: The condition for the possibility of habit's slowing entropy is its rootedness in substantial form; because man is by form the kind of thing he is, it is possible to regulate personal and social existence by forming a definite natural panoply of kinds of habit.

Take, for example, the mind-set of the city traffic engineer. He sees only the need to facilitate the throughput of motor vehicles, his favorite frame of reference being vehicular flow, illumined by the *Sein* of the world of traffic engineering into which MIT threw him. The opponents have tried to alter his world, arguing the beauty of the trees, the residential character of the street. He replies that it is an important provincial highway, so there is nothing to do. Although this mold is not as unalterable (within the relevant time frame) as the rootedness of the healthy maples or the serene beauty of the Victorian houses, the environmentalists are, in the occurrence, right to treat this decision as a given. So, intelligently, they invest their energies in going over back behind his world. They can see a certain logic in his position, from his point of view. In moments of generosity some mumble that it is just a conflict of values. Not only values, though, but habits informed by initial and continuing decision,

---

This is not the place to investigate what it is about the *Sein* of *ethnos* that makes some people in certain circumstances ready to sacrifice their lives for "my people." No one is willing to die for Rome, Ontario.

illumined by living in a different world. These worlds meet, to be sure, in the larger world of modern times and the planetary epoch of technology. These projects have been decided for various reasons, including what the different parties ultimately want out of life, which affects their choice of the worlds they want to live in.

When objective situations arise in which two kinds of *desiderata* cannot be accommodated, ends have to be sorted out, a choice will have to be made. (Such crises are graces and provide the occasion to step back behind our conflicting worlds, to probe more deeply into the ontological implications of the conflict. Inauthentic man refuses the offer and prefers to battle it out—may the strongest man win.)

Beware concluding that *Sein* is somehow deterministic and habit is simply a constraint on freedom: Effective freedom can only be exercised in a world; it demands consistency, but not just any kind of obdurate persistence. Freedom, to be genuine and authentic, must serve truth. Consistency of a course of action should harmonize with the objective thingly permanences (form) and social stabilities (including institutions) and steadiness in real processes by which we are affected. The fruits of good, free but intelligently consistent acts get deposited in the building up of good institutions and good habits, virtues. This is the *bilden* of sound culture. Unfortunately, bad fruits incarnate just as well, in oppressive institutions and vicious habits and degraded cultures. These are effective, too, in a bad way. When we consider the history of Being, we will see the importance to human existence of this form of incarnation,[77] and the need to step back behind *Sein* itself to reflect on the tensions between good and bad elements in the traditions.

As our imaginary car cruises one last time past the stately rhetoric-wrapped maples still lining Rome's Main Street, glance into the rearview mirror to see the various changes of frames of reference we have experienced on our tour. They were motivated by and revealed different modes of being of this municipality, stretching along a spectrum reaching from

1. the most spiritual being of this town (the juridical); through
2. the more incarnate habitual attitudes and physiognomic traits mixed together in the attitudes regarding ethnicity; to
3. that intermediate level of institutionalization, in which the conceptions governing the town—the operational fundamental projects—get incarnate in the enculturated role playing of many individuals in the bureaucratic hierarchy; down to
4. the most material reality, the physical structures and utility networks.

This has revealed the layers constituting the various modes of human existence, rooted in the form of human nature. All tend to lower entropy. All affect and

---

77. The question of good and bad traditions, and faithful and unfaithful institutions, is treated extensively in *T&A*, chaps. 4 and 5.

are affected by human culture. The history of being—*Sein* and *esse*—manifests a kind of body-soul, nature-culture interaction.

Layers or modes are related to territory, but note also the distinctive temporalities of each of these modes as time and space correlate. The juridical, for instance, depends for its existence on an inner recognition of human spirits, requiring a certain memory, and the sense of it has to be passed along; it will disappear when unwanted (for example, Rome is annexed, by provincial law, to Ouestmonde next door, whereas the physical existence of the sewer system is only slowly affected by lack of maintenance after the town is abandoned).

And note as well the difference between these intersubjective social realities and the distinctive rhythms of life of the individual. As an organism, I am conceived, gestate nine months, am traumatically projected into the world at birth, and follow a curve of organic rise and decline with its own given rhythms of lowering then rising entropy. Along its path come daily and seasonal cycles. And running through them, the cultural persistences: playing different roles and these with different intensities of application and interest, different lengths of tenure, and absorbing different portions of one's waking life. How all these relate to the maintaining of form, how they enter into the ultimate significance of man and of being itself, requires phenomenological-ontological exploration. We shall have to relate all these temporalities, cycles, rhythms, and intensities to the manifestations of permanence within them, because they are all important to the optimal exercise of our freedom in order to fulfill our greatest potential to be.

Throughout consideration of all this variety there runs a challenge of keeping proportion, of avoiding obsessive absorption in one activity or by one goal to the exclusion of others. Any ontology that neglects or downplays any of these modes will be seriously distorting reality. Language philosophy, indulging in an idealism of the ideational, tends to underplay the important role of objective spirit. A too thing-centered or overly empirical philosophy underemphasizes the role that social pressures, internalized as mind-set, play in our lives. The first neglects *esse*; the second, *Sein*. An existential philosophy, stressing freedom and time management, may neglect to examine unchanging principle. It may fail to recognize in the truths passed on by the traditions of revelation the challenge of thinking the possibility of infinite *esse* transcending *Sein* itself, though it offers indications of its reality within the historical horizons of man's interpretations, the *analogia entis,* the analogy of being.

Central to an adequate philosophical synthesis will be its ability to deal with this truth, becoming evident through our exploration: that reflection and creative projection are not of the same order of being as the organic. This points to claims embedded in the Occidental tradition of the possibility of a living contact with the Source of time, which somehow conquers death, a realm glimpsed within the *Seinsgeschichte,* but which cannot be com-prehended within it. Evidence of the transcendence of consciousness beyond the merely organic offers incentives for the philosopher to take claims of attaining a transmaterial Source seriously.

I have been mustering evidence to suggest that reflection and interpretation are not just manifestations of higher complexities as matter spontaneously moves against entropy toward ever-greater form. The dimension of spirituality and interior life introduces us to issues raised by the traditions of both philosophy and revelation, which themselves claim to mediate knowledge of man's status. We shall have to see how these claims from history articulate with our evolving self-reflection, appropriating the discoveries of modern science along the way.

7.

NATURAL HISTORY AND HISTORICAL AWARENESS MEET IN MAN

MAN, AN ORGANISM THAT THINKS ITS OWN HISTORY
Discovering the Objective Being of the Cosmos as Pre- and Post-Existing Us

What began as an exploration of how one thing, myself, can be interpreted according to various frames of reference came to a summit in the insight that this ability to change frames of reference is essential to the possibility of the coming to be of Being through human awareness.

Of course the *esse* of real cosmic entities existed from the first instance of the Big Bang, billions of years before evolution reached the point where man appears and interpretation and appreciation become possible, when a history of *Sein*, if only of a small, orally bound group, begins. But now that it has, and after perhaps seven hundred thousand years of human existence and two and a half millennia of critical philosophy, we have developed a science of the cosmos, and we are able to reason to the preexistence of the cosmos billions of years before the first human acts of recognition.

When human *Ek-sistenz* did at last appear on the scene, new kinds of being—symbols and cultural objects, and for the first time, the beginning of Being as world, hence meaning and history and culture—became possible.

Man, reaching out to his own birth and his own anticipated death, and to that even of his kind, finds thrust upon him the question of development: in the immortal words of Simone de Beauvoir, looking back over her life as existentialist guru, "La liberté, pour quoi faire?" Man is the only being challenged to build a better world for himself, to maximize possibility deliberately, and hence to ask, To what end?

I have promised to explore later the significance of the overall *Seinsgeschichte*, the coming to be of Being through man's creative deployment of interpretative horizons and his work that, through building up, transforms and spiritualizes his milieu and accumulates traditions of wisdom. At that point, we must probe into the future-opening dimension of *Ek-sistenz* that makes this all possible: potentiality, desire, need, projection, precisely as opening—the origin of the very possibility of transcending by going forward. But a too voluntaristic sense of *Bildung* can be treacherous. This newness must be shown to have its roots in the already-having-been-essential *(das Gewesene)* of the past, to be also therefore a *cultura*, a past that is effectively present as genetic and symbolic information, encoded in the genes, in neural paths, in language, and engraved in the cultural objects of objective spirit. These presence actively in the space we do not so much produce as, drawing on stored-up formed possibility, open up to allow the objects to present their thing. Out of all this comes new possibility: the challenge of what we can do, and the source of advances in culture and wisdom.

An Organism That Deliberately Searches Out New Forms of Information

The preprogrammed nature of organisms and their need to destroy lower life forms to absorb them seems to be increasingly (but never fully) transcended by higher organisms as one approaches the upper end of the evolutionary scale. All genetic coding appears to allow some adaptability. (Even cells have been shown able to adapt to new substances.) With consciousness, this ability to transcend the already coded takes a qualitative leap. What follows is evidence in defense of the claim that being *(esse)* of a kind radically different from all lower life forms emerges on the scene with human spirituality: There comes to be a process that, being aware of itself, can deliberately search out its information, and even form creatively new kinds of information. A certain kind of appreciative awareness allows deliberate adaptation, selection of what one will absorb, and care to preserve higher life forms from undue damage.

Indeed the scene itself in which subject plays off against object comes to be, in a critical sense, only with the advent of that phenomenon, deliberation, and so control becomes more creative and opens the way for the revolution of a relationship beyond control: appreciation, a new level of union, through love, the highest form of being. Deliberation, appreciation (with its essential relation to cultivation), and *Bildung* all belong together. The quality of the deliberation is dependent on the quality of the culture on which it is based, and on the grace of the new input of insight and breakthrough. The following, functions of one another, must be balanced in developing an adequate description of the way human finite freedom works: playing with the formation and use of information; dawning self-awareness, including awareness of subject-object op-position; increasingly aware shift of frames of reference; culture; appreciation; and deliberation. The spiraling progress of their interplay constitutes a growth in spirituality,[1] both in the development of the individual and in the

---

1. "Spirituality" is used in this book in two senses: first, as a relative term. Different kinds of entities show more spirituality and less materiality as one mounts the evolutionary chain. With increasing complexity goes greater centering, more interiority, and, thus, higher-quality operations, which we term "more 'spiritual.'" Second, at the highest level, in man, we speak of "a 'spiritual' life," meaning the higher capabilities of his reflective, self-aware, critical, creative, and interior life. The difference in spirituality in this second sense, in which we say Saint Francis of Assisi was a more spiritual man than Pope Julius II, comes from an exercise of the freedom available at this high point on the scale of spiritual operations, that is, the intensity and quality of their presencing in the interior life to the realities contemplated. It

progress of culture. Such progress is at the heart of what the human form and history are all about.

How Cognition Transcends Materiality While Remaining Dependent on It

The limits of material conditioning from below, and absolute dependence upon time-space conditions, are progressively rendered less confining. I am claiming here a new expression of a radical insight as ancient as Plato. The question is, though, whether the breakthrough to consciousness marks a mysterious new direction in the thrust of evolution, or whether it merely fulfills what we now understand evolution has been working toward all along. Does man, as a tradition of thinkers stretching from Plato to Teilhard de Chardin and Eric Voegelin has believed, achieve an overcoming of dependence on matter, "the divine calling the soul to immortality," in Voegelin's words?[2] The answer holds a key to what the universe is all about; it hinges on how one understands the gap separating properly human operations from those of the highest animals.

Consciousness, as Aristotle remarked, can become the thing known without destroying the object's in-itself reality.[3] The object can be taken up into the subject, as usable form *(in-formation)*, without ceasing to be itself. This degree of spirituality is already evident in the sensory perception of the higher animals. With human knowledge, new kinds of nonconsumptive being appear on the scene.

We should recall, in order to avoid the excesses of phenomenological idealism, that consciousness reaches out to the other without ever entirely producing its object. Finite consciousness retains significant elements of material dependence. In perception and in conceptual insight, consciousness lets be the object or the essential form of the object (or one of its accidental aspects) by providing a time-space horizon for it, focused in a frame of reference illumined by *Sein*, which permits the thing or abstracted form to evidence its in-itself reality and/or intelligibility and its own real place in cosmic time-space and its position in an intelligible context. Without the *Sein* deployed by the human knower's project of knowing, this reality and this ideality could not appear as they do, but each appears as what it is and how it is also because of its reality and/or intelligibility in itself. Even in the most creative acts of the imagination, the imaginer uses elements of remembered reality and, combining them in fresh ways, must respect both their inherent form and his own previous decisions that have begun to shape the object he is creating.

---

also comes in holiness, from the integrity and generosity with which the saints live out the implications of what has been given to them in the interior vision (provided it is, itself, great enough), which includes, centrally in the case of Christian spirituality, a call to love of other.

2. Voegelin, "The Beginning and the Beyond," in *What Is History? and Other Late Unpublished Writings*, vol. 28 of *The Collected Works*, ed. Thomas Hollweck and Paul Caringella (Baton Rouge: Louisiana State University Press, 1990), 224.

3. Aristotle, *De Anima* 424a17–27, 429a13–28.

The cognitive processes show, then, a kind of receptivity of structured energy, fruits of the deployment of energies on even a cosmic scale, as our receptors present to the mind facets of the universe from which we can build a model of the structure of the entire cosmos.[4] The knower's relation to the known, as reaching out, and his ability to appreciate it as it is, need not be at all ego-centered. The condition for the possibility of *benevolentia*—willing the good of the other, and thus uniting constructively with it (not destroying it), perhaps even enhancing it—begins with the formation of objective information. There is no genuine appreciation of the other without accurate knowledge of who and what he or it is, and there is no knowledge without humble receptivity. (Love begins in receptivity to the other.)

But I am never a mere supine receiver. As reflective consciousness, to some degree deliberately aware of what I am about, I can reach back into my past selectively to project explicitly the possibilities rooted in it that I choose to actualize, selecting that to which I choose to attend and elements of the contexts into which I wish to integrate it. Thus I can exercise a degree of command over previously accomplished storing and ordering of energy, over present reception of energies, and hence over time and history. The lower natures, however, are confined to instinctive mechanisms for the preservation of species, and hence rigid cognition.

Powerful as this freedom is, this interpretative capacity is not first and foremost poetic and dreamy but is like the best capacities of other organisms, at the service of survival and prosperity: It is devoted to knowing about the actual things and persons in interaction with which I must daily make my way in a particular world of intersubjective activity. The difference from higher animals is here: in what it is for humans to survive and prosper humanly. We are the creatures who need more than mere physical survival, indeed who need to love and to be loved[5] in order to prosper. Why ontologically this is so, and what it signifies about Being itself, we shall explore.

If this great human freedom is so spiritual compared to even the highest animals, then why put so much emphasis on its base in physical organism? For two reasons. First, if we neglect this fragile base, we get sick and die. And second: Because at our poetic best, we are constrained to work out from our base in objective time-space, which is always that of the individual human organic existent as it is. Part of that givenness is not only our ethnicity, our personal history and habits (including the damage from traumas and vice),

---

4. At the perceptual level, this occurs through the reception of actual formed (and thus in-formation-bearing) radiations. Where this results from a mere reflecting—for example, of light—the object expends no energy, but where it must take initiative of some kind to send (perhaps first encoding) information, there is some expenditure of the object.

5. The actual phrase Patrick Haggerty, then chairman of Texas Instruments, was reported to have used in addressing the security analysts in New York, was this: "Human beings require three things: to create, to love and to be loved. Any institution that provides the opportunity for this successfully will itself succeed." (Anecdote reported in private conversation by Mr. Bryan Smith, retired vice president of Texas Instruments.)

but our organicity (including psychosomatic pathology). We share with other organisms many of the aspects of all organic existence and so need to look after our bodily, as well as mental, health. We do not just love (and hate), we also breathe and eat,[6] the later interrupting our most contemplative activities, annoyingly, three times every day. We not only can dream of the cosmos and reach for God, we are obliged to keep up-to-date information about our crops—and that date with the therapist! There is much we can learn about ourselves and about being from study of this organismic substructure on which we are dependent, including the ecology.

We Need the World but Should Not Get Absorbed by It

Countless individuals and whole peoples have died through neglect of the limits of reality and indulgence in substantially false fantasies. Intellectuals seem especially prone to dreaming grand "gnostic" visions for reengineering mankind, leading to what Voegelin calls "pathological mischief," like Leninism, Stalinism and Nazism, and today's political correctness.

But the opposite temptation of absorption by the in-sistent solicitations of the practical objects of everyday and of species survival is itself a mortal danger for the spirit. Recall Pascal's sardonic comment on our being distracted from the highest contemplation by the buzzing of a fly. Recall the chart plotted in Part II: We must navigate the fragile bark of our lives, as individuals and as peoples, between the Charybdis of obsessive absorption and the looming Scylla, the rock of reality. Even at higher levels of contemplation, in the absence of any insects, there is a balance to be achieved, because there, too, a dependence manifests itself: the consciousness seems often to be *ravi* (again, Pascal's term) by the object, and we must never let loose of our re-sponsibility. A true lover gives man back to himself.

Ravissement is not per se a loss of freedom; it is not always the narcissistic projection of fantasies onto another, which happens in obsession. Just how healthy it is to be *ravi* depends on the fullness of being and hence of truth of the object that the soul allows to reveal itself. I can become absorbed in trolley cars or Beethoven's last quartets. To be *ravi* by an object incapable of satisfying our full need for growth is to risk falling into an obsessive complex. To the extent the object is not genuinely fulfilling, the obsessive potential in us tends to project onto it wishes (Freud: *Wünscherfüllung*), instead of reaching out lovingly to

---

6. I was tempted to add, "indeed our being able to love is conditioned on our being able to eat," but then one has to add a qualifier: Love transcends even normal bodily functions in special circumstances of intensity. The French mystic, Marthe Robin, bedridden from the age of nineteen, survived for twenty-three years on nothing but the Eucharistic wafer. This is as well attested as any historic fact. She died in 1982, and from her bedside has flowed one of the greatest influences of renewal in the history of the Church. The theist will explain this transcendence as grace reaching down to transform nature. The atheist will have to have recourse to the notion that hysteria can sustain a body for twenty-three years. You see, there are facts that are inconvenient for atheists as there are facts inconvenient for theists. In either event, facts must be respected.

envelop the person or thing with horizons bringing the wisdom necessary to allow the object to reveal its depths. Obsession builds idols—narcissistic constructions that hold deeper, more demanding reality at bay and do not give us back to ourselves. The same energy they drain from us goes out and returns unenhanced, de-formed by the lie, instead of becoming a source of enriching energy returning in re-sponse to the energy we expend opening onto them.

But to be *ravi* by that which can fulfill us completely, by wisdom itself, the Logos, has always been understood not as a loss of freedom but as joyful recognition of what first founded in us our freedom. To invest oneself in another who is source of genuine being is like "the bread [of charity] cast upon the waters [that] returns a hundredfold." Paradoxically, we reach out to it, directing our energy toward it, because we love it for its own sake; it is real, and a source of free creative ordered energy, and so it responds, sending us back new being, as a *comm-unio* is created or enhanced.

Obsession has no lasting fruit because it feeds on itself; what we project onto the object is not loving interpretative possibility destined to unlock its potential but a *pseudos*, part of our own substance designed to exploit some aspect of the object for our immediate gratification. Thus manipulated, the object is diminished, allowed to reveal minimally its own depths, if indeed it has any. If not, it is like the products compulsively consumed by the person who seeks gratification through pathological gobbling of food. This may satisfy momentarily a material or limited ego impulse, but never the subject's deepest need, never challenging him to discover the self that is called out by the profound object, e-ducated (hence cultivated), all of which demands something more creative than the kind of information that can be handled in fixed categories.

The most dangerous obsession is passionate love for another human being. Passionate love, which seeks narrow self-fulfillment and wants control so this can be guaranteed, is absorbed not in the true being of the significant Other but in projection around a selected core of that being. Moreover, the Other always brings surprise and delight, blinding one for a long time to the fact that, without true love, without genuine, unlimited commitment of true friendship, this play will come to an impasse, an inevitable collision of egos. True love tends not to be heated by passion, for the suffering (that is what the word means) is nurtured by some unfulfilledness in the passionate one. A trustworthy deep emotion is calmer, never hysterical, as passion always is. Mature love brings peace, not heat.

The polar contrast with the unfulfilledness of passionate love is the experience of being taken up by the living Source of all reality. The true lover—that God who is love—may be "a jealous God," wanting my will to be one with his, as the Old Testament says, but he, who alone knows me as I cannot know myself, gives me back to myself whole and entire, to my true self, as it is in its depths and very roots, which only he can e-ducate totally.

Ravissement and obsession are here contrasted ontologically, not just psychologically. I am describing two ways in which psychic energy can be deployed, the one a self-serving projection; the other, loving interpretation in which my projected opening of a time-space in which the other can appear is caringly attuned to what the other has to reveal, in humble, devoted receptivity. The fruit of past experience is vital: A baby can love its parent spontaneously and disarmingly, but it cannot bring the mature understanding that allows true adult interaction.[7]

It is harder to fantasize about a person in his presence than in his absence, when the imagination has free rein to pick and choose the features one desires to emphasize. The presencing of the object is usually, except in cases of pathology, a guide to the imagination. When we are building schemes out of sweeping abstract concepts, the danger of sailing far from reality is great. Silent Charybdis waits in the mists.

But this weakness of getting lost in dreams is the obverse of a strength. The human organism is not the source of its own energy, but a great recycler of solar radiations and of past codifications: It is thus incapable of generating entirely, interiorily, its own information.[8] But because it can creatively reshape the sense of that past, it can manage information, under the guidance of what it projects. Because of its ability to put those limits in question and then to conduct research, looking for precisely targeted information (while remaining open to surprise and always willing to dream a bit, too), it can shape further its destiny.

Human Freedom as Spiritual Activity

Decentering, objectivizing, symbolizing, researching, *theorein*, appreciating, and managing[9] are all related deployments of psychic energy that seek to understand better how it stands with things. Historically man has named this ability to soar and embrace all existence, and the ability to give over to the other while not ceasing to be oneself, and possibly even transcendence beyond the disintegration of organism, "spirit."[10]

---

7. The degree of experience and culture does not, however, determine the genuineness of the resulting relationship. A quite old, cultured gentleman can fantasize about a young woman, for whom he has no real love, and a baby cannot play imagination games with its mother.

8. Contrast our dependence with God's total freedom: God did not need to create the world to know himself. The creation does not diminish his *autonomia* but affirms it. For it is a purely gratuitous display of energy, a divine joy that he then shares with his creatures, for their own sakes. Because he loves his creation, it is an expression of the perfect love between the divine persons interior to the infinite life of God.

9. We cannot "manage" either God or a lover. The temptation to magical control is the wish to manage what cannot be managed, as in the technical wizardry of personnel management (which, Bruce Stewart says, "does not work, save only as a cybernetic *Wünscherfüllung*"). It is part myth, part charlatan evil, to the extent that manipulation can work on people. It is a reflection of the exercise of power rather than of appreciation. In an authentic cooperative working together, people can consent freely to a managed ordering that need not be either inauthentic or ingenuine. Like all true love, however, that is rare.

10. This inclination, in several traditions and many languages, to use as symbol of transcendence a material reality, "breath," or "subtle wind" *(pneuma, spiritus)*, itself eloquently bespeaks our material limits.

All these indications of spirit are, then, evidence that the organic frame of reference is too narrow for interpreting adequately all the givens of human existence. Perhaps it may be possible to cast adequately in the organic mode all that man can achieve at the highest levels of information processing, but that seems doubtful to me. Starting with the recent consideration that information is somehow beyond mere power understood as brute transformation of energy, that form itself is a lowering of entropy through the achievement of some new kind of permanence, a higher way of ordering power, and going on to the discovery that the ability to know and to create form is the highest power, we see that these are all points beyond the organistic model.

As we investigate this question of the material-spiritual spectrum, recall my earlier hesitations about the term "psychic energy." In physics, potential energy stands for a given ability to do work, and kinetic energy is that potentiality being actualized as any transformation takes place. Now I acknowledge that in the human organism, the condition for the possibility of deploying psychic energy is the availability of a conditioning physical energy. Still, the mind-over-matter phenomenon is familiar to us all. One can be dead tired, even very sick, and yet a spiritual determination energizes the person to do the impossible. He then mobilizes himself, managing to find the physical energy somehow.[11]

How can we bring better into view spiritual frames of reference in ways more adequate than the categories of present physics and information theory allow? What are their characteristic, distinctive dynamics, their ultimate *telos*? Is it advisable to speak in terms of a more spiritual form of energy at work in the higher animals and, supremely, in man? How would this relate to the divine energy, both that at the source of the whole cosmos, and that of any divine action on souls, in the form of grace?

There is a human phenomenon ready to hand, for introducing such a wider exploration. The material and the spiritual meet in that central human achievement, the summit of all information-processing activities in nature, symbolization.

SPIRITUALITY AND SYMBOLIZATION

Man's ability to symbolize is both an evidence for and a tool of that spiritual power he possesses to achieve a deliberate space-time conquering, storing, and steering of energy. Using a part of material reality to move beyond both the cosmic time-space of the particular object and beyond the particular subjective time-space point of his own present existence, he enters into a new time-space of meaning, illumined by *Sein*, and absent at all lower levels of being. One can enter this realm of signification—the world of *Sein*—either by adopting the

---

11. The mind may trigger, through a brain mechanism, a discharge of adrenaline, which has quick effects throughout the cardiovascular system, so that a burst of oxygen reaches to the muscles. But the gritty determination that is at the base of a renewed effort, while capable of being depressed by fatigue, can also overcome fatigue.

already constructed symbolization of an existing language (and with it, the *Sein* that particular language hands down, making accessible a culture [*Bildung*]), or (rarely) by beginning to constitute a new symbolization in response to the gift of *Sein* accompanying a new soliciting presence of an object giving of itself.

When we forge symbols, the formed sound or the engraved or inscribed lines endowed with meaning are a melding of physical and psychic energies, which mysteriously trans-forms the sound or line into a sign, as illumined by *Sein*, deployed only through the human soul *(Da-sein)*, as the sign takes its place in a context or world of meaning.

Because the signified things and relationships are all experientially encountered in larger settings and structures, such symbolic representation can be built up for any manner of large, complex system that we may come to know, bit by bit, and to model. This ability to express whatever the mind is able to distinguish involves re-sponse.[12] Preserving the information requires a deployment of the same kind of psychic energy we find in love, as we shall see.[13] This information can then be used to deal with those energies, and it can be shared with others, permitting action in concert, which further lowers entropy by building larger systems.

The moment is lifted from the flow of psychic time, from *Sein*, and held above it, for instance, by being inserted through work into a more enduring medium, recorded so long as, for example, a granite monument lasts. This transmits, to someone recovering the monument from the sand centuries later, potential information, permitting insight into the flow of energy through events long ago, offering perspective on how the present came to be, and hence into the sense of the flow of present processes.

DEGREES OF SPIRITUALIZATION

As one ascends the scale of entities and activities from more material to more spiritual, an increasing command over space and time is manifest, which allows longer-range and wider-horizon storage and as well greater imaginative manipulation (creation) of information, central to freedom. This all makes possible living more—greater perfection. (The *metron* of this "more" remains to be clarified, as does the sense in which it, too, shows materiality.) But at the same time, the ability to project also increases the possibility of getting lost in

---

12. *Spondeo* (commitment). The French term, *engagement*, is more reflective of the actual process.

13. Louis de Broglie observed: "If we wish to give philosophic expression to the profound connection between thought and action in all fields of human endeavor, particularly in science, we shall undoubtedly have to seek sources in the unfathomable depths of the human soul. Perhaps philosophers might call it 'love' in a very general sense—that force which directs all our actions, which is the source of all our delights and all our pursuits. Indissolubly linked with thought and action, love is their common bond. The engineers of the future have an essential part to play in cementing this bond" ("The Role of the Engineer in the New Age of Science," in *New Perspectives in Physics* [New York: Basic Books, 1961], 213).

the dreamworlds created by the imagination.[14] The sense of what it is to get lost will also require more exploring.

In a Teilhardian fashion, starting with the least aware building block, the atom, and following from there to the level of complexity that supports the life of the spirit in symbolization, let us observe what happens at each level, on the lookout for how increasing levels of power are organized, how a richer permanence (although not always greater endurance—these are not the same thing) is achieved, seeking glimpses of the dynamics of being as it has advanced up the evolutionary scale. What is it all for, this cosmic becoming, this striving for a more? We need to understand the *metron* of that more.

Our point of view, for now, will be as external observers of behavior, illumined by the contemporary science-informed *Sein*. But we are observers who, knowing from within their own experience the spiritual life of symbolization, are aware of what to look for.

The Materiality of the Atom

A free-standing atom[15] commands only a minuscule space;[16] and though, seconds following the initial explosion, a given hydrogen atom may have become disengaged from the primordial plasma, and may persist uncombined in any molecule until the end of the cosmos, its long endurance is mute and without memory.[17] Since the first seconds of the Big Bang, the coming to be and the destruction of atoms are relatively rare events in the cosmos (radioactivity excepted), whereas their combination into molecules and the breakdown thereof happens continually.

Enjoying, then, no degree whatever of memory or of anticipation, the individual atom commands no more than this instant of existence through which it is passing now,[18] and its form as hydrogen atom or gold atom, and so on,

---

14. No animal species has undertaken the systematic destruction of a subspecies of its own kind because of ideological daydreams.

15. Much that can be said about atoms can be applied to the current smallest unit, the quark. The reader should adjust his horizon of interpretation to reflect "atom" in its sense of smallest indivisible unit and in its sense of that entity bound by the strong and weak nuclear, and the electromagnetic forces, that is elemental.

16. One can barely call it "a space," so complex, almost to the point of being erratic, is the motion of its orbit-changing electrons, yet the nucleus possesses mass, and in larger entities, at least, mass cannot be separated from occupying space.

17. Although experiments now seek to determine whether protons have a finite lifetime. There exists among atoms something of an exception: Because the rate of disintegration (radioactivity) of the heaviest atoms is known, we can infer something of a minimal history in their case. But can we assume that all the heavier atoms are newer than the light ones? Many of the heaviest "cooked in the heart of stars" surely are, and perhaps so are all heavier than hydrogen and helium. Not enough is known about the initial formation of atoms to permit great certitude.

18. In one sense, as Teilhard de Chardin points out, in virtue of its given structure it knows to which other atoms it can bind. Teilhard's extension downward of the notion of knowledge here is as deliberate as it is questionable. It has to do with action guided by a given form, not, as in the case of DNA directing elaborate cell functions, of in-formation.

determines rigidly the possibilities of its joining with other atoms. Because the atom does not alter its essential form,[19] the lighter atom has no internal history, and though the events of its combinations with other atoms are theoretically intelligible, we cannot follow the course of one atom. Because the atom itself has no awareness of any of this, it cannot be, in any sense, either selfish or devoted, and so its couplings, essential for all higher forms of material being, are simply dumb.

Paradoxically, materiality here at its extreme degree does not entail any of the qualities common sense associates with it: impenetrability, solidity, or easy visibility by human eye. It involves, rather, a minimal ability to extend itself, persistence, and yet the atom does have that enduring structure provided by form that one expects of something material, as of all being, even the most spiritual. Another paradox: this mute, unchanging, almost spaceless building block of the cosmos is conceived in contemporary physics in terms of mass, that is, as a constant relation of charges, a balance of forces, and hence a potential energy, if the atom is trans-formed, and the energy released. (Changes of form always absorb or release energy.) The atom has a weight. The most permanent entity in a dynamic cosmos has a nucleus that can be blasted apart, releasing the energy that binds particles and sending radiation capable of introducing a disturbance that ripples to the confines of the universe. Mark a point for our belief in the unity of being: The smallest mass has cosmic implications.

These considerations drawn from present physical theory can provide metaphors for understanding being at levels of greater complexity, even at the very high level of social interaction. The thread that has emerged as a kind of analogue model—the notion of in-form-ation—finds in the atom a foundation: Form here is at its simplest, save only for the even more elemental, and more mysterious, particles and waves. The human mind fairly easily grasps the idea of an atom as an equilibrium of charges—a formed energy providing mass—in a given disposition that assures the greatest permanence that is representable as a general concept, an in-form-ation. It contributes to a larger form-ation, the molecule, its functions being altered according to objective context, by the nature of the other atoms. At the base of all information lies the reality of objective forms given in the cosmos by its very nature, which variety of forms, of structures achieved in nature and enjoying varying kinds of permanence, is a foundation for all the information man can compile and recombine.

THE LIMITED SPIRITUALITY OF A CELL

If space allowed, I would reflect here on molecular structure, moving from the simplest inorganic compounds, through crystals, to basic organic compounds—proteins—and then on up to prelife forms, especially those fascinating viruses. But we have to content ourselves with a contrast between simple life forms and that greatest simplicity, the single atom.

---

19. Once created, this little self-contained structure of energy is like a minuscule unmoved mover. But it is not God: It can be changed from without, by bombardment with particles.

In comparison with even the heaviest naturally occurring atom, the radioactive isotope of uranium, ^{238}U, the simplest cell commands an immense space, one occupied by the many millions of molecules coordinated by the mysterious organizing force we have been calling its form.[20] A cell is many billions of times heavier than a carbon atom. Whereas atoms can only attach to one another via the most probable shape giving the least strain as regards their electrical balance, cells actively discriminate among surrounding matter the forms they can use, absorbing them, breaking down those lower forms in ways dictated by their genetically encoded instructions, selecting what they need, discharging the rest, and then building and renewing themselves out of this atomic and molecular stuff. Since Margulis,[21] it has been recognized that cells host what were independent microorganisms contributing their own information as DNA, needed for the life of the cell.

Atoms are extremely difficult to smash, while cells, despite the organism's immune systems, are used up by predators. But some kinds of cells can recognize predators and fight them off by various devices. The information governing the ability to interpret the relevant data and then to act is likewise encoded in the cell. Because of that, the cell wins permanence both by continually reconstructing itself and by actively defending the integrity of its structured space, primitive precursors, at the lowest level of life, of those qualities we celebrate in human beings, self-development and appreciation, the ability to recognize another for what he is. In the cell, the purely defensive is not truly appreciative and lacks all altruism.[22]

The differentiated, specialized parts of the cell are coordinated by the heart of the cell, the information encoded in the nucleus.[23] Cells are even able to split, producing a progeny, with which they share identical genetic information,[24] to carry on the work for which they were structured. They will multiply themselves, rapidly spreading, occupying all available space, and absorbing all available nutrients unless forcibly contained by other organisms. In a sense, such a cell never dies out completely (unless another cell destroys it); it simply replicates and replicates, so a part always goes on living so long as the organism as a whole lives, and perhaps surviving the host organism, although it may pass through occasional mutations, the whole history being in theory traceable from the ultimate result.

Despite this permanence and rapaciousness, the question of personal identity of the individual cell does not arise. To be sure, this improbable event of

---

20. Justifiably we could here say "its soul," the term employed by Aristotle for that class of forms of living things.
21. Lynn Margulis, *Symbiosis in Cell Evolution* (San Francisco: Freeman, 1981). Eukaryotic cells contain microorganisms that contribute vitally needed DNA.
22. The microorganisms contributing DNA to eukaryotic cells show no signs of doing this altruistically either.
23. Increased specialization implies increased information flow. (At the level of human social structure, we recognize specialization—the division of labor—as a progress in being.)
24. There is redundancy in this information, probably allowing for some mutation in some progeny, the mechanism by which life evolves.

endurance through replication, moving against entropy,[25] establishes a genetic history, a lineage of cells, for which there is nothing comparable on the level of the individual atom. The cell's success establishes a minimal degree of futurity, of need, primitive *Ek-sistenz*, a structured reaching out, as the cell seeks what it must obtain (at all costs to the innocent other it unappreciatively uses) to fulfill the demands coded into its nature. But all this individual cohesion and permanence and self-aggrandizement and self-protection does not add up to the least degree of personality. For all its complexity and its distinctiveness of kind, this particular cell is so similar to another of the same kind as to be perfectly replaceable and without significant unusual events leaving traces, except when it mutates—but then it is no longer itself!

The Superiority of the Rabbit

Now move up the ladder of being and consider the spiritual superiority of Brer Rabbit to the single cell, however complex and sophisticated the cell may be. You may never have thought of that rabbit as spiritual, but its conquest of time and space is so much greater than that of lower life forms; its flexibility; and even its personality, though still limited compared to the highest animals, is already interesting. The cell, however, has no personality and exhibits, by comparison, rigid behavior. To achieve this high level of activity, the rabbit has to be made up of billions of cells, of hundreds of different kinds, flawlessly coordinated by its sophisticated soul to produce a beast about 10^9 larger than the cell. This organism not only occupies in itself a large space, it is able to run about over a considerable territory within which it enjoys much autonomy. (A cell circulating in the bloodstream cannot go far, and a preprogrammed sensor allows it to "recognize" only the organ or tissue to which it is meant to contribute.)

The rabbit's elaborate sensory system allows it to interpret a few molecules floating into its nose as data coming from an as yet distant enemy, or to interpret a few sound waves as information about an impending danger. A not very flexible or creative imagination and memory are yet enough for the rabbit to learn a bit from experience[26]—it stores up information.[27] Along with this enhanced information gathering and processing goes superior means

---

25. See, for instance, the recent work by the English biologist James Lovelock, *The Ages of Gaia: A Biography of the Living Earth* (New York: Norton, 1988). Lovelock points out, as Teilhard had, the universal tendency for things to be arranged in the least intricate, most probable way, but life goes against this, creating complexity where there was none.

26. So, too, perhaps can the cell, in a very limited way. Some research is pointing in this direction.

27. The rabbit's attention span is notorious. When fleeing an enemy, after a short while it forgets why it is running and just stops. But they do learn a little from experience. My brother's favorite rabbit, Shoo, has learned where the vegetable garden lies, and every day, about the same hour, projects himself in that direction for his herbal smorgasbord. He has also learned, from dire experience, to stay away from the cat—and vice versa. On the other hand, Shoo's experience cannot overcome his "hard wiring" when it comes to being *méfiant*: After five years of tender loving care, he is still terrified of his owner.

of locomotion: Look at those legs fly! (Transportation and communication develop together.)

Does the rabbit live in a world? Does a kind of rabbit-*Sein* come to be through him? At the risk of committing *lèse-majesté*, and in anticipation of the fuller discussion to come, I suggest yes. From external observation, I conclude that, the rabbit's range of freedom is so limited, compared even to higher animals, and the future it can open extending out not much beyond the meal in the herb garden, its world is illumined by a *Sein* with an extremely poor history. But if the rabbit can learn a few things and put them into practice, as they affect its future projection, then within its restricted little world, a harmony of bunny social behavior *(Mitsein)* with a highly selective milieu can be observed unfolding. Because the rabbit cannot symbolize (although it can express a few emotions), it cannot pass on what it has learned, and so no culture is being built up. Cats, however, can be observed teaching their young certain tricks of the trade, not through symbol, but by imitation. Again, there is apparently no great progress from generation to generation.

The Spirituality of Man

Even the highest animals innovate little compared to man, and appreciate mostly negatively. (I say "mostly" to leave a space for the "love" a female goose can have for her goslings and dogs for their masters.) Innovation and appreciation as a sign of spiritual superiority in man are at a point we can only describe as a radical difference in kind of spirituality, compared to all other life forms.

At the bottom of the quality scale of innovation would be trial and error, stumbling onto solutions through mutation, probably a key mechanism in evolutionary adaptation. Higher animals possess more innovative ability than this stumbling accident, although even the ingenuity of chimpanzees is limited compared to man. Man's ability not just to anticipate but to forge according to his will a new kind of future, deliberately and knowingly mutating himself within certain material limits, is linked with his ability to possess the past in a unique way—discriminatingly, critically—which entails the fundamental capability of appreciating.[28] This allows him to be present in the present in a remarkably far-reaching and deep manner, to enjoy a very large present. The new kinds of information and information processing this permits are part of a new kind of activity: being responsible.[29] Appreciation is an essential part of such maturity.

---

28. There is a detachment from self in appreciation that makes of it the highest manifestation of man's spirituality. Discrimination marks the lowest level of distinguishing; "critically" adds some note of awareness as to criteria for decision; appreciation suggests the possession of a freedom of point of view that allows one to grasp and treasure the other as other, not just as a function of self-centered criteria.

29. If we are truly responsible, why do so many of my students resist this notion of superiority? "We are not superior to the animals, just different," writes a young woman who, in the same comment, attacks the notion that anybody, especially the Church, should "impose laws." Who has any business telling her what might constitute self-destructive behavior on

One can build a biological case for the need to accept responsibility—the ability to respond to what the situation demands. Failure to face up to the situation is a sign of decadence in the organism, of increasing entropy, of impending death of the individual and perhaps of the race. In man such facing up is a free act—a large space *(die Freie)* is made available to it by its nature, within which it can make determinations, so it is not, at its best, merely dumbly reactive, but appreciative: a unique ability to decenter from himself, assume the perspective of the other, thereby appreciating him, not just as prey, but as friend. That is a tremendous force, even for survival,[30] as nothing succeeds so much as loving cooperation. The *Sein* projected by *Dasein* (the human *Eksistent*) can in this way be a *Mitsein*. When such an adequate human response is refused, as it is implicitly with every selfish act, then inevitably follows a distortion in one's willingness to see the whole scene (the world is not in fact centered just on me), which can grow pathological. The self-lie distorts our hold on ourselves and on reality. To the inevitable limits of the *Da* of *Dasein*, which restrict the illumining of *Sein* and account for its always also being an obscuring, comes the distortion of perversity. Man is the only entity in creation capable of such a perversion of his most precious capabilities, a sign of their inherent flexibility and freedom,[31] the devastating negative side of his great capability to build the world. The most constructive organism is also the most destructive. Such perversity is in a funny way a counter-evolutionary, entropy-increasing capability. Through such distortion man seems at once less powerful and more powerful than he is.[32]

Man reaches out, thereby allowing *Sein* to illumine a vast present landscape, by building into things cultural forms that will facilitate a future reading of what has been learned or achieved, and by teaching people, acculturating them,

---

her part? She says, "I alone have the right to determine what may be destructive or not for me, and that in terms of what I want." So much for the social dimension of man's wise mutation. This rather primitive level of libertinage is certainly one kind of expression of the life force surging through human beings. Its primitivity in the face of the more sophisticatedly evolved situation of man holds the key to an unhealthy rejection of the obvious. It shows, suggested my nineteen-year-old daughter (who, not incidentally, works at a group home for difficult teenage boys), "a fear of assuming responsibility." It is also an arrogance masquerading as humility. If the very possibility of knowing any superiority is skeptically denied, then with one blow the objector has excluded the possibility that anything or anyone might in any way be superior to her, leaving her absolutely autonomous.

30. It is a strength of the Israelis, who are caught in a survival situation, to have Arab experts capable of understanding the situation from the Palestinian viewpoint.

31. Some higher animals are cunning and capable of deception, but these are to some quite practical end other than self-deception.

32. The simpler the living thing, the less "give" and receptivity it has, and so it has a limited capacity to be imprinted by external forms. Among humans, the hugely complexed individual lacks this receptivity in important sectors of his spiritual life, and so remains blocked, impervious to reality's efforts to impinge on him. Paradoxically we say of such a person that "he is complicated; he lacks simplicity." In fact, he is impoverished as a result of his complexes and, to that extent, lives at a lower level of evolution. For examples of just how far such ideological complexes can go in refusing the obvious, see the classic by Leon Festinger, Henry Riecken, and Stanley Schachter, *When Prophecy Fails: A Social and Psychological Study of a Modern Group That Predicted the Destruction of the World* (New York: Harper Torchbook, 1964).

for instance, into institutional forms that will motivate them to cooperate in his enterprises, through joint deployment of appropriate *Mitsein*, without which this little cultural world over which he is ruling (for example, this bank) could not be.

THE SPIRITUALITY OF HUMAN OPERATIONS: INTERIOR LIFE

Every kind of central nervous system, in amalgamating the signals received from the various sensors, structures a perceptual scene, reflective (to some degree) of the organized energies of the things at work in the setting in which the perceptions take place. But when man reflectively observes himself observing, he can glimpse the whole perceptual system shifting focus and emphasis, thus actively seeking (the eyes, it is said, shift five or six times a second), and filtering differently, as we center our attention, in response to some need or interest, now on one thing or one aspect of the scene, now another. Sometimes we will go to voluntaristic extremes in this filtering: "Stop all the noise; I am trying to concentrate," says the man reading a difficult text.[33]

The human's ability to generalize concepts manifests a considerable freedom vis-à-vis the states in which the data are being received (while still allowing attention to the truth of what the data actually offer). The freedom this gives with regard to the imposed time and space of the present experiential moment seems, upon reflection, a strange kind of power for a material organism to possess. (By "imposed time and space," I mean simply here I am, ineluctably, at 1432 hours, on January 9, 1996, in this narrow windowless room in a basement in North Toronto, seeing and feeling what I can, period—a physical, cosmic fact.) Already the sensory and information-processing abilities of the higher animals are impressive in the power they grant the creature to go beyond the moment of his present operations, offering him a range of willful possibilities. This is useful for the cougar searching the forest for scarce prey. But what purpose of survival is served by our ability to reach out in imagination to the ends of the cosmos, to conceive apocalyptically the end of the world, and even to think of a transcendent Source beyond time and space and unconditioned by them, and by our ease in encompassing time itself as a concept?

This ontological capability reveals an interior life not possessed by any other creature: the grasp by what Plato named *psyche* of its own meaningful life. This seems somehow to leave behind the psyche's instrumental dependence on the material organism, since it can reflect critically on its own instruments and grasp not just itself, but Being, rising to the unique conceptualization of the *analogia entis*. Because this transcends the limits of mere physical survival, what is it all for? "La libérté, pour quoi faire?" (Simone de Beauvoir).

---

33. Gerald G. May, M.D., *Will and Spirit* (San Francisco: Harper, 1982), 219, provides an analysis of kinds of awareness, with a matrix relating "alertness" (dulled-alert) and "openness" (open-restricted), and both either "relaxed" or "tense," which illustrates very well the various ways of being aware.

I was told by a physician friend how, when he is attacked by "cerebral deficiency causing migraines" he takes consolation in knowing that "this will pass in a day or two and I shall regain normal functioning." We agreed that it is astonishing how "the real, central me," as he put it, can stand in some sense outside the whole process and watch it, "as though it were happening to somebody else." This does not reduce the pain, but puts it in a context that makes it more manageable. I told him about the beautiful death of Eric Voegelin. His wife and dearest friend for fifty years, Lissi, is reported to have commented, "Eric, you are dying, and, you rascal, you are lying there watching the whole process with great interest, aren't you?" Voegelin smiled and nodded approvingly. That was the great man's last gesture.[34]

Spirituality and interior life are not the same thing. Although spirituality exists in degrees, only at the higher levels of complexification does it make sense to speak of much interiority; only at the highest, of pursuing an interior life. I reserve that term for methodic development of self-awareness. Interior life arises at the moment when prophets and psalmists and philosophers begin to pursue the truth that is to be found in the depths of the soul. Even the achievement of analysis and reflection by early man did not entail self-aware discovery of psyche. Eons, perhaps hundreds of thousands of years, before the discovery of *philosophia* by the fifth-century Greeks, man engaged in symbolizing; and writing existed for a millennium before the invention of psyche, permitting a new time-space, a new kind of organization of information, the thought of being as such, which Plato named *philosophia*, an erotic seeking after the *sophon*, that totality of what is. This breakthrough to the thinking of *Sein* is not the beginning of *Sein*, as Heidegger misleadingly suggests. *Sein* began with the first interpretative act hundreds of thousands of years before in the dark of prehistory. Personal *Seinsgeschichte* and oral and tribal *Volksseinsgeschichte* (a people's Being-history) antedate the birth of history at Sinai, the writing of history and the thought of being as such. But the breakthrough to the thought of being as such is that development of *Sein* that also entails the will's discovery of itself. The breakthrough to the thought of *Sein*, to psyche, and to the will's awareness of itself is one e-vent.

We live, to an extent hard to exaggerate, in our symbols and artifacts, in which we build up the culture that becomes the basis of our wisdom. We live especially intimately in our language, but also in our intelligently formed houses and gardens, roadways, and so on, all of which express things about what we consider important and how we feel, even deep inside. But it is in words that we "gather together" *(legein)* what we have been able to understand.[35] *Anthropos*, defined Aristotle, is "the animal who possesses the Logos," the word.

---

34. Recounted to me by Dr. Paul Caringella, Voegelin's last assistant and his close friend.
35. Heidegger went so far as to declare, "Die Sprache ist das Haus des Seins" (Language is the house of Being). An overstatement if we take *die Sprache* as the sum total of *das Haus*: the institutions, the cultural objects, our habits constitute as well at least "rooms" in "Being's house."

Yet our freedom is very much bound up with what we learn through these words, what they permit us to express, even about our deepest interior, and how we act as a result of what they relate and help us work out. What can be more important to us than "I love you" or the tragic pronouncement "Get out of my life." In the Christian revelation, Jesus is presented as the Word of God incarnate. Although wordless prayer may constitute the mystic's highest achievement, we must first express in words and liturgical gesture what we mean in our relations with God before we can ever hope to arrive at such rich silence of adoration.

We get so caught up in the life of the symbols, we often forget to seek the reality to which they are supposed to give us access. This is the intellectual's plague, the narcissism generated by a gifted one's poetic play with symbols inviting gnostic dreaming, holding the key to mankind's beneficent reconstruction. When the intellectuals arm political fanatics with attractive symbolized dreams, the latter use them to march the masses down the path their power madness dictates.

Such dreams shatter—rather rapidly, as it turns out—against the Scylla of reality. Plato's philosophy endures, despite the ridiculous failure of his own Syracusan political adventures, because the admittedly captivating symbols expressing it refer to something beyond themselves, and with a considerable charge of genuineness. That vision is available no other way than in the poetic genius invoking an interweaving of dimensions of being attained as well nowhere else. The risk remains, as with all poetry enjoyed as pure music, that we become so enchanted with the vision, we forget to ask to what extent what these symbols proclaim is true. (It is a sin against Plato to reduce his work to literature.)

We can revel so much in the beauty of poetic expressions that their intentional transcendence toward the objects of which they speak becomes secondary. The enchantment of Plato's language, on the other hand, is clearly subordinated, following his philosophical intentions, to evocation of the things, actions, settings, feelings, and attitudes, the ontological relationships that make up the splendid light—the *Sein*—of his inexhaustible vision. It is impossible to separate the poetic effectiveness of the language from the full intended result, for it is a way of moving the reader emotively to deploy energies—of imaged experience, of conceptual insight, or even of action—in a certain way, producing in him the desired object. We are sufficiently programmed, both by nature and by virtue of sharing the same culture, hence the *Sein* of the same tradition, for certain symbols to trigger a roughly calculable response (the poet's art).

To illustrate how thoroughly we live within our symbolic systems, and something of how they work in their spirituality, I explore first, not a philosophical vision, but a more mundane materialistic (or so it seems) reality, touching the lives of everyone in advanced societies. In this example from an economic sphere of everyday life, all find themselves at home, and no one's complexes will cause him to deny the evidence of spirituality to be found in this materialistic marketplace.

An Example of Living in Our Symbols: The Monetary System

In Part II,[36] we examined the symbolic—the spiritual—nature of a monetary system. Here I recall how real symbols are to us, to show how the spiritual life of everyday human consciousness, lived in the midst of vast complexes of symbols, enjoying sometimes rather remote relationships with objective entities, yet enabling us to command resources over vast stretches of time and space, is something so familiar we hardly take notice of it. We take no note of the whole intelligible world's being illumined by the *Sein* that permits it to function as an intersubjective reality.

A first reaction, when the philosopher points out to commonsense man the imaginary nature of money, is defensive—as though one wanted to rob him of value as surely as inflation does.[37] He does not recognize that this abstract system of monetary value is rooted in the will.

The computer entries crediting the Calgary oil magnate's account with several millions in T-bills and ownership of many assets permit him to convince a syndicate of banks to grant him yet more credit (more entries on computer records), which permits him to buy control of more oil and gas properties, which now are his. Well, they become his responsibility, but they still in some sense belong to the banks that have lent the money to buy them.

All this takes place principally in the minds of those involved (indeed exclusively, except for the recorded entries, the objectivized symbols, which are an aide-mémoire, having force so long as a certain society continues to abide by what they take them to mean. So long as the respective agents live unquestioningly in the same world illumined by the same *Sein*, and so continue to want the same thing—the taken-for-granted set of values will prevail. These are not arbitrary, but related to a set of cultural objects that harmonize under the same epochal *Sein*. All this ownership can evaporate like the morning dew, come a revolutionary change of mind).[38]

The reality of these monetary assets is their ability, as a kind of information, to command our attention and our wills, and hence mobilize energies, so long as we are mutually enculturated (ourselves in-formed) to accept these terms. You are willing to give up possession and occupancy of your house in Pushthrough, Newfoundland, to me in exchange for a piece of paper signaling that the

---

36. Chapter 4.
37. I can still remember the astonishment of my brother and me when our father announced, at a time a loaf of bread cost fifteen cents, "You will live to see the day when bread costs a dollar." Not only did we believe he had lost his mind, but the thought invoked a sense of outrage—so real did the coin's purchasing power seem to us, and so strong is the hold of these symbols on us. Our father had intuited something of the essential dynamics of the political economic world of the Occident which allowed him to foresee the development of continued inflation. This represented a certain thinking back into the *Seinsgeschichte* of that world.
38. My wife, as a child, played with a steamer trunk full of Czarist Railway bonds, of great value in 1910 and none after 1918. Ask the Paulista holding a fistful of worthless cruzeiro notes about this.

proper computer entries have been made in some Registry Office, knowing that once they have been executed, you can command a further computer entry and, with it, buy a house across the inlet in Saint-Pierre et Miquelon, by approaching someone there willing to give up a property in exchange for such an internationally recognized credit, translatable easily from Canadian dollars to French francs, at a market rate.[39]

Information and people's desires are what make the international monetary system go. A common epochal *Sein* is what it presupposes, because that *Lichtung* is at once all-pervasive and elusive—so much so, it is rarely appreciated. The system is so complex, not even the most learned professor of international economics understands more than a fraction of the interweaving realities and symbols. (That is what makes the temptation to *Seinsmysticismus* so strong: The system works although no one fully understands it, despite the fact that it is a kind of massive human artifact. As I argue in Chapter 9, only by working away, from a set of resolutely realistic premises, at understanding how such a world operates can the philosopher demythologize *Sein* and the impression that the mysterious system is animated by something like a *Zeitgeist*.) The owner of the IoFood store in downtown Toronto understands next to nothing about it, yet manages within his sphere of daily operations to survive (for a while anyway) quite comfortably—he is not in a terror (as perhaps he would be if he knew more) all the time. That is because the immediate horizons of interpretation governing his daily operations are familiar, and the things and relationships he has to deal with do not change so rapidly that he has to inquire within a broader frame of reference. For instance, he sees that his market share in milk is declining relative to the SaveEasy supermarket out on Highway 2. He knows what his profit margins are, and so he can debate with himself whether to cut his prices to increase market share. He can do this without having to relate the Canadian dollar to the American dollar, or without worrying about the gold reserves of the Bank of Canada. Within this narrow, practical context, he does not even have to worry what the inflation rate will be next month. The thing-centered situations our merchant has to cope with on a day-to-day basis enjoy some degree of autonomy and hence intelligibility, within a given time span. (The Brazilian merchant, forced by rampant inflation to change his prices daily, may have his attention raised to the political level.)

Such familiarity is the fruit of relative stability, in the things, the habits, the language, and as a result the typical situations that arise again and again in the workaday world of a settled community. It guides desire, hence human energy, the work necessary to obtain what is wanted. Familiarity lowers entropy so long as the typical situations repeat themselves, by eliminating the need for creative thinking (which requires great mental energy, of a quality not easily

---

39. A Market is an information network, informing potential buyers and sellers about offer and demand. When these offers and demands are monetarized, that is, expressed in the symbol of a certain currency, they are easily compared, and these then reflect what the market is today. A market is completely free when no one intervenes between potential buyers and sellers to fix the price in any way.

stored up). The essence of the tradition reveals a consistency in the *Sein* that illumines it—in some respects, over centuries—and so personal, local, and national situations change slowly in certain basic respects. What Heidegger terms "calculative thinking"—moving the counters without questioning the sense of the familiar horizons—suffices to deal with the problems that surge up spontaneously, fortunately for practicality, because creative ("originative" *[anfängliches]*) thinking is hard to come by. But for appropriation in the service of authenticity, it is an obstacle, as *Tradition and Authenticity* shows—there can be no critical appropriation without testing the familiarity. Hence creativity (a grace)[40] is required.

HISTORY AND INTERIOR LIFE

The strong role of history in securing such a sense of stability—sedimentations, in both a subjective form (habit and memory) and an objective form (cultural objects, concrete spirit)—is now clear to us. What begins as will and projection becomes sedimented as the already having been, the past. It is the sedimented already-having-been reality *(das Gewesene)*[41] that guides future projection, with its determination, particularly strong in acts of "calculative thinking"—routine—and it is that ground in will projecting illumining *Sein* that appropriation has to bring to light.

Explicit awareness of history emerged hundreds of thousands of years after human existents were living personal and tribal (unwritten) histories. It was driven in part by breakthroughs in information processing: The invention of writing permitted the recording of experiences and interpretations beyond what was possible through oral transmission of traditions. Yet more than a half millennium passed before that invention was first used to record something like a sense of human destiny as having a beginning and an end, as going somewhere, as being a story, *historia*.[42]

This first happened in biblical revelation, in the Exodus account, now thought to have taken basic written form about the time of King David, perhaps some three hundred years after the horizon-opening events themselves happened at Sinai and in the Exodus from Egypt.[43] As reported, that event appears to have nothing to do with a leap in consciousness by the Hebrews themselves; it has nothing to do with information processing. Rather, in a total surprise, YHWH took the initiative, revealing himself to Moses as the leader God, calling to himself, on his own terms, a people, whom he chose to lead toward a particular destiny, linked to the meaning the Creator God had chosen

---

40. *T&A*, 13–15.
41. Hence the *Wesen* (essence), in the Heideggerian sense, of the tradition.
42. The title of Herodotus' investigations, meaning "researches." Consciously to search for significance is a result of becoming aware that there is significance to be found in the first place. Yet Herodotus himself was still far from the sense enjoyed by his contemporaries, the Hebrews, that mankind had an origin and a destiny.
43. The case for this is so ably argued by Eric Voegelin in *Israel and Revelation* (vol. 1 of *Order and History*), there is no point in taking here the long detour necessary to establish it.

to give to mankind: hence he gave as a gift a new self-awareness to a new kind of people. To them he gave an important in-formation, a set of commands frought with implications, a revelation of new profundity to the human condition, his commandments, or a new Law. With this came a new intense sense of what it means to be a people, to have a destiny.

It took five volumes of Eric Voegelin's *Order and History* to trace the developments of historical consciousness from the cosmopolitan empires of Mesopotamia and Egypt, through the event at Sinai, to Saint Augustine's time, and Hans Urs von Balthasar seventeen volumes of his (unnamed) trilogy to meditate on the truth found in the resulting "treasure-hoard of symbols" as it has come down to us.[44] Each step leading to this is itself an event, or a series of events, with a history: the awakening of human consciousness, the growing ability to analyze and symbolize, the invention of writing, the consciousness of the common mind of "a people," and of history, in the sense of a notion of a human destiny, the awakening awareness of the ego and of an "interior life" among the Greek poets and thinkers of the sixth, fifth, and fourth centuries B.C. This history is woven together in the history of the Church, through the Greek and Hebrew synthesizing and deepening work of the fathers, and then of all of Western civilization, a suite of events affecting, more than most realize, our everyday lives.[45]

We do not much notice this debt to tradition because the deployment of the relevant horizons is guided and our awareness of what we are doing is mostly absorbed by the insistent tasks of everyday life in the myopic particular setting in which we live, which we take for granted. All are enveloped by the same *Sein*.[46]

Much of this significance remains what Heidegger calls "the unthought in what is thought." Practicality's obscuring of our debt to history paradoxically

---

44. Balthasar by no means limits his appropriation to the main Christian traditions, but ranges widely over the whole of Western culture, from the Greeks to the present time, and even casts many well-informed glances at other civilizations, but always from a perspective rooted in living revelation as lived in the Church. The implications of his incredible accomplishment will demand decades to be appreciated adequately. The endeavor is bolstered by some sixty other books, and more than one hundred volumes of translations (his way of coming to grips with a text).

45. Eric Voegelin says he was put onto examining the symbols left by man's historic search for order when he read, in 1937, *Prometheus*, by the young Jesuit, Balthasar, where the notion of the gnostic deformation of symbols was first called to his attention. (*Autobiographical Reflections*, ed. Ellis Sandoz [Baton Rouge: Louisiana State University Press, 1989], 23, 65–66). Two works show well the kind of appropriation the present situation requires: Voegelin's *Order and History*, vol. 2, *The World of the Polis*, and vol. 3, *Plato and Aristotle* (Baton Rouge: Louisiana State University Press, 1957); and *Herrlichkeit*, vol. 3, *Im Raum der Metaphysik* (Einsiedeln: Johannes Verlag, 1965), in 2 vols., *Altertum* and *Neuzeit*), which Balthasar devotes to the foundations of metaphysics.

46. When a psychologist wants to see more clearly the depths of a patient's soul, he will encourage him into a situation where what he projects will become more obvious. The best way is to get him to interpret something vague, in which he has little investment, such as an inkblot (the Rorschach technique); also, when people speak or write about vague generalities, their prejudgments (prejudices) stand out.

hides our sense of our own forging the future, hence dims the full sense of the *autos*, self, and thus of response-ability. Heidegger is justified in terming everyday existence inauthentic—lacking in *autos*. Inauthentic, but not necessarily ingenuine, not "untrue."

Precisely because so much of our unthinking ("calculative") commonsense activity is largely genuine (in keeping with the facts of the situation), it works well. Only rarely do crises provoked by obstacles damming the flow of our projects invite us to become aware of the normal frames of reference deployed spontaneously under the direction of our ongoing natural faith. A "crisis"[47] is often just an awareness of the need for a new kind of information on which to base an unfamiliar judgment. When crises do come, we sometimes can search out the origins and depth of the realities lying at the base of the commonly shared horizons (raising questions of principle) and so perhaps start to become aware of the *Sein* and the history that is embedded in them, and of the steering effect these entail.

Enculturation in the institutions that have formed us contributes in two ways: doctrine, that is, the traditions direct our attention to certain realities, through transmitting the symbols that guide us to them; and role-playing, which helps to form good and bad habits, virtues and vices, needed to fulfill daily coordinated actions (roles).

Anyone who begins to examine the sense of our common projections ought to take seriously what Heraclitus first termed "the depths [*bathys*] of the soul [*psyche*]."[48] For it is only within that interiority (Saint Augustine's "great halls of memory"[49]) that we can find the living source of all historic interpretation, the principle of authentic ordering, indeed the fountain of those well-ordered psychic energies that give human spiritual life its vitality and direct it in lowering entropy.

It is there, too, in the depths of the soul that we discover the fundamental encounters of person to person, whether human or divine, at the center of our *Ek-sistenz*, which manifests itself especially in that power (will) of engaging the self *(spondere)* that founds every genuine re-sponse, so claim both the biblical and philosophic traditions.

In our busy everyday life, we are called rarely to much of that searching awareness, not just of the inner self but of its opening onto the more transcending and elusive dimensions of existence. One can even enjoy a fairly active prayer life without such reflection, praying rather mechanically and reading Scripture with little accompanying meditation. Even in meditation, one can be so absorbed in the divine objects presented through the symbols of Scripture

---

47. From the Greek verb *kritein*, to cut, as in de-cision; "cutting the Gordian knot" or "Fish or cut bait."
48. Fragment B.45: "You will not find the boundaries of the soul through traveling every path; so deep is its *logos*." He opposed deep knowing *(bathys)* to much-knowing *(polys)*. See as well fragment B.40.
49. *Confessions*, book X.

and the traditional teaching that the ongoing interpreting-loving *ek-sisting* of the soul goes largely unnoticed, and so its potential remains underdeveloped.

It is a supreme paradox of human existence that we are at once capable of an interior life and for the most part so little given to it. Too attached to our own desires and projects, the teachers of contemplation have always warned, as does a modern psychiatrist, Gerald May, examining the relation between contemplation and the wrecks we make of our lives.[50] A stupendous kind of information then lies fallow, the ultimate sources of the greatest human energies, the psychic strengths, are undeveloped, awaiting the few mystics and genuine (nonsophistic) philosophers to be exploited.

DIMENSIONS OF THE INTERIOR LIFE

Earlier we discovered the role of traditions in transmitting symbols. These symbols awaken in the recipient, among other phenomena, different kinds of spiritual life, conveying vicariously experiences of the spiritual dimensions of both *esse* and *Sein*, which have been matured over millennia. Without these to direct our attention, our lives would be incredibly impoverished.[51] Beyond the transmission of a language and the institutional arrangements—family, tribe, village, and so on—and everything else that goes into daily life in a given culture, there are the traditions—especially the religious—formative of the great civilizations. This very transmission by tradition marks a significant conquest of time.

What approach might offer hope of recuperating the main potential of the interior life in a way intelligible to common experience?

According to the Occidental tradition, what the interior life is all about is the quest *(philein)* for truth (the *sophon*), *philosophia*. Christian revelation transformed the sense of philosophy through its insistence that the Truth has its origin, not in the life of the human psyche, but in the interior interpersonal life of the three Divine persons, who are the creative Source of the reality and intelligibility of the exterior world, including our bodies, and Source of all energy, cosmic and psychic, Creator of Heaven and Earth and Font of Wisdom. That is why Saint Augustine saw the psychic life to be an image of the Trinitarian divine life. So recuperation of the interior life, where, in Heraclitus' sense, the deeper truths are pursued, and in Saint Paul's sense, where the power of love and the light of the world reveals itself, holds the key, not only to the sense of all history and all culture, but to the very being of the cosmos itself which has produced this human interiority as its highest form of created power.

---

50. May, *Will and Spirit.*
51. I find many of my students impoverished because these traditions influence them only superficially. They do not know what they are missing by being so cut off from the roots of the Occidental tradition. They have become so secularized, they float on the surface of an inauthentic, commercial, and manipulative popular culture, and are so preoccupied with surviving, they do not recognize the shallowness of their lives.

James Lovelock, in *The Ages of Gaia* comments, "Teleological explanations, in academe, are a sin against the holy spirit of scientific rationality, they deny the objectivity of Nature."[52] Extreme as this statement is, it does give a needed warning. The interior life, being an intentional life of meaning and ends, has its own forms. We must be careful not to project them onto the exterior, material world without adequately attending to the differences between natural form and culturally imposed purposes. On the other hand, we must avoid the materialist reductionism that refuses to recuperate the sense inherent in the distinctive life of the psyche. In-formation signifies a rather powerful kind of form, with an inevitable teleological dimension, but we must stay alert to differences between natural genetic coding and more spiritual human purposes in transforming information deliberately.

A further warning: In approaching the interior life, we must take care not to underemphasize either element constitutive of the activity we call *philosophein*—neither the importance of the information, the content of truth, the *sophon*, grasped through insight in *theoria*, nor the love of that truth, the *philein*, the *spondeo*, that deployment of psychic energy which is a creative reaching-out to embrace, without which the search for and the appreciative union with truth will not be sustained. Aristotle told us what the essential dimension of that *philein* is: the life of virtue, an accumulative ordering of intellectual and moral energies. This requires, the Christian tradition insists, a special nourishing, which itself comes only from love from beyond the soul, a uniting of appreciative beings, formative of the supernatural virtues of faith, hope, and charity, a purported ultimate dimension of psychic energy we shall have to explore. That love is openness to, and receptivity of, *Sein*, indeed of all being, total *Sein* and all *esse*; it is the needed radical attitude (*Verhalten*, as Chapter 9 will explain) and gratitude for every form of grace.

The interpenetration of *theoria* and praxis, of truth and life and love, is put forward, then, as a key to the reality of the inner life and, through it, to being itself. ("Not everyone who says, 'Lord! Lord!' will enter the kingdom of heaven," [Matt. 7:21]; "Blessed are those who hear my word and keep it" [Luke 11:28]; and "The truth will make you free" [John 8:32] are injunctions in the spirit of what I mean here on the part of a well-known master of the interior life—truth and life must not be separated.)

By What Method Discern the Dimensions of the Interior Life?

Eric Voegelin used a historical method to explore the dimensions of the interior life, archaeology of the texts in which first a sense of history emerges—those of Exodus and then the historical books in the Bible; next, a half millennium later, a sense of psyche, arising in the quest for the *sophon*, in the dialogues of Plato and the works of Aristotle principally; and, after merging in the fathers of the early Christian Church, moving toward that maximum of differentiation

---

52. Lovelock, *The Ages of Gaia*, 33.

of the treasury of symbols to be found especially in the spiritual giants, Saint Augustine in the early fifth century and Saint Thomas, marking the thirteenth-century summit of Christendom.[53]

Voegelin's is an approach heavily indebted to one great line of tradition, the Judeo-Greco-Christian, a limitation he later came to feel was too restricting.[54] It was motivated by the insight that throughout this history, man has been struggling to discover a way to order society, one that must reflect an inner order of the soul. To what extent the psychic energy came from sources beyond the soul, horizon-opening input of new insight making society itself possible, human destiny becoming an ordering object for the soul, is something Voegelin extensively explores.

Voegelin's is in many ways a good method, and I have followed a variant of it in my appropriation of the Catholic tradition, hoping, in the process, to make at least a start on that appropriation of the most differentiated treasure-hoard of symbols, which he was unable to complete.[55] In the present volume I consider friendship, something typical of all human existence, without reference to a particular tradition or epoch. After reflecting somewhat haphazardly on as many aspects of this experience as I can, I step back and hope insight highlights the basic structure, whence the energies, what is peculiar to them and how are they ordered. This is supposed to produce what Husserl calls "the eidetic insight," the grasp of form, of an intersubjective relation. This insight should be repeatable by the reader reflecting on like experiences of his own. This will help achieve at least a preliminary grasp of the dimensions of the interior life.

MUTUALLY SELF-AWARE FRIENDSHIP

The friendship we are examining goes beyond a sharing of information, of points of view, and even an offering to the other of a glimpse of what each holds inside; it is grounded in love for another person. By "love" I mean the ideal both of willing the other's well-being—*benevolentia*—and the desire to unite my being with his (which may or may not include some form of living together—one can live together with a roommate, with a spouse, or with God, and one can be very close to a friend without ever sleeping in the same tent).

Benevolentia is a commitment (*spondere*) of self to other for the other's sake, an appreciation of a separate source of energy, a freedom, an inexhaustible mystery not to be commanded, and a decision to direct energy toward the other in service of his need, so that he may realize his own truth, that is,

---

53. Voegelin was prevented by death from carrying out his full program, which called for methodic exploration of these immense Christian syntheses.

54. On this, see the introduction to vol. 4 of his *Order and History, The Ecumenic Age;* and *Autobiographical Reflections,* chaps. 18–20.

55. I differ with him, however, as to where it is to be found: not in the great syntheses of Saint Augustine and Saint Thomas, but in the full teaching of the living tradition, centered in the Church as Mystical Body of Christ. Voegelin was a Protestant, so he looks to theologians for the truth question while, as K. L. Schmitz reminded me, a Catholic looks to the Church, its entire history, and above all its *Magisterium* through the ages.

develop the potential of his own existence in good ways. If genuine, it is a commitment of energies according to an understanding of what is good—that is, being-enhancing—for the other. At its very best, it is accompanied by such con-fidence in the other, one is prepared to be *ravi* by him, allowing one's energies to be commanded by him in faithful *obedientia* (*there* is a notion lost in today's voluntaristic world!), vulnerably delivering oneself over to him, because one desires (a rational-willing appetition) to unite one's being with his, so far as this is possible without violating the nature of either, and at the cost of some of my *autonomia*. Whether such total con-fidence in another is ever completely justified except in our relation to a God who is perfect Good is another question.

Such a commitment, while it may be expressed more or less adequately to the other, and hence pass expressively into the objective domain, is lived first and foremost in the soul of the lover. It is an act of his *esse* traditionally named "will." It is a deployment of energies: there is no loving by us incarnate beings without repeated acts of animadversion, at least. It is hard work sometimes to keep the loved one in mind, to contemplate him, to listen to him, and to renew genuine acts of willing to be of service. This has to be rooted in some knowledge of the other, which starts with a wanting to be in-formed by the other as he really is; otherwise one is projecting one's desires around a nucleus of selected aspects of the other. When one loves, one desires to know everything about the beloved, and when it is authentic love, to know how he really is. Second, a commitment to direct attention and energy to the cause of the other, a confident accepting of the other's will insofar as it is good, becomes then an ordering principle, of *communio,* lowering entropy; and finally, to be with him in every way that our natures allow. As I said, to live with him ("Abide with me!" sings the psalmist), in fulfilling, not damaging or diminishing ways, fulfilling for both of us, in human relationships, and for me alone in love of God, who does not need me for fulfillment.[56]

In building a life together, we accumulate intersubjective, cultural form as we found, for instance, a home or a society, accumulating together understandings, memories, habits, putting an ever-enriching order into an extending time-space.[57]

Love understood as willful direction of energy distinguishes itself clearly from lesser forms of desiring: Either the desire to control another, so he will

---

56. The perfect perversion of this is when two mutually consenting adults shack up in order to exploit each other for self-satisfaction, without *benevolentia* and without commitment. When this replaces marriage, the parody is complete.

57. Since writing this, I have spent three days in an exceptionally well ordered environment, the Trappist monastery, Our Lady of the Genesee, near Rochester, New York. The experience of unparalleled peace is surely rooted in the monks' decision to pursue with total integrity a single, high goal—strictly to observe, out of love for God, the Cistercian rule and be obedient to the father abbot they had elected for life as final guarantor of the desired order—and the mature and cheerful way they went about keeping the spirit of this communal life, in silence and through singing the hours, from vigiliae (matins) at 0200 hours until compline at 1900, and off to seven hours' sleep at 1930 hours.

do my bidding, or to possess the other as object for satisfaction, say, of my sexual desires, deploys energies of force or manipulation, or seduction. Victim myself of the enthralling power of sexual appetite, I am more enslaved by the impulsive, consuming pursuit of the object than liberated by it. Devotion to the good of the other, in contrast, opens me onto a revelation of new being—the other in his freedom is a new perspective, a center of creativity, a source of rich experiences and traditions. I associate my energies with his, rather than consume him in a blind outpouring of poorly thought-through energy that seeks to capture part of him for use in my schemes. Enhancing his freedom paradoxically enhances my own as together we open a larger, more human space. Outpourings of passion do not encourage and allow him to deploy his own energies in the direction of his maximum growth; he operates on a superficial level dictated by my pleasure.

When the friendship is mutual, it is accompanied by reciprocal confidence and service: In that way, we share a mutual project of service and esteem, securing an enduring intersubjective time-space, an ambience in which our life together can grow. We share a *Mitsein*[58] in some ways unique to us.

Eros and *Benevolentia*

Such giving-over of self to the other while desiring union with him cannot occur without some kind of affective involvement. We remain incarnate beings even in the depths of our spiritual life. Affectivity is a manifestation of the body—source of our energies, or a flow-through of energies from the other[59]—being moved, wanting to move, and actually moving when we are acted upon, desire, and act.

I first have to be affected by the other to begin to have some disposition toward him; the commitment grounded in love, however deep within me it may lie, passes when the occasion triggers a relevant display of energy, to expression and through expression[60] to some kind of living relationship with the other, becoming dialoguing energies, spiritual but organic at the same time. This overworked word, "dialogue," is here just right: The medium of

---

58. Heidegger's notion of more than one *Dasein* being-together. *Sein und Zeit*, 8th ed. (Tübingen: Neomarius Verlag, 1957), 263 (¶53); *Being and Time*, trans. J. Macquarrie and E. Robinson (New York: Harper and Row, 1962), 308.

59. If, as we shall see later, that master of the interior life, San Juan de la Cruz, is correct, there is an important exception: Affectivity in every form, he declares, is first an instrument for drawing near to God and then a block to God's taking complete possession of the soul. This transcending affectivity would be ontologically a reality beyond the level of exchange of psychic and bodily energies.

60. The emotive depths of the soul are the source of the beloved expressions of music and lyric poetry. Wilhelm Dilthey remarks that Friedrich Hölderlin's poetry "expresses the exuberance of feeling, the non-objective power of mood which arises from the inner recesses of the mind itself, the infinite melody of a psychic movement which seems to emanate from indiscernible distances only to disappear in them again"; "Friedrich Hölderlin" (1910), trans. J. Ross, in *Poetry and Experience*, vol. 5 of *Selected Works* (Princeton: Princeton University Press, 1985), 376.

this bodily interaction, as human, is the merging of two logoi in one ongoing conversation. A logos expressed is a physical energy bearing (or standing for) a psychic energy, therefore transporting *(metaphorein)* a form, hence informing, triggering and partially enabling in the other, an answering (*Ant-wort*, an anti-word), acceptance and then release of psychic energy as he grasps its meaning, ordering the intention by integrating it into his wisdom, which must be recentered to accommodate it. He may or may not speak in return, he may merely blush, or deliberately maintain a stony face, which can be a devasting *Ant-wort*.

The bodily medium does not always entail sexual attraction.[61] Indeed, because of a certain self-centeredness in the erotic wanting to possess,[62] being in love (as opposed simply to loving) is usually an ambiguous mixture of *benevolentia* and erotic desire requiring constant sorting out. In that state, ideally, the *benevolentia* will motivate reason to keep the erotic from becoming destructive of the other's well-being. The resulting loving space mysteriously is always open to others, to the child who may be born when the relationship is also nuptial, to his friends and mine as well, even to the needy stranger.

The erotic element includes body chemistry, the mysteries of which are buried in the genetic depths of our organic being, orchestrated by our psyche's having processed certain past experiences in obscure ways. Not all profound bodily emotion need be sexual in this narrow sense. But it will be in the large sense: the way a woman experiences the affectivity involved in the expression of friendship and the way a man does will be different, colored by their distinctive biophysiological makeups and their distinctive gender-cultures. The fact that our bodies have been formed both genetically and culturally (second nature) influences the way we are, even to the depths of the soul. The mystical methods of San Juan de la Cruz seek to purify those depths, to the extent that the most foundational energies of our personal being can create resistance to the ultimate love and source of ultimate life, the divine energy, which is neither biological nor sexual nor cultural but radically other and originating. "In Christ there is neither Jew nor Greek, master nor slave, male nor female" (Gal. 3:28).

Sharing Horizons

Phenomenology is more fundamental than information theory, for it recognizes that prior to sender-encoded message-channel of communication-

---

61. "Sexual" in a focused sense, the kind of feeling that reaches its summit in the desire to engage in intercourse.

62. I am not sure whether a drive to possess and control the other is inherent and must be overcome by the higher desire of *benevolentia*. Perhaps the sexual drive is neutral as regards control, and the forms sexual activity takes when the person wants control are fed by other psychic factors—for example, personality deficiencies. Or perhaps the body, seeking reproduction, instinctively wants some kind of control of the mate. If that is so, such an instinct would have to be humanized, being transformed into the freedom that accompanies true love.

appropriate receiver, there has to be *Sein* embracing all, which is the condition for the possibility of that appropriateness.[63] The foundation of this commonality is human nature, and then common language, which the former makes possible.[64]

The symbols imply and invite on the part of the other deployment of relevant, suitable frames of reference-formed energies, based deep in memory, deployed by both coordinately to constitute a field of understanding, illumined by the same *Sein*. Expression reveals in every case something of what is going on in the meaning-generating and -storing center, the consciousness. This then becomes the occasion for a glimpse of the depths of each of the discussants.

Glimpses in Expression of the Life of Consciousness

Because so many of our daily communications are centered not on the state of soul of the interlocutor but on the object, usually the goal of some short-range practical action, they need not illumine too much of the subject's personal thoughts about his more intimate relations with others and his life in God. But even then, in the midst of our merely functional relationships, a skilled interpreter can build up some picture of this psyche, including its psychological type. The stored energies in the great halls of memory are socially conditioned in well-known patterns and subject to the (much studied and yet still mysterious) common natural and cultural structures of human psychodynamics. Many syndromes reveal the fashionable ailments, and all of us display conventional wisdom and conventional reactions.

Sharing of Selves: Self-Awareness and Commitment

Friendship is about sharing of selves. The self is much more than one's natural faith and the horizons of interpretation it founds; the horizons enfold considerable self-consciousness, and self-control (will) is necessary for this sharing to become profound. Further, appreciation, necessary for any mature response-ability, not to speak of authenticity, is required for full engagement of the *spondeo* to happen: "Love thy neighbor as thyself" is God's second law. The spontaneous, con-fident opening-up of the child is precious, fragile, and touching. It is so dis-arming, who could fail to respond? But its depth is limited; he cannot yet love himself, for there is as yet little he possesses to know and

---

63. In a cell's manufacturing DNA, into which are encoded the instructions for the new cell, one can say analogically that the typical receptors, the templates, function like horizons of interpretation in communicating humans, but without any self-awareness, so this is not full-fledged knowledge. The implication here, that the objective reality of common human nature is a fundamentum of *Sein*, is explicitly developed in Chapter 9. If the Heideggerians are shocked, they should await that discussion, which suggests that the *Ek-sistentialien* of *Dasein* are ontically grounded in the genetic reality of common human nature!

64. The natural faiths of those involved in an intersubjective situation may contribute not just truthful interpretive elements, making the common communication and/or action possible, but possibly also distorting, mendacious ones as well—disorder in the form of pathological ordering—whence the possibilities for not so innocent "misunderstanding" in all social situations, and for group actions of social delusion.

affirm. Feelings may run strong. But depth is different from strong feeling. Emotion's full flowering includes an element of reason: That is why emotional development can attain refinement, but feeling remains as it is from birth. Depth requires some degree of critical, reflective self-understanding as ground of the possibility of reading into the expressions and the other's whole way of being something of what he really is.

In friendship at its deepest, even where we cannot fully harmonize our worlds, where we (perhaps tacitly) agree to disagree, my respect for him demands that I appreciate his world; and he, mine. There must be commitment to bring these worlds together, to search for the fullest reality.

We average souls are, alas, always guarded. We have been too often hurt, especially as children, when that spontaneous, ingenuous con-fidence was misused. We tend to term "neurotic" those who are even more hurt and so distort reality further than we in their efforts to defend their most precious territory, the inner self.[65]

If my knowledge of the other's real self does not grow, then my commitment is not to him but to a projection of my own fantasy to which I attach some pathologically selected parts of his being. In his place, and using his existence as a nucleus, I build an idol. To the extent that I do, the friendship is a *pseudos*. The same happens intersubjectively when a group projects around some core of reality a mythology, in which they invest, and so develops a strain within a culture that is partly delusional.[66] Eros is rarely absent from such an act. The desire to possess and control this source of satisfaction can lead, for instance, to fabrication of the most absorbing of all idols, a homemade Jesus figure, to respond to our less than honest interpretation of our real needs.

Is it perhaps the deficiency of the other, his staying closed and his deception, that blocks progress in knowing? When an authentic person truly loves the real other, he is likely to learn to see through the lies and to penetrate a bit the defenses, however neurotically clever their design. The search for fullest, genuinely securest self-possession (authenticity), then, is a prime phenomenon of interiority.

Is Authenticity Essential to Friendship?

Obviously that fullness of self-possession which is authenticity[67] is not necessary for friendship to begin. Love seems to be a kind of grace that can

---

65. In *Morgenröte*, Nietzsche cries, "Give yourself grace!" (*Werke*, vol. 2 [Munich: Carl Hanser, 1969], 79). How and to what extent we are dependent on others for an infusion of psychic energy, especially on God's grace, is a large subject to be explored in an eventual anthropology. Failure to cooperate with such gifts of the other is condemned in Christian revelation: "You are neither hot nor cold. Because you are lukewarm I spit you out of my mouth" (Rev. 3:16).

66. Freud (*Moses and Monotheism*) thought that all religion was nothing but such projection, and of course he is right in believing that some of that goes on in all religious traditions and all cultures.

67. Penetrating the bastion of lies and some reality is not easy. The insincere other will use every artifice to keep even the best friend at a distance from the last redoubt. Balthasar had this in mind when he wrote his attack on Catholic ideology, *Schleifung der Bastionen: Von*

spring up in a soul, perhaps when it is *ravi* by the object, so that it is then attracted, at least to some extent, beyond the safe bastions of its self-protection system out toward the genuine core of the other. The other then has become a kind of grace nourishing the lover and unleashing in his soul the necessary generosity, a gift of attention, solicitude, service. To be able to give is to have received the ability to give; this particular kind of energy is allowed to flow through me. (A hated child is rarely a font of generosity.) But as one freely opens onto the other, he stands the best chance of receiving in return—the gift of beauty or of enhanced understanding of the other, perhaps even the supreme gift of response, for grace proffered can return as enhanced grace.[68]

While waiting for fuller knowledge of the beloved to develop, I open a credit, as Gabriel Marcel says in *Le mystère de l'être*, in the form of a willingness to accept the other whatever he does and however he comes to reveal himself—will preceding intellect, a con-fidence.[69] This does not mean that true love is blind.[70] Genuinely wanting the good for the lover motivates one not to be alert to evil, but to do everything to help him combat the destructive.

Such a generous commitment is rooted in the lover's *esse* as creator of new order—that is, new forms (a divine quality in us, made in the image of God). When the erotic is active, it can feed on fantasy, in oneself and about the other. Our ability to create new forms is rooted in that very power of fantasizing. Fantasy is not always happy with the constraints of physical reality, as you can witness when a child throws a tantrum to obliterate it or the old man drinks himself senseless or the young men talking politics in the café think they have improved the world. The primary goal of the sexual drive biologically, judging by its most basic result, is not the expression of *benevolentia*, for which it, along with other means, is also used, but the begetting of children, so that the species may continue, just as eating means a sound body, more basic than just having a good time. That good-time aspect is there as an imaginative human embellishment of nature's basic way of moving higher animals to assure that the survival goal will be achieved. Our imaginative orchestrations of the bare drive are manifestations of the creative humanization of everything we do: An element of fantasy, of wider expression and beautification, perhaps even of

---

der Kirche in dieser Zeit (Einsiedeln: Johannes Verlag, 1954); *Razing the Bastions: On the Church in This Age* (San Francisco: Communio Books, 1993).

68. *T&A* (chap. 2, but esp. 2–14, 30–33, 98–100) develops a sense of the self from a philosophic tradition, leaving for a later work the recuperation of theological dimensions and the psychological dimensions of spirituality to a projected Christian anthropology.

69. How are depth and greatness of soul related? There is certainly a kind of generosity implied in greatness of soul. And yet, a great soul can be in love with beauty or truth or even with its own experiencing-of-beauty (I am thinking of the tragic obsessiveness of Mahler's Sixth Symphony here) and yet not be very generous and loving toward others. Plato (the quality of *megaloprepeia* [Republic 491E]) and Aristotle (the virtue of *megalopsychia* [Nicomachean Ethics IV.3, 1123a34ff.]) launched this notion—great-souledness.

70. The erotic element in being in love can be blind, because it can be motivated by the desire to fulfill my needs—to achieve that end, one may overlook realities flagrantly obvious to everyone else.

appreciation, is added (but also sometimes, alas, an element of a grossification, which we insult brother animal by calling "bestial").

I am here using the complexity introduced by the mixture of the erotic with generous love as an example of the ambiguities that affect the interior life, making it difficult for us to understand ourselves. When we separate the enjoyment of the wonderful humanly orchestrated feelings and basic natural realities, with the danger that the feelings become narcissistically an end in themselves, then only the limits of the imagination put any restraints on the bizarre things people will invent to get all the titillation they can out of this realm of the body's feelings. Witness the ridiculous extremes to which the gourmet can go to find a new taste thrill. In the case of sexuality, the instrument is not inanimate food but one another's bodies, the prime medium of expression of each other's souls. These can too easily become objects of consumption rather than channels of love, as when we are treated in the workplace as mere manpower. When possession, physical abuse, obsession, the violation of children, and other forms of confusion reach extremes, the danger of detaching basic realities from their whole context shows its diabolical[71] destructive force. One becomes deceptively hidden from oneself. Rationalizing reaches extremes. When our psychically formed energies interact with naturally formed ones unharmoniously, the disturbance introduced by the collision affects both.

When, however, carnal desires are integrated into a fully human scene, they function as one essential motive and as a source of pleasure that completes the whole event. Friends sharing a good meal experience a kind of sensual-intellectual-loving action together, a sort of social sacrament of their mutual love, that appreciatively shows the fullness of the human. Similarly, the erotic driving toward a fulfillment of desire in copulation when integrated into a friendship between male and female, whose situation allows them to be genuinely open to the new human life this tends to produce, becomes an irreplaceable natural and completely constructive expression of the unlimited mutual commitment of a friendship. The *benevolentia* thus mutually manifest issues in and can be shared with the new human being who may result. (The public mutual commitments [*spondere*] and recognition of unrestricted responsibility for one another and for the children, so long as required—namely, for life—are called "marriage.")

The Other as Essential to One's Being and Self-Discovery

Psychologists have recognized the role of the other for e-ducating—"drawing out"—the personality of the child. Consider the ontological ground of their insight: friendship is an indispensable source of a humanly formed kind of energy necessary for proper development of man.

A friend challenges. He points out faults and false pathways, in-formation (a grace) of a special kind, essential for my continuing re-formation. He offers

---

71. *Diabolos* means "deceiver," from *dia-bolein*, which has a sense of division.

encouragement to improve, reinforcing the motivation that unleashes and forms my own energy, because, among other things, it helps me see for myself what is good in me (the *true* form). It is strange how a glance, a holding of the hand, a kind word can awaken new assurance. (Is it simply the form taken by a message, which, entering my soul, is the control key to unlocking fresh levels of energy already there as potential within me, or is there also a mysterious flow of psychic energy from one soul to another over and beyond the message form?)

Why, once past the infantile formative stage, does such e-ducation by friends continue to be essential, not just psychologically (instrumentally) but ontologically (fundamentally)? I shall argue in a moment that it is not sufficient, for there is much more to who I am than even the most devoted friend can know or what his effects on me touch. Authenticity requires historical depth to understand how our respective traditions have molded, at their deepest level, the horizons of interpretation that surge up from our natural faiths, but it requires still more. In the depths of the soul, claim the philosophers and the fathers of the Church, one encounters not just a chthonic nature but the presence of an Other that is more than human. How is that dimension incarnate? It is in part in the foundations and riches of what has been transmitted by the tradition—the oldest and deepest level of the culture's power of *e-ducere*—but then also in the very Source of the irreducible center of the ego.

But before addressing these fundamental ontological issues of the historical content of horizons and of the depths of the interior life, I would like to reinforce the suggestion that the interaction with the friend, though not sufficient, is nonetheless essential, not only to my self-discovery but to my very being.

I am the result of the meeting of two lines of genetic inheritance, reaching back through the first human beings to the formation of the cosmos. These inherited formed energies, tendencies, talents, and limitations of temperament are difficult to isolate in the cultural syntheses formed by my own interpretative actions and those of the society (including *ethnos* and social class). They are woven through the entire fabric of our natural faith, illumined by the common horizons of the *Sein* of our tradition. These culturally interpreted genetic dimensions have been reinforced by the family's culture. They are not part of my *essentia* (those aspects of our being we have in common with all humans—genetic traits with roots so deep in the becoming of the human kind as to be common to all), but they also help form my *Wesen:* The traits of my own personality are so fundamental to my second nature that there is no hope of knowing myself as I really am in any concrete way without discovering and confronting their upshot, the form of my personal life.

How do I start to become aware of myself as a kind of whole, to reflect on who I am?

The expression is accurate—"reflect." I become aware of myself when my actions bounce off an ob-stacle to my project and bend back *(re-flexio)* attention on myself, the wellspring of the frustrated energy. The nature of the ob-stacle[72]

---

72. As Fichte pointed out in the *Wissenschaftslehre* (Hamburg: Meiner, 1969), in developing his key notion of the *Anstoß*.

is essential. Just as light, reflecting off an object, bears information about that object, so it is when any obstacle forces the subject back upon himself and his projects. When the obstacle is a recalcitrant doorknob, I am not likely to be alerted to much about myself, except what I already know, that I am the fellow who wants to get through that door. But when it is a colleague blocking me for puzzling reasons from developing a new program—a conflict of desires and wills, a collision of perspectives—then I search more deeply in myself for understanding of what is going on, and I begin to see myself in contrast to that other.

Such opposition is a somewhat negative impulse (or *Anstoß*) to self-discovery. More positively, there is the joy and the pain of working together to achieve something, perhaps over a lifetime, as parents do in raising a family, or as co-researchers in discovering some truth, or artists in creating a beautiful building. I can of course encounter being in all these kinds of realities by myself alone. But with the other, there is always a complement of perspectives—hence, more form—that can make me aware of both sameness and difference, that I have indeed only one perspective, not the total picture, and that together our perspectives enrich the total discovery, building the form of a richer intersubjective social order.

When one gives in to the fear of having the inconsistencies and lies and just plain obscurities of one's soul too clearly revealed, then interaction, instead of self-revelation, can provoke new depths of self-deception. One rationalizes, and one finds security in ideological groups.

But through the sensitive ministering of an insightful other, we can lovingly be led out of our self-dug cave by his solicitude. (The unloving other is equally efficient at reinforcing our worst tendencies, encouraging refuge in that cave.) How an energy directed into the depths of my soul by the other penetrates to release there a creative, healing, energy requires continued investigation.

TRADITIONS AND EXPERIENCE AS PERSONALLY FORMATIVE

If one has never known anything but a milieu of mindless accommodation to the little demands of each day, the role of great formative traditions in that life will be minimal. I offer later an example of such a flat life. But where one has been profoundly formed by a great tradition, penetration of the sense of that tradition becomes essential to understanding one's story. I first illustrate just how fundamental this can be by an example, drawn from the recent experience of two of my students. It becomes clear how appropriation of tradition can be essential to coming to terms with a real-life situation.

An Illustration: The True Story of Adam and Joan

Adam, a twenty-nine-year-old pediatrics resident, has for four years been struggling with the decision of whether to marry a slightly younger physician, Joan. They seem compatible, and both are committed to raising children with the hope that they will grow up loving God and man. So what is the sticking point?

Adam was reared in a largely secularized milieu in Winnipeg, but his parents continue to attach importance to their Jewish cultural heritage. Joan is a committed Catholic. Through long discussions with Joan, and perhaps moved by her example, Adam began to believe in God. But the God he discovered is the YHWH of the Jewish people. So confronted by the obstacle represented by Joan's Catholic faith, Adam began for the first time in his life to move beyond fun conversation on the subject of what it means to be a Jew. Serious re-flection, hence appropriation, began instead. For three years he has been struggling with this problem of identity: What historically and religiously is a Jew? How do I, Adam, relate to this? What implications has it for my marrying a Catholic woman? He has read voraciously and even traveled to Jerusalem to consult a great Jewish philosopher.

Those close observers of this struggle who themselves shared no religious faith tended to find the obstacle of the young couple's differences in religious belief "a pity," "a waste." Those with a serious faith, Jews and Christians alike, viewed the pair's struggles as serious business, containing indeed an element of pathos, but not just a futile exercise of fantasy.

The unresolved difficulty of how the children should be raised led, after four years, to the single most painful event in their lives: the final decision to go their separate ways. The impact of this decision on the rest of their lives and, through the resulting lack of progeny, on human history, is considerable. I see three issues of reality here:

1. the psychological fact (the respective templates), which cannot be denied, led to the decision with its fateful results;
2. the validity of the truth claims entangled in the web of emotions and motives, which drove the decision (Joan has told me of her admiration for Adam's seriousness about the truth of who he is as a Jew, and I believe Adam respects Joan's refusal to give up her faith in Christ, to become a Jew, as Adam early on suggested);
3. and obscure psychological and sociocultural motives—for example, not wanting to offend one's parents or community, opposing prohibitions against intermarriage, racial prejudices inherent in one's upbringing, whether acknowledged or not, and so on.

On that second question of truth hangs the issue of whether this potentially rich life together was sacrificed for something real, or was merely the victim of confusion and illusion, embodied in the factors listed in point 3. To the extent that any of those truth claims that actually played a role in motivating the decision were ill-founded, cultural vestiges of a life that has lost its deeper meaning, templates that are effective but ill-formed to produce healthy reality, they had a destructive impact on reality.

If, however, Adam's conviction that he is called to have Jewish children and Joan's conviction that she cannot withhold from her children the truth about Jesus Christ are well-founded, at least as their respective communities understand and live Being, then their resolutely maintaining conflicting positions to the end would have considerable justification. Whether a *modus vivendi*, respectful of the clashing truth claims and able to come to terms with the emotional mix-up, could have been worked out is another—prudential—question we are not considering here. Clearly, Adam's unresolved and profound confusion about what it means for him to be a Jew did not help. Joan, apparently much more secure in her Catholic identity, seemed prepared to go a long way to meet Adam's needs, even to the point of agreeing that the children could be raised Jewish, provided only she did not have to hide from them anything she believed to be true. Joan once told me she was convinced that Adam was fearful that Christianity would win out, and that he himself was not that unattracted by it. Adam, on the other hand, told me that it was for him a great emotional concession to think about having a crucifix in his house. Untangling truth claims from emotional mortgages was so difficult, both moved to separate cities for a while to get distance from their families, so they could figure out what they felt in themselves alone. That did not help in the final analysis. These incarnate spirits are not emotionless thinking machines. The things that motivate them are buried deep in the flesh.

How they might have reconciled conflicting fundamental truth claims, or at least achieved a harmonious coexistence respectful of clashing convictions, once they sorted out some of the emotions enough to get clear what those claims really are, is a subject the surface of which we barely scratched earlier in raising the question of the possibility of a single wisdom (Chapter 5) and to which we return in Chapter 10. It is, indeed, at the heart of the truth question.

To know what happened and to assess the soundness of their decision—which they have had to do and, rightly, continue to do and will probably reflect on all the rest of their lives—one must enter into not just the dynamics of the two psyches but the sense of the traditions at work here, where alone one can find the larger perspective from which to judge the soundness of their more emotional reactions. (One glimpses here the difference between the work of the psychiatrist, seeking to help a person disentangle emotions enough to make well-grounded judgments, and the spiritual director, seeking to deepen one's understanding of the truths handed on by the tradition as wellsprings of life. Ideally, the psychiatrist should be nonjudgmental about the claims in the patient's tradition, assuming it is not some obviously destructive sect. The spiritual director, firmly believing in the foundational truths of the tradition that has formed both director and directee, will seek to bring out the life-giving potential he himself experiences in those truths.)

One's assessment will depend upon his own natural faith as to what is real. That is bound to be much affected by his being in the community to which the sympathetic observer himself belongs, illumined by the same *Sein*. (As the story of Adam and Joan unfolded, it was fascinating to see the different readings they got from a Reformed rabbi, an Orthodox rabbi, and a Catholic priest. Interestingly, the three advisers agreed in many elements of their assessment of the situation, and all three stressed the need for the couple to work this out, to clarify what they believe, and to make their own decision. All warned against their allowing their parents to make them feel guilty. All were respectful of the differing visions of the truth handed down by the respective traditions.)

A Contrasting Illustration: The Case of a Non-reflective Decision

At the other extreme, people will without much thought make decisions the results of which mold their entire lives. Sometimes this can be in response to a sudden grace, comparable to a conversion, but it can often be for frivolous, short-sighted reasons. I remember a conductor on the old New York Central who told me, as we roared along on the lamented Southwestern Limited, that he became a railroader for forty years because at eighteen he wanted to be on the local NYCRR semipro baseball team. Had the young hireling stopped to reflect, "Do I really want to spend my entire life working as brakeman on the New York Central, with the highest hope being to rise eventually to conductor?" he would have found himself asking about implications of a more sweeping theoretical nature, about the meaning of his vocation on earth. Or at least he might have wondered about the nature and future of the railroads.[73]

I contend as an ontological proposition that the person who makes some progress in deepening his understanding of what life is all about is more mature, because he not only raised the issue of the sense of his life, but he puts into action the principles that he discovers. For this, he does not have to be an intellectual: He may be a loving, artistic, creative person in good touch with reality and who does not run away from the more basic and challenging questions of life, but faces them with his intuitive wisdom. In contrast, I contend that the common impression is essentially correct that the unthinking person who avoids the tough issues and just muddles along managing life's little pleasures and pains on a daily basis becomes empty inside.

A certain seriousness *(gravitas)*[74] manifests the power of reflective engagement, an ability to perceive the depth of things, especially the foundations of one's own beliefs, and the courage to grasp how the particular formed energies one is unleashing on the world fit in with the largest and oldest formations of that world. Ultimately, and ideally, such seriousness leads today to the need for the appropriative act of taking the step back behind one's traditions in an effort to think the history of the *Sein* that illumines them. If one follows the questions where they lead, it becomes increasingly difficult to avoid a certain degree of intellectuality, because the very complexity of what reveals itself demands education to keep all the issues in order. That *gravitas* is a manifestation of the

---

73. As I did when I quit my beloved Frisco Railway to become a philosopher—the railroads' gain and philosophy's loss. Proof that I would never have survived on the railway is the fact that I actually did consider the implications for life. Long-range planning was not then a forte on the railway.

74. I discovered after writing this that Balthasar uses the same term, in the same sense: *intensio*. See *Theo-dramatik*, 3:92.

engagement of self that allows the other to be fully present. It is the will to allow the other to be. Here we find the key, paradoxically, to our own being more.

How is this being more related to being deeper? And how do both dimensions relate to that greatness of soul the tradition has recognized since Aristotle?[75]

They are not exactly the same manifestations of being. A certain intensity of life stemming from a clear view of an end to be pursued which one then goes after with all one's might may lead to the "greatness" of the "fanatic," analyzed by Gabriel Marcel. Such a person, lacking generosity, may be very little open, either to the reality and the good of the other, or to the sources of being in his own history and soul. If, as a consequence of this lack of genuine openness, the vision driving him is narrow, he will likely be merely obsessive, and so will repel others, whom he badly needs, and he will be dismissed as a crank. If, on the other hand, he brings his obsessive energies to a rather larger vision, but still lacks true love, he may prove to be a charismatic leader who can sweep many weak people into his train, or even a great artist who opens up new vistas onto being while leaving personal tragedy all about him, in the manner of Auguste Rodin or Pablo Picasso. Though he may basically live out of the spiritual capital that has been handed to him by a tradition, he may yet mix in a certain creativity with it. But his essential closedness on self, with the result that he never really listens, will block him from gaining much deep knowledge of either self or other. (From records of Hitler's *Tischrede*, one gets an impression of pompous pontificating, not dialogue.) That is because the reflective grasp of principle demands putting things in question, striving to reach the foundational levels of being where vast sweeps of energy are caught up in the very large formations or orders of nature and society; it is to step back behind the traditions to understand the mysterious and ambiguous unfolding of the *Sein* that illumines them. This is what the fanatic has sacrificed, by never listening.

Depth comes from consistent acts of the will that form virtues. They found the needed comportment (*Verhalten;* see Chapter 9) of receptivity, continuing deployment of formed psychic energy for the sake of openness to being. This comportment manifests itself both as the loving capacity to be *ravi* by the other—the ultimate depth of appreciation—and to respond to the "exigence de l'être," as Marcel would say, what is revealed by the life deep within oneself, which keeps *ravissement* from becoming obsession.

The failure to make an informed, long-range strategic decision in one department of life does not necessarily entail a complete absence of interior life. An individual might well believe that a job is a job, confine work to the bare necessity of earning a living, and then go on to pursue an interior life in a way that he does not connect with his job. Our brakeman, for instance, could be a pious Baptist, a daily reader of his Bible, a man of prayer, who finds the

---

75. See note 69, p. 230.

summit of his week the Sunday service. If he strives to be a man of integrity, then of course in his moral life, which includes his working hours, he will bring the light of the Gospel vision to his actions. But if he treats his work only as a necessary evil, since that occupies so much of his time, such work without deeper commitment is not likely to yield the full ontological fruit that it otherwise might. His culture *(Bildung)* remains somewhat compartmentalized. Moreover, suppose our good man becomes a great railway conductor. Is that not, by virtue of the intersubjective constraints of a high-tech railway, a lesser being than that achieved in his work by another conductor, say, Herbert von Karajan?[76]

I am not forgetting that many of the finest human beings one could ever hope to meet are to be found in the humblest jobs, and great saints are encountered among the chronically ill and handicapped who cannot work at all. As a Christian, I joyfully acknowledge that God sends calls to many to be sanctified in every position of honest service imaginable. But my intent here is to attack the nihilistic egalitarian prejudice of our populist times, that one work is as good as any other. That seems to me part of an obscurantism that shades the path to seriousness. Different people are called, by their whole personal history, to different kinds of work, but this difference implies graded positions on the scale of greatness, not as regards their personal devotion, competence, usefulness, or sanctity but as concerns the scope of human contribution in this world.

In some of his relationships with musicians, Karajan may well have had things to learn from our Baptist NYCRR conductor. How far does Karajan's soaring recorded interpretation of Mahler's Sixth go in redeeming him for his relationship with the flutist that virtually destroyed his effectiveness with the Berliner Philharmoniker at the end of his life? Greatness in one department of life can all too easily cohabit with pettiness or downright evil (remember Rodin's destruction of Camille Claudel) in another, and evil can undermine greatness in all, bringing the person to a tragic end. This human capacity to compartmentalize (which is related to our freedom in shifting frames of reference) holds implications for our understanding not only human nature but being itself. The pursuit of wisdom demands that we pose the question of what is fundamental. Indeed, "what *does* it profit a man to gain the whole world if he loses his soul?" (Matt. 16:20). And what does that mean, to lose one's soul?

PRESENCING AND ENGAGEMENT

As a way into the question, let us probe farther the nature of that deeper commitment to which we referred in considering seriousness. Imagine two pious Baptists, equally serious about their religion, and both working in routine industrial jobs. But the one also thinks about the importance of vocation and so tries to make the work department of his life an integral part of the meaning of

---

76. See the corresponding discussion of the technocrat and hero in John Ralston Saul, *Voltaire's Bastards* (New York: Penguin-Viking, 1992).

his being on this earth. In his daily work, he is, as a result, more present, because more of his being is consciously engaged in this part of his life. "More present" means more thoroughly and consistently engaged—he has his mind more on what he is doing. He not only strives to achieve maximum quality, he tries to be a good presence to his bosses and his fellow workers. Because the more *engagé* worker sees better what is going on, he responds more sensitively to the demands of each situation. He may even hear what his colleagues actually say, sometimes—rare event!

Or consider two persons who spend equal time in Bible reading, liturgical exercise, and personal prayer. One may achieve a different degree of spirituality and holiness. The difference in spirituality comes from the intensity and quality of their presencing in the interior life to the realities contemplated; in holiness, from the integrity and the generosity with which they live out the implications of what has been given to them in the interior vision (provided it is itself great enough), which includes centrally, in the case of Christian spirituality, a call to love of other.

Spirituality can exist with deficient interior life and with insufficient holiness —the recipe for hypocrisy and an invitation to fanaticism and cultlike excesses, which one sees in many occult groups and spiritism and among religious fanatics of all kinds. And holiness can exist without the depth of spirituality that comes from the intense reflection that interior life demands. One sees this in the simple faith, say, of the good peasant who lives out the vision that has been passed on to him lovingly and with integrity. The memorable giants among the saints who mark history by their greatness and holiness have usually gone beyond this relative shallowness. But the towering structures of interior life they reveal to us, in their splendor, take nothing away from the simple beauty of a humble life lived privately by a good and constant person.

Intensity is closely related to integrity. Integrity suggests not only consistency but a certain generosity, an integration of all there is (so far as one knows) to be brought together. Being intensifies with integration—the process, visible throughout nature, of creating form. Ordered energies can be brought together to achieve a new effect and a better-targeted effect. So dispersion in any way, including deficiency in moral integrity, and especially use of psychic energy defensively to hold at bay unpleasant realities, diminishes the possibility of presencing and dissipates being in disorder: Energy is lost in entropic disorder, or fails to maximize potentials through deploying lesser, simplistic orders— we might think as a kind of simile of the crystalline repetition, which cannot integrate with much foreign material (a "bad infinite"), versus the complexity of the organic, for instance, which can, and in the case of the highest forms, the spiritual, which can unite all that is positive and good, and knowingly discriminate against and reject the noxious (opening onto "the good infinite," in Hegel's terminology). In the unfortunate case of superficial spirituality, psychic energy, perhaps itself lacking concentration, could be expended defensively, not against the truly noxious, but against goods the weak person cannot face, thereby not accumulating consistent, meaningful results, either in the building up of habit, the increase of knowledge, or the building of richer interpersonal relationships. Intensity of psychic presence *(intensio)* requires the gifts that awaken awareness and the development of the set of habits—character—that allows concentration to happen, a consistent storing up of formed energy potential, the *Bildung* of the soul.

Presence holds a key to the spiritual existence of man. It is at the core of the human spirit's growing through successfully willing to reach out and unite with what is other than it, as other. Perhaps the highest degree of presence is what Gabriel Marcel describes as *disponibilité*, which adds a note of willingness to be generously devoted—service beyond just lending a friendly ear. True presence is nonconsuming; rather, through it, the soul lets the Other nourish the spirit as it will, both finding their own being enhanced through involvement in every way—emotionally, intellectually, lovingly—with the larger reality of being itself.

Presencing involves, first of all, an element of attention, but underlying that, of care.[77] This is not merely a psychological state, but a fundamental ontological condition, which allows new being to come to be, the fruit of uniting the caring consciousness with the cared about, involving seriousness *(gravitas)* that looks for depth, going as far as possible toward principle, and mindful of the farther reaches of the future, as *Sein* illumines them. In caring, in this ontological sense, the interpreter deploys the fullest horizons of interpretation he can, placing no arbitrarily restricted limits on the full play of Being that can be achieved, stretching his regard from birth to death (ideally, but rarely practically, even from beginning of the cosmos until its putative end, if at all relevant to the beings at hand). Thus is created a good quality of new actuality, a profound new bond, which founds new possibility limited only by the creative reach of the freedoms engaged.

My friend John called me on the phone for what at first appeared a casual chat. I was absorbed in reading, but I was at least polite, trying to disguise the fact that I was minimally present. He gradually begins telling me that he feels, in his present state, left out of things, it is a difficult period, and so on. I reply with a brief sermonette, elevating and irrelevant to what he is really after from me. He hangs up disappointed. (I subsequently felt bad about my failure and called John back. He was much relieved, saying, "I started to think I cannot depend on Tom Langan as a friend anymore. It was not what you said, but the way you said it that hurt.") Had I cared more for him and less for my own preoccupations, I would have been from the start more *sympathique* (the word says it well, "suffering with," a form of caring).

In more significant instances, when a person presences, a permanent disturbance in the soul can occur, a reordering of at least part of one's mental landscape, in some mysterious way a redistribution of psychic energies within

---

77. In invoking "care," we rejoin a long tradition, reaching from Saint Augustine's *cura*, through Kierkegaard, to the *Sorge* of *Sein und Zeit*. (See my *The Meaning of Heidegger* [New York: Columbia University Press, 1959], 28ff.)

the tense stability of the memory. In cases of psychic trauma, this can be fundamental and disruptive, because fragile but basic patterns of self-relation and self-understanding, of trust and openness, are shaken. In the case of the serious engagement of authentic love, it is fundamental and constructive, permitting a whole new region of orderly development in one's life. There is even the danger of obsession—everything tends to get referred to this new all-absorbing center, the beloved. But also (and here we encounter a principle of fundamental importance): new being is created beyond the soul, transcending the merely psychological, as a real relation is created between the other and that soul.

Relations of Presencing

We are such natural empiricists in our everyday lives, it is difficult for us to grasp that real relations, because you cannot touch them, are indeed being. Every act of presencing establishes such a relationship.

Yesterday, the thought of the unfortunate telephone exchange with my friend came back to mind several times. I decided to send a signal somehow that I really do care for him. Now, while that deliberation happened in my soul, yet without his even knowing this was going on, it affected his being, for he changed from being neglected (by me) to being cared about. He may believe himself abandoned by all. In fact, although he does not know it, he is not, for I, at least, do care. That is a truth about his being as cared for. He is in fact the target of psychic energy, just as I am absorbing cosmic radiation whether I know it or not. I have deployed the energy to open a field of concern that englobes him, and he is now standing in that field of concern. The world in which he exists has been altered, as has his place in it. Clearly, with the success of my second phone call, a rapport was set up between us knowingly. This canceled much of the effect of the doubt that had crept in. This two-way relationship is founded in each soul, my love for him reaching out from mine, and his for me from deep within him. There is mutual re-sponse at the base of this new intersubjective ordering.

The reality of such a bond is most apparent in a publicly expressed contract, which the state, defending the common good, will enforce. What starts in the souls of each party as directed psychic energy gets expressed into the public domain by this psychic energy in turn directing physical energy as each body states and swears an agreement; this meaningful physical energy (meaningful because psychic energy, supplying meaning, in-forms the physical acts to express an intention), is taken up into the public consciousness through its integration in the general field of ordered psychic energy that operates as a dimension of *Sein* in the collective understanding—inculturated habits that enable the rule of law.[78] What our commonsense empiricism makes it less easy

---

78. Recall the bank loan (Chapter 4). The parties concerned, those contracting and those witnessing, must enjoy the stored information allowing deployment of coincident horizons of interpretation without which neither the mutual commitment nor the witnessing could make any sense. This gives a hint as to how *Sein* works.

to see is that my friend's being is really changed when I love him, even though he does not know it.[79]

Another example may help make the point, which, it turns out, is revealing about being as such. An undiscovered text lies rotting and unappreciated in an old wine jug at Khirbat. Its existence is a fact, although no one knows of it. A goatherd discovers it and sells it to an archaeologist, who, after deciphering it, recognizes it to be a document of the Essene community. The core ontic reality of the text—the stable balance of physical energies that have been ordered to incarnate psychic energies of meaning on the surface of the parchment—has not changed. But it has been taken up into the world of Middle East archaeology by knowledgeful interpretation, even though the archaeologist has not yet communicated this to anyone. His act of interpretation has contributed, along with the possibilities inherent in the ontic fact of the objective spirit caught in the signs on the parchment, to bringing to be a new entity, in the order of psychic energies, hence of meaning, the interpretation of the text. What was an undiscovered and uninterpreted text has now become a discovered and interpreted text, although only one lonely archaeologist as yet knows this. The additional steps he will take to communicate this meaning to others will actualize possibilities posited in that initial interpretation, bringing about new knowledge: the growing awareness of the archaeological community. It would now be false to say that the text is undiscovered and uninterpreted. This change in its significance will likely have results in the physical world, too, because the parchment is going to be moved from cave to air-conditioned laboratory.

To return to our first example. My friend John may doubt my love for him. But psychic energy is directed toward him; lacking expression through a physical medium, it does not yet touch his center of awareness, and so does not change his inherent ontic, physical being or any of his mental states. But his situation changes the meaning of his existence. A one-way psychic bond is created between the agent and the patient, the patient is brought into a new spiritual field and is thus situated among those loved by Thomas Langan. Longer term, this could prove to be the basis of actions that will have other consequences for John. Suppose everyone around John has become suspicious of him: He is an object of rather negative regard. So long as he does not know it, his inner ontic reality does not change, but his situation is becoming dangerous, and his being totally unaware of it is itself dangerous ignorance; it constitutes an irrealism on his part—John is in the dark. It is often dangerous to our very survival to be ignorant of relevant facts, even when these facts are uniquely about others' state of soul. Profound changes can be happening to the Being of our epoch to which we remain blissfully oblivious, but they are happening nonetheless and will affect our most obvious ontic being one of these days.

---

79. This contention provoked heated discussion in my graduate seminar one year. It is, I agree, difficult to see, and in fact during the several weeks the discussion raged on, I stood hesitant on the sidelines.

To this it might be objected that so long as John is unaware of my love for him, the change is only a Cambridge change, if I may allude to a famous controversy on just this point. If a hundred years after Bach's death, Mendelssohn makes him famous for the first time, this is not a change in Bach's being—it can't be, for he is dead. It is a change in the fame of Bach, his image, which is in the minds of others. If John becomes aware of my love for him, this new knowledge and his reaction to it constitute a change in his being. Otherwise, *nichts*. But, as I have tried to show, the ontic reality is far richer than that which is physically—or self-reflectively—visible. It is filled with relations, including those of which we are not yet aware.

Nonreciprocating (One-Way) Relations

Why is the issue of one-way relationships worth insisting upon? A metaphysician who read this discussion in manuscript remained unconvinced of the whole point. On the other hand, I recently asked an undergraduate class what they thought of this, and a rather poetic young woman blurted out, "What it is really all about is that God can love me without my acknowledging it, and it is still the most important thing about my being." Bruce Stewart, who was a participant in the seminar, claimed that what is at stake is the most fundamental issue of all, What is being? He thought the issue so important, he drafted much of the discussion that follows.[80]

One is reminded of Gabriel Marcel's discussion in *Le mystère de l'être* of the garden that no longer exists, but continues to have being because it had existed—not just because held in memory,[81] but because it retains a stake in being, which, of course, goes on unfolding. I have never had much success getting undergraduates to see this point. Those who would insist on the reality of non-reciprocal relations are opposing an overly positivist notion of being, which would reduce being to actual space-time[82] material existence. Psychic energy would then be reduced to physical energy (or denied altogether), and the meaning of meaning, and all sense of stored-up form, would evaporate. That is why it is important to probe this issue further.

To the poetic student who might say, "God loves everyone. Although many ignore this, it is an important aspect of their being," the positivist riposte is quick in coming: "But that is different, for the divine love, if it were a reality, would be constitutive of our being. My love for John would be constitutive of a relationship if he acknowledged it; otherwise, it is a one-way relationship that changes nothing in his being."

When the disturbed person declares, with feeling, "I am garbage; nobody loves me," one can see that it is not true. The person feeling rejected is misdescribing, not his feelings, which really are low, but his own being, as well

---

80. He elaborated with examples in an appendix, which space constraints would not allow to be included. To anyone interested in pursuing the issue, we will be happy to send a copy.
81. Gabriel Marcel, *Le mystère de l'être* (Paris: Aubier, 1949), 2: chap. 2.
82. Recall, from Chapter 2, the distinction between time-space and space-time.

as misconstruing the larger situation, the bonds of love that come from others directing attention and love toward him. This misinterpretation of the situation is itself the product of disorder and a further disordering. It adds to the confusion. The love of the others may indeed remain (who knows?) ineffectual in his life until he accepts and acknowledges it, ordering this reality in his soul properly, in keeping with the way the world actually is. Maybe the psychic energies the others direct toward him have a mysterious effect on his being beyond the change we have acknowledged, the change of state to being loved. Sometimes a person will pick up a change in the atmosphere and gradually, within their inner being, react to it.[83] Is that just a reading of subtle signs, or something more mysterious, something like what Christians call a grace that works directly on deeper levels of the soul? Perhaps it is just an unreflective harmonizing with an ordered situation, such as I have seen happen when a psychologically disturbed person comes to live for a good while in a happy family. Such persons will often try to sow discord where there was little before, but I have seen them slowly but surely, mysteriously calm down, although nothing overt is happening, just from being accepted into a stable environment.

What will be required, to adduce evidence for the reality of nonreciprocating relations, is to show that a change in being occurs that is significant to the entity in question as a stable structure undergoing dynamic processes. Such a shift in its structure—whether recognized[84] by the being or not—would be sufficient to establish the reality of this type of relation. One example might well be the case at hand, the relation of being loved. Bruce Stewart volunteered this instance: As "the last true Tory,"[85] he shares enthusiasm for the arch-Tory, the late Canadian

---

83. Stewart adds: "The best example is the reading of the text itself. When an argument—say, this one—is first presented, it is *new*. Now, if I am in dialogue with you already—so that the intersubjective bond (two-way relation) is already operative—it is easy to see how the communication leading to understanding of the force of the argument is 'carried on the (communication) channel' thus opened. But with the text no 'dialogue' exists: There are two monologues, one from author to reader, and one (we trust) within the reader of re-flection. So how does the communication of the argument unfold so as to join these into a 'dialogue'—how do they become *spondeo:re-spondeo*? If they are not conjoined, then the positivist explanation of 'communication'—required to communicate 'the truth of positivism itself'—fails; if they can become re-sponsive then what passes in 'positivism' for a change in physical being was initiated by nonreciprocating deployments of psychic energy, that is, 'one-way' relations."

84. A subtle distinction: It is common to limit nonreciprocating relations, even as a possibility, to that sense so well expressed by my student that God loves us, whether we acknowledge or know him or not. We tend, therefore, to prejudge the outcome by putting the following conditions into play: The relation must be of emotional content only, and it must be recognized—a reaction to the original action—save only in this one (God) case.

Not all nonreciprocating relations are of emotional content. Relations of "use" change the dynamic structure of processes engaged in by a stability at a minimum. Not all relations should be presumed to follow the Newtonian action-reaction model, especially where psychical/spiritual content is concerned.

85. In the sense of a political philosophy and not to be understood as (a) a member of the Progressive Conservative Party, (b) a British Conservative, (c) a descendant of the United Empire Loyalists (the Tories of the American Revolution), and so on, and certainly not as a right-wing liberal.

philosopher George Grant.[86] He has told me, "I love George Grant." Because he never communicated with him, his love of Grant and his work constitutes a one-way relation, a love relation as active today as it was in 1988, when Grant was still alive.

The Jump into Relations

All openings of new horizons—of making possible the presencing of what is real to oneself—require at their heart a jump into relation without knowing in advance that it will be reciprocated (or even exactly what it will produce). A certain leap of faith must be extended to every framing of a hypothesis, every tentative starting of a friendship, every decision to explore a reality new to the knower. This is as true of the individual who is attempting to know himself by examining his own heretofore unreflexive natural faith as it is of our every attempt to reach out to others, and to understand things in the world more fully, completely, and responsibly.[87]

This is true in a most obvious manner of our reaching out to embrace the whole. Recall the discussion of the unity of being (Chapter 3): Although good reasons were found for believing that being is one, by the very nature of the case—our inability to transcend the whole and embrace it, as it were, from without—our opening to the whole remains an act of faith, including a confidence in being, a faith accompanied by hope, because we believe the good and order is more powerful than evil, that is, disorder will not prove ultimate.

To act (as opposed to react), we must take the initiative, which implies that inevitably a certain number of initiatives will not be reciprocated. (Not all wonderfully brave experiments work out!) The Christian claim of God's unqualified love for us without his waiting for our reciprocation (or even knowledge of his love)—revealed in his supreme freedom—is founded in God's being understood as *actus purus*. Indeed, one thing the Christian does not claim about God is the presumption we make for human affairs, as though they were governed by physics: for every action there is an equal and opposite reaction. God's action on us is not governed by the laws of physics or psychology; God's energy is neither capturable in $E = mc^2$ nor is it psychic energy. As absolute Source of all being, it is beyond the limits of every possible created re-sponse, which, not incidentally, he makes possible to start with.

The Importance of Nonreciprocating Relations

We are beginning to glimpse the philosophical significance of this claim that nonreciprocal relations call into question the transcendental validity of a physics of action-reaction. Hume's distortion of our understanding of relations has nowhere caused more difficulty to philosophy than in this business of trying to come to grips with nonreciprocating relations. Despite the positivistic,

---

86. Also self-proclaimed: Charles Taylor, *Radical Tories: The Conservative Tradition in Canada* (Toronto: Anansi, 1979).
87. See *T&A*, 23.

phenomenalist influence of Hume on much of modern-day scientism, the functional reality of relations is generally conceded (even where the nature of these functions as real entities may be denied). What is generally not accepted is the possibility of any relation that is not reciprocated. Hume's example of the billiard balls serves, I think, to reinforce this image. We find it hard to conceive of physical things not interacting in this manner.

Yet the sole justification for accepting only reciprocating relations is that one considers the psychical/spiritual life of beings epiphenomenal to biophysical life. Certainly this is not reasoned out by those oblivious to the possibility of nonreciprocating relations. If a psychical/spiritual life is not just epiphenomenal, directly constructed from chemical interactions, which would allow for libertinage on the grounds of determined behavior (a bizarre thought)—then relations beyond action-reaction should be considered likely.

As I noted earlier when discussing structure, processes are a network of shifting relationships that can be either open or closed. Once I have placed a stone in my Japanese garden, the change is complete; others are open. The plant continues to prosper because the relation with the caring gardener continues, not because it was in effect once upon a time. We have also seen that certain types of relations can be established in the absence of contact relations that inform all individuals as they are formed by traditions—for example, in the encounter between a person and another's work.

Recognition of the possibility of nonreciprocating relations—both nonreciprocatable and not yet reciprocated—is critical to understanding how authenticity is possible. Developing oneself authentically and genuinely requires that one enter into such relations, both with oneself and with others, in advance of any possibility of knowing myself, the full self, or the other as more than a vague preliminary target of my attention. This is the implication for those who accept and welcome man's psychical/spiritual life as it is, with all its complexity and venturesomeness, and its openness to possibility. For the purveyors of scientism, I leave one closing thought. Every interaction begins with an initiative that is itself nonreciprocating when it is launched—a truth open even to the epiphenomenalists, since all psychic results are, in their view, the result of a nonreciprocal physical change, a one-way relation from the physical to the epiphenomenal psychical. How true can this Hume-derived ideology be, when it founds the very thing it denies?

THE SUBJECTIVE LIFE NEEDS TRANSCENDING CONTENT

In the two cases of the subjective life we considered earlier—the archaeologist's interpretation of the text and my love for John—two principles were emphasized: (1) the life of the soul requires an object toward which its intentionality is directed; and (2) what happens in that life affects the object, because it creates a relationship with it. (We set aside for the moment the case of the soul's reflection on itself, where the larger, mysterious self is object to the reflective center of awareness—the ego—probing its depths.)

This emphasis on the being of the patient-object changing marks the transition in our analysis from the merely psychological to the ontological. This ontological point can be made clearer by returning briefly into phenomenological theory.

Recall the Husserlian insight that every intentional act necessarily has the structure *noesis:noema*, and that the *noemata* correspond in their being to the nature of the noetic act: seeing:object seen, fearing:thing feared, wishing:the wished for, and so on. The reciprocal is likewise true: The nature of the object affects the act—fearing a grizzly standing ten feet away on its hind legs is not the same act as fearing the dark in your bedroom.

The point is that the intentional act is always a relating to something, and that that something is itself a correlate of the act, permitted to be as it is (in part, as regards what Husserl calls its form [*morphe*]) by the act itself. The object is formed in part from the energy of the subject, deployed to make this in-forming possible. Only the noetic act of the subject can allow the object to take its place in a context, in a world of meaning; through that meaning-bestowing, object-producing act *Sein* is allowed to illumine, and thus let be *(Seinlassen)* as meaningful, the object.

The *noema* is not, however, entirely determined by the noetic act, for what has been allowed to presence makes its contribution, which Husserl terms the *hyle*—the matter,[88] source of the new data at the core of the new information the *noema* offers. That matter itself always reveals its inherent structure. Indeed, that revelation works dialogically with the noetic act of determining the range of appropriate stances of the subject's interpreting. (In the presence of a real menacing grizzly, imagining him as a Teddy bear would be fatally erroneous interpretation.) The resulting in-formation has the form it does, because the subject deploys the formed energy, say, of seeing, which is always an interpreting seeing, bringing the fruits of past knowledge, as the form the subject contributes (as the result of the illumining that *Sein* is allowed to achieve) and because the object allows a glimpse of its real form, what in it accounts for its developing as a tree, in a way typical of trees, or what in these molecules accounts for the consistency in a transformation that we recognize as fire, and so on. The *noema* is a dialogical product, a new in-form-ation from noetically contributed form and hyletic received form.

The matter comes from beyond (transcends) the *noein*, which opens onto its sphere and presence, and the matter's origin shows this otherness *(evidentia)*; the *hyle* is embraced by the *noein* so as to be in-form-ative in the *noema*, and

---

88. Those accustomed to Aristotelian terminology, take note: what in Aristotelian analysis is called "form and matter" belongs in Husserl's *hyle* as I am reinterpreting it. The entire being-there in consciousness of the thing is conditioned by the noetic act, and hence gets its form (in Husserl's sense) from it. The knower, however, receives the matter (form and matter in Aristotle's sense) from the transcending dimension in the *noema*.

it adds to the sense of the context into which it is received, which world of meaning has to be adjusted to accommodate its reality.

This insistence that the matter that presences is never structureless sense-data but is ordered, structured information combats the Humean-Kantian error, the mother of all voluntarism, that structure, and hence meaning, is the contribution of the interpreting subject. Rather, the subject in interpreting integrates the self-presencing structure into (necessarily relevant) larger structures of meaning, both objective (knowledge of things and settings that it retains in and supplies now from memory) and subjective (the inner flow of mental life of the subject). This is a further ordering of what presences as already having an objective order of its own.[89]

The objective givenness, within the self-presencing dimension of every *noema*, manifests real relatedness to other things, which lines of implication the knowing subject is free to follow up or not, but must always to some extent re-cognize. Otherwise, the mind would not know what are the possible relevant horizons of interpretation to apply, and so to what relevant past knowledge to refer the now-presencing *noemata*. The abstracted general objective forms held in memory can be (and most are) about the real world, they are founded in real relations within that cosmic world, and as such they are mostly about real general structures, supported by lines of causal process.

The objective exteriority of the *noema* to the *noein* does not necessarily entail, however, that the *hyle* be always exterior to the spiritual life. The matter of the *noema* is inside the soul, whether received from the senses or generated there imaginatively.[90] But the *noema* is the presence in consciousness of something the being of which may evidence—often with unmistakable clarity—its transcending the soul, in the sense of existing in itself independently. This is true whether my present knowledge of it is from an ongoing perception, or from reading symbols that invoke it, or recalling one or the other in memory.

When the *hyle* is generated largely from within the soul, the matter itself still transcends the conscious, reflective center—the ego—as that which that center grasps. Even when the ego is reflecting on itself, it can distinguish the center of present awareness from the ongoing, larger cognitive life that it is now contemplating reflectively and thereby to some extent ob-jectivizing.

When I open a new relation to a real thing or person, the nonreciprocal real relation effects a change not just in the form of the *noema* but in its *hyle*. I begin to think of John, as I mull over the unfortunate telephone conversation, and I reanimate an old love I had for a now rather neglected John. I affirm that I do, indeed, care for him; he is present not only as an object in my imagination but as the object of my care. (That is why I resolve to phone him again, to make this clear, to in-form him of this truth.) But at the moment I am directing the psychic

---

89. See the work of the psychologist of perception James J. Gibson, *The Senses Considered as Perceptual Systems* (Boston: Houghton Mifflin, 1966). He establishes not only that the senses grasp structure but much about the physiology of how this is accomplished.

90. The imagination uses matter received at least once upon a time from outside the soul.

energy of thinking-about-John-as-cared-for, the *hyle* changes, evidencing John the beloved.

Imagine a debt-free person who believes that he is crushed under a million-dollar debt. The object of his fear is the imaginary million-dollar debt. This contains three intelligible notes or distinguishable elements in its matter: debt, modified by "million dollar," here probably meant to symbolize huge. To this is added the feeling of insupportable burden, the emotive sense of that "huge."

Now each of these notes signified refers to kinds of states of affairs *(Sachverhälte)* that we commonsensically recognize as having a socioeconomic reality. Consider the notion of monetary debt. "Debt" signifies a fiduciary relationship between a person, real or legal, and another person or persons, real or legal. It is a contractual relationship, an agreement between wills (mutual *spondere*), in which a sum, commonly calculated in an agreed-upon monetary unit, is borrowed and is to be paid back at a time and rhythm stipulated by the contracting parties.

There is no thing, in the sense of a tangible space-time-occupying physical entity that is the debt. Yet failure to pay can result in the state sending a very tangible space-time thing, the sheriff, to seize one's assets, and these may include things in the empiricist sense—jewelry, car, and so on.

All well and good. But in this concrete instance, there is only the delusional crushing debt, an image nourished by a fear that is a mere disturbance in this fellow's soul which he is projecting, in the psychologist's sense. When he expresses his concern, this ordered energy of expression is not received as intended, it creates disorder—confusion. There is no re-sponse, or at least not the hoped-for response. The thing evidenced in the *hyle* of his delusion cannot enter into the *hyle* of another's noetic-interpretative act, becoming the node of an intersubjective deployment of world, because it is not real evidence—or, rather, it is evidence of mental disorder. The soul is feeding on itself, deploying its in-formed energies without correct in-forming from the object; the fantasy is therefore unhealthy. The marriage of energies from subject and object is incestuous. What should be a dialogue with reality is in fact a monologue.[91]

For all that, however, this disturbance of this man's soul does have an intentional content—it is about debt. It is different, by its matter, from a delusory snake. A psychiatrist can grasp the sense of its *hyle*, but he cannot affirm in cosmic time-space its reality. The *Mitsein* in question is conflictual. The patient says, "It *is* real," and the doctor re-sponds, "You are delusional." The psychiatrist will find it significant that our subject is afraid of an imaginary debt rather than an imaginary tornado. The matter of the imagined *noema* fails

---

91. Is all truth then dialogical? According to Balthasar, there is one instance when it is not: when the knower, in total obedience, accepts and understands the unique image revealed by God, the Word that is Jesus Christ, the living image of the Absolute who calls us to follow his total obedience to the Father. In this case the monologue is not pathological, because it is not a projection but a reception in faith of the wholly Other, the wholly originating, to whom the knower owes the very possibility of his understanding. Balthasar, *Love Alone: The Way of Revelation* (London: Sheed and Ward, 1968), 66.

to link directly to other things in the world but does to the subjective context, that is, to other things in the patient's soul and in his history, and then indirectly through the events in that history to the larger outside world. There is indeed significance here, but it is psychic, not physical.

In even this brief reflection, we can discern a number of principles:

1. Human interiority or subjectivity is content full;
2. that content is caught up in contexts, subjective and objective; which
3. are affected by what happens in every subject's interior,
4. by the interior act's altering being itself through its coming to be in the soul (the sphere of nonreciprocal relations); and, potentially,
5. by eventually guiding action and thus by what happens outside.
6. Disorder is introduced in the soul through its relating a form to the exterior world incorrectly, that is, in a way that will not harmonize *really* with what exists in the world.
7. When, rather than a simple mistake, this is the result of a *Wünscherfüllung* (wish-fulfillment) projection, the disturbance is unhealthy, a moment in a process of the psyche's closing on itself. This makes correction from the outside more difficult, because the subject does not want to be corrected.

IN WHAT SENSE IS THE INTERIOR LIFE INTERIOR?

With my realist's hat on, I have so emphasized the transcendence of all intentional activity, and the *hyle*'s significance for the objective world, one could lose the sense that the interior life is somehow inside the soul. Even the example of the delusion drove home the point that the wider public recognizes it for what it is because the demented man's object cannot be integrated into our *Mitsein* in the way he would like. A distinction may help assure the subject-object balance.

By "interior life" is meant not the subject's entire psychic life (his interiority, which all organisms have to some degree), but rather that important part of interiority constituted by self-conscious, reflective efforts to recover the ultimate significance of the life of the soul itself, with its own characteristic form and order, its energies. "Interior life" is concern for what accounts for the soul's participation in being, not just *Sein*—the world of meanings—but *esse*, real relationships of existence, including the largest meaning of intersubjective relationships, our foundations in nature, and our life in God and him in us.

Different masters of the interior life discover and interpret that life in ways guided by the wisdom of their distinctive traditions. (The richness of the interior life is manifest in the existence of so many traditions. To point out that this means that man sure has an active imagination is not per se an objection against the objectivity of what is discovered in the soul.) A Yoga master explores dimensions of the soul in ways quite different from the dialectical disciplines of Plato or Saint Theresa of Avila or a Sufi master. To know what these distinctive spiritual traditions have in common, how their ways differ and how they may relate, nothing less than appropriation of each of them and then a comparison, followed by their eventual integration into an ecumenic wisdom, is called for.

Even within one tradition, such as the Christian, there will be different emphases, distinctive subtraditions of orthodox (and heretical) Christian spiritualities. If, with a San Juan de la Cruz, faithful to the Neoplatonic, Augustinian subtradition, there is found in the innermost being of the soul the active presence of the God who is Source of its life and of whose own Trinitarian life the soul is revealed to be an image, then indeed everything that makes up our distinctive personalities, our concrete historical being, our particular loves and friendships, is to be set aside as one pursues God's direct love and operation in our soul.

If, on the other hand, with the phenomenologists, with Teilhard de Chardin, Karl Rahner, Bernard Lonergan, and Hans Urs von Balthasar,[92] one insists that the essence of the person is not to be divorced from its concrete being-there *(Dasein)*, which includes its insertion into history and the intersubjective reality deposited in it as an essential part of its own makeup, then emphasis must be put on the nature of the noetic act as in part determined by the hyletic content of its object. When the reflective ego takes as its object the soul, then, because it is constituted not just by the interior life but by the form of the whole person, which is the source of the order of its life, reflection must grasp both the organic foundations of the interior life and its nourishment by exterior events. The whole man, inserted in history, is the *imago Dei*—for this is part of that total creation Christ came to assume unto himself and thus redeem. The fullest revelation of God is found neither in his creation (natural religion), nor in his active presence sustaining our psychic being, discoverable in the depths of the soul (the Augustinians), but in that perfect icon in which he chose to reveal himself, and hence is, as Jesus of Nazareth, himself man in situation, cosmically evolved body and reflective soul acting on each other, "das Ganze im Fragment."[93]

These two examples within just one of the great religious traditions hint at the vastness of the spiritual worlds waiting to be appropriated.[94]

---

92. Hans Urs von Balthasar, *The Glory of the Lord* (San Francisco: Ignatius Press, 1989), 1:219–316, esp. 308–9.

93. This is the title of Balthasar's theology of history (Einsiedeln: Benziger, 1963), poorly translated as *Man in History*, trans. William Glen-Doepel (London: Sheed and Ward, 1968). Those in this subtradition of theology (influential in today's Church) insist, then, that appropriation of the sacramental reality of Christ, including the Old Testament preparation for his coming and his post-Resurrection life in the Church, is essential to the fulfillment of the interior life.

94. My undertaking—*T&A*, this volume, and subsequent ones—is motivated by my faith that this appropriation is life-giving and today indispensable. I tremble at the thought of those, alienated from all the great spiritual traditions, impoverished in a secular world, who have no master's help into the depths of the interior life. But I shudder, too, at the thought of those caught in the prison of a sect, misdirected by a pseudo-master of an ideologized method, inviting one to feed on oneself in a spiritual misadventure—Scientology or Jonestown, to cite

This tension within our own Occidental Christian tradition of theological ways into the interior life, with their difference of ontology, touching the nature of man and his incarnation, runs deeper even than the important tensions between Plato and Aristotle, partly contributory to the varieties of religious experience within Catholicism. Their differing appreciations of the significance of the incarnation of God in Christ hold implications for the understanding of God, and hence, underneath, for the epistemologies that go with their ontological differences. In my belief, this is important not only as a key to the Occidental civilization but as a motor at the very heart of the truth. That is why, eventually, I shall seek, following Balthasar, to offer a synthesis of the truths of both positions: This labor of love begins in Chapter 8 and becomes focused in Chapter 10.

Whichever of these ontologies—the more interior or the more incarnational—one argues for, the criteria for recognizing the interior life are the same. The interior life in the specific sense just outlined is measured by:

1. intensity of presence;
2. degree (or breadth) of awareness (which is related to the scope of that leap of faith embracing the whole, including the step back behind, to think the history of *Sein*);[95]
3. the truth of the resulting self-knowledge (which, too, will be affected by the scope and quality of the *Anstoß* provided by the object permitted by the leap, as well as by interferences from unconscious elements);
4. the reflective, critical quality of the appropriation of one's situation and the traditions that have formed one; hence
5. the reflective, critical penetration of one's natural faith; and
6. openness to the gifts of what nature offers us to know of it, and of the graces of love offered by other persons and the divine, the *Gunst des Seins*,[96] the mysterious outpourings of insight offered by the illuminations of *Sein*.

INTERIOR LIFE AND ORDER IN THE SOUL

All Greek and Christian masters of the interior life[97] agree that the being of the soul is both moral and intellectual. The Augustinians, insisting on the Trinity image in the soul, would add this precision: that life is made up of

---

only extreme examples. Then there are those practicing Catholics who never seek spiritual direction and so appear to stagnate along what is basically a correct way.

95. Because "interior life" is here defined as willful, reflective, critical quest for being, within the soul, the unconscious dimensions of subjectivity, to the extent operable, are not central. Rather, pursuit of the interior life seeks to extend the light of reason as far as possible to illumine them, when and if they retard the soul's search for truth. Obviously, when factors operating in the soul of which the conscious center is not or cannot be aware, work their effect, distortions in one's views will unwittingly occur. Unerring grasp of all truth is just not on for frail human beings.

96. The term used by Heidegger, in his essay "On the Essence of the Work of Art."

97. I dare not speak here of the Oriental masters, as I do not know these traditions well enough.

intellect, memory, and will (mirroring Father, Son, and Holy Spirit), the virtues of each—faith, hope, and charity—affecting the other.

All would agree, as well, to the need for order in the soul, a notion introduced by Plato and embraced by thinkers from the time of the Academy right up to Balthasar, Rahner, Lonergan, and Voegelin. Just as nature is observed to unfold with a certain order, so what happens over time in the finite soul requires ordering. Meaning *(Sinn)* is found only when energies are properly formed. This is assured, first, by acquiring a true understanding of things, including a correct knowledge of the order revealed by nature: Memory is then in-formed thanks to the forms and relationships found in nature,[98] which also requires forming those capabilities of soul through building up formed power (virtues intellectual and moral) as the result of repeated correct actions of knowing and of external action. The virtues are rightly ordered in good character. Finally, one achieves order through the prudential management of one's life, personal and social, in keeping with true knowledge and character, an ordering work carried out jointly with other *spoudaoi* (mature persons),[99] which disposes the environment to enhance human existence *(Bildung)*.

One can sum up the criteria for discerning interior life in a phrase that brings out the moral as well as the intellectual dimension: Seriousness about the meaning of life—*gravitas*, again. The serious person is the one who faces earnestly the reality that life engages the person and requires adequate response. He accepts responsibility for who he is, a life in the midst of life, an existent in a situation, a powerful ordering energy in the midst of the ordered energies of nature and the order and disorder of cultural life.[100]

As the other is allowed to presence, unlocking its potential, I can then appropriate its being, bringing it into a right order within my soul, reflective of the whole of reality. Without commitment, there will be no sustained relationship deep enough to allow the needed level of mutual self-revelation to occur, and there will be no consistent building up of the being of either, and hence no culture of a friendship.

"La vérité sans la charité est un idole." Pascal is right: Profound truth comes from revelation, and the free other will not (perhaps, cannot?) reveal himself without a free act of loving commitment on my part. Without that, projecting (in the psychological sense) we build narcissistically an idol that we then (safely) worship.

---

98. Which, not incidentally, the soul is able to do because of its own rightly formed biophysiological natural energies.

99. *Spoudaios* is usually translated "good man." Voegelin argues, from the context, that perhaps "mature man" would be better. *Order and History*, vol. 3, *Plato and Aristotle* (Baton Rouge: Louisiana State University Press, 1957), 300. See Aristotle, *Nicomachean Ethics* 1095b6.

100. Nature seems wonderfully ordered compared to the chaos introduced into human life by perverse acts of destruction, and even all the silliness of our trivialization of what could be an incredibly noble human life. When Alexander Leman did a systematic study for UNESCO, "Impact of Natural Disasters on Human Settlement" (1984), he was surprised to see that the impact of war exceeded that of any natural disaster. It should also be mentioned that many of the deaths resulting from natural disasters could be avoided by proper use of foresight.

It is also true that charity not guided by truth is no charity at all, but a lie. It is not devotion and service to the other, and risks turning into aggression, as I force the object providing the nucleus of my delusion to fit the mold I am building for it. (Hence the three supernatural virtues, faith, hope, and charity, form one supervirtue. Without love, there can be no con-fidence in the other; there is no faith, however, without commitment to that in which one believes, but where there is such belief and such love, then hope will be present, that con-fidence in Being to prevail over the forces of destruction.)

The fanatic (or the insecure, damaged person of whatever type) is not completely open to the other as he is. The fantasy he projects around the hyletic nucleus provided by pillaging the other, interwoven with some real attributes, carefully chosen so as not to disturb the delusion, is energy directed at reinforcing what the projector wants to hear about himself. It introduces disorder into the real world as well, because the erstwhile friend will react to this distortion.

The being of the other can only be accommodated to mine by my appreciatively allowing that difference to be grasped in its difference and then, at a higher stage of appreciation and dialogue, allowing a mutual, critical enlarging of horizons of interpretation and consequently ways of being to grow together.

In what sense is such reaching out and letting in and building up a vision of the truth a sign and a fruit of interior life? Encounter with the living other demands that I enter the depths of myself to criticize my basic convictions, at a level where my natural faith is so identified with me that only my brute ontic facticity, founded in my biophysiological givenness, is as basic. It is that fundament where my *esse* and the *Sein* illumining my personal life interpenetrate.

When I am driven to discover the foundations of my being, what is revealed is not just an encyclopedia of ideas but the character and molded temperament—formed potential—that are the fruits of a lifetime of being a certain way. More accurately: what I discover is that my world, my *Sein*, is an interpenetration of all the light made possible by whatever has been stored in memory and all the virtues and vices that are formed by this ongoing interpreting and that in turn guide its deployment.

As I am not a Mother Teresa, my being is not a wonderfully consistent dynamic structure, resplendent in its clarity and in the balance of its order. It is more the somewhat confused product of a dark and ambiguous bumbling along, a mix of old commitments and fears (some carefully examined along the way; most just allowed to work their effect like complexes or, worse, to fester as resentments) that have woven virtues and vices into an ambiguous style of life, an elaborate chosen and imposed and oft-reinforced setting of home and family and friends and books and musical instrument and wine cellar, rhythms of life, the way my time is blocked out, a set of institutional involvements, with distinctive roles, as well as notions (often spotty and vague) about the politics, economics, and religion of the immediate society and of the world. A *Bildung* on shaky foundations, but one that would be far poorer if I were not the recipient of the fruits of a community illumined by a marvelous tradition.

Culture, unless it is soundly based in moral virtue, does not save the soul. Indeed, the temptation of a San Juan de la Cruz to say in effect, "Away with all this buzzing confusion of my life, these obscurities and fantasies of my soul, which only block the coming into it of the sweet peace of God's love," is understandable. Heidegger, in stark contrast, searches for the sense of Being's revelation and obscuring of itself squarely in the mediocre everyday existence of *Dasein*. This buzzing confusion is, he claims, nothing less than Being revealing and obscuring itself.

It would be premature (and unfair to either spirit) to suggest that we must choose: the way of Heidegger or of San Juan de la Cruz—appropriation *(An-eignung)* or renunciation *(Ent-eignung,* expropriation by Christ), immersion or purification. For the moment, let us just acknowledge, as we did when we contrasted the Augustinians and Balthasar, that there are different ways, different spiritualities, different traditions of *bilden,* holding open the possibility they may have something to offer one another.

For now, we shall attempt to understand better *Geschichtlichkeit* (historicity) in the Heideggerian sense, which presupposes a decision on our part at least to this extent: that the buzzing confusion that is our existence in the final analysis somehow really matters, that it has ontological significance. But I am reluctant just to drop the sense of the purity of San Juan's experience of God. So we shall return to that challenge in Chapter 8, and then hope in due course to give some idea of how one might fit the core truths of both experiences into one wisdom.

HISTORICITY AND INTERIOR LIFE: THE ROLE OF THE FUNDAMENTAL PROJECT

In *Sein und Zeit*'s phenomenological structural analysis of the existential dimensions of inauthentic everyday existence of *Dasein,* Heidegger emphasized the unifying role of the "fundamental project" *(Ur-entwurf),* which, opening a long-range future, gives direction to an existence. It is this fundamental source of a course of action throughout long stretches of life, or, in the case of the deepest levels of a natural faith, throughout all of conscious life, which, taking up possibility from what has been handed to *Dasein* by the tradition and situation, builds for him his own past. What one most basically aspires to make of his life, active as our primary love or desire, plays a central (but, given our inconsistencies, our tendency to yield to passions of the moment, not all-determining) role in how one orders his life. This, in turn, should be reflected in our basic institutional commitments. These help give flesh to our more limited intentions, through our consistent, daily putting them into practice socially. But these institutional involvements also have a way of commanding a substantial portion of our time and attention, often more than we would ideally wish, and they pull us in all sorts of directions, some of them animated by bad intentions, or at least a dulling averageness.

A San Juan de la Cruz would short-circuit all these problems by leading a monastic institutional life totally reinforcing of his fundamental project, one designed uniquely for searching for inner peace. (We should not forget that in San Juan's own life this never in fact meant leaving this world. He was so faithfully immersed in the everyday life of his community, he landed in jail.)

What might change the course of a life, resulting in a radical turnabout in fundamental project, a conversion—adoption of a new set of guiding notions and accompanying institutional shifts? For one, it may be falling in love, followed by the lifelong commitment of marriage—this can certainly bring a sea change. Likewise religious conversion, or ideological engagement, or falling in love with a vocation. To bring out the ontological implications of the commitment of one's life we shall examine how each—falling in love and religious conversion—can affect to its foundations, not just one's existence in the world, but the interior life, the whole building of the self.[101]

Ontological Revelations in Falling in Love and Committing to Marriage

If one falls in love and decides to marry, this definitive and radical kind of opening up reveals something of who one really is down deep—both the quality of the commitment and the choice of partner.[102]

Falling in love is an ambiguous phenomenon, the treacherousness of which is well signaled by the opprobrious verb, "to fall," as in the Fall of Adam and Eve, the market has fallen, and so on. He fell for her like a ton of bricks: Next time a truck is unloading a ton of bricks at a construction site, contemplate the phenomenon—it is not a good symbol for freedom.

But assume an ideal instance of a man and a woman who generously will the well-being of the other, a free gift of self through devotion to the other's very person, a will to unite, "to form one body," as Saint Paul would say (1 Cor. 6:16), not altogether metaphorically. There is in this case a certain merging of beings to form a new intersubjective social *esse* and *Sein*.

Of its very nature, such a gift of one's whole being to another can have no conditions, for, at this fundamental ontological level, the self is supposed to be all of a piece, or if such integrity is a pipe dream, then let us say that the *esse*, the very source of one's existence, as will, is freely, unconditionally engaged. That is what unconditional commitment is: the free act to engage with the express intent of not disengaging.

---

101. One can also just drift away from earlier commitment through lack of character, as a series of little acts of infidelity undermine the reality of commitment. One passes from lukewarm, to cool, to complete dissipation. Observe the cooling of a once passionate marriage through failure to take regular steps to help the relationship flourish. And many who have been raised in the church and may have gone through phases of some fervor can drift away in this fashion.

102. As with any thoughtful vocational choice, willingness to make such a commitment is a sign of being a deeper person than those who just live together, following the feelings of the moment and only so long as the arrangement is mutually convenient. In marriage, the ordering of energies is more generous, longer term, potentially more challenging, if we let it, and fraught with large consequences for new life.

Despite all that, and glancing nervously at a divorce rate approaching 50 percent, should we not ask whether there may sometimes be reasons for taking back one's word, one's fundamental gift of self? A friend experienced in counseling married people put the case for the need to avoid believing such commitment should ever be forever: People do change, at times so greatly or so unequally that even with a couple's very best efforts to stay together, they may do more harm to leading holy lives by obdurately maintaining what has become an unfulfilling marriage merely for the sake of good form or because of dogmatic prohibition by religion. This is not a question of truth, but of the Church flexing political muscle.[103]

The counselor, I believe, misses the point. Forget the question of the Catholic Church, which is bound by the unequivocal prescriptions of Jesus himself. But even the Church acknowledges the legitimacy of separation when a spouse becomes abusive, and it declares marriages to have been null and void from the start when subsequent behavior shows that there was neither psychological maturity nor moral commitment. Here is the ontological point: In accepting to unite freely with the being of the other until death do us part, one makes an ontological commitment, based not just on my present view of just who the other is,[104] but to the real him as he is in truth—and will become—a free gift of myself and an embracing of his very *esse*.[105] There will be periods when the marriage is not fulfilling, to use my friend's words—indeed, it cannot be ultimately, totally fulfilling. Does one love another and bring new human beings into the world just to fulfill *oneself*?[106]

My counselor friend tries again: Suppose Frank and Mary, both practicing Catholics, fall in love and marry. After a time, Mary converts to Buddhism. They had promised to share destinies, but their notions of these destinies are now radically distinct. Frank believes that the most important thing in life is to be open to the grace that will prepare a life with God in eternity; Mary, to follow the way that will empty her, leading to Nirvana. The original commitment, he argues, is not fundamental or ontological; it is not to some unchanging substrate in the person. It is more a commitment to a mutually agreed-upon

---

103. The foregoing is the actual marginalia written by my counselor friend at this point in an earlier draft.

104. Whatever that view may be, it is necessarily severely limited, surely flawed, and bound always to lead to surprises, because he will change.

105. Living together before marriage to try the other person out is basically irrelevant, once one is beyond the convenience of mutually consenting adults. If you commit to the person as being, then you accept to share destinies, even when you are both old and bearing little resemblance to the sexy young couple now seeing how it goes. Not incidentally, and also not surprisingly, recent studies show the divorce rate is twice as high among couples who lived together before marriage.

106. In *Manhattan*, Woody Allen's latest girlfriend announces she felt better with her old lover, and Woody heads back to try to seduce the seventeen year old who "makes me feel better." But she is leaving for England for six months, sent by her parents, to get her out of Woody's clutches. "Six months! But that is a very long time! You will have changed." "Six months is not long," replies the obviously more mature seventeen year old. And on *that* happy note, the prophetic film ends.

arrangement, to share a way, even for life, which now, because of events, has become impossible. Now one or both see that it was a mistake. (The very words of my friend, commenting on this situation, and he added, "Would you say once committed to the Nazi Party, one should stay because a commitment is a commitment?")

This argument reflects, I believe, the natural faiths of many who now cohabitate and even large numbers of those who marry. Bluntly, there is a fundamental ontological disagreement between them and me on the position I am putting forth here. I disagree with those who do not see any sense to the very notion of unconditioned commitment, of a gift of self that results in being that is deliberately willed into existence to last, an act that constitutes a definitive *conversio* (not in the sense that it cannot be taken back but that it ought not be taken back). This new being can subsequently be destroyed, obviously, but then I see this to be will reversing itself perversely and smashing the beautiful thing it freely brought into being and agreed never to smash. It is free to do this, in the sense that either partner has the power to walk away from the solemn commitment, just as they in fact have the power to murder each other.

In addition to the element of will—an act of endowment, of instituting *(stiften)*, a directing of psychic energy that is the human creative moment par excellence—commitment involves a cognitive content: I must know to what I am committing and how, in what sense. Does the marriage promise imply a mutual effort to work for a common wisdom, so those destinies will not be allowed to diverge too much? If they do, one risks allowing this new being-together to be slowly undermined through daily frictions. Perhaps that is why, when the *Ek-sistenzen* of the two are founded in fundamental projects that have little to do with one another, such as individual careers, and there is no mutual commitment to serious pursuit of the same way, as there is when a couple share a profound commitment to a great religious tradition, then, when the one important remaining source of common interest—the children—start to leave the nest, they drift apart.

Mature love endures, in part, because the lovers, knowing what they are getting into, accept the danger and commit to help each other grow and to put up with each other's failings. That in no way entails allowing the other to indulge himself to the mutual diminishing of both. No one is justified becoming the equivalent of what AA calls "an enabler."[107] One can direct untold loving energy toward the other and sometimes not budge a bad will or a sick psyche. A human being is always free to spurn grace.

How much interior life is actually involved, essentially, in all this mutual commitment in love? There can be, in marriage, very little. A couple could commit themselves and then muddle through, letting the accidents of the moment set the agenda. Still they can accumulate positive results—children,

---

107. Recent work on enabling and co-dependency has shown that the enabling individual is disordered, making it likely that he will seek out situations in which enablement is possible.

home, memories—but also a certain resentment, all the while building character through consistency of action, guided by the structure of their situation, especially the institutional demands made upon them. With little intellectual depth, and almost no explicit, searching discussion between them, they still can achieve a moral solidity, a kind of consistency, in the best case marked by honesty as they live it, a practical holiness without much explicit philosophizing.[108]

The image of the happy peasant comes to mind. Such a life is imaginable in a socially stable setting, like a pre-industrial agricultural society, but not so easy in our turbulent cities. Anyway, I have my doubts about how widespread is the phenomenon of the happy peasant. But this much is sure: Most people in the urban setting find life too broken up to permit a successful "bumbling through" devoid of any searching reflection.[109] One is confronted with sufficient serious crises to invite at least occasional confrontation with one's sense of it all. If he looks at the situation at all honestly, he will at least glimpse Being.

But he should see that Being is more than the concrete reality of chairs and bodies, that it has to do, too, with the sustenance of a monetary system, with the fabricating of the bonds of every institution, with the lien of friendship, and with the sense of family and ethnic continuity, with history. He may begin to understand that the act of contract is creative, like the fantastic projects of the artist—creative of being. It is the process of such fundamental questioning that makes conversion possible.

Conversely, every cowardly act of sticking one's head in the sand or of failed commitment adds another lie to the situation, obscuring and eventually destroying being, because the lie de-forms and confuses, letting the situation slide slowly then precipitously into disorder. If this were not so, why would so many people be engaged in "running before Being,"[110] in every form, from chemical addictions to the socially acceptable workaholism?[111] If one is not finding oneself, then generally one is losing oneself. And when that happens, interior life and depth are destroyed, or never come to be.

Tradition as Resource for Life and Its Abuse through Everyday Mediocrity and Mindlessness

Two negative conclusions and one positive result from this reflection on marriage for understanding the interior life. First, under "happy peasant" cir-

---

108. Caution: Many couples marked by pathological disorders also can come to an "all of a piece" consistency in which not verbalizing what is going on becomes central: to the world it looks all right, when in fact it is not.

109. Two psychologists have advanced the theory that HTX society itself has adopted co-dependency structures: The number of dis-ordered individuals has grown, they have affected society, dis-ordering it, thus assisting in the development of more dis-order in individuals, and so on. (This is not unlike the process of natural faith adoption: We are formed by and in turn re-form the traditions, institutions, and so on, that feed natural-faith creation in children.) See Anne Wilson Schaef and Diane Fassel, *The Addictive Organization* (New York: Harper and Row, 1988).

110. Heidegger terms it "Flucht vor dem Sein."

111. See Schaef and Fassel, *The Addictive Organization*, on this point.

cumstances, people could feasibly lead a viable life with little reflection (implicit here is life buoyed along and caught up in an *ethnos*). Second, living together without a proper commitment could produce an ambiguous and confusing situation hiding a lie. When matters are too unclear, there is a disincentive to reflection, lest one open a can of worms. (A paradigm for much daily living without critical thought, adapting to circumstances without commitment, opportunism, inviting game playing, as one seeks to adapt to the shifting currents, and manipulation by the anonymous them.) Third, and positively, mature commitment gives rise to occasions inviting searching reflection about the sense of what one is engaged in and so who we each are, and what we are about together. Such mature commitment often grows out of a conversion, a moment when one has been brought to confront squarely the meaning of life.

Given this positive possibility, what are the resources upon which one can draw to answer the kinds of basic questions that arise at the critical points in life? What do culture, traditions, and situation have to offer that will assist the quest for the sense of existence?

When in Part II we examined the role of the great explicit traditions with a view to the kinds of truth claims they pass on, we did not yet consider them as resources for the proper conduct of life, traditions spawning supportive communities, living together in truth. They can also be menaces: when traditions degenerate into ideologies, they become closed sects, damaging of fruitful being. The time has come to consider both. My example is the contribution a healthy religion and the devastation of a stifling ideology in influencing the actual being of an individual. What effects may it have on the being of a person to be reared in a particular religious or other ideational tradition?

The importance of critical reflection in pursuing authenticity has been stressed. Most culture and traditional wisdom is passed on through unreflecting acculturation, so we need to understand better how this works, as background for appreciating the ideal of a more mature, reflective stance toward being.

Consider someone who has been reared in a home where a structured religion is practiced, and he has something like this as vision for life: God created the world and placed man in it, wanting from him obedience to the divine law, a struggle, but with God's help, obtainable by prayer and which may lead to his saving his soul. Church provides ongoing disciplined contact with the Word of God, the sacraments, an encouragement to good works. It also provides beautiful rites of passage.

In making fun of the Catholic ideologue with all the answers in the back of the book, one can easily overlook the following truth: However routinely and unthinkingly the kinds of things just outlined have been enculturated into our member of a churchgoing family, they nevertheless provide a fund of experiences, an ecclesial and sacramental life, generating innumerable invitations and opportunities for reflection. What the mediocre may abusively take as answers can more maturely become sources of fertile questions, which may never have occurred to him in such elaborate and profound forms without this patrimony. Holy Scripture, for instance, is an inexhaustible treasure of symbols crying out for searching, thoughtful reflection; a structured prayer life is a constant invitation to enter the depths of the soul to contact the Source, which is found there and which the words and the attitudes of prayer invoke. The commitment of the churchgoers should itself be a cause for thought, and the hypocrisy—the gap separating what is professed and what is done—is a scandal, especially when placed alongside the undoubted examples of heroic sanctity one finds in the Church. This clashing reality would, you might think, force deeper searching for understanding of how we humans operate and, through that, questioning of being itself.

Not, of course, on the part of the worst hypocrites. The fact that, confronted by the brimming fountain of spiritual riches pouring forth from a millennial tradition, so many of us "church people" seem nonetheless able to go mindlessly through routines demands explanation. My psychologist friend stands ready with many illuminations. The phenomenon is such a contradiction to what the traditions preach, yet so common, I believe it rife with psychological and ontological implications. (Heidegger described "everyday averageness" *[alltägliche Durchschnittlichkeit]* as one of the *Ek-sistenzialien* of inauthentic fallen *Dasein*).[112] Because of the glories of the vision, the tawdriness of everyday inauthenticity that pervades much of human existence is in this particular form—religious inauthenticity—especially unaesthetic. It is counter-ontologic, pointing to a structural disorder deep in finite being itself. Kierkegaard, Nietzsche, and de Lubac were masters at exploiting these paradoxes to illumine the tragicomedy of being itself.

Like them, I seize on the Christian religion for my investigation, because, revealing the complete emptying of ego by the Son of God himself, it so blatantly and dramatically detests mediocrity. "You shall become perfect as your Heavenly Father is perfect" (Matt. 5:48). Here is a claim of redemption from fallenness, original sin and that aspect of it described by Heidegger as everyday averageness. Failure to re-spond brings drastic consequences: "You are neither hot nor cold. Because you are lukewarm I spit you out of my mouth," thunders its judging divinity (Rev. 3:16). Yet Christ consorts compassionately with big sinners—"He prefers the company of prostitutes and tax collectors," complain The Pure; in the presence of the mediocre he shows anger and frustration—the big sinners are not lukewarm. Though he is the incarnation of God, he cannot work miracles in the unbelieving town (Mark 6:4). The scribes and the Pharisees— who become symbols of us all in our self-contented puritanism—are his despair.

Complacency with mediocrity is a profound ontological mystery found throughout human life. Average and below-average performance is found in animal and plant life, too, but the struggle for survival purifies. Given human freedom to create, there is something ontologically different about human

---

112. *Being and Time*, ¶9, p. 69. The *Ek-sistenzialien* are the dimensions of the structure of *Dasein*.

mediocrity, to the extent that it is the result of choice: a series of decisions to be much less than what one knows one could become. In the concrete, we cannot rightly judge of any specific person, other than ourselves, for we do not know what struggles go on in the soul of another, we do not know its real limits, nor are we party to the graces—natural and supernatural—proffered and refused. Even in the privileged instance of my own life, this is not always all that clear, and I must constantly struggle for honesty—which is strange, too, when you think about it. But as an ontological principle, failure to be all that one can is counter-evolutionary, a mysterious perversity revealing of fallen human nature and of that realm of psychic energy we have been exploring.

What is being invoked here is nothing less than the fundament of that fundamental ontological reality, the fallenness of inauthenticity,[113] a major dimension of which is mindlessness, and cowardly going along with peer pressure that lies behind much "lack of application," as schoolteachers put it on report cards. Mindlessness is a (literally) deadly combination of lack of reflection and a failure to be present (lack of *intensio*)—the polar opposite of *gravitas*. This troubling phenomenon of failing to be all one could has its source in the realm of psychic energy, which is why it has no counterpart anywhere else in nature. It is a phenomenon of human freedom. (Sometimes called "lack of will power," then "lack of energy," or "I didn't think," or "I have no time." Each of these expressions touches on part of the ontological structure of mediocrity, the realm of manipulation.)[114]

Plato offered a hint: Cherchez le *pseudos* derrière l'affaire. The *pseudos*: the living lie, refusing and deforming reality, the dark side of that fantasy necessary for human creative freedom.[115] This is not inculpable ignorance, inevitable companion of our finitude, nor mental illness, which may cause an involuntary

---

113. There are several superb analyses in the philosophical literature, beginning with Plato's attacks on the Sophists, continuing in Augustine's attacks on himself in the *Confessions*. continuing throughout Kierkegaard's work, with many insights to be culled from Pascal, Nietzsche, and reaching a summit in two great analyses of the inauthentic mode of everyday mediocre existence, Max Scheler's *Ressentiment* and Heidegger's *Being and Time*. There are also many insights throughout the work of Gabriel Marcel. The few pages here provide only a hint of what is to be found in this rich literature.

114. Manipulation requires a cunning com-prehension—a taking in hand of the other, by playing on his emotions to bypass his reflection, that ground of the possibility of his acting genuinely freely. Imagine in this a spectrum of possibilities, running from manipulation, through persuasion, to rational, critical argument. But also remember Freud's warning in the *Traumbedeutung* about overdetermination: One's motives for doing anything are never simple, and even when one attempts to be as clear and straightforward with oneself or another as possible, there are undetected overtones of motivation operating. This sense is caught better in the German term: *überbestimmung*.

115. Lies can be onetime acts of weakness, a neurotic dimension of the persona, or psychotic delusion, with varying degrees of self-deception mixed in. In psychogenesis, the form-ation of psychic energy patterns, there is a chicken-and-egg situation. The child comes to awareness having already been formed in a mediocre situation, where some degree of confusion and disorder is both maintained through lies and caused by them. Even in the most loving family, he is to some extent manipulated, and in turn responds, to some extent freely, to both genuine love and manipulation with a mixture of love, lie, and manipulation

incapacity to face certain realities; rather, something more mysterious: deliberate perversion, well-maintained hypocrisy and the deception implied in all moral evil. These are effective blocks to thought and are thought's disorderer. This capability of choosing the lesser, perhaps even a patently destructive path, of destroying and dissimilating with the very powers meant, by their nature, to construct and reveal, is an ontological mystery, not to be reduced to the structure that allows it to happen.

By the "liar" I mean here everyone insofar as we are all tempted to try to get something without paying the price—the commitment of disciplined, ordered energy—everyone who at some point lacks the discipline to do what he knows, on some level, is needed,[116] perhaps because he is simply afraid. What is needed includes all thinking worthy of the name.[117] When one is not free oneself, and allows himself to be controlled by others, controlling seems all he knows. Control is a lower form of energy deployment than love and appreciation, which hold open the field of free exchange, requiring continual mutual creativity. The user has no respect for the freedom of the other, because he has little for his own.[118] The manipulator plays on the emotions of the other like a musical instrument, seeking to bypass genuine dialogue which invites that healthy reflection which leads to genuine decision.[119] The unfreedom in inauthentic society is the builder of bad elements in the traditions. It is a principal source of such horrors as race and class hatreds, religious fanaticism, and ethnic strife.

The *pseudos* is the source of what Plato calls "disturbance" or psychic disorder—*akosmia*[120]—whether self-induced or traumatically caused by the aggressive other. The disturbance sets energies, which should be working together harmoniously, against one another (internal conflict), or takes away their proper rational reference to one another (dissipation). Sometimes our energies are uncoordinated and even work at cross-purposes, not because we are pursuing some sick fantasy, but because we fail to think. To be fair, we

---

of his own. Sorting this all out is the work of a lifetime, the core of sound spiritual formation, which may need to be accompanied, where patterns are too pathological, by psychotherapy.

116. What the Christian means by "the will of God." Motivated by the supernatural virtue of faith (con-fidence) in the Source of Being in His revelation and hope in His benevolence, the Christian sees in the needs and possibilities of his concrete situation a loving call to participate in his own manner in the building of the Kingdom. That is why he is supposed to be patient in adversity, because he believes that a loving ordering principle is at work, and that such difficulties can become especially efficacious occasions of growth as a person. This is supernatural hope.

117. On this, see the wonderful reflection, *The Intellectual Life: Its Spirit, Conditions, Methods*, by A. D. Sertillanges, O.P., trans. Mary Ryan (Westminster, Mo.: Newman Press, 1959).

118. The problem is that he fulfills the commandment, "Love thy neighbor as thyself." His own lack of self-respect, or his parents having retarded its development, has something to do with the deficiency of that love.

119. Inauthentic everyday society is a tissue of utilitarian relationships, grounded in routine and secured by emotional mortgages, relieved, fortunately, by occasional moments of free exchange and even strands of committed love.

120. *Republic* 504A. See also Voegelin, *Order and History*, vol. 3, *Plato and Aristotle*, 36, 63, 69.

should admit that frequently our situations and motivations are so complicated and loyalties conflicting, it becomes difficult to sort out. Mindlessness can result from pulling back from situations one finds so confused, he does not know how to begin to deal with them.

If what I am striving for is a delusion, it can only be sustained at the price of insupportable destruction of something or someone else, manipulated to play the role demanded by my fantasy, the disturbance of fruitful relationships, or the morally unacceptable dismantling of an entity. (Going through the motions—for instance, engaging in signs of friendship where there is no commitment—is a form of lie, appearances substituted for reality, signs that have no contact with the signified.)

Going through the Motions and the Reality of Everyday Living Out of Truth

This last point raises an ontological issue about the fabric of everyday existence. Is not going through the motions a rather minor form of lie, without which daily life as we know it would be rather impossible? Just how destructive can something so common, so banal, really be?

When one gives the appearance of being what in reality he is not, he deceives himself, the way a routinely religious person, by rather effortlessly fulfilling all the rules, gives himself the assurance he is earning heaven. Pseudo-religion is a classic form of escape from the world (and one of the most effective blocks on the Way to God. It puts an idolatrous God-figure, tailor-made to fit our narcissistic notion of our needs, in the place of the genuine living Source).

Second, the liar offers a disturbed witness, which can lead others to conclude that the entire sphere of activity in which he is engaged is illusory. Fanaticism can discredit the greatest causes,[121] especially devastating in politics and religion, because both deal obligatorily with ultimate issues that do not permit scientific experimental control. Because the religious symbols are about being itself and about the very meaning of life,[122] they place the utmost demands upon us. Our failing to live up to them is to some degree inevitable. (The greatest saints express their unworthiness for the love God bestows upon them.)

I have been very rough on going through the motions. Ontological balance demands that I put in a word here on behalf of a proper place for some routine. For us incarnational creatures, the social and religious forms are frameworks provided by the traditions and institutions, invitations to perform in certain ways, which may be good or bad. A considerable capital is transmitted in

---

121. Since that is always the case, one cannot judge the truth of any tradition through brandishing the excesses of its fanatics. This is a tendency in Eric Hoffer's *True Believer*, which makes it in some ways a seriously distorting account.

122. Dr. Edwin Hersch points out to me how frequently grave psychic disorder is expressed in religious or moral terms—the patient, for instance, instructed by the voice of God. In conversation, we agreed that this is probably because a matter disturbing the depths of the soul requires the most absolute language the person knows.

those forms. Those intersubjective fruits of past discovery require personal appropriation if the good is to be separated from the bad and their full sense enjoyed. Still, the routine motion is a gesture and, as such, a witness. It need not be as mediocre or as hypocritical as adolescents think when they seek to get out from under the tradition. I might go regularly to visit an old friend in the hospital, and nothing much may happen between us; yet my very coming there says something. It creates an intersubjective fact. The person who drags his weary bones to Mass every Sunday says something too, even if he daydreams when he is there.

One should not to be too quick to equate what strikes us as mediocre and the downright hypocritical. In the spirit of Christ's admonition, "Judge not lest ye be judged" (Matt. 7:1), remember that often people are doing the best they can, in all honesty. Descending from a high pharisaical level of criticism, we may judge them harshly, ignorant of the integrity their (to us) pitiable effort represents. Recall Christ's parable of the rich Pharisee who boasts of giving a tenth of his great wealth to the Temple while the humble widow gives her mite, which, it turns out, is all she has (Mark 12:42).

In sum: Enculturation into an explicit tradition leaves one with a set of practices that call for at least going through the motions. In art, they are technique and style. In association, the rules of the game. In science, method and mind-set. In the case of a religious tradition, they may be motions of a liturgical and perhaps private prayer life (say, morning offering and evening act of contrition and grace before meals) and meditation, and certain practices of almsgiving or social work. The tradition, second, hands on a treasure-hoard of symbol. In religion these would be found in the sacred books, in the teachings of the fathers, in the catechism and documents of ongoing Magisterial teaching. These symbols are forms that not only encapsulate the Being won from many past encounters with reality but the power to move us to action and to direct us in our ways. Mediocre religious education can hand on a more or less pat worldview; some forms of living teaching authority, such as a catechism, might strike one that way, although they can represent an authentic effort to transmit clearly, for the use and benefit of the whole faithful, profoundly meditated-upon truths.

The teachings of any explicit tradition can easily be turned into an ideology, answers held in such a neat way as to become a block to challenging thinking. (Consider, for instance, the close-minded positivism of many university science teachers.) In the case of Christianity, one can say that this kind of ideological deformation requires a curious distortion of the revelation, which confronts us with the greatest possible paradoxes,[123] hardly the stuff for pat answers. But the ideologue's talent for turning the Cross into a crutch and then using it, when the occasion demands, to beat people over the head with "The Truth," is widespread.

---

123. One of this century's greatest theologians, Henri Cardinal de Lubac, wrote no less than three books on paradox.

But let us turn to the positive side to see in more depth what typically such a tradition offers as nourishment for interior life—as a Way to being.

The Offering of Institutional Forms of Religion

The Church (and the synagogue, not to forget similar institutions in other traditions) is the only institution in our society that at least tries to get people to reflect throughout their life. Schools and universities do this too, but we are not enrolled in them from birth to death, nor do most school programs attempt these days to cover the essential life issues. Sermons, retreats, meditation on Scripture, on the mysteries of the life of Moses or Jesus or Mohammad, and, at the extreme, the disciplined life of contemplation in the monastery or the yeshiva or Sufi school, not to mention the existence of perhaps four thousand Christian seminaries, colleges, and universities throughout the world, represent an enormous effort of *Bildung* by seeking to cajole and discipline people into reflection on the last things. The more than four hundred thousand Catholic priests in the world are required by canon law to engage in an hour of structured reflection daily (the Holy Office, or canonical hours, an obligation over and beyond saying Mass, and that puts them in contact systematically every day with the entire sweep of the four-thousand-year-old tradition).

In what ways do the symbols, liturgical practices, sacraments, and specific forms of virtue nurture a deeper life of the soul? How may the divine presence to us through these means? What does this reveal about Being?

The genuine divine, being infinite freedom, cannot be magically forced, any more than the true freedom of another person can, by any kind of incantation, be manipulated by the individual ego to presence in the depth of the soul, revealing the soul to itself. To believe otherwise is the worst of "gnostic" distortions.[124] There are, on the other hand, many means of inducing in oneself a delusionary psychic state, perhaps even hallucination, so one may entertain his psychiatrist by telling him what the voice of God has announced.

The divine presence, beyond what anyone can sense in nature, is not an abstract idea but—at least as it is experienced within the Abrahamic communities—a concrete Word. The commanding presence as Person takes definite initiatives, placing demands upon us (Abraham, asked to sacrifice his son!), just as the relations we take up with any person are always demanding, too. If we elect to be open to that presence, then we must be receptive to his being with us as he is, as he elects to be present, and as he elects to be absent—precisely the opposite of what Freud thought of all religious sentiment, that is, precisely not as a projection of our imagination.

---

124. Even in the midst of the Sinai experience, Moses seemed, by asking God His name, to be trying to get some kind of control of Him. YHWH's reply—these letters mean precisely the lack of a name for Him, *ehye asher ehye*, which the Middle Ages interpreted as "I am pure existence"—carries as well, according to Martin Buber, the sense "I shall be present as I shall be present." See the profound pages in Buber's *Moses* (Oxford: East and West Library, 1946).

How, according to the witness of these different traditions, does one know, how does this concrete presencing of the divine actually occur, when, unexpectedly, it does happen?

The holy books of each tradition are inexhaustible treasures of symbols expressing different kinds of knowledge of the divine. The various Hindic traditions, for instance, offer claims about how the divinity presences that are quite different from any of the Abrahamic traditions.[125]

The *Mahayana* and the *Hinayana*—the Great and the Little Vehicle—present their own negative ways of emptying out all that separates us from the Nothing, but popular Buddhism differs from the more intellectual and the purer traditions, in some forms becoming a kind of polytheism.

Judaism testifies to God's prophetic presence in his chosen people, as a leader God, and to the gift of the Law as the way God has elected for his people to follow him.

Christianity claims that the divine Word came into history not just through the prophets but by dwelling among us as a gift of love. This fleeting instance of unique presencing in Jesus Christ teaching the Father's will showed us how to live and, manifesting the Father's supreme power through his total emptying out of self, offered his body as a redeeming sacrifice for our sins. Gloriously defeating death itself, he withdrew to allow the continuing presence of the Holy Spirit of Father and Son working, until the end of history, in the Church.

Islam, accepting its own version of the prophets of the Old and New Testament, including Jesus—according to the Qur'an, not Son of God but the greatest among them—finds the Word in its entirety in the Qur'anic revelation, and draws inspiration from the example of the life of Mohammad, putting the Truth of the Qur'an into practice.

Greek natural theology, the center of philosophical speculation, certainly for Plato, Aristotle, the Stoics, and the Neoplatonists, strives to discover the divine presence in the depths of the soul.

The nonreligious person cannot help wondering, with Feuerbach and Freud, how much of all these vast inquirings is mere human projection, impressive perhaps but still mere wish fulfillment lacking in objective ontological substance. But if one so suspects, should he not, in all fairness and in his self-interest, ask: How is it, and in what ways, all this illusion seems to have provided over the millennia some genuine nourishment for the interior life? (Freud's appropriation was terribly negative.)

The religious person is confronted by just as demanding a critical task. He, too, needs to sort out genuine spiritual nourishment from unhealthy wish fulfillment. There is no hope of doing this so long as one stands outside these traditions, making no effort to see what those who live steeped in these ways

---

125. Hindic is shorthand for all the many varied and complex traditions of religion and spirituality in the vast Indian subcontinent for the past three thousand years. Although most of the Hindic traditions are polytheistic, certain developments move toward monotheism. The whole complex story of the Hindic traditions is poorly known to me.

purport to have experienced and, through their witness, invite all to see. Nor is there any hope of doing it so long as those within the tradition refuse to see how much illusion creeps into every religion.

The notion of way is central. As *ek-sisting* builders we develop, following some process, demanding a modicum of direction and consistency. Greek philosophy speaks of following the disciplined way (*meta + hodos*, whence the word "method"). It is intended as an exercise of the soul. Gautama the Buddha invited his followers to imitate, to continue in his way. The Christ declared, "I am the way—unless you follow me you will not have life—you can only *go* to the Father through me." Even with Descartes' introduction of modern essentially secular psychic inwardness, very different from religious interiority, there remains emphasis on following a way. Descartes introduces his subjectivist revolution in *Discours sur la méthode*, but now *méthode* is depersonalized completely, a far cry from "Come follow me, the living Word." With Descartes, Kant, Freud, or Marx, it is "Come follow my scientific method." (Comte and Marx at least provided for a community: respectively, the Positivist Temple and the Communist Party.)

The assembling of many persons into technological institutions requires method. But it also requires common goals, consistent intersubjective willing to coordinate energies, which results in building the social habits without which neither institution nor community could exist.

How One Way Nourishes the Interior Life

Because each religious and other ideational tradition presents its distinctive experiences, caught in its own symbols, and lived out in different forms of institution, thus meriting treatment as a kind of grand personality, none should become the model for understanding the others. Appropriation of the truth places different demands on us from one kind of tradition to another: Interpreting scientific truth claims is something quite different from sorting out the associational truth of an industrial corporation and that is something quite different from following the development of impressionist painting and what it reveals of the world. There are lessons for ontology in general and for better understanding of the interior life in particular in an examination of each of the great traditions: artistic, religious, and scientific/philosophic.

To this suggestion that there is a need to appropriate each of the great traditions in its own terms three objections might be raised. The first is an implication of relativism; the second is the difficulty of bringing them together in a single wisdom—the challenge of translation; the third is the seemingly endless nature of the task. Although *Tradition and Authenticity* and Chapter 5 of the present work deal with all three, a word of reminder is useful.

Integration of the truth won from any particular tradition into one's wisdom will be guided by one's natural faith, formed by the traditions one believes to be most true. Still, this basic canon of rationality, which no one of good faith and sound mind can reject, applies: Criticize Islam (for instance) for what Islam believes, not for propositions you, out of ignorance of Islam, put in Muslims' mouths. Honest confrontation of differing experiences should lead to inquiry into the grounds of one's own natural faith, and not to distortion of the other's experience to make it fit easily.

The objection about the endlessness of the task is well founded: Respectful study of all the great traditions would be an inexhaustible undertaking. I know this painfully from the fraction of the task which I have worked away at for twenty-five years. It is a task exceeding the ability even of a large collegial group of dialoguing searchers. But it is a task the ideal of which needs to be pursued nonetheless: Just as the physical and biological sciences are confronted with a never to be achieved ideal of understanding the cosmos and the processes of life, so the reflecting community should be seeking to think being as revealed in all the traditions, to find the essence of what *Sein* has illumined and obscured in each of the traditions, and the whole human endeavor together. In both cases the challenge is not only theoretical (Know it better because it is here to be known) but practical. Out of the sciences grows technology; out of appropriation of the traditions grows the chance for a more meaningful human existence and a more peaceful world.

The challenge of translation is more a moral than a theoretical problem. From my own experience seeking to understand other traditions, and from participation in Islamic-Christian dialogue, I have seen that the issue is motivation: wanting to hear the other. Living in a great tradition is already learning to listen to the witness and revelation of others, proffered us in their Word. A Catholic, for instance, lives from the treasure handed down from the prophets, from Christ ("not by bread alone" [Matt. 4:4], "but by every word that comes forth from God" [Deut. 8:3]), and from the reflections of the fathers and doctors of the four thousand years of lived experience. If I want to hear the word from any of these, I have to want to listen to the "stille Stimme des Seins" (the quiet voice of Being) illumining the world of his discourse, and integrate it into my own in a way totally respectful of what the other wants to tell me.

For present purposes, I shall look into only a couple of aspects of one tradition, probing examples of what it means to be nourished by handed-on experience. I shall remain with the one I know best, which, fortunately for our ontology, is a fundamental one, inexorably mixed up with our Western culture and life. Even a brief examination of this history will help us begin to understand what it means to claim some kind of encounter with the divine as ultimate Source of being.

At the same time, this will serve as a first step toward consideration of the divine. I prefer this approach to the more classical philosophical one of launching first into examination of proofs for the existence of God, because it seems to me truer to the way we come to know God. Characteristically we encounter the divine by being reared in the life of a community claiming acquaintance with the divine or, later in life, by encountering the witness of such a community.[126] Formal philosophical proofs play a restricted and special role only in certain intellectual traditions; they are not how the divine is encountered as Being. We shall discuss all this later.

The first consideration I intend to raise is rather paradoxical: The condition for the possibility of the interior life—the most intensely personal—is its being nourished by a way that is life in a community. For example, Plato founded a community, the Academy, to search for God. Aristotle founded his community, the Lyceum. The Neoplatonic philosophers were all functioning parts of communities that not only sought the divine theoretically but attempted to live together a life of wisdom. Plato's Academy, in one form or another, lasted more than half a millennium, until Justinian closed it in A.D. 529. Judaism is the religion of a people. Islam is the religion of the *umma,* literally, the great "mother folk," gathered about the revelation transmitted through the Prophet. Christ founded his *ecclesia,* his gathering, and he built it on Petrus, designating the leadership of his flock, and promising that his spirit would be sent to guide it. In the sixth century, Benedict of Nursia wrote a rule of community life to assure intensification of interior life, the start of a vast monastic movement in the West lasting until our own day.

Is that to imply, then, that the interior life starts (and ends?) somehow outside? A vision leading to community life may begin deep within the soul of the founder of the tradition, but for those who come after, it is communicated from outside, in the community into which one is enculturated, it is sustained by the community's life, and its object—in the case of the religion, the divine with which the soul seeks union—is supposed to ravish the soul, drawing it out of itself (to e-ducate it), without its becoming alienated.

The ontological implications of all this go beyond reflection on our necessarily social nature as incarnate beings: The Abrahamic religions, as do the philosophies flowing from Plato and Aristotle, see Being revealing itself as one displayed in many. Time-space is experienced as radiating from a center, which for Plato is the fertile Idea of the *Agathon* (the Good), for Aristotle the attraction of the self-thinking Thought, and in Hebrew revelation manifests the character of a creation and a Leader God, further revealed in Christ as a life, indeed ultimately as a body into which each of us personal thinkers is to be gathered in love to become its living members. This one-in-many freely divides and multiplies, bringing new life to the created many, who are intended to be knit together, as are the divine Persons of the Triune God themselves, by bonds of love.

It is the ontological meaning of the order of this life of the one-in-many that has to be penetrated if one is to grapple with the Christian, Hebrew, Islamic,

---

126. Even in our society, where atheists, dominating the media and the universities, make a disproportionate noise, census figures show that still, in 1992, an overwhelming majority of children are brought up in families with some theist tradition. The last census saw 92 percent of Canadians report themselves as being Christians. See *Statistics,* Canada's summary report on the 1992 census (Ottawa: Queen's Printer for Canada, 1993).

or Greek philosophical traditions,[127] and their various senses of the interior life. (A life, after all, is a unity out of many, whether natural or cultivated [*Bildung*], always form guiding process, Apollo conquering Dionysus, but Dionysus impelling always to new forms.)[128]

In the Platonic traditions, God is sought dialectically, dialectic being the way for plunging deep in the life of the soul seeking the source of unity, a method developed by Socrates, perfected by Plato, and continued for a half millennium in the Academy by his disciples, erotically[129] seeking the *sophon*. The mnemonic element—the soul recalling its previous dwelling in the presence of the divine forms—plays a central role.[130]

In the Abrahamic traditions, the temporality of the community is also founded in memory, but not of visions in another world, rather of historic acts, God's mighty deeds calling into existence and leading a people. It is they, the faithful members of that historic people, who keep alive the memory and anticipate the eschatological fulfillment, promised by God and toward which, by his continuing presence, in which they have faith—con-fidence—he is leading them. From such an eschatological temporality—fruit of a breakthrough on Sinai, and missing in Platonism—is born, in fact, history.[131]

In Christianity the people of God expands from the people of Israel through active embrace of all mankind: God wills that all be united in a single family of love, under his divine fatherhood, not in theory but through consistent and persistent acts of solicitude exercised already in this world and continued, perfected, in the next, together constituting the Kingdom of God. Here *Bildung* receives a definite social realization, the progress of the Church. This coming together in love is the work of God's own spirit moving among us, introduced in the fullness of God's revelation about his being, through the divine Word, and realized in history only through our cooperation. The Word was sent into history to found the new covenant with God; then, after conquering death for all mankind, he deliberately withdrew in order to send forth, under the guidance of the Holy Spirit, this concrete, real apostolic people to gather all creatures into one definitive family, the ontological achievement of the creative process, the lasting form.

---

127. The interpenetration of persons has influenced modern physics. James Clerk Maxwell discovered field theory while reflecting on the creative work of the Holy Spirit. Thomas McCormick explores this in "The Field and the Spirit" (manuscript in progress).

128. That is why those who hate their own lives want to sow disorder, to divide *(diabolein)* class from class, intensifying social-pathological tendencies such as incipient racism or sexism while preaching that they are against it.

129. For Plato this is eros always guided by the Apollonian.

130. For an analysis of this teaching, see Voegelin, *Order and History*, vol. 3, *Plato and Aristotle*, and also his epistemic reflections, *Anamnesis* (Notre Dame: University of Notre Dame Press, 1978).

131. Voegelin, *Order and History*, vol. 1, *Israel and Revelation*. Voegelin demonstrates that the sense of going somewhere, of having a destiny, was born in mankind first with the revelation on Sinai.

This is a symphonic vision: *Die Wahrheit ist Symphonisch* is the title Balthasar gave to one of his books. Architecture and painting, being static, even at their most effervescent rococo best, cannot capture adequately the pluralism of manifestations of God this essentially living vision plays out for us in the harmony of God's unfolding living Word, working polyphonically through distinctive spiritualities.

How is this people empowered to make Christ present, so that individuals, with their distinctive personhood and spiritualities, are brought together in an effective Christ-centered community of love, a many-voiced[132] Kingdom destined to spread to the whole earth? There are three dimensions to this:

1. passing on the Incarnate Word, not just Christ's teaching but witness to his mighty deeds, a vision of how that culture is to be built up in the members, through the supernatural virtues of faith, hope, and charity;
2. assuring the sacramental presence of Christ and prayer life as *communio* with him and through him with the Father, and through them with all the saints—a community that spans time and space, reaching beyond this world; and
3. the works of love (Eucharist, not just as remembering-thanksgiving, but as "doing this . . ." as the operations of charity, form of all the other activities of man, *forma virtuorum*) by which "you shall know I am with you." ("What you have done for the least of my brethren you have done for me" [Matt. 25:40].)

In Part II, we considered these as aspects of a way in which a kind of truth could be handed down. Now we shall look at them again, but this time as dimensions of a way of being, the being of interior life, which as ultimate created form throws light on Being itself.

The Teaching. As one is reared in a Christian tradition he encounters the Word of God in sermons, in Bible-reading sessions, in catechism instruction, and in formal prayer (the psalms, for instance; and readings from the Scripture are a substantial portion of the Eucharistic liturgy). If it was an active Christian milieu, he will probably have at his fingertips a wealth of biblical images, illustrating most of life's basic situations; he will have before his mind's eye the figure of Christ and his main disciples, Mary his mother, the early Church community. Woven throughout this treasure of images will be a quite concrete prescription for how the Christian is to conduct his life, in love, which is the point of the whole teaching, after all. He will be so well and specifically instructed, he will generally know in most situations how he is expected to

---

132. As Christianity interacts with various preexistent cultures and unfolds in local and national Christian communities, it is bound to produce many Christian cultures (*Bildungen*); but to the extent the one people of God is obedient to God's will, follows Christ on his way, and thus becomes as perfect an image of Christ as possible, an underlying universal Christian culture should become apparent.

give of himself. (That is true of many other traditions as well: they offer a rich pedagogy.) The question before us now, though, is how these riches actually feed the interior life, understood as a way of being.

Although meditating on scriptural or patristic texts or papal and conciliar documents is clearly a method of internalizing what these sources have to say, normally most Christians encounter the teachings in a liturgical and prayer setting. In fact, that turns out to be appropriate. When they approach in a humble receptive spirit of discipleship—"Teach me Lord!"—where one is experiencing the presence of Christ among a group of worshipers, this is a most fitting way to interiorize the Word. Liturgy (literally, "work of the crowd") is a public act, and good works are social realities. Yet they are so essentially bound up with the kind of revelation of being we are here investigating, we must probe deeper into how the Word, the liturgical and prayer act, and good works relate to one another, before we can grasp their impact on the interior life.

Liturgical and Prayer Life. "Wherever two or three are gathered in my name, there I am" (Matt. 18:20). The role of Christians is sacramental, to make Christ present everywhere in the world, by themselves being an icon—imperfect but striving for sanctification—of him whom they believe to be the perfect icon of God. This disposition is more perfectly realized in society than by lonely saints because the interior life of the Triune God is revealed to be a loving commerce of three persons.

But that social reality of the Mystical Body of Christ does not sound very interior. Remember, though, we are not trying to invent an interior life that does not exist. Remember the incarnate intentional nature of our consciousness—the interior life is nourished only by the content given it in experience. Now, if God has revealed that within the absolute simplicity of the Godhead, there is a life consisting of the knowledge and love the three divine persons have of each other,[133] the Son being dependent on the Father's total gift of himself, and the Son obediently receiving and giving back that love; and that it is this life which, by the divine will, is exteriorized in creation and in the sending forth of the divine Logos, "in the fullness of time," into the created world, then the liturgy is appropriate Christian prayer precisely because incarnational and social as well. The central Christian liturgy, the Eucharist, is *agape*, a love feast. That is why the kiss of peace, just before receiving the Body and Blood of Christ under the signs of bread and wine, is so appropriate, and why every Christian preacher repeatedly insists that participating in the Eucharist without its flowing over into good works is hypocrisy.

A certain routinization of the sacramental-liturgical life is part of the strength of the system: the regularity and endurance of the liturgy over millennia has assured an effective presencing, it provides a body *(liturgia)* into which the spirit

---

133. The early Church fathers' use of this term, *persona*, to express these distinctions transforms the term from the theater and Roman legal usage, a step in the evolution of its sense to our present understanding, which derives from the theological reflections on the personhood of Jesus, as one of the three aspects of the divine life.

can—indeed, if it is to come to something, must—be breathed. Think of this routine as a kind of form that must be constantly enlivened by the breathing in of spirit. The long and arduous work must be directed inward, to the seat of psychic energies, seeking then to transform hard hearts to render them more pure (of crippling egoism) and more generous, *sanctification* requiring an enduring discipline and a limitless outpouring of grace to feed both the contemplative inner life, where the intimate love in Christ is nourished, and the exteriorization of its fruits in good works. The Bible emphasizes "doing the word," which is about "loving one another as I have loved you." The object, whatever it is, always makes its demands. But when the object is another horizon-opening, Being-projecting person in turn reaching out deliberately toward me to enfold me in his world, a complex meeting of interiorities, through the mediation of the separating and joining materiality of our bodies, our body language, our linguistic symbols, and all the things we are working on together, is at play: *symphonisch,* including the instruments we play. To the extent that each avoids mindlessness, this should challenge him to a deeper interior life. As interior life is grounded in the social being of a community, what, then, is entailed in such Being-with *(Mitsein)?*

SOCIAL BEING

From a brief encounter, an event with no lasting significance, a new social entity comes into existence, as it does in a friendship that may last beyond death. Social entities can range in time from minutes to eternity, and in scale from a relationship between two individuals to the vast reality of the nation or the Catholic Church, which would embrace all mankind under God.

The friendship of the minimal two already establishes a very complex being, which can compound indefinitely as the friendship is enlarged to a group of friends, a family, or any other form of larger association in which love relationships can still exist. But the intensity and depth tend to remain at the one-on-one level. (Hearts do not often open up on committees.) There are plenty of put-downs between brothers and sisters in a family, but it is difficult to rise far above the level of purely occupational or professional relationships in larger groups. The need, fed by our insecurities, to read carefully the other's signals and to keep control of emotions is too urgent for intimacy to occur.

Lovers are most interested in what is going on in the other's soul. How many times does one spouse ask another, "What are you thinking?" And because confidence between humans is rarely perfect, many a time the spouse may not care to tell.[134] Indeed, does one not sense that the interior life of the other is where his real self is to be found, in his deepest convictions, in his heart

---

134. An interesting question to pursue, but not here: Does one have a right to retain a little corner of privacy from even the most intimate companion? Or is the desire to do so prima facie evidence of lack of confidence, hence of a blemish in the relationship, a lack of being where being is due, hence a moral evil?

of hearts, and that hardness or purity of heart matters most? "Show me his loves and I will show you the man," said Augustine, that is, the hidden source, deeper than all *Bildung* and even chafing at the constraints of nature, from whence all fantasy and indeed all *Sein*, save for the mysterious input from Beyond, surges up.

Because acting in common cause is out there in the shared time-space, the public square, a certain tension appears to exist between the intimacy of the interior life and all social action. Are we glimpsing here, too, something of the dialectic of God's nearness and transcendence, that *Nähe und Ferne* (near and far) Balthasar sees manifest even in the sudden appearings and disappearings of the Incarnate Christ?[135]

Our actions, however, do not just reveal who we really are down deep. They are at the same time a further development of our being. Even a contemplation in which, for instance, I reflect upon some aspect of the life in Christ, although it may not at this moment have any exteriorly observable result, still to the extent that it changes my being,[136] it is bound—if it is serious—to affect my actions, and so change the material energies of the exterior world.

Can God Be Found in the Soul?

So the interior life is always a going out by the soul toward its object, the form of which has already been e-ducated by a community. But what about the claim of the mystic to find God deep within the very workings of the soul? By "God" he does not mean, of course, the presence of Christ in the Church, in those living icons, the people of true love we encounter. Rather, he is referring to an intimate relationship of the soul with its own ultimate Source.

Because "God" in this sense is involved in every push in nature and even the most arbitrary and fantastic productions of the human brain, it is necessary to clarify our understanding of the ways in which God can be known and our appreciation for the nature of the various kinds of evidence of God's working in all reality.

Few are closed to the consideration that some sort of Source stands at the initial surge of cosmic energy and is also in some way at work in the complexifying becoming of the world in and about us. But how to discern this ultimate dimension of dynamic reality, how to distinguish it from its effects—cosmos and culture—what to attribute to it, how it is experienced and evidenced, these are matters of dispute among thinkers of good will.

We shall turn, then, in the next chapter to this challenge of how and what we know of God, the context for the question whether there can be an encounter with God deep in the soul.

---

135. Balthasar, *Die Wahrheit ist Symphonisch* (Einsiedeln: Johannes Verlag, 1972), pt. 2, chap. 3, "Ein Gott der Nähe und der Ferne," 105–15.

136. Both the *inesse* of my habits and the *Sein* of my outlook.

The Breakthrough to Consciousness and Evolution

I remind the reader of the question asked initially: "Is the breakthrough to consciousness a mysterious reversal of the thrust to evolution, or the fulfillment of what it is now understood to have been working toward?

Throughout I have been hypothesizing that psychic energy is somehow different from the energy deployed in the rest of nature in all changes of state. By describing the process of *bilden*, I have invoked a sense both of what distinguishes man's higher, more spiritual operations from all lower forms of energy, and of the thrust of the development that has prepared the way and upon which the human is still dependent.

But before the final assault on these issues, at least within the limits of this volume, I must face directly the question of evidence for and the nature of the *archē*. Only then will we be in a position to pose the basic questions of an ontology, not just the issue of clarifying and situating matter and spirit, but what is meant by being and what have been discovered to be the fundamental dimensions of our human, finite experience of it.

8.

THE ULTIMATE GROUND

> The argument [for the divine], of course, is not a "proof" in the sense of a logical demonstration, of an *apodeixis*, but only in the sense of an *epideixis*, of a pointing to an area of reality that the constructor of the negative propositions [vis-à-vis the Divine Ground] has chosen to overlook, or to ignore, or to refuse to perceive. One cannot prove reality by a syllogism; one can only point to it and invite the doubter to look. The more or less deliberate confusion of the two meanings of the word *proof* is still a standard trick employed by the negators in the contemporary ideological debates [on this point]; and it plays an important role in the genesis of the "proofs" for the existence of God ever since the time of Anselm.
> —Eric Voegelin, "The Beginning and Beyond"

According to Heidegger, since the beginning of metaphysics some notion or another of a *Grund*—whether understood as the greatest entity, cause of all other entities (the Beginning, or *archē*), or as somehow beyond all limits and hence thought as entity only inappropriately (the Beyond)—has been the way *Sein* has revealed itself in the thought of the West, as grounded.[1] Voegelin asks whether for Plato and the early Gnostics, the Beginning and the Beyond are to be thought as the same God.[2] We saw earlier how naturally the question of

---

1. This is why, according to Heidegger, *Sein* has dissimulated itself, being missed then as the horizontal, ecstatic time-space world opening in which, historically, *Sein* comes to be. The thought either of ground as *Ur-sache* (the German word for "cause" means literally "fundamental state of affairs") or of the most general concept, being as transcendental predicate, distracts attention from *Sein* as worlding world of *ek-static* time-space of revelation. Here the symbol, being, includes all three: the transcendental concept, predicable analogously; *Sein* as *ek-static* opening of world; and *esse*, being as real existence independent of what may be thought about it.
2. Eric Voegelin, "The Beginning and the Beyond," in *What Is History? and Other Late Unpublished Writings*, vol. 28 of *The Collected Works*, ed. Thomas Hollweck and Paul Caringella (Baton Rouge: Louisiana State University Press, 1990), 202.

the unity of being occurs to us, and how inevitably this raises the issue of the ground of that unity and, Voegelin would add, of the unity of the ground.

Meantime, while the metaphysicians busied themselves with questions of ground, unmoved mover, first cause, self-thinking thought, and the One, ordinary mortals found in their belief in a personal God[3] some sense of a foundation, not just to the universe, but to their personal and social lives. "You, O my God, are my refuge and my strength!"

Complicating this already mixed and ambiguous picture of metaphysics and of popular striving to conceive of a personal God or gods, the Abrahamic traditions of revelation confront the thinker with prophets claiming that through them God is revealing himself, and in such a way as to transcend the limits of all metaphysical and popular religious stretching toward God. The good news is proclaimed: He has reached down from his infinite transcending Beyond to reveal his personhood, his intimacy to all being, and his loving plan for man.

Because of the sense of unity accompanying the thought of Being, a contemporary ontology should undertake more than some kind of Feuerbachian or Nietzschean critique of naive or anthropological notions of God, and more than just a warming over of the Kantian notion of the need for a concept of God as a regulative principle of thought. Rather, it should probe, as Heidegger himself did, the evident need in a deeper sense to which this thought of God responded, in order to understand better why, in the history of *Sein*, Being so revealed and obscured itself. Such a probing reflection led, in Heidegger's case, to a critique of what he conceived of as the metaphysical function of God as ground, distracting from the sense of *Sein* and the transcendental origin of the notion of ground. One should not be so disappointed with Heidegger's personal failure, his unwillingness to consider seriously the prophetic claims of God's self-revelation, that he does not see the truth that every ontology should reply to his challenge[4] of appropriating the history of *Sein*, but being sure to include in its development all thinking about Being and God, especially the prophetic claims.

The Christian tradition has looked on atheism as an aberration, from Saint Paul's recalling the psalmist's assertion, "Only the fool says in his heart there is no God" (Ps. 14:1),[5] to the declaration of the encyclical of Pius XII *Humani generis* (1940), "Human reason can, without the help of divine revelation and grace, prove the existence of a personal God by arguments drawn from created

---

3. Whether in One God, as with the Abrahamists, or in many gods under a Supreme God, as with the Greek Pantheon under Zeus or the Roman under Jupiter.

4. Heidegger's challenge is that either we rethink the nature of ground or at least situate the discovery of the Source within the *Lichtung des Seins*, the time-space historical world opening. I attempt this in Chapters 9 and 10. A response to Voegelin's challenge follows, with particular attention demanded, the Christian philosopher would say, to the dangers, in his profound analysis, of undermining the objective dimension of revelation. See below.

5. On the sense of the Hebrew *nabal*, see Voegelin's excellent discussion in "The Beginning and the Beyond," 199.

things."[6] (It should be added, however, that the First Vatican Council was careful not to assert that fallen man does always in fact recognize the God who is implied, as the Absolute, in all reasoning, or that revelation is not important to knowing who God is. And the Second Vatican Council took an attitude respectful of the sincerity of atheists.)[7]

Now, the Church is not alone in insisting that, properly understood, God is included as the ground and end of all thinking. Many philosophers have contended that man of his very nature seeks to relate consciously to a transcendent Ground, implied by the very quest for truth. Some, like Eric Voegelin and Mircea Eliade, would also then see the atheists to be the exception requiring explanation: What cultural events have invited such "gnostic" individuals to become "agnostic" regarding God, in the name of a gnosis deemed by them superior to what lies naturally in the human heart? Why have they "closed the apophantic field" that was opened, in our tradition, at Sinai, in the breakthrough founding history and that, as a result of this event, became a central dimension of the revelation of Being (Voegelin)? Writing off all the evidence of encounter with a divine Other as mere human projection (Feuerbach) and trying to replace any transcendent notion of *Grund* as essentially different from that based in a monistic principle like will to power (Nietzsche) constitute severe constrictions of the field of what is to be considered.

The atheist of course will see it as a healthy surgery rather than a kind of forgetting. Freud's view of religion as neurosis has come to dominate much of the university, a phenomenon Voegelin sees as itself the serious pathology.[8] (It leads to wonderful dialogue to have both sides squared off, hurling mutual accusations of mental disorder. The university is such a peaceful milieu, ideal for loving dialogue and reflective meditation.)

Cultural anthropology weighs in on the side that says thinking of God is natural to man. All the mythologies show man's imagination striving to attain a dimension beyond death. Anyone developing a theory of being has to account for this pervasive wanting to reach beyond time and to believe in and even to pray to such a Source.

How one conceives of the foundation permeates the thought of the rest of being, and it colors the conduct of our lives. Even were one, like Marx

---

6. The First Vatican Council even anathematizes anyone who says that natural human reason cannot know "Deum unum et verum, creatorem et Dominum nostrum" (Denziger, 3026). See Bernard Lonergan, S.J., "Natural Knowledge of God," in *A Second Collection* (London: Darton, Longman and Todd, 1974), 117–33.

7. Henri de Lubac, who has studied the phenomenon of modern atheism as intensively as anyone (see, for instance, his *Drama of Atheist Humanism*, trans. E. M. Riley [London: Sheed and Ward, 1949]), makes this telling remark: "The antitheist—and every militant atheist is one—pretends to know God, since otherwise he could not oppose Him. But, by that very fact, and whatever he may say, it is not God he opposes. For God would not be able to be known in this way" (*Sur les chemins de Dieu* [Paris: Aubier, 1956], 208).

8. Voegelin, "The German University and German Society," in *Published Essays 1966–1985*, ed. Ellis Sandoz, vol. 12 of *The Collected Works* (Baton Rouge: Louisiana State University Press, 1990), 9ff.

and Freud, to follow a Feuerbachian[9] explanation of projection, this liberating discovery has implications for how one should live and how society should be built—the most superficial glance at the extremes of atheist humanist society going on about us shows that. The popular need for such an illusion, and the heroic struggle to divest mankind of it, should be accounted for in ontological, not just psychological terms. Nietzsche, Freud, and Heidegger all attempted such a radical critique.

We have discussed the tendency on the part of man to project onto objects of many kinds, especially onto the image we have of our friends (and our cats and dogs) what we would like to find there. Such wish fulfillment (*Wünscherfüllung*) mythmaking is one of the most serious blocks to truth. Pseudo-being, emerging from the human imagination as it molds debris of the real world to fit our desires, absorbs into itself obsessively the eros that should be in pursuit of the genuinely transcending, which, because it is real, can challenge us and nourish us indefinitely. (Trying to feed off our fantasies is a kind of ontological auto-cannibalism.) Not all the genuinely transcending may transcend the cosmos, but it does go beyond my ego as center of creating fantasies; that transcending other may be food, sex, the beauties of nature, or human friendship, whatever responds to genuine needs within.

The fact that humans appear to have naturally divine desires for immortality and for relations of adoration to a personal transcending ground of some kind, the glory of which they seem at least dimly to perceive if only in intracosmic beauty, and that they feel the need to fulfill these desires in some reality that is Other, tells us something about being itself.[10] At the very least, we have to acknowledge that the world has developed so as to produce a kind of thing, man, who has such divine desires. What does this say about being?

I shall begin answering this in an indirect way, by recalling two dimensions of the needed correction to our mythologizing: (1) An ever-renewed will to allow every sort of genuine object, through its matter—through every form of givenness—to surprise and in-form us. (2) The other corrective to projective de-form-ation is to allow a friend who knows both me and the object I am embellishing to point out the danger that lies in the ingenuineness of the fantasy, whether it be some form of projection or a stubborn refusal to examine entire realms of human experience. This fraternal correction can be institutional: my superior at work, or a spiritual director, or simply the ordinary teaching of the Church can pull me up short.

It is difficult to open someone's eyes to the harm they are doing themselves through pursuing an ideology or losing themselves in some gnostic dream.

---

9. Ludwig Feuerbach (1804–1872) influenced the young Marx with his teaching that God and the gods were human projections that must be rooted out if man is ever to achieve freedom.

10. Cardinal Balthasar, no less, argues for the need of contemporary man (he includes Christians, to be sure) to recover something of the sense of what the ancients experienced in the gods.

Pseudo-religions can become gross blinders to the truth. When the object being mythologically embellished is nothing less than the Source and End, the Alpha and Omega, the question becomes where to find the objective givenness of the true foundation of all reality, the Source of our sources, including our very ability to know, to allow its own evidence to correct the childish fantasies we weave about the holy name of God.[11]

According to Heidegger, intent on showing that metaphysics is *Sein*'s obscuring of itself as the *ek-static* time-space of world and meaning, metaphysicians think of the all-founding, all-encompassing Source as though it were itself just another thing albeit, as Heidegger scornfully put it, the "thingliest thing" *(das Seiendste des Seienden)*. This they conceived alternatively, and inconsistently, as "the highest" *(Ur-sache)* and "the most general" *(das Höchste und das Allgemeinste)* thing.

K. L. Schmitz, critical of Heidegger in this, points out, "The great metaphysicians never thought of God as merely the highest." He cites, for instance, Anselm's reply to Gaunilon. Schmitz paraphrases: "I do not speak of the highest—that in itself relativizes God and is a foolish notion—but I [says Anselm] speak of that than which none greater can be conceived, and which itself cannot be conceived." Schmitz further reminds us of Nicholas of Cusa: God is not other from his creation; not that he is simply the same, but he absolutely transcends his whole creation. He cannot be caught in Plato's categories (Sophist). That is the Christian breakthrough. That is the sense of St. Thomas on *esse absolutum*.[12]

Heidegger's glaring mistake is that he construes metaphysics as an all-inclusive modern system, even as do those who deny system. The disease is still in their blood. In *Der Satz vom Grund*, Heidegger thinks he is speaking to Aristotle, but, Schmitz contends, he is speaking mostly to Leibniz. "Heidegger no doubt inherited this conflation from the bad scholasticism to which he had been subjected in the seminary. Neither Christian *creatio* nor pagan cosmos is a system in that sense."[13]

Hans Urs von Balthasar, recuperating the history of mankind's efforts to struggle to some kind of knowledge of the Source and End, suggests that there have been three bases of knowledge of the Source: reflection on his effects—his handiwork, which God is understood to sustain and animate, resulting in cosmological conceptions of the divine (today a trace of this remains in the popular concern for the environment); discovery of his working deep in the soul, the very light of spirit itself. This can range from anthropological conceptions of God, to experiences of genuine grace when the vision is directed by prophetic witness to his interventions in history, where the issue is not what

---

11. See Robert Sokolowski, *The God of Faith and Reason* (Notre Dame: University of Notre Dame Press, 1982).
12. K. L. Schmitz to the author, October 1991.
13. Ibid.

does man think of God but what does the Infinite Freedom elect to tell us about the inner reality of the Source itself, and how does it elect to do this.[14]

More recently, thinkers in the phenomenological tradition have underscored a fourth kind of consideration, a reflection of the implications of what we know of the operation of mind, not psychological but ontological implications, developing something earlier thinkers had already touched on in the form of "thought of that than which no greater could be conceived."

After a brief consideration of the most modern form of what has been called the cosmological argument, I shall look at the last of Balthasar's three suggestions and then the more traditional ways men have discovered God. Full exploration of "the way of revelation, love alone," as Balthasar calls it—in my conviction the most definitive—requires entering into a tradition and community of revelation, to appropriate its lived wisdom. That is for a future work. The purpose of the present reflection, however, is more modest, and the results will be provisional. It is to enhance our understanding of what thinkers in our Occidental traditions have meant by God and, in the process, to garner some credibility for the contention that any contemporary ontology should address the following two questions: the nature of the Source of the developing cosmos, and the religious experiences of a transcendent Person, knowing and willing and providential, the seriousness of such experiences being attested to by the great religious traditions in which live the majority of mankind. The seriousness of their derailment has to be faced, too, either as pathological forms of religion or as a kind of refusing, closed atheism that "shrinks the apophantic field" (Voegelin).

LONERGAN'S TRANSCENDENTAL ARGUMENT FOR THE EXISTENCE OF GOD

One category of argument for the existence of God[15] that has preoccupied many philosophers from Saint Anselm in the late eleventh century, through Descartes at the origin of modern philosophy, right up to influential contemporaries such as Alvin Plantinga, are various forms of what is commonly called "the ontological argument," based on reflection of how the mind conceives the greatest that can be. Sorting out important variants of this argument is complicated because Saint Thomas's important riposte to Saint Anselm is not based on the best version, as he did not have the whole text of Anselm. Today, because we do, a more defensible version can be reconstructed.[16] Crudely put,

---

14. Although detailed mustering of the evidence is the work of the seventeen volumes of Balthasar's trilogy, he sums up the essence in a succinct statement: *Love Alone: The Way of Revelation* (London: Sheed and Ward, 1968).

15. Embedded in the varieties of which are, of course, somewhat different notions of what is meant by "God."

16. Thomas had only a *florilegium*. Barth points out that one needs to take into account the whole work, the prayer that sets out the task of the proof, and the chapters that follow upon it, as well as the controversy with Gaunilon. One must also take care not to read Anselm through the eyes of Descartes or the other modern proponents, whose formulation is subject

Thomas's valid point was this: From the undoubted fact that the mind can form the notion of an entity than which no greater can exist, and that the mind sees that to exist is greater than not to exist, it does indeed follow logically that to be the greatest, this entity would have to exist. But it simply does not follow from this that the mind thus somehow has access to the actual, real existence of what the Christian understands by God, an existing infinite Source of all finite things. No move from the seeing of logical connections between mere concepts can establish the actual real existence of what is conceived.

That riposte is indeed devastating to the Cartesian version of the proof. But Anselm objected precisely to the term "greatest" in his controversy with Gaunilon. He pointed out that he affirmed "that than which none greater can be conceived." There is, I believe, a modern version of the argument that captures something closer to what Anselm intended.

Bernard Lonergan, in *Insight*,[17] unfolds an argument prepared by the entire elaborate categorical analysis in the book. I cannot presume to sum up Lonergan's whole transcendental philosophy here; I only wish to indicate the kind of argument that can be generated by a transcendental philosophy, working in the wake of Kant, yet escaping Kant's making of God a mere regulatory idea. Fortunately, David Tracy has adapted and simplified the argument in *Blessed Rage for Order* and applied it to scientific reasoning.[18] I shall be dependent here on that version.

Prior to chapter 19 of *Insight*, Lonergan sketches out the pattern of "invariant" human cognitive activities: experiencing data (whether of sense or of consciousness); questioning the data; grasping the concrete intelligibility of the data; perhaps conceptualizing—that is, formulating this concrete intelligibility, expressing it apart from concrete instances and hypothesizing about the data; and judging the truth about those concepts and hypotheses. Note, however, that the intelligible content of the concept is first grasped in the particular instance. So judging is primarily a question not about concepts but about the intelligibility expressed abstractly in the concept. Lonergan asks the reader to make his own phenomenological verification that this is indeed the invariant pattern in knowing: experiencing, understanding, judging. One cannot even assert that an alternative pattern exists without employing this invariant transcendental structure of inquiry and response.

This implies that a tension can manifest itself between one's cognitive performance and one's conceptual and theoretical schemes. When one maintains

---

to a Kantian sort of criticism. I am grateful to Schmitz for pointing this out to me. Eric Voegelin insists that Anselm never intended to prove the existence of God, but from within faith, to point, in the spirit of what Plato termed *epideixis*, to the transcendent glory. "The Beginning and the Beyond," 202.

17. Bernard Lonergan, S.J., *Insight: A Study of Human Understanding* (London: Longmans, Green, 1957), chap. 19.

18. Tracy, *Blessed Rage for Order* (New York: Seabury Press, 1975), 96–99. I am grateful to Duane Falconer, S.J., for calling this to my attention, as well as for help in condensing the argument and to Michael Vertin for further suggestions in clarifying my presentation.

"a counter-position," the problem is not one of contradiction, as between two statements, but of a deviation between actual cognitive performance and what one says one is doing, rather like my declaring, "I am utterly unconscious."

Such counter-positioning runs all through the history of thought, including philosophical discussion of the existence of God. Some hold that the very question is meaningless, that it cannot be legitimately asked. Others, conceding its meaningfulness, maintain that one cannot establish the existence of God objectively—John Wisdom comes to mind. These positions are, for Lonergan, contrary to what is in reality implied in and by our implicit, unthematic, undeterminate, preconceptual activity of "intelligent and reasonable intending." The ground for saying that is his conviction that the question of God is meaningful and that the existence of God is implied by and in our implicit, unthematized, yet undetermined activity of knowing. How does he make this contention convincing?

I shall follow, now, Tracy's summary of a more complex argumentation. No sane person would seriously entertain the thought that scientific questions are meaningless, that they cannot legitimately be raised. Scientific inquiry leads one out of the world of commonsense immediacy and into the world of meaning. There are what, why, where, and how questions and there are whether questions. The first kind seek understanding; the second, truth and, through truth, reality. But even before understanding and truth are achieved, one yearns toward them, one is driven by an eros to know, one intends them. Intelligent intending is one's intending of understanding; reasonable intending, of truth. When the scientist asks, for instance, what something is, he seeks understanding: he is on Lonergan's second cognitive level. When he asks, for instance, "Why is it so?" he is trying to move beyond mere concepts and hypotheses to a mediated reality and truth independent of himself and his questions. His reflection is not about his concepts or his questions, but about the reality into which he is inquiring. This, the third cognitive level of reflection, is the level at which one can establish the act of existence.

What, though, are the implications of all this for the existence of God? On the second cognitive level, which Lonergan calls that of "intelligence," the scientist is trying to grasp some intelligibility in the data under investigation. Now, if he is a thorough questioner, he will see the need to wonder what grounds the intelligibility of his answers. This is really to ask about the ground of the very possibility of scientific inquiry itself. That is a philosophical question, and as it is about ultimate ground of possibility, at once also a religious question.[19] Perhaps he will be tempted to say that his answers are intelligible because the world is inherently intelligible, but that begs the question. Can the world be intelligible without an intelligent ground of that intelligibility? So scientific

---

19. In recounting the argument, I do not wish to hide a certain disquiet I have with this equating ultimacy and the religious. I fear that one may pose certain kinds of ultimate questions with no sense of either transcendence of the ground beyond this cosmos or of a God who could respond.

inquiry at the level of understanding leads inevitably to the God question, in the sense of the question about the intelligent ground of the world.

The third level in the process of cognition, judging, including scientific judging, also leads to the question of the existence of God. A scientist, again if he is consequent, should wonder about the ground of his virtually unconditioned judgments—that is, judgments about conditioned existence, statements whose conditions have been fulfilled to some degree of probability.[20] Can there be virtually unconditioned judgments without a strictly unconditioned? But that is to ask whether God exists, for that is what is meant by the unconditioned.

This kind of move along the implications of the scientist's very acts of intelligence and judgment, this move beyond the scientific into the philosophic and religious horizon, is not, the Lonerganians argue, extrinsically imposed, the question arises legitimately from within the horizon of scientific inquiry itself. So, they further argue, one denies the legitimacy of the question of God only at the expense of maintaining an irrational counter-position. If it is meaningful to inquire scientifically, then it is meaningful to inquire about the ground of that meaningfulness, and that is what is meant by the question of God's existence.

At this point, it may appear that Lonergan has established only the legitimacy of the question, but nothing of the existence of God. Lonergan claims that in fact more has been established: The scientist by his inquiring activity implicitly acknowledges the formally unconditioned and intelligent ground of Being. It establishes that, provided he proceeds to the level of spelling out the implications of what he inevitably presupposes in his asking questions and achieving answers, he seeks to recuperate phenomenologically and transcendentally the very implications of his cognitional activity, he will discover the unconditioned reality, the unrestrictedly intelligent intelligible, which combines the implication of there being both an object and a subject involved in all inquiry. This unrestricted intelligent intelligible is that toward which all inquiring tends: the totally known, or being. This ultimate goal transcends every cognitive content—that is, everything actually achieved by any given cognitive act—as condition for the very undertaking of such an act being meaningful. And since the inquirer never doubts that what he is undertaking is meaningful, he is implicitly grasping that ground, he is judging to exist the ground of what I called in Chapter 3 "the unity of being," that Being itself is intelligible and absolute.[21]

This brief condensation does not do justice to Lonergan's long preparation through most of *Insight*, which carefully leads the reader to see that much is

---

20. Lonergan makes this equivalence in *Method in Theology* (New York: Herder and Herder, 1972).

21. In a speech in Parma, Josef Cardinal Ratzinger spoke of Christianity as a fervent defender of rationality, precisely because faith holds that the origin of the cosmos is not an irrational outburst of energy but an intelligent and intelligible ground. See *Thirty Days in the Life of the Church and the World* (May 1990), 50. It is basically the same point Stanley Jaki makes in many of his works on the history of science: Science developed in the Christian West, in the thirteenth and fourteenth centuries, because of faith in the inherent intelligibility of all reality.

implied when we operate as though the very being into which we inquire is itself, through and through, an ultimately unconditionally intelligible, that what we experience as intelligence at work is indeed manifest by being itself beyond anything man or any one thing does or can do, the ultimate object of all our striving to integrate what we know into ever larger intelligible settings and, ultimately, into a setting of all settings.

For my part, admiring as I am of this endeavor, I remain quite hesitant about the key move: the equivalence of the unconditioned with God. At best this seems grounds for acknowledging the unity of being as cosmos, but falls short of demonstrating God as wholly transcendent. If this is so, then Saint Anselm would not be happy with the argument, either. The way "intelligent" is slipped in, at the point at which it is argued, because the cosmos is intelligible it must be, in its origin, intelligent, would probably be convincing to someone who already believes in God, but not to someone for whom that is precisely the crux.

EVIDENCE FOR GOD IN HIS HANDIWORK

As we proceed now to examine another way thinkers in our tradition have thought of God—the Greco-Christian version of the cosmological—we shift gears methodologically from the phenomenological, which has characterized our own ontological reflection and underlies Lonergan's transcendental philosophy, to the objectivistic, pre-subjective-turn way of thinking of classic metaphysics.

As we search through the evidence, gathering glimpses of how thinkers in these Occidental traditions of metaphysics found God and how they conceived of the God they found, we shall have to raise and respond to the inevitable question, Are they just captive to the unexamined encultured thought patterns of a particular tradition, one now surpassed and subsumed into the philosophies operating from the transcendental viewpoint, or have these traditions, whatever their own peculiarities, garnered evidences available to all human beings, which any honest soul is therefore responsible to take seriously? Beyond that lies the question of the strengths and limitations of natural cosmological thinking.

Different philosophers in the Occidental traditions have pointed to three kinds of purported "evidence of God's handiwork": from the design of the universe; from motion; and from the very constitution of Being itself. We shall see the kinds of considerations that have been raised about the Source with the help of each of these, and how they tend to flesh out the tradition's notion of the Source.

Evidence from Design: An Evolutionary Perspective

In earlier eras, when the universe was looked on more as a harmonious but static whole, the wonders of design were remarked in a somewhat different way than now, when Western science emphasizes evolution. The earlier arguments, different versions of which can be found in thinkers as diverse as Plato, Cicero, the Stoics, and Abélard, taking the cosmos as a complete whole are synchronic, whereas any modern discussion will provide a diachronic reading. Because our goal here is not antiquarian but to see what remains valid, I shall consider a modern version, in the most attractive form, the best glimpse of God to be had from the cosmological.

The modern debate has centered on efforts to explain a process of natural complexification driven from a single initial source of energy and reaching, on this planet at least, that level of self-referencing and reproducing entities we call "living," showing an ingenuity in finding breakthroughs to successfully surviving and even prospering higher life-forms.

Contemporary microbiology, able to decode in part the genetic information governing the development of cells and (through cells) whole organisms, shows the deficiency of trying to work out an adequate explanation for the whole evolution of life on the sole basis of the Darwinian principle of natural selection by fittedness to conditions. Computer modeling suggests that the time the planet is known to have existed would not suffice, and by a good measure, for such a process of mere chance to have arrived where we know we are.[22] Were it to turn out that the universe is a great deal older than we now believe, the argument would be weakened, but it would have to prove to be almost unimaginably older before the main point would be destroyed: that achieving these complex combinations by mere chance statistically requires spans of time that themselves are incredible. Thaxton, Bradley, and Olsen calculate the probability of one protein of one hundred one amino acids forming spontaneously in five billion years—about the length of time it is thought such molecules have existed on earth—would be 1×10^{45}.[23] Although the principle of accidental mutation and survival of the fittest could well explain how some mutations, proving durable, prevailed, it is difficult to extend the theory credibly to cover some of what, on the basis of incomplete evidence, appear to be rather large leaps within the unfolding process, or if not leaps,[24] solutions of such ingenuity that explanation merely by utterly random trial and error strains our faith. It is believable at the level where the combining of one kind of atom with another might take place under the influence of a lightning stroke, but it becomes increasingly difficult to believe as one contemplates a vast series of such developments leading to nature's more ingenious inventions needed to solve some very complex problems, like the development of the

---

22. See, for instance, Lester King and Thomas Jukes, "Non-Darwinian Evolution," *Science* 164 (1969): 788–98; and the discussion in Jeremy Campbell, *Grammatical Man* (New York: Simon and Schuster, 1982).

23. Charles B. Thaxton, Walter L. Bradley, and Roger L. Olsen, *The Mystery of Life's Origin: Reassessing Current Theories* (New York: Philosophical Library, 1984), 146, point out that G. Steinman (*Arch. Biochem. Biophys.* 121 [1967]: 553) and A. G. Cairns-Smith (*The Life Puzzle* [Edinburgh: Oliver and Boyd, 1971]) likewise conclude that "chance is insufficient."

24. In the absence of complete evidence, we are never sure whether a large gap in the upward course of complexification represents a real leap, or just a black hole of our ignorance.

more advanced eyes as instruments for great extension of an organism's range of information gathering.

The gap that has recently been subject to the most intense scrutiny, about as frantic as the older search for the missing link between the highest anthropoids and man, is that which separates the perhaps chance production of certain amino acids and the first DNA. I cannot pretend to reproduce here the two hundred pages of analysis found in a work like that by Thaxton, Bradley, and Olsen, and certainly not the details of their chemical arguments, which I follow only up to a point. One thing they do seem to show well is that the efforts to reproduce in the laboratory conditions under which, out of a given biotic soup, amino acids, the building blocks of DNA, might have formed spontaneously, are all flawed because of the illegitimate interference of the experimenter, an intelligent agent choosing and ordering a complex set of conditions that they have reason to suspect would produce the desired results. They also argue that the experimenters forget that even if the unlikely concentration of prebiotic chemicals necessary for the production of the sought-after amino acids were to exist in some hypothesized pools of concentrated soup (for which, incidentally, there is no geological evidence), these soups would also contain many of the chemicals destructive (often in short order) of these larger prebiotic molecules. But that is not the most telling argument. That comes when the authors, reminding us that before "natural selection" could begin to "do its thing," the "metabolic motor must form," and that means DNA must first evolve—evolve before natural selection becomes a factor. The early earth conditions appear to offer no intrinsic means of supplying the configuration work required—the "selecting" and "coding" (the task of arranging the selected monomers in the proper sequence in the polymer for biological function) to make the macromolecules of life.[25] Efforts to produce proto cells in the laboratory have yielded structures with a crude resemblance to cells, but without the "internal cellular machinery," such as enzymes, DNA, or phospholipid cell membranes. The few "cell" functions manifested by protocell systems typically arise from simple physical forces.

Michael Polanyi is quoted as opining that the appearance in the cosmos of DNA (even if somewhere far from earth, which adds the problem of how it could reach our planet) required "a profoundly informative intervention."[26] A complex message sequence such as the DNA code, if it were picked up by a radio telescope searching the galaxy for signs of intelligent life, would instantly be hailed as evidence for its existence. The only reason there remains resistance to recognizing in the DNA code an intelligent arrangement is, claim Thaxton et al., "metaphysical." There is a will to keep creative intelligence out of science.

The information encoded in DNA is now being discovered to be more like a set of grammatical rules than actual, determined sentences, arming the cell

---

25. Thaxton, Bradley, and Olsen, *The Mystery of Life's Origin*, 146, 184.
26. Polanyi, *Chemical Engineering News* (August 21, 1967): 54; cited in Thaxton, Bradley, and Olsen, *The Mystery of Life's Origin*, 185.

with a possible set of solutions, somewhat adaptable to changing situations. Jeremy Campbell cites by way of illustration the experiment by Dr. Edmund Lin and associates at the Harvard Medical School in which several billion bacteria, deprived of the carbon compounds they normally utilize for nutrients, were given a quite different carbon compound, xylitol. In the DNA of the bacteria, there is information for producing an enzyme called ribitol dehydrogenase, which can metabolize another compound, ribitol, with a structure similar to xylitol, although with much less affinity. And when confronted with xylitol, the enzyme is able to convert it into another usable nutrient. But there was a problem. Ribitol needed to be present for the required structural gene coding to be switched on. The challenge for the poor bacteria: find a way to produce ribitol hydrogenase in the absence of ribitol. It turns out that in such a large population, there are a few mutants, not with the full instructions but with "a meta-statement" in the DNA, altering a regulatory program so that the gene coding for the needed enzyme is expressed whether ribitol is present or not. Under continued selection, the structure of ribitol hydrogenase is modified in such a way that it can metabolize xylitol more effectively. Such mutants would grow faster on the substituted xylitol. In a matter of days, organisms with new capabilities arise by a change in the programming of gene expressions and by improvement of existing compounds in their genetic makeup, rather than by construction of a completely new component. Mammals possess a DNA text thirty times as long as that of sponges, "but the extra length does not consist of genes which code directly for protein—Britten and Davidson think the extensions to the text contain new sets of control programs."[27]

I am not suggesting that biologists are getting in a mood for a general renewal of teleology. The evening before I wrote this, however, a friend who is a distinguished endocrinologist, and not a religious believer, told me, "Only when I introduce teleology can I begin to make some sense of many processes. There is a great thrust for the organism to perpetuate itself and for the species to look after itself."

In works like James Lovelock's *Ages of Gaia: A Biography of the Living Earth* (1988), scientists are at pains to detach the sense of *telos* from the notion of a God setting the goals. Still as one reads much of the more imaginative popular biological literature, one becomes increasingly appreciative of just how foresighted was Teilhard de Chardin, who himself sought to unfold from the evidence a theory of evolution that scientifically required some sense of a destination as well as an origin to the processes becoming visible to us. Teilhard de Chardin examines the (very incomplete) evidence with a view to bringing out the inherent thrust of the cosmic process toward ever-increasing "complexification,"[28]

---

27. Campbell, *Grammatical Man*, 133.
28. Teilhard de Chardin made the order:complexity distinction fifty years before Thaxton et al., but they do not offer him so much as a footnote. Perhaps they are frightened of arousing the ire of those with what they misname a "metaphysical commitment" (meaning ideologically committed positivists) against the very notion of creative intelligence.

indices of reorderings on higher levels of operations occurring at certain points, breakthroughs requiring ingenuity as well as chance, and giving the impression that the highest operation yet achieved, reflection and "hominisation" of the noosphere, was somehow a goal programmed from below.

Today the once lonely voice of Teilhard de Chardin (by his time, most had forgotten Schelling's suggestions along the same line a century before) is joined by some biologists supporting a theory called the "anthropic principle," which maintains that since the entire evolutionary process has produced this highest entity, the human being, perhaps one can best make sense of the many steps along the way by seeing them in terms of their contribution to the high result.

Such an admission demands acceptance of an intelligent factor at work within the cosmos, but acknowledgment of such a factor does not rigorously entail affirming the preexistence of a transcendent intelligent Source who, knowing what it would take, creates all the necessary conditions at the start. On the other hand, the hypothesis of something like a transcendent God is certainly not excluded by this way of looking at evolution, and indeed those who have other grounds for believing in such a transcendent creative source will see in this cosmic principle of intelligence evidence of that Source's being itself intelligent and deliberate.

What strikes us as the sheer ingenuity of many of nature's solutions to very complex operational problems—more, the overarching inventiveness of the whole system of nature—suggests something at work analogous to what we experience in ourselves as mind. Such a principle seems to transcend any one solution or any one part of the overall system, as well as the system itself, being a manifestation of the design of the system. This would have had to be present before even the most rudimentary fruits of it, in the form of the earliest complexities, themselves still very primitive, came onto the developing scene. Otherwise, they would not have contained (and themselves could not have known they should contain) all that which, in retrospect, we now know to have been necessary for all the subsequent development to have been possible.

In the phases when only the simplest compounds are thought to have existed, the things that have to carry the evolutionary process forward show nothing of the complex ability we see in mind: the capacity to anticipate, to reach out to embrace the other in a structuring embrace. One has to await the higher developments before beginning to see traces of something like intelligence. Yet, for the later very complex phases to be produced, the thrust had to be in the right direction, and all the elements that would be necessary for the things destined to appear only hundreds of millions of years later had somehow to be present.[29] An atom of a certain kind has structured into it the

---

29. As proponents of the anthropic principle never tire of pointing out, the slightest deviation in a whole chain of conditions would have rendered life on this planet impossible—for instance, a very slight (on the order of 1 percent) difference in the distance of the earth from the sun, or in the sun's temperature. In fairness, two points against this interpretation:

ability to combine with only atoms of certain other kinds. These, however, can combine into very complex molecules that are able to build cells, capable of supporting complex operations, elaborate instructions for which are encoded in RNA. The atoms could never know they are to build to such results, and yet, it turns out, they possess from the start just the needed ability to permit the higher molecules to be built.

It is hard to avoid thinking of what looks like a rather simple explanation (too simple, perhaps): A creative mind (granted, of unimaginable power) conceiving of the building process from the start could have so structured the most basic building blocks, the very atoms, as to make possible the hierarchy of material entities as we now see them. Is not the only other alternative to declare that it was an immense series of sheer chances, thus declaring the irrational to be at the origin of the rational?

I recall the conclusion of the Yale engineering professor, William R. Bennett, Jr., cited by Campbell, who calculates that if one trillion (10^{12}) monkeys were to type ten keys a second at random, it would take more than a trillion times as long as the universe has been in existence merely to produce the one sentence, "To be or not to be: that is the question."[30] But by applying certain rules of probability, based on a knowledge of the language, so that the keys were not struck at random, imaginary monkeys could turn out in minutes passages that resembled lines in Shakespeare's plays. Passing through four levels of programming, the results got closer and closer to Shakespearean blank verse. The point here is to suggest that evolution was carried forward not by complete randomness, but through the emergence of different levels of instruction, in the form of "grammars" of transformation.

Human mind is powerful, in the sense of the ability to concentrate and control energy. By this simple materialistic criterion, the human being is the most powerful kind of entity on earth, indeed, so far as we know, in the cosmos. Other things contain more brute force but show no evidence of being able to direct it sustainedly toward an end, as can the simplest cell. Recent developments suggest we have barely begun to tap the potential of the mind, through grasping how other structured forms of power work, to bend them to our purposes. Yet, look how far we still have to go to penetrate the secrets of nature. After hundreds of thousands of years of employing the mind,

---

(1) Lovelock's Gaia hypothesis takes into account the increasing radiation (hence effective heat and ultraviolet delivery, which is what is meant by "sun's temperature") output of the sun, and (2) the anthropic principle starts by saying, "Examine the end result." We are the result of just these conditions; to say that a slight unfavorable chance deviation wouldn't yield the path to us doesn't establish quite as much as one would like. Suppose that deviation would have led, not to us, but to silicon-based anaerobic avian intelligences instead. That world could have an avian principle, whose unfavorable chance deviation labeled life "impossible" merely because it led to us. Although the anthropic principle points to considerations of great interest, we must be careful not to employ it in a circular form.

30. Campbell, *Grammatical Man*, 116–18.

someone has only now been able to model one virus completely. The X-ray-gathered information was so vast, it took a Cray supercomputer days of number crunching to produce the final picture: With each atom represented by a small ball, the physical model took up the whole end of a lab room. What we observe in the virus is a life-form most able to achieve what is necessary for its own survival. It is a nuisance to the host cells. But what role does it play in the larger picture of the organic sphere of nature? We do not know. It could be an offshoot of the evolutionary building process, a wayward accident that now perpetuates itself, causing harm and no good, except for itself.[31] But the virus could also be a key to understanding aspects of the whole biosystem necessary to its functioning, aspects we do not now understand.[32] We do know that certain bacteria have invaded cells to contribute their DNA, necessary to the functioning of the cell as we know it.

Now, what to make of all this? Honesty about what we know of the cosmic evolutionary process and the unfolding of life prohibits concluding definitively one way or the other whether something like an intelligent plan is being deployed.

But does such hesitation come from inadequate information about what actually happened? Or is the reason something deeper, perhaps this: The intellectual effort of embracing in one vast scheme of understanding any immense system will always involve an element of faith. If, for whatever reason, one is impressed by the evidence for intelligence in all of man's experience, one could then set out to read the huge and inconclusive evidence that way, as Teilhard de Chardin did. Or if one is more impressed by the role of sheer chance, and perhaps resistant for other reasons (for example, positivistic prejudice) to the idea that a Great Intelligence rules over the cosmos, he will try to explain the evidence as much as possible in terms of a process without guidance from before or outside itself.

Be that as it may, I share the scientists' *eros theoreticos:* It is intellectually compelling to seek to understand in all possible detail how step by step there is a building up throughout evolution, from within the process itself. But I do not see this as in any way inconsonant with a spontaneous religious reaction of marveling at what continues to look, to many throughout the tradition, like an intelligent plan unfolding, pointed and furnished from the start with all the necessary conditions—immensely complex themselves and precariously balanced—to produce the highest known effect, man. To the religious person, the conviction of mindful authorship seems the intellectually less demanding hypothesis. The difficult demands that God makes are more in the moral order.

---

31. There are plenty of indications that the evolutionary process is not so designed as to avoid all dead ends and seriously disruptive nuisances. If that is so, there are implications for the way the creative spirit operates in the evolutionary process, not without what appears to the human observer to be waste. Teilhard de Chardin had many interesting observations on this in *The Phenomenon of Man,* trans. Bernard Wall (New York: Harper, 1959).

32. Some of what we have taken to be wasteful has turned out to be more ingenious than we thought.

Evidence from Motion

The difficulty for a modern person assessing the classic proof from motion for the existence of an unmoved mover is that the Aristotelian physics, founded in a theory of act and potency, is a different conception from the idea of motion at work in Newtonian mechanics. If one starts as the modern inertial analysis does, the other way around, positing motion (understood, reducibly, as mere *vis activa*, energy) rather than rest as first, then what is needed is not an explanation of how motion begins but how it stops (countervailing forces in balance, and finally the second law of thermodynamics, the law of increasing entropy, which removes any need for a last stopper). Energy, the changing of states, is simply posited as always having been and as going on until equilibrium is reached in the informationless rest of final entropy.[33]

Assessing the Aristotelian proof demands coming to terms with the mixture of physics and metaphysics at work in his entire act-potency analysis. If indeed all change is motion from potency to act, then the need for a first mover which itself is not moved and hence is pure act is intellectually compelling. For my part, I have always found the act-potency analysis to correspond with everyday experience, and this proof from motion, for the existence of an unmoved mover, to be convincing.

Modern physics, with its reduced sense of motion as force, confronts us with another problem: entropy. This consideration might be called the "no free lunch" principle. It hinges on this: Do we ever in our experience observe the greater coming from the lesser? Normally there is input from a higher form when a superior form emerges from lesser parts. This experience is not of motion in a narrow sense but of becoming (it was this larger sense Aristotle meant in developing the act-potency theory), where what is generated is understood to be of higher being—that is, of greater complexity—than the elements of which it is composed.

The basic insight here—if it be a genuine insight—is that the higher form of the more complex entity possesses, so to speak, more being than is found in the elements without order. If this is so, this complex form must either be imposed on the elements to order them in their present configuration (as the builder does when he brings lumber, bricks, and so on, together harmoniously to form a house); or an intelligence knowing what is wanted has to see to it that some elements are somehow endowed with the intelligence-bearing instructions, perhaps in many instances unreflectively present, the way the genes are structured, analogous to a computer's being hard-wired to process incoming elements and order them in complex series aimed at producing a complex final result. Obviously, put this way, the "no free lunch" argument is just another variant of the argument from design.

---

33. Formulated long before the theory of the Big Bang, thermodynamics nonetheless fits well with it. Thanks to Arturo Portoraro for help in formulating some of the ideas in this section.

There is a great debate raging among theorists of biological development about the way evolution toward ever more complex forms moves against entropy. Two opposing forces are at work. Does all matter have inherent in it a tendency to combine and build larger and more complex wholes *ad infinitum*?[34]

Those who (for no good reason that I can see) have left behind the Aristotelian principle, "Nothing is moved from potency to act except by a principle in act," remain with a great mystery in the form of this entropy-defying developing characteristic of matter. I refer the reader to an intriguing discussion by the Nobel Prize–winning chemist Ilya Prigogine, *Order Out of Chaos*,[35] whose quite technical arguments drawn from physics and biochemistry I cannot assess, but which cause me to hesitate, given how the discussion stands today, to assert that the argument for God's existence from design is "compelling." The sense in which the complexifying motion is moved is most obscure. The contemporary considerations are too complex to justify anyone's accusing anyone else of prideful not wishing to see. Every honest person should admit, I believe, that the mystery of evolution's movement against entropy remains almost total. The person who already believes in the existence of a mindful transcending Source of what appears to him an incredibly cunning designed process finds his faith confirmed at every discovery. The person who insists that the process is rooted in an essentially meaningless explosion of energy developing into matter seen to be inherently complexifying has to struggle to make sense of sense emerging out of senselessness.

Whereas complexification develops exquisite order the forms of which become, at a high level of development, the base of flows of information, this counter-entropic development is only local and temporary. All such complexifying work takes place at the expense of burning up higher-grade energy, reducing it to more diffuse and less usable states, with the result that something like this wonderful planet supporting higher life, the theater of the divine-human "theo-drama," is really only a window of opportunity. (One is reminded of Christ's insistence that "the hour has come," and Saint Paul's cry, "Now is the acceptable hour! Now is the hour of your salvation!" Physics informs us that there really is an hour for mankind.) If out of it results no spiritual life capable of being subsumed into a transcendent sphere, not dependent on the created energy of this cosmos we know, then nothing will remain, all will have been in vain, once the pleasures of the moment no longer exist. That is the point of Teilhard de Chardin's remark that if humanity were to come to believe all is lost finally in entropy, "it would go on strike."

---

34. Some will argue that complexification is indeed occurring on this planet, but because this is not a closed system, the sun is burning huge amounts of fuel to produce the radiation being absorbed by the complexifying life-forms on earth, so that what we observe here may be nothing more than a very local eddy in a vast sea of energy moving toward entropy. But what grounds are there for suggesting that entropy-lowering complexification is not visible in the whole galaxy-building process of the cosmos?

35. Ilya Prigogine and Isabelle Stengers, *Order Out of Chaos* (New York: Bantam Books, 1984).

God and the Constitution of Being Itself:
Is the Supreme Being Love?

When the mind necessarily sees that, given being, reality must be thus and so, the suspicion, since Kant, hangs heavy that such insights have more to do with the way the mind is structured (and so in turn structures the evidence) than with the totality of reality as it supposedly reveals itself as it is in itself. Kant claimed to have shown the practical reasons for the mind's having to posit the existence of the great context-consolidating entities—God, World, and Soul—and the utility of the data-organizing functions of the time-space forms of the aesthetic constitution of the world and of the categories of the transcendental understanding. Because of Kant's influence, insights into being as such are henceforth suspected to be nothing more than mind grasping its own structure.[36]

I have been seeking to make credible, on the contrary, knowledge of certain principles of Being as such, not mere expressions of mind's organizing function. I see mind's organizing function working successfully to organize because it is constituted to achieve a realistic grasp of being, bowing to that which it discovers in opening onto being, which it is capable of knowing as it is in itself. A most unskeptical faith, which you have seen at work throughout my descriptions. But our context at this moment, recall, is one of searching for evidence of, and about the meaning of, the divine: Does the mind's grasp of such principles lead to some understanding of God? And what sort of God might such knowledge of the principles of Being yield?

The mind, so goes this position, is so constituted as to produce objects able to presence offering compelling evidence that they are existing things and persons, or relations between things and kinds of things as they are in themselves, responding to and using the data without necessarily distorting the sense of those things. In knowing the other as other, the mind is able to distinguish itself and its own cognitive instruments from the larger reality presented by these presencing things-in-settings.

Now, although the mind and the realities present themselves as only a part of what is and can be, they reveal enough, at both poles, subjective and objective, about being to enable the mind to assert some truths about Being as such. The mind does not have to be acquainted with every being, not even with every kind of being, to be able to grasp and hold as principles some aspects of Being as such.

An example: by experiencing things and persons coming into and going out of existence, we are able to see that it is different to possess *esse* or not to possess *esse*. Observing things change while remaining the same substance, we come to distinguish substance and accident. We are able to build up knowledge of what it is for a thing to be a kind of thing. We contrast natures.

---

36. For a summary, see my chapter on Kant in Etienne Gilson and Thomas Langan, *Modern Philosophy: From Descartes to Kant* (New York: Random House, 1963), 411–48.

Observing substances, we see them interacting causally, and we watch them gradually decline and then finally disintegrate into elements, which continue their separate existence. Saint Thomas asserts that "what falls first into the mind is being." He means not that the mind grasps itself, but that it is essentially ordered to grasping the surrounding otherness. In this spirit, I am suggesting more attention be paid to our learning of being through ob-jective encounters with the things-in-the-world. The mind distinguishes itself as knower from the object known, experiencing and distinguishing the different rhythms of life, subjective from objective context, and so on. Through this interaction, through this observation of me knowing it, of my knowledge scrambling to keep up with the object's changing, or of my abstracting a formal idea of a way of being from experience of an entity that has just changed, I build up a complex, nuanced, and reflectively possessed knowledge of being as such. But what, then, does Aristotle mean in asserting that the mind knows certain first principles of being "of and in itself," such as the principle of identity ("a thing is what it is") and the principle of contradiction ("a thing cannot both be and not be in the same respect at the same time")? He means that the mind is the brute given power to grasp being, but it also experiences these truths, so to speak, at work in the world. They are verified in experience, when I deal with things that have and maintain an identity, and when I live through what it is for things and persons to be born, develop, and die.

We build up in this way, too, a notion of the good. Again, this is not to deny the existence of an innate sense of the good: As knowing-willing beings, we have a sense of pursuing that which will fulfill the need that surges up in the *ek-sistent*, that "good" which might satisfy the hunger. And then, of course, we experience fulfillment of desire, we achieve certain goals, which turn out to be good solutions to the problem as it posed itself to us. Moreover, as we come to know in detail what is expected of different kinds of things, we learn to recognize deficiencies in their operations and assaults on their integrity. It is not good for the pine tree in the back of my garden to be struck by lightning. The apple tree is no good at producing apples, but it remains an excellent shade tree; it would be better now to cut down the magnolia, as it is rotting at the core. In each of these judgments, reflectively and critically we can recognize, were the issue to arise, the standpoint from which the judgment about what is good—good in itself, in that other—is being made.

But what about a transcendental judgment like this: "It is better to be than not to be" or, another formulation of the same principle, "Being is good"? This can be defended as a condensed expression of the experience that, first, unless an entity comes into existence, organized so as to stake out for itself an identity, there is nothing, and hence no progress, so no interest in it is possible. And when some thing or idea does somehow come into existence, it shows itself to be some kind of thing or idea, it manifests itself as a center of interest and concern, it may have an impact on or be available to help other things, it needs defending against possible aggressors, and so on.

In sum, then, to be is to be a center of interest. When some thing or idea is proven more noxious for its surroundings than helpful, this evil is a reflection of a deficiency in its being, like the tree that has ceased to bear fruit, or the virus that is attacking hogs, evil from the standpoint of the hogs' well-being, though the hogs are a good host, from the virus' standpoint. From such judgments follow utilitarian considerations, which, when they enter the realm of human action, become full-fledged moral judgments: The hogs ought to fend off the cellular parasite.[37]

But how to move from the recognition that being is, and that being is good, to consideration of the ground of all being, the good as such?

Typical of the way this is argued is Saint Bonaventure's discussion in *The Soul's Journey into God*. The whole argument, with its being-embracing sweep, is circular but, for all that, useful. It was never intended as a proof, in the apodeitic sense, but as *epideixis*, Plato's sense of pointing to a reality we know of otherwise.[38] There is achieved a meditative pulling-together of the experience of the religious person whose life in God directs his attention to a certain understanding of being. That puts us far beyond a bare metaphysical notion of the unmoved mover, and Bonaventure takes us into the charmed circle of personal religious experience.[39] What we find here is not Saint Thomas's analogical notion of being but Bonaventure's meditation on what Pure Being would be in God. This is worth considering at length, as it will help us see an ultimate implication in the very notion of the good.

In contemplating God in "His first name" in the Old Testament, where God revealed himself to be "I am"—that is, as being—and according to his first name in the New Testament, the Good (for Jesus' revelation was principally about love), one begins by recognizing that being itself is so certain in itself that it cannot be thought not to be. Since nonbeing is the privation of being, it does not come into our understanding except through being; but being does not come to us through something else, because everything that is understood

---

37. Note here the potential for a position on the supposed impossibility of moving from is to ought, another type of Humean reductionist fraud (see Chapter 4, "Hume on Causal Relations," and Chapter 7, "Presencing and Engagement") wrought by the empiricist analytic philosophers. When the "is" is seen to stand for the existence of a recognizable kind of thing, and one realizes that judgments can be formed about what supports or is noxious to the well-being of that thing, then the move from this knowledge of what is, to an understanding of what ought to be done to preserve it, is a genuine and defensible intellectual move. But note, too, there are many kinds of goods. Only those are moral that engage the free human will.

38. See the epigraph from Voegelin, "The Beginning and the Beyond," 202, which opens the present chapter.

39. "What man, starting from his own initiative, calls 'God' is an *élan,* a last summit of the world from which the call beyond issues, a threshold for the leap of faith. But if one contents himself with that and gives it a definitive value, then there results the *'religieuse'* deception *[tromperie]* in which nature or any old ideal finds itself deified. Such a divinity, to start with the *numina* of natural religions, up to the absolute being of religious philosophy, does not exist. The God 'who is given' *[qu'il y a]*, 'He Who Is,' the true and the living, is the one who shows Himself in revelation. Man has to deal with Him, whether he wants to or not, for all time and for eternity." Romano Guardini, cited without reference by de Lubac, *Sur les chemins de Dieu,* 196.

is understood as nonbeing or being in potency or being in act. If, therefore, nonbeing can be understood only through being and being in potency only through being in act, and if being signifies the pure act of being, then being is what first comes into the intellect and this being is pure act. But this is not particular being, which is limited because mixed with potency; nor is it analogous being, which has only a minimum of actuality because it has only a minimum of being. It remains that the being in question must be divine being.[40]

The finite being of the things of our experience is mixed with nonbeing, the presence and limits of which we can only know because of the being. But we fail to notice the pure being, which is like the light which illumines the things we see, but they then absorb our attention, and so we fail to notice the light itself. We are blinded by the busyness of the limits and connections and thresholds, and so fail to see the centrality of being itself, which sustains all these things and their busy interactions. Because that being of itself simply is, with no nonbeing mixed in it—as that would be against its very meaning. Being as such, then, simply is and hence is ground and substance of all limited things and of their very limitations.

Bonaventure does not mean the all-englobing cosmic process out of which things and persons and ideas surge, which sustains them and into which their elements return to be reformed as other entities; for this process itself, vast and long-lasting as it is, transcending every other thing, is itself but one huge thing, a finite actuality limited by potency. The expanding universe, becoming more being, is itself therefore grounded in and sustained by being as such, unlimited and unqualified source of its energy, which, unlike the cosmic process itself, neither comes into being nor goes out of being, neither increases nor decreases. "Behold then purest being itself and you will realize that it cannot be thought of as received from another. From this, it must necessarily be thought of as absolutely first since it cannot come from nothing or from something. For what exists of itself, if being itself does not exist of itself and by itself?"[41] With no nonbeing inmixed, it is absolutely simple, hence eternal.

But what is to be said of this pure, simple, eternal being? For some understanding of its "emanations," Bonaventure would have us turn to contemplation of it as good.

Bonaventure, who sets out to contemplate the Trinitarian life in the Godhead, begins by recalling Dionysius' principle, that the "good diffuses itself."[42] Understanding what thinkers in this tradition, the Christian Neoplatonists, meant by this is critical to Bonaventure's reflection here, which is key to understanding

---

40. Saint Bonaventure, *The Soul's Journey into God*, trans. E. Cousins (New York: Paulist Press, 1978), chap. 5, ¶3, 96.
41. Ibid., chap. 5, ¶5, 97.
42. Dionysius the Areopagite, thought in the Middle Ages to be the companion of Saint Paul, was a fifth-century Eastern monk whose Neoplatonic speculations enjoyed great authority among the medieval doctors.

being as it has been experienced in the central Occidental biblical and philosophical traditions.[43]

Essentially Dionysius' formulation recognizes that being is self-affirming. In the case of beings capable of any degree of reflection, this entails a desire to perpetuate self and kind. In the unique case of infinite being, this entails its total grasp and appreciation of itself, which introduces a play between Being as divine mind knowing itself as its own infinite object and affirming that being through the absolute mind's love for itself as infinite content. This self-affirmation of the goodness of being is source of its willing to give of itself in creation in a great demonstration—a showing forth. Through the divine Logos the finite good of creation is poured forth, and embraced by the Source's love, as the Holy Spirit working in the world through the Logos, a world to be capable of appreciation, "of giving glory to God," and hence of re-sponsively loving back. This love fulfills the knowing creature through a rich union with the Godhead, producing perfect joy in the creature.

The highest possibilities within this finite good are reached when created minds recognize the goodness of being and want to join themselves to it maximally. This reaching-out runs the gamut from physical desire's wanting to absorb an object to assuage its natural appetite, through the friend's wanting to unite with the other to form a common bond, a new entity, to the offering of self to the most splendid other in adoration. The greater the being, the greater the good to be attained through union. The divine Logos helps us to this fuller understanding of the highest reality by coming into history to provide salvationary guidance. Only with this help can we know ourselves, because we find revealed the Source and sustenance of our spirit and bodies. So the being and the good we are talking about here are not abstractions but, at the summit, vivifying love relationships.

The diffusion in time in creation is no more than a center or point in relation to the immensity of the divine goodness. Hence another diffusion can be conceived greater than this, namely, one in which the diffusing communicates to the other his entire substance and nature. It would not be the highest good if it could lack this, either in reality or in thought. If you can behold with your mind's eye the purity of goodness, which is the pure act of a principle loving in charity with a love that is both free and appropriate and a mixture of both, which is the fullest diffusion by way of nature and will, which is a diffusion by way of the Word, in which all things are said, and by way of the Gift, in which other gifts are given, then you can see that through the highest communicability of the good, there must be a Trinity of the Father and the Son and the Holy Spirit.[44]

---

43. This takes us for a moment beyond what we have called the cosmological speculation, based merely on natural reason, because that same reasoning power goes to work on hints about the nature of the Absolute being derived from revelation.

44. Saint Bonaventure, *The Soul's Journey into God*, chap. 6, ¶2, 103–4.

I have offered this paraphrase, at the risk of irritating all readers unsympathetic with the Trinitarian nature of our Occidental thought traditions,[45] because it reminds us wonderfully that the experience of being enjoyed and reported by some of the most influential souls, from the prophets, through all the fathers and doctors of the Church,[46] for two thousand years has been an experience of life centered in love, of an essential relationship between knowledge and will, of self-giving, diffusion. From that experience, contemplation of the good is no mere intellectual demonstration, but a reflection on the experience of being as love.

It seems obvious that this sort of experience of God goes beyond logical analysis of everyday givens to which all minds must assent in good faith. Without meaning to diminish either the validity or the worth of metaphysical analysis, I point out that what we have here, as the believer sees it, are expressions by persons who have encountered divine love in their lives, in ways other than through dispassionate analytic thought, of what they have lived through. They seek to integrate their experience of this life-giving, foundational force into their global understanding of being, which must be founded on and mold their metaphysics.

This kind of consideration recalls the difference between "the God of the philosophers" and "the God of religion" discussed so beautifully by Etienne Gilson.[47] When the philosopher is also a religious man who has experienced the love of God and who loves God, he cannot in all truth stand still for reducing God to a function of source or unmoved mover in a system of thought; he must go on to witness to the full reality, the glory of this *theos*.

PROPHETIC WITNESS TO GOD'S INTERVENTIONS IN HISTORY

Because of the ontologic importance of the truth claims involved, and their formative influence on Occidental traditions, the question of prophetic witness to God's action in history occupied our attention in Part II.[48] I shall not repeat all of that here, nor consider supernatural faith's role in one's willingness even to take such witness seriously.

---

45. Not being open to some understanding of this core of the Occident's very history, one will not understand very well the great medieval doctors, or the modern Christian thinkers like Descartes, Malebranche, Pascal, and Kierkegaard, or post-Christians like Hegel, Nietzsche, or, for that matter, Feuerbach and Marx. So many of our intellectuals cut off from the roots of our tradition is a catastrophe. That is why in *T&A* I mount an argument for the urgent need to appropriate the Catholic tradition as a responsibility for all thinking people in the Occident. Reject it if you will, but know what you are rejecting—a major part of your own roots.

46. The extent to which the Trinitarian revelation surrounding Jesus is foreshadowed in the Old Testament, and the further question of the ways Plato, Philo of Alexandria, and Plotinus see love as an integral part of being, are issues requiring exploration.

47. Etienne Gilson, *God and Philosophy* (New Haven: Yale University Press, 1947).

48. The reader may want to review Chapter 4, "Traditions," 100f. and Chapter 5, "Communicating Public and Private Experiences," 130f.

But I do wish to go a bit farther than the preceding reflection, on Saint Bonaventure's sense of the supreme good, and consider the essence of what these traditions and particularly Christianity claim about God, especially about the way he elects to relate to us, discoverable in the experience of God which emerges in the history of that tradition. This claim of God's coming to encounter us is a key to a critique of what we shall study next: one mystical tradition's claim as to how God is present in the soul.

The underlying questions are these: What in such knowledge of God in the soul is natural (hence "anthropological," in Balthasar's sense),[49] and what is the result of initiatives of God, over and beyond creation, intervening in history ("supernatural," in de Lubac's sense)?[50]

I shall return later in this chapter to ontological consideration of God's being. The goal for the moment is to prepare ourselves for a fuller understanding of being by looking at dimensions of the life of the soul that historically manifest themselves, according to the witness of the masters of interior life. Such witness proves valuable to the theist and the atheist alike. The theist expands his theoretical ontology to open onto a transcending reality thus found. The atheist, like Freud, interprets such experiences in terms of imagination and psychodynamics, perhaps bracketing out the transcendent truth claims, but acknowledging their imaginative creativity and their personal and social impact, and even their potential as escape mechanisms.

When we think of mysticism we usually imagine some of the more unusual experiences of those masters who devoted their lives to exploration of the interior life. But we should be aware that everyone has the potential for mystical experience,[51] and that reflection, efforts to heighten our awareness of the depths of conscious life, and indeed every form of prayer are part of mystical experience, which can be quite ordinary. The great masters offer a fuller and deeper exploration of this potential (along with evidence, as they would say, of fruits of special supernatural gifts from God).

Since mystics cannot be understood apart from rich and long traditions, be they Hindic, Platonic, Sufi, Talmudic, or Christian, if we are to follow the writings of one of these masters as he leads us into the inner chambers of the soul, we shall have to possess enough understanding of his particular tradition to be able to interpret the language in which he expresses these experiences.

Obviously, much would be learned about being by comparing and contrasting the different ways of great mystical figures in each of the rich traditions. In what are they grounded? Is there something common to all, an anthropological or psychological reality? What distinctive dimensions of being does each reveal

---

49. Balthasar, *Love Alone*, chap. 2. The anthropological would be an experience traces of which are found in all cultures, in all of mankind's strivings toward God.

50. For an introduction to the difficult debate on the relation of the natural moment of God's creative initiative and the more personal encounters in history, see the classic by Henri de Lubac, *Surnaturel: Etudes historiques* (Paris: Aubier, 1946).

51. On the distinction between philosophy and mysticism and the need for both in us all, see de Lubac, *Sur les chemins de Dieu*, 167–76.

particularly well? But that is a task exceeding both my poor capabilities as a neophyte student of mysticism and the scope of the present volume. I am obliged to stay with the one tradition I know reasonably well from the inside.

The Central Abrahamic Claim: God Is Love

The evidence in one's own life of the presence of a personal, loving divine providence is something one is inclined to notice only if he already believes the prophetic witnesses historically active in the tradition. Failing that belief, one can easily interpret away such experiences as projections of the imagination or, if a sense of providence is at work, as good fortune or one's own cleverness. Evidence from the tradition, the witness of prophets, apostles, and saints, which, after all, has to be dug out through hard reading, meditation, and prayerful reception, will scarcely be sought after if one is indifferent to the idea that the Ground can make some kind of personal intervention in history.

I do not mean to imply that experience of God is private, unable to be shared through discourse pointing the other toward the sources of these experiences. Any experience can, but only so far. To deny that is to embrace the most reductionist positivism, which would limit shared reflection on the truth revealed in experiences to the repeatable, measurable, and experimental. But without a larger belief, there is no incentive to pay attention either to claims of prophetic events or to difficult and allusive inner realities, intimate and personal[52]—personal, but not esoteric, not totally uncommon to human beings.

Some of what the Abrahamic traditions ask one to believe seems almost too good to be true. That God, through his prophet, called into being a people, Israel, and personally, by encountering and instructing Moses, led them to freedom and through a series of prophets, kept calling at least a remnant back to the true path; and that all this hard work was undertaken to prepare for a supreme moment in a redemptive plan; that God "so loved the world that ["in the fullness of time"] he sent his only begotten Son for our redemption" (John 3:16), this Messiah who forgives sins and overcame death, preparing the way for everlasting life; that God sent a prophet in Mohammad to complete his revelation. These are the kinds of propositions that, when nonbelievers cannot bring themselves to embrace them, believers should not take offense, for they themselves acknowledge them as miracles of unexpected and inexplicable divine love. Gratuitous acts of generous freedom are unpredictable and, in that sense, irrational. There is no reason why I love you, why I freely decide to reach out to the ones I love. The ability to reach out to embrace these gifts in an act of

---

52. Of the most intimate of these experiences, the mystic is loath to talk, for fear that the inadequacy of his language will give a misimpression and that he will betray or besmirch such a precious intimacy. "Le vrai mystique ne fait pas de confiances. Ce n'est pas de tout prudence ou dédain. Ce n'est pas seulement humilité ou amour du secret. Il n'a point de confiances à faire. La vie de la conscience échappe à toute psychologie et, plus que tout autre, sa plus haute forme, la vie mystique" (de Lubac, *Sur les chemins de Dieu*, 190).

free loving re-sponse is itself part of the miracle. These claims are so demanding of our power to believe, the only reason for possibly embracing them would be that we become convinced that what they report actually occurred. But then one can say that of the foundational idea of creation itself.

Because he is already thankful for the wonders of creation (gratitude is the religious reaction par excellence, a grace, at least of natural faith), the Abrahamist is prepared to believe these wonderful historical claims. (He is helped along by the record of Holy Scripture: There it stands, a great pile of evidence of God's unpredictable and marvelous interactions over two thousand years with the people he was so laboriously preparing as instrument of his work; a story of fire and gentle breezes, of angry blasts and timely seductions, which he finds hard to believe the human imagination would invent all by itself.)

There is only one exception, a claim much harder to believe than the creation and all the prophetic interventions combined and so rejected by Jews and Muslims: God's ultimate *kenosis*, as Saint John the Evangelist calls it, his emptying himself out to become, in Jesus, one of us. That the Infinite Source of this vast cosmos should lower himself to come into the womb of a virgin, having first to submit himself to her decision, and delivering himself into the condition of human fragility, and suffering and dying for us on the cross, assuming all the effects of our perverse revolts onto himself, next to which act of sacrifice and pardon the Resurrection's conquest of death itself pales in significance—all of this is staggering in the audacity of what is claimed. Because the Abrahamist believes that God is already in every atom and cell of his creation, structuring and relating them coherently; and because he has experienced in the people of God, amid all their sinfulness and mediocrity, enough of God's gifts of holiness and love to nourish his belief in the goodness of providence and God's sustaining graces (de Lubac testifies that an encounter with one genuine saint is enough, like the ray of light penetrating through a tiny window into the dungeon),[53] he is able to live with these mysteries and struggles to secure his grasp on them.[54]

The leitmotif in this entire discussion, obviously, is love. Saint John declares simply, "God is love" (1 John 4:8). But the appreciation of love is not a monopoly discovery by Abraham's descendants. Surely the atheist experiences love and can believe just as firmly as any Abrahamist that love is central to human being. So what is the ontological point of difference, the distinctiveness of the Abrahamist-Christian revelation?

---

53. "Atravers la plus épaisse muraille du plus sombre cachot, l'étroite fente d'une meurtrière suffit pour attester le soleil. Ainsi de ce monde, maintenant opaque et lourd: la rencontre furtive d'un saint y suffit pour attester Dieu" (de Lubac, *Sur les chemins de Dieu*, 180).

54. For the religious person, the miracle of one Mother Teresa outweighs the grinding discouragement of massive mediocrity daily experienced. The miracle is found in the positive; the negative is experienced as the dark mystery of our electing, again and again, incomprehensibly to abuse our liberty by choosing the lesser way, or even straight destruction. Counter-evolutionary.

Love Is Divine

Consider first of all this fact of experience: The experience of love demonstrates (*monstrare*—"shows forth") that being itself, in its highest manifestations within human reality, can diffuse itself through a self-giving that neither diminishes the giver nor disorders the receiver. This is per se divine, in at least this sense: Loving solicitude is the highest form of being we can experience, so superior in the reach and flexibility of its constructive abilities as to constitute a category of existence unto itself. It provides us with a direct personal experience of genuine creativity. Its fore-sight in concern for the other's well-being (*pro-videncia*) (and in genuine love of self, fore-sight for one's own good); its imagining of solutions and the arranging of means to reach ideal ends, and, potentially, its co-creativity as the new being of friendship, family, and society is formed (a creation of order and dependability, its open-endedness and commitment)—all this transcends the power and domination patterns of all in nature that can be tyrannical. It permits something unique in nature: loving cultivation of a part of nature as our garden, and domestication—a home is created within it. It allows of the playfulness of the gods. At its best, a taste of Paradise.

Acknowledging all this, the atheist might still ask, "Divine in this sense, sure. But is there anything in this pattern that suggests a reality superior to the (admittedly wonderful) side of human nature you are describing?"

My theistic response starts in a roundabout manner. When we sin against these highest possibilities, our infidelity and perversion of order leads to death—not always directly to death of the body;[55] rather, to death of the spirit, de-struction of relationships that seem by their very nature meant to last forever. Quite naturally we wonder if such vital relationships do not perhaps have their origin and (when they do last) sustenance, and their ultimate fulfillment in purely positive and constructive being, of itself purely faithful, never perversely destructive. (Being, as that which is building up, seems to exclude deliberate, perverse destruction of what is good. It should cultivate and preserve what has proven good. Indeed, we are bewildered by the human phenomenon of sin against what is holiest. How can our dearest lover, in a moment of selfish, unrighteous anger, turn on us so viciously? Of course, he soon says he is sorry—unless he is so weak that he can never acknowledge that he has been wrong.) All this seems contrary to the very essence of what is revealed by love, the love that is so counter-entropic, while outbursts of destructive aggression reverse the building-up thrust of unfolding being, giving us a foretaste of the entropic, of death.

Is this a fantasy: From the experience of what by its nature should be unlimited, one moves to the thought that perhaps there is an unlimited ground

---

55. The inevitability of biological mortality already seems to run counter to the thrust of these constructive love experiences. In *Love Alone* (chap. 4), Balthasar, examining "the limits of human love," shows the devastating effects of our finitude, especially death, on the realization of the projects inherent to love. This, along with C. S. Lewis's *Four Loves* (London: Collins, 1963), is the most profound brief reflection on love I know.

to this being, which for now, in its limited form in us, proves so patently and mysteriously deficient, indeed destined to tragic frustration (a central Greek experience)? The Christian sees through this experience of love to the Source, the origin of all that is fructifying and renewing, of being coming to be and enjoying an ever-refreshing permanence because the energy of the Source continually flows into it as the gift of its nature promises. He sees the loving author of our being seeking to pull all our timid human tentatives into a *communio* of everlasting being, the union of the essential *energeia* at work in us, the Alpha flowing through the pluralism of time and space back to a final rich unity in the end, the Omega, which is that very Alpha recovered and the point of the whole vast spreading-out exercise of creation.

The Abrahamist is mindful that there is much more than the evidence of creation and of human love experience; there is evidence in human history of a transcendent Lover actually at work among men. The believer argues that the public evidence is indeed rather massive. In the Abrahamic tradition alone, it stretches from the recording of the experience of Abraham, called by God to lead his tribal confederation from Harran toward what was to become called Palestine, events written down centuries later by persons who still experienced in their own lives enough of something similar to this divine guidance to be struck by, and able to formulate, the phenomena; through the record of God's deeds at Sinai, some centuries later, in calling a people into being, by leading them from captivity to freedom, an event never repeated anywhere else in human history; through the love songs of the psalms and the Song of Songs, and the great interventions of the prophets, calling the faithless people to remember and repent, again a phenomenon, in duration, variety, and intensity unparalleled in history;[56] through the Gospels, the meditations of the fathers and the mystics and the doctors of the Church, down to our own day.

The Muslim sees in the Holy Qur'an the summit of this generous self-giving by God, and in the example of the Prophet, on which he ceaselessly meditates, the flowering of saintly human acceptance of God's gifts. The many other mysterious outbreaks in other traditions enrich this testimony to the Source at work among us. Every particular element of that evidence can be disparaged—it can all be psychologized and explained away. But then so can every act of genuine human love, if one has a mind to do it.[57]

I consider it an imperative scientific responsibility for all thinking persons of our time to undertake careful examination of the record of purported evidence

---

56. Many studies demonstrate the historical nature of much of what is recorded in the biblical records. I cite only two: Voegelin's *Israel and Revelation,* vol. 1 of *Order and History* (Baton Rouge: Louisiana State University Press, 1969); and, more popular, Werner Keller, *The Bible as History* (London: Hodder and Stoughton, 1956).

57. One of the central aspects of the mystery of our freedom is our denial of evidence of every kind. But so, too, is our capacity to invent, not just wonderful realizable ideals, but pure fantasies, in which we invest with utmost insistence (in Heidegger's sense of an obdurate ingenuine hanging on). Those perversions enflame the critical sense of anyone confronted with testimony of realities with which he has had no contact.

for transcendent love at work in history. I hope to make eventually a contribution to the methodology for doing this. Here I want to deepen our understanding of what the interior life is like when it is given over as completely as possible to this love of the divine. I do not pass critical judgment at this point whether what is reported is genuinely an experience of the transcendent coming into the soul or of the soul's ultimate experience of its own being. My personal belief in one rather than the other of these possibilities is neither here nor there. In any event the master of the interior life will enrich our understanding of being.

Let us listen awhile, then, to a chosen master, San Juan de la Cruz, a sixteenth-century contemplative friar, a man dear to Christians and non-Christians alike because of the supreme beauty of his poetry, and spiritual director of Saint Theresa of Avila. We shall consider here, not his artistry but his more technical treatise on how the soul can mount toward God, *The Ascent of Mount Carmel*.

THE DEEPEST LIFE OF THE SOUL

San Juan's *Ascent of Mount Carmel* was requested of him by those Carmelite contemplatives who, having devoted their lives to the utmost intense quest for God, turned to this master for help in reaching the highest summit.

Does man attain that summit by turning deep within the soul? From the beginning, San Juan treats us to a startling ontological reversal. We have been contemplating love taking us out of ourselves to the other, who then enriches us by impressing his being on ours. Now San Juan, who in no way invalidates the soundness of such in-tentionality, tells us that letting the ultimate reality, God, come into the soul to the maximum extent possible in this fleshly life is a matter, at the summit, of setting aside everything with any content whatsoever, including the most ethereal spiritual consolations. This looks very much like a deliberate move against the transcendence of intentionality. The least one can say is that this would obviously not be easy to accomplish. Indeed San Juan tells us that it requires careful guidance and enormous discipline. Who will be our guide?

Again, a surprising answer, which at first seems to contradict what I have just termed the "anti-intentionality" of the goal: Jesus Christ himself. Working through the things that normally absorb the soul—by his teaching, sacraments, his Church—he, and he alone, can bring us, by means of these gifts, beyond them all.

The normal way to God is through following Christ by leading a good life in this world, as Jesus himself put it, by "keeping all my commandments." These are revelations by God of what is demanded by our nature, as God, the author of nature, intended, commandments that are perfectly reasonable, when we deign to think of them. (And, recall, the first of these commandments is "that you love one another.") Experience of the mystical presence of God in our souls, over and beyond what are normal as the soul's own operations, is not a condition for salvation, but an altogether exceptional gift. There follows a sentence no student of the interior life should ever forget: "One act done in charity is more precious in God's sight than all the visions and communications possible—since they imply neither merit nor demerit—and how many who have not received these experiences are incomparably more advanced than others who have had many."[58] Love is the revealed norm, and love is in-tentional.

But if God is to grant the special gift of his presencing maximally in our souls, then we have to be taught, through discipline, to become cleansed of the soul's preoccupation with the legitimate things of this world; they can lead us to, but cannot themselves become, that empty interior time-space (which San Juan calls "the night of the soul") in which God finally can presence directly.

In a middle chapter of book II, San Juan summarizes the steps through which we are led. He places the whole discussion under the guidance of three principles. The first, from Saint Paul's Epistle to the Romans, has it that whatever humans accomplish is ordered by God; the second, from the Book of Wisdom, "Disponit omnia suaviter" (God disposes all things gently); and third, "from the theologians," "Omnia movet secundum modum eorum" (God moves things according to their own modes). *Suavitas,* we shall see, not only does not exclude discipline; properly carried out, discipline is sweet. Being is inseparable from order, and in the sphere of human action—of freedom—order demands self-control.

Let us put aside our own preconceptions, then, and listen to this master of the interior life, hoping to get a glimpse of his experience of a dimension of being unknown to us:

> Since the order followed in the process of knowing involves the forms and images of created things, and since knowledge is acquired through the senses, God, to achieve his work gently and to lift the soul to supreme knowledge, must begin by touching the low state and extreme of the senses. And from there he must gradually bring the soul after its own manner to the other end, spiritual wisdom, which is incomprehensible to the senses. He first perfects the corporeal senses, moving one to make use of natural exterior objects that are good, such as: hearing sermons and Masses,[59] looking upon holy objects, mortifying the palate at meals, and disciplining the sense of touch through penance and holy rigor.
>
> When these senses are somewhat disposed, he is wont to perfect them by granting some supernatural favors and gifts to confirm them further in good. These supernatural communications are, for example: corporeal visions of saints or holy things, very sweet odors, locutions, and extreme delight in the sense of touch. The senses are greatly confirmed in virtue through these communications and the appetites withdrawn from evil objects.
>
> Beside this, the interior bodily senses, such as the imagination and fantasy, are gradually perfected and accustomed to good through considerations, meditations, and holy reasonings, and the spirit is instructed. When through this natural exercise they are prepared, God may enlighten and spiritualize them further with some supernatural imaginative visions from which the spirit, as we confirmed, at the

---

58. *The Ascent of Mount Carmel* (London: Baker, 1928), bk. I, chap. 22, ¶19.
59. Does this rather passive sense of the Eucharist suggest a deficiency in the incarnational theology of this great mystic? If so, it runs counter to his sound advice to value a single act of charity above all mystical favors.

same time profits notably. This natural and supernatural exercise of the interior sense gradually reforms and refines the spirit.

This is God's method of bringing a soul step by step to the innermost good, although it may not always be necessary for him to keep so mathematically to this order, for sometimes God bestows one kind of communication without the other, or a less interior one by means of a more interior one, or both together. The process depends on what God deems expedient for the soul, or on the favour he wants to confer. But his ordinary procedure conforms with our explanation.[60]

Spirit and senses are here clearly distinguished. God may bring us to spirit gradually through the senses, but to the extent we have been allowed to grasp spirit, to that extent any representation of it will prove unsatisfying. What happens then?

When people have finished purifying and voiding themselves of all forms and apprehensible images, they will abide in the pure and simple light and be perfectly transformed in it. This light is never lacking to the soul, but because of creature forms and veils weighing on and covering it, the light is never infused. If individuals would eliminate these impediments and veils and live in pure nakedness and poverty of spirit, their soul in its simplicity and purity would then be immediately transformed into simple and pure Wisdom, the Son of God. As soon as natural things are driven out of the enamoured soul, the divine are naturally and super-naturally infused since there can be no void in nature.

Little by little the divine calm and peace with a wondrous, sublime knowledge of God, enveloped in divine love, will be infused into their souls.[61]

What to make of this? I asked earlier, Is the emptied-out soul simply discovering its own being? "This light is never lacking to the soul" could refer to the natural infusion that is God's being sustaining the natural spiritual operations of the soul—that, in us, which is truly "made in God's image," as Genesis says. (It is God-like because it is that in the human form which allows the deployment of psychic energy in the future-opening, newness—in-breaking deployment that allows *Sein* to come to be. This creativity [more properly, co-creativity, because of its essential dependence on the already having been of possibility generated in the past] and the will-to-deploy involved in it, source of love and appreciation, is the image of God in us.) It would be "infused," in the sense not of first coming to be there after the clearing of all distractions, but of first having a chance to be noticed when we put aside our absorption in objects of all kinds.

But the supernatural, with its overpowering sense of God's love as the sustaining other, is experienced, San Juan might reply, as the supernatural light that comes into the soul in the form of a rarer gift, a light without knowledge content—San Juan says that "we know not what we love"—but experienced above all as possibility of limiting representation of knowledge because surpassing all other being and all our hopes.

Another objection may arise: If this supreme loving knowledge is without detailed content, what good is it to us—for instance, how might it help lead us in life? San Juan's answer is straightforward: It is not useful, it is not supposed

---

60. San Juan de la Cruz, *The Ascent of Mount Carmel*, bk. II, chap. 17, ¶4.
61. Ibid., chap. 15, ¶¶4–5.

to lead us. (Remember, this is about love, not utility!) Its good is in itself; it is the (very exceptional) presence of the highest good, next to which the sweetness of all else pales. When one returns from what seems like an instance of rapture to discover that he has been absorbed in God in fact, according to companions, for hours (which happened more than once to San Juan, as it did to his spiritual daughter, Saint Theresa of Avila), this is obviously not something that has much to do with the laws governing the practical conduct of life. It will not contribute directly to making the monastery, let alone democratic civic society, run any better. But will it not come, through the stirring example given by the great mystic (and through his teaching, such as this very text, the *Ascent*) to permeate the monastic community, and thus transform the monks' lives together, and so indirectly improve life in the convent and through it—for the monastery functions as spiritual resource center—the world?

For that needed guidance, however, we have already the supreme gift of the Word of God, given in Jesus Christ, which is meant to help us gradually transform our lives to be capable of standing in the presence of the Supreme Love, and which helps us to live better together, because more lovingly. The Gospel and Christ's Church are all we need; we shall need no additional detailed direction. He spoke everything to us at once in this sole Word—and, San Juan assures us, giving proof in the process of being a self-assured master: "He has no more to say."[62] To want secret revelations is to despair of the fullness of truth in Christ. San Juan has God speak hypothetically: "If you desire me to declare some secret truths or events to you, fix your eyes on Him [Christ] and you will discern hidden in Him the most secret mysteries, and wisdom, and the wonders of God, as my Apostle proclaims: '*In quo sunt omnes thesauri sapientiae et scientiae Dei absconditi.*' "[63]

San Juan is in no way encouraging escape from this world. On this he agrees with Balthasar, who reminds us always that the fullest—indeed, perfect—revelation of God is in that icon he has fashioned and set into "the public square," Jesus Christ. In San Juan's words, "We must be guided humanly and visibly in all by the law of Christ who was human and that of His Church and His ministers. This is the method of remedying our spiritual ignorances and weaknesses." More than that, San Juan is suspicious of much that is reported in the mystical life, for it can easily be spurious. "One should not believe anything coming in a supernatural way, but believe only the teaching of Christ, who became human, and of His ministers who are human. So true is this that Paul insists, 'If an angel from heaven should preach to you any gospel other than that which we humans have preached, let him be anathema.' "[64]

Only to the thus well ordered ecclesial soul—well ordered because obedient to the full teaching of Christ handed down and lived out by his Church—is

---

62. Ibid., chap. 22, ¶3.
63. Ibid., ¶6. "In whom are hidden all the treasures of the wisdom and science of God" (Col. 2:3).
64. Gal. 1:8. San Juan de la Cruz, *The Ascent of Mount Carmel*, bk. II, chap. 22, ¶7.

there any hope of genuine divine experiences being granted. "An unsettled soul, which has no foundation of moral good, is incapable as such of receiving spiritual good. For this spiritual good is only impressed on a restrained and peaceful soul."[65]

If the whole world were to crumble and come to an end and all things were to go wrong, it would be useless to get disturbed, for this would do more harm than good. The endurance of all with tranquil and peaceful equanimity not only reaps many blessings but also helps the soul so that in these very adversities it may make a better judgment about them and employ the proper remedy.[66]

Such tranquillity is a manifestation of Christian hope, which itself is founded in faith, that is, con-fidence in Christ who, as the Good Shepherd, leads us to the Father. The visionless loving presence of God is not that guidance but rather the foretaste of heaven granted to those who, having striven mightily to keep all the commandments, have allowed themselves to be steeped in the inexhaustibly contentful reality of Jesus Christ. Nevertheless, it is the sweetest recompense God can grant in this life, to allow us for a moment to be in eternity with him. Its effect is substantial:

> Some of the divine touches produced in the substance of the soul are so enriching that one of them would be sufficient not only to remove definitively all the imperfections that the soul would have been unable to eradicate throughout an entire life, but also to fill it with virtues and blessings from God.
>
> [God] affects in the soul what it is naturally incapable of acquiring. God usually grants these divine touches, which cause certain remembrances of him, at times when the soul is least expecting or thinking of them. Sometimes they are produced suddenly through some remembrance, which may only concern some slight detail. They are so sensible that they sometimes cause not only the soul but the body to tremble. Yet at other times with a sudden feeling of spiritual delight and refreshment, and without any trembling, they occur very tranquilly in the spirit.[67]

I would underscore an important principle of Christian spirituality which San Juan here invokes, a dimension of interior life that, I venture to suppose, Christians have in common with the other Abrahamists: the experience of the limits of what the human soul can do for itself, or, put positively, the experience of grace as a gift from God healing and purifying the soul of its debilitating psychological and sinful limits, expanding it in a way that we cannot will into being ourselves. We cannot make ourselves more generous, capable of allowing a greater *Sein* and love to be deployed through it. As I grow old, I am ever more astonished at how hard it is for any of us to grow, to break out of those personality and character limits which are painfully obvious to our friends, and against which we seem to struggle all our lives. The experience of masters of the Christian spiritual life is that we cannot change ourselves; all

---

65. Ibid., bk. III, chap. 5, ¶3.
66. Ibid., chap. 6, ¶4.
67. Ibid., chap. 26, ¶¶6, 8.

we can do is struggle mightily to hold open the space in which the Holy Spirit of God can work slowly, but given our freedom to be perverse, not necessarily surely.

So there you have a report of a kind of experience I'll wager few of my readers have enjoyed, any more than I have. Two important ontological points from this reflection: (1) These divine touches, being without intellectual content, coming from a God whom the favored soul knows through the Gospels and the life of the Church, add no new knowledge, yet they are infinitely precious, because they are favors of love; they are, in other words, realities revealed in the order of will, not intellect. Recall Pascal again: "Le coeur a ses raisons que la raison ne connaît point." Yet, without defined content because flowing directly from the unlimited life-source, they strengthen the virtues of the soul, at the operational center, and they swell therefore human being with an affirming sweetness. So, when we read that "being is love," we may start to realize that is not just an expression of sentimentality, but an ontological claim of the most fundamental kind, about the dynamic energy that founds all things. The source of the possibility of all in-form-ation is not itself information.[68]

(2) We are brought to the threshold of this quality and intensity of love only by being led knowledgefully along a certain way ("methodically"). A fullness of love requires more than the generosity of the giver; it requires orderly preparation of the receiver, whose soul has to be led out of itself, educated so as to form a big enough time-space to receive the great gift. The child can love its parent disarmingly. But the contemplative's renouncing each and every created thing, each being only one limited form of expression of the inexhaustible source, is an activity on the subject's part for which he needs assistance and guidance. Only the disciplined mature person can be seized as the recipient of the greatest love. It is as though the soul, through educated remembrance and hope, has first to be made into an ample space, and then emptied of all the things that helped expand it, to be filled by the ultimate gift.[69]

Balthasar, who has studied the Christian mystics and who has meditated on Plato, Plotinus, and Buddhism, believes that there are two distinct genera of mystical ways, those aimed out beyond the soul to grasp the supernatural realities in the historical events and words (the ways of the Bible and of the mystics guided by the Church's theology), and those that concentrate on the experience (like the Spanish mystics). These latter, such as San Juan and Saint Theresa, are more like non-Christian mysticisms and tend to find the same reality of soul as do Platonists and Buddhists. The following text brings out Balthasar's hesitations about mysticisms that are not as united to the revealed teaching of the Church as he thinks they should be:

---

68. In a human love affair what is most precious and central is not more information about the beloved or furnishing him with more knowledge of oneself. It is the outpouring of commitment, solicitude, fidelity, the bonding of wills.

69. Again, on the everyday human level, we see that *disponibilité* has to be achieved, that it requires the building of a certain character, and then ultimately the sheer grace of the event of willingly being present.

The mystical states are, of course, the objects of John of the Cross' and Teresa of Avila's descriptions; roughly speaking, the external objects are derived from the state which reveals them. In this respect, Spanish mysticism is in strong contrast with that of the Bible: from the mysticism of the Apocalypse, where the seer, in ecstasy, is wholly oblivious of himself *in his office of transmitting the revelations*;[70] from the mysticism of the patriarchs and prophets; of Mary and Joseph, Paul and Peter, where the inner graces all serve the single act of revelation. It is very different, again, from the dogmatic mysticism of Hildegard of Bingen, of Matilda, Bridget and the two Catherines, with whom it was pre-eminently a question of serving the Church *in conveying an objective message*, itself no other than an interpretation of the one revelation for contemporary needs. When the main emphasis is transposed to an inner experience, to its degrees, laws, sequences, variations, dogmatic theology is relegated to the background. A close connection with the doctrinal teachings on God, the creation and the redemption ceases to be evident; whereas, often enough, the connections, parallels and analogies with religious phenomena outside Christianity are correspondingly more frequent and prominent.[71]

THE ONTOLOGICAL CONTEXT OF THE OCCIDENTAL (CHRISTIAN) EXPERIENCE OF GOD

This warning from the greatest of contemporary theologians does not dampen my appreciation for what this brief study of our chosen Spanish witness to the depths of the interior life has accomplished for us. We could achieve a similar opening of the spiritual eye by following Plato in his profoundest moments or Plotinus or the greatest Sufi masters of Islam. If we did, we might not find each time the same form of reality. I do not know how similar or how distinct they may prove to be, for, unlike Balthasar, I have not undertaken such research. I suspect, however, that we would find in every instance much in their symbols that remains ambiguous and troubling for us.

This exploration, limited though it may be, will help me expand a bit on my earlier summary of the ontology that is implied and expressed in this rather typical Christian form of inner experience of the Spanish or more Platonic type, and in this way make a last effort here to consolidate a hold on this most important dimension of our eventual ecumenic wisdom, that of the

---

70. Emphasis added.

71. Balthasar, *Explorations in Theology,* vol. 1, *The Word Made Flesh* (San Francisco: Ignatius Press, 1989), 190–91. (Originally, *Skizzen zur Theologie*, vol. 1, *Verbum Caro* [Einsiedeln: Johannes Verlag, 1960].) The contrast with Voegelin is evident—it is precisely the loss of objectivity, of sense of office of revelation, of the legitimacy of strict dogmatic formulation, which opens the Voegelinian "experience in the *metaxy*" to the charge of undermining objective history, event beyond the soul. He clearly and consistently affirms God's transcendence of the soul but not so clearly his incarnation that transcends the soul by happening in the cosmic time-space of objective history. That is why Jesus' divinity appears in Voegelin mythologized. That is why there is no sense of Church as objective office founded by Christ, of Eucharist as real presence of Christ, or of the Resurrection as victory over death. Voegelin, despite the influence of the young Balthasar upon his thought, was too Protestant and too Platonic to appreciate the full range of the objectivity—the transcending in the experience of reality—of both what revelation is about and the mode of its happening. Vol. 4 of *Order and History, The Ecumenic Age*, is a great disappointment to Catholics.

divine. Now we can sketch more meaningfully the belief context in which such experiences occur.

I have warned of a circularity in the way we have been proceeding. Complaint of circularity would be legitimate if my purpose here were to prove apodeictically the existence of God.[72] Rather, if one has been reared in a tradition within which the sense of God's presence and his gifts of creation and revelation and sacrament are such a part of life that one's natural faith includes a rich and deep faith[73] in God, then he readily sees some point of the traditional ways to God. Their inadequacy for capturing the full living experience of God in his Church, which is what leads to disparaging remarks about the God of the philosophers, is not the point. If, on the other hand, for whatever reason, one believes that the cosmos of our experience has to be dealt with only in terms of what is intrinsic to it and accessible to experimental verification, what we have seen of the sense of God will likely not prove compelling of belief. It is not meant to. Rather, these meditations point epideictically to the experience in which the meditator bathes. When we listened to a mystic's experience of how God can work in the soul, this helped us appreciate the sense of being that is necessary to accommodate such experience, the full impact of which the atheist cannot accept and still remain an atheist. In the attempt to provide here the sketch needed to consolidate some grasp on this Occidental traditional onto-theological framework, I must be simplistic. Fuller appropriation must await completion of a work in progress.

The Christian Onto-Theology

The revelation (itself a gift from God) of creation shows all being coming from a unique and unbounded Source, which the philosopher symbolizes as pure energy (not the energy of physics, or the limited psychic energy of human experience, but that from which both come through infinite creative will) that existed before all boundaries were set in place by the creator. So the Source itself is no entity, because unconditioned by time and space, which are its free creation, it cannot be properly expressed by calling it even the

---

72. "The ways [*voies*] reason borrows to go to God are proofs, and, likewise, these proofs are ways. That does not take away their character of proof—although they are often incomplete proofs—but their Object, unique among all the objects of thought, gives them a special character. They do not deliver up to us their object the way other proofs deliver their objects to us. They do not cause us to penetrate it. Only, on the one hand, God is present already with an intimate presence to him who proves Him, as He is to him who denies Him. But at the same time, on the other hand, with a presence so ungraspable [*insaisissable*] that, unique among all objects, we cannot hold onto Him" (de Lubac, *Sur les chemins de Dieu*, 92–93). De Lubac cites the Thomist, Fernand Van Steenberghen, on the incompleteness of Saint Thomas's five ways in the *Summa theologica*: "None of the *quinquae viae* constitutes, in their literal form, a complete and satisfying proof for the existence of God. The first and second need to be prolonged; the third and the fifth need to be corrected and completed; the fourth is unusable" ("Le problème philosophique de l'existence de Dieu," *Revue philosophique de Louvain* 45 [1947]: 168).

73. "Faith," says Balthasar, "here means my response to the love that has sacrificed itself for me" (*Love Alone*, 82).

Seiendste des Seienden (the thingliest thing) in Heidegger's terms, or the Greatest or the Highest or most general *(Allgemeinste)*. Rather, it contains, in a manner surpassing our understanding, as the cause contains the effect, every capability we find in nature and man, but without their evident (and frustrating) limits, for it is also source of that nonbeing of limits that only makes sense when finite being is set into time and space. Hence it includes in its being the activity we experience as mind and love, but as unlimited self-knowing and perfect self-affirmation and unbounded pouring forth of its being, love "that surpasses all understanding." In sum, a life of Infinite Mind knowing itself as its own object and affirming itself as a love that flows from this eternally begetting-begotten relationship, that knows not in and of itself the hesitations, the ambiguities, and the death of finite minds and wills and relationships. It does, on the other hand, know our hesitations, ambiguities, indeed perversions and sins, but only because it, the author of human nature, lovingly wills to associate itself intimately with its creation and to the depths, even the dregs, of it by entering into its troubled history. The whole cosmos is but its effect, the stage setting for a drama of divine interaction with its creatures, on the highest level an affair of mutual love, but also, and therefore, a play, a struggle of freedoms, infinite and finite.[74]

The whole point of creation (so far as the Source allows a glimpse of its motives) is to allow creatures to share in the glory *(doxa)* of the Source, to be loved by him and to love him. Belief in such a source is tantamount to accepting that creation has not just a unity but a point, in the sense both of a meaning and a focused end, a truth unknown to science but compatible with what has been discovered by it. The ontological claim inherent in that point, which the tradition believes is put forward by the infinite Source itself, is overwhelming. The immense power of the cosmos and the brutishness of nature have as their origin and goal the realization of what appears the very opposite of their forceful thrust (and so requiring a reversal, a *metanoete, conversio*): appreciation, unending enhancement, love. Hence, in the language of recent biological speculation, the profound meaning of "order out of chaos": Scientists are hypothesizing, as a property of matter as such, an inherent tendency to complexify, which the Abrahamist cannot but see as an effect, at the lowest level of created being, of that loving-creating which revelation long ago uncovered for us. The achievement of form—the holding off of entropy—and from lower forms, higher permanences, culminating in the in-formation that makes life possible, and amid life-forms, that highest information, Word, is what matter is for. But at the lower levels, complexity is achieved at the cost of the independence, even the life, of the gobbled-up elements. Out of the struggle and pain evident in finite existence, and despite the profligacies of evolution and, worse, the treacheries at the highest created level of the perverse use of

---

74. In capturing in one sentence the subject of the seven volumes of the middle third of Balthasar's trilogy—the part he called *Theo-dramatik*—I have bested the editors of *Reader's Digest*. For a bit of further nuance, I can only refer the reader to the original.

finite human will, comes the reversal: union without destruction, love. The triumph of Job is a sound experience.

To this end—the realization of the maximum of love—the summit of creation, man, is made "in the image of God." That is, these highest creatures are mind and will, although dependent for operations on the bounded material energy we call body, and the divine interior life is sustaining them with something of its very own Mind, to be found especially pure in the depths of the soul, through which *Sein* comes to be, and everything can be appreciated.

If this is indeed the underlying ontological reality, then you would think that it should be obvious to those created minds, which are, after all, sustained in their very being by the life of the Spirit. Why, then, do so many seem oblivious to it, if not proudly proclaiming themselves agnostic, at least living as though they were atheists?

It is not our incarnation—our having to work through a body—that blocks the obvious, for it was meant to be part of the instrumentality of our being and hence of our knowing ourselves and God. The body puts us in contact with the world of things, every aspect of which "tells of the glory of God"—if we care to see it. But we in our freedom are capable of converting every one of those means into an end, in the sense of a dead end, or at least into an instrument of our own (false) self-aggrandizement—an idol we can manipulate at will—so that instead of feeding us, of truly in-forming us, they become grist for our narcissistic mill.[75] Again, revelation informs us: What happened was the abuse of the God-like liberty that was given to us as central to our very being. The ontological condition for the possibility of love existing within creation was the setting into being of creatures who are genuinely free. To be free means to be able to appreciate and to affirm, to direct energies co-creatively with the structures provided in reality by the creative Source of all, and to give of self in an act of uniting that enhances, rather than destroys, what already exists, forming it into a glorious totality.

But instead of loving God and themselves in this way, the first men were misled into wanting to be, not images of the loving true God, co-creating with him, but little gods of their own—dead ends—enjoying a relative autonomy and the illusion of absolute sovereignty, hence deploying power for control, a state that could not last. They attempted to supplant God, acting—pneumopathologically, as Voegelin says—as though they were the ultimate reality instead of infinitely beholden and called to gratitude for the gift of life. Ingratitude remains the foundation of all sin and the dam to the current of life.

The lie—dis-information and de-formation—was thus introduced into creation, distorting, disordering and obscuring it. The foundation of all lies is man's convincing himself of the supreme absurdity—that he is the ultimate reality. Such perversion remains an existential mystery of the most baffling

---

75. For an excellent analysis of the difference between things of this world as icons of God and our perversions of them into idols, see Jean-Luc Marion, *Dieu sans l'être* (Paris: Presses universitaires de France, 1991), 15–36.

kind, because it is palpably anti-evolutionary, entropy advancing instead of entropy resisting, the free twisting of the greatest power in creation into a source of ultimately unproductive domination, breeding hatred and war.

What is most disturbing is this experientially observable phenomenon: That through the abuse of liberty, the lie gets lodged at the very heart of human existence, from which it must be purified. This is a methodical struggle to achieve and keep order as the systematically installed obscurity of the divisive (*diabolein*) lie is combated.[76]

This proper leading back along the disciplined way is impossible for damaged man to achieve by himself. He has destroyed the principle of good order within, and so he is dependent upon a fresh initiative from the loving Source beyond. Because His is the love of the infinite Father, he has indeed undertaken to lead us, suavely restoring order, gently because of our damaged nature— he has to work his way around our perverse self-bondage, our not wanting to see—lovingly (although wrenching change is not painless), because he is love and loves his own creatures as himself. His forgiveness is a making whole again what we have disrupted.[77]

Such a love-centered ontology may seem difficult to reconcile with the struggles for survival in nature, the power-politics reality of social existence, and the pathology found in everyday human existence. None of these negative dimensions is passed over by the tradition of revelation; rather, it is that "sinfulness of the flesh [*sarx*]" that Saint Paul contrasts in detail with the life of love. What he describes is an anthropology of struggle: flesh and death versus spirit and life. The moral distortion is the source of that evil which God took on himself—he does not just know it, so to speak, theoretically. By allowing his Son to experience it to the full in his human life, even to the point of suffering an unjust death at the hands of the power-brokers of the time, God tastes the bitter fruit of the worst infidelities of his creatures, drinking the cup to the dregs. Here is the most central and profound mystery: that God so (freely) wanted this creation of a cosmos of love, he called it into existence knowing and accepting that he would freely offer himself, in the person of his Son incarnate at a moment in history as "this Jesus whom you have killed" (Acts 2:23). (Reflecting on this brings out the seriousness of the creative act.)

From such a recognition of the full force of evil follows an attitude of tempered involvement with the world. Accept what legitimate state authority demands, do not fight it, its authority comes from God, counsels Paul to the Romans, writing of a regime that has already arrested and will soon martyr him. "My Kingdom," Christ told the representative of the all-powerful Roman

---

76. A rich thesaurus of symbols about and reflections on evil is to be found in that classic, Paul Ricoeur, *La symbolique du mal*, in *Finitude et culpabilité*, vol. 2 of *Philosophie de la volonté* (Paris: Aubier, 1960); *The Symbolism of Evil*, trans. E. Buchanan (New York: Harper and Row, 1967).

77. But without effacing every trace of the damage we have wrought. It is as though God wants us reminded of our responsibility. His miraculous freeing us from ourselves is not an unmaking of who we are; it is a slow, painful pedagogy, and we continue to bear some scars.

Imperium, "is not of this world." Saint Augustine's *De Civitate Dei* is a vast reflection on the difficult relationship of the two cities. The Christian, caught in this life in the earthly city of flesh, is above all a citizen of the City of God, which is reflected here below while having its center in heaven.

Nietzsche saw clearly the need to evacuate this entire ontological faith if man was to be delivered over to himself, to be able, as Nietzsche exhorted, to "Give yourself grace!" *(Morgenröte)*. Programs of human self-redemption abound in this civilization, as secularized versions of the Christian eschatology.[78]

How is God's love leading his people to fulfillment continued down through the centuries? Through his ongoing Eucharistic incarnation in the Mystical Body of Christ, the mystery of the Church, the gathering of those who respond to his call for holiness, who congregate in love to help one another, and all God's creatures. But that is another and long and very intellectually challenging story, part of the appropriation I am working on.

In sum, what we find in this tradition is an affirmation of life, a life that can achieve lasting fulfillment in a world that is not a mere accident, but rather a manifestation of being as ultimately in-formed and informing. The revelation that the all-powerful Source of the cosmos can be addressed as Abba, the most familiar form of Father, that Being at its core is capable of response, not dumb fact, and that we are called to a response of love, faith, installs all Abrahamist-inspired ontology in a personalism and focuses the philosopher's attention on phenomena of freedom and the infinite worth of the person.

---

78. Recall my earlier recommendation of the best analysis of these secular schemes for self-salvation: Eric Voegelin, *The New Science of Politics* (Chicago: University of Chicago Press, 1952); and Etienne Gilson, *Les métamorphoses de la Cité de Dieu* (Louvain: Publications universitaires de Louvain, 1952).

9.

THE HISTORICITY OF BEING (*SEIN*)

THE CHARTER FOR A POST- (AND ANTE) HEIDEGGERIAN METAPHYSICS

To all that we have just seen about a Christian experience of God a Heideggerian might reply: "The God known in any one tradition is an interpreted God. He can only reveal himself in and through a cultural setting; what is revealed is expressed in the particular symbols most meaningful within one tradition at a given epoch." Our Heideggerian may be hinting as well that because God is no thing, our notions of him must result from more mysterious happenings within the obscure unfolding illumining of *Sein* than anything like an encounter with some kind of entity. Although such a suggestion underscores the truth that the divine is no entity, it risks reducing God or the gods to mere expressions of the diaphanous *Heilige* (the Holy), which for Heidegger is one of the four dimensions of *Sein*.[1]

As a Christian, I confessed that I find the matter a bit more complicated, but I showed in Part II that I am prepared to concede this basic Heideggerian point: Because all knowledge of being is the work of a subject, it is necessarily interpreted knowledge, and hence necessarily historical. As Heidegger would say, it is subject to "historicity."

"Historicity" is a translation of the barbarous German neologism, *Geschichtlichkeit*, created recently to express this insight because the discovery of the historicity of *Sein* is new and radical. This discovery, prepared by the subjectivist turn that began with Descartes, became possible only in the perspective of the transcendental turn, begun by Hume and crowned by Kant. It was further developed by Hegel, who went the whole way in historicizing being, considering the unfolding of nature and the gathering up into spirit of its sense to be absolute thought itself unfolding with necessity.

Heidegger sees this Hegelian necessity to be too rigid and, worse, as a manifestation of the end of metaphysics. It is a thinking of *Sein* as an Absolute entity,

---

1. *Das Geviert*—the Fourfold—a notion inspired by Hölderlin's poetry, is one of the more obscure among many obscure Heideggerian symbols. I have always taken the "four" to stand for the three temporal *ekstases* plus facticity (earth), but my student, David White, who wrote a doctoral dissertation on this subject, was not convinced. He did the best anyone has, to my knowledge, to make sense of this, but again it all remains obscure. See David White, "The Fourfold in Heidegger's Philosophy" (Ph.D. diss., University of Toronto, 1990).

Absolutes Wissen, or the Absolute idea, which indeed embraces all illumining, but in a grounded way, as metaphysics always thinks. This misses the mystery of the opening of the *ek-static* time-space of significance, which is the very illumining-obscuring of *Sein* itself. It fails to capture the freedom of *Sein*'s revelation and dissimulation of itself—the errance *(Irre)* of Being's becoming, wandering through time, *Sein* always obscuring as it illumines, as the very happening of history occurs through free but necessarily finite gifts (*Schicken*, sendings) from the mysterious Source beyond all horizons of interpretation of the *Dasein*. It is Heidegger's accomplishment to have opened the question of the way in which *Sein* actually unfolds in time with a radicality, amplitude, and ambiguity more worthy of the richness of reality itself than previous transcendental idealism. Or—interrupts the classical metaphysician, a critic not altogether sympathetic to Heidegger—should we say simply "the way the knowledge of being unfolds in time"?

Speak of ambiguity. This "simple" question brings out the radical ambiguity in the use of the term "being." I hope I have laid the foundations for accommodating in the same wisdom both sides of the ambiguity: the truth about interpretation, and the commonsense experience of the reality in themselves of things. This requires three symbols: (1) "being" in the all-inclusive sense of everything that is, was, or can be, whether real, in a cosmic time-space, real in infinity, or subjective, in consciousness; (2) *esse,* the actual factual existence of things as they are in themselves, including their stake in cosmic time-space and their having a definite nature, and of the infinite *esse* of God, and of the existence (*inesse,* accidental existence) of real relations between them—all of this independently of what anybody thinks about them; and (3) *Sein,* Being-interpreted, the meanings to be found in things, always within subjective and intersubjective discourse, which is always in a context and always subject to historicity. *Sein* and the world(s) of signification, introduce us to the human world of culture and imagination. The creative, future-opening projecting of *Dasein* is indeed how the breakthroughs to new *Sein* occur, as the mysterious source sends *(schicken)* its gifts *(Geschicke);* but this interpreting is healthy and true, the source of constructive new being rather than destructive fantasy, when it is rooted in the fullest possible appreciation for the already having been (demanded by authenticity). This includes the unchanging essential being of God, reasoned to (if not conclusively, at least requiring some appreciation) and revealed by God in history; the principles of the cosmos and the real natures of things, as we know them in everyday experience and through scientific inquiry; and the accomplishments of culture as they presence and reveal themselves to us, freely in the case of God and other persons, and necessarily in the case of the givens of natural structure and process and the accomplishments of cultures that have been inscribed through work in things (objective spirit).

I am obviously seeking to bring into communion a transcendental (in the phenomenological sense) philosophical tradition with one that acknowledges the transcendental in the objectivist sense of the *analogia entis*. With each comes certain philosophical baggage.[2] I have had to reshape both to develop this interplay, inevitably deforming some aspects of the two traditions. The complaint that Langan has ignored Heidegger in this, or that Saint Thomas would never have said that may be historically illuminating, but does not count against the truth of what I have reformulated: Both interpretation and existence revealed in thought as independent of thought can be harmonized in the way I am proposing. Here now is a fuller elucidation of the two cardinal symbols.

Sein. The illumining of world through the deployment of the suite of time-spaces historically unfolded through the human existent as interpretative horizons, the possibilities of which are rooted in and fashioning of cultural things and symbols, and natural things as interpreted. The results of past interpretative illuminings of *Sein* in the form of the concrete possibilities of the already having been *(das Gewesene)* are handed on principally through the enculturation of new generations of *Dasein*, whose natural faith is molded by the anonymous, average them *(das Man)*, passing on traditions and language inauthentically,[3] governing the way epochs continue to come to be through intersubjective interpretation *(Mitsein). Seinsgeschichte* (history of *Sein*) means the suite of epochs growing out of the dialectical relationships between the brute facticity of the in-itself (the ontic, including the cultural forms embedded in transformed natural

---

2. An effort to develop a notion of *Sein* does not entail accepting Heidegger's reading of the history of metaphysics. Acknowledging that "*Sein* has been forgotten," in the sense that only after the transcendental turn and indeed ultimately in Heidegger's own work has the "taking the step back to think the history of *Sein*" become a possibility, does not entail devastating diminution of the classical metaphysicians, none of whom—not Plato, Aristotle, Plotinus, Augustine, or Thomas—in fact tried to reduce thought of the Source to "the highest and most general thing." To take just one instance, Saint Thomas says that the infinite *esse*, as Source of all being, hence of all meaning, including all that man may interpret, is clearly understood to escape all finite meaning. Rather, it supplies its foundation, both through the creation of natural form, and especially through setting in place the natural possibility of human interpretation through human nature. It rules providentially and even intervenes prophetically in the formation of human traditions and the building of their treasures of symbols. Although before Kant and Husserl the thought of human cognition as an *ek-static* opening of time-space of world was forgotten, the profound thought of infinite *esse* provides a clear metaphysical priority even when interpretation is discovered. In this understanding, infinite *esse* and even created finite *esse* come before *Sein* ontologically and, if you will, chronologically, as condition for its possibility. Or consider this text:

> Plato: The sun, I think you will agree, not only makes the things we see visible, but causes the processes of generation, growth and nourishment, without itself being a process.
> Glaucon: True.
> Plato: The Good therefore may be said to be the source not only of the intelligibility of the objects of knowledge, but also of their existence and reality; yet it is not itself identical with reality, but is beyond reality and superior to it in dignity and power. It really must be devilish superior, remarked Glaucon with a grin. (Plato, *Republic*, 509).

3. The English "inauthenticity" as a translation of Heidegger's *Uneigentlichkeit* has a pejorative flavor missing in the German. The technical term expresses the everyday state of affairs in which I am molded to the outlooks and fashions of the time which are properly no one's, they do not constitute my ultimate *autos*, but they form massively my public persona.

THE HISTORICITY OF BEING (SEIN) 321

carriers) and the sense-making activity of the interpretation (the ontological). These are not to be confused; the thinker should not forget this ontological difference between *Sein* and *Seienden*. As these interpenetrate, the socially shared interpretative horizons account for what is allowed to stand in the attention of our individual and collective dealings with the world. The facticity responds, by presencing within the opened space-time and by being altered by man's action, to become a guide to future cooperative interpretation and action.

Esse. The in-itself reality of all entities and relations between entities *(inesse)* includes the inherent givenness of their forms, understood as real regulative principles governing the development of the thing, and hence real foundation of their potential intelligibility. This is true of the infinite being of God (whose "form" is his infinite *esse*), the divine ideas, or the fleeting existence of the most ephemeral of entities, regardless of whether or how they may in fact happen to be known. Even images and concepts have accidental being *(inesse)* in a mind, as psychological entities.

We just saw that classical metaphysicians find it difficult to see that *Sein* adds anything to what a Thomist would mean by historical knowledge and by knowledge of the whole *(Totalitätsbegriff)*. The Heideggerians say that this shows the great difficulty with metaphysics as such: "Being has been forgotten." This would be a ridiculous charge, if by "being" were meant all that has or can have *esse*, for metaphysics is nothing more than the exploration of every aspect of being in that sense. But the charge, in my view, is true if one means by the forgotten Being, *Sein*. The entire tradition, from Parmenides to Nietzsche, has failed to see the importance of *die Lichtung,* the time-space of world, the opening of a context of meaning that gives *Sein* to the epochal reality, and hence holds the key to the meaning of the particular historical understanding of the world characteristic of an epoch and its cultural organization. Having forgotten the ontologic (in this sense, of historical *Sein* interpretation), the metaphysicians misinterpret radically and fundamentally the ontic, failing to see that things are indeed *Seienden*, that is, things interpreted, *noemata*, into the essence *(Wesen)* of which enters that meaning which is brought from the horizons of the interpreting ontological time-space opening affected by *Dasein*.

This illumining is, in one, noncausal sense, fundamental: for instance, the technologically efficient organization of society and the coming into being of research and industrial institutions, technosciences, and myriads of technical entities,[4] indeed more fundamentally yet, our being molded as technical men, with a unique mind-set and our inculturated habits formed a certain way, all this distinguishes our epoch radically from, say, the Baroque era or the feudal arrangements of the Middle Ages. Its being *(Sein)* is indeed different.

The epochal *Sein* is a mysterious and dense weave of considerations, subjective, intersubjective, and objective (there are, after all, many cultural objects

---

4. It is estimated the technical vocabulary in English includes ten million words, a measure not only of language's importance in all this but also of the fertility of technical invention in the epochal light of *Sein*.

characteristic of this era and collectively necessary to it, all enjoying *esse*), harmonizing in a kind of Zeitgeist fashion. What is more, the suite of these epochs manifests ex post facto a certain intelligibility, a necessity *(Not-wendigkeit)*, but one that, as Heidegger's explorations of the *Irre* and the *wenden* in *Not* (the wandering in need) of the *Seinsgeschichte* show, is essentially free, thoroughly un-thing-like, that is, the creative breakthroughs are totally unpredictable—*Sein* is always surprising. The past does not rigidly determine the coming to be of the future but does "attune" it *(be-stimmen)*.[5] There is a mystery about the input of the always new element from beyond the circle of interpretation—it is more than just fresh presencing of the already-having-been things of the world.

I believe a will to recuperate the fullness of the objective, and especially the core of consciousness-transcending reality that offers itself, is operative in my ontological project more consistently than in Heidegger's. That is why I urge caution about getting swept up into the idealistic language obsession of so many post-Kantians, Heidegger included—the royal road to the kind of fantasy land where thinkers as brilliant as Heidegger move from inventing a secret Germany in and around the dreams of Hölderlin, to illusions of preempting the National Socialist revolution and turning it toward authentic *Denken*.[6] With just a twinge of glee at turning the tables on certain Heideggerians, I make the following claim: Our epochal interpretative horizons make possible such a scientific project as this "will to recuperate the full spectrum of objective data,"[7] and my own natural faith motivates the will act of fundamental projection that realizes this ontological interpretation of objective reality, of things indicated by and transcending the language we use to speak of them—in short, recuperation by our meditation of all that is gathered up under the symbol *esse*.

This is indeed a claim about the accessibility of form—hence, permanence—in the midst of process, and of the possibility, therefore, of directing action (more change) in ways not de-structive of but preserving *(wahren)*[8] good structures, enhancing the order they incarnate. My will to do so, "to dwell in the nearness of the things" in this objective sense, as the beginning of a recuperation of genuine

---

5. See the fine play on this acoustical image in "Die Erinnerung in die Metaphysik," the last essay in the Nietzsche volumes, Heidegger, *Nietzsche,* vol. 2 (Pfüllingen: Neske, 1961), 481–90. *Stimme* means "voice"—I attune *(stimme)* my violin. *Be-stimmt-heit* means "determination" with the sense not of limit (term) but of harmony of voices. "Truth is symphonic" (Balthasar).

6. See Frank Edler, "The Significance of Hölderlin for Heidegger's Political Involvement with Nazism" (Ph.D. diss., University of Toronto, 1992), for the whole frightening tale.

7. See Voegelin, *The New Science of Politics* (Chicago: University of Chicago Press, 1952), for an explanation of why the scientific horizons have become healthier since the reductionist days of nineteenth-century positivism. In Heideggerian terms, then, Being has come to be in our epoch at what he means by "the end of metaphysics," in a way that begins to overcome the metaphysical forgetting of *Sein,* but without necessarily undermining our sense of the in-itselfness of things *(esse)*. The triumph of post-Kantian voluntarism, despite the reign in the universities of its present form, deconstructionism, is not complete. Indeed, it is being challenged on many fronts.

8. Heidegger recalls the sense of truth *(Wahrheit)* as preserving *(wahren)* the already having been illumined *(das Gewesene)* as gifts of *Sein.*

order, natural and cultural, toward the responsible exercise of finite human freedom, is foundational to the claimed objective metaphysics and illumines the true goal of all science. Science is not about science but about objective reality, with implications for how we ought respect it—yes, "is" leading to "ought." Metaphysics, understood in the Heideggerian sense as the forgetting of *Sein*, is dead; but a *Sein*-recalling metaphysics that thinks the origin of *Sein* in the infinite *esse* and in *Dasein's esse* as human nature is alive and well. The will to pursue it is no *Seinsvergessenheit* so long as the post-Heideggerian metaphysician recalls that this project-founding will is itself a gift of *Sein*. The present study is offered in evidence of at least a faint pulse of such a post- (and ante) Heideggerian metaphysics.

To put the metaphysical priorities bluntly, then, I claim that the condition for the possibility of the *esse* of the first man is the real cosmic process of evolution, with whatever causal dependence this cosmic becoming can be shown to have on the infinite divine *esse* as its origin.[9] Further, the condition for the possibility of the first act of interpretation by *Dasein* was the coming to be of the human *esse* of the first man, that *Geistnatur* to which Balthasar refers. I believe it a mistake to confuse the coming to be of *Sein* with the philosophers' first raising the historically retained question of the sense of the whole, the *Seinsfrage*, or even with any earlier effort to raise the question of overall meaning. I suggest, rather, that *Sein* came to be with the first interpretative act, however primitive, however implicit the sense of it all may have been. With the emergence of a conscious subject over against objects and with some sense of being in a world of meaning, *Sein* has already given the gift of a world- and meaning-founding illumining. From this it follows, too, that a history of *Sein* happened, both within the consciousness of the first *Dasein*, as he deployed more and more interpretative acts within a consistent developing world, and in the expressive interpreting-together *(Mitsein)* of the first two or more *Dasein*, as a certain remembered and culturally inscribed continuity of meaning was achieved, basically through language, but also later through cave painting, and so on. That is a history lost to us in prehistory except to the extent we recover artifacts and are able to read them. The continuity of the tradition of Occidental thought flowing from the breakthrough to history on Sinai and from the breakthrough, almost a millennium later, to the explicit thought of "being" as the meaning of the whole is another matter. That is the foundation of the history of being of our tradition, the Occidental tradition of *Denken*, which the art of writing has allowed to remain continuous since the prophets and the philosophers, indeed even from the earliest Egyptian religious texts.

Heidegger can make a nice pun with the German word for mystery, *Geheimnis*. The *Ge-Heim* is what keeps us from being at home *(Heim)*, the uncanny

---

9. Chapter 8 showed the challenge of making such a dependence plausible. It showed that binding conclusive proof of such dependence was not, at least in my summary, achieved. But it also pointed to faith's loving acceptance of revelation as an ultimate source of such a Light, which illumines the proofs as so many signs of God's loving authorship of the cosmic process.

(as English translators have put it) destroys the taken-for-granted sense of the familiar. Let us inquire more deeply, and rather realistically, Where do we find the source of new breakthroughs?

First, consider the already having been. We are the recipients of the generous gifts of the sedimented results of all previous illumining that is passed down in the collective memory of our tradition: my own personal memories; all the symbols of the language, mathematics, liturgy; every kind of cultural object; all the institutional arrangements we find in our situation, even on a planetary scale; in sum, all the traditions in everything they pass on in whatever way. All this has a history, all this comes together to form a world, and many little worlds[10] within the epochal world, all providing gifts of concrete possibility of unimaginable richness, a seedbed of future breakthroughs.

Then the present. This working together as world of such a vast variety of kinds of *Seienden* is itself a mystery, although we have allowed familiarity to render us mindless in accepting it, until Angst reveals its groundlessness, in the sense that the Light which ties it all together is no thing, or any concatenation of things, or a cause. The mystery of its harmonious *(be-stimmende)*[11] working together as world unfolds before our eyes at every instant, an ongoing outpouring of little gifts of meaning the generosity of which we take for granted.

This mysteriousness of the present worlding of world, of the consistent intelligibility of the whole and the mutually reinforcing contributions of billions of agents, drawing on nature, culture, and religious in-spiration, becomes more startling still when we contemplate the mystery of the future. Into the hermeneutic circle of *Mitsein* interpreting world, breaks the element of newness that occurs with every interpretative act.[12] Most of the time the mass of the automatically presented possibilities stored in the past absorbs the element of newness in every act of interpretation sufficiently so that we do not notice it. The weight of the past may even successfully cause to resist some of the newness being offered. (In the neurotic person this can form a closed-mindedness of tragic proportions.) In the case of those interpretative acts that achieve epochal breakthrough, the new is dramatic and radical, in rare instances even founding whole new traditions, and always advancing what Marcel calls "l'exigence de l'être," that *Anspruch des Seins*,[13] the demands Being makes of us to respond to its word. In the greatest leaps the mystery of the new at last impresses even the most jaded, who speak then of "paradigm shifts."

---

10. There are as many worlds as there are individual *Dasein* (He lives in a world of his own; each possesses a personal and idiosyncratic history). And every sustained cooperation of human beings founds *Mitsein* worlds—of IBM, of the Catholic Church, and the epochal world in which every modern man, to the extent he is modern, participates.

11. See note 5 above.

12. When I come to understand for the first time what is a banality or an old experience for others, it nevertheless constitutes a newness in my life, a coming to be of being, which affects the *Sein* of the world, as at least a slight inflection in public opinion. Newness, however minor and banal, is new and mysterious, a gift of *Sein*, from nowhere.

13. Heidegger, "Die Erinnerung in die Metaphysik," 482.

Another aspect to this mystery lies in the discovery that the illumining achieved by *Sein* is always also, because of *Da-sein*'s finitude, an obscuring. We can glimpse this truth on two levels: (1) When I focus on the cardinal on the magnolia, I push everything else to the horizons of my world; (2) after the coming to be of certain insights, experienced as a gift *(Gunst)* of Being, the previous epochal understanding of things now appears to have been definitely deficient—the Roman philosopher had no notion of genetic codes. On the other hand, fascination with what is revealed through new insights leads us to forget what he may have known—for example, he may have had a stronger sense of the importance of heredity than we have. Most significant, the epochal *Sein* influences even the typical kinds of questions we are likely to ask, and the language in which we express them. But it also influences the evolution of the real things in the world itself: Guided by our transcendental notions of how it stands with Being—our collective natural faiths—our work transforms the face of the earth. It is becoming difficult to glimpse the nature beneath the colossal transformations worked upon it by activistic contemporary high-tech culture.[14] The most fundamental obscuring of all: As *Sein* illumines and thus brings to be the *Seienden*, it dis-tracts all attention away from its own giving as source.

We should be open to the grace necessary, and first available in this epoch, for stepping back behind the entire suite of epochs that forms the Occidental *Seinsgeschichte*, in search of its ultimate meaning. "Ultimate meaning," however, is not to be understood in the overly demanding sense of Hegel's absolute *Wissen*. Taking what Heidegger calls *den Schritt zurück*—the step back, as opposed to Hegel's *Aufheben* (the uplifting synthesis that accommodates and relates all to all)—remains the challenge of thinking *Sein* in its essence *(Wesen)*,[15] returning to the beginning *(Anfang)*, including re-membering *(An-denken)* as we enter into the sphere of the *Seinsgeschichte (er-innern)* the obscuring and forgetting of *Sein*.[16] It acknowledges the need for a much more tentative, open, nontotalizing structure of thought than that achieved so impressively by Hegel, and one

---

14. If it is a culture. Bruce Stewart suggested dubbing this planetary phenomenon "the HTX," leaving open the sense in which this is an altogether new kind of social reality, neither a culture one can live in, nor a civilization bound to a prime-symbol region (geographic, religious, and so on), more than the world system, which undoubtedly forms part of it, with its weave of planetary-scale institutions. This High Tech X is more about doing, about manipulating, than about living. It is massively instrumental, suggests Stewart.

15. For Heidegger, *Metaphysik* gives way to *Philosophie*, which now yields to *Denken*, and *Denken* leads even to the cancellation of any notion of *Sein* that might harden it into something. As will become evident in this chapter, I do not follow Heidegger in such a radical critique of metaphysics, and I shall explain my nervousness about a tendency in Heidegger to *Seinsmystizismus*. For me, *Denken* means the effort to think together both the evidence, in what presences, for its objective otherness with all the distinctiveness of forms that present themselves, while remaining aware that this evidence is interpreted, so that we must strive to embrace the largest possible context of meaning, extending to the fundamenta of time and space, and even transcending them, to the divine Source. This will all be explored later in the present chapter.

16. Heidegger, "Die Erinnerung in die Metaphysik," 481.

more guided and anchored in the gifts of presencing reality ("des données qui sont des dons")[17] than Heidegger's Kantian propensities seem to have encouraged. It reveals the need for a new *Sein-denkende* metaphysics, embracing the discoveries of the sciences, the wisdoms transmitted by the traditions, and the recent experience of seeking to achieve a political order on a planetary scale. It must be a *Denken* that does not avoid the metaphysical questions of causal grounding, just because it remembers that *Sein* itself is no cause, and that God is no thing.

That returns us to the subject with which we began, in transition from the last chapter: How does this attempted balance of interpretation and objectivity of a new-old metaphysics affect the question of our knowledge of God, who is not an empirical object, indeed in some sense not a *Gegen-stand* at all, but more an *Um-stand*, where circum-stance refers not only to the e-vent of revelation but to the *Um-greifende* (Jaspers) all-encompassing reality of the divine? God can only be thought in the categories available to a tradition at a given time, and he can only reveal himself in and through a cultural setting: What is revealed must be expressed through the prophet (or the Logos itself made flesh) in the particular symbols most meaningful within one tradition. But before crying victory for the subjectivism of interpretation, consider three needed objectivist correctives: (1) the Christian claim about revelation. The absolutely transcending God, whose infinite free reality can never be adequately inferred from the finite effects of his creation, even with all the superlative adjustments to analogous predication, nevertheless has found the (human) language to reveal that he is sovereignly free to communicate to man as he will. The Christian garners evidence from the history of revelation—the witness to how God has actually elected to interact with the concrete, historical people, Israel, and then, through Jesus Christ, with all mankind—becoming a *Seiendes* of his choice within ontological horizons he prepared from the beginning of time, so as to be a witness inscribed in objective historic events as reported by his chosen witnesses, under his inspiration. What the believer hears in these words reveals the success of the transcendent God in forging over time the symbols to express what he wants revealed of his sovereign majesty. As Hans Urs von Balthasar says,

> God speaks his word within man [using the totality of human reality as his language]. Not only what man utters but *all that he is* becomes God's organ of communication. What man is and can be is only revealed in its fullness when God makes of him his alphabet, his sounding board and sense organ. God in his freedom decided to become man, chose His creature's mode of expression in order to reveal the hidden things of divinity in a way that could mean something to man [otherwise, what is the point?], and resolved to pour Himself out into the abyss of emptiness and indigence caused by sin; from the beginning His word regarded man's whole existence and experience as an aspect of the mode of expression.[18]

---

17. For this sense of *don*, see Jean-Luc Marion, *Dieu sans l'être* (Paris: Presses universitaires de France, 1991), 250–58. This Christian rereading of Heidegger provides an important corrective to the great German thinker's philosophy.

18. An essential aspect of revelation is the realization of how much guidance God has given the long process of forging the grammar of symbols necessary to express the fullness

THE HISTORICITY OF BEING (*SEIN*)   327

Consequently, in receiving God's revelation, we are confronted, not just with what went on in the depth of the souls of prophetic individuals, but with the concrete expressed teaching of the prophets, of Jesus, of the Church, and their mighty acts, worked pedagogically and as seal of the genuineness of the prophetic source; and finally with the comportment of the entire people of God, the splendors of sanctity that result from their reception of God's Word, and the depths of their infidelity and the destructiveness of their sinful acts when they reject it, or at least do not live up to it. These are all events in history, acts *(Seienden)* for the ontic givenness of which mountains of evidence exist; but as with any order of evidence, one has first to believe that that order of reality is worth investigating before he will elect "to dwell in the nearness of the *Seienden*."

(2) As we have argued, these symbols in which the teaching is couched are still translatable. Many Hebrew and Christian symbols express experiences of objective events involving real persons and things; and others, experiences common to human nature. For this reason the truth they reveal can, when properly expressed, be appropriated by persons in other epochs and even other traditions, integrated interpretively (hopefully not arbitrarily or distortingly but correctly, in keeping with the intended sense) into their language and hence their worlds. (If this were not possible, neither continuity of tradition, ecumenism, nor conversion would make much sense.)

(3) If a transcending Source exists, none of our interpretations can either exhaustively express (any more than they can any great reality) or affect what God is in himself. But then it is also true that what I may think of the tree in my garden does not affect it, unless I act on it in consequence, nor can my knowledge of it ever exhaust its potential intelligibility. Even when the interpretations are true (as far as they go), they can only point to aspects of God as he is in himself. All traditions have acknowledged this from out of their experiences of God, those with the strongest sense of transcendence have always recognized that what we know of God through our own interpretative striving is the merest drop in the ocean. Moreover, God reveals himself as subject, and so, as with any subject, he can always surprise us. One surprise is his fidelity: God freely deigns to enter into covenants with his creatures, because he loves them, and so engages himself to remain faithful—the only personal freedom in which a human can have complete con-fidence. The teachings of Jesus Christ, like those of Einstein, are in the public domain, but, because of their prophetic nature, he backs them up with publicly witnessed mighty works (the miracles) to which the biblical texts witness. Our interpretations become a living dialogue with his teaching, with himself, and as we find them lived out and meditated upon in his Church. If I may put it somewhat picturesquely, it then becomes the Incarnate God-man's job to make out of all of human existence in history the acts and the symbols to which all, in every generation and every

---

of Truth vouchsafed mankind in the coming into history of the Logos himself. Balthasar, *Explorations in Theology*, vol. 1, *The Word Made Flesh* (San Francisco: Ignatius Press, 1989), 85. (Originally, *Skizzen zur Theologie*, vol. 1, *Verbum Caro* [Einsiedeln: Johannes Verlag, 1960]).

social class, coming from whatever culture, can relate,[19] and to inspire his chosen apostles to teach these to all nations. He is, down through history, as Balthasar says, "His own exegete."[20]

There is danger that the very concepts we forge to grasp a bit of understanding of God, even those faithfully formed by Christ himself but taken into our own interpretation, become idols rather than icons.[21] That is why they must be permeated with the light flowing from acts of love. The loving acts of re-sponse, of keeping the commandments, as will giving itself, are not just interpretations, but engagement, devotion. *Sein* must not be understood in too much of a theoretical mode. Obviously, we have to know what to do, and that involves interpretation, but the actual willingness to do it is realizations of love. They are not just new revelations of *Sein* as knowledge giving but increases in *esse*, and hence they, like any *esse*, are what they are, whatever we may, rightly or wrongly, subsequently think of our actions and however they may be reacted to by other human agents.

This, then, is a capital ontological principle of objectivity: The fullness of the human *esse* comes to be and flows out into the world through action, which, as fully human, is conscious will. An action must begin in an interpretation as to what to do and it may end in an interpretation of what was done, but it itself as act is no interpretation.

That insight may seem to suggest that the soul may finally just be (admiringly) with itself in the discovery of its Source vitalizing it. If that were so, how in that moment would it distinguish its own *esse* from that of the infinite *esse* which continually sustains it? However one answers these questions, the essential point here should not be lost: Interpretation guides and deploys the regard and interpretation integrates into the larger structures of meaning what is revealed in the looking (producing thereby information), but what reveals itself at the core of the seeing (the data) is the reality of a being in its raw presencing.

THE FINITUDE AND AMBIGUITY OF *SEIN*

Sein, then, is indeed elusive. It is impossible to com-prehend because it is no thing; it is, rather, the encompassing light within which all things are allowed

---

19. The Christian believes that the divine pedagogy has not been found wanting. It takes a form that is most concrete, enjoying historical continuity, and flesh and blood. But even when the transcendent God freely elects to involve himself with our affairs, and allows us to lay hands on his incarnated Son and put him to death, and when he allows the agents of his Church "to teach with authority," he is never captive of mankind. We may represent the Godhead suffering, but that is only insofar as he elects to enter our history. We cannot lay hands on the Source itself, and either tarnish or destroy it, and the glorified Son remains, so to speak, "His own man," and "the Spirit bloweth where it will." See the work of Balthasar mentioned above, all of which is devoted to this theme.

20. Balthasar, *Does Jesus Know Us? Do We Know Him?* trans. Graham Hunter (San Francisco: Ignatius Press, 1983), 73.

21. This distinction is superbly explored by Marion, *Dieu sans l'être*, chap. 1.

to stand, hence the Source of com-prehension itself. We are reminded of San Juan de la Cruz's search to empty out of the soul all the objects that catch the light and thus are illumined by it but then distract us from noticing the light itself, so that we must struggle to rid the soul of them if the pure light is to be allowed to flood the soul.

But, unlike San Juan's gift from God, the Light that is the interpretative time-space of a world is not formless. On the contrary, being epochal, *die Lichtung des Seins* is no light in general but always bears the stamp of its place and time within the unfolding *Seinsgeschichte*; it is always the bearer of considerable already having been, including the perennial structures given with human nature, reflected in the permanent *Ek-sistenzialien* that characterize all *Dasein*'s projection of world. Heidegger expresses it as "das Seiende im Ganzen und als Solches," the thing in general (characterizing the epoch) and as such.

Heidegger throughout his long search is not always clear about this, for later, desperate to get thinking to re-call *Sein*, he sometimes seems to want us to imagine a kind of contentless *Sein* as pure possibility of temporal meaning. In the present meditation, I want to stay closer to the Heidegger of *Being and Time*, as I distance myself from any temptation to *Seinsidealismus* there may be after the turn he takes following the early work; rather, I think of *Sein* as a kind of unfolding *(entwickelnd)* all-forming form of forms, symphonically in-forming the weave of concepts essential to the *Mitsein* projection of an epoch.

In a Heideggerian mode of thinking, it is difficult to keep clear as one moves back and forth between several notions of *Sein*. All the following are at work:

1. *Sein* as the light deployed in each act of interpretation;
2. the *Mitsein* of intersubjective cooperative deployment of interpretation (which requires, obviously, mediation and achieves social horizons of many little common worlds);
3. the epochal *Sein*, which is made possible by the accumulated results of personal and intersubjective acts of interpretation embedded in acculturated symbols, habits, and institutional arrangements, a vast mediation of the already-having-been forming to some degree all acts of interpretation insofar as they are epochally relevant;
4. *Sein* found in the posing of the question of the sense of it all *(die Seinsfrage)*; this raises the question of the all-englobing *Sein* of the entire *Seinsgeschichte*, the entire *Not-wendig* (necessary) unfolding of the becoming of *Sein*.

The first—the act of interpretation of the individual *Dasein*—is foundational to all the others.[22] But once *Dasein* has deployed his first act of interpretation, drawing on the already having been of his natural capacities, the *Sein* deployed through him is ever thereafter formed in part from the fruit of that past experience, offering, along with the presencing of the thing as other, an already

---

22. That entails, as well, the principle that the *esse* of a human being was condition for the possibility of the first and all subsequent acts of interpretation.

contentful, historically informed light, that of his own history and his own little world.

A good antidote to the temptation to mystify the concept of *Sein*, which is inherently mysterious enough, and a way of grasping better how *Sein* unfolds is to ask, as I did above, Where is *Sein*? I am quite aware that the question is guaranteed to turn Heidegger in his grave. But in my resolutely realistic refashioning of the notion of *Sein* for a pre- and post-Heideggerian metaphysics, we have seen that this question can be meaningfully asked and at least partially answered. Found first and foremost in the interpretative horizons *Dasein* deploys (in which deployment language plays a key role), *Sein* will always display some aspects of common humanity,[23] to be found then equally in the interpretative horizons deployed by the lawgiver Solon in sixth-century Hellas and those deployed by an IBM engineer—in other words, deployment of an epoch-transcending natural foundation.

But there is much going on in the contemporary horizons that would have been totally incomprehensible to an ancient Greek, and there is much about the Greek world that is for us now forgotten, never to be recuperated from reinterpretation of the fragmentary concrete spirit that is left to us by bits of texts and broken monuments formed in the spirit of that ancient Zeitgeist. It is not only because these carriers, these things of objective spirit, are so fragmentary; even with more recent epochs for which we possess massive documentation, there were dimensions of the epochal *Sein* transcending the common natural, and inadequately caught in the thingly carriers, the sense of which we shall never suspect.[24]

Commenting on what I have just written, K. L. Schmitz wrote: "The challenge facing metaphysics today is to introduce 'historicity,' not into 'Being as such,' which is an abstraction, nor into God, who has no history, but into the 'meaning of being as act,' as Joseph de Finance, S.J., and others (Lonergan?) have been trying to do."[25] I agree with the basic thrust of the remark, but with this caveat: natural things have their *esse*, which is that of this thing's own kind of being (its essence), but they have in themselves no historicity. Historicity applies only to human interpretation of them; there is historicity in each and every human knowing of them, but that historicity arises from human nature only, and consists in the known things' being included in a context and being illumined

---

23. Heidegger's exploration of the *Ek-sistenzialien* in *Sein und Zeit* as the ontological structure of *Dasein* is a superb beginning of the necessarily phenomenological recovery of these human dimensions.

24. Not every milieu produced a Marcel Proust to capture its *Sein* so evocatively. Not everything is caught in the language and other cultural objects. There are large questions of atmosphere that have to be lived to be known, matters of implicit tradition passed on by daily imitation which fade out, never to be reinvocable. With the help of what has been passed down remembered continuously in our traditions, and thanks to our common nature, we reenter the ancient epochal horizons as best we can. But it is never the same as having lived as Plato's student or as a direct disciple of the Buddha.

25. K. L. Schmitz, personal note to the author, February 1992.

by it, while the thus illumined things contribute to the further *bilden* of *Sein*. Only to that human nature is it given to be *ek-static*, to deploy energy formed by the peculiar spiritual human soul—psychic energy. I call it that to bring home that this kind of action is governed in part by laws other than those of physics. It is through deployment of psychic energy that *Dasein* reaches out to the other to embrace it in a cultural time-space. Natural history itself is a human construct, true to the extent that our interpretations of how this or that thing or species or the cosmos as a whole corresponds with the facts about the in-itself becoming of the things of nature.

The relation of *Sein* to psychic energy can thus be clarified. Psychic energy is deployed by a human soul, in virtue of the form of its *esse*. One central capability of that *esse* is to be able to open an *ek-static* field, allowing the knower to reach out and com-prehend the other, as it allows the other to presence and show a profile of its own essence actualized by its *esse*. We have seen in Part II that this projection of an informed future is a willful "standing in the presence of," which allows the other to in-form the knower. So this psychic energy is a reader, receiver, and processor of forms, as the new form is integrated into the already having been of the knower's previously acquired knowledge. But because every interpretative act, opening a new moment of futurity, hence a new present, involves the mysterious input of the new from beyond the store of possibilities brought by the knower, this deployment of psychic energy and reception of the gift *(Gunst)* of *Sein*[26] as new meaning are intimately linked. Deployment of psychic energy is a necessary but not sufficient condition for the possibility of *Sein* coming to be. It remains a mysterious, natural process, spiritual at the highest end of the created scale, in the sense explained in Chapter 7.

One especially impressive form of such deployment of psychic energy *ek-statically* to open the new is an act of imagining what has never been: the projection of an ideal. Even in the most prodigious flights of fancy, this is never a pure leap, but always to some extent a recombining of pieces drawn in the past from the real world. Nevertheless, the soul's ability to extend the already given sense of these parts in a new configuration of a thing or a state of affairs that has never existed and indeed may prove totally unrealizable is an astonishing reception of new *Sein*.

I emphasize that it is a reception, not a voluntary act. The thinker acts, working out of the concrete possibilities he has inherited in the nature that surrounds him, the nature that he is and the culture that has formed him, to prepare the place for the possible reception of the gift of creative intuition through meditation; but he experiences the coming of the vision, the leap of insight, as a surprise and as a gift received. He can never force it to come.

---

26. These mysterious gifts of the new range in scope from the individual's first insight into what many others have known, but which is new to him, to epoch-founding breakthroughs, like the great leap that occurred through Einstein into a new way of conceiving of the physical universe.

The distinction between unrealizable, perhaps even unhealthy fantasies, and ideals, perhaps worth working a lifetime to help realize, is a life-and-death matter. The first is a voluntaristic projection out of already possessed resources of what turns out to be a pseudo-future, because it never manages to achieve a healthy hold on cosmic time-space; it may persist for a while by inserting itself into reality violently, wreaking undue destruction.[27] The second, the reception of a new vision, is a gift. The test of the difference always lies in contact with the wider world, not just the realities of nature, but the culture lived in common, intersubjectively by the society. It is often necessary to challenge aspects of the *Bildung*,[28] because it is inadequate or counter to nature or to God's law, because too much collective fantasy has been mixed into it; or conditions may have changed, demanding an upgrading of the culture. Persons possessed of a genuine vision will meet resistance from the defenders of pseudo- or dead elements in the culture. They may themselves become the victims of violence. Christ told his disciples to expect persecution; tens of thousands were put to death, but the Christians themselves remained nonviolent. But the vision ended by transforming the Hellenic-Roman empire. Only when Christians adopted unhealthy worldly ideals from this success did they themselves become at times violent, in pursuit of a pseudo-future. Objectivity, as regards what can be learned from the givens in nature, and as regards the sociological facts, so one at least is aware what one is up against, and clarity about the grounds of the ideal vision one is working to achieve are essential. Pseudo-visions are characteristically accompanied by what Voegelin so well characterizes as "corrupt language."[29]

When within interpreted *Sein* one distinguishes in that which presences its in-itself reality, rooted in its *esse*, one then relates *Sein* and *esse* as follows: From within the historically transmitted possibilities of interpretation offered by *Sein*, a *Dasein* opens a time-space of interpretation enveloping a thing in a setting. But if his intention is to know it, and not simply fantasize in and about it—in such a way as welcomingly to receive its true presence in all that is other and permanent and wonderful about it, as it is in itself—the interpreter must

---

27. An ethical-ontological judgment, in which we see that the disorder outweighs whatever short-term gain of order may have been achieved. Hitler built Autobahns, gave the economy a lift, and made the trains run on time. But thirty-five million dead later, does anyone believe these gains were worth the destruction inflicted?

28. Eric Voegelin is justifiably critical of the use of *Bildung* to excuse the search for the truth of nature and "the opening to the divine." He rightly remarks that the great subjectivists, like Alexander von Humboldt in his gnostic dreams for education, can play with *Bildung* as they like. See "The German University and German Society," in *Published Essays 1966–1985*, ed. Ellis Sandoz, vol. 12 of *The Collected Works* (Baton Rouge: Louisiana State University Press, 1990), 26. *Bildung* is in the realm of the subjective, and to the extent that the subjective, the realm of meaning, turns in on itself instead of being devoted entirely to knowing what is and can and to be, it becomes "pneumopathological" (6).

29. See Voegelin's discussion of corrupt language, in "The German University and the Order of German Society: A Reconstruction of the Nazi Era," in *Published Essays 1966–1985*, 1–35.

be willing to accept that other. Since the *esse* of each thing is a particular act of existence of a given kind of thing, this willingness to receive must include a decision to search among one's concepts for the categories and distinctions necessary to hold the thing in mind correctly. One will have to search in the language, poetically extending it if necessary, for the means to express accurately what one has thus been allowed to see.[30] Knowing is a dialogical cooperation.

The *Sein* Idealists stress language and neglect objective spirit in cultural objects, as well as ignoring acculturation through the building of habits allowing institutional form. This obsession with language should not distract us from the contribution of these natural and objective-cultural and institutional dimensions to the ability to grasp form. The *Sein* of a world and the *Sein* of a *Dasein* interpreting a world illumine in a harmonizing way the relevant images, concepts, symbols, and culturally formed things and habits, and are in turn further incarnated in them, *Sein* itself receiving its in-formed character from them. The epochal *Sein* does not somehow float above the persons and things and relationships that make up the world, but escapes being mere fantasy only to the extent that it is a faithful illumination of them, as they really are in themselves. Hence the fundamental metaphysical importance of the presencing of every manner of real form.

■ ■ ■

The consistent weaves of attitude, images, concepts, words, and habits have overwhelming influence in our lives:[31] They establish family atmospheres, social class atmospheres, company cultures, religious milieus, political orientations—in brief, the matters that concern us the most. I keep reminding: These worlds all interpenetrate to some degree in the larger national and finally epochal *Sein*. They are passed on as traditions, mostly implicitly, and people in the respective milieus or worlds begin absorbing the commanding language by imitation, becoming gradually familiar with the culturally formed things and the dominant images and learning the roles expected of them. They are

---

30. My student, the late Mr. Edwin Alexander, wrote of his experience—a severe stroke that temporarily deprived him of speech. As the ambulance careened toward the hopital, Alexander thought, "Well, I cannot find any words, but my thoughts are clear—concepts and the words to express them are not the same." Later he showed me a letter from Professor D. Laplane, neurologist at the Salpêtrière in Paris, agreeing with him: "Concepts are much larger than are definitions of words because of the personal experience of each person. [This] very simple [observation] is an explosive one able to blast out all language philosophy stemming from Wittgenstein and the 'deconstructionism' of Derrida, because the first assumes that 'the limits of my language mean the limits of my word,' that is, there is no idea without language; and the second lays on the assumption that significant and signified are the two sides of the sign." Laplane to Alexander, April 22, 1992.

31. I am surprised that my friendly critic K. L. Schmitz does not see the need for a term to sum up this notion of a weave. Calling it *Sein* is convenient, and each such world, from my own personal one, through the little world of my sporting club or my family, to the great planetary-scale epochal world of high-tech culture, has *Sein*. The inconvenience in calling it "being" is that more is covered—*esse*, even (and especially) the infinite *esse*, which is something other than meaning and world.

illumined by *Sein* and *Sein* is illuminating the world through them, without their having perhaps any conscious awareness of *Sein* as such. To be sure, it is indeed—most unfortunately—forgotten.

The illumining time-space that makes possible a given milieu and the things and expressions of all kinds molded by it lies somehow back behind all these things and the language itself, which provides the peculiar light of that milieu. It is at this level Heidegger speaks of the "sendings" or "gifts" of Being (*Geschicke*, a word he links to *Schicksal*, destiny, because these fundamentally mold the historical epochs and the relations between them).

This *Sein* enjoys an essence (*Wesen*, not *essentia*): The atmosphere of IBM is elusive but consistent enough as a set of long-developing processes (one is tempted to say also definitive enough) to make it possible in almost every case to discern whether an event, a person, or a thing belongs. (One determines this by performing something like Husserl's imaginative exercise, "eidetic variation.") Enough intrusive, jarring facts can alter the sense, just as in an organism when enough invaders are accommodated and the immune system can handle them no longer, the organism's comportment alters visibly. It can first begin to act in a strange way, and if that goes far enough, the organism will even die. Dramatic events—such as Apple's marketing the microcomputer—can suddenly and radically alter the situation, forcing the giant organism to react with unaccustomed rapidity and vigor, thus rapidly changing its *Sein*, or see its relative position in the world of information processing diminish, dangerous where survival and market share are intimately linked.

Where the temptation to *Seinsmysticizmus* becomes almost irresistible is on the level of the largest world. The temptation has good grounds: There is much that goes on in the chemistry between attitudes, symbols, actions, and things embodying concrete spirit that is unperceived and unappreciated by us, but effective all the same. It can seem as though a Great Spirit—the Zeitgeist, or whatever—hovers over the whole affair.

Heideggerians fall easily prey to *Seinsmysticizmus* because children of a post-Kantian age, they neglect to recover the full charge of the objective ontic core (the *hyle*) in the *Seienden* incarnating *Sein*, and they overextend the sway of the epochal *Sein*—in this becoming unwitting children of the *Abendland* as well. They do not pay enough attention to the fact that in any epoch only certain societies, those most formed by the commanding traditions in their sphere, are fully under the sway of the epochal *Geschick*. The Occident[32] does not hold sway even now over all the planet. The Indians up the Rio Putumayo in Colombia, untouched by civilization, are deploying completely different horizons of interpretation, with only their basic humanity in common with the citizens of the high-tech Western world. Large parts of Africa and Asia similarly escape its sway.

This consideration does not reduce the legitimacy of the issue of the relative power of the globe-invading Occidental HTX, its destabilization of most other

---

32. "The evening land," as Heidegger, fond of the German word (*das Abendland*, land of the setting sun), puts it, relishing the note of decline as the West slides further into nihilism.

worlds, with all the problems this raises at the many hot points of encounter between civilizations. But it does remind us that the *Sein* of even this powerful globe-encircling set of traditions is neither the Holy Spirit nor the sole "ultimate dimension of being." Being, after all, includes both *esse* and *Sein* (including the different noncommunicating *Sein* of distinctive traditions) and a God who is never reducible to the interpretations that *Sein* illumines in every possible tradition.

WHY IS THINKING INTO THE ESSENCE OF THE HISTORY OF BEING VITAL?

The last remarks are in no way intended to diminish the importance of thinking back into the history of *Sein*, difficult as it may be. Indeed, it is most difficult to achieve the step back behind the history of our own epoch, in an effort to understand our situation in this large planet-spanning dimension. It cannot be accomplished, and the essence of the epoch thought, without some grasp of the history of *Sein*—that is, the antecedents of the present epoch, considered in terms of the all-englobing illumining and obscuring by the *Sein* of our Occidental tradition.[33] One must seek to see something of the ways in which the present epoch is different from the preceding ones in our civilization, and the ways in which it continues to draw from old roots, from the now past mother civilization. We can only comprehend the essence of the technological age by thus contrasting it with the essence of other ages and also following the threads of common tradition throughout the history of the West. Moreover, by comparing and contrasting these with the unfolding essences of other civilizations, we can begin to discern outlines of a common humanity, as well as what separates civilizations and cultures.[34]

In all this, the thinker will be learning about the ways of *Sein*, how it reveals and dissimulates itself, in the one tradition in which Being inspires the explicit thought of itself and also in those non-Occidental traditions within which *die Lichtung* is also necessarily an effective animator of the horizons of those worlds, even if *Sein* never becomes an explicit theme. That it has not revealed itself elsewhere as explicit thought of the highest and most general thing, or as the *analogia entis* (in Balthasar's sense of the term) in the metaphysical traditions, takes nothing away from the principle that every epoch in every tradition is formed by Being itself.[35]

Throughout the forty-five years of his career Heidegger experimented in inspired ways with the challenge of thinking *Sein*. In my judgment, the most

---

33. Is there one all-englobing *Sein* that somehow embraces the *Sein* of the many distinctive traditions? Given the commonality of human nature, *Sein* in the sense of common human horizons could embrace all the others. But a *Dasein* would have to have access to the *Sein* of every existing tradition, and that will never happen.

34. For an excellent recent example of such thinking, see Remi Brague, *Europe: La voie romaine* (Paris: Criterion, 1992).

35. I say traditions in the plural, because it may be possible to see in some Buddhist traditions something quite close to the Occident's metaphysical way of thinking being. I am not sure about this.

revealing moments in his long research came in two forms. First, Heidegger reflected on the art object, thus revealing the dialectic of *Seiendes* and *Sein* even better than in his description of instruments (*Zuhandensein*) in *Sein und Zeit*, with the contribution of the facticity of the *Seiendes* more clearly described than usual for a post-Kantian. Second, he would "dwell in the nearness of *Sein*" as it revealed itself in a given text, supremely, for instance, in certain poems by Hölderlin and a few fragments of Heraclitus, Kant's works, and fuller texts on Friedrich Nietzsche in the two volumes of essays devoted to that radical thinker.

I have suggested some of the lacunae in the Heideggerian thinking back into and back behind the history of being. It is useful to make them as explicit as possible, for they bring out deficiencies I hope in my own "thinking back" to strive to overcome. I shall mention five such areas here.

1. Instead of carefully following the full course through all the essential moments—events of crisis, bringing epochal change—of a consistent central tradition, he was only able to accord us glimpses of the overall structure, as in his outlines for a history of metaphysics. These offer some brilliant insights into the essence of certain epochs, though others are neglected, and glimpses of some moments of crisis, though he is silent about others. My proposed remedy: The community of thinkers must strive for critical appropriation of the essence of the entire tradition, of all the traditions central to our civilization, with due attention to institutions, events, and processes as well as symbol systems.[36] These appropriations become material for the more englobing, wisdom-achieving task of thinking the revelation-obscuring of *Sein* itself.

2. Apart from the superb pages of "The Essence of the Work of Art," he pays far too little attention to the details of the unfolding of being in symbol, other than language (for example, liturgy), and not enough to language as capturing knowledge of things. Nor does he attend sufficiently to institutional arrangements, and their interplay, emphasizing the ways these processes are guided and anchored by the things themselves, natural (*Vorhandensein*) and cultural (*Zuhandensein*). The brilliant insights of *Sein und Zeit* might have led one to expect more on this. Institution and world and regional process, as well as event, not just as the *Ereignis* of *Sein*, but as factual, determining historical happening, are three elements of the world situation Heidegger underplayed, although he talked a great deal about the essence of the present epoch. He was so eager to fix that essence, he neglected to study what is happening precisely to analyze it into the various essential processes and institutions and traditions and their intricate interweaving; his treatment of all this was summary and largely negative.

3. This has led to temptations to that *Seinsmysticizmus* I have been troubled by, which reach their climax in the late essay "Time and Being," where the mysterious unfolding of *Sein* takes on a life of its own, too removed from the

---

36. See *T&A*, pt. II in its entirety and pp. 205–11, on a method of appropriating.

things and the people (and divine initiatives in history) through which and in which *Sein* alone can incarnate itself by taking up existence as *esse*. This temptation is not unrelated to the fourth lacuna, in many ways the gravest.

4. Heidegger was unwilling to examine the development of the symbols and institutions of the central tradition of the post-Roman Occident, at least until modern times, the Catholic tradition. For years I have pondered this gaping emptiness at the heart of Heidegger's thought, and I can offer only one unsatisfying explanation: a personal crisis feeding this unwillingness to face the issues raised by what he dismissed from "the thought of Being" as *Glaubenssachen* (matters of faith).[37] *Sein* shines as much through matters of faith as upon the rocks of nature. The entire history of the Occident is unintelligible without the thought of being as "onto-theo-logical," in Heidegger's somewhat disparaging terms, giving the impression that *ho theos* can only be thought, as he calls it, "metaphysically" as "the highest and most general thing." (I trust that our short foray into the sanctuary of Carmelite mystical experience, and the caveat above that the great thinkers of the Occident refused to think God as a thing, even as *das Seiendste des Seienden*, has insulated us from this mistake.)

5. Heidegger does not appear to have been very impressed by the accomplishments of science and technology. His endeavor to capture the essence of the epoch in a single symbol, the *Gestell* (framework, invoking the peculiar manipulative-calculative form of contemporary organization), is audacious and not without truth, but reductionistic in its ambition. A much more appreciative and carefully receptive building-up of a knowledge of how the world system operates and how the new symbols signify and the new institutions are in fact managed, leads[38] to a necessarily much more elaborate set of symbols as minimal evocation of the epoch's HTX *Wesen*.[39]

In undertaking to appropriate the Catholic tradition, I have sought to counteract the effects of the first four of these limitations. In a projected work, Stewart and I are working on the fifth. Throughout, the effort is to recuperate all the essential sense embedded in the symbols and institutions and to understand the weave of processes unfolding over the millennia. The *Sein* of the Catholic tradition manifests, of course, an epochal character (not the same before and after the Council of Trent), but the tradition also manifests an essence *(Wesen)*,

---

37. For the relevant texts, see Jean-Luc Marion, *Dieu sans l'être*, 91–109; *God Without Being*, trans. T. A. Carlson (Chicago: University of Chicago Press, 1991), 61–72. Marion points out the confusion that emerges from these texts.

38. Such has been my experience working on this with my students.

39. In my Philosophy of History seminar, after elaborating a very long list of relevant factors operating in the HTX (the high-tech *Sein*-planetary phenomenon), we eventually reduced it to the following essential ingredients and considerations: ideas (product, plan, what do you want to do and control?); thought of the whole, temporally (eschatological, progress) and spatially (global, gigantic); centralization-decentralization (in bureaucracy); management, manufacturing, and marketing techniques; creativity vs. imitation; investment capital; personnel (staff, workers, customers, citizens); mobility (interethnic); education vs. manipulating public opinion; population explosion; family and personal breakdown; social welfare net; materials and energy; and information (needed about all of the above).

such that the Church is also the same, faithful to the founding vision throughout, because of its ability to adapt to the changing demands of the epochs through which it passes, without losing the essential truth that it was founded by Christ to hand down and to live out. In no other way can the full charge of givenness, of objectivity, and the sense of the tensions between interpretations and what is interpreted be adequately explored.

But that achieves at best the beginning of an appropriation of only one tradition. It has to be integrated in a balanced way with all the others, including those whose institutions drive the workaday technological world, a vast, communal undertaking. In the next chapter I shall reflect on the various dimensions of being we have discovered in terms of a strategy for the pursuit of an ecumenic wisdom, seeking to illumine one last time the sense of that daunting symbol, "being," as it is meant in the title of this book.

CODA

This chapter and, indeed, this book leave the perplexing sense of *Sein* and its relation to what I am calling *esse* insufficiently explored. Because we are here confronted by mystery, this is not surprising. But we need to understand better what is at stake in the *Sein-esse* distinction. We can use the example of the Christ event to attempt one more step of clarification.

Jesus Christ, who as a human being enjoyed *esse*, with all that that implies of a stake in cosmic, historic time-space—being acted on and acting upon other persons and things—is not, as *esse*, the product of *Sein*, although what he said and did in his mighty works took place within a *Sein* epoch, and we, when we interpret the reports of what he said and did, are illumined by *Sein*. That is one sense of Jesus' repeatedly underscoring the need to wait for the "fullness of time": The long dialectic of God interacting with his chosen people through his prophets and his own theophanies to individuals in history, prepares a history into which, "in the fullness of time," the Son is sent, when the illumination of *Sein* will allow some understanding of the discourse and works of Jesus. And that Son, once conceived and born into a family, a people, a historic situation, must live out in time, through a series of progressive steps, his own human development, and the steps of the redemption.[40] Nor is the Church first and foremost a concept or an abstraction, it is a concrete institution, a people of God, an intersubjective time-space reality, which incarnates itself through the cooperative acts of many persons, praying together and working together, responding to promptings of the Holy Spirit to forge symbols and inculturated habits adequate to the task of passing on the truth God has revealed in Jesus Christ. Again, "in the fullness of time," at a moment "known only to the Father," the destiny of this people, with all mankind gathered into it, will be fulfilled, the glorified Christ will return and make "a perfect offering" to the Father.

---

40. Balthasar insists on this temporality of the redemption. This is a central theme of *Die Wahrheit ist Symphonisch* (Einsiedeln: Johannes Verlag, 1972).

But acknowledging that the sense of those symbols and of those evolving intersubjective structures is illumined by *Sein* through every Christian *Dasein*'s interpretation of them and through the collective *Mitsein* interpretation of the Church is not tantamount to suggesting that the Holy Spirit is *Sein*. Rather, he is believed to be one of the three divine (and hence in a preeminent sense real) persons in God, a manifestation therefore of the infinite divine *esse*, effective in history when he intervenes to inspire the prophets, Jesus, and the members of his Church to do (action-*esse*) the will of God (which has to be correctly interpreted, for *Sein* and *esse* to meet). The fruits of the Holy Spirit are felt in cosmic time and space through the work of the human beings he inspires. However, what we know of the Holy Spirit, and of God the Father, and of the divine Logos is itself illumined by *Sein*. When a Saint John the Evangelist interprets these realities for us in the text of his Gospel or the Book of Revelation, what is going on deep within his soul—the Holy Spirit inspired deployments of formed psychic energy that is his writing down the Gospel—is illumined by *Sein* as he draws on all the genius of the Greek language and all his experience of the Hellenistic Hebrew milieu in which he grew up. He combines it with what the Holy Spirit did in John's encounters with Jesus and by his working now in the mysterious depths of his soul, as he interprets what he has experienced, in daily commerce with Jesus and in prayer, and in the supernatural visions given to him of the mysterious things of which he tells us.

All this forms, at any one time, in any epoch, a world, and a history of a world, a *Seinsgeschichte*, that is, the sense of the unfolding treasure of meanings in the symbols, in the institutional arrangements, in the inculturated habits, in the interpretations of those symbols that keep re-forming their sense, interpretations illumined by all that is going on in each epoch beyond the inner confines of the Church itself. The immense dynamic of this interpretative ek-sistential interweaving of meaning factors of all kinds is here symbolized as *Sein*, and from this dynamic we can spring to think back behind, but it always partially eludes us, especially as this very thinking of Being is illumined by Being and changes it.

Why, then, as I struggled to appropriate critically this tradition was my attention on the key persons, the events, the institutional structures, and the actual meanings rather than on the illumining of *Sein*? What has been lost in my appropriation as a result of such a *Seinsvergessenheit*—a forgetting of Being?

I have indeed been guilty of a normal *Seinsvergessenheit*, for the usual, basic reason: One's interest is always directed toward the things illumined and away from the illumining. What has been lost as a result is the fruit of a deeper thinking into the gift of Being, which makes possible the very thought of Jesus Christ and his Church, the history of the gifts of breakthroughs in ways of seeing the world, without which the interpreting of Christianity as I have done it would be impossible.

In the effort to think Christianity, then, more in terms of what must be presupposed if it is to be thought—the whole language-culture-history complex in which it occurs—one must beware, on the other hand, and as I have cautioned in this chapter, not to forget the full charge of the ontic reality that has been illumined, the facts and permanences about the Hebrews and their prophets, the facts about Jesus, his preaching and his works, especially the incomparable, incomprehensible mystery of his eucharistic gift of himself—the *don* that is the ultimate *donnée* of this tradition, as Marion so well explains in *Dieu sans l'être*—the facts about the apostles, and their development of the Church. An *Essevergessenheit* is just as disastrous as a *Seinsvergessenheit*.

PART IV.

BEING AND TRUTH

10.

THE ULTIMATE STRUCTURES AND THE OVERCOMING OF IDEOLOGY

Tradition and Authenticity issued a call to arms: Come to grips with the emerging world system. The Faustian element in Western man has produced the high-technology concentration of power, centered in an emerging world-scale system of intertwining institutions. As a consequence, the great traditions have come into a new intimacy of contact, one that sees the HTX penetrating many cultures from within, working out from a series of urban nodes, transforming them. This is leading to resistance on the part of many peoples and generating resentment against the West. All the while the local cultures and the civilizations behind them are changing, setting up a multitude of conflicts, the more dangerous because of the concentrations of power.

At the same time, the worldwide scope of the phenomenon is raising hopes for a New Age, and not just a New World Order, a humanistic universalism, borne by HTX, though many are repulsed by the environmental damage the HTX is wreaking. This mishmash catholicism is based in syncretic elements of very old paganisms, forging a new, man-centered religion, marketed with all the manipulative skills of the HTX. (The HTX's more creative will-to-power people know how to manipulate New Age symbols to their benefit as adroitly as Protestants believe the priests did those of Roman Catholicism.) The New Age is in tense relation to the new canons of scientific truth (HTX movers and shakers care as little about scientific truth as they do genuine revelation) and mortally opposes the Christocentric Catholicism out of which the West has grown. It collides head on with a third catholicism,[1] Muslim universalism, itself provoked by the HTX peril to take refuge in hardening antimodern positions, of which fundamentalism—a marriage of religious and political fanaticism, terrifying to my intellectual Muslim friends—is the most dangerous form.[2]

---

1. Marxist ideology constituted a fourth catholicism, but although Marxist anthropology has seeped into much of the Western world, as a coherent ideology incarnated in strong institutions—the Soviet and the Chinese states, prime among them—it is so on the wane, I expect that most of its initial attractions have been successfully absorbed into looser New Age recipes. The present HTX transformation of Russia and China is fascinating to watch.

2. Fundamentalism exists among Christians, too, but the Catholic Church knowledgefully rejects it (but no more casts into outer darkness pathological fundamentalists among its billion members than it does progressive liberation theologians. The Church understands as its God-given mission, not the rejection of sinners, but their conversion. Except for Jesus and Mary, there is no one in the Church except sinners).

Because the Church both helped spawn and continues to hold a dialogue with the modern world—and has every intention of leading the world toward what it believes to be the path of its salvation—it does not simply reject the HTX revolution, the way the more neo-hippie among New Age people reject it. Rather, the Church seeks, as it has since first confronting the great Roman civilization of the first century, through what it today calls "the new Evangelization," to espouse what is good in these new developments and to transform HTX society by enhancing those and working against the bad aspects, rooting it in the perennial tradition. The Church believes that Christianity—the longest continual tradition—can provide criteria for a critique of the widest swings of new epochal Being, and accommodate the good in what has been discovered. Whereas New Agers lacking perspective on the HTX adopt and reject elements of it with insufficient critical distance, the Church is developing a methodic critique of contemporary social phenomena based in well-thought-out principles of being that permit some sort of step back behind the epochal *Sein*. (It is a great pity that most outside the Church do not suspect what a vast and rich dialogue with modernity this has become in the form of the social teaching of the Church.)

Once one becomes aware that our time is one of titanic clash of these catholicities, he has just two choices regarding the ultimate planetary context: ignore it as too vast and too rapidly evolving, or, working with others, struggle to come to grips with it as best he can.

Ignoring the planetary context means, in world affairs, the kind of *Seinsvergessenheit* that would have us pragmatically limit our efforts (personal and social) to an ad hoc region-by-region response, issue by issue, run to put out fires, the mode of the pluralistic democracies. (The General Agreement on Tariffs and Trade, signed by one hundred seventeen trading nations, admirable as it is as an HTX structure, cannot respond to the questions raised by the clash of catholicities.) A believer in providence might say, in all humility: "It is beyond our capacities, it is in the hands of God"—far from an irrational reaction. A world system with five and a half billion cells, each with a unique perspective on the world, all capable of some creative innovation, presents one with an object of knowledge of incomprehensible complexity, boundless dynamism, and endless surprise. But we are obliged to try to manage the world system the best we can. So before throwing our theoretical hands in the air, consider the other possibility.

We can set about to learn how to study the planetary situation of mankind, step by step, methodically, following a way developed as a function of "a strategy for the pursuit of truth,"[3] within a multidimensional ultimate context, kept open by remembering-thinking of the *Seinsgeschichte*. This choice equally requires humility: Acknowledged is the inadequacy of our conceptual tools

---

3. The title of my 1975 Presidential Address to the Metaphysical Society of America: "A Strategy for the Pursuit of Truth," published under the title "Searching in History for the Sense of It All," *Review of Metaphysics* 32:1 (September 1978), 37–52.

for grasping the dynamic essences of the vast systems and processes[4]—the great traditions, their interaction with the planetary-scale institutions, forming distinct cultures and entire long-lasting civilizations that produce rich symbol systems. Foremost remains the challenge of how the separate wisdoms of the different great traditions are to be integrated into an ecumenic understanding of being.

The second option can be defended by the religious man as well as the secularist, if he has thought through a theology in which "fides quaerens intellectum" and the "intellectus fidem quaerens" is understood rather like this: Providence has endowed us with broad information-gathering faculties that enable us, given the light of revelation—a vital source not just of hope but of information[5]—to know the meaning of life as the author of nature intends it, and to think through strategies for the pursuit of truth and the direction of worldly systems of power, in keeping with what God has manifested of his will, indispensable both for a decent daily life and the fullest development of human potential. The *essential center* of our meditating[6] on the *Sein* of the present planetary epoch has to be what God reveals of his intentions for mankind.

That is a hopeful faith, a con-fidence that it makes sense to search because there is sense, that its Source wills that we should discover, and that, because at its core it is for our good, we in managing the world's affairs should cooperate with His founding and guiding intentions. As Balthasar explains, the claim that the present opens "vertically" to the eternal, so that the fullness of time is opened to us, not in an ever-elusive future, but from an everlasting present now, creates a special understanding of time. The quest for a future perfect time on earth is rejected, but we are set on a *missio* toward a genuine, hopeful future, fulfilled eschatologically by God alone, already redeemed but only at the end to find its full sense.

> Faith alone contains a fulfilling hope—and no empty clinging to some future thing—because, beyond all intermediate stages in time, faith grasps the Fulfilling itself,

---

4. Consider, too, the obstacle formed by the unevenness of our information, which, though massive, is also spotty and often unclear.

5. Does one not have to believe to access it? I have shown that this is true of every source of information. Look how many people either ignore altogether science or choose not to take it seriously. What in each case is embedded in the individual's natural faith motivating either indifference or, worse, hostility to sources of challenge is a matter for spiritual direction.

6. There are important differences separating the Heideggerian *Denken des Seins*, the Voegelinian "reflective meditation in the *metaxy* in response to the invitation of the divine," and the Balthasarian "theologizing in response to the Word fully revealed in Jesus Christ." Each is centered differently, because grounded in a somewhat different faith. My own way of theoretical inquiry has been influenced by all three, but I am not as yet prepared to thematize my own synthesized way sufficiently to clarify the exact impact of those influences on me, or to assure that they even meet as harmoniously as I hope in the work of writing *T&A*, the present volume, and projected books. I follow Voegelin in believing that method is worked out as one proceeds, in intimate contact with the object of meditation. As I proceed from *T&A*, the center of the meditation shifts somewhat, from the question of bringing the several traditions into dialogue to the *Sein-esse* tension in doing so.

nay, *is grasped by it*. Faith reaches for the goal that has already reached it. (Paul, Philippians 3, 12–13.) Faith grasps the whole unconditionally *(unbedingt)* in every fragment because it is already grasped by the incarnate whole [Christ] and articulated into its body. Faith, therefore, has no occasion, like all the idealisms, to fly from time into an "eternal moment," for it is in time itself that it holds the whole, as the whole holds it in time. But faith has just as little cause to fly from an unfulfilled present to a more fulfilled future, for it would lose with the present, which it had let go as of little value, the eternity dwelling within it. Faith fills itself with this eternity only by fulfilling eternity's mission in present time: only in the today do time and eternity fall together. But mission unfolds with happening *(sich ereignenden)* time.[7] Mission means and requires future. Self-fulfilling mission is one with the prayer "Thy kingdom come, thy will be done *(ereigne sich)* on earth as it is in heaven." With the self-fulfilling mission comes on the way to the future the Eternal into time and, therefore, time strides toward a rendezvous with eternity, in which the fulfilled time is *already waiting as resurrected*. Praying, obeying we hasten the arrival of Christ.[8] "For salvation is nearer to us now than when we first believed; the night is far gone, the day is at hand" (Rom. 13:11–12).[9]

Man has been endowed by his creator with freedom, and he has been fully instructed by him as to the ends toward which that freedom is to be exercised. But man's revolt against God's will is a basic ruinous aspect of the reality in the midst of which those ends are to be pursued.[10] Hence the pressing need for a critique of actual society, always (including the Church, *semper reformanda*). For my part, I abhor the form of latter-day gnosticism, contrary to God's intentions, suggesting that we take refuge in an imagined purity: Because worldly power is always sinful power, the Pure throw up their hands and either abstain from exercising any responsibility or organize peace rallies to condemn every use of coercion or armed force, however vital to maintaining in the midst of sin and pathology a minimum of order and to protecting vital interests.[11] It is easier to

---

7. As Balthasar knew Heideggerian thinking well, and so I suggest that the full force of the Heideggerian sense of *Er-eignis*, as both the surprising e-vent of *Sein* and of its ap-propriating the *Seienden* to itself, is here appropriately re-called.

8. Christ *kunftet sich* (announces himself) from the *Zukunft* (future). Recall Heidegger, "The past announces itself out of the future." I do not remember the origin of this text, perhaps *Das Wesen des Grundes*. In the case of Christ, that future fulfillment is assured by the eschatological founding event, the resurrection, the conquest of death as ultimate future limit.

9. Balthasar, *Man in History*, trans. William Glen-Doepel (London, Sheed and Ward, 1968), 334. This translation is unfortunately poor, so I have corrected it. Emphasis is added.

10. Two biblical texts—both quoting Jesus himself, and both from Matthew's Gospel—stand in dialectical tension: "Be wise as serpents" (Matt. 10:16) and "See the lilies of the fields, they neither spin nor weave, yet Solomon in all his glory was not arrayed as one of these" (Matt. 6:28). God gave us our intelligences and our hands to use, and he made us masters of the earth. But we must remain realistic about the narrowness of our horizons and our need to respect the fragile structures of the world; whatever our contribution, God's guiding hand is most important, the fullness of truth is to be sought in his Word, and he has the final say always.

11. Dreamers are suspicious of all interests, and not unjustifiably. But they fail to see that masses of people, societies, nations, and economic systems inevitably have vital interests, never Simon Pure in nature, that they will in any event—and indeed, within limits of justice, should—defend. The Church in its social justice teachings acknowledges this. See

roll one's eyes in pain whenever interests have to be defended than to engage in the analysis and discussion needed to discern what in a concrete situation is right, or at least less wrong.

Against the background of that hopeful and critical natural faith, rooted in a central supernatural faith—my confidence in the revelation of that fullness of reality, of which Balthasar speaks[12]—I propose to conclude by pulling together what I see to be the fundamental dimensions of the present intellectual and existential context of mankind. This constitutes my final effort here to clarify the relations between what we have seen emerge as the ultimate structures of being.[13]

If any one of these dimensions is ignored, mankind's efforts to find the way forward will work only from a disastrous conflict of ideologies, rather than within the full sphere of Being's illumination. Ideology is yet another form, different from that of the Pure, of gnostic response to the challenge of the planetary situation. Instead of fleeing into a never-never world of irresponsible purity, the ideologue tries to obtain security through a closed system of thought, which has to be neat to attain its goal, control. On the grounds of a pretended grasp of the sense of the whole planetary structure of Being and, as Voegelin says, "the end of history," the ideologue sets down an unambiguous course of action for producing the perfect society, "the gnostic dream."[14] In its name, the gnostic superman activist, whether Communist, National Socialist, Arab nationalist, Muslim fanatic, or whatever, considers himself justified in perpetrating the worst atrocities, which always have as their real goal the bolstering of his power position. This includes every form of Christian ideologue who deforms the divine promise, sealed in the Resurrection, into some idol of possession by us of "the end of history," a step all too easily taken if mystery is forgotten, which it always is when faith is weak.

---

the encyclical of Pope John Paul II, *Centesimus Annus* (1993), on the world economic situation and the way forward.

12. From this perspective within the oldest and, I believe, richest (I also believe truest) tradition of mankind, it is for me an immense sorrow to observe in many of my intelligent students the ideational and experiential poverty that results from their having no profound life in a community committed to exploring and passing on truth. Even many of the science students seem to have little sense of belonging to a serious scientific community. Many ideological Catholics do not reflect richly or deeply on what has been handed down to them. And many students stand in no explicit traditions at all, but just move with the crowd.

13. In my study of the HTX, now reaching completion, these ultimate structures are explored in the concrete reality of the present planetary epoch, and the complex realities of the HTX are shown in their roots and in the challenges with which they confront us in our daily lives.

14. What an irony that Heidegger, dreaming in 1933 of getting the German nation to move forward by a radical thinking back behind the history of *Sein*, was tempted for a while to link up with the craziest ideologues, the Nazis, believing that he could transform their revolution in the direction of his *Denken*. My hypothesis is that such a blindness to reality was fed by *Essevergessenheit* on his part, a temptation endemic to a thinking that is pulled toward *Seinsmystizsmus* and that turns away from any question of what might be the revelation of God's will.

The question here, then, is this: What is the appropriate attitude (*Verhalten*—a way of holding oneself [comportment] in engaging the world) to adopt in order *to think the large structures we cannot adequately comprehend*, and how do we relate ourselves—the whole person—toward them? What would constitute the essence of a wise, humble, realistic, prudent, resolutely nonideological comportment toward the world?

THE ULTIMATE STRUCTURES

The two distinctive foci operative in our experience are the existential and the scientific. The results of their having been deployed interpenetrate, of course, because consciousness is one: the fruits of both are in the "great halls of memory" somewhere and intermingled. Despite the englobing illumination of epochal *Sein*, we seem able to compartmentalize our mind frighteningly, not just separating theoretical and practical, but within each sphere forgetting what may lie in another compartment as we concentrate on one challenge at a time. But even as we willfully, perhaps pathologically, shut out one set of considerations or another, they still subtly, involuntarily contaminate one another, so the compartmentalization has an element of living a lie. (The most successful hypocrite probably knows on some level that he is living a lie—the still, small voice of conscience is hard to root out altogether.)

The existential focus is that of the primarily concrete approach one takes in everyday life. It is dominated by a narrow time-space scaled to the demands of everyday human affairs, and so tends to be too dominated (but not exclusively) by the practical. It is more about doing than being—"running life's errands."

The scientific focus underlies the work of theory (*theorein*, to see), which is rooted in the project of wanting to see. Theorizing began methodically only a few thousand years ago, with the gift of the opening in which the question of Being is first posed as such. It is evident in some early Egyptian texts, erupts into historical awareness at Sinai,[15] and achieves a self-conscious earnestness with the birth of philosophy, this last only twenty-six hundred years ago,[16] although less thematized theoretical meditation emerged much earlier.

---

15. I here assume that the Exodus text, with its dis-covery of human existence as directed to a fulfilling end, opens history, not just as a practical "follow me," but with evidence of a reflective sense that YHWH is Source of Truth. This assumption requires more analysis of the text. Voegelin, in *Israel and Revelation* (vol. 2 of *Order and History* [Baton Rouge: Louisiana State University Press, 1987]), sees Sinai as an amazing breakthrough in consciousness, resulting in a new sense of political order, implying, I believe, a new sense of truth.

16. This tells us something important: for the first half million to a million years of his existence (we are no surer than that!), man has been driven by the existential demands of everyday life. With the spread of theory in the last few thousand years, and the growing proof of its potential existential power, only this has changed: A few men have grown wise in the recognition of the need for the good exploitation of this power. More have exploited it in lesser ways. The masses have remained largely untheoretical. The brevity of the theoretical epoch confronts the researcher with a problem: Recorded human self-consciousness reaches back perhaps only six thousand years, and historical consciousness only thirty-five hundred years since the Sinai experience, and scientific study of history, as a large-scale enterprise (anticipated by the occasional genius—a Herodotus, Livy, Augustine, Otto von Freising,

In deploying the theoretical focus of attention, one seeks knowledge of things for their own intrinsic interest. It is rooted in a love for the thing in its otherness. Because inviting attention to real contexts as they suggest themselves, rather than contexts set by narrow practical projects of the moment, the genuine theoretical quest, inevitably, by virtue of being itself, tends toward the ultimate dimensions of reality. *Seinsvergessenheit* should not itself be forgotten here, however—a forgetting that operates at all scales of *Sein*, from the personal to the *Seinsgeschichtlich:* The intricacy and depths of the things studied pull attention into them, distracting us from their fuller meaning and their larger contexts, their wider involvements, and from the mystery of the light of enveloping meaning. But if the researcher's opening onto the objects is rooted in love (contrast with research driven by desire for prestige), this *ravissement* should interest him in the thing's or person's receiving and giving, and hence lead him to grander horizons, first to the immediate context that proposes itself, then to the context of that context, and thus onward and outward. We are stopped only by fatigue and (more sinisterly) by our (often hidden) decisions not to see—there is much we have mortgaged through self-centered decisions and thus there are things we do not want to hear about. The commitment of true love should provide the antidote to the closure to which *Seinsvergessenheit* at all its levels tempts one. But even openness to ultimate context will not lead automatically to the repeated taking of the step back behind the whole history of *Sein*. How to renew this *Sein*-consciousness at the heart of our *Verhalten*?

Theoretical discoveries about ultimate structures have important longer-range practical implications and so, paradoxically, turn out to be more powerful than many a practical pursuit. But that is not the theoretical goal. On the other hand, the fact of our searching and how we search are existential, carried out only by particular situated individuals and groups, whose motives are rarely pure (they have, for example, career goals). As we acknowledged, because the human agent is one, the existential and the theoretical intricately intertwine. Nothing in either assures thinking of *Sein*.

The essential time-space of the theoretical as such is not that of everyday human affairs but ultimately of the universe itself. And because the cosmos includes evidence suggesting a time-space-transcending Source, and human history evidence of revelation, theory seeks to reach beyond the cosmos to its origin out of time (as Greek philosophy did), and to remain receptive to hearing what that Source, in reaching down to us, has to reveal through its incursions into history (four thousand years of Judaism and Christianity and fourteen hundred years of Islam attest to such willing listening). For this reason, *Sein*, when interpretation is not distorted by a gnostic lie, arbitrarily "closing the apophantic field," does indeed have a center (I am thinking of Derrida's concern here, when he rejects the notion there is any center of meaning. Here is

---

or Vico) not more than two hundred fifty years. So we have neither accumulated much experience with the large-scale realities—cultures, civilizations, traditions—nor have we had long to learn how to study them.

a reply neither he nor Heidegger would like): *The center of attention, the base of theoretical motivation, should be to let the totality of* esse *appear.* The *Seinslassenheit* (*lassen*, to let be) is letting all *esse* and every kind of *esse*, every thing and every genuine manifestation of God, presence. Totality of *esse* is intended to invoke not a *Totalitätsbegriff* but openness to every sort of evidence of every sort of real being (including the significant differences in each free person), and a patient search for the order revealed by real relations, avoiding deductions from pseudo-concepts of the Ground. Because *Sein*-illumined consciousness opens onto the real cosmos, and because *Sein* only comes to be through and is conditioned by the given human form of man, *Dasein*, authentic *Dasein* seeks the transcending Source of its own *esse* in all its relations (including every form of causality) to all other *esse*, and, to the extent that the lines of relationship lead to it, the infinite *esse*. The centering of that interpretation that is the quest of theory, the center of *Sein*, is then on the evidence of the ultimate source of all order, following whatever may be found "of His handiwork" and "every word that comes forth from the mouth of God," if the genuineness of a revelation can be satisfactorily established.

With the center secured, we consider the ultimate structures themselves. I start with the existential. *Synchronically*, the ultimate structure to be found in existential Occidental experience in every epoch has been until recent centuries a world that stretched barely beyond Europe, North Africa, and the Middle East. But (starting in the sixteenth century) it has become the planetary situation, dominated since the late nineteenth by the emerging world system. Today science (theory), through the space program, is opening our existential system out practically toward the larger cosmos, and we realize certain practical results from probing deeper, wider, and farther back into cosmic time-space. The field of practical, even everyday experience is enlarged and deepened, becoming cosmic (raising dilemmas of general relativity).

Diachronically, a similar expansion is happening. We are normally inhibited existentially from thinking about the truly relevant ultimate frame because of our undue absorption into the demands of the immediate practical setting. Both this volume and *Tradition and Authenticity* have warned about how dangerous this pragmatic foreshortening is. Heidegger showed how difficult it is to raise our sights. He explored in a rare thinking back beyond these practical settings to the ultimate diachronic context, with its hidden but real influence (*Gewensein*) forming aspects of the present situation out of the ancient past.

In the present epoch, Being's illumination that makes science possible is driving reflection back behind the beginning of the Occidental tradition of thinking itself,[17] back behind the very history of the thought of what Heidegger

---

17. I agree with Heidegger that an overarching tradition of *abendländisches Denken* stretches from the birth of philosophy to the present epoch of "the end of metaphysics," although I would not reduce the contribution of the tradition of Jewish and Christian revelation only to what is combined in a metaphysicizing theology. Nor would I agree that this *Denken* is so of a piece that it forms as neat an essence as he describes; a neatness he achieves by

means by *Sein*.[18] The way *Sein* has unfolded has brought to birth science, which penetrates back behind the time when Being itself was first explicitly thought. So now the thought of human prehistory and the natural history of the cosmos itself gets latterly enfolded within the light of the history of Being.

At the same time, the intimacy between cultures brought on by technology, fruit of the illumining of *Sein*, is inviting thought to enfold the once distinctive time-spaces of the other great traditions into a single planet-wide scheme of critical appreciation. But with what center—that is, on the basis of which tradition's sense of time? Having answered the question, Where is theoretical inquiry centered—on *esse*—we now ask, where is *Sein* itself centered?

Granted all that has happened—discovery of the cosmic dimensions in science, development of the HTX, the spread of its mind-sets and characteristic organization through Europe and North America, and its penetration from many nodes within other civilizations—has indeed come out of the Occidental tradition that has both thought and forgotten Being as the mysterious opening of an illuminating time-space in which the suite of characteristic epochs could happen. Out of this *Seinsvergessenheit* (Occidental "metaphysical") has come paradoxically the present possibility of thinking the prehistoric, the transtraditional (including the possibility of placing the limits of the tradition itself in question while thinking back into all the world's traditions), and ultimately the cosmic ontogenesis. This growth in perspective is a great positive achievement, a "Gunst des Seins," a kind of gracious outpouring of light, but given the finitude of *Dasein*, it also distracts and obscures. How do we center our *Denken*?

Heidegger has been, on balance, too negative toward the present scientific-technological epoch to appreciate fully its accomplishments, not in spectacular practical results alone, which he acknowledges, but in thought. His effort to think the essential characteristic of the epoch as what he calls the *Gestell* is, I have suggested, problematic.[19] This notion of a narrowly organizing efficiency, while pertinent, does not do justice to the immense opening of horizons, in time and space, macro and micro, that science has achieved.

To sum up, we need to understand better how our cognitive approaches succeed in relating ultimately in a single wisdom the following ultimate structures (centered how and where, I have begun to suggest):

---

arbitrarily discerning a main line stretching in modern times from Descartes through Kant and Hegel to Nietzsche, thereby marginalizing Pascal, Vico, Newman, and everything that was being learned by living the life of the Church, the invention of industrialization, and the construction of liberal society.

18. Which thought of *Sein* as such only began with the philosophers' posing "the question of the Sense of Being" (die Frage nach dem Sinn des Seins). *Sein und Zeit*, 8th ed. (Tübingen: Neomarius Verlag, 1957), 1; *Being and Time*, trans. J. Macquarrie and E. Robinson (New York: Harper and Row, 1962), 19.

19. A *Gestell* is a framework. In this symbol, recall, Heidegger seeks to express the essence of the epoch as characterized by the technological mentality, the ordering of society and objective spirit through calculative efficient will-to-power. *The Question Concerning Technology and Other Essays* (New York: Harper and Row, 1977).

the history of Being (*Seinsgeschichte*) (the center lies in Occidental thinking, where first and, to date, still, only the *Seinsfrage* has been posed, methods of thinking Being developed, and criteria for judging all truth proposed);

the HTX, driven by the pragmatic world system with its various traditions, whose institutions' molding of masses of human lives constitutes a fact of life (this system, too, finds its genetic and still its present institutional center in the Occident, although the enthusiastic embrace by Japan and the Asian Tigers is forcing the first serious challenge by a non-Occidental version of this weave of institutions and mind-sets—a decentering trend);

the scientifically reconstructed cosmos of the ontogenesis (centered in Occidental physical and biological sciences);

transcendence: the question of the opening to that which lies beyond the time-space of daily or cosmic experience, and is (if Abrahamist thought is true) the ultimate, all-embracing Source (Creator) of all of it—*ens creatum*, including the "game,"[20] of *Sein-Seienden*. (The most developed form of such a challenge is found in the Abrahamic family of traditions of revelation, with the Christian claim offering the most centering version: The Center is not an idea, nor even an ideal; it is a Person [in Balthasar's term, "a Fragment"] eucharistically present and active in continuing human history, the Church, manifesting the transcending whole. (*Das Ganze im Fragment* is the title of Balthasar's theology of history.)

In *Tradition and Authenticy* and in the present volume, I have commented on the stumbling block (*skandalon* and folly, recall, are Saint Paul's words for the claims about Christ) nature of the questions raised by these last claims. Not that the galloping imperialism of the HTX or the revolutionary fallout from the breakthroughs of contemporary science are without challenge! To be sure, mediation of accumulated differentiated experiences of the transcendent is the work of distinctive theological traditions, difficult of access to those outside. But then so are the traditions of science, and so is the struggle to get a responsible hold on what is happening in the explosive becoming of the HTX. Difficult for the appropriator or not, the breakthrough of the transcendent into consciousness is nevertheless a fact, a fundamental achievement within human history, formative of the biblical and the Occidental traditions, and of Islam, and hence an essential aspect of the history of *Sein*'s illumining-obscuring in the West. The *skandalon* of Christ and his Church remain embedded in the HTX epoch. To deny or fail to take this adequately into account—if only to attack it, like Feuerbach, Marx, and Freud did, calling it mythical delusion—leads, again in Voegelin's terms, to "mischief."[21] Resolute refusal to regard this central fact can be a phenomenon of sociopsychopatholgy, as Voegelin demonstrated.

Integrated into the Occidental history of the illumining and obscuring of Being has been, then, the encounter with and subsequently the theological

---

20. *Spiel* is Heidegger's word.
21. Voegelin to Schütz, January 1, 1953, in *The Philosophy of Order*, ed. P. Optiz and G. Sebba (Stuttgart: Kleitt-Cotta, 1981), 454.

thought of God, which encounter first occurred in the pretheoretical (thus pretheo-onto-logical) time at the origin of biblical revelation, when the thought of history was born. But it was at first conceived as *eskaton,* not history.[22] The Source revealed himself objectively as Logos, not the Logos of the Greek philosopher but the *Dabar* that speaks the world into being. By virtue of the *analogia entis,* an achievement of thought, responding to a gift of Being, Abrahamist consciousness has been drawn up into an opening-out beyond and above the sphere of daily social and natural commerce. This relativizes, whether we like it or not, our own and all other histories. The eruption into history, at the start of historical consciousness, and at a point in time and space, of the divine has lifted human consciousness to an awareness of what transcends all history.

This breakthrough to transcendence is not, as enlighteners such as Feuerbach claim, a case of humanity pulling itself up by its bootstraps; it is not a human initiative; it is not our own mysteriously leaping beyond. Rather, it is about a human response to initiatives coming from beyond the sphere of human control, horizon-opening confrontations within history, infinite freedom encountering and calling forth finite freedoms, using the whole of human accomplishment as its instrument of expression. These e-vents begin at Sinai,[23] founding history, and prepare, through a first centering in a chosen people led by the jealous God who reveals himself to be above all other gods, the definitive centering in the Christ.

Voegelin solidly establishes the credibility of the fact of the beginning of history with the Sinai experience as a scientific datum. The datum is not that YHWH confronted Moses at Sinai—acceptance of this claim has never been thought possible apart from a gift of grace, founding supernatural faith, confidence in the (human) witness to the (divine) Word manifest there. The claim is, rather, that historical consciousness begins with the Hebrews and their witness to the Sinai events. To ignore that is to ignore the origins of the entire Occidental tradition, almost a thousand years before the philosophers. Finally, it is in the christological claims, founded in the experience of the power of

---

22. That term, *istoria,* was the title given to his "researches"—which is what the word means—by the father of history, Herodotus. It is thus intimately bound up with the Greek origin of *theoria,* and happened seven hundred years after Sinai.

23. The evidence for this is mustered by Voegelin in *Order and History,* vol. 1, *Israel and Revelation.* Sinai is where it began, and not in philosophy's "breakthrough to the soul" (Voegelin, *The New Science of Politics* [Chicago: University of Chicago Press, 1952], 69). Heidegger, mistakenly (and it damages the truth of the Heideggerian *Denken*), places it in philosophy. Voegelin agrees that the beginning of philosophy in the discovery of the soul is of greatest importance, and does indeed constitute the beginning of the thinking of the history of Being, in the Heideggerian sense of *Sein*—the thought of the totality as such. But the breakthrough to transcendence is an event apart, which becomes integrated into philosophy's theoretical way only in the theology of the fathers of the Church. Is that to say that the glimpse of absolute transcendence is a revelation and hence not attained by philosophy, in the sense of natural reason operating alone? I take that to be Voegelin's sense, and I believe he is correct in this. This realization introduces the question of the relation of theology of history to every possible philosophy of history, a question brilliantly explored by Balthasar, in *Das Ganze im Fragment* (The whole in the fragment), which much more accurately signals the subject of the book than the title of the English translation, *Man in History.*

God in Jesus Christ, that the horizon-transcending dimension reached its apex, founding a new epoch in the thought of freedom and feeding two thousand years of analysis and differentiation by Church fathers and scholastics in the "extraordinary co-operative enterprise" that resulted in the inexhaustible "store of religious experiences," as Voegelin says in his letter to Alfred Schütz.

This is not to suggest that only in the Moses-prophets-Christ-Church tradition has there been a breakthrough to transcendence. Critical rapprochement of all the traditions in which a claim is made to an experience of transcendence is vital.

But a critical rapprochement on whose terms, in keeping with whose criteria? How is the *metron* of what is real to be furnished? And how would such dialogue (assuming that this is the appropriate term for this kind of exchange of experiences in friendship) articulate with the thought of the ontogenesis that is fed by the discoveries of science? The question is really this: How does the thought of transcendence and the exploration of the cosmos relate to the history of Being *(Seinsgeschichte)*?

TOWARD A NONIDEOLOGICAL ATTITUDE *(VERHALTEN)*

My approach to these questions aspires to be grounded in the attitude *(Verhalten)* that I earlier presented as resolutely nonideological. The appropriate attitude is dictated in part by natural faith and partly by character, especially the courage and the generosity necessary to allow the other to be other—easier said than done!

Everyone tends to reshape his beliefs about Being to fit the comfort level of his own character. Then, our natural faith will in part determine what we allow to presence, and hence what can be for us at all. When collectively entire institutions, such as the modern university, refuse to take seriously fundamental dimensions of reality, or at least purported ultimate structures, some of which have fundamentally shaped history, this is more than a phenomenon of mass pathology: It comes to affect (and is itself affected by) the coming to be of *Sein* itself, understanding *Sein* now on the fundamental level of the *Seinsgeschichte*.

Thanks to the fact that in open society one is not a prisoner of a single community's mass pathology, one can hope to be enlightened from beyond one's most formative community. But what about the need to search for truth within community, which for the Christian means that dialogue with other traditions is to be encouraged but always in union with the mind of the Church? Why is this not tantamount to another form of ideological conspiracy, fatal for the coming to be of being as is the conspiracy of silence in the university? Is there not a need, even within the Church, for the free individual conscience to criticize the limits of the community's thinking?

A loyal attitude, a confidence in what the tradition hands down, rightly understood, because of the nature of Christian revelation, should be resolutely anti-ideological. Christianity is supposed to be about receptiveness to the transcendent, which love should produce in the soul receptivity to all being, including each person's efforts to live out his life according to the vision that has been given to him, insofar as it shows itself to be fruitful (this entails loving criticism of what is not good). Christians have a word for such a comportment: *charis*—love with an overtone of graciousness. Christianity, rightly lived, opens a true catholica, the ecumenic par excellence. It is not an accident that the drive toward ecumenic wisdom originates in the Christian West, although it took the Church a long time to develop that degree of collective charity, a nondefensive respect of others, necessary to recognize fully freedom of conscience, although it was implicit in the revelation that was handed them. That loving vision is sinned against in practice; the struggle to live it is never ending.

The appropriate attitude is the will to remain alert to the full scope of historical development; to the importance of epochal differences; to the ecumenic reality of a multiplicity of great traditions; to phenomenological grasp of the dialectic interpenetration of image-concept-symbol on the one side and person–thing–institutional arrangement–cultural object on the other; but *surtout*, all these dimensions should be viewed as englobed in the tension between the different ultimate dimensions. From this all-embracing phenomenologically aware attitude, a number of aspects of the present situation, which we brushed past, now become clearer and merit greater elaboration.

Extreme Nihilism Helps Recall Being

The first is Heidegger's point: The very radicality of the forgetting of *Sein* in this period, which Heidegger calls "the end of metaphysics," has led to the beginning of a recovering thinking of the Mystery. Although I agree with Heidegger that neither philosophy nor theology has ever, until now, thought *Sein*, and that *Sein*, in the sense just invoked, is fundamental; and although I agree that the present extreme of this "forgetting of *Sein*" has much to do with the activistic voluntarism of the "efficient organization" characteristic of our epoch, enemy of all graciousness, I am encumbered in my use of the Heideggerian insights because I have certain disagreements with his ontology (explored in the last chapter).

By "metaphysics," recall, Heidegger means the effort to think Being as grounded in a highest and most general thing, the thingliest of things (the God, the Idea of the Good, *actus purus*, absolute knowing, will for the sake of will), which is also somehow supposed to coincide with the most general concept, "being" as the emptiest term. Now while I agree that this is no way to glimpse *Sein*, there is something inadequate in this Heideggerian reading of the history of metaphysics. First, it is neither untrue nor harmful, indeed it is natural and at some stage in the development of science inevitable, to form an abstract concept of "being" as the most general term, meaning nothing more than mere opposition to nothingness. Again agreed, it is a mistake to confuse such a most general concept with *Sein*, which has nothing to do with it. But it would also be a mistake—Heidegger's error—to confuse the most general and the highest with the *analogia entis*, which, properly constructed, is not a general concept but a thought-form *sui generis*,[24] designed precisely to protect the mystery of the Source, which is no thing. Second, it is not simply wrong to conceive of God as first cause, but it is wrong to conceive of this Source as though it were just another thing, even the thingliest of things; for, as the greatest philosophers and the fathers of the Church knew, the infinite God has no restricting essence, and no setting in time and space, as do all things. But the infinite Source is not *Sein* either, not for Heidegger (for whom the Source lies beyond horizons of interpretation as the *Nichts, die Quelle, das Ge-heimnis, SeXyn*, and so on—in brief, the unnameable from which all possibilities of interpretation, all *Sein* and hence all names, surge up), and not for Saint Thomas, for whom *actus purus* is the infinitely transcending Source of the possibility of all nature, including human nature, and, as Jean-Luc Marion establishes, is also Source of the finite *Sein-Seiendes* circle of world *(ens creatum)*.[25] I earlier criticized Heidegger for not remaining clear about the priority of *esse* over *essentia*, and *essentia humanae* as ground for the possibility of *Da-sein*. *Sein* cannot be source of the *esse-essentia*, the factical existence of human beings.

Now, although it is not simply false to think being (in reality *esse*, in our sense) either in terms of *analogia entis* or as the Source, Heidegger is right to clamor that so thinking has as one of its effects the distracting of thought from that horizonal time-space opening of the epoch, which is a fundamental aspect of *Sein*. Neo-Thomists and classical metaphysicians today overlook this. It is within this *Lichtung*, this characteristic epochal illumination, that things are allowed to appear as they do, for example (in our time) as technological objects or (in Greek times) as filled with gods. When metaphysics appears to have explained everything by grounding all in the activity of the highest cause, distracting from the critical inquiry into the nature and content of the common horizons of interpretation, or they are relegated to historical sociology as though of lesser importance, the forgetting of *Sein* is most complete.[26]

---

24. Here I remain the Gilsonian evident in my doctoral dissertation, "Construction in Philosophy" (Institut catholique de Paris, 1956), the second part of which is devoted to exploring the uniqueness of this thought-form, forged to avoid thinking being as a general concept. I showed that philosophers tend to flesh out such a general concept by selecting some part of reality as explanatory principle (root metaphor) and then try to imagine all reality in terms of that part, which soon shows the strain of trying to make one kind of thing stand for all things. That moved philosophers to advance from more restricted to less restricted parts, but Nietzsche's Will for the sake of Will remains as much a thing as Thales' water. The analogia of proper proportionality developed by Saint Thomas neither posits the Source as highest thing nor thinks being as a general concept. It is a set of relations that point toward, but cannot com-prehend, the mysterious Source.

25. This is an important theme in Marion's *Dieu sans l'être* (Paris: Presses universitaires de France, 1991).

26. To what extent this "end of metaphysics" thinking of Being is rooted in a lack, in the late philosophers, of interior life grounded in a holiness itself nourished by grace-filled communion with the living God is not something Heidegger appears to have considered. But, then, as I have already complained—indeed, since my negative remarks in *The Meaning of Heidegger* (New York: Columbia University Press, 1959)—he uncritically sought to marginalize the

Heidegger sees this dark night of the extreme forgetting as itself a gift of Being, which has made possible the step back behind the whole history of the suite of Being's epochal gifts *(Geschicke)*,[27] so that we may begin to think the mystery of the *Seinsgeschichte*. The step back (which Heidegger contrasts with the error of Hegel's *Aufhebung*[28]) is constituted by that phenomenological thinking of the situation in terms of its essence *(Wesen)*.[29] Thought of the essence of the situation demands recovery of the sense of the epochal opening. If we take up Heidegger's challenge and, against the backdrop of the whole history of the suite of epochal openings, seek to discern the character of our own epoch, what do we discover? Again, my own answer is not strictly in harmony with Heidegger.

First, and with this he would agree, we should struggle to glimpse in it whatever has permitted the scientific thought of the world as we now have it. But also we must ask what is there about this present epoch that continues to permit the opening toward the transcendent, or, better, the breaking into history of the Transcendent, particularly of the kind I shall term "the christologic" (explored below)? The eucharistic presence of Christ in history as the *ecclesia*, remains, in my judgment, an essential aspect of the epoch,[30] which is then not reducible to its HTX-like organization but reveals severe tension between the HTX and the christological at the fundamental ontologic level. The enduring presence of vital communities (including some of the most intelligent and

---

whole claim of revelation by treating it as an affair of faith, as though this had not permeated the thinking of the Occident, saving it from the worst effects of *Seinsvergessenheit*. Consider how much closer to a sense of *Sein* Augustine is, compared to Karl Marx, Augustus Comte, or Herbert Spencer.

27. From *schicken*, "to send"; in English translation, often rendered by the rather strange term "mittance." Man does not create the overriding, all-illuminating, all-forming epochal horizons. They shine forth (*Scheinen*, "to appear," that is, to make manifest, and to seem somewhat other than what something is. All phenomena are, in some sense, *Erscheinungen*, appearances, and never the thing-in-itself). *Das Geschick* permits a pun on *Schicksal* (destiny), because the suite of epochal horizons is indeed what seals the destiny of the tradition. For the fullest play on the sense of *erscheinen*, *Schein*, and so on, see Martin Heidegger, *Einführung in die Metaphysik* (Tübingen: Niemeyer, 1958); *An Introduction to Metaphysics*, trans. Ralph Manheim, (Garden City, N.Y.: Doubleday-Anchor, 1961.)

28. There is a definitive character to the thought process as Hegel unfolds it in "the System" that too hastily reduces the pluralism of dimensions, of varieties of entities, of distinctive traditions. The step back behind the whole history of Being more easily can resist the natural tendency of the mind to want definitive answers, the emphasis being on the mystery of the coming to be of Being, of the Light that springs from the transcending Source, favors respectful dwelling in the proximity of the rich variety of things, persons, events, and histories.

29. Heidegger, "Die onto-theo-logische Verfassung der Metaphysik," in *Die Frage noch dem Ding* (Tübingen: Niemeyer, 1962); *What Is a Thing*, trans. W. B. Barton and V. Deutsch (Chicago: Henry Regnery, 1967). Excerpts are to be found in *Martin Heidegger: Basic Writings*, ed. D. F. Krell (New York: Harper and Row, 1977), 247–82.

30. I believe that the continued existence of "God's first love," as Saint Paul calls the Jewish people, is an aspect of the "sign of contradiction." But what of the *umma* of Islam? That it witnesses to a vital relationship with the divine is evident. What a Christian makes of this massive reality from the perspective of his faith will be the complicated subject of a later volume.

most openly thinking persons) witnessing to the glory of the transcendent and adoring it, not only in non-European societies but even in the heartland of Europe, is a sign of contradiction between the continued existence of the life of the Spirit and the HTX kind of organization, including the narrowest forms of ideological manipulation, from herding mass opinion for consumption, to terrifying the innocent through political correctness. Heidegger's efforts to marginalize this spiritual life ("Here and there exist little communities of love")[31] does not correspond to my community's experience of a vibrant and massive reality.[32] The Christian faith's role in the recent collapse of the Soviet Empire[33] and the coming world crisis with Islam do not suggest the impotency of "little communities of love."

Avoiding a *Seinsgeschichtlich* Reductionism

Neither the Transcendent's reaching into history "to experience us," as Balthasar explains it,[34] nor the objective discoveries of science should be reduced merely to the *Seinsgeschichtlich*. The present work puts into place elements of a theory of knowledge and being to resist the *Seinsidealismus* that results from a certain interpretation of Heidegger.[35] In a moment we shall return to the nub of the issue: the ontological difference and the dialectic between Being and the beings. There I recall the full essential[36] contribution of the ontic, of the things presencing in their otherness and eliciting and providing the *metron* for correct interpretation. It took a long preparation in human

---

31. See Heidegger, "Nietzsche's Wort, 'Gott ist tod!,'" in *Nietzsche*, vol. 1 (Pfullingen: Neske, 1961); "The Word of Nietzsche: 'God Is Dead,'" in *The Question Concerning Technology*, 53–112, esp. 98.

32. There are 1.1 million practicing Catholics in the Archdiocese of Toronto. Recent studies show that 65 percent try to go to Mass every week, 18 percent several times a week. Not such a little community of love, or at least a rather large number of people trying to love. Of the 1.3 billion people in the world who call themselves Christian and the 700 million who call themselves Muslim, or the 12 million Jews, or the 500 million Hindus, how many really allow their lives to be in-formed in some essential way by receptivity to the transcendent, and to what degree, no one can judge. But in the face of the sociological reality of their apparent efforts to lead some sort of religious life, it seems arbitrary, to say the least, to speak dismissively of such little communities.

33. Especially via the pope's role in Poland and with *Solidarnosc*, widely recognized as the beginning of the end of the Empire.

34. Balthasar, "Experience God?," in *New Elucidations*, trans. M. T. Skerry (San Francisco: Ignatius Press, 1986).

35. Whether it is a misinterpretation by certain Heideggerians or not, I shall not here pause to argue. The interpretation in my *Jugendschrift*, *The Meaning of Heidegger*, suggests a way of reading Heidegger that avoids idealism. But even then I expressed some doubt, because of ambiguities in Heidegger's writings published to that point. His writings published since 1957, when my study was completed, offer more grist for the mill of the deconstructionists and other nihilist idealists, if one is determined to read him that way. Fighting the whole question through would require another book on Heidegger.

36. In the sense that *Wesen* contributes to *Sein*'s illumination of *essentiae*, and the factical givenness of the *essentiae* constitutes the given core of what is illumined in the already having been.

consciousness before the *Geschick* of *Sein* made the thinking of mathematics a possibility. We have examined something of the *Geschichtlichkeit* of theology, too. The effectiveness of the Transcendent working in human lives through grace (love in deed),[37] the objectivity of events of divine initiatives in history as witnessed to, and the objectivity of the genuine discoveries of science are not mere functions of the horizons of interpretation through which we grasp their meaning and in terms of which we examine the evidence for them. The Transcendent is effective in the lives of those who harken to God's word, however it is offered to them, a *Geschick* that can have objective as well as consciousness-inhabiting aspects. The Transcendent's effectiveness is almost palpable in the saints and in the common experience and thought of the Church. An ontic relationship between one person and another does not have to await, so to speak, permission of the particular ontological horizons of the epoch to happen. This person and that already possess a common human nature, on the shared grounds of which they can meet in *Mitsein,* just as God knows how to address that nature and make use of it as his instrument of expression. To be sure, the way any event, any thing, any fact is interpreted and taken up into the whole fabric of meaning will be partially conditioned by the epochal horizons of interpretation—partially but not entirely, for there is also this important element: that which here and now actually offers itself to be taken up. Certain kinds of relationship can only happen when the situation is prepared, that is, when the setting and the context are ready in which they can happen.[38] But then happen they do, factically, here and not there, now and not then, thus and not otherwise. Other kinds of relationship, rooted in the core of human nature, happen typically in every epoch. Of course, the forms of medieval spirituality will be different from those of the spirituality of the fathers of the Church, and an Opus Dei spirituality will differ from the charismatic in today's Church.

The Dialectic of Being and Beings

Epochs change and horizons of interpretation expand radically because of breakthrough. New things are revealed, and new cultural objects become possible. The importance of this Heideggerian insistence on the mysterious breaking into well-established and familiar worlds of the new nevertheless reveals upon reflection a multiform meaning of newness. (1) Something may be (objectively) old hat to those in the know but a revelation to me (or us). (2) A new insight into the nature of real things or real relations between certain

---

37. See Balthasar, *Love Alone: The Way of Revelation* (London: Sheed and Ward, 1968), chap. 6.
38. For example, the relations between the pharaoh's chief architect and the slaves who built the temple at Karnak were in no way like those of the production engineer at IBM and his workers, who hold over his head the threat of unionizing. An Amalgamated Brotherhood of Pyramid Constructors and Temple Renovators is inconceivable. And, in turn, the relationships among IBMers are quite different from, say, those among fairly independent consultants and analysts in a research firm such as Gartner Group, even though a significantly large minority (more than 30 percent) of Gartner Group's research staff are ex-IBMers of long service.

kinds of things that have been there in the cosmos all along may revolutionize (for example, science), and these new insights may lead to (3) new kinds of work on the environment which change it, but the base is the discovery of the already having been of nature. (4) On the other hand, there may occur in the soul of a creative-poetic sort the summoning into being of a new form, a new artwork, for instance, or a kind of social structure ("association," as *Tradition and Authenticity* put it), or a poetic religious myth that has much more to do with the state of feelings in that person than with anything out there in the objective world. Finally, (5) God or his Christ may utter a new Word introducing a new Time, instituting a previously unheard-of kind of organization—the Church—with a new Law, proving its authority with mighty works, the conquest of death being the mightiest of those that have been witnessed.

Given the spectrum of possibilities ranging from founding a new Time, or from new discovery of the objectively already having been, to pure poetic fantasy, and the projection of ingenuine ideals, one should always be careful in celebrating breakthrough or breaking in or that breaking out *(Aufbruch)* so dear to the reckless Hölderlin-adoring (and partly inventing) German conservatives,[39] so easily manipulated by the crazy ideologues of National Socialism.[40] And in the transcendent sphere, false prophecy remains a great danger. "Test everything," warns Saint Paul.

Sein unfolding through *Dasein* either indifferent to truth or seeking truth with inadequate grounding in objectivity leads to personal and social pathology. It is experience with the devastating results of such pathology that has motivated me to stress the strong ontic component in every genuine breakthrough, which is the breaking-in of reality to consciousness, as opposed to the breaking-out *(Aufbruch)* of poorly founded leaps of imagination stewed deep in the soul. These can sometimes prove subsequently to have been nurtured by sick communities, like the Stefan George circle, and all the ilk that cooperated with the illumining of *Sein* in the way that contributed eventually to the epoch of National Socialism.

Genuine breakthroughs happen concretely, involving particular persons who accept responsibility for individual acts, and most often are centered on the discovery of a new kind of real thing, or a new objective aspect of things, or on a responsible re-ordering of institutional structures that stay close to

---

39. In the Dilthey-Michel-Georg-Heidegger circle from just before and after World War I were those dreaming of a secret Germany summoned up from within their souls. Voegelin, too, uses the term "outburst" to speak of the sudden surprising manifestations of the divine. I assume that he is thinking of the German word, *Aufbruch*. I have signaled the dangers in Voegelin's situating this in the *metaxy* in such a way as to render ambiguous the sense of any objective encounter with the divine that is clearly a confrontation, not in but *to* the soul, which is summoned to come to meet the Lord, particularly in the sense of an event that could be witnessed by many, such as Christ's preaching and his miracles.

40. The recent dissertation by Frank Edler, "The Significance of Hölderlin for Heidegger's Political Involvement with Nazism" (University of Toronto, 1992), traces this pathological development and shows the philosophic depth of the error of poetic dreaming that gave rise to it.

real demands.[41] The case of the pure work of art is more complex.[42] There are two kinds of truth of art objects, more basic to their reality as art than any theses the work may put forward about the world: the integrity of the work in terms of the little cosmion it opens—the work is created to express itself; and, second, how it fits into a tradition from which it draws, and to which it adds, a language of expression, without which it would be simply unintelligible. It is here in the element of pure subjective creativity that we find the bewitching character of pure art—it is really very much about itself. But because artists interweave at least suggestions about the larger world, about the realities of nature and human history, one gets the dangerous and unsavory George circle kind of phenomenon, where one no longer knows what is fantasy and what transcends toward a larger reality.

A Beethoven's drawing the *Aufbruche* of Mozart and Hayden into new realms of expressive possibility to achieve the unexcelled leap of the Eroica Symphony may be innocent and exhilarating as a great emotional extravaganza that fires us to *Entschlossenheit*. But remember the bad old joke about the Heidegger student stumbling out of the Freiburg Seminar in 1927, eyes shining, exclaiming, "Ich bin entschlossen . . . aber Ich weiss nicht wozu" (I am resolved . . . but I don't know to what). Just as poorly directed *Entschlossenheit* of the "Dasein soll seinen Helden wählen" kind (The human existent shall choose his heroes)[43] was, to put it mildly, dangerous in an epoch with Hitler and his gang offering themselves as ready-made heroes, so a certain kind of exaltation in 1803 with Napoléon's propagating of his version of la Revolution française was not without its quotient of potential mischief. (Remember the scene of the disillusioned Bonn master ripping the title page off his score to replace the Napoléon dedication with one reading "To the Unknown Hero." The first choice of hero turned out to be a bad one. An unknown hero, on the other hand, is not much use.)

But even in the case of the pure work of art, there is a dialectical[44] relationship between the ontic and the ontologic. The previously established epochal horizons (the past) make possible the (present) presencing of certain entities in certain ways. But this presencing is more than mere effects of the already established ontological light: It is the self-giving of things with internal structures of their own, partially revealed in the epochal light favorable to their revelation, but always able to impose, in their presencing, more than the already having been horizons—the anticipation—could have called for, offering surprise, and thereby engaging a new future, changing where we go

---

41. Revolutions, such as the Protestant Reform, responding to extreme abuses, tend to rip apart rather than refashion structures. This is typical of the nebulous gnostic dreaming by ideologues of all kinds.
42. I already wrestled with the issue of the kinds of truth claims to be found in artistic traditions. See *T&A*, 69–72.
43. *Sein und Zeit*, 371, 385; *Being and Time*, 422, 437.
44. "Dialectical" is a term not to be used imprecisely in philosophy. The exact sense intended here is, I trust, clear from the description that follows.

from here. For the discoverer to receive this gift of ontic revelation, he must be *disponible*,[45] and that requires receptivity to the gift of expanded horizons of understanding needed to grasp and hold the new ontic, objective treasure.

Those of a subjectivist bent tend so to emphasize the extent to which only the deployment of certain interpretive projects can even allow particular kinds of things to be in the first place, they undermine credibility for objectivity, because the *noemata*, the things known, are made to seem entirely products of consciousness. The phenomenological idealists thereby weaken the sense of the phenomena as transcending consciousness to reveal the real natures of things.

Of course, what we receive through the senses is received in the mode of the knower, and hence it is never the totality of reality; indeed, it may barely penetrate the surface of what is presenting. But it is received as data, as givens, partial and to be interpreted, but nonetheless definite and explorable, and hence potential information about the things and about the transcending setting of those things, and transformations going on between things consistent enough to be grasped as processes. One sure sign that the senses do yield knowledge of the things as they are in themselves, partial but true, is that within these limits we have been able to learn that there is more than what is readily accessible to unaided sensation, and to fashion instruments to extend the range of our perception. And when we penetrate at the microscopic level, we are able to integrate this surprising new knowledge with the familiar understanding of common experience.

An example illustrates this *Sein-Seienden* dialectic. A dialectic can be observed between epochal horizons of interpretation, influenced both by Greco-Roman thought and by Christianity, which directed the attention of the fourteenth-century Franciscan Neo-Augustinian philosophers of nature to look for the numbers in things, which then revealed measurable aspects of themselves. This suggested pointedly the need for further observation and experimentation of a new kind, which turned up further aspects of the things of modern physics, which in turn called for creative modifications in how one should conceive of the world. Newly altered ways of looking at things directed research in new directions, and so on and on.

We are all aware today of how persons enamored of familiar, traditional horizons resist change, and of the conditions of what Thomas Kuhn calls abrupt "paradigm shift." What one must not lose sight of in all this, however, is the continual and massive role of the ontic givens. The artist enjoys a degree of creative license the scientist does not; he is free to express himself as he wants, because this self-expression is central to what the pure artwork is all about. But from the moment he makes his first choices, he has posited in the medium of his choice, say, by means of a line drawn by pencil on fine paper, an ontic reality, which his further working on the object must respect. And because he cannot work in a historical vacuum, he has inserted the coming-to-be artwork

---

45. Gabriel Marcel, whose term I have borrowed for this, possessed an excellent sense of just the point being made here. It is a central theme in *Le mystère de l'être* (Paris: Aubier, 1949).

into a tradition. The force of that "must" is clear: It is imposed by the already-having-been *Wesen* of the work so far; he can ignore it completely, but under pain of a certain incoherence, which, in Dada, may be the very violence the artist wishes to express. If he has chosen, like Hans Hartung, to scribble a busy spaghetti on a vague bed of rosy background, the further development of the work can go only certain directions. But if he has drawn a fine classic torso seen from the back, it would constitute a voluntary break with the inherent vector of the work's becoming, were he suddenly to draw a Hartung spaghetti. If he did so, the work would jump from a classic tradition of nude design to the nihilism so worshiped today.[46]

It would be wrong to believe that theology is more like art than science. Theology, especially in a tradition of revelation, is a positive science: The first requirement for the theological scientist is respect for the givens, the events witnessed to. In this sense, theology is even a strict science, where *streng* does not mean kowtowing to a narrow canon of the physically measurable and experimentally repeatable,[47] but, as in the historical sciences, a strict adherence to the facts about what the tradition has handed down. Just as in any other science, the faith of the investigator will affect what he makes out of the facts; it ought not, ideally, move him to ignore or alter the givens. An atheist studying the facts about the transmission of the words and acts of Jesus will likely indulge in a great exercise of explaining away, while a believing Christian will be receptive to the claims about the revelational character of what has been transmitted. But if either of them denies that the tradition, from the earliest Scriptures down through the consistent witness of the believing Church, has transmitted claims, for instance, that Jesus rose from the dead on the third day, they would be in fundamental violation of the most primitive demands of the science.

Transcendence, Cosmogenesis, and Prehistory within History

The horizon growth within physics and biology has allowed the discovery of facts demanding the objective interpretation of the world as older than we thought, and as grander—and more dynamic and complex—than heretofore imagined. By "objective interpretation" I mean that the cosmos is interpreted as being in itself like this, independent of the thought that has laboriously, and after much twisting and turning *(Irre)*, come lately to discover these realities about it. We understand why certain givens of ordinary sense experience led to the ancients' erroneous (but not stupid) interpretations. Even those exceptional Greek thinkers who imagined the cosmos to be enormous had no way of knowing its real size. When we say we now know it to be at least many

---

46. So much so that the Hartung drawing a friend of mine paid $800 for twenty years ago is now valued at $80,000—ah! the force of the voluntaristic element in *Sein*.

47. Any more than *streng* meant that for Husserl, who used the term in his early, mathematics-inspired work, *Philosophie als strenge Wissenschaft* (Frankfurt: V. Klostermann, 1965).

billion light-years in radius, that does not mean either that our imaginations can adequately encompass such a cosmos or that what we know is subject to no correction. That knowledge is based on elaborate inference from complex data that is difficult to interpret (like the "red shift").

Although inferential, demonstrated from patchy, difficult to interpret data, that which the astrophysicists do conclude is an intentional object: They are predicating the existence of an objective reality, an ontic complex of interrelating things—stars, planets, galaxies, asteroids, comets, gases—and of relationships between them—fields, forces, black holes, expansion, radiations of all kinds, and so on—including the still disputed dimensions. Although present as a noetic totality only in their minds, and not comprehensible sensibly as a whole, like the nail I roll between my fingers, nevertheless whatever is predicated, even hesitatingly, is predicated of the cosmos as real.

The certainty of their knowledge of these things varies with the things—of the existence of some suns, some planets, some galaxies, some comets, there can be no reasonable doubt, and the yet superficial knowledge we have gained of their *essentiae* contains many sound elements. Certain particles and even certain forms of radiation and certain relationships may later prove to have been invented imaginatively to handle certain data within the standard model at a certain stage in its development. Some of these things are subject to a high degree of perceptual confirmation—any doubts about the existence of our sun and that it is an ongoing thermonuclear reaction?—and others are entirely inferred at certain moments in the development of the theory, and hence subject to subsequent correction.

Today the thought of Being should[48] be extended to embrace the ontogenetic and the prehistoric. Long ago, thought opened a radically different kind of place for the Transcendent, particularly as it revealed itself on Sinai, through the prophets, and in Jesus Christ. And thought opened a space for creation, as it came to be known in revelation—not a Greek discovery, not at least in the radicality it came to enjoy in the fathers' *creatio ex nihilo* doctrine.[49]

Like the other great missionary Abrahamic religion, Islam, Christianity has been, throughout much of its past, aggressive in spreading the Gospel.[50] At a time when the message of scientific socialism is imposed by arms on ungrateful populaces (the citizens of the USSR have managed to say, "No thanks," those of China and of Indochina have not been similarly smiled upon by *Sein*); and elements in Persian and Arab Islam, for instance, show few signs of a liberal

---

48. The force of this "ought" is both logical and moral: Thought, to be true to itself, should (logic demands) loyally accommodate facts in keeping with their reality in themselves. And the human agent, to be true to his nature, ought (moral) to accept and respect the facts.

49. See Balthasar on the radical change in lived temporality itself this requires and affects, in his remarkable reflections on time in Saint Augustine, "The Fragmentary Nature of Time," in *Man in History*, trans. William Glen-Doepel (London: Sheed and Ward, 1968), 1–42.

50. As, indeed, some branches of the Christian community remain today, even to the extent of poaching—as, for example, Pentecostal missionary efforts in Latin America and North America.

outlook, the Church has accepted from the Enlightenment an appreciation of freedom of conscience, which is, paradoxically, more Christian than some of the Church's own earlier behavior. This constitutes yet another expansion of thought, revealing a further initiative of *Sein*. The anti-Church establishment enlighteners (many of whom were still in varying degrees Christian believers) have helped the Church realize certain implications of its own understanding of man. Now this new understanding has to be incorporated into the attitude with which the Christian approaches the challenge of dialogue, in the mutual search for truth.

On Maintaining a Space for Genuine Dialogue

Neither atheist socialism nor liberal humanism, both driven by hedonistic will-to-power, shows the slightest intention of indulging seriously in live and let live. In dealing with the agents of both, one must learn to discern genuine respectful tolerance for the other from tactical maneuvers of coexistence. Anyone convinced that open society is the best we can hope for in social order, and that a regime of genuine dialogue is the only solution for mankind, paradoxically must be prepared to struggle to enlarge, almost contra-culturally, a space for dialogue. Secular materialism degenerates into wars for markets, and totalitarianisms destroy all public openness. In contrast, awareness of the need to think *Sein*, to accept the grace to open horizons to enfold the full mystery of the gift of the Light, is the challenge of a mature quest for wisdom. It must not, of course, ignore the obscuring that accompanies the always finite illumining—including every form of rejection of the Light, sinfulness, and every form of pathology. It must be critical.

This dark note brings us up short. We appear desire driven and seem to suffer from complex and not very clear conflicts of desires. Ego, defensiveness, put-down, driving ambition, self-indulgence, the clearly pathological—the catalog is long of aspects of human behavior that hardly encourage generous, loyal dialogue. Every society continually struggles against these destructive and negative tendencies. The effort requires a common faith, rooted in the genuine. No social struggle can be maintained effectively without a sound common faith.

Eric Voegelin laments the erosion if not the destruction of the "civic theology" of the West. Is such an ideal as a nonideological civic theology credible for the planetary epoch in which we now live? It would have to be rooted in a *Denken* that respects the objectivity of science, and in a belief in gathering the family of man, the two together—the *Denken* and the political (ecclesial?—see below) together acknowledging the need for the most open and respectful dialogue between traditions. To be civic, even when the *civitas mundi* one seeks is planetary, such a widely accepted set of beliefs would have somehow to be effective in organizing the public spaces, academic and political, in which the body politic works out its compromises. Never would a uniformity of belief be achieved, and legitimate conflicts of interest would always persist, so compromises remain necessary. As a people, we the members of the best-functioning open societies have not renounced the search for a working consensus among sometimes—in the case of the U.S.A.—hundreds of millions.

For the Christian, the ground of his belief in both the possibility and the need for such a loving gathering of all mankind is the reality and mission of Christ. The concept is ecclesial, with all the immensely rich eucharistic sense of that term. The Jew awaits the Messianic era for such an in-gathering to be possible. The Muslim would see the only adequate in-gathering to be the conversion of all to Islam, although more liberal Muslims embrace the ideal of a peaceful coexistence between the unachieved *umma* and the non-Muslims. The secularized liberal places his hope in a basic humanitarianism, which, to him, requires no acknowledgment of the Fatherhood of God to achieve an adequate brotherhood. To what extent all these impulses contain the actuality or the potentiality of love can only be determined through concrete efforts to achieve dialogue and through it understanding. Talk of civic theology seems premature at best, and perhaps altogether meaningless. In all events, the road ahead promises to be difficult.

Still, I would contend that the model of civic representation that best permits hope of genuine dialogue, however defective it proves to be in practice, is representative democracy. I say this fully mindful of the danger, inherent in it, of degeneration into demagoguery. The severe danger is from within: Internal pathological elements can make immature use of their liberty, those who, miserable with themselves, feel a compulsion to wreck the society in which, because of family and personal disintegration, they have been unable to feel at all at home.

On the theoretical level, the greatest challenges facing the humanistic democratic thinker are (1) coming to understand the truth claims of the major traditions, seeking to glimpse something of how they relate in light of the maximum field of meaning, that of the broadest *Sein*; and (2) representing the pragmatic situation—the relative *jeu des forces*—clear-sightedly, without ideological distortion, and then thinking about it in light of the truth to be gained from the entire history of *Sein*. Genuine dialogue is indispensable (but not sufficient) for both.

A central task at the heart of this theoretical challenge is the achieving of a nonideological view. This, as is the thought of Being of which such a nonideological comportment is a necessary condition, remains, of course, an ideal: Interpretation is always from a point of view; no one possesses an adequate critical appreciation of the limits built into the biases of his own position, and no transcending view of the limits of Being's epochal horizons of interpretation is possible. But humbly acknowledging the finitude of our knowledge does not imply an inevitably defensive ideological attitude. Quite the contrary.

Finally, there are methodological aids—gifts of Being—that help to approach the ideal. First, written appropriation of the kind I am attempting permits others to criticize the worst limitations of one's biases while encouraging clarity in thinking out his views and to understand better the source of its founding experiences. One is forced to confront more earnestly and honestly the living source of one's life in faith.

In attempting to translate the truth claims of others, we develop hermeneutic sensitivity to the character of the symbols being translated. To deny in principle translatability is to deny the very possibility of meaningful dialogue and with it the project of truth and indeed faith in the unity of being. Destruction of the very project of truth is a denial of the tradition of philosophy and theology, and I am convinced that it leads to the abandonment of the hope of a free society. Skepticism delivers us to pure power struggles.

Because our thoughts and perceptions transcend interiority, out to the opening in which the things themselves, and their relations and settings, can reveal aspects of themselves, thus becoming reference points for our discourse and anchors for our thought and action, we can communicate.

Why do people ever resist this, which is obvious to common sense? Because objectivity entails our being beholden to things, we are brought to acknowledge our dependence on the others, to respect them, to be grateful—all guides to the proper use of our freedom. We can share feelings about things, not only because we have the same human nature, but because that human perceptual and knowing ability opens onto a common world of real things, commonly accepted laws, functioning institutions.

My work is rooted in a natural faith that remains resolutely hopeful that mankind can progress in peace toward an ecumenic wisdom. Such cross-cultural cooperation requires the rejection of nihilism and every form of skepticism and the embrace of all evidence of objectivity, common human nature, and the ability of mind to reach insight. Guided by insight and anchored in objectivity, the human community can work together to govern a liveable world in which our best energies may yet be devoted to the discovery and admiring contemplation of Truth.

GLOSSARY

Abschattung	A profile or limited point of view.
Affectivity	Accompanies everything we do, as it is experience of the body moving and being moved, when we act and are acted upon.
Appropriation	Taking responsibility for what one is by critically examining the vision according to which one leads one's life, working to purify it of unfounded elements, and to bring one's actions into line with what one has been able to know is true—that is, making it properly one's own.
Common Sense	The core of experience common to a culture.
Consistency	The recognition that, in the midst of change, in a process, there is an intelligible unfolding of phases, so that as the mind's eye scans the process it can grasp the sense of these phases, following one another. Compare with **Stability**.
Crisis	Greek, *kritein*. The German parallel is *unterscheiden*, which should be compared to the English phrase "fish or cut bait."
Critical	An explicit, aware, maximally responsible judgment of *what is*.
Dasein	Human existent as the place through which *Sein* illumines.
Depth	A willful *in-formation* of virtues to deploy psychic energy for the sake of openness to Being.
[The] Divine	Whatever is not just beyond Man (and the angels) but more perfect in its mode of being than Man (and the angels).
Eksistenzialien	Permanent structural elements in *Dasein*'s interpreting, reflective of givenness of human nature.
Ens rationis	Being of reason, like an idea that exists only in the mind.
Essentia	To be of a recognizable species, genus, or order, that is, one's form is part of a persistent set of propertied identifications. Connected to *esse*. Contrast with **Wesen**.
Ereignis	The e-vent of Being happening.

Experience	The source of any incoming information, any awareness of something other than the center of awareness itself, which calls itself to the attention of the awareness center of the experiencing self.
Experimental Knowledge	What is accessible to us as a result of our willful probing of nature.
Form	A structured equilibrium of effective, directed energy recognized as typical by insight.
Friendship	Love for another person.
Gravitas	Latin: seriousness, depth, especially as a way of being.
Handeln	German, from Heidegger, *Sein und Zeit:* dealing with things.
Holiness	The integrity and generosity of one's living out what one has been presented in the interior vision. Related to, but not the same as, spirituality.
Horizons of Interpretation	The opening provided by consciousness which permits an object to stand in awareness. They are formed by our natural faiths and are in part the product of traditions in which we have been educated.
Humanly Present	More completely and intensely present, more thoroughly and consistently engaged.
Ideal	A vision of a longer-range goal, conditions for the realization of which have yet to be created, at least in part.
Ideology	The tendency to fabricate imaginatively holistic explanations poorly grounded in evidence. In other words, a set of pat answers to the deeper questions life poses, held in such a neat (and superficial) way as to block challenging thinking.
Indiscipline	The evil fruit of an insufficiently or improperly structured upbringing, of indulgence, conflicting motives, and mixed-up signals.
Indulgence	The vice of following the most immediate and insistent impulse, instead of rising judgmentally to a broader, more ordered view of needs.
Institution	A conjunction of people playing coordinated roles in view of a basic common end.
Intelligibility (of a situation)	Literally, our ability to read into each situation its sense.
Intensity	The result of integration—the process of creating form. Intensity of psychic presence requires, to happen, the

	gifts which awaken awareness and the development of the set of habits (character) which allows concentration. A consistent storing-up of formed energy-potential.
Interiority	The life that goes on within a living being: The more relative spirituality it enjoys, the more complex and rich is its possible interior life.
Interior Life	A self-conscious, reflective effort to recover the ultimate significance of the life of the soul, in what accounts for its participation in Being, including the largest meaning of intersubjective relationships, our foundations in nature, and our life "in God and Him in us."
Lack of Motivation	A failure, caused by disorder, to see what there is to see, leading to a loss of faith in Being.
[The] Liar	Everyone, insofar as we are all tempted to try to get something without paying the price—the commitment of disciplined, ordered energy—everyone who at some point lacks the discipline to do what he knows, on some level, is needed.
Living	At some level of complexity it becomes clear that the specialization of functions and the working together of these various parts permits the thing to absorb energy and materials from its surroundings and, following a source of information built into it, order these to its own overall benefit, and ultimately it can reproduce itself, again following the information contained in the ordered materials that we now call the genetic code.
Love	A willing of the other's well-being—a *benevolentia*—which is a commitment of self to other, a willingness to accept the other as genuinely himself, and a disposition to be at the service of that other so that he, too, may realize his own truth, that is, develop the potential of his own existence in good ways.
Manipulation	Playing on another's emotions to bypass his reflection, the ground of the possibility of his acting genuinely freely.
Martyrein	Greek: bear witness. (This need not involve dying for the cause; indeed, misapplication of death is a primary underpinning of all revolutionary ideologies.)
Methodos	Greek: meta + hodos—following along a way, or method.
Metron	Greek: measure, especially as objective standard of judgment.
Mitsein	Being-with (intersubjective being).

Noema	The objective correlate of an act of *noein*.
Noesis	The particular act of consciousness that produces some kind of object.
Objective Context (of knowing)	That larger structure or setting of which any idea or thing is part.
Philosophical Categories	Large-scale concepts chosen to play the role of attempting to mediate all experiences, as one seeks to bring them together intelligibly in a single wisdom.
[The] Philosophy	Discourse aiming at universality of assent.
Presencing	Being present and engaged with the other; an openness to it as other, founded in the element of care.
Pseudos	The source in the soul of what Plato calls "disturbance," *akosmia*, psychic disorder, whether self-induced or traumatically caused by the aggressive other, setting energies, which should be working together harmoniously, against one another, or depriving them of proper rational reference to one another.
Realistic Principle	The principle that human knowledge *in-tends* things with a reality in themselves and intelligibilities with a sense in themselves.
[Recipe for] Hypocrisy	A pursuit of the spiritual without an adequate interior life and/or without holiness. Particularly found in institutional settings.
Sachverhalt	German: state of affairs.
Seienden im Ganzen	German, from Heidegger: things as a whole, that is, all-englobing context, or world we live in.
Self-Control	A kind of personal territorial imperative, in which, life-long, the individual strives to extend the imperium of his conscious center of awareness over the darker and more unyielding aspects of his givenness, to the extent these seem to be brakes or obstacles to his fullest development.
Setting (objective)	A real disposition of objects in material, cosmic time-space, which remain even if there is no consciousness to become aware of them.
Situation	The personal or intersubjective living-together of subjects, at different scales, from personal and familiar to national and civilizational.
Spirit	The ability to soar and embrace all existence—to give over to the other—while not ceasing to be oneself. Transcendence beyond the disintegration of organism.

Spirituality	The intensity and quality of one's presencing in the interior life to the realities contemplated. Related to, but not the same as, holiness.
Spirituality (of man's highest operations)	The mind's ability to embrace all being and to pull everything together into a single wisdom.
Spirituality (relative ordering)	Speaks of increasing psychic and interior life as complexification increases—for example, "A man is more spiritual than a rabbit, is more spiritual than a cell, is more spiritual than an atom."
Stability	The recognition of nonprocess, that an object, in some respect over a significant time span, does not change. Compare to **Consistency.**
Subjective Context (of knowing)	Every act of knowledge is that of a concrete subject who himself is in a time-space situation.
System	A network of interactions between things that nevertheless maintain their distinctiveness.
Time-Space	Denotation of a presencing. Contrast with the space-time of physics. Time-space is always a relation; hence, the emphasis upon deployment over and in time.
to ti einai estin	Greek; from Aristotle: essence, "that which is as having been."
tradere	Latin: handing-down. Also the root word for tradition.
Transcendental	The principle that the formative influence of consciousness goes beyond every particular object, every aspect of an object, and all relationships between objects, as the condition for the possibility of their appearing in consciousness in the first place.
Truth Question	The quest for the foundations of wisdom in a unified knowledge of being.
Valid	Reflecting some aspect, level, or part of the underlying reality one experiences as the source from which the abstraction is made and to which I can return for renewed experience.
Verhalten	Comportment for example of genuine openness permitting philosophical exchange. The term is from Heidegger.
Wesen	Reflecting the already-having-been contribution of its epochal *Sein*, as in the school of a work of art. Can be either static or dynamic. Connected with *Sein*. Contrast to *Essentia.*

Wesen als das Gewesene	German; from Heidegger: essence as "the having been."
Zuhandensein	Things as instruments.

INDEX

Abba, 317
Abrahamic tradition: and revelation, 5
Abschattung: as profile, 48, 369
Absolutes Wissen: an impossibility, 319
Abstraction: process of, 54–56 passim; of form, 61
Accompagnement, 107
Acculturation, 260
Act: as intentional, 14, 247; rooted in horizons, 14; illumined by *Sein,* 14; transcending consciousness, 15; knowledge of context of, 97; intelligible in two ways, 97; as revelatory, 275; and potency, 293; as gratuitous and free, 302
Affectivity, 369; and body, 226
Agathon, 270
"*Agere sequitur esse,*" 70
Akosmia: as disturbance, 263
Allgemeinste: God as, 281, 314
Ambiguity, 111; of sin, 328–35 passim
Analogia entis: and being, 197, 214, 319, 335, 353, 356
An-denken, 325
Anfang, 325
Angst, 324
Anspruch des Seins, 324
Anstoß, 233, 252
Anthropology: as cultural, 279
Anti-being, 128
Anti-Christian: thought and hostility, 109
Anticipation, 44, 361
Anti-egalitarianism, 169
Anti-intentionality, 306
Ant-wort, 227
Apodeixis, 277
Apophantic field, 279, 282; closing of, 349
Apostles: Symbolon of, 103–4, 131, 133
Apostolein, 104
Appreciation, 212, 314, 415, 319; as critical, 366

Appropriation, 317, 336, 338, 366, 369; and critical self-understanding, 6; of who we are, 173; of truth, 268; of tradition, 268–69
Archē, 121, 276, 277; as biblical, 184
Atheism: as aberration, 278
Atom, 291–92; materiality of, 208–9
Attention: focus of, 349
Aufbruch, 360, 361
Aufheben, 325
Authenticity, 319; and holiness, 129; and fullness of self-possession, 229; and friendship, 229–32 passim
Autonomia, 225
Autonomy, 175, 190
Autos, 221
Averageness, 255
Awareness: centers of, 125; breadth of, 252

"Back behind": as method, 173–74; in cosmos, 178
Bad faith, 139
Bad institutions, 255
Balthasar, H. U. von, 311–12, 326, 345; and history of mankind, 281–82
Behavior: as consistent, 74
Beholdenness: to reality, 60; reflection upon, 61
Being: defined, 8, 319; as working through us, 22; as guided by *Sein,* 22; as whole, 23; not a product of our collective wills, 23; revealed through form, 46–47; incomprehensibility of, 127; coming to be of, 199; "as such" and thinking, 215; quiet voice of, 269; as social, 274; and the good, 296; emanation of, 298; diffusion of, 298–99, 300; as self-affirming, 299; as building up, 304; instrumentality of, 315; and truth,

343–67 passim; recalling of, 356–58; as abstract concept, 355; gifts of, 366
Benevolentia, 111; possibility of, 202; and eros, 226–29
Be-stimmen, 322, 324; as attunement, 321
Big Bang theory, 168–69
Bildung, 171, 199, 200, 253, 266, 271, 275, 322
Bohm, D., 174–75, 177
Bonaventure: on God's being, 297–98
Breakthrough, 324

Care, 240, 240n77
Cathalou: as universality, 131; as whole truth, 137
Cell: limited spirituality of, 209–11; *Ek-sistenz* of, 211; evolution of, 287
Certitude: of objective realities, 10; apodeictic, 10
Charis, 355
Charity, 306–7
Choice of worlds: as reflection of smaller worlds, 17; as principle, 17, 18; role of traditions and culture, 17, 18
Christ: as revealer of humanity, 116; truth claims of, 132–38; as *skandalon*, 134; and three ways of presencing, 272; teaching of, 272; "mystical body" of, 273, 317; as Logos, 273; in Church, 309–10; *kunftet sich*, 346n8
Christianity: as "treasure-hoard of symbol," 136
Church: as mystery, 317; *semper reformanda*, 346; and anti-church establishment, 365
Civic theology: destruction of, 365; as *civitas mundi*, 365
Codification: of Catholic tradition, 114
Cognition: transcends materiality, 201–3; process and receptivity, 202
Commitment, 255; and self, 228–32 passim; and friendship, 229, 231; generous, 230
Commonsense: man, 43; presence of things, 43; unthinking, 221; defined, 369
Communio, 305; in liturgy and good works, 114; sacramental prayer life of, 116; *ecclesia*, 118; and entropy, 225; as community of thinkers, 336; as community, 354; and communication, 367
Communio sanctorum, 107

Complacency, 261
Complexification, 160, 289, 294; of man, 169–70; and matter, 294; tendency toward, 314
Concept: formation process of, 60; stability of, 61; own life, 90; generalization of, 214; inadequacy of conceptual tools, 344–45
Concrete universal: as concrete totality, 70; as cosmion or little world, 71
Confidence, 229, 230, 345; as "faith together," 129; as comportment or *Verhalten*, 129; in other, 254; in tradition, 354
Confusion: and scientific spirit, 39
Connectedness: reality of, 91
Consciousness: as finite, 201; of itself, 201; and reflection, 202; expression of, 228; breakthrough and evolution, 276
Consensus: and search for truth, 18; relation to *communio*, 18
Consistency, 369; as moral, 259
Context: and cosmos, 26–29 passim; man in, 151–98 passim; spatial, 156–57; temporal, 157–58; social, 158–59; ultimate, 175, 344–45; and world of meaning, 207; planetary, 344, 351; real, 349; objective, of knowing, defined, 372; subjective, of knowing, defined, 373
Contextuality, 330; as principle, 13; affirming connectedness, 13; subjective vs. objective, 16, 19; structure and setting, 17
Conversation: possibility of, 125
Conversion: as fundamental change, 7; as turning of heart, 116; as *conversio*, 314
Cooperation: and building the kingdom of God, 21; as cross-cultural, 367
Cosmiota ("little world"): and *Sein*, 98
Cosmos: concept of, 25; and Kantian transcendental consciousness, 25; and our understanding, 26–29 passim; and *telos*, 168; and wholeness, 168; unfolding purpose of, 168; truths about, 178, 179; as setting, 180; beginning of, 183; end of, 184; objective being of, 199, 200; and cosmogenesis, 363–65
Courage: and virtue to change, 37; to carry through, 74
Creatio ex nihilo, 364
Creative: leap, 173; thinking as *anfängliches*, 219; intuition, 331

Creativity: and imagination, 89; defined, 89–90; and emerging *Wesen*, 90; and co-creativity, 308
Crisis: defined, 221, 369
Cultura, 200
Cultural transformation: of natural things, 88

Dasein: and human soul, 207; limits of the "da," 213; reality depicted in, 251, 255; as future-opening, 319, 321; *esse* and, 323; finitude of, 325, 351; and symbols, 329, 334; and *Sein* unfolding, 360; defined, 369
Death: vanquishing of, 107. *See also* Entropy
Decision: basic and fundamental projects, 37; of practical life, 38; genuine, 263
Deconstructionists, 120
Deep grammar, 141n32
De-formation, 315; projective, 280
Denken, 351, 365; as authentic, 322, 323, 325, 326
Depth, 369
De-structive, 322
Diabolein, 316
Dialectic, 30; of *Sein* and *Seiendes*, 336; of Being and Beings, 359–63
Dialogue, 226–27, 263; and space, 365, 366
Difference: and spiritual dimensions, 80
Dionysius the Areopagite, 298–99
Dis-information, 315
Discipline, 274
Discourse: universal, 125–28 passim
Disponibilité, 110, 112, 240, 362
Distance: spirituality and spatiality, 57
Dis-traction, 325
Divorce rate, 257
DNA and RNA, 162–65, 288–89
Données: des dons, 326, 340
Doxa, 314
Dreams, 49–51 passim
Dwelling, 327

Ecclesia, 357; of lovers, 132
Ecumenic: dialogue, 127, 128; wisdom, 338, 367
E-ducere: of culture and friends, 232
Egoism: as defensive, 128
Eidetic: insight, 224; variation, 334
Ek-sistenz, 199, 221, 222, 296
Ek-sistenzialien, 228n63, 329; of *Dasein*'s projected world, 75; defined, 369
Ek-static: and Heidegger, 277n1

Enculturation, 265; in institutions, 221
Energeia: as essential, 305
Energy, 164, 293; as forming, 154; deployment of psychic, 205, 206, 241, 276, 308, 313, 331
Engagement, 238–40 passim
Ens mentis: and structure, 58
Ens rationis, 192, 369
Entropy, 155, 293; as death, 157, 304; lowering of, 196
Entschlossenheit, 361
Entwickelnd, 329
Epideixis, 277, 297
Epistemology: vs. ontology, 7
Ereignis: of *Sein*, 336; defined, 369
Erfahrung: as "traveling," 119n108
Er-innern, 325
Erlebnis, 119
Eros: and *benevolentia*, 226–29; and friendship, 229; *theoreticos*, 292
Erscheinung: as particular experience, 70
Eschatology, 317; as *eskhaton*, 353
Esse: defined, 8, 319, 321; and formal insight, 15; precedes *Sein*, 47; as "material existence," 48; and God, 106, as reality, 196; history of, 196–97; and human spirituality, 200; as lover's commitment, 230; and relationships, 250, 295, 296; infinite and God, 321; as recuperation, 322; and love, 328; of natural things, 330; and *Sein*, 332–33, 338–40; totality of, 350
Essence, 269; as *to ti einai estin*, 20n1, 187; as *Wesen als das Gewesene*, 20n1, 373; recognition of, 187–89; defined, 373
Essentia, 369
Essevergessenheit, 340
Ethnos, 191, 193
Eucharist: living sacramentality of, 115–18; as *agape*, 273; and Incarnation, 317; as gift of self, 340; and presence, 357
Everyday averageness: as *Durchschnittlichkeit*, 261
Everyday existence: as inauthentic, 221, 261
Evidentia, 247, 367
Evil: force and recognition of, 316–17
Evolution: and God, 286–92; of cells, 287
Existential myopia, 156
Experience: as changing, 60; as translatable symbol, 125–28 passim; genuineness of, 129; as public and

private, 130; of objective events, 130–34 passim; as dynamic equation, 142; as rich and varied, 151; as mystical, 311, 313; defined, 370
Experiential grounds: critical possession of, 3; and ultimate structure, 6; and ecumenic wisdom, 6, 10; as *natus*, 7

Facticity, 320
Faith, 313; as living, 123; as hopeful, 345
Fanatic, 254, 264
Fidelity, 327
"Fides quaerens intellectum," 119, 345; and mystery, 104
Flexibility: of perception, 56; as indication of freedom, 56
Foreknowledge: as prejudice, 71
Forgiveness, 316
Forgottenness of Being, 321, 323. See also *Seinsvergessenheit*
Form: seeing, 46; regulative operation of, 190, 191; and capital, 264; defined, 370
Formal cause: as principle of being, 121
Foundation: in experience, 3; of everyday life, 72; and particular experience, 119
Frame of reference, 43, 121; defined, 52n21; as "many," 152–60 passim; scales of, 157–58; as organic, 168; and spirit, 206
Free: meaning of, 315
Freedom: affection of our knowledge, 18; finite, 18, 56, 353; as first foundation, 57–60 passim; and truth, 111; at low degree, 167; and man in context, 170–74; and *Sein*, 172–74; and spirituality, 202–7 passim; concepts of, 214; and words, 216; as engagement and disengagement, 256; to create, 261; and genuine divine, 266; infinite and finite, 314; of conscience, 365
Freie, die: as large space, 213
Freud, S.: view of religion, 279; projection and Feuerbach, 280
Friendship, 277, 354; mutual self-awareness of, 224; and *benevolentia*, 227; as sharing of self, 228; as *pseudos*, 229; eros, 229; defined, 370
Fundament, 40
Future, 345; as projective, 43; attending acts, 43

Galileo: and Aristotelian cosmology, 179
"Ganze im Fragment," 251, 352
Gegen-stand, 326

Geheimnis, 323–24
Geistnatur, 323
Generosity, 310, 324
Geschichtlichkeit: as historicity, 255, 318
Gestell, 337, 351
Geviert: in Heidegger, 318n1
Gewensein: as real influence, 350
Gift, 299, 300, 303, 334
Gilson, E.: parts as wholes, 37, 147
Givenness: of objects of consciousness, 13, 14; of informing, 280
Glaubenssachen, 337
Gnosticism, 347; vision of, 203
God: in classical tradition, 5; and incomprehensibility, 127; and fulfillment, 225; as *actus purus*, 245; nearness and transcendence of, 275; *Nähe und Ferne*, 275; found in soul, 275; as unconditioned, 286; evidence in handiwork, 286–92 passim; evidence from design (evolution), 286–92; evidence from motion, 293; as constitution of being, 295–300; as love, 295, 302–6; in history, 300; as healer, 310; and ontological context, 312; co-creating with, 315; as *theos*, 300; private experience of, 302; as renewing source, 305; as alpha and omega, 305; ontological context of, 312–17; glory of, 315; co-creativity with, 315; as revelation of source, 317, 327; not an entity, 318; as man, 327; as *ho theos*, 337
Goethe, J. W.: *Farbenlehre*, 177
Good: of being, 296; diffuses itself, 298; finite, 299
Gospel: and objective events, 130–32
Grace: as salvation, 20; as nourishing and enhancing, 230; natural and supernatural, 262; graciousness, 355; as love in deed, 359
Gratitude, 303, 315, 367
Gravitas: as seriousness, 4, 236, 240; and life, 253, 262; defined, 370
Greatness of soul, 230n69
Ground: need for, 32; in objective experience, 32–34 passim; ultimate, 277–317 passim; transcending, 280
Grundlegung, 152
Gunst des Seins, 252, 325, 331, 351

Habit: as critical appropriation, 37; functioning in faith, 37; requires virtue, 37, 38; of categorizing fellows, 77;

of enculturated people, 98; cultural and bodily, 161; formation, 171, as ontological ground for social patterns, 195–98 passim; not a constraint, 196
Hallucinations, 50–52 passim
Handeln, 41, 370
Hawking, S., 182
Heidegger: and error of Source, 281; and metaphysics, 318–28 passim, 355, 356; post and ante, 318–28 passim; and "thinking back," 336; and lacunae in thought, 336–40; and *das Nichts*, 356–58
Heilige, das, 318
Heraclitus: and flux, 46
Herrlichkeit: of God's body, 106
Hierarchy: organic, 166–71 passim
Historia, 219
Historicity: and interior life, 255–76 passim; of *Sein*, 318–40
History: natural, 199–276 passim; awareness and man, 199–276 passim; God's intervention in, 300–306 passim; end of, 347
Holiness: as ground for witness, 104–9 passim; and acceptance of truth claims, 104–9 passim; defined, 105, 370; and integrity of being, 106; natural communication of, 107; followers of, 108; in the Church, 108; ignoring of, 110; formative experience of, 110; and authenticity, 129
Hope, 308, 310; Christian virtue of, 107
Horizons: and natural faith, 7; as informing, 7; as frames of reference, 15; as shared commonalities, 98; deployment of interpretative, 199; sharing of, 227, 228; new and presencing, 245; as interpretative, 322, 330; defined, 370
HTX, 146, 334–35, 337, 434–44, 352, 357
Human being: different from other entities, 70; interiority of, 70; as "choice," 152; power of, 291
Humani generis, 278–79
Human nature: basic and common knowledge of, 75–88 passim; commonality of, 78; and scientific evidence, 79; sameness of, 80–81; vs. culture, 84–88 passim; and social concerns, 88
Hume: critique of causal connectedness, 63; and bundle of perceptions, 77; on causal relations, 92–93

Humility: virtue of realism, 109
Hyle, 248–49, 250, 334

Icon, 328; as archetypal just man, 109; living in Church, 275
Ideological commitment, 30
Ideology, 265; voluntaristic and hedonistic, 27; overcoming of, 343–67 passim; anti-ideology, 354; defined, 370
Idol, 253, 328
Imagination: deconstruction and reconstruction in, 62
Immortality: as natural drive, 280
Inauthenticity: as fallenness, 262
Indiscipline, 370
Indulgence, 370
Inesse: defined, 319; as accidental being, 321
Information: external and received, 61; chronology of command of, 165–66; as "usable form," 201; objective and benevolential, 202
In-forming, 51, 156; givenness of, 280
Innovation, 212
Insight, 367; defined, 42; importance of, 42–43; and situation, 53–54; and structure, 57–60 passim; as not intellection, 58; as process, 59; as pervasive, 95; as ideationally and eternally valid, 95; summary of, 96; reflection and responsibility, 160; new, 359; and relations, 359
In-spiration, 324
Instituting: as *stiften*, 258
Institutions: defined, 98, 371; recognition of, 98; truths of, 99–100; as forms of religion, 266
Integrity, 129, 171, 239; of being and holiness, 106. *See also* Holiness
Intellect: conflict with will, 20
Intellectus fidem quaerens, 345
Intelligibility, 327; gain and loss of, 38; of things, 39; "of itself," 201; defined, 370
Intensity, 240; defined, 370
Interior life, 152, 214–76; and history, 219–76 passim; recuperation of, 222; as intentional, 223; dimensions of, 222–24; interiority of, 250–76 passim; order in the soul, 252–76 passim; measurements of, 253; nourishment of, 268–72; and inside and outside community, 270; and *ravissement*, 270; grounded in

socializing, 274; of a community, 274; and going out of soul, 275; defined, 371
Interior terrain, 174
Inter-legere: as reading into, 78
Interpretation, 319, 339, 355, 366; and familiarity, 43; and new data, 43; as collective (*Verstehen*), 173; of theory and praxis, 223; of truth and life, 223; ontological, 322; as act, 324; and subjectivism, 326; as guiding, 327, 328
Intersubjective, 233; possibility of discourse, 18; structure, 339
Intuition: as vague, 130
Irre, 322, 363

John of the Cross: and soul, 306; on love, 307–12 passim
Judgment: of existence, 15; correction of fallible, 63; critical vs. ongoing, 120

Kant, I., 295
Kenosis, 107, 303
Knowing: rooted in acts of will, 15; related to frames of reference, 15
Knowledge: impossibility of total, 9; recuperation of, 10, 11; different kinds of, 39; past, 46n12; and synthesis, 48; common fund of, 82–89 passim; not abstraction, 95; of acts, 97; of context, 97; as objective, 124; experimental and revealed, 180–83; of natures, 187; of kinds of things, 189

Language, 330; *an sich*, 128; theory of, 140–45; as House of Being, 215
"Letting in," 254
Liar, 371. See also Pseudo
Libertinage: drive toward, 59; as ideology, 169
Liberty: God-like, 315, 316
Lichtung: and *Sein*, 321, 328, 356
Life: and social relations, 96; affirmation of, 317
Life principle: presence of, 82
Limits, 366; as agglomerational, 192; of understanding, 314
Link: causal/*tradere*, 190
Liturgy: as work of God, 114–15; and prayer, 273
Logos, 353; revealed in history, 135; as fullness, 273; and flesh, 326
Lonergan, B.: and the existence of God, 282–96; levels of cognition, 284–85; counter position, 284; intending and intellect, 284
Lorenz, K., 162
Love: before faith, 33; and science, 33; and image of God, 33; in short supply, 129; as receptivity, 202; and commitment, 226; erotic and generous, 231; falling in, 256–59; one and many in, 270, 271; and God, 295–302; and God's transcendence in history, 306; as revealed, 307; as intentional, 307; maximum, 314, 315; act of, 328; defined, 371
Lovelock, J., 289, 291n1

"Making whole again," 316
Malum, 170, 177
Man: in context, 151–98 passim; and organic hierarchy, 168–69; superiority of, 169–70; and freedom, 170–74; from a subjective point of view, 186–87; as type and essence, 187–89; "to what end," 199; and history, 199–276 passim; spirituality of, 212–16; perversion in, 213; values and, 217; as *imago Dei*, 251, 308; and Creator, 346
Man, das, 320
Manipulation, 262n114; defined 371
Marion, J. L., 326n17, 340
Market: as information network, 218n39
Marriage, 256–59; and natural faith, 256
Martyrein: to witness, 131, defined, 371
Material conditioning, 201
Maturity, 212
"Maximum of differentiation": experience of, 135–38; and Church, 223
Me: real and actual, 215
Meaning: of human existence, 269; of tradition, 269; ultimate, 325; maximum field of, 366
Mediocrity, 259–65 passim; as ontological mystery, 261–62
Memory: of things and settings in perception, 55; as *memoria*, 166; as interiority, 221
Metanoete, 314
Metaphorein, 227
Metaphysics: description of, 277–78; as *Sein* recalling, 323; as *Sein denkende*, 326
Method, 268; importance of, 3; as *meta ton hodon*, 151; defined, 371
Metron, 354, 358; and judgment of truth, 18; and body, 57; and commensurability, 128; as inquirer, 152; and hierarchy, 169;

and whole understanding of being, 169; and more, 207, 208; defined, 371
Mind, 295–96; structures of, 56; opening of onto reality, 123; infinite, 314
Mindlessness, 259–64 passim
Missio, 345
Mitsein, 213, 249, 226; *ethnos* and institution, 194; sharing of, 320, 323, 329; interpretation of, 339, 359; defined, 371
Modus vivendi, 235
Monetary systems, 217–19; existing in mind, 64; and intersubjective objectivity, 65; and *Sein*, 65
Money: extraction of as spiritual process, 142–44; system, 217–19
Morphe, 247
Motivation, 269; lack of defined, 317
Municipality: as institution, 193–99 passim
Myself: as biophysical organism, 153; as material thing, 153; as manifesting complexity, 153–54; and psychic energy, 155–56; as information processor, 160–66
Mystery: as *mysterion*, 117; of God's freedom, 316; of the new, 324; recovery of, 356–58
Mysticism, 301

Natural faith, 367; as starting point, 3, 6, 12; as horizon, 7; defined, 7–12 passim; and epochal *Sein*, 8; and the hermeneutic circle of interpretation, 9; as intersubjective, 228n64; and wisdom, 268; collective, 325
Natural selection, 288
Nature: meaning and purpose of, 166–70 passim; as organism, 166–70 passim; role of man in, 166–71 passim; and hierarchy, 167–71 passim; as foundational to ontology, 174–86 passim; and meaning of "mean," 168; as damaged, 316
Nearness, 327
Need: for the love of a particular, 77; as universal love, 77; and pleasure drive, 85
Newness, 359
Nihilism, 356–58; reflection of, 366–68
Noema/noein: and Husserl, 14; dialectic of, 14; transcendence of, 60; and noesis, 247, 248, 249; and *noemata*, 321, 362; defined, 371

Not-wendigkeit, 322
Obedientia, 225
Object: never appears alone, 14; as present to consciousness, 14, 15; appearing in itself, 15, 16; as other than consciousness, 16
Objective: spirit, 89, 319; conveying of message, 312; context of knowing defined, 372; setting defined, 372
Objectivity, 332, 367; of our knowledge, 31; Kantian response, 31–32; as ground, 32; enjoys some reality, 41; role of, 125–26; of principles, 328
Obsession: and idols, 204; and passionate love, 204–7 passim
Ontic vs. ontological, 320–21, 359–63; and art, 361
Ontogenesis, 352, 354
Ontological balance, 264
Ontology: and epistemology, 7; and classic optimism of truth, 20; as classic embracing of reality, 20; as classic survival and making sense of the world, 20; and history, 37; as love-centered, 316
Onto-theology, 337; Christian, 313–19 passim
Order: foundations of, 103; out of chaos, 154, 314; enfolding of implicit, 175; as intra-cosmic, 176; in soul, 252; and higher form, 293; and self-control, 307
Other: as essential to one's being, 231

Paradigm shifts, 324
Paradox, 265
Past: projective and recuperative, 44
Pathology: and dreams, 56n25; and mischief (Voegelin), 203; in man, 354; internal, 366
Perception: as starting point, 42; things of, 42–49 passim; of real things, 44–49; includes setting, 44; and limits, 48; as waking vs. perceptions vs. hallucinations, 49–50; and profile (*Abschattung*), 48; material reality of, 51–52; permanence of thing in, 52; and memory, 55; and flexibility, 56; physical to spiritual, 62–68 passim
Permanence, 79; and human species, 81
Person, 273n133; as projection, 274; as horizon opening, 274; and freedom, 317; infinite worth of, 317
Personal identity, 159–60

Perspectives: and human ability, 171
Phenomenology: as neutral, 12; as guiding ontology, 41; and recovering clarity, 48n17; as foundational, 227–28; attitude, 355
Philein, 128
Philosopher: task of, 37; view of, 37
Philosophy: as erotic striving, 20, 215; moral base of, 128; *philein/sophia*, 128; and truth, 222; defined, 372
Physics: as reductionistic, 176–80; as ontological, 179
Pleroma, 109
Pluralism: of planetary situation, 3, 5; of situation, 37; and "live and let live," 125
Polanyi, M., 288
Postmodern subjectivism, 4
Prayer, 261; defined (Trent), 115; Christian not isolated, 116
Presencing, 238–42 passim, 326, 361; and attention, 240; relations of, 241–43; failure of, 262; as person, 266; knowledge of divine, 267; of source as mystical, 306
Pride, 109
Principle: possibility of, 9; and natural faith, 9; of realism, 13, 14, 15, 16; of contextuality, 16, 17; choice of world, 17, 18; as transcendentally possible, 21, 22; defined, 42n6; importance of, 42–43; as *archē*, 121; insight, 121, 122; as transcendental, 123; as guide, 124; of being, 295; of and in itself, 296; realistic defined, 372
Process: of a character, 70; knowing roles in, 70; recognition of, 145; understanding of, 145
Prophetic witness: and God, 300–306 passim
Pro-videntia, 304
Prudence: related to habit, 38; defined, 38
Pseudo: as living lie, 262, 263, 264; and being, 280; religion, 281; future, 332; visions, 332; defined, 372
Psyche, 214, 221

Rabbit: superiority of, 211–12; and *Mitsein*, 212
Ravissement, 237, 349; of relation, 11; not a loss of freedom, 203–7 passim; and obsession, 204–5; and interior life, 270
"Reaching out," 254
Real: setting, 39; systems, 39; defined, 41

Realism: principle of, 13; as foundational experience of perception, 13; in symbol of language, 140; and flux, 148
Reality: two kinds of, 11; subject-object, 48; greatness of, 123; juridical, 192; geographical, 192
Reason: as ability of intellect, 123
Rebelliousness, 20
Receptivity: defined, 37, 38; as love, 202
Recuperation, 322; of itself knowledge, 10, 11; of past, 44
Reductionism: as capital sin, 37–38
Reflection: as beholdenness, 61; as "reflect," 232–33; critical, 260
Relations: importance of, 39–40; network of implications, 40; and fundamental ontological investigation, 40; and frames of reference, 52; as spiritual, 67; proper descriptive, 92; social relations and their representation, 96–97; and institutions, 98; between organisms, 168; parental and personal, 190; one-way, 243–47; of presencing, 241–43; importance of nonreciprocating, 245–47; and Source, 275
Relationship: with things, 32; and interpretative initiatives, 32
Relativism: vs. absolute, 121
Relativity: theory of, 185
Re-sponse, 328; as *spondeo*, 111, 249; and mind, 207; failure to, 261
Responsibility: shuffling off of, 169; 203; as *spondeo*, 228–31; and mutual commitment, 231
Revelation: fullness of, 347
RNA. See DNA and RNA
Roles, 221

Sachverhalt: as state of affairs, 91, 249, 372
Sacrament: routinization of, 273
Sacrificium intellectualis, 123
Sanctification, 274
Sarx, 316
Schmitz, K.: critique of Heidegger, 281
Schritt zurück, 325
Scihcken, 319; as *Schicksal*, 334; as *Geschick*, 334
Security, 129
Sedimentation: and ideational cores, 49
Seienden: and *Sein*, 98, 321, 352, 362; *im Ganzen*, 101, 372 (defined); "im Ganzen und als Solches," 329
Seiendste des Seienden, 281, 313, 337

Sein: defined, 8; epochal and natural faith, 8; and source of agenda, 8; elusiveness of, 8, 195; and illumination, 8, 195; and *Ek-sistenz,* 47; epochal and imagination, 47; of modernity, 59; and monetary systems, 65; transcendentality of, 75; continuity and personal history, 78; and depth of familiarity, 88; as illuminating *cosmiota,* 98; and symbols, 138–40, 141; critical seriousness and, 148; epochal, 152, 321–22; being and information, 160; and Logos, 160, 163; and *Verstehen,* 163; becoming of, 172; of personal world, 172; of larger world, 172; and freedom, 172–74; and critical interpretation, 174–77, 197; gifts of, 187; history of, 188, 199; as not deterministic, 196; and *esse,* 196–97, 332–33, 338–40; and project of knowing, 201; and *Bildung,* 207; as science-informed, 208; projected by *Dasein,* 213; and man, 213; and tradition, 219; *Gunst des Seins,* 252; as grounded, 277; Heideggerian, 277n1, 278n4 (*Lichtung*); as obscuring, 281; historicity of, 318–40 passim; as *das Heilige,* 318; *Irre* of, 319–20; and historical interpretation, 321; as project-founding, 323; as gift, 323; finitude and ambiguity of, 328–35 passim; at work in, 329; "Where Is Sein?" 330; *bilden* of, 331; reception of, 331; and weave, 333n31, 336, 339; as *Wesen,* 334; revelation and obscuring of, 336; mediation and, 345; consciousness of, 349

Seinsmystizismus, 177, 218, 325n15, 334, 336

Seinsfrage, 329, 352

Seinsgeschichte: and being, 197, 199, 215, 320, 322, 329, 339, 344, 349, 352, 354; avoiding reductionism, 358–59. *See also* Historicity

Seinsidealismus, 329

Seinslassenheit, 350

Seinsvergessenheit, 344, 349, 351, 355; as forgetting of being, 323, 339–40

Self: control, 171, 307, 372; reflection evolving, 197; awareness, 228; sharing of, 228; commitment, 228; understanding, 229; aggrandizement, 315; redemption, 317

Self-centeredness: as centrifugal, 159; and illusion of self-importance, 181

Sex: consent to, 86–87

Sin: meaning of, 253; of flesh, 316

Sinai: events begin at, 353; experience of, 353–54

Situation: understanding of, 27–29 passim; as network of relationships, 28; as concentric circles, 28–29; as embracing subjective and objective, 29; intelligibility of, 29; external and internal, 29; objectivizing, 172; and space, 172; defined, 372

Skanadalon: Christ as, 134, 352

Small-scale mindlessness, 30

Solicitude, 233; as loving, 304

Soul: as principle of development, 122; and *telos,* 122; life of, 306–12; emptiness of, 308

Space: for genuine dialogue, 365, 366. *See also* Time-space

Spirit: communication of, 176; defined, 205–7 passim, 372; and organic frames of reference, 206; as in Holy Spirit, 311

Spirituality: of highest operation, 176; growing of, 200; defined, 200n1, 372; and symbolization, 206–15 passim; of cell, 209–11; of man, 212–17 passim; of human operation, 214–19 passim; and interior life, 215; and deficient interior life, 239, 240

Spiritualization: degrees of, 207–12

Spoudaoi: as holiness, 129; as "mature people," 147, 151, 253

Stability: of spiritual systems, 66; two types of, 76; classification of levels of, 81–82; social, 191–98 passim; defined, 373

Stellung im Kosmos, 178

Streng, 363

Structure: defined, 57; as *mixtum gatherum,* 58; as *ens mentis,* 58; static or dynamic, 58–60 passim; grasped by reflecting mind, 121; ultimate, 343–63 passim

Suavitas, 307

Subjective vs. objective: considerations and assertions, 8; and situation, 29; context, 47; intersubjective, 55

Subjectivist turn: and truth, 21; in Kant and Descartes, 21, 22

Subject-object: distinction, 19; language, 40, 41; meaning, 248

Supernatural: community of faith, 103

Symbol: and concepts, 60–69 passim; written, 67; clarification of, 72–75 passim; and systems, 82n57, 146, 216; of tradition, 101, 127; transmission and transfiguration of, 101; as translation of experience, 126–38 passim; as fruits of religion, 130; of other traditions, 138–40 passim; as subject and object, 140–41; and *Sein*, 140–41, 329; as representation of unperceived, 141; and Trinity, 163; manipulation of, 180; pointing beyond itself, 216; living in our, 217; religious, 264; as form, 265

Symbolization: by mind, 61; own life, 90

Sympathique, 240

System, 54; world and ontology, 145–48 passim; world, 343. *See also* Symbol

Technology: as mentality, 120

Teilhard de Chardin, P.: and phylogenesis, 182; and omega point, 183; and cosmogenesis, 289–90, 294

Telos: and soul, 122; vs. finis, 158–59

Territoriality: and social context, 158–59

"Test everything," 360

Theo-onto-logia: of wisdom, 132

Theory: and practice and interpretation, 32–34 passim; as *theoria*, 160; *theorein*, 205–7, 348

Things: as having sense in themselves, 16; and relations, 16; and *Selbst-ständigkeit*, 19; inherent coherence of, 38; internal and external sense, 39; and setting, 39; and intelligibility, 39; and imagination, 39; as self-presencing, 43, 44, 46; and form, 46; and self-giving, 361

Thinker: challenge to, 366–68

Thinking: the history of being, 335–40

Time, 214; and fullness, 273. *See also* Time-Space

Time-space: role of, 57–59 passim; experience of person, 57; three kinds of, 57; as structural insight, 57–60 passim; spiritual, 67; collision of, 68–69; entrance of transcendence, 137; center of, 186, 270; engaging of, 192; conditions of, 201; of meaning, 206–7; as cultural, 331; essential, 349; and transcending source, 349; defined, 373

Tonus, 8

Totalitätsbegriff, 321, 350

Tradere, 190; defined, 373

Tradition: as vital, 81, 336; as life-molding, 100; implicit and explicit, 100–102 passim; translation between, 128; as *tradere*, 190; debt to, 220; as formative experience, 233–38 passim; abuse of, 259–60; as resource for life, 259–64; as ideology, 260; integration of, 268–69

Transcendence, 352; defined, 38n2, 373; content and subjective life, 246–50

Translatability, 269; perfect is impossible, 144

Trinity: symbols of, 163

Truth: urgency of question, 3; not disincarnate, 4; as guiding vision, 4; and skepticism, 4; relativism and voluntarism, 4; undermining of, 5; meaning of, 6; claims, 9; as principle, 9–10, 18, 19; pursuit of, 10; and freedom, 18, 19; that is God, 20; not merely *theoria*, 21; as community/*ecclesia*, 21; and subjectivist turn, 21; as transcendental predicate of being, 38; and analogous predication, 38, experience of transcendental, 38; plurality and chaos, 38; as way, 38; as revealed *Wesen*, 71; of institutions, 99–100; as knowledge of being, 101–2; and holiness, 104–9 passim; essence of, 111, 172–73, 174; and Revelation, 113, 126–28; rooted in divine, 113; grounded in enfleshed spirit, 118; as difficult to conceptualize, 119; and dialogue, 129; security in, 129; and foundation, 129; demythologization of, 134; as revelation and love, 253; going through the motions of, 264–66; everyday reality of, 264–66; interpretation of, 268, 269; as symphonic, 272, 274; three symbols of, 319; revealed, 327; and being, 343–67; strategy for, 344; pursuit of, 344–54; of other, 367; destruction of, 367; discovery of, 367; admiration of, 367; question of defined, 373

Types: recognition of, 187–89

Tyranny: of crowd, 169

Um-greifende, 326

Um-stand, 326

Uneigentlichkeit: inauthenticity defined, 320n3

Union: without destruction, 315

Unity: and wisdom, 37

Unity of being: as scientific assumption, 21–22, 23; grounds for the assertion of, 24–30 passim; as ontogenetic, 25; and cosmological evidence, 25; as ecological

and psychological, 29–30; wisdom of, 39; critical understanding of, 39; occurs to us, 278
"Unthought of thought," 220
Ur-entwurf: as fundamental project, 255
Ur-sache: and Heidegger, 277n1

Valid: defined, 373
Value, 217; as relativistic: 5
Vector: of change, 59; informing others, 167
Verhalten: as comportment, 111, 237, 348, 349; as nonideological attitude, 354–58, 366; defined, 373
Verification, 180
Virtue: supernatural, 254; cultural/soul, 254
Vis activa, 293
Vocation: Christian, 112
Voegelin, E.: "maximum of differentiation," 135–38
Volksseinsgeschichte, 215

Voluntarism: as ideology, 27; plausibility of, 30; and limits of consciousness, 30–31; objection of, 31; and need for consistency, 31
Vorhandensein, 336

Wahren, 322
Weltanschauung: as guide, 37; and natural faith, 37
Wesen: Gewesen defined, 20n1, 373; hiding behind, 173; *das Gewesene,* 200; *Sein* and, 321, 325, 363
Will: conflict with intellect, 20
Will-to-power, 174
World: not a clutter of things, 189; projection of, 329
Writing: and alphabetization, 166
Wünscherfüllung, 250, 280

Zeitgeist, 218, 322, 334
Zoon politikon, 190
Zuhandensein, 336; defined, 373